PERSONALITY DISORDERS

301.00	Paranoid
301.21	Introverted
301.22	Schizotypal
301.50	Histrionic
301.81	Narcissistic
301.70	Antisocial
301.83	Borderline
301.82	Avoidant
301.60	Dependent
301.40	Compulsive
301.84	Passive-Aggressive
301.89	Other or mixed

PSYCHOSEXUAL DISORDERS

Gender Identity Disorders

Indicate sexual history in the fifth digit of Transsexualism code as 1 = asexual, 2 = homosexual, 3 = heterosexual, 4 = mixed, 0 = unspecified.

302.5x	Transsexualism
302.60	Gender identity disorder of childhood
302.85	Other gender identity disorder of adolescence or adult life

Paraphilias

302.81	Fetishism
302.30	Transvestism
302.10	Zoophilia
302.20	Pedophilia
302.40	Exhibitionism
302.82	Voyeurism
302.83	Sexual masochism
302.84	Sexual sadism
302.89	Other

Psychosexual Dysfunctions

302.71	with inhibited sexual desire
302.72	with inhibited sexual excitement (frigidity, impotence)
302.73	with inhibited female orgasm
302.74	with inhibited male orgasm
302.75	with premature ejaculation
302.76	with functional dyspareunia
306.51	with functional vaginismus
302.79	other

Other Psychosexual Disorders

302.01	Ego-dystonic homosexuality
302.90	Psychosexual disorder not elsewhere classified

DISORDERS USUALLY ARISING IN CHILDHOOD OR ADOLESCENCE

This section lists conditions that usually first manifest themselves in childhood or adolescence. Any appropriate adult diagnosis can be used for diagnosing a child.

Mental Retardation

Code a 1 in the fifth digit to indicate association with a known biological factor

317.0x	Mild mental retardation
318.0x	Moderate mental retardation
318.1x	Severe mental retardation
318.2x	Profound mental retardation
319.0x	Unspecified mental retardation

Pervasive Developmental Disorders

Code in fifth digit, 0 = full syndrome present, 1 = residual state.

299.0x	Infantile autism
299.8x	Atypical childhood psychosis

Specific Developmental Disorders

315.60	Specific reading disorder
315.10	Specific arithmetical disorder
315.32	Developmental language disorder
315.39	Developmental articulation disorder

Indicate course in the fifth digit as 1 = primary, 2 = secondary, 0 = unspecified.

307.6x	Enuresis
307.7x	Encopresis
315.50	Mixed
315.80	Other

Attention Deficit Disorders

Code severity in fifth digit as 1 = mild, 2 = moderate, 3 = severe, 0 = unspecified.

314.0x	with hyperactivity
314.1x	without hyperactivity

Conduct Disorders

Code severity in fifth digit as 1 = mild, 2 = moderate, 3 = severe, 0 = unspecified.

312.0x	Undersocialized conduct disorder, aggressive type
312.1x	Undersocialized conduct disorder, unaggressive type
312.2x	Socialized conduct disorder

Anxiety Disorders of Childhood or Adolescence

309.21	Separation anxiety disorder
313.21	Shyness disorder
313.00	Overanxious disorder

Other Disorders of Childhood or Adolescence

313.22	Introverted disorder of childhood
313.81	Oppositional disorder
313.23	Elective mutism
313.83	Academic underachievement disorder

Disorders Characteristic of Late Adolescence

309.22	Emancipation disorder of adolescence or early adult life
313.82	Identity disorder
309.23	Specific academic or work inhibition

Eating Disorders

307.10	Anorexia nervosa
307.51	Bulimia
307.52	Pica
307.53	Rumination
307.59	Atypical

Speech Disorders

307.00	Stuttering

Stereotyped Movement Disorders

307.21	Transient tic disorder
307.22	Chronic motor tic disorder
307.23	Tourette's disorder
307.20	Atypical tic disorder
307.30	Other

REACTIVE DISORDERS NOT ELSEWHERE CLASSIFIED

Post-traumatic stress disorder

308.30	acute
309.81	chronic

Adjustment Disorders

309.00	with depressed mood
309.24	with anxious mood

309.28	w
309.82	v
309.30	w
309.40	w ti
309.83	w

DISORDI NOT ELS...

312.31	Pathological gambling
312.32	Kleptomania
312.33	Pyromania
312.34	Intermittent explosive disorder
312.35	Isolated explosive disorder
312.39	Other impulse control disorder

SLEEP DISORDERS

Non-organic

307.41	Temporary insomnia
307.42	Persistent insomnia
307.43	Temporary hypersomnia
307.44	Persistent hypersomnia
307.45	Non-organic sleep-wake cycle disturbance
307.46	Somnambulism
307.47	Night terrors
307.48	Other non-organic dyssomnias
307.49	Unspecified non-organic sleep disorder

Organic

780.51	Insomnia associated with diseases elsewhere classified
780.52	Insomnia with central sleep-apnea
780.53	Other organic insomnia
780.54	Hypersomnia associated with diseases elsewhere classified
780.55	Hypersomnia associated with obstructive or mixed sleep-apnea
780.56	Other organic hypersomnia
780.57	Organic sleep-wake cycle disturbance
780.58	Organic dyssomnias
780.59	Unspecified organic sleep disorder

OTHER DISORDERS

Unspecified mental disorder (non-psychotic)

V40.90	Unspecified mental disorder (non-psychotic)

Psychological Factors Affecting Physical Disorder

316.10	Psychological factor probably affecting physical disorder
316.20	Psychological factor definitely affecting physical disorder

No Mental Disorder

V71.00	No mental disorder

CONDITIONS NOT ATTRIBUTABLE TO A MENTAL DISORDER

V65.20	Malingering
V71.01	Adult antisocial behavior
V71.02	Childhood or adolescent antisocial behavior
V61.10	Marital problem
V61.20	Parent-child problem
V61.21	Child abuse
V62.81	Other interpersonal problem
V62.20	Occupational problem
V62.82	Uncomplicated bereavement
V15.81	Noncompliance with medical treatment
V62.88	Other life circumstance problem

Note: The traditional neurotic subtypes are included in the Affective, Anxiety, Somatoform, and Dissociative Disorders.

Diagnostic and Statistical Manual of Mental Disorders, Third Edition (DSM-III), draft version January 16, 1978. Reprinted by permission of the American Psychiatric Association, Robert L. Spitzer, M.D. Chairman APA Task Force on Nomenclature and Statistics.

1981

ABNORMAL PSYCHOLOGY

ABNORMAL PSYCHOLOGY

Kurt Haas
State University of New York, New Paltz College

D. Van Nostrand Company
New York Cincinnati Toronto London Melbourne

Cover illustration by Mark Williams.

D. Van Nostrand Company Regional Offices:
New York   Cincinnati

D. Van Nostrand Company International Offices:
London   Toronto   Melbourne

Published by D. Van Nostrand Company
135 West 50th Street, New York, N.Y. 10020

10 9 8 7 6 5 4 3 2 1

For

ARJ

PREFACE

Abnormal psychology is a field experiencing rapid growth and change. Advances in medicine, psychology, and the social sciences continually introduce new concepts and treatments. It is important, therefore, to present contemporary abnormal psychology as it is: not with any favored theoretical slant, but rich with new information and divergent viewpoints. But we also do not overemphasize disagreement. We believe it is important for our audience—psychology students and those in related fields—to begin their study with a solid core of information.

Because our goal is to inform, we carefully provide full descriptions of the various clinical conditions. We want students to fully understand the different symptoms, causes, and treatments of abnormality. After students have learned psychopathology, we introduce critical questions. Our discussions of causes, for example, often contrast different explanatory models. At other times, we use boxed materials in each chapter to examine pivotal issues and stimulate discussion.

In addition to the primary purpose of giving a substantive account of abnormal psychology, there are several other goals. We believe it is important to introduce the topics of multiple causality, prevention, community and ethnic mental health concerns, and many other recent subjects. We hope also to leave students with skills and attitudes they will find useful in their later professional lives. Relating to skills, we present, for example, the terminology of the Diagnostic and Statistical Manual because it provides a working vocabulary.

Since at this writing the final version of the DSM-III is not complete, some DSM-II nomenclature is still used. Both DSM-II and DSM-III diagnoses are also reproduced on the endpapers of the text as an additional aid in making the transition from the older to the newer concepts.

Our goal relating to attitudes is advanced by including research that examines areas such as diagnosis, vulnerability, aging, hyperactivity, and depression. In this way students can develop an educated, critical ability to evaluate future investigations, treatment, and theory.

There is a final purpose. We firmly believe that the study of abnormal behavior is part of the larger scientific enterprise. But we try not to present people and their problems in a cold, detached manner. Case histories often consist of patients talking about themselves. Discussions of prognosis and treatment are as positive as reality will permit. It is our hope that readers, by getting to know people who are termed abnormal, will increase both their expertise and their humanity.

A word, too, about style. We have tried whenever possible to speak, for example, not of "a schizophrenic" or a "retardate" but of a mentally retarded person. Though we are limited by language, we want readers to be reminded that whatever the diagnostic label, we are talking about human beings.

The text is divided into six sections and eighteen chapters. Readers can progress from the first to last chapter in easy steps; or all the sections and most of the chapters can be studied independently. Instructors can thus omit any area or can design sequences to suit their special needs. An *Instructor's Resource Manual and Test File* that includes suggested topics for lectures, discussions, questions, and essay and objective test material is available.

A text is built upon the work of countless scholars and practitioners, both eminent and relatively unknown. Their contributions and ideas are gratefully acknowledged in the bibliography. I thank the reviewers whose suggestions have been so helpful in the development of the manuscript: Professor Robert Sollod, New York University; Professor Richard Price, University of Michigan; Professor Bernard Gorman, Nassau Community College; Professor Roger Cox, University of Indiana, Evansville. Additional thanks are due students and patients whose efforts and suggestions have added considerably to this work. A very special note of gratitude is owed Judith Joseph, Jeannine Ciliotta, and Harriet Serenkin of D. Van Nostrand Company for their editorial help and to Adelaide Haas for her encouragement and contributions.

Sources for all photos are credited in the captions. Those labeled "Scribe" are the property of the author. Special thanks are due the author's patients, students, and friends for several of the pictures.

CONTENTS

II | NEUROTIC AND PSYCHOTIC DISORDERS

III   DEVIANT AND ALTERNATIVE BEHAVIORS

IV CHILDHOOD AND DEVELOPMENTAL DISORDERS

V   ORGANIC AND ADJUSTMENT DISORDERS

CHAPTER 15   ORGANIC DISORDERS   311

CHAPTER 16   ADJUSTMENT REACTIONS: TRAUMA AND AGE   328

VI   TREATMENT

CHAPTER 17   MEDICAL, COMMUNITY, AND BEHAVIOR THERAPIES   343

ABNORMAL PSYCHOLOGY

1 HISTORY AND VIEWPOINTS

1 The Legacy of the Past

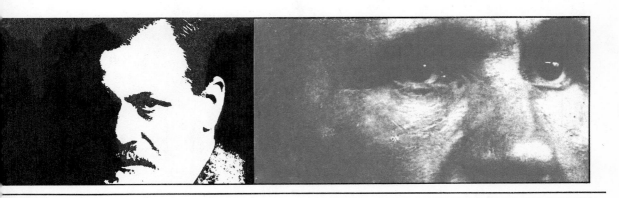

2 The Medical and Psychodynamic Models

3 The Behavioral and Social Models

1

The Legacy of the Past

For hundreds of years, until well into this century, people who were psychologically abnormal were considered outcasts. Mental disorder was not treated as just another illness; it was looked at as a personal failing or even an affliction to be mortally feared. In this first chapter we will review a little of the history of our attitudes toward abnormal behavior so that we may better understand many of today's mental health practices and issues. Before we begin, however, we need to know what is meant by the term mental disorder. We also need to know the major diagnostic categories it encompasses—the working vocabulary used by mental health professionals.

WHAT IS MENTAL DISORDER?

Mental disorder is a general term used to describe many different kinds of psychological,

emotional, and behavioral disabilities. Some disorders, like schizophrenia, severely restrict a person's ability to understand reality. Others are marked by deviant sexual behavior, excessive alcohol consumption, or profound attacks of fear or depression. But in all instances, whatever the symptoms, the effect is the same: a **mental disorder** seriously impairs an individual's ability to function. In the past, efforts were sometimes made to distinguish among descriptions like mental illness, nervous disorder, abnormal behavior, and the like. Such distinctions have now fallen into disuse. In this book, and for professionals generally, a number of overlapping terms all refer equally to the entire group of mental disorders: mental illness, emotional disorder, abnormal behavior, psychopathology, nervous disease, psychiatric illness, psychological abnormality, mental deviation, and nervous disorder. ("Nervous breakdown" is the vague phrase used by nonprofessionals to describe any mental disorder whose onset is usually sudden and disabling; it is not part of the clinician's or therapist's vocabulary.) The general category of mental disorder is subdivided into major types, some of which are these:

MENTAL RETARDATION: Below normal intelligence and reasoning, and other deficiencies in learning and social ability. Retardation is described as *mild* to *profound,* depending on the degree of impairment.

PSYCHOSES: Conditions in which mental or emotional faculties are so impaired that the person loses touch with reality. Psychosis is frequently called insanity in everyday language and may include one or more of the following symptoms: hallucinations, severe depression or elation, memory loss, inability to communicate, and false beliefs.

ANXIETY DISORDERS: These disorders are often referred to as *neuroses* and are characterized by symptoms such as anxiety, feelings of inadequacy, headaches, and fatigue. Unlike psychotics, neurotics do not lose touch with reality.

PSYCHOSOMATIC DISORDERS: Physical illnesses such as asthma, ulcers, and high blood pressure that may be caused by emotional problems or life stresses.

BEHAVIORAL AND PERSONALITY DISORDERS: A large range of maladaptive responses that cause difficulties for the person and/or for society, such as addiction, antisocial behavior, exhibitionism, and delinquency.

This list is by no means complete; nor are these categories universally accepted. As we shall see in subsequent chapters, the debate concerning causes, symptoms, definition, and treatment of mental disorder continues. It is a debate fueled in part by attempts to change attitudes and beliefs whose roots go far back into the past, to a time when people had far less control over the environment and far less knowledge of its workings.

FROM THE DEVIL TO MESMER: A BRIEF HISTORY

Demonology and witchcraft: persecution

Our conflicting reactions to mental disorder—suspicion, hostility, awe, and dread—have been shaped over thousands of years. Archeological evidence and historical records demonstrate that the mentally disordered were seldom simply considered ill and in need of treatment or respected for their differences and left alone. If they were fortunate, their peculiarities were honored and they were held to be especially powerful and gifted. More often, however, those who were different or who behaved abnormally were cast out or put to death. We can still observe both reactions among existing primitive groups all over the world, and even in some of our own "instinctive" responses to those who are different.

Figure 1.1. Among many American Indian tribes, an individual who hallucinated or exhibited other behaviors we would call psychotic was believed to be gifted. Such persons were held to be specially endowed and often looked up to as sages or healers. (Photo: Alan Carey/ Kingston Freeman)

In medieval Europe, people who behaved strangely were believed to be possessed by devils. In response, the clergy and self-appointed healers developed a technique called **exorcism** for casting out evil spirits. Exorcism sometimes persuaded an occasional hysterical or depressed person that he or she was being helped and did bring about some improvement. But all too often, exorcism was based upon the belief that the body must be made so uncomfortable that the demon is driven out. Along with prayers and curses, the victim was given whippings, burned, or otherwise abused physically (Figure 1.2).

No medieval cruelty, however, matched that inflicted during the centuries of witch hunting. Early in the fifteenth century, clerical authority, which until then had been nearly absolute, was threatened. Intellectual dissent, social unrest, and several waves of epidemic disease that eventually halved the population of Europe produced a climate of fear and instability. The blame had to be leveled against someone. In many countries, the masses were incited against Jews and other minorities. When this violent persecutory mania had run its course, a new scapegoat was found: the witch.

The medieval attitude toward sexual drives had been that they were evil, temptations of the Devil. Now the social turmoil and fear of disaster led to a new chain of reasoning: Lust was evil; women aroused men's lust; therefore, women were evil. Women's souls were possessed by the devil; they were "witches" who defiled men. (Notice how our language still reflects these beliefs in phrases like "She's bewitching" or "She's charming.") Then in 1487 two Dominican monks, Johann Sprenger and Heinrich Kraemer, published *Malleus Malefircarum* (The Witches' Hammer), which explained, in copious sexual detail, the seductive and evil work of witches, the means for detecting witchcraft, and the appropriate remedies. Ambitious women, Sprenger and Kraemer noted, were more deeply infected by the devil and "more hot to satisfy their filthy lusts."

This antifeminine, antisexual witchcraft fever eventually claimed hundreds of thousands of lives. Women were mercilessly tortured to extract confessions and then burned at the stake (Figure 1.3). At first it was only noteworthy women or those who were envied or disliked who became victims. Soon, however, any woman, man, or child who was different, or whose behavior puzzled or frightened others,

Figure 1.2. This illustration shows a priest curing a man believed to be possessed by demons. The devil-like figures can be seen flying away from the victim, who was probably what we would call psychotic. Patients treated by prayers were fortunate; but many of those believed possessed were exorcised by beatings and torture, on the theory of making the body so uncomfortable that the demons would flee. Such treatment frequently resulted in the person's death.

Figure 1.3. Those accused of witchcraft rarely escaped with their lives. The victims were usually women but men and children who were considered "deviant" were also tortured till they "confessed," then burned at the stake.

was accused of witchcraft, a charge against which there could be no defense. The result was that nearly every behavior we now think of as indicating mental disorder or even eccentricity was believed to be a manifestation of Satan's power, against which the only remedy was capital punishment (Neaman, 1975).

The witch-burning crusade, which received the approval of Pope Innocent VIII in 1484, lasted into the eighteenth century mainly because of Cotton Mather, a New England minister. Mather's two books on witches reignited the demon-hunting frenzy in America. Mentally disordered or nonconforming but innocent women were tortured and murdered after "trials" to which they could bring no defense.

Asylums: treatment

Despite the popularity of beliefs in demons and witches, many physicians and scholars suspected that what was called possession or witchcraft had in fact a rational explanation. They saw the mentally disordered as people in need of help rather than punishment. From the end of the twelfth century, mentally disordered persons began to be sheltered in monasteries, prisons, and hospitals. Institutions for the insane were begun in Metz, France, in 1100; in Uppsala, Sweden, in 1305; in Florence, Italy, in 1385; in Mexico City in 1567; and in many other places throughout Europe and the Americas. In most cases, these shelters began with noble goals. Founders proclaimed their intention to provide every person with "light, fresh air, and sustenance" in order to enable them to get well as rapidly as possible. But the medieval attitude that the insane were in league with the Devil was difficult to eradicate; and sooner or later most asylums became little more than prisons. Patients were often chained or locked in cages. Sometimes they were displayed like animals in a zoo. At the Bethlehem* hospital in England, the Lunatics Towers in Vienna, and many other such institutions, patients were exhibited to visitors for a small fee. On a Sunday afternoon, ladies and gentlemen of leisure amused themselves by watching the "demented ravings" and "shocking" behavior of lunatics (Figure 1.4).

Although by the eighteenth century nearly all enlightened men and women recognized mental illness to be the result of natural and not supernatural processes, mental hospitals continued to be little better than prisons. It took until well into the nineteenth century before the more severe abuses such as starvation and beating were eliminated. The "father" of American psychiatry, Benjamin Rush (whose face appears on the seal of the American Psychiatric Association), wrote in 1812:

In reviewing the slender and inadequate means that have been employed for ameliorat-

* The contracted name of Bethlehem Hospital, Bedlam, gave a word to English indicative of conditions there.

COMPASSION FOR THE MENTALLY ILL

While abuse and torture for those considered mentally ill was common throughout Europe for hundreds of years, there were also many brilliant instances of intelligence and compassion. Often as not, a few intrepid and humane clergymen or scholars spoke out for decent and effective treatment.

In 1509, the renowned scholar Cornelius Agrippa wrote a vigorous defense of women, *On the Nobility and Pre-eminence of the Feminine Sex.* Furthermore, in 1519 he put his beliefs into practice by rescuing a woman who had been accused of witchcraft in the town of Metz, in France.

The Swiss-born physician Paracelsus (1490–1541) argued forcefully against the notion that the mentally ill were either evil or possessed. For Paracelsus, the abnormal were simply sick people in need of treatment. Further, he believed that since the disturbance was psychological, patients could be reached by talk, persuasion, and counseling. Paracelsus may have been among the first to practice psychotherapy as we know it today.

In the fifteenth century, stories of a religious miracle brought mentally disturbed patients from all over Europe to the town of Gheel in Belgium. There, with the help of humane clergy and townspeople, many patients remained, living and working with local citizens. Kindness and responsibility became the theme for the community, and eventually a therapeutic colony, which is still functioning, was founded.

Following the French Revolution (1789), Phillipe Pinel, a physician imbued with the hope of "freedom and equality" for all men and women, took the bold step of unchaining the inmates of the asylum he administered. Pinel also demonstrated that not only were mental patients more likely to recover if they were unshackled, but that they should be given useful work and their problems listened to with care and understanding.

Figure 1.4. The eighteenth-century painter William Hogarth depicted conditions for those confined to "Bedlam" in England. Revelations such as this initiated a wave of reform during the nineteenth century.

In North America, many humanitarian changes were due to the work of Dorothea Dix (1802–1887). Despite her own fragile health, Miss Dix, a Massachusetts school teacher, raised money, petitioned, and testified before countless legislatures. Her efforts resulted in many states prohibiting the ball and drag chains and punishment then routinely inflicted on patients. (Photo: National Library of Medicine, Bethesda, Md.)

IS THE PAST, PAST?

For thousands of years, the mentally ill were thought to be possessed by demons. In 1973, a motion picture called *The Exorcist* portrayed a child who acted in a violent, abusive, and insane manner because she was possessed by the Devil. After medical and psychiatric therapy failed, a clergyman correctly diagnosed her disorder and through prayer and rituals exorcised the demon, making the little girl well again. In a survey of 212 moviegoers who saw the film, 14 percent stated that they believed in possession and exorcism and that what they saw in the film could in fact happen.

For centuries the mentally disordered were locked away, imprisoned in asylums because they were thought evil and therefore feared. In 1978 a halfway house was scheduled to open in a small city in New York State. Halfway houses are facilities for formerly hospitalized and other psychotic patients who need a place to live and receive minimal treatment before they are ready to be independent. Residents are free to come and go, just as if they lived in a hotel. The halfway house in the small city never opened. Influential citizens and political leaders opposed the project, citing reasons such as expense, taxes, traffic congestion, and property values. At a public meeting, one of the opposition leaders, speaking very honestly, pointed to the more likely source of opposition. He said, "Speaking for the majority of this community, I know I can tell you that frankly we believe these people are dangerous and ought to be locked up."

---

ing the condition of mad people, we are led further to lament the slower progress of humanity in its efforts to relieve them of their suffering than any other class of the afflicted children of men. For many centuries they have been treated like criminals, or shunned like beasts of prey: or, if visited, it has been only for the purposes of inhumane curiosity and amusement. . . . Happily, these times of cruelty to this class of our fellow creatures and insensibility to their sufferings are now passing away. In Great Britain a humane revolution dictated by modern improvements in the science of mind, as well as of medicine, has taken place. A similar change has taken place in the Pennsylvania Hospital, under the direction of its present managers. The clanking of chains and the noise of the whip are no longer heard in their cells. . . . In consequence of these advantages, they have recovered the human figure, and with it their long-forgotten relationship to their friends and the public. Much, however, remains to be done for their comfort and relief. (p. 16)

Causes: body and brain

Twenty-five centuries ago, the great Greek physician Hippocrates argued that mental illness is the result of bodily imbalances and deficiencies. Hippocrates theorized that our mental and physical well-being is determined by a delicate interplay of "humors," substances we might roughly think of as hormones today. An excess of, for example, the yellow humor caused confusion and violence; too much black humor produced depression. For several hundred years doctors both believed in and argued about this theory. The hypothesis was wrong, but during the golden ages of the Greek and Roman civilizations it linked psychological abnormalities to physical functions and rightly led human beings to be viewed as unions of body and mind.

But when these great civilizations declined, the knowledge accumulated over centuries was lost for a time in the West. Science, learning, and reason were replaced by mysticism, superstition, and ignorance. For more than a millennium, the Western world appeared to abandon intelligence and willingly lock itself into the grip of supernatural delusion and ideology. It was not until the seventeenth century that the body could once again be explored and studied. During the eighteenth century, the link between behavior and the nervous system was given an enormous boost by Franz Josef Gall's theory of phrenology, which held

Figure 1.5. During the eighteenth century, many scientists were convinced that the brain could be divided into specific functions and that each trait supposedly left its characteristic mark or bump on the skull. Consequently, an individual's personality or mental well-being could be "read" by studying the contours of the head. By the nineteenth century serious doubt had been cast on this theory, prompting a contemporary artist, George Cruikshank, to caricature this alleged science. (Photo: National Library of Medicine, Bethesda, Md.)

that personality traits, conduct, and emotion were located in specific regions of the brain.

Whenever one characteristic, say laziness, dominated a personality, it was bound to be physically evident in the contours of the skull (Figure 1.5). A bump low down and to the right, where the intuition area supposedly is, suggested more than ordinary intuitiveness. A shallow region high up in back and to the left, where sympathy allegedly resides, indicated an underdevelopment of this faculty. Most important, it was possible to localize mental disturbances. Gall insisted that symptoms we now call hallucinations, anxiety, and amnesia could all be traced to specific and visible over- or underdevelopment of parts of the brain.

Gall's hypotheses were eventually disproved, but other evidence of the role of the brain in mental illness was mounting. Of particular interest was the discovery by A. Bayle (1799–1858) and J. Calmiel (1798–1895) that psychotic individuals frequently had sizable lesions in their brains. Findings such as these led eventually to the suspicion that a serious psychological disturbance known as general paresis (the symptoms of which include paralysis and delusions) was related to a venereally transmitted infection, syphilis. The symptoms of general paresis usually include memory loss, tremor of the lips and tongue, irresponsible behavior, overactivity, and delusions of grandeur. But how is mental disorder related to syphilis? The symptoms of the disease seem totally nonpsychiatric.

Syphilis is almost exclusively transmitted through sexual intercourse. Several weeks to several months after infection, a small and usually painless chancre appears on the genitalia. The chancre soon heals; weeks later, it is followed by a rash and mild feelings of malaise. After recovering from this short illness, most eighteenth-century sufferers believed they were cured. In reality, the microorganism may remain in the body for a very long time. In a very small number of people, anywhere from ten to thirty years later the syphilitic spirochete may attack the central nervous system. When the brain is involved and blood vessels and tissues destroyed, the end result is often the mental disorder called general paresis.

Because it can be cured by antibiotic therapy, syphilis is now uncommon, and general paresis rarer still. But during the eighteenth and nineteenth centuries in Europe, paresis and the other late consequences of syphilis were frequent. By the late 1800s, several medical practitioners who had followed syphilitic patients for many years had noticed the likelihood of a connection between the venereal disease and mental illness. In fact, autopsies of those who had had syphilis but never manifested mental symptoms often showed brain damage similar to that noted in general paretics. Finally, in 1897 Kraft-Ebbing conducted an ingenious experiment. It was known that if a person had syphilis in any form he or she could not get it again. So Kraft-Ebbing took nine brain-injured and disturbed paretic patients, all of whom denied ever having had syphilis, and inoculated them with virulent microorganisms. None developed any of the early signs of syphilis, proving to Kraft-Ebbing and his colleagues that these same patients indeed had, and were still carrying, syphilis. In short, these patients were mentally ill because of the damage syphilis had inflicted on their brain.

Syphilis provided a *medical model* for all psychopathology. For nineteenth-century psychiatrists and for many mental health professionals today, the brain is seen as the physical source of all psychological illnesses. Even if the exact biochemical or structural failures cannot be detected or pinpointed, specific brain malfunction is believed to be the cause of psychosis, retardation, addiction, and possibly all other mental disorders.

Causes: magnetism and mind

At the same time that the search for the neurological causes of mental illness intensified, doubt about the role of the brain increased. For many patients with severe psychotic symptoms, lesions in the brain were often found. But for a great many others, particularly those suffering from neurosis, depression, and sexual aberrations, the closest scrutiny of their nervous systems revealed no damage. However much physicians searched, impairment in the brain and other organs could explain only a few mental disorders.

Theories about the causes of mental illness took a new direction because of the activities of Franz Anton Mesmer (1734–1815), an Austrian who had become interested in magnetism. By experimenting and reading the ancient literature, Mesmer became convinced that magnetism involved more than known physical and electrical properties. He saw it as an all enveloping force that dominated the universe. Each individual was filled with magnetic fluid; balance equaled health, but disequilibrium caused mental and physical ailments.

Mesmer's views were unpopular in Vienna, so he moved about Europe, eventually settling in Paris at the end of the eighteenth century. There he established a clinic for the treatment of medical and nervous disorders where he used a technique he now called *animal magnetism.* One popular variation of his treatment was to assemble patients around a large wooden tub with protruding metal rods. The patients held on to the rods, and Mesmer circulated among them, waving a magnetic wand. He touched here and there and announced that each person's magnetic fluids were being restabilized. In fact, the more Mesmer talked and coaxed and suggested, the better his patients felt. Often there were even dramatic moments when patients wept, shouted, or laughed hysterically as they felt health being restored to them. But Mesmer's methods and his personality irritated the physicians of his day, and several professional groups investigated his claims and cures. Almost without exception, the various scientific commissions, one of which included the visiting American inventor Benjamin Franklin, denounced animal magnetism as a fraud. It was only several decades later, after his death, that Mesmer's work was explained as **hypnotism.*** Mesmer was putting his patients in a trance. Though unaware of what he was doing, he was using the powerful dynamic that makes hypnosis work—**suggestion,** ordering people who were extra cooperative.

By the 1900s, when psychiatrists had become aware of the possibilities of hypnosis, it became a major tool both for investigating and for treating mental illness. What was particularly interesting was the announcement by Pierre Janet (1859–1947) that under hypnosis his patients were able to recall painful memories which seemed to be at the root of their neurotic symptoms. Janet was declar-

---

* *Hypnosis* comes from the Greek and means sleep. Sometimes it is still called mesmerism.

Figure 1.6. Hypnosis seems to work best in persons who are highly suggestible. Here a hypnotist is asking people to imagine their hands are glued together in order to pick out those most susceptible to hypnosis. (Photo: Scribe)

ing, or more accurately reviving, a new causal explanation for abnormality—the *psychodynamic model*. Unhappy psychological experiences, hidden conflicts, or wounded emotions often led to mental illness (Figure 1.6).

PERSONAL AND SOCIAL ATTITUDES: THE LEGACY OF THE PAST

With few exceptions, throughout history the mentally ill have seldom been treated either kindly or wisely. Consequently, both individually and as a society we have been left with many invalid ideas, a host of unresolved issues, and very likely some personal fears concerning mental disorder. In this section we will examine some of this legacy.

Nonconformists: sick or just different?

It is commonly believed that anyone whose conduct significantly deviates from the social norm is either a criminal or mentally disturbed (Figure 1.7). If a person scorns material possessions and dresses and lives in his or her own nonconventional fashion, the common-sense diagnosis is that this person is "a little nuts." People are even more likely to label

as abnormal anyone who is very introverted, who has a rich fantasy life, or whose sexual, religious, or social activities are out of the ordinary.

Hallucinations, delusions, acute anxiety, bizarre thinking, disorientation, and emotional extremes all suggest some kind of abnormality. But if the only distinctive feature of an individual's conduct is that the person's sexuality, vocation, living arrangements, hobbies or life style is different from that of the majority, it is *not* a symptom of mental disorder. We personally may not want to share in, or approve of, another's conduct; but neither our distaste nor our perception that the behavior is different necessarily makes it abnormal (Kittrie, 1973). Thieves, rapists, and other felons are also different from the norm, and almost no one approves their behavior. Yet just because the criminal breaks significant social and legal restrictions does not automatically make him or her mentally ill. It is true that some lawbreakers may be disturbed, retarded, or psychotic. But we must not fall into the trap of thinking that every felon is deranged and that any person whose conduct violates legal or moral standards is "sick." Such false labeling confuses ethical judgments and often makes it difficult to plan effective punishment or rehabilitation. Further, calling anyone and everyone whose actions are different or harmful ill extends the concept of mental disorder so much that it becomes meaningless.

Would you label any or all of the individuals in the following case examples as mentally ill? Or just different?

Edna, age 17, was caught shoplifting and tearfully admitted to stealing ever since she was 14. Edna's lawyer and the court decided that since she came from a good family and was truly remorseful, she was sick and needed psychotherapy instead of punishment.

Howard, age 34, has left his wife and children, taken up the guitar, and is singing in bars to earn a meager living. He was arrested on a streetcorner for carrying a small quantity of marijuana.

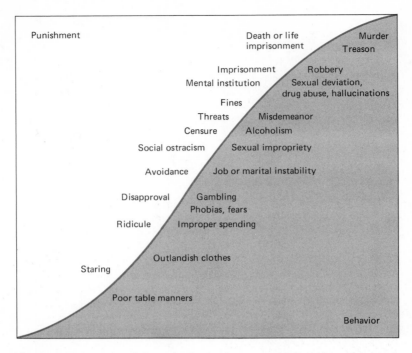

Figure 1.7. Every society defines what it considers acceptable behavior and appropriate punishment for violations. At the bottom of the chart are behaviors that deviate from our standards in minor ways and as a result have mild punishments. As we go up the chart, responses vary from ridicule to confinement. (After: K. Haas, *Understanding Adjustment and Behavior.* Englewood Cliffs, N.J.: Prentice-Hall, 1975, p. 455)

Miss Winters is a fiftyish high school teacher, never married and without any known friends. She is a good teacher but is also disliked because she is strict and demanding. She can become enraged at a student whose paper is late or sloppy and can be very punitive. She collects dolls as a hobby and often talks about it in class. Students both fear and ridicule her.

Jack and Louise have an "open marriage." Both have intimate friends of the opposite sex and sometimes spend a night away from home with them. Louise is bisexual, and occasionally she and Jack together have relations with another woman.

None of these people are in fact mentally disordered. Their conduct may or may not conform to society's or to our own personal expectations, but since they have no obvious psychiatric symptoms, we are not justified in calling them mentally ill. Thomas Szasz (1974), a leading critic of many current mental health practices, has pointed out that by calling everyone whose behavior is unconventional "sick," we are in danger of creating a mental health standard for proper conduct that labels as ill anyone who fails to conform.

Different and dangerous

The caricature of the "madman" plotting destruction and violence is continually reinforced by the entertainment and communications media. How truthful is this picture? Are those who are psychiatrically abnormal as ridiculous as comedians who try to depict men-

Figure 1.8. Many people falsely equate behavior that is different with abnormality. Unless we recognize that well-adjusted people may also be unconventional, we are in danger of creating a mental health standard by which to measure all conduct. (Photo: Alan Carey/Kingston Freeman)

tal illness by brushing away imaginary butterflies? In these social stereotypes, there is a small, in fact a very small, kernel of truth. A few people may be potentially violent and a few may behave in bizarre or absurd ways. But this is by no means typical; patients in mental hospitals are ordinary men and women who are perhaps a little more distressed and bewildered than the rest of us.

In terms of danger, mental patients may be slightly more likely to act irrationally. A few markedly paranoid individuals may be assaultive, some very depressed patients are suicidal, and alcoholics and other addicts have a better than average chance of coming into conflict with the law. The result is that compared to normal people of similar age and background, mental patients have a marginally higher arrest record. But as these carefully qualified statements show, regarding everyone who is mentally disordered as dangerous is a serious error. The great majority of mental patients are law-abiding and peaceful (Wilber, 1975; Zitrin, 1976).

In terms of the mentally disabled being different from normal people, *the distinction is one of degree.* In most instances there is no sharp boundary, no discernible gap, between

DANGER: MADMAN

Because many people are frightened by individuals they correctly or incorrectly believe to be mentally ill, involuntary hospitalization is still common. Consider the case of 44-year-old Robert Friedman, reported in the Chicago *Sun-Times.* In February 1975, Friedman was arrested for begging near a Chicago bus station. He protested to the police that he was not a vagrant and opened an attache case he was carrying to reveal $24,000 in small bills. Later the court ordered that Friedman be examined by a psychiatrist, who diagnosed him as paranoid schizophrenic and had him committed to a hospital.

The case came to the attention of Edward Bennet, an attorney who volunteered his services and argued that his client was merely a harmless eccentric. With diligent effort, Friedman had saved the money by working as a speed typist for over sixteen years. He had a number of peculiar habits, including extreme thrift and begging. The lawyer argued that these were insufficient reasons to label him schizophrenic and put him in an institution for the rest of his life.

This case raises a number of questions, none of which are easily answered.

1. What are the differences between mental illness and eccentricity?
2. Who decides who is abnormal—a judge, a police officer, a doctor, or the person?
3. Should a person have to be proved dangerous, incompetent, or otherwise a menace to society before being hospitalized?

psychologically healthy and unhealthy people. The healthy person can feel quite low; the disordered person may simply feel even lower. A healthy man or woman can be fearful; the mentally ill may have a wider or deeper range of anxieties. In fact, very often the feelings of relatively healthy people and those diagnosed as ill actually overlap. As Figure 1.9 shows, the amount of anxiety experienced by some normal people is as great as that felt by some labeled mentally ill. The difference is the normal person may be a little incapacitated in one area but can still carry out ordinary routines and responsibilities. The mentally disordered person is so handicapped, usually by a constellation of symptoms, that he or she is no longer able to function effectively.

Nomenclature and numbers

Throughout this book we will be using terms like schizophrenia and anxiety disorder. This

16

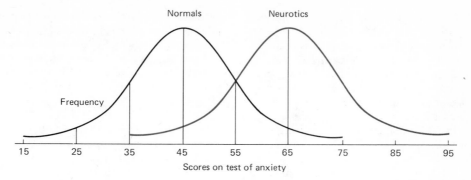

Figure 1.9. Scores on an anxiety test for normal adult subjects and those diagnosed neurotic. Although the neurotics do have generally higher scores (neurotic average is 65; normal average is 45), the scores of both groups shade into one another. Like most symptoms of mental disorder, anxiety is on a continuum, so that it is difficult to pinpoint where normality ends and abnormality begins.

nomenclature is the legacy of centuries of medical effort to bring some sense and order to what otherwise seems a jumble of disconnected signs of mental distress. But the diagnostic labels we use today are based on a medical model that many critics do not believe appropriate to describe psychological disorders. It is argued, for example, that the symptoms we believe supposedly constitute a single disorder called schizophrenia actually point to two, three, or even more different and distinct conditions (Chapter 7). Others believe that the entire psychiatric labeling process, in addition to being inaccurate, is just the counterproductive heritage of an inhumane past. The mere act of pinning a label on someone, they say, so alters the perception of that person for himself and for those around him that the diagnostic term becomes a "self-fulfilling prophecy." (Phillips and Draguns, 1971).

Despite the substantial criticisms of our diagnostic process, most mental health workers do use the current nomenclature. For them, and for us, it is a functional convenience enabling us to communicate. But even though there is sufficient agreement on most terms, precise definitions differ. For example, just what is alcoholism? How often and how profoundly must an individual be intoxicated to be called addicted? According to the World Health Organization, an alcoholic is a person who is "dependent" on alcohol or shows the "prodromal" (beginning) signs of such dependence. This leaves the door open to classifying anywhere between 5 to 25 million Americans as alcoholic. The conventional definition of mental retardation is anyone with a valid IQ score below 70. This figure suggests that nearly 7 million American children and adults are intellectually deficient. Tarjan and others (1973), however, propose that true mental retardation begins lower on the IQ scale and involves far fewer persons. According to their calculations, there are only about 2 million intellectually disabled individuals in the United States.

Just who is ill and what the proper diagnostic term is are unresolved issues that will be explored again in subsequent chapters of this book. But we do need some estimates of the number of people who may require care and treatment so that the health services, communities, and schools can be more adequately prepared. Many different agencies, such as the National Center for Health Statistics and The American Psychiatric Association, have released approximations they believe reliable. But there is considerable variation among these figures; one source may count 20 million mentally ill, while another suggests 40 million (*The New York Times,* February 13, 1977). Based on a population of about 220 million Americans in 1980, we have chosen fairly minimal estimates. Conservative counts show that the most common abnormality is mental retardation, and that about 6.5 million persons suffer from this disorder. Alcoholism is next, with about 4 million severely addicted drinkers. Disorders of childhood and adolescence account for 3 million, and there are about 2 million psychotic patients, about a fifth of whom are hospitalized. Adding the other categories of psychological disorders, as shown in Figure 1.10, the total number approximates 25 million people, or over 10 percent of the American population.

Single and multiple causes

Human beings have a long history of thinking in terms of single cause for events, and explanations of mental disorder have been particularly susceptible to single-cause arguments. Throughout history, investigators have

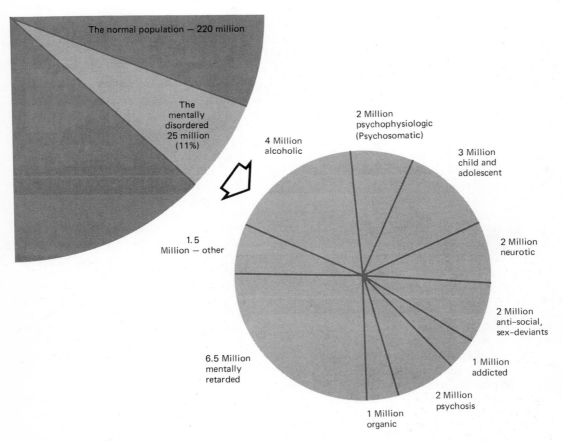

Figure 1.10. Of a total population of about 220 million in the United States in 1980, 25 million are estimated to be mentally disordered. Most of the disordered are not in treatment. (Sources: U.S. Public Health Service, Department of Justice, National Association of Mental Health, American Psychiatric Association, Alcoholics Anonymous)

Sex has continued to reappear for several millenia in one guise or another, as the *single* cause of mental disorder. The early Greek physicians hypothesized an unfullfilled uterus (Gr.: hystere) caused mental illness. Two thousand years ago the Roman physician Galen wrote that sperm which is not discharged damages the brain. More recently, during the last century, an Austrian physician, Richard Von Kraft-Ebbing put the blame on masturbation. His book, *Psychopathia Sexualis* (1886), richly detailed how "self-abuse" triggered a chain of perversions ending in madness in cases similar to the following:

Case 9: A young girl had an increasing sexual desire which she satisfied by masturbation. As she grew older, because of her habit, she developed insane and violent sexual excitements at the sight of any man. Since she could not be answerable for herself she used to lock herself in a room for a time until the storm had subsided. At last she gave herself to various men, in order to get peace from her torturing sex-urge. But neither coitus nor masturbation brought any relief, so that she went into a madhouse.

Sigmund Freud also singled out sex as the primary, if not the only cause, of mental disorder. The analytic version suggested that *repression,* the denial of sexual feelings, motivated neurosis and psychosis. Paranoid schizophrenia, for example, was attributed to latent homosexual impulses.

We are aware today that sexual motives and capabilities both reflect, and play a vital role in, mental health.

But it is unlikely that sex occupies a uniquely

The Frightful Consequences
of
ONANISM

The Heinous SIN of
Self Pollution,

The evil results
madness and lunacy
weakness and pallor
Advise to those who have already
injured themselves

Prevention of this abominable
practice

---

searched for *the* cause of abnormality. Continually, to this day, announcements have proclaimed that the single cause has been found. Note the following newspaper headlines, which appeared during the last decade:

Crime Caused by Faulty Gene
Schizophrenia Caused by Blood Chemical
Sex Crimes Tied to Mother Love
Low IQ Due to Poor Food

Every headline is, of course, untrue. In some instances no relationship has been verified. In others, such as IQ, poor diet has been found to play only a very small role in the intelligence of most children. In nearly all cases, as will be evident in subsequent chapters, mental disorder is the result of a number of causes that together produce symptoms and disability.

The historical tendency to search for a unified description and a single cause for mental illness has left us with a number of different explanatory "models." As we shall see in the next chapters, there are today at least three major viewpoints. The medical or organic model attributes the cause of abnormality to malfunction of the nervous system or brain.

These somatogenic (meaning due to the body) views can be traced back several thousand years to ancient theories that body fluids, or humors, determined whether a person was ill or well. In contrast, psychogenic and sociogenic models include a number of explanations suggesting that mental illness is due to inadequate family experiences, faulty learning, or social and cultural stress.

We will examine each approach in Chapters 2 and 3 and in subsequent chapters weigh the evidence from each as it applies to specific disorders. We will find that in the majority of instances, it is far more meaningful to think of cause as multiple rather than single. Even when a disorder like schizophrenia seems to be traceable to a single organic cause like heredity, many more factors are likely to play a role as well. Kety (1975), Schulsinger (1976), and others have found, for example, that children from schizophrenic mothers given up for adoption at birth may or may not develop schizophrenia depending on a large number of psychological and environmental circumstances. Being the child of a schizophrenic parent apparently makes one more susceptible to this psychosis. But whether or not abnormal behavior eventually results is also a product of relations with parents and with brothers and sisters, school adjustment, and many other variables. What we are saying is that despite our legacy of thinking in terms of a single cause, our commitment should be to look at all the possible causes that could contribute to mental illness.

Medical students disease

For thousands of years, ever since students have been studying abnormal mental and physical processes, they have become the victims of their own scholarship. As they learn the details of physical or psychological ailments, before too long they begin to suspect they have some of the symptoms. Medical students studying the heart soon become extra alert to some of the strange sounds they think they now hear in their own chests. Abnormal psychology students reading about the charac-

teristics of neurasthenia—fatigue, headache, and indigestion—suddenly think they recognize these symptoms in themselves or their friends. Relief for this mild type of medical student's disease comes through being aware that we are all quite suggestible. When the symptoms of any disorder, whether voyeurism or schizophrenia, are spelled out in graphic detail, many people temporarily believe they have what they are reading about.

There is a second form of medical students disease, and that is a loss of objectivity. Some new mental health workers become so concerned about their patients that they act like a suffering parent or spouse.

The opposite of overidentifying with people who are emotionally disordered is treating them almost as if they were nonhuman. Sometimes beginners in mental health feel so anxious about clients that the only way they think they can continue working is to keep patients at a very great distance. Students too have a

Figure 1.11. The ability to communicate with and understand people who are different from ourselves is an indispensable trait for anyone interested in working in mental health. At the same time, a proper balance needs to be maintained between sympathy and objectivity. (Photo: Alan Carey/Kingston Freeman)

tendency to think of the people they are studying about as "them," as opposed to "us," who are allegedly all right and acceptable.

The cure for loss of objectivity is twofold. First, we should know that some identification with abnormal processes and with patients is good. To have a few of the feelings that patients experience not only increases our understanding but makes it unlikely we will treat the mentally disordered as objects or people to be shunned. But what is most needed is a balance—enough compassion to enable us to continue to act as concerned human beings, coupled with sufficient objectivity to help us maximize our contribution.

A second possibility, if we are not able to strike a compromise between sympathy and objectivity, or if our exposure to the field arouses continuing anxiety, is personal counseling. Many people in mental health were attracted to the field partly because they themselves had psychological difficulties. With good treatment, such individuals often make excellent professionals.

SUMMARY

Mental disorders are characterized by psychological symptoms that together seriously handicap an individual's ability to function. Throughout most of history, people considered abnormal were believed to be wicked or in the grip of evil forces. There were also instances of the mentally disordered being considered supernaturally gifted. Attitudes of awe, fear, and hostility toward abnormality reached a violent culmination in the witch-hunting frenzy that began in the fifteenth century and lasted nearly three hundred years. Slowly, however, psychological impairments came to be looked at as illnesses. Patients were confined to asylums, and doctors began to look for the causes of abnormality in bodily processes.

In the eighteenth century, Gall proposed the science of phrenology, and asserted that mental disturbances were localized in specific regions of the brain. Though the ideas behind phrenology were wrong, discoveries of brain lesions seemed to point to a neurological cause of insanity. At the same time, the work of other investigators resulted in psychological explanations for mental illness. Mesmer suggested that animal magnetism caused disorder, and other analysts attributed mental problems to emotional conflicts and unhappy experiences.

The history of our attitudes toward mental disorder has left us with a legacy of suspicion and misunderstanding. Nonconformity is frequently still equated with psychiatric abnormality. Many still believe that the mentally ill are different and dangerous, although in both dimensions the disordered are divided from the normal only in terms of degree.

Our historical heritage has also resulted in disagreement concerning diagnosis, frequency, and cause. Although it is popular to think of mental illnesses in terms of single organic or psychological causes, in most instances these conditions are the result of many different physical and psychological circumstances, as we will see in the following chapters.

The Medical and
Psychodynamic Models

The search for an understanding of abnormal behavior has led to a variety of explanations. The various views of the causes and treatment of mental disorder are referred to as **models.** The medical model developed from work such as that of Hippocrates and Franz Gall (Chapter 1). Hippocrates believed mental illness was due to an imbalance of humors, and Gall pointed to the improper development of the brain. Both investigators were wrong, but they originated hypotheses that culminated in the view that mental disorder may be physically rooted and due to brain damage.

Psychological and social models of abnormality can be traced to people like Anton Mesmer and Pierre Janet (Chapter 1). Their work with hypnosis increasingly suggested that mental problems were the outcome of conflicting emotions and unhappy experiences. In this and the following chapters we will discuss several psychological models. The psychodynamic

position holds that abnormal behavior results from conflict and struggle within the personality. The learning view (Chapter 3), another psychological model, believes that abnormal as well as normal behaviors are learned. The social view, (Chapter 3) heavily emphasizes environmental experience as a determinant of mental illness. We will discuss all of the major models in terms of their proposals concerning diagnosis, cause and treatment.

THE MEDICAL MODEL

One of the first "scientific" views of mental disorder suggested that mental illness could be accounted for in much the same way as physical disease. If someone is breathing badly, probably his or her lungs are damaged. Similarly, if someone's thinking or behavior is deranged, it means that his or her brain is injured. The explanation of mental disorder that hypothesizes an underlying physical cause we will refer to as the **medical** (or **organic) model.**

Diagnosis

Beginning with the 1800s, most doctors agreed that symptoms such as extreme periods of elation, paralysis of an arm without actual physical damage, or talking in confused sentences were all signs of emotional abnormality. But what these symptoms meant and how they related to one another were the objects of intense debate. A clue finally came from physical medicine, for doctors had found that symptoms group together to indicate specific diseases. Each cluster of symptoms, called a **syndrome,** points to an underlying cause and thereby suggests a logical treatment. As a result, when tuberculosis is treated doctors do not try just to alleviate symptoms like cough or fever; they direct their efforts instead at controlling the tuberculosis bacillus.

Modeling his efforts to understand mental illness on this apparently successful medical approach, Emil Kraeplin in Germany carefully and meticulously catalogued the behavior of thousands of his patients. At the turn of the century, Kraeplin, often credited with being the founder of modern psychiatry, asserted his observations proved that *psychological symptoms occur together with such regularity that they clearly define specific emotional diseases.* A patient who was withdrawn, hallucinated, and disoriented had dementia praecox (now called schizophrenia). A patient who was exceedingly depressed and had had previous periods of extreme elation was likely to be manic-depressive. Kraeplin's observations were so thorough that his *Lehrbuch der Psychiatrie,* first published in 1883, went through nine editions. By 1927 it totaled 2,500 pages and was used in the United States and throughout the world as the definitive guide to symptoms and diagnosis.

From this medical point of view, it is the job of the psychologist or other mental health professional to examine each patient, establish

Figure 2.1. Emil Kraeplin (1856–1926), more than any other scientist, came closest to the goal of integrating the mental illnesses into medicine. Kraeplin was determined to show that psychiatric disorders, like physical ailments, had a specific cause and could be effectively teated once the proper medication was found. (Photo: National Library of Medicine, Bethesda, Md.)

the symptoms, and then attach the appropriate diagnostic label. Today, in a clinic or other psychiatric facility, such a final diagnosis is often determined by a staff diagnostic conference several days or weeks after the patient is first admitted:

PSYCHIATRIST. My examination of Mr. Y showed some paralysis of his right arm, speech loss, and confusion. He seems not to know where he is or what is happening.

PSYCHOLOGIST. My tests definitely point to brain damage. He is rigid, perseverates, has very poor visual-motor coordination, and his speech seems aphasic.

Figure 2.2. In most mental hospitals and clinics, a diagnostic conference is held some time after the patient is first admitted. Psychiatrists, social workers, psychologists, and other members of the mental health team who have examined the patient discuss their findings. The purpose of the meeting is to make a diagnosis and set up treatment plans. (Photo: Scribe)

SOCIAL WORKER. His wife told me he had been very depressed and irritable before being admitted. He was also forgetful.

PSYCHIATRIST. We'll need some more neurological information. But so far his symptoms, taken together, point to cerebrovascular psychosis.

But Kraeplin's work was not the final word on mental disorder; our information about, and understanding of, abnormal behaviors continues to evolve. In addition, social expectations and standards change, so that what was considered abnormal yesterday may not be thought so today. Alcohol and drug abuse were, until relatively recently, not even considered psychological problems. Now addictions form a major class of mental disorders. Conversely, some behaviors believed only a few years ago to be abnormal, such as some forms of alternate sexuality, are currently no longer viewed as necessarily pathological.

Because of the constant need to update our understanding of the conduct considered disordered and to bring unity to our descriptions, the American Psychiatric Association has periodically assembled experts from many nations and published a guide, the *Diagnostic and Statistical Manual* (DSM) (Figure 2.3). This booklet describes behaviors currently defined as psychologically ill. Each mental disorder in the DSM is defined in terms of the presence or absence of a cluster of psychological symptoms. The individual who is withdrawn but otherwise not particularly maladjusted is probably normal. But the person who is withdrawn, hallucinated, and disoriented exhibits a constellation of symptoms, a syndrome, that points to schizophrenia.

In this book our definitions and terms will generally follow those in the latest edition of the manual, the DSM III (1978). In fact, today nearly all professionals use DSM terminology, and most clinics and institutions require that this vocabulary be employed to define the status of every patient. The DSM occupies such a central place in clinical practice that whether or not a particular symptom or behavior is listed has critical significance for law, insurance, and treatment. At the same time as we use the diagnostic terms of the DSM III, however, we recognize that not all scientists agree that the medical concept of diagnosis, cause, or treatment is applicable to psychological disorders. As we shall see in this and the following chapter, the medical approach may not provide the most appropriate model to explain mental disorder. In short, the DSM-III may not be the final authority describing mental disorders with uncontested validity. But we and most clinicians use it since it does make it possible for mental health workers to understand one another, to communicate, and to conduct research.

Causes

HEREDITY Since its inception, proponents of the medical model have contended that heredity plays a critical role in mental illness. In the past, evidence was spotty and often based on unreliable family genealogies and personal recollections. Now, however, twin studies have given an enormous boost to the

definitions   38

295   Schizophrenia

These disorders are characterized by disturbances of mood, thought, and behavior. Misinterpretations of reality, hallucinations, and delusions are common. Other symptoms include: loss of empathy with others, withdrawal, constricted and inappropriate emotions, and bizarre behaviors.

295.10 Schizophrenia, Disorganized Type (Hebephrenia)

This psychosis is typified by shallow and inappropriate emotion, disorganized thinking, mannerisms, giggling, regressive behavior, and sometimes fragmentary hallucinations and delusions.

295.30 Schizophrenia, Paranoid Type

The outstanding symptom is persecutory and/or grandiose delusion. Patients are frequently hostile, excessively religious and aggressive. Personality of these patients usually seems more intact than those found in other types of schizophrenia.

Figure 2.3. The DSM III. This page illustrates the style and content of the latest edition of the *Diagnostic and Statistical Manual of Mental Disorders,* published by the American Psychiatric Association. Since there is some disagreement about which behaviors are abnormal and which symptoms define particular kinds of mental disorder, the DSM III provides a standard enabling practitioners to use a common vocabulary.

Figure 2.4. Monozygotic (MZ) twins come from the same fertilized egg. If they are raised apart so that their environments are different, the ways in which they remain the same suggests that similarities are inherited. Many studies have shown that separated identical twins frequently share schizophrenia, similar IQs, and other psychological characteristics. Such research has given considerable support to medical-genetic views of mental illness. The twins pictured live in different parts of the United States, and have individual life styles and different ways of dressing. Yet their fundamental similarity is apparent. (Photo: Scribe)

THE BRAIN

Medical models suggest that the explanation of mental disorder lies in the workings of the brain. Abnormal behavior is postulated to be largely the result of genetic or acquired neurological malfunction. So far, however, searching the brain for physical evidence of tissue or chemical damage has yielded only limited results. The brain is an enormously complex organ composed of more than 10 billion cells, each interacting with up to 50 thousand others. As a result, many brain activities are shared, and pinning down the function of specific areas is extremely difficult. It will take many years before more of the physical role of the brain in mental health and illness is understood. But a beginning has been made. A small sample of what we have learned follows:

Most of the brain, the *cerebrum,* is composed of two large *hemispheres,* which are almost mirror images of each other. The hemispheres are interconnected, in part, through bundles of nerve fibers called the *corpus callosum.* Both halves share many mental and motor functions. The hemispheres themselves interact with opposite sides of the body, the left hemisphere controlling the right side, and vice versa. For this reason, damage to one side of the brain usually results in losses on the opposite side of the body. *Split brain research,* that is, investigations of persons whose hemispheres have been surgically disconnected, has revealed that the two halves can also work separately. In most people the left hemisphere is considered "dominant" and in control of several complex functions such as language, logic, and mathematical skills. The right hemisphere

Frontal lobe

Corpus callosum

Occipital lobe

Parietal lobe

Central fissure

A human brain viewed from above. The deep middle groove separates the two hemispheres.

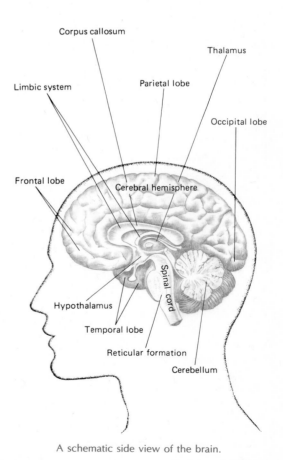

Corpus callosum

Thalamus

Limbic system

Parietal lobe

Occipital lobe

Frontal lobe

Cerebral hemisphere

Spinal cord

Hypothalamus

Temporal lobe

Reticular formation

Cerebellum

A schematic side view of the brain.

seems to excel in motor-visual tasks such as drawing three-dimensional figures.

The surface of each hemisphere is a 2-millimeter thick layer of cells, packed and folded upon one another in convolutions and called the *cerebral cortex.* The cortex, which is divided by *fissures* into four *lobes,* receives sensory and motor impulses from the eye, skin, and other receptors. In turn, it sends out motor impulses to the fingers, legs, and other muscles. In addition, the cortical lobes seem to be responsible for the following psychological activities:

Frontal Lobe: Motivation, abstract thinking, inhibition, sorting information, planning ahead

Temporal Lobe: Memory, verbal and perceptual behavior, and appropriateness

Parietal Lobe: Learning, organizing ideas, abstract thinking, coordinating information

Occipital Lobe: Visual memory and insight

Damage to the lobes may cause confusion, loss of self-control, poor motivation, and disturbances in thinking and perception, as well as various physical disabilities.

A cross section of the brain permits us to go beneath the cerebral cortex and see some of the deeper areas. The *thalamus* seems to act as control center, channeling messages to the proper places in the brain. It may also be involved in the perception of pain, fear, and anxiety. The *hypothalamus* helps regulate basic drives like sex, hunger, and thirst. Closely linked to both areas, the *limbic system* incorporates other brain structures (amygdaloid nucleus, hippocampus, fornax) to play a crucial role in emotional behavior. Both pleasant, pleasurable feelings as well as aggressive and fearful ones seem to originate in this system. Damage to any of the limbic structures could result in feelings of euphoria, emotional overactivity, or even extremely disordered moods and feelings. The *cerebellum* is involved in balance and motor coordination; damage usually results only in physical disability. The *reticular formation* filters sensory messages,

and controls alertness, consciousness, and attention. Injury here may result in disorientation and confusion.

If we took a long, shallow slice of the cortex and were able to pinpoint its motor and sensory functions, we would see the illustration below.

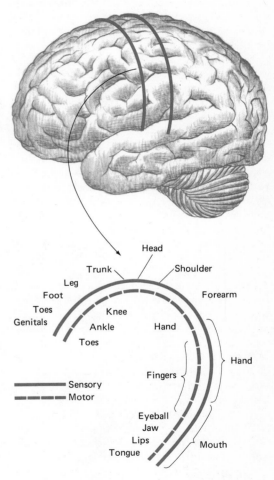

In this inside schematic view a few motor and sensory cortical areas are localized. The sensory cortex, the solid line, registers electrical changes whenever the corresponding part of the body is stimulated. Activation of the motor areas, the dotted line, causes responses in the specific body parts involved. Notice how much cortical space is given important organs like the fingers and mouth.

genetic argument. Identical twins come from the same fertilized egg. They are *monozygotic* and thus share nearly identical genetic components. Fraternal twins are *dizygotic;* they come from two different fertilized eggs, and thus are not much closer genetically than ordinary siblings. If monozygotic twins are raised apart so that their environments are different, the ways in which they nevertheless remain the same suggest that these similarities are inherited.

Twin studies dating back for more than fifty years have shown that if one identical twin develops schizophrenia, the chances are better than 40 or 50 percent that the other will also. These findings have held up in research conducted in several countries, even when the twins were separated at birth and raised by different families in very different circumstances. In contrast, among fraternal twins the rate for simultaneous schizophrenia has usually been about one in ten and for ordinary siblings even lower. Although this kind of evidence has not convinced everyone, it has suggested to many mental health professionals that schizophrenia is hereditary (Wahl, 1976).

BIOCHEMISTRY Hippocrates guessed that depression and other mental illnesses resulted from a disturbance in the body's humoral equilibrium. Contemporary research has, in fact, pointed to several biochemical substances that may be responsible for mental symptoms. For example, Meltzer (1976) has shown that serum creatine phosphokinase (CPK) is closely related to a number of psychotic symptoms. It has been found that the higher the serum CPK, the more intense and disturbed the psychotic symptoms, the longer the period of necessary hospitalization, and the more medication required to moderate abnormal behavior.

INJURY Perhaps the most obvious and least debatable cause of mental disorder suggested by the medical model is brain injury. Whatever damages the brain may cause not only physical symptoms but also mental problems. We have already mentioned syphilis. Other infectious diseases, toxic substances such as lead or gasoline, drugs such as alcohol or amphetamines—in fact almost any chemical inhaled or swallowed—can destroy brain tissue.

Brain injury may also occur through accidents, "strokes" (usually a blood vessel breaking within the brain), the degenerative changes of aging, tumors, or surgery. In any of these instances, depending upon the location of the damage and the amount of tissue involved, psychological symptoms may occur. Although the symptoms vary enormously depending upon the injury, frequent signs of abnormality include memory defects, confusion, false beliefs, and emotional instability.

PREDISPOSITION Even the firmest advocates of organicity recognize that in many instances mental disorders seem unrelated to brain damage or any other physical disruption. People who have a neurotic animal phobia clearly seem to have learned to be extraordinarily afraid of cats and dogs. Alcoholics frequently appear to drink just to escape from conflict or guilt and not because they have some neurological disease. In such instances, ardent believers in the medical or organic view of mental illness argue for *predisposition*.

It is agreed that brain injury, or some other biophysical disruption, may not be the immediate cause of all neurosis, psychosis, and personality disorder; stressful experiences, personal conflicts, and maladaptive habits may stimulate a mental illness. But these situations can only trigger disorder in a predisposed, vulnerable individual. The person who becomes mentally ill is genetically, biochemically, or otherwise more than ordinarily susceptible to the stresses of life. Often the immediate cause of mental abnormality can be found in brain damage or other neurological deficiency. When it cannot, we need to look for a predisposing cause hidden in the defective structure or function of body and brain.

Treatment

From the medical point of view, mental illness is the result of injury, biochemical deficiency, or some other physical cause. Emotionally disturbed people are therefore biologically ill and may need to be hospitalized, medicated, or treated with any of the medical techniques that have proved useful for physical illnesses. People with psychological impairments have thus been treated with surgery, vitamins, electric shock, whirlpool baths, carbon dioxide, bed rest, artificial fever, and chemicals. Many of these approaches have proved worthless or even harmful. But **chemotherapy,** that is, psychiatric drugs, seems to offer considerable promise. The following is a typical investigation researching the effectiveness of a drug for treating a major neurotic symptom, anxiety.

Does Trazodone Relieve Anxiety?

Eighty-three patients measured as very high in anxiety on the Hamilton Anxiety Scale and the Hopkins Symptom Check List were administered Trazodone. To rule out the effect of suggestion neither patients nor physicians were informed whether Trazodone or another medication was being employed. Evaluations of anxiety level for each patient were performed five successive times, and results showed that Trazodone was highly effective in significantly reducing anxiety (Wheatley, 1976).

Currently, the major mode of treatment prompted by the medical model is chemotherapy. Many dozens of drugs are available to help relieve the symptoms of schizophrenia, depression, and other psychological disabilities. The medication may not result in a "cure," but it does seem to greatly assist the rehabilitative process, as we will see in later chapters.

PSYCHODYNAMIC MODELS

During the nineteenth century, the once-promising medical model began to seem insufficient. Sigmund Freud (1856–1939) and other pioneering thinkers suggested that mental illness might involve the person's motives. Abnormality might be not the result of physical disease, but the outcome of mental and emotional turmoil. This model of mental disorder emphasizes the importance of *dynamic factors*.

That is, it postulates that both normal and abnormal personality is the result of a conflict of conscious and unconscious memories, drives, and desires.

Sigmund Freud

Freud, who had studied the theory and use of hypnosis in France, brought the method back with him to Vienna. There, along with Josef Breuer (1842–1925), who helped establish Freud in practice, he began to specialize in the treatment of hysterical conversion neurosis (a neurotic disorder in which there are physical symptoms, such as a paralyzed arm, without actual physical damage). Freud's

Figure 2.5. Though much of what he wrote is now disputed, Sigmund Freud was one of those rare geniuses whose insights and observations reshaped our understanding of human motivation and conduct. There are only a very few traditional Freudian psychoanalysts today, but nearly all mental health professionals have been significantly influenced by Freud's viewpoint and outlook. (Photo: National Library of Medicine, Bethesda, Md.)

method was to hypnotize patients and encourage them to talk about or relive the circumstances that led to their symptoms. The result was that often patients virtually exploded with emotion, reexperiencing the guilt and pain that caused their disorder. This outburst of pent-up feeling was called the **catharsis,** from the Greek word meaning purge, since it seemed to cleanse the patient's psyche.

FREUD'S THEORY AND TECHNIQUE Eventually Freud found hypnosis unnecessary and simply encouraged his patients to talk, to say whatever came to mind. Freud called this uninhibited talk **free association** and named both his theory and treatment of dissecting the mind **psychoanalysis.** By listening to what his patients told him, Sigmund Freud was able to create a very complex, almost poetic, theory of human behavior and abnormality. Central to his view was the hypothesis of **unconscious conflict.** Freud believed that most of our actions are the result of a motivational struggle, a dynamic interaction taking place in the mind without our awareness. This unconscious battle pits raw sexual and aggressive drives against morality, practicality, and civilized restraint.

Freud was ridiculed and opposed by the ultraconservative Victorians of his time. Sex was certainly not mentioned in public, and it could not be believed that any well-bred woman, let alone a child, shared the kind of "base animal desires" he described. In actual fact, it was probably because of this prudish denial of biological needs that Freud found hidden sexuality to be so prominent in the disorders he treated.

The complex of biological urges that seek immediate and total gratification Freud called the **id.** Competing with id demands are the practical requirements of reality, the **ego,** and the forces of conscience, the **superego.** The id energies are immediate. "I want that woman, now!" The ego counsels, "Be practical. If you seize her you may be caught. Instead be friendly and invite her to your apartment." The superego admonishes, "Carnal desires are evil. You must wait till you marry." The result

of this unconscious, psychodynamic turmoil is that when you do speak to the woman, you feel fright and guilt and do not know why.

DEFENSE MECHANISMS The unconscious conflict between id demands and superego controls often produces a pervasive feeling of fear, called **anxiety.** The anxiety, in turn, calls into play any of numerous **defense mechanisms,** unconscious techniques intended to help us maintain psychological peace. The foremost defense mechanism is **repression,** an almost complete hiding from oneself of any id or superego needs or conflicts. For example, a husband who believes extramarital sexual feelings to be wrong may eventually experience so much conflict and anxiety about his urges that he represses all sexual stirrings. Ultimately he may become so repressed that he is no longer even aroused by his wife. When his impotence finally brings him to a psychologist, he truthfully says: "I don't know why. I used to have a good sex drive. My wife is good looking. But after we got married I just seemed to gradually lose interest. I just can't understand it."

A single defense mechanism, or a combination, can become so prominent that it dominates the personality and impairs effective functioning. Extreme projection, for example, may result in paranoia; repression and displacement together may become so severe and extensive that the result is schizophrenia.

PSYCHOSEXUAL STAGES Based on what his patients recalled during free association, Freud believed that psychodynamic conflicts began in childhood. The nature and intensity of the id, ego, and superego clash were determined by child-rearing practices and parental attitudes. Supportive, affectionate, and reasonable parents were likely to raise children with few damaging defenses who were well able to handle their own contentious drives. But fathers and/or mothers who were punitive, inhibited, or seductive were likely to raise children who made excessive use of defense mechanisms and were quite likely to manifest mental disorder.

During the growing years, according to psy-

THE DEFENSE MECHANISMS

According to psychoanalysis, the ego develops ways of preventing the expression of impulses it considers dangerous or threatening. The means of guarding against danger, or feeling anxiety, may be conscious or unconscious and are called defense mechanisms.

Repression: Blocking from recognition disturbing thoughts, desires, or experiences. (The mother who hates her children is unable to recognize these feelings in herself.)

Projection: Attributing to others feelings we have ourselves. ("I like the people I work with. The trouble is they all hate me.")

Displacement: Channeling id drives toward a substitute. (Since aggression toward a father may not be possible, a child may become a bully and beat any child who even mildly threatens him.)

Reaction formation: The unconscious anxiety-producing impulse is turned into its opposite on a conscious level. (The person who vigorously crusades against pornography is sometimes unconsciously fascinated by it.)

Denial: or *suppression:* Consciously rejecting feelings, ideas, or experiences that are painful. (The child who refuses to admit he or she made a mistake may be trying both to fool others and himself or herself into believing it did not happen.)

Undoing: Engaging in action that undoes or "disproves" one's true feelings. (The adolescent who feels guilty about sexual experiences becomes an extra-devout churchgoer to prove his or her morality.)

Rationalization: A "sour grapes" explanation to others or oneself. (The student who is afraid of people explains his or her social isolation by the alleged need to study while others are busy with friends and dates.)

Sublimation: Transforming sexual energies into constructive nonsexual activities. (A woman with very few sexual outlets becomes artistically very creative, vigorously painting and sculpting.)

Isolation: Compartmentalizing threatening motives or feelings so that one is not normally aware of them. (Whenever he became significantly intoxicated, one patient became aware of his homosexual feelings and tried to pick up men.)

Fixation: Remaining at a less mature psychosexual level. (The person afraid of the responsibilities of marriage and a job continues to act like an adolescent although he is 38.)

Regression: Returning to an earlier level of functioning. (Under stress, a 26-year-old patient began to cry and whimper, demanding her way, in much the same manner that she did when she was an infant.)

choanalytic theory, the child passes through a number of pivotal physical-emotional stages that can fuel psychodynamic stress. If parents overindulge a particular developmental need, or do the opposite and not sufficiently satisfy it, permanent personality damage may occur. During infancy, for instance, the mouth is supposedly critical for future personality development. Too much sucking, crying, and eating during the oral (mouth) stage could produce a dependent and clinging individual. Too little of these oral satisfactions, however, might result in a tense, mistrustful personality. Parents needed to guide their children carefully through each successive **psychosexual stage**

lest some undesirable personality trait become fixed and ultimately lead to some form of psychopathology (Table 2.1).

Freud theorized that each child passed through several biologically rooted stages before attaining adulthood. If the psychosexual challenges of each stage were not correctly handled by parents, many different abnormalities could result. Eric Erikson (1963), a present-day psychoanalyst, has described similar stages in terms of developmental tasks. At each age the individual has the possibility of assimilating healthy attitudes or unhealthy ones, depending upon the parents and the social environment. But note that, unlike Freud,

TABLE 2.1
DEVELOPMENTAL STAGES

Age	Psychosexual term (Freud)	Task (Erikson)	Possible abnormal outcome
0–1	Oral (mouth activities—sucking, eating)	Trust vs. mistrust	Schizophrenia
1–3	Anal (toilet training experiences)	Independence vs. shame	Anxiety disorders
3–6	Phallic (sexual and aggressive feelings learned)	Initiative vs. guilt	Phobias
6–12	Latency (period of sexual repression)	Identity vs. confusion	Hysterical disorders
12–18	Genital (adult sexual and love feelings)	Intimacy vs. isolation	Sexual disorders
Adulthood		Leadership vs. self-absorption	Neurosis
Senior years		Integrity vs. despair	Depression

Erikson sees personality continuing to evolve throughout life.

Freud's followers

Once Freud opened up the possibility of explaining abnormality in nonmedical terms, dozens of other practitioners and theorists followed suit. Countless modifications and additions to Freud's viewpoint were proposed by his own students, and then by their students. Psychodynamic theorists continue to revise and add to the psychoanalytic model. Describing their work is beyond the scope of this chapter. Here we will look at only one briefly.

ROGERS AND HUMANISM Carl Rogers (1902–   ) has become the focus of a loose grouping of psychologists, the so-called humanistic school, who reject strict psychoanalytic explanations. In the 1940s Rogers first questioned the authoritative role of the therapist, the significance of unconscious motives, and the potency of the id. By the 1960s, humanists had also begun rejecting learning explanations for human behavior and emphasizing instead the self-directing nature of feelings, consciousness, and experience.

For Rogers and humanistic writers such as Abraham Maslow (1971), the critical premises of their approach are these:

1. Human beings are free, aware, and responsible. Unlike animals, their behavior is not totally the result of environment or conditioning. Humans are conscious of alternatives; they can understand their own needs and experiences and analyze their own behavior. They can make choices and must accept the responsibility for their decisions.
2. The way people see their milieu is the way it exists for them. Therapists do not need to dig into supposed unconscious depths to find the truth. Instead, they should try to enter the patients' *phenomenological* world, seeing and experiencing it the way they do.
3. People are born with positive motives to grow, share, love, and develop. Each person, no matter how old or apparently ill, retains at least some striving, some need to *self-actualize* and make the most of his or her potential.
4. Given a favorable psychological climate, meaning warm, supportive parents and the like, each person discovers his or her true self and all his or her creative energies and potentials. But when a person has suffered emotional mistreatment and been denied important life experiences, the self emerges wounded and scarred. The good potential within has been im-

TESTING PSYCHOANALYTIC THEORY

Biological and medical formulations can often be experimentally investigated, but psychoanalysis, and dynamic theories in general, are difficult to evaluate objectively. James Halpern (1977) of the State University of New York at New Paltz devised an intriguing experiment in order to assess the validity of *projection.* Projection, attributing one's own feelings to others, is a defense mechanism central to Freudian thinking and plays a large role in disorders such as paranoia, phobias, and other neuroses.

Halpern tested 188 college students on the Sexual Defensiveness Scale, an instrument designed to tap feelings concerning erotic arousal. Next, all the subjects were handed six photos of people they did not know and asked to pick the portrait they liked least. In the third part of the experiment, half of the subjects, the experimental group, were shown erotic pictures of nude men and women. The other half, the controls, did not see the sexual photos.

According to psychoanalytic theory, in this experiment students who were most defensive about sexual arousal would both deny their own interest and attribute their feelings to others. To ascertain whether this happened, at the end of the investigation Halpern gave all the subjects a list of 20 adjectives and asked them to rate words that described themselves and the portrait photos they had picked at the beginning. Careful statistical analysis of the results clearly revealed that the most defensive students did the most projecting. Students with the higher scores on the Sexual Defensiveness Scale and who were shown the erotic pictures, in comparison to controls and those low on the defensiveness test, described themselves as less "lustful" and attributed the most "lustfulness" to the photo of the person they liked least. Halpern concluded that his findings supported the classical Freudian hypothesis of projection. People who are threatened by their own sexual, aggressive, or other powerful impulses are likely to defend themselves by denying the drives within themselves and attributing their own feelings to others.

---

paired, and what we see instead of a self-actualized person is an individual who is defensive and disordered.

For Rogers, the formation of personality is best described as the development of the self. The self-concept is formed out of experiences with others. Children who grow up in a home filled with **unconditional positive regard,** whose parents unreservedly love and value them, develop a firm, positive self-concept. When parental love is almost always *conditional* ("Mommy doesn't love you when you do that"), a weakened and fragmented self emerges. As children learn that in many respects they are liked "only if," a *condition of worth* emerges. Gradually they adopt these conditions of worth into their self-image: "I am good, I like myself only if I . . . finish my work . . . or do what others tell me to do . . . or act meek and unaggressive . . . or don't expect any love from anyone . . . or remain sexually pure . . . or see the world just like my parents want me to."

A self filled with introjected conditions of worth frequently conflicts with inborn actualizing tendencies to experience all of one's psychological and biological heritage. The result of such conflict is despair, denial, and distortion:

Jon is 34 years old and feels unhappy, lonely, and self-destructive. He grew up believing himself strongly independent, unemotional, and distant. Conflicting with this self-image is his healthy desire to experience love. But whenever a woman became affectionate and Jon tried to respond, he soon became uncomfortable and fearful. Then he would distort the intent of the relationship till he convinced himself that the woman was only "out for a good time" or in some way trying to manipulate or control him. It was necessary for the preservation of his self-image that he deny the genuineness of any offer of mutual caring and love.

PSYCHODYNAMIC THEORIES

Psychoanalysis	Sigmund Freud	Bioenergetics (Orgone therapy)	Wilhelm Reich, Frederick Lowen
Individual psychology	Alfred Adler	Analytic play therapy	Anna Freud, Melaine Klein
Holistic analysis	Karen Horney	Developmental analysis	Eric Erikson
Ego psychology	Heinz Hartmann, Ernst Kris, Rudolf Loewenstein	Existential analysis	Ludwig Binswanger, Medard Boss
Analytical psychology	Carl Jung	Transactional analysis	Eric Berne
Will therapy	Otto Rank	Logotherapy	Victor Frankl
Cultural analysis	Harry Sullivan, Clara Thompson, Erik Fromm		
Primal therapy	Arthur Janov		
Gestalt therapy	Wilhelm Koehler, Fritz Perls		

The psychodynamic model originated by Sigmund Freud has generated many different viewpoints concerning the psychological origin of abnormality. Many of these positions actually differ very little from one another in terms of theoretical concepts, but they do use different vocabularies.

The more life experiences need to be distorted to conform to an unhealthy self-image, the more likely the symptoms of mental disorder such as anxiety, guilt, confusion, and the physical signs of tension. When even such neurotic devices fail to maintain a seemingly coherent self-image, total personality disintegration, or psychosis, may be the result.

Diagnosis

Those who adhere to a psychodynamic model of mental disorder frequently disagree with one another. Their theoretical explanations, terms, and definitions often diverge in so many respects that it is difficult to summarize where they all stand on diagnosis, treatment, and causes. In terms of diagnosis, for example, positions range from acceptance of the current symptom-based nomenclature to rejection of all labels. Freudians and their allies frequently use the present classification of mental disorder. In contrast, Rogers and the humanists reject terms like schizophrenia and

neurosis. They believe such designations unfairly prejudice therapists and handicap a person's self-perception and potential. As a general rule, it may be closest to the truth to say that all the dynamic approaches question the medical diagnostic model, although no one has developed an alternative descriptive system that has been widely adopted.

Causes

The dynamic position emphasizes childhood and family experiences as critical to mental health and disorder. The child who is raised in a supporting, reasonable milieu is likely to emerge psychologically intact. But the child subjected to frustrations, domination, conflicts, and other sources of parental and environmental stress is bound to be psychologically disordered. Each psychodynamic school tends to emphasize its own favorite source of pathology, but generally the following family experiences are held to be particularly destructive to mental health:

DEPRIVATION: Denial of normal paternal warmth and affection either because of rejecting parents or impersonal care in an institution

INCONSISTENCY: Parents who are unpredictably lax or strict or confusingly ambivalent

SIBLING RIVALRY: Competition between children for parental favor or status

PUNITIVENESS: Frequent physical or psychological punishment or serious abuse

DEMAND: Unrealistically high family expectations for performance, ranging from toilet training to learning to read

SEDUCTION: Psychological, emotional, or actual parental seduction of the child

BIOLOGICAL FRUSTRATION: Insensitive or inhibitory parental responses to physical needs

such as food, bodily contact, and sexual pleasure

ROLE CONFUSION: Family insistence that child act a role other than that appropriate to sex, age, or ability

PARENTAL MANIPULATION: Forcing the child to take sides between father and mother or attempting to control the child's feelings and affections

JEALOUSY: Parental competition with child, rivalry and power struggle

Most of the evidence for the dynamic models comes from clinical practice. Freud, Rogers, and other psychodynamicists often verify their claims concerning the causative role of family interactions by the work they have done with

Figure 2.6. Critics of Freud contend that even if his theories were correct for his patients, they would not be applicable today. Freud's observations were based on early twentieth-century, middle-class Western European families. Generalizations based on such family interactions may not adequately describe current parent-child relations. (Photo: Scribe)

PSYCHODYNAMIC AGREEMENTS

I. At least some important behavior is the result of motives and conflicts of which the person him or herself may not be aware.

II. The early childhood years and its parental and environmental interactions have a vital influence on personality and mental health.

III. Mental health problems typically involve anxiety and repression and other defensive adjustment techniques.

IV. Encouraging patients to talk freely and reveal themselves, and establishing a warm, helping relationship with the therapist, are the essentials of psychodynamic treatment.

The psychodynamic view is marked by many important disagreements. Yet there are several major areas of concordance. Nearly all psychodynamic theorists would generally affirm the statements above.

---

patients. But there is also some research evidence. One of the best, though older, studies was an investigation of 379 mothers conducted through the Harvard University Human Development Laboratory. After careful analysis of parent and child interactions and variables like punishment, acceptance, negativism, and aggression, the importance of the mother's attitude clearly stood out. It was discovered that mothers who are emotionally warm and loving produce children who are highly motivated, more obedient, and generally better adjusted. Maternal coldness is associated with feeding problems, bed-wetting, fighting, and emotional instability (Sears, Maccoby, and Levin, 1957).

More contemporary evidence has come from a survey by Rothchild and Wolf (1976), reported in their book, *The Children of the Counterculture*. The authors traveled throughout the United States, visiting communes where young adults were pursuing alternative life styles. The communities included stable groups, religious establishments, and those almost totally without any structure. There were even a few communes where there were virtually no restrictions of any kind; children did not wash or attend school or had sexual relations with adults and relatives. In addition, the degree of affection and respect accorded children covered the entire range of emotions. In some communes, children were loved, valued, and respected. In many others, they were considered a nuisance, subjected to severe discipline, forced to work in the fields under abusive conditions, or totally neglected. As might be expected, the psychological well-being of the children was closely correlated with their treatment. A critical reading of the book suggests that most of the abused and maltreated children may be well along the path toward developing mental disorder.

Evidence for the psychodynamic view sometimes comes from animal studies. For over a decade, Ruppenthal and colleagues (1976) have been investigating the maternal behavior of motherless mothers. When female rhesus monkeys raised without mothers themselves become mothers, their behavior is typically inadequate. Does the negligent and sometimes even hostile behavior of such monkey mothers affect their infants? There is little doubt. The rhesus children cry, cringe, experience digestive upsets, and act frightened and withdrawn. The monkey youngsters raised by rejecting and abusive mothers exhibit symptoms that in humans we might call anxiety, confusion, and misery, and even seem to escape into fantasy.

Treatment

Perhaps the strongest contribution of the psychodynamic models are their treatment techniques. From Freud on, all the psychodynamic approaches have emphasized the necessity for each patient to talk freely and establish a positive relationship with the therapist. But techniques do vary. Freudian psychoanalysts do a great deal of questioning of their patients to dig out unconscious meanings. The Rogerian approach is *client-centered* and deemphasizes the role of the therapist as interrogator or expert. Patients are encouraged to lead the way; the therapist often just lets the patient talk and express feelings while he or she listens attentively. Bioenergetic practitioners frequently require their patients to do vigorous exercises. Primal and Gestalt adherents may exert a great deal of psychological pressure on their patients in order to get them to "open up." But whatever the technique, dynamically oriented psychotherapy has become such a universal tool that sooner or later almost every person with emotional problems will have at least a brief exposure to it. We will discuss these techniques in greater detail in the final chapter.

SUMMARY

Over the centuries, different viewpoints concerning mental illness have developed. The medical model suggests that abnormality is the result of brain pathology. Diagnosis is established on the basis of syndromes, symptoms that regularly occur together. The current symptom descriptions and definitions of mental disorders are brought together in the APA's *Diagnostic and Statistical Manual* (DSM). Though the medical view of abnormal behavior and diagnosis is not universally accepted, nearly all mental health professionals find the DSM nomenclature useful.

The medical view postulates the causes of mental impairments to be genetic, biochemical, the result of brain injury, or of biological vulnerability or predisposition. Since emo-

tional disturbances are seen as physical problems, the appropriate treatments are believed to be hospitalization, medication, and other medical remedies.

The psychodynamic model was originated by Freud, who believed that mental illness was largely the result of unconscious conflicts which result in anxiety and emotional defenses. Freud believed the conflict began in earliest childhood and pitted raw biological urges against social restraints. Following Freud, many other psychodynamic theorists have revised the original psychoanalytic view, but all still maintain the importance of conflicting needs and drives as central to mental illness. Carl Rogers, for example, has rejected psychoanalytic postulates concerning unconscious conflicts and the like, but still affirms the importance of the childhood years. He and other humanistic psychologists believe people have positive motives to grow and self-actualize and to make responsible, conscious choices.

Many psychoanalysts and psychodynamic therapists accept the current diagnostic system, but humanistic psychologists often object to any sort of labels. Causally, the dynamic model postulates satisfactory childhood and family experiences as critical to mental health. Since there are many different dynamic viewpoints, there are also differences in the approaches to treatment. Nearly all agree, however, that encouraging patients to reveal themselves and establishing a warm, helping relationship with the therapist are the essentials of treatment.

The Behavioral and Social Models

Almost contemporary with Freud's development of psychoanalysis, another psychological model emerged that emphasized the role of *learning*. This position suggested that instead of trying to work with alleged mental conflicts hidden in the mind, our attempt to understand mental disorder should focus on *observable behavior*. If somone is abnormal, the explanation lies neither in the biology of the brain nor in the unconscious. Mental disorder is simply the result of faulty learning.

A fourth explanatory outlook can be called the *social model*. Since the last century, many psychologists and social scientists have remarked on the apparent tendency for all sorts of abnormal behaviors to be correlated with poverty, racism, cultural change, and other social stresses. Two decades ago these suspicions were given impressive support by a careful investigation of mental illness in the core area of a city. The findings clearly seemed to sup-

port the position of the social model that mental illness is in large part a reflection of social pathology (Srole et al., 1962).

In this chapter we will examine the behavioral and social models and also take note of how the different explanations overlap and contribute to our total understanding of mental illness.

BEHAVIORAL MODELS

At about the same time that Freud was advancing psychoanalysis in Europe, John B. Watson was proclaiming **behaviorism** in the United States. Watson, a Johns Hopkins University professor, asserted that the mind and its alleged hidden drives and conflicts cannot be scientifically studied. Psychoanalytic concepts such as the id or repression are nothing more than imaginative guesses, inferences about activity that cannot be directly measured or evaluated. The proper subject of study for psychologists is **behavior.** What people actually do, that is, their *responses,* can be measured and recorded. Further, the visible conditions that lead to the response, the *stimuli,* can also be objectively described. Watson's rejection of speculative explanations and demand for positive, scientific rigor were given substance by two important discoveries about learning. The announcements of the principal ways in which organisms learn were based on solid laboratory investigations in which both stimuli and responses were clearly visible.

In his Russian laboratory, while exploring the digestive processes in dogs, physiologist Ivan Pavlov stumbled upon **respondent conditioning.** Pavlov had noticed that dogs not only salivate when food is actually given them, but also tend to salivate when any activity associated with the food occurs all by itself. In order to test this, he rang a bell just prior to giving food. After only a few pairings of bell and food, dogs salivated at the sound of the bell alone. Their food response, salivation, had been conditioned to a neutral stimulus, the ringing bell. Soon it was found that almost any "natural" response such as an eye blink or withdrawing a paw could be conditioned to nearly any stimulus, like a musical tone, seeing the color red, or even a voice command.

While Russian dogs were being conditioned, American cats were being required to find their way out of a latched box. E. L. Thorndike reported that in his laboratory cats confined to boxes scratched, bit, and clawed in attempts to get out. Finally, by accident they found a loop of string, pulled it, and were free. On subsequent confinements, the unsuccessful responses slowly dropped out. Eventually, as soon as the cat was put in the box it made the right response; it pulled the string and was freed. Starting with these data, Thorndike continued his investigations and announced the **law of effect,** which states that successful responses are learned. If pulling a string gets a cat out of a box, that act is repeated and learned. Or if a temper tantrum gets a child a toy, it is similarly likely to be learned. Today we call the phenomenon Thorndike described as the law of effect, **operant conditioning.**

Right from the beginning, attempts were made to apply the new scientific discoveries about learning to psychopathology. Pavlov himself had noticed that conditioned dogs could be made to exhibit "neurotic" symptoms. For example, animals were conditioned to salivate when a drawing of an ellipse was shown. They were taught *not* to salivate when a drawing of a circle was placed in view. Once the animal had learned both responses well, the ellipse was gradually rounded, with each subsequent presentation looking more and more like a circle. Finally, a point was reached when the dog could apparently no longer distinguish between an ellipse (salivate) or a circle (do not salivate). As the discrimination became more difficult, the once cooperative dog acted confused, barked, whined, and bit the experimental apparatus. The animal, once peaceful and adjusted, had begun to behave abnormally.

Watson also used the early knowledge of respondent conditioning to simulate phobia. In one experiment, an infant previously fond of animals was made fearful of a white rat. Whenever the child reached out to play with the animal, an experimenter behind the infant banged vigorously on a steel bar (Figure 3.1). After only a few such associations, the child cried and acted disturbed whenever the animal was presented. Even more revealing, the child **generalized** his response. He became fearful whenever he was near other white and furry animals, or any stimuli closely resembling the original one.

Several other attempts to use learning experiments as a means to understand abnormal behavior followed. One investigator taught cats to open a box and expect a food reward inside. After learning to open the box, an electric shock was substituted for the anticipated food. Hungry cats reacted to this conflict (to open or not to open) by evidencing many of the symptoms of what in humans we call anxiety. Another set of experiments revealed that animals which had learned to escape from shock and other noxious stimuli but were then forcibly kept in the stressful environment be-

Figure 3.1. This child was conditioned to be afraid of a white rat. Every time the animal was presented, the experimenter banged vigorously on the steel bar. For behaviorists, this experiment demonstrates that fear, anxiety, and related mental symptoms are learned—and can therefore be unlearned.

came dazed, apathetic, and sometimes violent. Subjected to stimuli that were unavoidably painful, the responses of many animals resembled that seen in psychotic human beings.

Despite these promising beginnings, early in this century the investigation of learning and behavior became largely an academic enterprise. Attempts to tie in human conduct, to demonstrate or explain how both normal and abnormal behavior is learned, were few. Watson himself left psychology, and for several decades behaviorism faded. The psychodynamic and medical views became dominant. Learning explained how animals behaved and possibly accounted for some human conduct, but it was not believed to be relevant to psychopathology. In fact, so prominent was the psychodynamic view that psychologists using be-

havioral concepts to explain mental disorder usually pointed out that they were only translating accepted psychodynamic concepts into the language of learning theory. Thus, in 1950 Dollard and Miller, in *Personality and Psychotherapy*, carefully explained how such psychoanalytic concepts as repression could be explained as a type of response extinction.

The current learning or behavior models to explain mental disorders are probably in greatest debt to Burrhus F. Skinner (1904–). Taking up Watson's decades-old demand for concentrating on the observable, Skinner and his allies have rejected most dynamic and medical concepts. For them, mental disorders are specific learned behaviors. In their view, DSM III is an imprecise collection of generalizations. If diagnosis is indeed neces-

Figure 3.2. B. F. Skinner, a Harvard University professor of psychology, is usually credited with being the founder of modern behaviorism. In hundreds of articles and books, Skinner has called for the objective understanding of learned human behavior as the basis for all psychological explanations and treatment. (Photo: Therese Statz)

sary, much more behavior-based and specific descriptions are needed.

Diagnosis

For most learning therapists, diagnosis simply means specifying the exact responses to be altered. From this perspective it matters little whether we are talking about someone who might be labeled manic or mentally retarded. All behaviors, except those physically determined by the capacity of the organism, are learned and can thus be unlearned. To cite an example, when a patient diagnosed as an anxiety neurotic is referred to a behavior therapist, a procedure different from that used by most psychotherapists is followed.

For psychotherapists, the diagnosis of anxiety neurotic immediately suggests medication or counseling sessions talking over the patient's feelings. The behavior therapist, in contrast, needs precise definitions of behavior. He or she wants to know from the patient what behaviors the person finds distressing. Does he have difficulty falling asleep? Does he feel sweaty and his heart pound? Exactly what does he mean when he states he feels frightened most of the time? The symptoms complaints are only the beginning. The learning therapist wants many more questions answered, such as: What are the present reinforcers for the behaviors? Why do they continue? What are the antecedent cues and might there be some internal mediators such as needs or motivations? What past learning has contributed to the present behavioral symptoms or complaints? Finally, after determining as best he or she can just what responses are to be reduced or changed, the therapist, together with the patient, defines reasonable targets. The aim is not to "cure" an "anxiety neurotic" but to work toward specific behavioral goals.

Cause and treatment

From the learning-behavior viewpoint, there is only one explanation for abnormality: All behavior is learned. It follows, therefore, that the same principles of learning responsible for the acquisition of undesired responses can become treatment techniques when they are directed at modifying behaviors. Although learning is both explanation and therapy, there are several different learning approaches.

COUNTERCONDITIONING For Joseph Wolpe (1973) and H. J. Eysenck (1976), behavior is in good part the result of classical conditioning. In fact, human disorders are very similar to experimentally demonstrated animal neuroses. Symptoms, for example, are usually acquired by the pairing of particular responses

THE VOCABULARY OF LEARNING

Respondent or classical conditioning: By pairing any neutral stimulus with a behavioral response, the neutral stimulus alone may eventually evoke the response. In a typical demonstration, a buzzer may be sounded just before a subject's hand gets a mild electric shock. The shock causes hand withdrawal, perspiration, and other signs of discomfort. After several pairings with buzzer–shock, the buzzer alone will produce nearly the same response previously elicited only by the shock.

Operant conditioning: A rat imprisoned in a box attempts, by trial and error, to release itself. Eventually it happens upon a lever that opens the door. The response that is successful in reaching some goal, or satisfying some drive, tends to be repeated and learned. In operant conditioning the response learned is that which is selected, consciously or accidentally, by the subject to help him or her reach an objective. Much of human learning is operant: when in an unfamiliar automobile, for example, we fumble with switches and buttons till one of them starts the wipers.

Reinforcement: A response or behavior that is reinforced, or put in a very loose and general way, rewarded, persists and is learned. Often the reinforcer is an obvious one such as a pellet of food for a dog when he sits up. At other times, the "reward" may be subtle and complex, such as the reinforcers involved in learning neurotic symptoms.

Extinction: Behavior that is no longer reinforced gradually disappears. A dog taught to sit up and never again reinforced for it will gradually no longer perform. Many responses or behaviors can be eliminated simply by finding the reinforcers, which may be hidden, and stopping them.

Generalization: A response taught to a specific stimulus may spread to similar stimuli. A child who burns his finger on a hot stove may become fearful of other appliances that are tall, enameled, and white, like the stove.

---

with anxiety-provoking conditions. A punitive mother may condition fear and withdrawal responses in her children. Like other well-conditioned responses, these behaviors can persist and generalize so that when these children become adults, they find themselves isolated and afraid of people. But since conditioning results in the learning of symptoms, **counterconditioning** can be used to alleviate distressing behaviors. The infant who was made fearful of a white rat was subsequently made unfearful by pairing the rat with a pleasant response. While the child was eating, feeling pleased and relaxed, the feared object was presented at a distance great enough for the child to tolerate it. Gradually, day by day, the rat was moved closer till the child was able to respond to it without fear.

Abnormal behaviors can also be counterconditioned. For instance, a patient may be anxious and impotent in the presence of sexual cues. In treatment, progressively more intense sexual fantasies of the feared situation can be coupled with relaxation until the impotence is eliminated. This procedure, a form of classical conditioning, is called **reciprocal inhibition** and is a widely used treatment technique devised by Wolpe.

MODELING For **social learning** theorists, a great deal of distinctively human behavior is acquired by **modeling.** Children observing adults or even television cartoon characters behaving aggressively themselves become more aggressive. Originally, some imitative behavior may have been reinforced by an indication of adult approval such as a smile or a nod. Eventually, however, modeling responses may generalize so that a great deal of adult behavior serves as a stimulus for similar responses in children. To bolster this contention, many investigators have noted the frequency with which hypochondriacal children come from homes preoccupied with sickness, addicts from alcoholic backgrounds, and psychotics from parents who were themselves disoriented and delusional (Mischel, 1973).

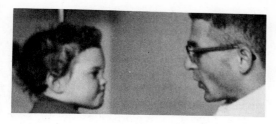

Figure 3.3. According to social learning theory, a good deal of behavior is the result of modeling, of children imitating the behavior of adults. Although such modeling can result in learning important skills, it can also be responsible for the acquisition of abnormal behavior. (Photo: Scribe)

OPERANT CONDITIONING Many behavior therapists insist on a strict operant conditioning or Skinnerian approach to treatment. For them, behavior is learned by reinforcement and extinguished through nonreinforcement. It is agreed that many behaviors do not seem to be the direct product of reinforcement. But, it is argued, this may well be because we do not always examine the situation carefully enough to find the reinforcers. The case of Rodney is an example.

Rodney, a 14-year-old boy, had a serious weight problem. Medical and psychological examiners both concluded that obesity was simply the result of eating too much. A careful study of Rodney's habits showed that at breakfast and in school his diet was conventional. But at home, during dinner, he ate enormous amounts, justifying his eating by saying he was ravenously hungry. Observation of the household routine showed that this was the only time Rodney, a lonely and inhibited child, had both parents present in a warm, rewarding situation. The longer Rodney was able to keep his parents at the table, the more his needs for affection and companionship were reinforced. In more exact behavioral terms, Rodney's eating was reinforced by parental smiles, touches and attention.

SOME MODIFICATIONS Skinnerian learning theorists represent an extreme; they insist on

the primacy of reinforcement and reject all notions about drives, motives, feelings, and other internal states. But many learning theorists now include such variables and recognize their importance in the formation of abnormal symptoms and in treatment. Bandura (1969), in particular, has broadened the definition of social learning theory to include motivation and thinking in the acquisition of behavior. While even complex responses, such as modeling, are often explicable as operant or classical conditioning, there is a third possibility:

Thought processes, emotions, expectations and many other feelings often play a critical role in learning. These internal events, or mediators, become *personal hypotheses* about the principles governing the occurrence of rewards and punishments. They are developed and tested on the basis of differential consequences accompanying the corresponding actions. "In this conceptual scheme man is neither an internally impelled system nor a passive reactor to external stimulation." Psychological functioning involves an interaction between behavior and its controlling environment. The type of behavior that a person exhibits partly determines his environmental cues and alternatives, and these, in turn, influence his behavior. (p. 63)

How such internal mediators may act as reinforcers can be illustrated by considering our own self-evaluative tendencies. Humans frequently stand aside to criticize themselves. When they believe they have done something good, they pat themselves on the back. When they feel they have been bad, they reprimand themselves. This kind of mental self-reinforcement cannot be laid out in immediately visible stimulus-response terms. Nevertheless, it appears to be an important determinant of behavior. Through self-reinforcement, some people are kept away from mathematics or from the opposite sex. Their anticipation of failure is such that when they get close to mathematics or someone of the opposite sex, they tell themselves they are doing badly and failing. Almost inevitably, their prophecy is self-fulfilling. One recovered paranoid patient described his self-reinforcement as follows: "I was sure everybody else hated me. Whenever anyone said anything to me at all, my mind interpreted it as something hateful. Whatever anyone did or said, I just always followed it in my mind by saying, 'see you're no good, they hate you.' " This kind of self-reinforcement may account for the persistence of several symptoms of mental illness otherwise difficult to explain in terms of classical or operant conditioning.

THE SOCIAL MODEL

Until well into the twentieth century, psychiatrists were called *alienists*. The term derived from the belief that mental patients stood apart, were in violation of cultural norms, alienated from the standards of society. After World War I, the social view of mental disorder took the next step. Not only was mental illness defined in terms of alienation, but society itself was held responsible for abnormality. Proponents of the new medical discipline, called **social psychiatry,** suggested the idea that the definition, cause, and cure for mental illness lies in society.

Support for the social psychiatry position came from many directions. Anthropologists like Malinowski, in his *Sex and Repression in Savage Society* (1927), pointed out that definitions of abnormality are the product of each individual culture. Unlike physical disease, what is considered mentally sick in New York may be thought of as normal in New Guinea. Malinowski particularly pointed to the lack of universal acceptance of Freudian notions like sexual repression. In many of the island societies in the Pacific investigated by anthropologists, abnormal symptoms common among Europeans and Americans (like paranoia and neurosis) are quite infrequent. The early twentieth-century middle-class Viennese family structure Freud was familiar with could not be counted on to provide a model of mental health and illness for all human beings throughout the world.

Additional support for social models came from **epidemiology,** studies of the distribu-

tion of mental illness. Since the end of the nineteenth century, physicians have noted the high frequency of psychiatric disorder among poorer people. As early as 1885, Edward Jarvis had pointed out that both "insanity" and "idiocy" were far more common in recent Irish immigrants to Boston than among native populations. In fact, the more carefully the various social and economic groups were studied, the more apparent it became that poverty and discrimination actually gave birth to abnormal behavior. Mental illness seemed as much an outcome of the way human beings live together in groups as politics and government.

Diagnosis

The traditional social view of mental illness is that most behaviors which deviate from cultural norms are either criminal or mental problems. Scheff (1970), in a critical look at our labeling tendencies, has pointed out that the social model calls mentally abnormal a wide number of behaviors relegated to a *residual category.* All societies give their members a set of norms governing conduct. Offenses against these norms have conventional names; for example, an offense against property is called theft. But the public order is also made up of countless unnamed understandings, unspoken norms for acceptable conduct. For instance, during a conversation one looks at another's eyes or mouth, and not at his or her ear. Or during a dinner party one chats pleasantly rather than humming quietly to oneself. Offenses against these unnamed understandings are usually lumped together:

If people reacting to an offense exhaust the conventional categories that might define it (e.g. theft, prostitution or drunkenness) yet are certain that an offense has been committed, they may resort to this residual category. In earlier societies the residual category was witchcraft . . . or possession by the devil; today it is mental illness. The symptoms of mental illness are, therefore, violations of residual rules. (p. 16)

CULTURAL DEFINITIONS OF MENTAL ILLNESS

Many mental disorders, such as schizophrenia, depression, and severe mental retardation are found in all nations of the world. But some of the diagnostic labels used in our own culture are not found in other societies. Our conceptions of neurosis, alcoholism, drug abuse, and some sexual deviations are not universally shared. On the other hand, a few forms of mental disorder described by other societies are not identified in our own. In every country people express their symptoms according to the physical and social conditions of their individual lives. (Source: *A Psychiatric Glossary*, APA, 1975)

Disorder	Culture	Symptoms	Disorder	Culture	Symptoms
amok	Malaya	Screaming, violent, homicidal attack on people and objects	piblokto	Eskimo	Attacks of screaming, crying, and running naked through the snow; suicidal or homicidal tendencies
koro	China, Southeast Asia	Fear of death and/or retraction of penis into abdomen; continual anxiety	susto	Latin America	Anxiety and panic due to fear of the evil eye, magic, or possession by evil spirits
latah	Southeast Asia	Extreme suggestibility, disorganized thinking and behavior; extreme automatic obedience	windigo	Canadian Indians	Fear of being possessed or devoured by a cannibalistic

Our current diagnostic nomenclature, standardized in DSM III, is heavily influenced by the social model. Although many of our diagnostic labels are distinctively medical, several clearly show the imprint of cultural standards. What we define as anxiety disorder other social groups may not categorize as a unitary disability at all. The Eskimos, for example, who have many different words for mental illness, have a term for psychosis, *nuthkavihak*, but nothing for what we call anxiety disorders. And many African countries like Senegal recognize the individual symptoms of anxiety but do not think of them as together constituting a single disorder (Beiser et al., 1976).

The area in which the social model has most clearly influenced current psychiatric nomenclature is in the category called personality disorders. In these "illnesses," the symptoms are much more social than psychological. Personality disorders such as addiction, gambling, and sexual deviations describe behaviors that society considers harmful, disruptive, or otherwise culturally counterproductive. The person who gambles does not contribute useful work to society and by failing to support his family forces the group to take up the responsibility. The individual who is a sexual fetishist may be harmless, but he or she offends religious and moral standards and threatens the culture's ability to prescribe appropriate sexual conduct.

Those who uphold social models of mental illness have difficulty agreeing on whether the unconventional behaviors seen in personality disorders are criminal or sick. In our own past, alcohol abuse was considered a criminal offense. The local alcoholic was tolerated up to a point, but after continued bouts of intoxication he or she was likely to be put in jail. Today social viewpoints have changed; alcoholism is treated as a "sickness," with hospital confinement rather than jail the likely outcome. But the social model still is not unanimous about whether several other behaviors are illnesses or crimes. There is great inconsistency, for example, in our treatment of homosexuality and drug addiction. Until quite recently, homosexuality was listed in the DSM as a mental illness. Now it is no longer invariably considered a psychiatric disorder, but it is still viewed as criminal in many communities. Homosexual activities, even by consenting adults in the privacy of their homes, may be punished by lengthy jail terms, a ruling upheld by the Supreme Court in 1976. Social views regarding drug usage are just as conflicting. The social model now considers heroin addiction both a mental disorder (it is listed in the DSM) and a criminal violation. At the same time, many psychiatric critics see it as neither and call for an end to legal and social prohibition.

Causes and treatment

The social model emphasizes the causative role of society. Most abnormal behaviors, like normal activities, are held to be the result of the culture in which each person lives. As long as the milieu is supportive and frustrations are minimal, the individual is likely to be mentally well. When conditions are unfavorable or erratic, deviant responses occur. A few of the factors that may lead to mental illness include change, urbanization, and social class.

CHANGE It has long been observed that people who undergo important changes in their lives are likely to get sick. One of the pioneers of American psychiatry, Adolf Meyer, early in this century began keeping "life charts" on his patients and thus was able to correlate important life changes with symptoms of both psychological and physical illness. More recently, Holmes and Holmes (1974), applying the life chart idea, combed through more than 5,000 case histories to construct an adjustment scale listing the most to least disruptive life changes. The scale shows, for example, that losing a spouse by death requires the greatest amount of readjustment, and is therefore assigned a value of 100 (Table 3.1). The investigators next correlated the readjustment challenge with sickness and found that

Figure 3.4. The social model suggests that personality and mental disorder is in large part the result of societal and cultural practices. In India, grandparents participate in raising children. This effects the adjustment of the child and gives older people an important social role, contributes to their feeling of usefulness and their mental health. (Photo: Scribe)

the more change a person undergoes, the greater the likelihood of illness. For example, a person who had accumulated over 200 points in one year had a fifty-fifty chance of illness. Someone with over 300 points was practically 100 percent certain to become sick. At the opposite end, people whose lives were stable, who accumulated fewer than 20 or 30 points, had a much better than average chance of remaining physically and psychologically healthy.

If change is related to health for individuals, does it have implications for society as a whole? One of the more persistent notions is that since today we live in a rapidly changing environment, there is also more mental illness. A generation ago marriages lasted a lifetime and few people ever lived in more than one or two different places. Since 1900, divorce rates have doubled, and people now change jobs or residence well over a dozen times dur-

TABLE 3.1
THE READJUSTMENT SCALE

Event	Scale Value
Death of spouse	100
Divorce	73
Marital separation	65
Jail term	63
Marriage	50
Fired at work	47
Retirement	45
Pregnancy	40
Death of a close friend	37
Mortgage over $10,000	31
Son or daughter leaving home	29
Beginning or ending school	26
Trouble with boss	23
Change in social activities	18
Vacation	13
Christmas	12

Holmes and Holmes, 1974.

ing life. But the frequency of mental health problems does not seem to have increased. In a careful review of hospital records in Massachusetts from 1840 to 1940, Goldhamer and Marshall (1953) found little actual increase in mental illness. When such biases as public attitudes, improved facilities, and the like were taken into consideration, there was no real climb in the apparent incidence of mental illness in over a hundred years.

A more revealing study involving an entire community was conducted among the Hutterites (Eaton and Weil, 1955). The Hutterites are a strict religious group of over 8,000 people. They have lived a stable commune-type existence for a century in north-central United States and Canada and earn their livelihood through farming. Rarely if ever do Hutterites leave the community, and divorce is virtually nonexistent. All Hutterites work hard and are self-disciplined; if anyone is incapacitated or handicapped, he or she is taken care of by the community. Social observers have noted that the Hutterites are almost a model of "cradle

to grave" security and stability. The Hutterite record of mental illness shows that this highly stable society has about the same amount of psychosis and organic and psychophysiologic disorder as the rest of the population. But there is a marked difference in personality disorders. Addiction, antisocial behavior, and the like, disorders common in our own society, are virtually nonexistent among the Hutterites. In sum, the evidence suggests that on an individual basis, change may lead to health problems. In terms of a broader social outlook, many mental illnesses have apparently not shown a true increase. Whether or not personality disorders have increased in reality, or by definition, is a question open to further exploration.

URBANIZATION More than half of the population of the United States now lives in cities. In some nations such as Great Britain and The Netherlands, the proportion may climb to as much as 80 percent. Not all cities are alike, and many provide their residents comfort and security. But more typically, city living means crowding, poverty, discrimination, and crime. Reasoning that these stresses were most likely to be encountered in the heart of a huge metropolis, Srole et al. (1962) interviewed over 1,600 residents in midtown New York City. Each subject was individually evaluated. The findings revealed extensive psychopathology. Up to one-fourth of all those surveyed had at least some serious symptoms of mental illness. Further, the more stressful and disadvantaged the person's life, the greater the proportion of abnormality. Thus, emotional well-being was worst and impairment greatest for those who were oldest, had the least money, or held the poorest jobs.

In a comprehensive review of ten studies of urban-rural psychopathology, Dohrenwend and Dohrenwend (1974) found that, just as the Hutterite data partly revealed, the higher city pathology focused on personality disorders. Investigators in North America, Africa, Asia, and Europe found the incidence of schizophrenia and manic-depressive psychosis nearly the same for urban and rural areas. But five out of six studies revealed neurosis and personal-

Figure 3.5. Several studies have shown that the rate of mental disorder is often far higher in large cities than in suburban or rural areas. Many believe the disproportionate amount of urban psychiatric disorder is due to the congestion, isolation, fear, and competition of city living. (Photo: Scribe)

ity disorder to be much higher in the city. The reviewers conclude:

On the basis of this evidence—and it is the best that we have available—the most reasonable hypothesis appears to be that total rates of psychopathology are somewhat higher in urban than in rural areas, due at least in part to an excess of neurosis and personality disorder in the urban areas. Whether these differences are a function of harsher stress on residents of urban settings, however, is quite another matter. (p. 435)

SOCIAL CLASS   Though the epidemiological data are not without contradictions, for over five decades studies have shown that people in the lower socioeconomic classes have more of nearly every kind of mental disorder. In contrast with middle- and upper-class adults, those from lower-class backgrounds are more likely to be admitted to a mental hospital and stay longer; have a higher frequency of schizophrenia and depression; have a higher pro-

portion of mentally retarded children; and have a disproportionately high rate of alcoholism, addiction, and social-legal problems (Wechsler et al., 1970).

The explanations for this phenomenon range from genetic to economic. It may be that the least capable members of society drift down the socioeconomic scale and then pass both their physical and their social disabilities on to their children. Srole and the other authors of the midtown New York City study believe, however, that psychosocial factors are much more likely to explain the high degree of psychopathology. They particularly single out childhood deprivation as a likely culprit. Children of poor parents who are busy struggling for survival are likely to be deprived of adequate food, attention, housing, education, and family love and care. The outcome is that they grow up intellectually and psychologically handicapped, much more vulnerable to mental health problems than middle-class children. Other support for a psychosocial explanation for the greater frequency of mental

STRESS, RESOURCES, AND SYMPTOMS

By taking a little liberty with the more orthodox versions of the medical, psychodynamic, and other models, we can conceptualize symptoms as the result of stress balanced against individual resources. So long as his or her physical and psychological resources are sufficient to cope with whatever stresses he or she is exposed to, the person continues to function well. But when stresses outweigh resources, signs of mental disorder may result. At this stage we can only make educated guesses at the exact processes involved, but what may be happening seems to follow this schematic sequence:

Stress: Hans Selye, (1975) has outlined a physiological explanation of stress that can also serve as a psychological model.

1. The alarm stage. The stressor alerts the organism, resulting in biological and psychological changes enabling the individual to cope with the stressor.
2. The resistance stage. The person defends against the stressor and thus restores psychological and physical equilibrium.

3. The exhaustion stage. Prolonged exposure to the stressor and inadequate resistance eventually depletes the person's resources causing a complete "breakdown" in resistance.

Stressor and resource: Stressors and resources could be symbolized as weights on a scale. So long as resources outweigh stressors, relatively good mental health continues.

Symptoms: Symptoms have a dual origin. First, like anxiety, they are the initial response to stress, alerting the person that something is wrong. Second, they are attempts to cope with, to resist, the stress, however poor and inadequate they may be (for example, alcohol abuse). When stress is serious but does not totally outweigh resources, only the initial and milder symptoms appear, such as phobias, headaches, and rationalization. If stress becomes more severe or all resources and responses are exhausted, more serious symptoms may emerge, such as depression and loss of contact with reality.

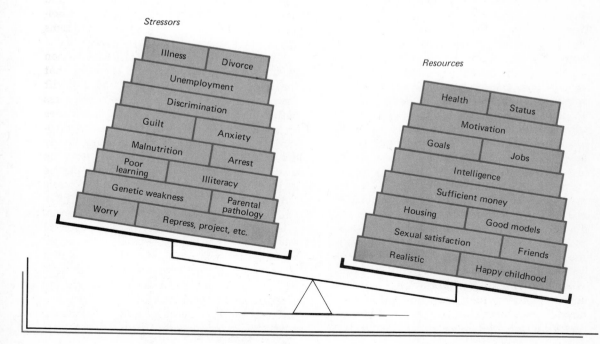

49

health problems among lower-class subjects has come from a study of over 300 women living in London, England (Brown et al., 1976). In this investigation, women from different classes but similar in ethnic background, family status, and age, living in the same area of London, were compared for psychiatric problems. One-fourth of the lower-class women, compared to only one-tenth of the middle-class subjects, were suffering from some sort of chronic psychological disability. Depression was most common and seemed related to a number of distinctive socioeconomic factors, including unemployment, a large number of dependent children, and serious housing problems.

There is usually a constellation of possible reasons for the high rate of nearly all mental illnesses among lower-class people. From the perspective of the social model, the most likely explanation is the most obvious. People who live in the city, lower-class and poor, are subjected to more of the strains, instability, stresses, and frustrations of life. Mental illness is often the result.

COMMUNITY TREATMENT   Proponents of the social model have sought to shift the focus of treatment from just the person alone to the entire community. In large part due to the work of George Caplan (1974), what is now usually called *community mental health* includes several overlapping therapeutic approaches: (1) protest, legislation, and other social action to improve housing, education, nutrition, employment, opportunity and all social services; (2) storefront and drop-in mental health treatment facilities located in the areas where they are most needed; (3) crisis intervention centers so that by telephone or in person, people in suicidal, homicidal, or other desperate situations can make immediate contact with a trained professional; (4) education of community members and leaders to the role of both prevention and treatment. These activities may range from teaching reading and writing to illiterate adults to demonstrating to unwed mothers how to take good physical and emotional care of their infants.

Therapists who work in a community setting, whether in a storefront or a fully equipped clinic, may come from psychodynamic, medical, behaviorist, or other backgrounds. No one form of psychotherapy is exclusively used in the community intervention model, which focuses on the recognition that more than just a single individual needs treatment. The abnormal person is a representative of a *sick society,* and therapists' efforts need to be addressed to both. A therapist who volunteers two days a week in a community clinic described his view:

When I'm working with a middle-class person, say a teacher, and he says he's not getting along with his boss, his principal, then I have mainly a relationship problem. But here, when

Figure 3.6. The social model suggests that more than individual treatment may be necessary in order to alleviate mental disorder. Community action and social protest may be required to improve the chances for good mental health. (Photo: R. Haines/Kingston Freeman)

you have a laborer and he tells me the boss doesn't like him, you have an entire class phenomenon.

The teacher and principal are intellectual and status equals. Their difficulty is one of interaction, behavioral nuance, unconscious needs and the like. The laborer is in a different boat. He doesn't have tenure. Anytime he talks back he can be fired. Can you imagine him saying to his boss he would like to discuss their "relationship"?

Here we have a class situation. The boss has high income, high status and almost life and death power over the laborer. . . . What we have to do in therapy is help the man work out his anger towards his boss in a non-threatening way. The boss is just another one of the

frustrations he has to learn to live with. . . .

We have to start motivating this man to improve his chances. Literacy tutoring, education for a better job, get his wife in and try to explain what he has to put up with every day. We got to do a lot more with a man that labors eight hours a day and comes home to four children and a pregnant wife than we do with a neurotic school teacher. The man who labors needs intervention at every level, educational, economic, political and everything else, not just psychological.

MODELS AND VIEWPOINTS

Why models? Would it not be better to just look for the causes of mental illnesses and let

TABLE 3.2
FOUR VIEWS OF MENTAL DISORDER

	Medical	Social	Learning	Dynamic
Definition	Diagnosis based on symptom grouping	A personal manifestation of the sicknesses and stresses of society	Labels are unimportant; the person's adjustment, potential, or specific behaviors define well-being.	
Cause	Probably genetic, metabolic, biochemical, or other physical	Social change and stress; poverty, discrimination, unemployment	Disordered behaviors are learned	Conflict, repression, frustrated self-actualization; parental mistreatment
Treatment	Hospitalization, drugs, and other medical techniques	Social action to improve socioeconomic well-being of people	Behavior therapies	Individual and group dynamic therapies
Goal	Treat mental illness as just another disease	Bring about a healthier, fairer society	Extinguish nonfunctional behaviors	Free people of repression and let them achieve their potential
Contribution	Diagnostic terms, drug therapy	Understanding of role of social stress, effects of hospitalization and social values	Understanding of how behavior is learned, behavior therapy	Understanding of motivation, and the unconscious; dynamic therapies

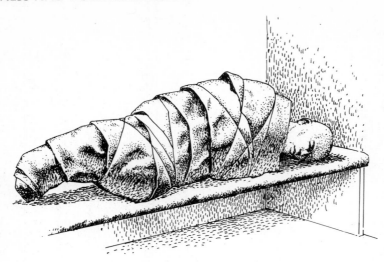

In the Soviet Union, persons suspected of disloyalty to the regime are sentenced to prison camps. Some of the more prominent political dissidents have frequently been forced into mental asylums run by the secret police. Two former inmates now in the West, Leonid Plyushch and Vladimir Bukovsky, told *Time* Magazine (February 21, 1977) of their treatment while confined. Among many other forms of punishment, patients were wrapped in wet canvas which was then allowed to dry, causing severe pain.

the chips fall where they may? The problem is where to begin. Those who have chosen a model have given themselves a frame of reference in which to operate. A model provides researchers, students, and clinicians with guidelines and coherent sets of explanations, enabling them to focus their work (Table 3.2). But models can also be disadvantageous, particularly when they insulate an advocate of one approach from understanding the worth of another. Thus, some behaviorists are extremely critical of psychodynamic beliefs. For them, such pivotal psychoanalytic concepts as repression are mentalistic inferences with no more validity than demonic possession. At the same time, psychodynamic proponents accuse behaviorists of dealing in superficialities. They agree that some symptoms may be altered by learning therapies, but they contend this does not mean any real change has occurred in the person's true conflicts, feelings, or motivation. Given a little time, symptoms will reemerge in a different form. The social model also has its critics, with most commentators particularly disturbed by the tendency to diagnose unconventional behavior as abnormal. So long as social standards are the sole or most important determiner of mental health, anyone whose sexual, recreational, or even political activities are unconventional risks being labeled sick. A clear, although extreme, example of this is the tendency in autocratic nations like the Soviet Union to treat political dissidents as mental patients. Prominent Soviet citizens who have called for free speech, the right to emigrate, and other civil liberties have frequently been diagnosed as psychotic and forcibly institutionalized.

The antipsychiatry movement

None of the present explanations of mental disorder is complete, and all have weaknesses and inconsistencies. The result has been the emergence of what can loosely be called the "antipsychiatry" movement. If there is one person whose comments and efforts typify this approach, it is Thomas Szasz, a psychiatrist who calls for the dismantling of our present mental health structure. Szasz has written dozens of books and articles and is probably best known for *The Myth of Mental Illness* (1974), which argues vigorously against the notion of mental disease.

In terms of the various models, Szasz states that first of all, mental illnesses are in no sense medical diseases. In only a few cases is there any real evidence that a germ or brain lesion caused the supposed malady. Further, the medical belief that symptoms hang together to make up disorders like schizophrenia is more the result of our biased perceptions than it is a description of reality. Szasz is equally critical of psychological models:

Psychoanalysis now functions as a religion disguised as a science and method of treatment. As Abraham received the Laws of God from Jehovah to whom he claimed to have had special access, so Freud received the Laws of Psychology from the Unconscious to which he claimed to have had special access. (*The Second Sin*, p. 96)

Commenting on social explanations of mental illness and present treatment approaches, Szasz states that a mental health power establishment has evolved and now functions much as the Church did hundreds of years ago. Mental health workers are called upon to arbitrate disputes, determine right and wrong, and rule which conduct is safe and which in need of incarceration. Szasz writes that our lives are ensnared by the "therapeutic state," whose aim is not to provide favorable conditions of life, liberty, and the pursuit of happiness, but to repair the alleged defective mental health of its citizens. This arrangement, he charges, gives meaning to the lives of countless bureaucrats, physicians, and other professionals but it robs the so-called patients of the freedom and meaning of theirs: "We thus persecute millions—as drug addicts, homosexuals, sui-

Figure 3.7. Born in Hungary in 1920, Dr. Szasz has lived in the United States since he was eighteen. He has written more than a dozen books and hundreds of articles, and is a founder of the American Association for the Abolition of Involuntary Hospitalization. Dr. Szasz, a psychiatrist, is an outspoken civil libertarian. He argues that every person, no matter how different his or her behavior, has the right to live as he or she pleases, so long as he or she does not do injury to others. (Photo: Gabor Szilasi, Montreal)

cidal risks, and so forth—all the while telling ourselves that we are great healers, curing them of mental illness. We have managed to repackage the Inquisition and are selling it as a new, scientific cure-all" (*The Second Sin*, p. 134).

The Szasz and antipsychiatry position is that what we call mental illness is really a way of coping with problems of living. Psychologists, sociologists, and other scientists who attempt to explain such problems as mental illnesses are "peddling" personal opinion as fact. What passes for valid explanation in the social sciences is little more than "familial and social policies disguised as empirical observations and promoted as scientific laws." The government also does not have a right to intrude on the personal challenges or problems faced by individuals. Neither the state, a doctor, nor a police officer should have the authority to tell people how to solve their problems or run their lives, so long as they do not actually harm others.

Szasz's criticisms strike many as exaggerated. The view that psychiatry is a modernized anti-witch crusade may in fact be more metaphorical than actual. But Szasz's insistence that mental illness and unconventional behavior are not necessarily diseases or crimes has brought about important changes in mental health practices in the past twenty years. Today far fewer people are hospitalized, and most of those who are, are admitted voluntarily rather than being forcibly committed. Psychiatric workers and the courts have also become sensitized to the civil rights of patients. By court ruling, hospitals must show they are treating and helping patients or else discharge them. It is now also obligatory when patients are admitted to inform them of their legal rights, including the privilege of refusing any treatment. Like many intellectual pioneers, Szasz takes strong, often unpopular positions, but his criticisms seem to have helped improve the position of those who are mentally ill.

How many models of madness?

Four views of mental disorder have been described, but just how many different viewpoints there are is fairly arbitrary, since differences can be minor or major. Psychodynamic views could easily be subdivided into Adlerian, Jungian, Existential, and so on. There are also divisions within the behavioral, medical, and social approaches. Our primary objective in presenting the four models has been to suggest that explanations for most mental disturbances are probably multidimensional. To draw a more complete picture, we need to mention a few other viewpoints:

THE PSYCHEDELIC MODEL   Mental illness is a mind-expanding "trip." Psychotic people see things more clearly; they are innovative and original, and others falsely label their creativity an illness. We have no right to diagnose or hospitalize people or try to make them conform to our narrow-minded standards. The mentally ill need a "guide" through their alleged madness to help them achieve their own unique potentials.

THE FAMILY MODEL   The patient is representative of an entire family that is sick. The family needs help in order to end their mutual manipulation and maneuvering. The patient is cured when a harmonious and productive psychological climate is restored in the family.

THE MORAL MODEL   Mental illness is very close to, if not the same as, bad or immoral behavior. Such people need the help of medical, psychological, spiritual, legal or other authorities in order to develop socially proper conduct. Hospital or other confinement may be necessary both as treatment and punishment.

THE IMPAIRED MODEL   The mentally disordered are poor unfortunates who are usually permanently handicapped. Society has to protect itself from such people but also offer them care and shelter. It is frequently thought best to keep mentally disabled individuals apart from society in institutions where they can be looked after.

THE CONSPIRATORIAL MODEL   The mentally ill are the victims of sociopolitical labeling. Treatment is often just punishment or a kind of "brainwashing" intended to coerce those who are different to conform to the ideological structure of society.

THE STATISTICAL MODEL   In this view, anyone whose behavior differs too greatly from a mathematically calculated average is likely to be abnormal. Consequently, there are no behavioral absolutes: What may be deviant in one culture could be the majority pattern, and therefore normal, in another.

Each model of disorder defines and treats abnormal behavior from its own theoretical perspective. But while there are many differences concerning causes, diagnosis, and treatment, there is also an increasing amount of agreement. As more and more is learned about mental illness, the different explanatory positions are continually being brought closer to one another (Siegler and Osmond, 1976).

OUR VIEW

Four models to understand and treat mental disorders have been presented. But in our view, neither medical, dynamic, behavioral, nor social explanations account for all abnormalities. All these theories explain *some* psychopathology. In fact, most practicing clinicians would agree to such a compromise, for relatively few take a doctrinaire stand for or against a particular viewpoint. For the majority of psychiatrists, psychologists, and other specialists, judgments of which model to use are based on substance and applicability. Valid, practical information and techniques can be derived from every viewpoint (Gallagher, 1977).

We find the descriptions and terminology of the medical model, the DSM III, imperfect but usable. They allow us to communicate, to agree on the disorders and symptoms we are talking about. Some of the causes of mental disorders described by the medical model, such as that German measles can cause mental retardation, are incontestable; other causes proposed by this model, such as the role of heredity and biochemistry in schizophrenia, are often backed by research that is not definitive but is substantial enough to be taken seriously. We agree too that psychodynamic insights and social explanations, though they may sometimes be imprecise, are often revealing. It looks very much as if unemployment, bigotry, a disordered childhood, serious motivational conflicts, and a wide variety of other psychological and social stresses can lead to mental illness. And despite reservations about the depth of their explanations, behavioral theorists have pointed out the ways in which many symptoms are learned and can be unlearned.

As a result, in each chapter of this book we will describe the relevant medical, psychological, and/or social explanations that seem to best account for the particular disorder being discussed.

Our discussion of treatment also recognizes that frequently more than a single approach proves useful. Depressed patients often respond remarkably well to electric shock, or to better housing and a new job. Sexually incompetent clients may be helped by behavior therapy and neurotic patients by psychotherapy, medication, and relearning techniques combined. In each chapter, when the treatments for disorders are discussed we will outline the therapies that have proved useful, regardless of their theoretical origin.

The mental health sciences are evolving rapidly. Much of what we accept now will be changed tomorrow by new research and insight. In appropriate chapters we will include current criticism and innovations so that we will be aware of present limits and future directions. Though mental health is an unfinished business, we have some suspicions about what a more final product will look like. We suspect that both our descriptions of causes and our prescriptions for treatment will be multidimensional. We will know the extent to which factors such as heredity, biochemistry, motives, life experiences, and learning play differently weighted roles in each disorder. We sense, too, more careful definitions of what constitutes mental illness so that several behaviors now regarded as psychiatric problems will be seen as social or ethical issues and resolved as such. We expect advances in the proper use of medication, and that social, learning, and dynamic therapists will increasingly work together to construct healthier lives for their clients.

SUMMARY

From the behaviorist viewpoint, nearly all human responses are learned by conditioning, reinforcement and similar processes. As a result, abnormal behavior is as much a product of learning as is normal conduct. Behaviorists generally reject most diagnostic concepts and prefer instead to focus on specific responses. Treatment consists of techniques like reciprocal inhibition or more advanced social learning methods to unlearn abnormal behaviors and substitute desired responses.

The social model emphasizes that the definition, cause, and treatment of abnormal behavior usually lies in society. Many people are considered ill only because they deviate from cultural expectations. Many others are disturbed because of the unique pressures and stresses of their society. In nearly all nations, rapid change is an adjustment challenge often resulting in abnormal symptoms. Other correlates of mental illness have been found to be disadvantaged city living and lower socioeconomic status. Individual psychotherapy is therefore often insufficient; treatment must involve efforts to bring about improvements in housing, employment, and income and should be immediately accessible to members of the community.

None of the models we have presented provides a totally satisfactory explanation of mental disorders. All are open to criticism for being rigid, superficial, mentalistic, or inappropriate. At the same time, however, all the viewpoints—medical, behavioral, dynamic, and social—seem to have some validity. In clinical practice most professionals use the techniques and insights of the models that appear applicable. It also seems that with time, overall explanations and treatments of abnormality will include elements of all approaches. In this text we will report the explanations and therapies that have proved substantial and useful, regardless of their theoretical origin.

4 Neuroses: The Anxiety Disorders

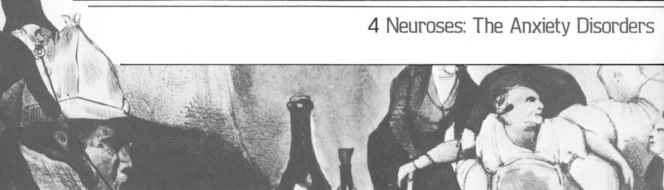

5 The Causes and Treatment of Neuroses

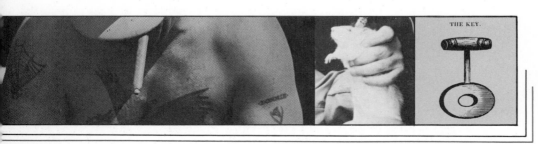

6 Psychosomatic Disorders

DISORDERS

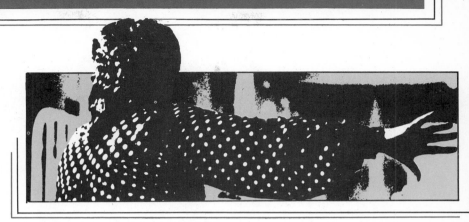

7 The Diagnosis of Schizophrenia

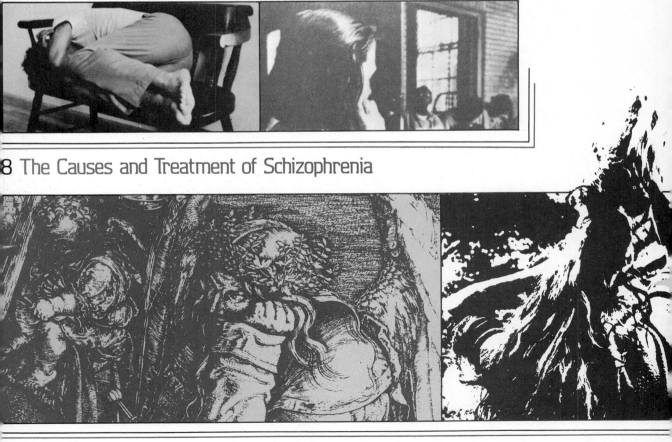

8 The Causes and Treatment of Schizophrenia

9 Depression and Suicide: The Mood Disorders

Neuroses:
The Anxiety Disorders

In everyday language, we tend to describe anyone whose conduct is peculiar as "neurotic." But **neurosis** has a specific psychiatric meaning: it is a pattern of maladaptive behavior accompanied by disruptive symptoms and feelings of distress. The neurotic person usually feels "miserable," has physical and emotional symptoms such as continual worrying and heart palpitations, and has difficulty getting along with others.

Neurosis should be distinguished from psychosis, which we will describe in Chapters 7 and 8. In *both* conditions people may subjectively feel unhappy and their conduct may be erratic or ineffective. Those with **psychosis,** however, are described as lacking contact with reality. They are likely to be hallucinated, and their emotional and physical responses so disordered that hospitalization is necessary. Neurotic people are in contact with reality. They *can* distinguish between fantasy and actuality,

and although their symptoms may be quite uncomfortable, they rarely require hospitalization.

For nineteenth-century psychiatrists, the symptoms of neurosis were due to neuron damage. A person was compulsive, frightened, or fatigued because his or her nerves were fragile, hypersensitive, or otherwise impaired. Twentieth-century psychiatrists, influenced by the psychoanalysts, adopted the view that neurosis was caused by anxiety. Until the 1970s, the DSM II stated: "Anxiety is the chief characteristic of neurosis. It may be felt and expressed directly, or it may be controlled unconsciously and automatically by . . . various . . . psychological mechanisms." But the accuracy of this assumption was also questionable. Compulsive and phobic neurotics typically feel anxious and may show signs of fear such as trembling and perspiration, but in hysterical neurotics, indications of anxiety are minimal.

The latest edition of the diagnostic Manual, DSM III, has recognized that anxiety may not play a significant role in every neurosis. In fact, all the psychiatric disorders commonly diagnosed as neuroses may actually be fairly distinct conditions. For this reason, the manual deemphasizes the all-inclusive label "neurosis" and instead calls for the use of the terms anxiety, somatoform, and dissociative disorders.

Here, we will continue to use the term neurosis to cover all these conditions. Despite the debatable applicability of the label, it has been used for two centuries and will doubtless continue to be generally employed to describe mental conditions that are nonpsychotic but nevertheless seriously handicap adjustment. In this chapter we will look at the symptoms and diagnosis of neurotic conditions; in the next, we will examine causation theories and treatment methods.

SYMPTOMS

Emma R is 27 years old, single, and works as a sales manager for a large department store. She describes herself as a person with very high standards for herself and other people. She is very demanding of her co-workers and is frequently verbally abusive. She appears domineering, rigid, irritable, and manipulative but complains of feeling frightened, lonely, self-conscious, confused, tense, and unhappy. She also has frequent "tension" headaches and on some mornings feels so "weak and depressed" that she stays in bed and does not go to work. Emma has recently begun to see a therapist and wants him to "make some reasonable plans" for her so that she "can get more out of life."

Everyone who is neurotic does not necessarily have the same personality traits or clinical symptoms. Even people who show the same symptom respond very differently, and no two people ever display exactly the same combination of symptoms and responses. But neurosis is typified by a number of fairly characteristic

Figure 4.1. The neurotic is generally an anxious, defensive person who has great difficulty getting along with others. (Photo: Scribe)

signs. Most people who are neurotic will show at least some of the behaviors that together point to the presence of the kind of disabling mental disorder we call neurosis: they will be anxious, they will be defensive, they will have trouble maintaining interpersonal relationships.

Anxiety

Traditionally, all neurotic disorders have been believed to share **anxiety**: a general physical and emotional feeling of fear. Freud and the dynamic theorists suggest that the maladaptive behaviors of neurotics are always attempts to cope with conscious and unconscious fears. Although this view is no longer universally accepted, anxiety—both as a physiological reality and as a personal feeling—continues to be a major feature of most neurotic patterns.

PHYSIOLOGICAL ANXIETY   The human neurological network is made up of two fairly separate divisions, the voluntary and the involuntary nervous systems. Skeletal muscles, which move our limbs and which we consciously manipulate, are under the control of the voluntary or *somatic* system. The involuntary or *autonomic* nervous system regulates activities over which we have little or no conscious control, such as the beating of the heart, the operations of the digestive system, kidney function, and glandular activity (see Figure 4.2). Any situation that evokes fear, anger, or other strong emotions produces autonomic activity.

The autonomic system is itself divided into two branches, the sympathetic and the parasympathetic, which work in reciprocal ways. The sympathetic branch stimulates "fight" responses. It causes the heart to beat faster, deeper breathing, and perspiration. The parasympathetic part works to conserve body resources in a defensive way. It constricts blood flow (to prevent excessive bleeding), speeds up digestive processes, and decreases metabolism. The two branches, acting together to control vital body organs, make us very aware that we are frightened. Their activities may produce involuntary trembling, urination, perspiration, fainting, cramps, and other physical signs of emotional arousal:

I've just gotten very afraid of crowds I guess . . . Tuesday night when I got out of the movies, I was caught in this mob of people leaving. My heart started racing, I was sweating all over, I felt nauseous and dizzy and I had to rush to the bathroom.

PSYCHOLOGICAL ANXIETY   Subjectively, the person who is anxious experiences fear, foreboding, and apprehension. Some psychologists have attempted to distinguish two subjective feelings, fear and anxiety. Fear is held to be specific and anxiety to be general. The person who becomes agitated and uneasy only when confronted by the boss, a member of the opposite sex, or a medical doctor is exhibiting fear. But an individual who is almost always frightened, worried, and tense—and usually cannot pinpoint a cause—is described as displaying **free floating anxiety.** Such people may occasionally ascribe their anxiety to some fairly ordinary life event, but they are almost always frightened. Their ever-present anxiety readily "attaches" itself to a situation and intensifies—for example, when they have to take a trip, talk to a strange person, or take an examination.

In actual clinical practice, the neat distinction between fear and anxiety often does not hold up. Most neurotic patients have periods of general anxiety as well as specific fears. They also show a range of intensity. Anxiety may be fairly minimal, with just intermittent feelings of disquiet. It may also be exceedingly strong, with feelings of desperation, severe agitation, even terror and panic. Because of the overlap in meaning, we will use the terms anxiety and fear interchangeably. When we refer to either experience, we will be indicating a condition manifested by a number of objective physiological symptoms and subjective feelings such as the following:

Feelings of nervousness, tension, worry, and dread
Inability to concentrate, preoccupied thinking, self-consciousness, irritability, sleeplessness, and lack of appetite
Feelings of inadequacy, helplessness, discouragement, gloom, dismay, and uselessness

MEASURING ANXIETY   Unlike many of the subjective symptoms of neuroses such as unhappiness, anxiety can be objectively measured. Probably the most commonly used physiological measure of anxiety is the galvanic skin response (GSR). When a person becomes emotionally upset, perspiration causes an in-

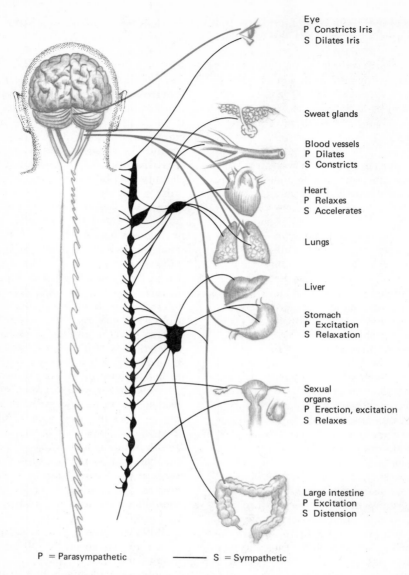

Eye
P Constricts Iris
S Dilates Iris

Sweat glands

Blood vessels
P Dilates
S Constricts

Heart
P Relaxes
S Accelerates

Lungs

Liver

Stomach
P Excitation
S Relaxation

Sexual
organs
P Erection, excitation
S Relaxes

Large intestine
P Excitation
S Distension

P = Parasympathetic ———— S = Sympathetic

Figure 4.2. The autonomic nervous system. Most organs of the body are supplied with parasympathetic and sympathetic nerve fibers. These two branches of the autonomic nervous system work together, reciprocally regulating each organ; the sympathetic branch tends to stimulate "emergency" responses, whereas the parasympathetic triggers more ordinary maintenance reactions.

crease in the electrical conductivity of the skin that can be measured by attaching electrodes to the fingers (see Figure 4.3). Many investigations have shown that persons afraid of snakes, spiders, and the like will show sizable changes in GSR and other measures when exposed to these objects. As a rule too, many people diagnosed as neurotic consistently have

Figure 4.3. The GSR, galvanic skin response, is a frequently used measure of anxiety. Electrodes attached to the fingers and palm evaluate the electrical conductivity of the skin caused by perspiration.

generally higher physical indices of anxiety.

The subjective measurement of anxiety is more difficult. Several pencil and paper questionnaires are available, but they are not always accurate. One of the better tests is the State-Trait Anxiety Inventory, by Charles Spielberger. This test attempts to measure anxiety both as a fairly constant personality *trait* and as a temporary *state* in response to a fearful situation. Each part of the test consists of twenty statements. Subjects circle their response to items like the following on a 4-point scale.

	Almost never	Some-times	Often	Almost always
I feel moody and blue	1	2	3	4
Little things upset me	1	2	3	4
Trembling and perspiration bother me	1	2	3	4

Although the evidence is not conclusive, many neurotics often seem to have both higher trait and higher state anxiety. In fact, because of their constantly high level of trait anxiety many neurotics may be more vulnerable to stress and react to state-anxiety-provoking situations with greater intensity and for longer periods of time (Martin, 1976; Shedletsky, 1974; Spielberger, 1972).

Defensive behavior

Neurotic individuals tend to respond ineffectively to environmental challenges. Instead of coping, they try to avoid confronting their problems; they make excuses, hide, or run away. This 34-year-old man, for example, was still living with his parents because he was frightened of being on his own. He had developed a number of avoidance patterns to "explain" his behavior:

I've developed a whole life style around avoiding being responsible, on my own. I could have moved out and been on my own many times. I always had a reason not to. Sometimes it was because I was afraid I might lose my job so I couldn't afford my own place. Another time I had the flu, and other times I just felt sick so I had to stay home and be nursed. Another time I actually leased an apartment but then I decided it was a bad neighborhood and my mother would worry. . . . Then twice my mother said she didn't feel well so I just couldn't leave her in the lurch.

In the psychoanalytic model, the neurotic person employs defense mechanisms to avoid coping: Unable to face the sources of the anxiety, he or she represses, projects, rationalizes, regresses, and uses all the other psychodynamic ego defenses in order to continue a maladaptive pattern.

Defensive behavior does help such individuals avoid a measure of anxiety, but it may also produce different kinds of fear and discomfort. The 34-year-old man who remained at home avoided the unpleasant conflicts and emotions that might be aroused by becoming independent, but staying at home was also distressing. In other words, his behavior was self-defeating. This tendency for neurotic actions to lead to additional anxiety has been called the **neurotic paradox.**

It occurs because however ineffective defensive behavior is in the long run, it offers some immediate relief. Whenever the dependent 34-

year-old man made arrangements to live on his own, his feelings of fear and apprehension became vastly intensified. As soon as he managed to find a reason to stay at home, however, he felt immediate relief. On their own, neurotics usually make only feeble efforts to face their problems and become caught in a vicious cycle. It begins with attempted resolution, which then stimulates anxiety, and finally ends with the reestablishment of maladaptive, but paradoxically comforting, defensive behavior patterns. Transactional analysts (see Chapter 18) see neurotics as persistently following the same "script." They have written scenarios for themselves, and despite supposed efforts to the contrary, they play out the game they have set up, every time.

Interpersonal conflict

Neurotics are often described as rigid, unbending, narcissistic, hostile, and manipulative. Because of their maladaptive behaviors and anxiety, they are usually extremely demanding and self-centered persons who have great difficulty maintaining a relationship with anyone. They have little real idea of what in fact they are like, cannot put themselves in another person's place, are extremely self-indulgent but intolerant of others, as the examples of Penny and the neurotic husband show.

Penny is 23 years old, intelligent and attractive. She has been engaged twice and had two friends she lived with for about four months each. All of her relationships ended with violent arguments and accusations. Her last relationship with Matt was typical. Penny was almost always late for appointments and very unreliable. But she quickly became incensed at Matt's criticisms, accusing him of being too possessive. On the other hand, she often berated Matt for not kissing her hello or goodbye and also accused him of neglecting her feelings.

Penny had many periods when she was "down" and felt useless, when she demanded that Matt make extraordinary efforts to cheer her up—although nothing ever worked to her satisfaction. She also completely neglected her

Figure 4.4. Neurotic individuals usually have great difficulty maintaining a relationship with other people. As a result, many become overly attached to pets. (Photo: Scribe)

own appearance but expected Matt to be spotlessly neat and groomed. One of the last demands Penny made which caused Matt to leave was that he call her from work, once every hour, since she was afraid to be alone in their apartment.

Neurotic individuals have poor interpersonal relations not only because they are excessively demanding and egotistical, but also because they frequently lack insight and are conflicted. As a result, many of their actions are erratic, and others are confused by their unpredictable behavior. All of us assume a measure of consistency in the conduct of others. When this consistency is upset, we find it difficult to continue a relationship. A woman living with a neurotic husband described him this way:

You never know what to expect. I've been married to him a year and a half and I don't know him yet. He'll be sweet and gentle and then he is sour and he wants me to do everything for him. . . . Then another time, I'm interfering in his life and he wants more independence. Then he's scared to apply for another job and then he blames me for holding him back. . . . I told him if he wants to be free then just tell me. Then instead he comes crying to me. I'm his mommy. He can't live without me. He needs me. He loves me. Then he forgets all about it. I'm a drag. He doesn't need anybody. He's the macho hero and he spends hours in the bathroom dressing himself just so, and he wants all the women to fall all over him. . . . He's got very little understanding of himself, and he certainly doesn't understand me or my needs at all.

Specific symptoms

In addition to the anxiety and interpersonal difficulties most neurotics display to at least some degree, they also have fairly specific symptoms. Many complain of physical impairments. These may be vague, such as aches and pains, or localized such as headaches, diarrhea, and even paralysis of an arm. Obsessional thoughts or fears, thinking about the same thing over and over again, are also frequent. Some neurotics complain they are constantly worrying about "going crazy" or "doing something desperate," or even carrying out a seemingly silly or trivial act.

A few feel burdened by conduct they believe they cannot control. They are "compelled" to keep listening to themselves breathing, to steal some minor object, or to avoid stepping on cracks in the sidewalk. They realize their compulsions are foolish or irrational but assert that they are unable to stop themselves. Some neurotic patients experience disorders in their self-awareness, or consciousness. They have long memory gaps, periods when they feel like someone else or are unable to perceive themselves as self-controlled human beings. (Extreme instances of such behavior result in amnesia or in very rare cases in multiple personality.)

Nearly all neurotic individuals complain of misery. They state that they feel unhappy, tense, and inadequate much of the time. For a few others, indifference, apathy, disinterest, and resignation are common. For nearly all, however, there is also a good deal of emotional **lability**: their feelings are likely to shift with some rapidity. They may feel apathetic, useless, or sad most of the time. But then they meet a new friend or read a book that promises relief from their troubles, and they become pleasantly optimistic. Such enthusiasms are temporary; sooner or later, what is often called the typical neurotic misery will return.

DIAGNOSES

Once symptoms have been identified and measured in some way, the person is given a diagnosis—a descriptive label. Some of the more common diagnoses we will discuss here are anxiety neurosis, phobic neurosis, and hysteria. Neurotics often display a number of the same symptoms, but in differing degrees. Rather than classifying by causes, the DSM III diagnostic categories are based on the predominant symptom. For example, if obsessions and compulsions are primary, in addition to misery and aches and pains, the disorder is called obsessive-compulsive neurosis. Such categorizations or diagnoses based on the major symptom facilitate description and communication. But since symptoms can change, diagnoses may also shift. Over the course of time, as a neurotic's behaviors fluctuate, different diagnostic labels may be applied to the same person.

The reliability of neurotic diagnosis is low. Studies have shown that professionals disagree about the correct diagnostic label in as often as seven out of ten cases (Zubin, 1967). So much disagreement can be caused by any one or several of the following factors: (1) Early psychotic symptoms, such as those found in schizophrenia or depression, may sometimes falsely suggest neurosis. (2) Neuroses seldom present themselves along the classic, neatly distinctive lines suggested by DSM and psychiatric definitions. Most neurotic patients have a mixed variety of symptoms, with sometimes one or another feature appearing more prominent. Consequently, some clinicians prefer to use the term *mixed neurotic reaction.* (3) Neurotic patients frequently have little insight into themselves and resist treatment even when they are being seen by a therapist. Hence they often present one list of behaviors and complaints to one clinician, and another to a second. (4) Environmental events, family support, or conflicts can change fairly rapidly and affect the symptoms the neurotic person experiences and exhibits. Often a person may seem to be an anxiety neurotic, but then when a family friction is resolved, his or her condition may more closely resemble that of an obsessive-compulsive.

Anxiety neurosis

More than half of all neurotic patients are said to have **anxiety neurosis.** Most are young adults, and women outnumber men. The majority have also had at least several months of chronic anxiety and perhaps one or two acute attacks before seeking treatment (Noyes, 1976).

During periods of chronic anxiety, which may last for several years, patients complain of mild to moderate feelings of fear, accompanying physiological symptoms, and adjustment difficulties. But none of these signs are likely to interfere with work, social activities, or family life. During acute attacks, however, fear becomes intense and symptoms so severe that normal activities are drastically curtailed.

The acute anxiety attack is the hallmark of this neurosis. Many diagnosticians believe that without such climactic episodes, the condition cannot properly be called anxiety neurosis. The anxiety attack is typically a brief, almost explosive, experience of sheer terror. It begins suddenly and unexpectedly at home, in a store, in the street, or even during sleep. One moment, everything is normal; the next

moment, the person becomes deeply apprehensive. Something terrible or catastrophic seems about to happen. The heart beats faster and faster, the lungs labor for breath. He or she is mortally afraid of choking or having a heart attack. Perhaps his body feels strange and not like his own, a sensation called **depersonalization.** Or the person may experience **derealization**—that is, believing the surroundings have been transformed and he or she is in some unknown, unreal place.

Within a few minutes, the attack subsides; the patient, left faint, perspiring, and nauseous, knows he or she has survived. For most anxiety neurotics, such attacks occur only a few times. But for others, they may be almost daily events. The attacks usually motivate anxiety neurotics to seek treatment. Because many believe they have a physical problem, they often seek medical help; relatively few are aware of the psychological origins of their anxiety. They believe instead that they have a serious heart, digestive, or respiratory problem.

ANXIETY AS A DISTINCT NEUROSIS   Whether or not anxiety neurosis is a distinct disorder remains controversial. Because of the pessimism and gloom characteristic of anxiety neurotics, many clinicians believe it to be a type of depression (see Chapter 9). Others suggest it is more like a phobic neurosis. But in phobias the stimulus that triggers the attack of fear is known, whereas in anxiety the catalyst is essentially unknown. Some argue that in anxiety neurosis the provocative stimulus is unconscious or subtly related to a previously learned anxiety response, as the cases of Mona L and the programmer seem to show.

Mona L was 27 years old, married, and had recently resumed working as a hairdresser since her child was now in school. She described herself as a person inclined to "worry and fret about most everything." Ever since last year, when she knew she would return to work, she had become particularly apprehensive and concerned. One week before seeking treatment, Mona had talked with the cosmetic salesman; as he left, she had experienced an acute anxiety episode. Her heart started racing, she felt dizzy and thought the "shop was about to collapse" about her. She went to the ladies room, felt more and more terror, vomited, and gradually regained her composure. Mona had two other acute attacks during the next month. The first occurred as she opened a package the cosmetic salesman had left and the next as she was opening a TV dinner for her husband. Since Mona had hesitatingly revealed some sexual fantasies concerning the cosmetic salesman, the therapist explored the possibility that the anxiety attacks were perhaps triggered by guilt feelings concerning a contemplated affair.

A 35-year-old programmer reported several anxiety attacks which he finally traced to the color blue. His boss had a deep blue carpet in his office and he apparently reminded him of his own alcoholic and abusive father. The patient believed that seeing a deep blue curtain or carpet triggered long-suppressed hostile feelings toward his father and boss. These feelings conflicted with his image of having become a self-controlled, independent, and mature individual.

ANXIETY TRIGGERS Any number of serious challenges, such as loss of a job, major illness, or death of a family member, may leave even the most well-adjusted person quite anxious. It is normal to be concerned with one's well-being and to respond to fear by taking constructive action. But the anxiety neurotic becomes upset for no apparent reason, or when causes are uncovered, they seem remote. More important, the fear does not usually lead to adaptive responses.

Many anxiety attacks may be precipitated by hidden conflicts, decisions, impulses, or feelings that the person finds threatening. Whether it is a fairly frank or disguised aggressive wish, a hetero or homosexual desire, a need for affection or dependency, the person is made uncomfortable by the intrusion of the thought. The impulse or motive is inconsistent with the person's self-image or challenges his or her self-esteem or capabilities, and the response is fear. Mona L apparently had an acute

attack whenever she was reminded of her sexual feelings for the cosmetic salesman. For the programmer, hostile needs were eventually found to stimulate anxiety attacks.

Notice that we may explain anxiety neurosis and its triggers in terms of psychological dynamics or learning. From the psychoanalytic view, any number of situations can directly or symbolically release repressed urges. A psychoanalyst, for example, pointed out that Mona's anxiety attacks occurred upon opening the cosmetic and TV dinner boxes. This was supposedly a representation of making herself sexually available to the salesman. Symbolically "giving in" to her id triggered a superego anxiety reaction. From the behavioral perspective, similar anxiety responses can be explained in terms of generalization. The programmer's boss physically resembled his

Figure 4.5. A student described frequent paniclike attacks of anxiety while in her dormitory. She found that sitting quietly all alone in the stadium helped resolve her frightening emotions. (Photo: Scribe)

father. The fear of his abusive father the programmer had learned as a child generalized not only to his boss but to prominent fixtures in the boss's office, such as the carpet. We will say more about these and other ways of explaining neurosis in the next chapter.

Phobic neurosis

Phobias, heightened fears of an object or situation, are fairly common. Many people are afraid of lightning, snakes, or closed spaces. Such fears are usually moderate and do not interfere with the person's life. In contrast, when a stimulus causes a severe anxiety response *and* the phobia seriously impairs functioning, it is properly called a **phobic neurosis.** Phobias account for less than 5 percent of all neuroses. But although phobic neuroses are infrequent, mild to moderate phobias often accompany other mental disorders.

SPECIFIC PHOBIAS   A good proportion of depressed patients and half of all anxiety neurotics, for example, also have specific phobias (Agras, 1969), such as fear of a particular animal or travel. These are not usually intense or disabling enough to be considered neurotic.

The most common phobia is *agoraphobia,* fear of open places, which is found in over half of all patients, most of whom are women. This is actually not just one fear but a constellation involving crowds and large areas. Many fears are probably not as specific as they appear on the surface; we label phobias with terms that imply great precision, but in actuality each phobia may represent only the surface of a number of related fears. Agoraphobia usually starts during adolescence and intensifies as the person grows older, eventually becoming disabling, as in the case of Kristine M. Or a limited phobia may suddenly become disruptive, as in the case of the golfer.

Kristine M had been afraid of "big impersonal places and swarms of people" since the age of 14. "I was in the A&P and all of a sudden it seemed so big, and all those people around me. I got very scared and I guess I fainted."

The next year Kristine had several other phobic episodes in a movie theater, a discount store, and at a track meet. As a result, she avoided stores, theaters, and other places where there were likely to be many people or that were large. She managed to hold on to her job as a typist till she was 24 years old. She avoided crowds by coming to work an hour earlier and leaving an hour later. Recently she was forced to leave her job since she had become frightened of the room in which she worked. The room was about 20 feet by 25 feet, but several desks had recently been removed, making the area seem more cavernous and open.

A talented and increasingly well-known young golfer was intensely afraid of flying. As he became more expert, games were scheduled with increasing frequency in different areas of the country, so that he was unable to meet his schedule by bus. Because he absolutely refused to fly, he was forced to give up his career at an early and promising stage.

Well over three hundred different specific phobias have been named. Since intense fear may be attached to any object or situation, the list could be expanded into the thousands. Some of the more common ones are shown in the accompanying box.

CHILDHOOD PHOBIAS   Nearly all children have some specific phobias, such as a fear of dogs, cats, insects, or imaginary monsters. As might be expected, children from disordered, abusive homes retain such fears longer and experience them more intensely. Those from psychologically healthy environments usually overcome their fears as they get older (Martin, 1976). One fear that can be very disabling is school phobia: Being in school or just preparing for it makes the child tense and sweaty, the heart races, and vomiting is frequent. As many as one-fifth of all children may have this fear to at least a mild degree; a much smaller portion are seriously afflicted.

Careful analysis of school phobia shows that this fear is more than just one specific anxiety. For most children, school phobia is the result

COMMON SPECIFIC PHOBIAS

animals	zoophobia	insects	acarophobia
bees	apiphobia	lightning	astraphobia
buried alive	taphephobia	marriage	gamophobia
being looked at	scophophobia	money	chrematophobia
being touched	aphephobia	mouse	musophobia
blood	hemophobia	naked body	gymnophobia
choking	anginophobia	robbers	harpaxophobia
confinement		sex	genophobia
(small rooms)	claustrophobia	sin	harmartophobia
darkness	nyctophobia	sleep	hypnophobia
death	thanatophobia	snakes	ophidiophobia
dirt	mysophobia	spiders	arachnephobia
dogs	cynophobia	strangers	xenophobia
failure	kakorrhaphiphobia	thunder	brontophobia
fire	pyrophobia	travel	hodophobia
ghosts	phasmophobia	walking	basiphobia
God	theophobia	water	hydrophobia
height	acrophobia	women	gynophobia
insanity	lyssophobia	work	ponophobia

of a number of anxieties (Gittleman-Klein, 1973), including:

SEPARATION ANXIETY: Being without one's parents
AUTHORITY FEAR: Fear of teacher
PEER PHOBIA: Fear of other children, fear of fighting
PERFORMANCE ANXIETY: Fear of being called on to speak or recite

Obsessive-compulsive neurosis

Obsessive-compulsive neurotics are dominated by persistent, unwanted, usually frightening thoughts and actions that seem senseless or irrational. They may be preoccupied with the notion that they are going to injure someone and so stop driving a car and remove all knives and scissors from their homes. Or they may be afraid of catching a disease and scrupulously avoid touching doorknobs, shaking hands, or handling money.

Compulsions usually accompany obsessions, although either may exist alone. A per-son may just be obsessional, thinking over and over again about his mother and father having intercourse. Or she may have a compulsive need, without any accompanying thought, to keep touching a particular object, arranging and rearranging her clothing in a detailed manner, or stamping her foot every time the word "I" is uttered.

Obsessive-compulsive neuroses are not common. In clinical practice, less than 5 percent of all patients are given this diagnosis, and many of these often show the symptoms of other neurotic disorders as well. It is important to note that although many obsessive-compulsives are made extremely anxious by obsessional thoughts that they will become insane or commit a violent act, very few actually do. The likelihood of psychosis or actually carrying out the feared obsessional thought is extremely low (Kringlen, 1965; Akthar, 1975).

The symptoms of obsessional-compulsive neuroses differ a good deal from one individual to the next. Which thoughts are endlessly repeated or acts compulsively carried out depends on the person's own life experience and interests. Religious individuals frequently have blasphemous thoughts. Sexually inhibited persons may be preoccupied with libidinal ideas. Often the most peaceful and retiring are obsessed with violent ruminations and images. Some of the more common symptoms often take the following forms:

Compulsive counting. Patients count words, fence posts, people, or cracks in the sidewalk in order to reach designated goals. Or they preselect particular numbers as stimuli to perform certain rituals. "Every sixth step I touch my heart twice, every twelfth I shake my head. . . ."

Compulsive cleaning. Patients wash hands, empty garbage or ashtrays, or remove dust dozens of times daily. "Every time I go to the bathroom, I have to come out completely clean . . . so it ends up that I scrub myself like crazy eight or ten times a day."

Obsessional ideas. Frightening, obscene, silly or unwanted ideas continuously intrude into thinking. Sometimes the ideas are no more than rhymes or parts of a song; sometimes they may be bizarre: "I keep getting the idea they crucified Jesus because he was a flasher. . . . This keeps rolling around my head, all different versions of it. I can't get rid of it."

Obsessional images. Realistic, detailed, and usually frightening scenes keep reoccurring. Usually the scenes are violent events, accidents, or involve sexual or excretory functions.

Obsessional fears. Patients are preoccupied with fear that they will injure themselves with common machinery, eating utensils, or that they are going insane or will commit suicide or homicide. Sometimes the fear is of doing something embarrassing or foolish, like kicking their boss or standing up in church, disrobing, and shouting obscenities.

Obsessional indecision. The person continually ponders a hypothetical question or common everyday act. One patient was relentlessly bothered by the question, "Is God one or three?" Another found he needed to do nearly every simple everyday chore over and over again because he could not decide whether he had turned the water off, signed his check, changed his socks, and so on.

Most people display a combination of obsessional thoughts and compulsive acts. Usually too, the neurosis begins during childhood but is tolerated since it does not interfere too much with adjustment. For many people, however, symptoms become worse and seriously interfere with their ability to function as they grow older and family or environmental stresses increase. In some instances, patients can usually point to a specific event ("my parents got divorced,") that intensified their symptoms. In other cases, no specific life stress is evident. As the person grows older, it becomes increasingly obvious that the numerous preoccupations and ritualistic acts are embarrassing, cause the person to avoid other people, and interfere with adjustment. It is at this point, when symptoms have become severe enough to frighten and depress the person, that most people come for treatment.

Many clinicians have observed that obsessive-compulsive neurosis tends to occur in particular personality types (see Figure 4.6). As adolescents, such people tend to be unusually orderly, obedient, and dependable. As adults they value punctuality, rules, and procedures. Some may also be superstitious, carrying amulets or believing in lucky signs or omens. It is possible that these personality types are predisposed to obsessive disorders and will manifest them when stress becomes severe enough.

Freud pointed out that in some ways the rituals and beliefs of obsessives resemble religious practices. He even suggested that some mystical convictions and the function of prayer may have originated in obsessive-compulsive behavior patterns. Other psychodynamic writers see this neurosis as evidence of the persistence of primitive magical thinking. The obsessive-compulsive individual often reasons, "If I stamp my foot whenever anyone says 'I,' then I won't become insane." For modern behaviorists, in contrast, obsessive symptoms owe their origin and persistence to avoidance learning and operant conditioning (Carr, 1974).

Figure 4.6. Self-portrait by an obsessive-compulsive young woman. She saw herself as determined, neat, and organized. In actuality, she had a considerable number of obsessive thoughts and compulsive rituals that greatly interfered with her adjustment and left her feeling miserable. (Photo: Scribe)

Hysterical neurosis

Conversion or hysterical neurosis is an ancient disorder. Over four thousand years ago, the Egyptians described it in very much the way modern clinicians do today. Two thousand years ago the Greeks attributed the condition to a displaced uterus, and early in this century Sigmund Freud's diagnosis and treatment of it helped catapult him into prominence.

Until recently, hysteria was distinguished from conversion hysteria. **Hysteria** was used to describe disorders characterized by a large number of medical complaints and pains particularly involving the gastrointestinal, reproductive, and cardiovascular systems. Such patients were usually able to convince physicians

to prescribe medication and even perform surgical procedures. **Conversion hysteria** was used for patients who asserted they suffered primarily neurological losses. They had difficulty walking, felt their limbs were numb or tingled, lost their sight, hearing, or speech, suffered periods of unconsciousness or memory loss (see Figure 4.7). But although both hysteria and conversion patients may describe their symptoms with realistic and even dramatic intensity, careful medical evaluation shows very little or no actual physical damage or impairment.

The DSM III makes further distinctions among the hysterical conditions—now called *somatoform* disorders. But, in keeping with everyday clinical practice, we will refer to all of them as hysterical neurosis. Although hys-

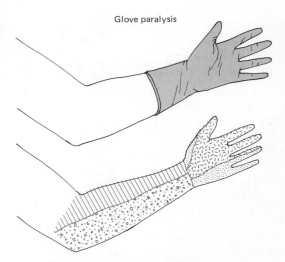

Glove paralysis

Schematic presentation of areas supplied by different nerves originating in several neurological control centers

Figure 4.7. Hysterical symptoms can often be distinguished from actual physical disease because they are "anatomical nonsense." In glove paralysis, the disability involves just those parts the patient's faulty understanding of neurology leads him or her to believe should be disabled. To obtain a paralysis shaped like a glove, several different nerves would have to be damaged in many different regions, as the lower drawing shows. This is a very unlikely possibility.

teria was once a fairly common disorder, today it is relatively infrequent. Only about 2 to 3 percent of neurotic patients are diagnosed as hysterics, the majority being women and from lower socioeconomic groups. Most patients have more than a single hysterical symptom; pain is usually the chief complaint, and the condition is often triggered by psychological stress (Stefansson, 1976):

The patient was admitted to the emergency room complaining of severe abdominal pain radiating into her left thigh and leg. She had been rehearsing her wedding and as she was walking down the aisle, tripped or collapsed. She cried out in pain and said she could not get up or walk. Initial examination suggested a lesion or herniation in the lumbar area of the spinal cord. Subsequent examination showed no physical or neurological damage of any kind. Psychodiagnostic examination was ordered and led to the conclusion the patient was suffering from hysterical neurosis.

Over the last hundred years, our understanding and description of hysterical neurosis has changed a great deal. Woolsey (1976), who traced the psychiatric history of this diagnosis from 1875 to 1975, found some of the more important contemporary dimensions to be these:

1. Hysterical patients are highly *suggestible.* Their symptoms can be made to disappear, at least temporarily, by almost any medical placebo (a "fake" pill or treatment), hypnosis, religious or faith healing, or any other technique that is convincing to the patient.
2. Hysterical symptoms make *little physical sense* and are *peculiarly selective.* The patient may complain of a pattern of arm and leg paralysis that does not correspond to any known neural distribution. Many symptoms are also oddly selective: "I can read the newspaper all right, but I can't see the writing in my schoolbooks."
3. Some hysterical patients exhibit *la belle indifference;* they are seemingly unconcerned about what appear to be disabling physical symptoms. This indifference was once held to be a hallmark trait of hysteria,

but it is now common to see patients who are depressed and anxious about their physical limitations.
4. Most patients obtain *secondary gains* (attention, sympathy, financial help) from their symptoms, and some may even be motivated mainly by the benefits their disabilities bring. For nearly all patients, secondary gains such as not having to work and being fussed over tend to prolong the hysterical condition.

In clinical practice, the diagnosis of hysterical neurosis is far from simple. Most patients list a number of typical somatic symptoms like chest pains and digestive upsets, plus more typical hysterical signs such as visual blurring and peculiar sensations in the arms or legs (Table 4.1). To make matters even more complex, Stefansson (1976), in a careful evaluation of the record of several hundred hysterical people, found that most actually had real physical disorders along with hysterical symptoms. Often the real organic disorder helped to trigger or suggest additional psychological pains and complaints.

In the past, the diagnosis of hysteria was applied freely; one reason for the decline in the number of hysterical neurotic cases today is that medical diagnostic procedures are far more exact. Many an older physician can recall cases of multiple sclerosis, brain tumor, or endocrine disturbance that were called hysterical for years before their true organic nature became known. Slater and Glithero (1965) followed up patients who several years earlier had been diagnosed as having hysterical neurosis. They found that the majority eventually developed related physical disorders, and very often neurological diseases. It seems as though what had been called hysteria is actually the preliminary signs of very real organic disease processes. As a result, most diagnosticians now insist on the most careful medical evaluation before reaching a conclusion of hysteria.

Dissociative neuroses

Dissociative neuroses are uncommon conditions in which the main symptom is memory loss or a related disturbance in consciousness.

TABLE 4.1

ANXIETY AND HYSTERICAL NEUROSES: COMPLAINTS
Anxiety and hysterical symptoms are similar, so that in actual clinical practice it is sometimes difficult to distinguish between the two conditions.

Anxiety neurosis	Hysterical neurosis
Most common	
Apprehensiveness	Pains (chest, back, limbs)
Heart palpitations	Dizziness, weakness
Headaches	Nervousness, unsteadiness
Weakness, fatigue	
Unhappiness	
Less common	
Sweating	Nausea
Nausea, diarrhea, lack of appetite	Difficulty breathing
Breathlessness	Fainting
Trembling	Visual problems
Fear of death	Poor appetite
Insomnia	Discomfort in genital organs
Least common	
Fainting	Paralysis
Loss of feeling in limb	Loss of feeling in limb
Lump in throat	Hearing loss
Uncontrollable trembling (seizure)	Lump in throat
	Amnesia
	Convulsions

Sources: *Marks, 1973; Martin, 1976; Noyes, 1976; Stefansson, 1976; Spielberger, 1972; Woodruff, 1972, 1975.*

These neuroses may take any of several related forms: amnesia, somnambulism, fugue, depersonalization, multiple personality.

AMNESIA In this condition, people suddenly realize they have lost their memory. The period lost may be as little as a few hours or days or an entire life. Some people have a type of amnesia called continuous, in which they forget every successive event as it occurs. Contrary to popular myth, the amnesia of dissociative neurosis is rarely due to a blow on the head. Most people tend to retain basic habits, recalling at least vaguely such intimate facts as religion, marital status, and from which region of the country they originate.

SOMNAMBULISM In these states, the person seems to be in a stupor and living in a private world. Such episodes, which may arise while the person is asleep or awake, are *not* ordinary sleepwalking. Instead, the person seems to be in another reality, speaking incoherently, upset about what is happening in that world and unaware or seemingly unconcerned about what is happening in the actual environment. The somnambulistic period seems to be a reliving of an imaginary or actual event, the conscious memory of which might be disturbing or painful. Upon "awakening" from the somnambulistic trance, which may take minutes or hours, the person usually cannot remember the experience at all.

FUGUE The Latin word for flight is used to describe a condition in which people wander away from home for days or even months.

SOMATOFORM DISORDERS

In this chapter we use the historical term hysterical neurosis, since clinicians and scholars still employ this diagnosis. But the latest DSM (1978) suggests several new classifications to replace terms such as hysteria. It will probably be a full decade before the new nomenclature fully replaces the older familiar terminology.

Somatoform Disorders Conditions that resemble physical illness but are psychological rather than organic in origin. The following are specific varieties of somatoform disorders:

Somatization Disorder Chronic and numerous physical complaints often coupled with depression.

Conversion Disorder A loss of sensory or motor function often resembling neurological disease.

Psychalgia Frequent and consistent complaints of pain.

Malingering All the somatoform disorders need to be distinguished from malingering. A malingerer is a person who deliberately fakes physical symptoms.

These people are frequently not aware they have forgotten who they are or where they live. They go to a new location, manage to find a job, and before long seem to establish a new identity and life for themselves.

DEPERSONALIZATION This symptom, found in many different mental disorders, refers to feelings of unreality, lack of control over self, or the belief that one is living in a dream or movie. If depersonalization is the only symptom, or associated only with other memory disturbances, the person is likely to be diagnosed as having a dissociative neurosis.

MULTIPLE PERSONALITY In this variety of dissociative neurosis, the person becomes two, three, or even more distinctly different personalities. Each identity may be very different from every other; for example, one aggressive and assertive, another shy and retiring, a third intellectual and scholarly. The entertainment media frequently portray such people and convey the impression the condition is common. Actually, multiple personality is rare in the extreme; most psychologists and psychiatrists never actually see such a patient.

Amnesia and other memory defects may arise from brain damage, drug overdose, and other physical causes. These are *not* neurotic dissociative states, but are due to brain tissue damage. Dissociative memory losses appear to be due to repression or avoidance behaviors: Memory or awareness seems not to be lost, but instead subdued. In fact, investigations have verified that what is supposedly lost is highly recoverable. Coe and several co-workers (1976) used hypnosis and found that "forgotten" material could be elicited as readily from amnesic patients as from those who were normal. The dissociative states seem to be the result of an active interference process. Patients appear motivated to block personal disappointment, conflicts, or anxiety from recognition, or physically and intellectually flee from difficult circumstances. Mr. L. C. C. is a case in point.

Figure 4.8. The fugue patient is an amnesic who wanders away from his home. Such persons often go to a new location and establish a new job, life style, and identity for themselves. (Photo: Scribe)

Like many dissociative, hysterical neurotic patients, Mr. L.C.C. was motivated "to get away from it all" and had a history of amnesic symptoms. He was generally forgetful, sometimes felt himself very unreal, and often complained of a tingling in the back of his neck and head which accompanied very brief periods of somnambulism. Mr. L.C.C. was 37, married to a successful businesswoman, father of two children, and frequently unemployed since he was a free-lance illustrator. At home the patient felt powerless, unhappy, and frustrated. Mr. C. came to the clinic in San Francisco with the following story. "I have a home and a family outside of Boston . . . This morning at 7:30 A.M. I put on my shoes. They were Hush Puppies. I don't own Hush Puppies. I had tan jeans, a tan striped polo shirt . . . I was in the Y in San Francisco . . . I left home in November. Just before Thanksgiving. I remember I got on a bus. Now its December 19 and I am in a strange city, and I don't have the vaguest recollection of what I have done these past four weeks or where I have been or how I got here. I got new clothes . . . I have money in my wallet. I don't have my credit cards or anything else. I have checked and I registered at the Y as Brewster L.L. but I don't know anything else. I need help and then maybe I should go home.

Other neurotic conditions

In addition to the more prominent neurotic disorders we have discussed, there are a number of other conditions that are less distinct, or for which a label is no longer listed in the Diagnostic and Statistical Manual (see Figure 4.9). We include a sampling of these to give a more complete picture of the diversity of disabilities included in the category of neurosis.

DEPRESSIVE NEUROSIS This condition is characterized by excessive emotional reaction to an identifiable event or internal conflict. The most common precipitants are marital separation, death of a relative, or the onset of disabling illness. Internal conflicts such as whether or not to stay at a difficult job or remain in college may also trigger depression.

Because this type of depression (unlike the varieties we will discuss in Chapter 9) is a response to a specific event, it is also called **reactive depression.**

Unlike normal grief or despair, which clears up in several months to a year, reactive depression becomes chronic. Depressive neurotics have continual feelings of apathy, melancholy, loneliness, and isolation. They feel "down," lose interest in the world around them, and believe no one else really cares. Physically they are likely to look glum, lifeless, fatigued, and worn. They may also complain of various bodily pains, sleeplessness, and digestive disturbances.

What is particularly characteristic of neurotic depressions is that sometimes they are masked by an aggressive or stoic appearance. After a serious loss or conflict, these individuals at first appear surprisingly unflustered. But later on their stoical acceptance melts away as gloom and pessimism take over. More commonly, some depressives hide their unhappiness by seeming to be bitter, sarcastic, and cynical. They become hypersensitive and irritable, and their speech and manner biting and aggressive.

For many people, the depression is in large part the outcome of a *loss of self-esteem.* The loss or environmental challenge has confronted them with their own limitations and they find it difficult to readjust. For some others, the marital separation or the death of a parent signals the end of a dependency relationship. The person is now thrown on his or her own, responsible for himself or herself, and finds it difficult to make the transition from dependency to autonomy.

GANSER'S SYNDROME Ganser's is a rare condition most often found in prisoners and seems to be the result of the person consciously or unconsciously trying to mislead others about his or her mental health. It is sometimes called the "prison neurosis" or the "syndrome of approximate answers." The major symptom is that the patient acts or responds in an awkward, off key sort of way. If you ask such an individual how he is feeling, he is likely to reply, "Well, I guess, so-so, really, maybe OK."

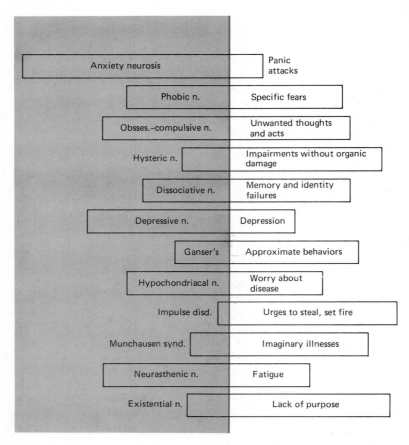

Anxiety neurosis	Panic attacks
Phobic n.	Specific fears
Obsses.–compulsive n.	Unwanted thoughts and acts
Hysteric n.	Impairments without organic damage
Dissociative n.	Memory and identity failures
Depressive n.	Depression
Ganser's	Approximate behaviors
Hypochondriacal n.	Worry about disease
Impulse disd.	Urges to steal, set fire
Munchausen synd.	Imaginary illnesses
Neurasthenic n.	Fatigue
Existential n.	Lack of purpose

Figure 4.9. The neuroses. The left side of this summary diagram suggests the degree to which different neurotic conditions share the same general symptoms. On the right, the symptom that uniquely defines each particular type of neurosis is indicated.

If asked how much is five and five, he may answer, "about nine, more or less, like that." Many clinicians consider Ganser's a type of dissociative neurosis, although in some extreme instances Ganser patients may even appear psychotic.

HYPOCHONDRIACAL NEUROSIS   This condition is more often found in older people, but it can occur at any age. Hypochondriacs are preoccupied with their bodies and particularly anxious about a presumed organic disease. Only after continued and persistent medical reassurances are they convinced they do not have a "bad heart," an ulcer, or cancer. Of course, after one dreaded illness is disposed of they quickly develop another fear—they have diabetes or kidney failure. By continually, self-consciously monitoring their own bodies, they develop one medical anxiety after another.

IMPULSE DISORDERS   Disorders such as pyromania (compulsion to set fires) and kleptomania (compulsion to steal) are themselves rare but sometimes accompany other mental disorders. One or the other is occasionally seen, for example, in mentally retarded individuals or in schizophrenics. But either pyromania or kleptomania may also be found in an otherwise relatively normal person. Though essentially well adjusted, the person has an overpowering urge to set fires. Or though mentally healthy and prosperous, the kleptomaniac steals inexpensive and useless objects. Many clinicians believe that pyromania is frequently rooted in sexual pathology. The disorder is far more frequent in men and seems a symbolic way of experiencing potency. Kleptomania is more frequent in women and is sometimes traced to a need for affection, love, and attention.

MUNCHAUSEN'S SYNDROME This condition derives its name from the mythologized German Baron Von Munchausen, who like Paul Bunyan was noted for his tall tales. Munchausen patients wander from doctor to doctor telling dramatic stories about imaginary and dangerous illnesses. They actually make up symptoms indicating intestinal blockages, hemorrhages, and circulatory disruptions, all with the intent of convincing the doctor to perform surgery. Many of these people have had a large number of unnecessary surgical procedures.

Munchausen's syndrome differs from hypochondria: Hypochondriacs do not make up symptoms; hypochondria is also relatively frequent and accompanied by anxiety, whereas Munchausen's syndrome is rare and patients are quite hostile, aggressive, and demanding people.

NEURASTHENIA Neurasthenia was once a favorite psychiatric diagnosis. In recent years it is found less and less, though whether this is a result of the condition becoming uncommon or the term unpopular is difficult to judge. The chief symptom of neurasthenia is *fatigue*. Patients feel tired, dragged out, lacking in energy and motivation. Associated with this are complaints about vague aches and pains, dizzyness, feeling rotten, and having poor digestion. Although neurasthenic persons are not really depressed, their spirits are generally low and they seem genuinely distressed by their symptoms. Because this condition was found with some frequency among married women who were unhappy with their role as mother and/or wife, it has also been called the "trapped housewife syndrome."

Through the years, theories of the causes of neurasthenia have undergone radical transformation. For Freud, neurasthenia was the result of excessive masturbation or nocturnal emissions; the symptoms were caused by too much sexual activity. Later psychoanalytic writers saw neurasthenia as the consequence of sexual frustration. Because the "trapped housewife" was sexually dissatisfied, her frustrations sapped her of energy and initiative (Cohen, 1974).

EXISTENTIAL NEUROSIS This relatively recent concept was originated by a psychologist, Salvator Maddi (1967), and describes a person who believes life is meaningless. Such people have usually grown up with fairly rigid predetermined role expectations, set to become a lawyer, mother, or corporation executive, but at some point were confronted with the fact that they did not choose but instead were pushed. They believe that since childhood their life patterns have been set for them by parents, friends, teachers, and society, and now they are seeking to free themselves, to rebel against the "establishment."

The result of the existential neurotic's rebellion is that he or she becomes impulse ridden ("I will do only what I want to do"), chronically bored, and listless. Nothing matters, nothing is sacred or valuable. Pleasures are only momentary and fleeting. Ethics and goals are "hangups," and if there is any objective it is to be "mellow." In terms of actual emotional tone and observable behavior, those who are called existential neurotics could also be described by the much older term neurasthenia.

SUMMARY

Neuroses are defined as patterns of maladaptive behaviors accompanied by disruptive symptoms and feelings of distress. Most neurotic patients experience anxiety, behave defensively, and have conflicted relations with other people. Neuroses are now generally diagnosed by the predominant symptom, although the diagnosis may often be changed or disputed because of changing symptoms and circumstances. The major categories of neurosis today are these: Anxiety (attacks of severe anxiety), phobic (specific fears), obsessive-compulsive (recurrent thoughts and rituals), hysterical (physical symptoms), and dissociative (memory losses). Other less frequent categories are depressive (reactive depression), Ganser's syndrome (vague behaviors), hypochondria (preoccupation with illness), impulse disorders (compelled behaviors), Munchausen's syndrome (fabrications to induce surgery), neurasthenia (fatigue), and existential (purposelessness).

In this chapter we have looked at how neurosis is defined and categorized and diagnosed; in the next we will examine causes and treatments, as well as the effectiveness of various kinds of therapy.

The Causes and
Treatment of Neuroses

If the diagnosis of neurosis is difficult and often subject to revision or challenge, the search for causes is even more open to interpretation. In the century since psychology has been a science, theories and hypotheses have proliferated, been refined and changed, gone in and out of fashion. Today we are still faced with variety and uncertainty; there is no one generally accepted explanation that adequately covers the great range of behavior called neurotic. Taken together, however, the theories and hypotheses give us some understanding at least of aspects of the disorders we group together under this label.

Treatment techniques for neurotic disorders are equally varied. They range from traditional analysis to new dynamic therapies such as primal or play therapy to behavior modification and learning therapies based on objective rather than subjective criteria. Here again, we cannot point to one method as being correct or best. They are all, depending on the disorder and the circumstances, effective. Our review of treatment techniques here will be brief; a fuller discussion appears in Chapters 17 and 18.

CAUSES

Like their medical colleagues, mental health professionals search for causes of disorders as well as for accurate descriptions and diagnoses. The psychological explanation proposed by Freud has now been supplemented by organic, social, and learning theories, each of which expands our understanding of the many factors that may play a role in causing neurotic disorders.

Psychodynamic causes

THE FREUDIAN VIEW For Freudian psychoanalysts, anxiety is the key to understanding all neuroses. The **birth trauma,** the supposed pain and fear associated with one's own birth, is believed to provide a model for all later feelings of insecurity and apprehension. Following the initial birth trauma, anxiety becomes aroused whenever the ego experiences **threat,** an attack of some kind. If the threat is the result of actual physical danger, anxiety responses can be realistic, life-preserving behaviors. In neurosis, however, the ego, (meaning the person) feels anxiety as a result of unwarranted guilt, shame, or moral conflict. Such ego anxiety emotions are most likely to occur when biologically rooted impulses, sexual and/or aggressive drives, are opposed by superego needs. The id says "do it, it feels good," the superego says, "it is wrong, wicked and sinful."

The id-superego conflict originates in childhood. Parents *and* society teach infants and children that their inborn needs for sexual experience, self-assertion, and acquisition have to be limited and perhaps even eliminated. In fact, the more punitive and restrictive parents are, the greater the potential for future neurotic conflict and anxiety.

When the id and superego clash, intense feelings of fear and dread are aroused, and the defense mechanisms are called upon to relieve the anxiety. In phobic neuroses, for instance, the major defense mechanism is avoidance. The person builds his or her life around staying away from the anxiety stimulus, which is usually a symbolic representation of the "real" source of the fear. One patient, for example, reported claustrophobia, a severe fear of small and enclosed places like elevators. His analyst determined that his true fear was the possibility of arousing homosexual feelings. He was attracted to men, a drive his superego totally rejected. Consequently, he avoided situations in which his physical closeness to a man might provoke erotic id needs.

Dissociative neuroses are seen by analysts as a consequence of the massive use of the defense mechanism of repression. The person, no longer able to tolerate the id-superego conflict, erases parts of his or her identity, or in extreme instances his or her entire existence, and starts a new life as a different person. Hysterical symptoms are also believed to be a form of dissociation. In this instance, anxiety is symbolically focused on a body part which is then dissociated, cut off, or otherwise rendered useless.

The patient recalled strong Oedipal feelings, that is, sexual and emotional needs for his mother, beginning in earliest childhood. Afraid of punishment by his father, he repressed these Oedipal drives, but as is usually the case, this left him preoccupied with sexuality. Beginning at the age of five, he satisfied part of his curiosity by pressing his ear to his parent's bedroom wall, which adjoined his own. In this way, for several years he guiltily listened to their lovemaking. At the age of 27, when his wife brought his own first child home from the hospital, he developed hysterical deafness. His explanation was that the new baby's crying made his ears ring and become deaf. The psychoanalytic hypothesis is that when his wife gave birth and became a mother, it rearoused the early Oedipal feelings and the related guilt. All these anxiety-producing associations were focused on his ear, so that by defensively cutting it off, making himself deaf, the ego was able to relieve some of the apprehension and fear.

A second source of maladjustive difficulty, according to analytic formulations, lies in the parents' unsatisfactory handling of the psychosexual stages. Mothers or fathers may not recognize the importance of permitting children to work through their oral, anal, and other developmental needs. As a result, they produce a person anxious about and **fixated,** meaning developmentally arrested, at an immature psychosexual stage. Obsessive-compulsive people, for example, are described as fixated at the anal level. Their parents either denied them adequate anal pleasure, or else gave them too much satisfaction. In either case, as adults they retain the perfectionistic, ritualized behaviors supposedly originating in early excretory functions.

THE NEO-FREUDIAN VIEW The classic Freudian view of neurosis is but one of many dynamic explanations. In Freud's own day, some of his students dissented and formulated their own descriptions. Carl Jung (1961) saw neurotic behavior as the result of an intricate and complex conflict between personal unconscious feelings and the **collective unconscious,** the alleged accumulated wisdom and motives of the entire human race. Alfred Adler (1929) assumed neurosis was a kind of widespread and debilitating "inferiority complex," a result of the person's unsuccessful attempt to achieve mastery over his or her environment and life.

A contemporary analyst such as Erik Erikson (1963) proposes that anxiety is the result of a failure in the child's psychosocial development. Like Freud, Erikson says it is necessary for each child to pass through several developmental stages in order to learn self-control, initiative, trust, and most of all to define his or her own identity. But if instead of being raised by caring, concerned parents, children suffer neglect, rejection, hostility, and ambivalence, they grow up distrusting others, the environment, and most particularly their own capabilities. Such individuals, confused about their own identity, suffer continual anxiety and develop neurotic defensive symptoms to help them cope, however inadequately, with the world as they see it.

THE HUMANIST VIEW For Carl Rogers (1961) and other theoreticians in the humanistic tradition, neurosis is a failure of growth. Every person has the need to *self-actualize,* to experience his or her own capabilities. But when children are raised by parents who attack the *self,* their feelings of competence and value, they grow up sensing a large gap between what they can and should do. This incongruence between self-concept and self-expectations ultimately produces anxiety that leads to defensive measures, particularly rationalization, regression, and avoidance.

THE TRANSACTION VIEW Transactional analysts see neurotics as confusing their roles of parent, child, and adult. In order to cope with their disorganization and anxiety, they

construct rigid, defensive personal role and life patterns. This leaves them with a neurotic **script,** a life game they play over and over, all the time wondering why they are in such a rut. The perennial bachelor, for example, age 38, has supposedly looked for a bride since he was 18. He says he does not expect perfection. But analysis reveals that because of his anxiety he continues to play the role of child, searching for the "beautiful princess." His fairy-tale script permits him to avoid the anxiety aroused when an ordinary, suitable woman is actually available.

THE GESTALT VIEW Gestalt advocates be-

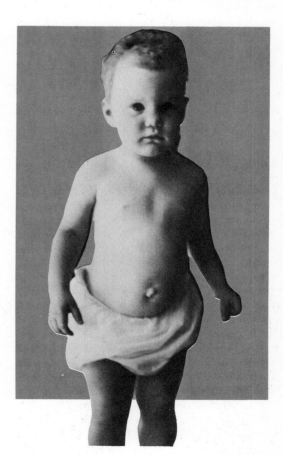

Figure 5.1. Nearly all psychodynamic theorists agree that neuroses originate in unsatisfactory parental relations during childhood. (Photo: Scribe)

Many women—and many men—concerned about psychological and social equality have accused Freud and psychoanalysis of helping to perpetuate gender discrimination. They point out that Freud's description of personality development overlooks or dismisses the psychological growth and problems of women. For example, Freud based some of his theory of neurosis on an unresolved oedipal conflict. Little boys supposedly "fall in love" with their mothers; unless this crisis is worked out, anxiety symptoms follow. The same age period for little girls is almost ignored, as if nothing very important is happening.

But when Freud does describe female psychodynamics, he frequently does so by looking at women as imperfect men. Freud asserted that women spent all their lives either trying to be like men or compensating for the fact that they were not male. This striving was called *penis envy*. Supposedly, little girls notice that they do not have a penis and feel flawed, mutilated, deprived. This envy generates great anxiety and results in women becoming sexually incompetent, self-pitying, narcissistic, and vain. With very few exceptions, women remain intellectually, emotionally, and socially less capable people.

Scholars who defend Freud point out that he also wrote that the "inferiorities" attributed to penis envy were the result of social conditioning. Women were born neither envious nor innately inferior. Freud was aware that in his male-dominated early twentieth-century European society, and perhaps to an extent in our own, women were consciously assigned a subservient role. Further, in his own life Freud treated women with what was then considered extraordinary equality. Although in 1920 women professionals were very unusual, he encouraged a number of women to become doctors and psychoanalysts, the most well known of which was his own successful daughter, Anna Freud.

lieve neurosis is the result of the person's inability to integrate his or her existence. The person does not live in the here and now but instead persists in carrying all sorts of rigidities, inhibitions, expectations, and disparate life goals carried over from childhood. In a somewhat similar vein, Erich Fromm (1973) has written of each person's need for relatedness and rootedness, to be in touch with other people and feel one belongs. To achieve these goals, people develop a social character. If childhood has been good, this will result in adjustment and competence. But if the person is weakened by years of parental mistreatment, if he or she grows up anxious and uncertain, the result will be a neurotic character structure. Two very common types in Fromm's formulation, the hoarding and the necrophilous personality, are roughly the same as the obsessive-compulsive and the depressive.

Organic causes

The evidence that neuroses, or that at least some neurotic symptoms, are physically caused begins with the results of animal investigations. Traits such as fearfulness, for example, can be genetically emphasized. Careful selection, breeding only the most "anxious" rats with each other, has led to generations of laboratory animals each increasingly exhibiting this trait. In fact, as horse breeders and dog fanciers know well, personality characteristics such as dominance, emotionality, and aggressiveness can be selectively bred in most domestic animals. But whether or not such data reveals much about the heritability of human characteristics remains an open question.

Among people, temperamental differences are often evident from birth. Some babies are noticeably relaxed and placid and others tense and easily upset literally from the time they are born. Such observations suggest that if neurosis is not inborn, perhaps the inherent structure of each individual nervous system makes some individuals more likely than others to manifest traits like anxiety. Twin studies of anxiety have actually supported this contention.

Slater and Shields (1969) studied 45 pairs

of twins where at least one of the pair was diagnosed as neurotically anxious. Seventeen of the twin pairs were monozygotic, that is, genetically identical. For these, the concordance rate for anxiety was 41 percent. When one of the twin pair was rated high in anxiety the chances were 4 in 10 that the other was similarly evaluated. For the 28 dizygotic, or fraternal pairs, the concordance for anxiety was only 4 percent. In this study, it looked very much as if inborn factors play an important role in determining anxiety, but subsequent genetic explorations of anxiety have yielded less impressive concordance rates. In several investigations in Japan, Europe, and the United States, the shared rate for anxiety for identical twins has remained high, but that for fraternal twins and ordinary siblings has also been fairly high. Marks and Lader (1973), in their review of several decades of family genetic studies, conclude that although the hereditary transmission of anxiety is far from a certainty, it is a low to fair probability. It seems that anxiety, a trait which may be at the core of the majority of neurotic behavior, may be in at least some small part genetically determined.

Evidence for the innateness of neurotic symptoms other than anxiety is far less certain. There is a slight tendency for hysteria, phobic and dissociative conditions, and neurasthenia to run in families. If one parent has obsessive-compulsive neurosis, for example, as few as 2 percent or as many as 20 percent of the children have been found to have similar neuroses (Eaves, 1973; Miner, 1973). But such results, of course, raise the question of heredity or environment: The child raised by obsessive-compulsive or other neurotic parents is just as likely to have learned neurotic behaviors as to have had them genetically transmitted.

Many other organic factors may play a role in the causes of neuroses. Animal studies have suggested that hazardous prebirth conditions may lead to psychopathology. Pregnant mice placed under stress, electrically shocked, or exposed to bright lights often give birth to offspring that act "emotional" or "fearful." In humans too, it is suspected that mothers whose pregnancy is subjected to serious, prolonged trauma, or who are nutritionally deprived or sick tend to have babies psychologically and physically less healthy (McClearn and DeFries, 1973). This is particularly true for premature babies or those who suffer possible oxygen deprivation at birth. Such infants are far more likely to have many serious physical, emotional, and intellectual problems (Fieve, et al., 1975; Martin, 1976; Rosenthal, 1970; Spielberger, 1972).

Diet and physical illnesses may also play a role in neurosis. Several investigators have noted the frequency with which actual physical disease coexists with neurotic disorders. The presence of organic illness both increases anxiety and also suggests additional psychological symptoms. For example, people with backaches caused by an actual muscular sprain are often so fearful about their disability that they become depressed and feel continuously fatigued. Some nutritionists suspect that chemical additives, lack of nutrients, or the typical American diet high in carbohydrates and sugar could lead to fatigue, depression, and other feelings frequently diagnosed as neuroses. Along this line, Greden (1974) has shown that many people drinking only four or five cups of coffee per day may get over 300 mg of caffeine. For susceptible persons this is enough to stimulate anxiety symptoms like nervousness, insomnia, irritability, and heart palpitations. At present, however, the role of diet, vitamins, drugs, and maternal health in neuroses is lacking in reliable scientific documentation and largely unexplored.

Social causes

Neuroses are frequently viewed as exclusively the product of industrialized societies and middle-class life styles. Supposedly, people become anxious, compulsive, or phobic because of competition, loneliness, and the other stresses said to typify life in the modern world. Although this seems a plausible hypothesis, investigations of the **epidemiology** of neuroses, the relationship of social factors to disease, have not confirmed this view. Rather, it seems that neuroses are found throughout the world. To cite

NEUROSES CAUSED BY SHOCK?

Early psychiatrists were convinced that neuroses were caused by a shock, by a single traumatic event. If patients did not spontaneously report the critical episode, their recollection and honesty were pressed until finally the trauma was produced. Thus, at the beginning of his practice Sigmund Freud announced that the root cause of hysterical neurosis and several other conditions was parental seduction. Little girls were apparently particularly vulnerable, for in every case analyzed, the female patient reported sexual abuse by her father during childhood. As case after case piled up, Freud became suspicious. Perhaps his own psychiatric attitude and theoretical expectations had something to do with the inevitable tale of seduction by every patient. Searching carefully, Freud found that nearly all the seduction traumas were false. He called them *screen memories,* stories that were personal fantasy or unconsciously made up to suit particular psychological needs, including the wish to please the therapist.

Psychological shocks, accidents, and other traumatic events sometimes precipitate neurotic, psychotic, or other mental disorders. But in most instances such conditions are temporary reactions, transitory disturbances that clear up with time and a minimum of treatment. People with anxiety, hysteria, compulsions, phobias, and the like frequently come from family backgrounds characterized by pain, dissension, unhappiness, and mistreatment—but usually no single event, however difficult, is responsible for neuroses.

---

just one example, a study of Yoruba women in Africa found that in this largely rural culture depression and anxiety were common neurotic problems, just as they are in the United States (Dohrenwend and Brown, 1976; Dohrenwend, 1974, 1975).

Surveys by the World Health Organization and other investigations indicate that neuroses occur in all countries regardless of the degree of industrialization, size and composition of the population, or cultural history. But there may be some differences in the total number of disorders and in the prominence of various symptom patterns. Such differences are usually a function of several of the following factors (Dohrenwend, 1974, 1975):

1. Childhood and family life may be a more stressful experience in some nations, particularly those suffering serious internal unrest, high unemployment, or similar disruptions.
2. Traditional beliefs, religious customs, and personal ideals play a role in determining the form many neurotic symptoms take. For example, a society that idealizes obedience and limits self-expression more often produces obsessive-compulsive neuroses.
3. Diagnostic criteria for what constitutes emotional illnesses vary greatly. In many less urbanized societies, anxiety and hysterical symptoms are more likely to be considered tolerable handicaps rather than being counted as emotional disorders requiring treatment.
4. The prevalence of neurosis, unlike that of the more seriously disabling psychoses, often appears related to the number of psychotherapists. It might seem logical to conclude that an increase in therapists results from a growing need for more such services. The opposite may be true. The greater availability of mental health treatment opportunities tends to encourage the self-report of neurotic symptoms that might otherwise remain undiscovered.

The operation of some of these factors can be seen in the case of a 22-year-old man who was diagnosed as an anxiety neurotic. He was born in India and lived there until the age of 15, when he was brought to the United States with the help of his uncle.

If I was still in India I would not have been expected to go to college, get high grades, and struggle to get into graduate school. I would have continued in the tradition of my father and brother and worked on the railroad. . . . It is true that I have always been fearful, ever since I was a little child. . . . I was known as the fearful one. . . . In India I would be very worried about our poverty. But I would not have thought to complain nor would my parents send me to a doctor. Now I have been here seven years. My studies are very upsetting to me and my counselor says that I have anxiety neurosis.

NEUROSES AND SOCIAL CLASS   In the United States attention has centered on the relationship between neuroses and social class. In a comprehensive epidemiologic study, Hollingshead and Redlich (1958) reported that neuroses were as much as two to four times as frequent in the middle as compared to the lower classes. It seemed that the supposed special conditions of middle-class life, the quest for school grades and later on for better salaries, houses, and other material possessions, could be blamed for the apparent high incidence of neurotic disorder. But support for this contention, like that for the assumption that neurosis is exclusively the product of industrialization, has been weak at best. Hollingshead and Redlich themselves noted that the overall rates for *all* mental illness could be described as roughly the same for both lower and higher socioeconomic groups. The lower groups, however, were more often *labeled* psychotic, whereas the middle-class people were more likely to be diagnosed as neurotic. There was a distinct tendency for psychiatrists and psychologists to see lower-class people as sicker than those from middle-class origins, perhaps because of the differences in the diagnosticians' own backgrounds and values.

Two people with anxiety but from different class backgrounds express their fear and discouragement in distinctive ways. The educated one may appear at a clinic well groomed, and complaining about "gastrointestinal distress," and "lack of initiative." The lower-class, uneducated patient may be poorly dressed and unkempt, talk about "bad bowels," and act

suspicious and fearful of professionals, before whom he or she feels inadequate and intimidated. This person is likely to be falsely classified psychotic, possibly paranoid schizophrenic.

Our evidence today suggests that the proportion of all neuroses in general may be almost the same for both lower and middle classes. But because of varied life styles and socioeconomic inequalities, there are some differences in the distribution of neurotic diagnostic types (Figure 5.3), such as hysteria, hypochondria, anxiety, and phobia.

HYSTERIA AND HYPOCHONDRIASIS   Hysteria and hypochondria seem to occur with greater frequency in people with less schooling and fewer economic advantages. In fact, the extent to which neurotic symptoms involve physical complaints is inversely related to socioeconomic level. The relationship is by no means perfect, but there is a rough tendency for people with poorer intellectual skills to have more neurotic complaints about digestion, heart palpitations, headaches, and many other physical grievances.

Hypochondriasis is found with fairly high frequency in poorer older people and in ethnic groups of European origin. Among older people, increasing attention seems to be drawn to the body and its functions. This apparently

Figure 5.2. Neuroses are found in every nation of the world regardless of the degree of industrialization or urbanization. But in countries with greater unemployment, civil unrest, or other stresses, the incidence of neuroses could be high. (Photo: Scribe)

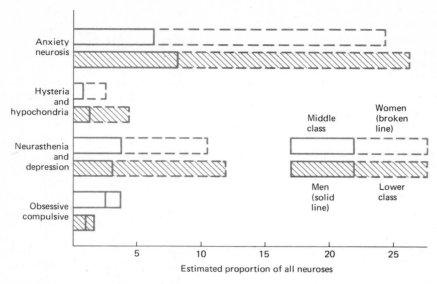

Figure 5.3. Neuroses and social class. (Sources: Agras, 1969; Brown, 1976; Dohrenwend, 1974; Hollingshead, 1958; Kenyon, 1976; Srole, 1962; Stefanson, 1976; Woodruff, 1972.)

Figure 5.4. This Daumier (1808–1879) lithograph caricatures a hypochondriac imagining illness, death, and burial. (Photo: National Library of Medicine, Bethesda, Md. 20014)

makes it easy to transfer many of the anxieties and stresses of aging into physical symptoms. Among a few ethnic groups, hypochondria seems to represent a cultural style. It is a means of expressing discontent or uncertainty that is learned and passed from generation to generation. Supporting this observation is the very high frequency of hypochondria in families. In a large proportion of patients their own hypochondria seems to have been modeled after that of their parents (Buss, 1976; Goldstein, 1976; Kenyon, 1976).

Hysterical symptoms seem to depend to a good extent on relative ignorance of anatomy and physiology. The socially limited and poorly educated person may believe his hand could be paralyzed because he is masturbating. The better-informed individual knows this an impossibility.

Hysteria is also a "social" disorder. Because hysterical people are often very suggestible, groups of people often "infect" one another with hysterical symptoms. Such copying is more likely in high-stress situations; in wartime, for example, a whole company of soldiers may develop certain symptoms. But it may also occur under milder anxiety conditions such as in a college dormitory, a small town, or an urban housing development, as the following case shows.

On May 3 an unemployed couple living in a three-year-old public housing complex appeared at a neighboring hospital clinic and complained of headaches, stiff neck, and tingling in their arms and legs. They thought that a new wall covering recently put up in the hallway caused their symptoms. The patients were examined and no physical correlates for their complaints could be found. Two days later two more housing residents appeared with similar symptoms. The next week the number of afflicted patients increased to 16. The following week there were 12, and then only 5 more came before the "epidemic" ended in June. All the patients were given a mild tranquilizer, reassured, and recovered completely.

In order to check on all possible causes, the wall covering, glue, and all other plausible contaminants were analyzed. The results were negative. The manufacturer was contacted and was able to show that in fifteen years of similar applications of the covering in hundreds of schools, apartment houses, and other facilities there was absolutely no evidence of any toxic or allergic reaction. The inescapable conclusion was that the proper diagnosis was hysteria.

A finding somewhat similar to this case of group hysteria was reported by Mucha and Reinhardt (1970). They investigated an unusually high frequency of hysterical symptoms among student naval aviators. In one year 56 patients appeared for treatment with symptoms such as visual blurring, double images, hearing losses, and other sensory impairments. The authors considered psychoanalytic interpretations of the massive outbreak of hysteria. But their data did not support the contention that the conversion neurosis is the result of unconscious sexual fantasies. As may have been the case with many of the public housing patients, an "escape" hypothesis seemed likely. The cadets had a previous record of success and achievement in high school and college. Their flight training was highly

demanding and even hazardous. But since quitting was personally unacceptable, and they had examples of physical ailments leading to termination, hysterical symptoms seem to have provided an honorable way out.

ANXIETY NEUROSIS   Anxiety, the most common diagnosis, is found with about the same frequency in all social classes. Woodruff and his associates (1972), however, have noted it to be more than twice as common in women than in men. A similar tendency has been observed for neurasthenic and depressive neuroses, which also seem to afflict women more frequently. Various reasons have been proposed, but one of the hypotheses that seems to have held up a little better than others may be the "helplessness" description. People whose lives seem static, who feel caught by responsibilities and burdened by demands, often seem to retreat into fatigue, fear, and depression. In our society women may much more often feel, or be, trapped by an unsatisfactory marriage, stereotyped roles (housewife or secretary), or lack of education and equal opportunity (Brown, 1976; Cohen, 1974; Crago, 1972; Udell, 1976).

The research data supporting the helplessness hypothesis is scattered. Investigations in industry have suggested that workers who have some control over their work—for example, the speed of the assembly line—are less likely to feel trapped and develop neurotic symptoms. Animal studies have also shown that monkeys who can exercise some control over whether or not they will receive an electric shock are less fearful than monkeys totally helpless in avoiding pain (Seligman, 1975). In one interesting experiment, Geer et al. (1970) asked whether being in control mattered as much as *believing* you were not helpless. Subjects were given electric shocks lasting several seconds. Control subjects were simply informed how long each shock would last. Experimental participants were told that if their reaction time in pressing a switch was fast enough after each shock began, they could reduce its duration. Actually, the shocks for both control and experimental groups lasted equally long. But the experimental subjects who thought they were partially in control, who felt less helpless about the source of their stress, exhibited fewer signs of anxiety and emotionality.

PHOBIAS Phobias are found in all social classes, appear a little more often in women than men, but are most closely related to age. Serious animal and school phobias may be seen in 2 to 5 percent of all children. Erythrophobia (fear of blushing) is occasionally found among adolescents and agoraphobia is usually limited to adults. At each stage in life, objects or situations that play an important role or perhaps symbolize a developmental challenge can become phobic stimuli.

There is still another factor, and that is that society often and usually unwittingly encourages some phobic behavior. School phobias, for example, are sometimes initiated or complicated by the confining appearance and impersonality of a particular educational system. To a small child, the separation from parents may seem a threat to existence and the vast hallways and crowded classrooms a nightmare come to life:

My school was only three blocks from home. The first day my mother brought me and I was scared. She left me in the classroom and I was sure I would never see home again. . . . It was awful, all the children were so noisy and I was so scared and the teacher was yelling at everyone. . . . I threw up and had to be taken to the nurse who sent me home. My mother sent me for a few more days but I always got sick. . . . Then I refused to go. . . . So in the morning she would push me out the front door and lock it behind me. . . . She did this for about a week. I would stand there and I would cry and I would throw up but she wouldn't let me in. . . . That was one of the worst experiences of my life.

Starting school is a bewildering experience for all children and can easily become the focus for many fears; but many schools seem unaware of the fear potential of children and do nothing to help ease the transition from home to institution. Some systems may even contribute to the development of phobias by their indifferent and bureaucratic handling of pupils (Agras, 1969; Gittleman-Klein, 1973).

Neuroses as learned behavior

It is popular to contrast the psychodynamic viewpoint with the learning or behavioral position in explaining neuroses. But making too rigid a distinction may misrepresent both explanations of neuroses. Many current psychodynamic theories such as transactional analysis recognize that maladaptive life styles are learned, and even early psychoanalysts were aware that neurotic symptoms like phobias and compulsive rituals are the product of experience:

In 1909 Sigmund Freud reported the case of *Der Kleine Hans,* little Hans, who had a terrible fear of horses. The phobia dated from the time Hans was riding in a coach with his mother and one of the horses fell and was injured.

According to Freud, the child's phobia involved two elements. First there was a large reservoir of anxiety related to the child's Oedipal fantasies. He was dreadfully afraid his father would discover his incestuous longing for his mother and punish or even castrate him.

Figure 5.5. Mild to moderate school phobias are common in young children. Often schools contribute to children's fears by their massive, confining, and impersonal appearance. (Photo: Scribe)

The second vital element was that an incident needed to occur which could serve as a symbol and crystallize these fears. In this instance the precipitating event was the injured animal who was beaten and prodded in order to make him pull again. Hans was ready to become afraid, and learned to be phobic of horses.

The Freudian "learning" explanation is dependent on assumptions concerning motivation, previous experience, and personal feelings. Contemporary behavioral positions describe the same animal phobia without reference to any psychological processes. The classical conditioning model sees phobias as learned fear responses acquired in much the same way as that seen in the child who was made afraid of rats by banging on a steel bar. This youngster developed a fear of rats, and following the laws of learning, the phobia generalized to all furry animals (Chapter 3).

In order to explain a wider range of neuroses in addition to phobias, Eysenck (1976) proposes different predispositions toward anxiety. Freud spoke of a reservoir of fear; Eysenck believes some people are more innately anxious. The child whose nervous and endocrine systems give him or her a high anxiety potential is *prepared* to learn a number of phobias, compulsions, and other neurotic symptoms. People with anxiety and other neuroses have both generalized specific fears and also a large number of particular anxiety cues. Their fears and/or symptoms are thus always ready to be activated by a variety of social, personal, and environmental conditions.

OPERANT CONDITIONING The operant view is that behavior which is reinforced persists. Since anxiety reduction is reinforcing, any behavior that results in a decrease in anxiety is likely to remain. This is seen most clearly in obsessive-compulsive neurosis. Here the compulsive ritual is an act that often reduces the fear-laden obsessive thought. Hence no matter how silly or irrational it is, it continues. For example, Roper et al. (1973) studied compulsive checkers. These people continuously check and recheck that their door is locked, their clothing properly folded, the light off, and

so on. They are obsessed by the need to do things "right" in a determined, ritualistic way. Roper arranged his research so that he could provoke a checking response. The subjects were evaluated before and after their ritual and showed a clear increase in anxiety before checking and a decrease afterward. Their compulsive checking behavior was reinforcing.

The neurotic behavior that is learned through reinforcement may "make sense" or it may be the result of chance. Naval aviators who have hysterical symptoms such as double vision seem to have a symptom directly connected to the sources of anxiety. In contrast, many compulsive symptoms are the result of little more than capricious accident. A kleptomaniacal client illustrated this when she recalled her first shoplifting:

Whenever I had a fight with my husband I would go shopping. That usually made me feel better. . . . That time when I went shopping, I was still very upset and I just took this little 89-cent hair ribbon and I remember I felt a lot better. That was the first time but then I went back more and more and it had nothing to do with whether or not Bill and I had a fight. I just stole things because I felt I had to.

SOCIAL LEARNING The social learning position broadens the reinforcement concept and states that neurotic behavior may involve many different and subtle rewards. Neurotic behaviors may "pay off" because they evoke sympathy, attention, and other social reinforcers. Some people may unknowingly structure their environment so that only maladjusted behavior and sick self-perceptions are reinforced. They may interact with others in such a way that they are rejected and made to feel undesirable and anxious.

Coyne (1976) conducted an experiment in which female college students were asked to speak on the phone for twenty minutes to either a depressed or a normal person. In contrast to their response to the normal person, the depressed one made the students very uncomfortable. Probably because the depressed

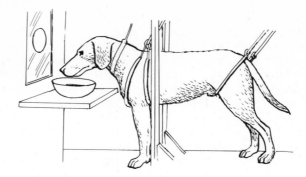

Ivan Pavlov (1927) the Russian physiologist who is credited with the discovery of classical conditioning, was among the first to explore experimental neuroses. Pavlov taught his dogs that food would be given whenever a circle was flashed on the screen. When an ellipse was presented, there was no food. When the dogs had been successfully conditioned, salivating for the circle and not salivating for the ellipse, Pavlov began to decrease the difference between the two shapes. At the point when the animals could apparently no longer make out the distinction in the two shapes, they showed experimental neurosis. The dogs behaved as if they were in the throes of a terrible conflict; they barked violently, bit at the apparatus, and otherwise acted agitated.

Wolpe (1973) gave electric shocks to cats and so thoroughly induced fear that the animals showed their anxiety even when they saw the experimental apparatus. Wolpe was able to eliminate this fear by feeding the cats, at first far away from, and then closer and closer to the apparatus. By slowly coupling a desirable stimulus with a feared one, he removed anxiety by counterconditioning. Wolpe has made this observation a basis of his therapy. He believes that if a response antagonistic to anxiety can be made to occur in the presence of a feared stimulus, the bond between the stimulus and anxiety can be gradually weakened and eliminated.

Over the years, many forms of anxious and neurotic behaviors have been demonstrated in animals. Sheep, monkeys, and cats have been placed in situations where they could not avoid pain, had to learn complex escape procedures, or needed to choose between not eating and receiving a shock when they did feed. Such experiments make it possible to evaluate the effects of conflict and of other disturbing conditions that it would not be ethical or practical to explore with human beings. All animal studies, however, leave open the question of how applicable the findings are to human behavior.

individuals talked a great deal about death, illness, and conflict, the experimental subjects wanted as little contact with them as possible. Neurotic people might have become disordered partly because they interact in such an aversive way that normal people avoid them. As a result, they get very little social reinforcement for good-natured and positive responses. Instead, almost the only time their behavior is reinforced is when they manage to extract sympathy for depression, anxiety, and other complaints.

Another possible variable that may interact with the kind of neurotic reinforcement just described has been reported by Klein (1976). In this experiment, control subjects could end a painful loud noise by pressing a button, while experimental subjects could do nothing about it. In a follow-up situation, all subjects were tested for their response to a new noise. The control group quickly learned to diminish the sound by moving a knob. The experimental group, which had previously experienced inescapable noise, reacted with anxiety and helplessness. It could be said that those who had previously been unable to escape the painful stimuli had been reinforced for apathy. Some neurotic symptoms, particularly those in neurasthenia, depression, and even hysteria, could arise from situations which have taught the person that there is nothing to do but suffer.

MODELING Just as children learn language, table manners, and even subtle personality traits by imitating their parents, so too are they likely to acquire neurotic behaviors. Many types of neurosis, including hypochondriasis, hysteria, and phobias, appear to run in families. Since there is little evidence for genetic transmission, the likely explanation is that children model or copy the neurotic styles of their parents. Two clinical descriptions and a study illustrate the importance of modeling:

Whenever my mother felt bad she went to bed. She said she was tired. That's exactly what I do. I guess that's why I feel so tired so much of the time (patient was diagnosed neurasthenic).

Mrs. V. W. complained of several phobias, including bearded men and medical doctors. Her history revealed her mother was very phobic and would often hide in the basement with the child during thunderstorms.

Adams (1973) studied 49 obsessive-compulsive children and their families. He found an assortment of rituals including counting, tics, and touching. The families were middle class and well educated. By parental example and admonition, the children had to be exact, clean, and above all correct. The child continually risked psychological discomfort and anxiety if he or she did not behave in precisely the right way. Ultimately, compulsive rituals arose out of the constant desire to be correct in order to avoid anxiety.

TREATMENT

Many different treatment techniques have been and are being used with neuroses, but the variety breaks down into two basic groups: psychodynamic therapies and behavior therapies. Medication is frequently used as well, but usually in preparation for or along with other techniques. The discussion here will be a brief overview; each of these techniques will be treated in fuller detail in Chapters 17 and 18.

Dynamic therapies

Dynamic therapies seem to be effective with a variety of neurotic disorders, although techniques vary depending upon the theoretical training of the therapist. Psychoanalysts tend to concentrate on the person's childhood and family relationships. They analyze their clients' recollections, dreams, and fantasies, looking for clues to unconscious conflicts and motives. Client-centered therapists are more likely to work with present feelings. They want to know how their clients perceive themselves right now in order to help rid them of negative emotions that impede self-actualization.

Variations of the dynamic approach are almost infinite. Clients may be asked to take part in a **psychodrama,** a theatrical acting out of problem situations. Or they may be asked to isolate themselves in a quiet, darkened room, as is frequent in **primal therapy.** Young patients may be encouraged to express their feeling using toys and dolls in **play therapy.** Very often too, patients are asked to work together in a group. **Group therapy** has many advantages, but most of all it permits people with similar difficulties to share experiences and give one another helpful insights and encouragement.

Behavior therapy

This type of therapy is usually aimed at the relief of symptoms. For example, **systematic desensitization,** a type of classical condition-

TREATING PHOBIAS BY FLOODING

A commonsense and often effective treatment for phobias is to force the person to endure contact with the feared object. Curtis (1976) and his associates used this technique, called *flooding,* with twelve patients. Before the sessions, patients were told that the major reason their phobia persisted was because they always *avoided* contact with it. In learning terms, their avoidance acted as a reinforcer for the anxiety. If they could maintain contact with their phobic object for a long enough time, the fear would diminish. Therapists then brought the feared object into the room, slowly bringing it closer and simultaneously keeping every patient informed and reassured. For most patients, anxiety was at first intense. They trembled, felt nauseated, and their hearts raced; many could be kept in the situation only by cajoling, negotiating, and stern orders to stick with it. Soon, some patients switched from anxiety to anger. Two who had been afraid of spiders, for example, once they overcame their initial anxiety, became angry, wanting to crush and destroy the spider.

Eventually all the patients who stayed in treatment, which ranged from two to seven hours, experienced dramatic relief from their phobias. But although this technique may work for many patients under professional supervision, it may not be effective for those who have several related anxieties or whose adjustment is generally less than adequate.

---

ing method in which patients are taught to associate relaxation with the cues that usually evoke fear, may be tried to relieve specific phobic and other anxiety disorders (Goldfried, 1975). A more complex behavioral technique that touches upon dynamic therapies is Meichenbaum's (1972) **cognitive restructuring,** a self-instructional procedure. Originally designed for phobic behaviors, the technique has been used to treat many other neuroses, including neurasthenia, depressive, and existential conditions. Meichenbaum contends that internal events, thoughts and motives, obey the same laws of learning as externally visible responses. The therapy requires three steps:

1. Patients are instructed that neurotic fears and behaviors are mainly a result of what the patient tells himself about the situation, rather than being due to the situation itself.
2. Clients are trained to recognize their self-defeating, symptom-engendering verbalizations, of which they were previously unaware.
3. By using behavior techniques such as modeling and reinforcement, new and constructive self-verbalizations, which are incompatible with the previous disordered responses, are encouraged.

Medication

Probably the most frequent form of treatment for neuroses, as for many other mental health disorders, is medication. Anti-anxiety drugs such as Librium and Valium or more potent tranquilizers such as Mellaril are usually rapidly effective in relieving severe obsessions, anxiety, and related symptoms. Antidepressants such as Elavil are often used for treating depression, neurasthenia, hypochondria, and many other neurotic conditions.

But effective as it is in helping patients feel and "look" better, psychiatric medication is not thought of as a cure. The drugs help diminish symptoms so that clients can resume their functions and responsibilities. Often medication is also used to facilitate either dynamic or behavioral therapy. It diminishes some of the neurotic person's complaints and makes him or her more cooperative (Begrin, 1971; Iverson, 1975).

Effectiveness

In addition to the therapies we have mentioned, many other techniques are often useful in particular instances. Hypnosis has been found effective with many hysterical and amnesic patients (Kihlstrom, 1976). Vitamin, endocrine, and dietary treatment may also be worthwhile for some neuroses (Ross, 1974). Not surprisingly, since some neurotic patients are literally desperate for help, almost any intervention in their lives often appears useful. Ricalla (1975), for example, has found that the "laying on of hands" may give some neurotic patients enough of a boost to help them work toward a more adequate adjustment.

Neuroses, like other mental disorders, tend to be cyclical. There are peaks of discomfort and symptoms, called **exacerbations.** With time there are also **remissions,** a decrease in distress and neurotic behaviors (Figure 5.7).

Figure 5.6. In relatively healthy individuals with fairly limited phobias, fear can sometimes be successfully treated by flooding—forcing the person to endure the phobia. An acrophobic hiker treated by flooding was eventually able to become a rock climber. (Photo: Scribe)

Because the intensity of neurotic symptoms fluctuate and almost any type of intervention seems to help, it is difficult to evaluate the effectiveness of the various therapeutic approaches.

Two decades ago Eysenck (1965) startled the therapeutic community by announcing research findings demonstrating that two-thirds of neurotic patients got well within two years *without* treatment. Possibly this number was even larger than those who recovered *with* treatment. Additional doubt has been cast on the value of treatment by the behavior vs. dynamic debate. Psychodynamic therapists criticize behaviorists for treating only symptoms. They agree that a particular symptom can be removed, but assert this will only lead to another, a process called **symptom substitution.** The behaviorist position is that the symptom is the problem, and once it is removed the patient is well. The conflict may be a result of two valid therapeutic positions dealing with different neurotic disorders (Figure 5.9). Blanchard (1976) has pointed out that dynamic practitioners are speaking about hysteria when they validly point out the possibility of symptom substitution. Behaviorists are talking about phobias or anxiety disorders when they correctly claim that curing the symptoms is curing the disorder. Both methods, then, can be effective if used appropriately.

Eysenck's criticism that more patients are cured by time than by treatment has not been substantiated. Careful examination of recovery criteria suggests that significant improvement without therapy is probably not much greater than about 30 percent. With a well-trained behavior or dynamic therapist and a client who is young and in relatively good socioeconomic circumstances, the chances for significant improvement or recovery may be as high as 80 percent. In fact, even with people who are not in very favorable life situations, improvement rates are good. Neuroses are probably the most therapeutically responsive of all mental disorders (Begrin, 1971; Beiser, 1976; Eysenck, 1965; Iverson, 1975; Lambert, 1976; Sloan, et al., 1975).

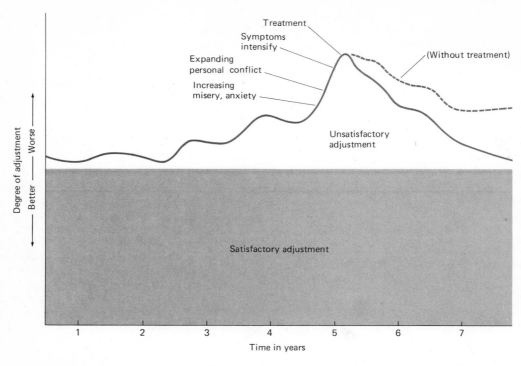

Figure 5.7. The course of neuroses. The solid wavy line represents the experience of many neurotic patients. Although their adjustment is usually unsatisfactory, only occasionally does it become uncomfortable enough to motivate treatment. Even without treatment (dotted line), most neurotic people get better over the course of time. But effective therapy often brings about greater and more enduring improvement.

Figure 5.8. The "nerve" pills advertised in this 1890's litograph sometimes helped neurotic patients feel better. Many neurotic persons, particularly those diagnosed hysteric, can be quite suggestive and seemingly improved even by ineffective treatment. (Photo courtesy, National Library of Medicine, Bethesda, Md.)

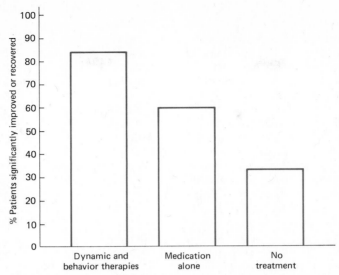

Figure 5.9. Measuring effectiveness. One of the major obstacles in determining the effectiveness of treatment for neuroses is deciding what constitutes improvement. Is it a decrease in symptoms, returning to work, or the therapist's or patient's own estimate of emotional well-being? We have chosen a combination of criteria based on a number of studies. Our conclusion is that skilled dynamic and behavior therapists, treating appropriate neurotic conditions, are about equally successful. We estimate too that both approaches are more effective than medication alone or no treatment *(Sources:* Begrin, 1971; Eysenck, 1965; Iverson, 1975; Lambert, 1976; Malan, 1975; Sloan, 1975).

Figure 5.10. The picture shows a new member being introduced to Neurotics Anonymous, an organization of people helping each other adjust more adequately. (Photo courtesy, Robin West and Neurotics Anonymous, Washington, D.C.)

PSYCHOANALYSIS VS. BEHAVIOR THERAPY VS. NOTHING

R. Bruce Sloan (1975) and his associates compared 31 patients with whom behavior therapy was used with 30 receiving psychoanalytically oriented treatment. Another 33 patients were assigned to a clinic waiting list and received no treatment. Most of the patients were diagnosed as having anxiety neurosis and a few had personality problems. Four months after treatment began, all three groups had improved, but those receiving behavior therapy showed the greatest reduction in symptoms. At one year, all three groups still showed improvement, but both treated groups now significantly outdistanced the nontreated control group in several adjustment areas. After two years, the treated groups maintained or continued their improvement.

David Malan et al. (1975) evaluated 45 neurotic patients who were seen for consultation but never received treatment. Of these, 11 patients were judged very substantially improved despite their initial complaints of anxiety and hysterical neurosis, sexual difficulties, and childhood deprivation. Malan found that those who improved by themselves were unusually insightful and motivated to work through their difficulties. These personality traits may have been assisted by one professional consultation which encouraged them about their own potential, although some could probably have helped themselves without any psychiatric interview at all. This study suggests that the people who improve without treatment constitute a small but unusually capable proportion of the population. Their recovery is not an indication that therapy is useless, but shows instead that some individuals can take the responsibility for managing their own lives.

SUMMARY

Psychodynamic theorists attribute neuroses to id and superego conflict, which leads to anxiety and subsequent defensive behaviors. According to Freudian analysts, fixation at infantile psychosexual levels may also contribute to neurotic character traits. Other psychodynamic theorists believe neurosis is the result of poor parental relations that result in identity problems or an inadequate and impaired self-image.

Animal breeding studies and genetic investigations of human twins have suggested that neurotic traits such as anxiety could have some hereditary component. Diet, disease, or some other condition in the mother or child may also leave some individuals more prone to neuroses.

Neuroses are found throughout the world, although the frequency of particular diagnoses may vary somewhat according to educational, social, and other environmental conditions. Hysteria and hypochondria are often related to educational level, and the former is more common among suggestible individuals. Group outbreaks of hysteria are sometimes encountered. Anxiety and related neuroses are found more often in women and could be related to feelings of helplessness. Phobias are related to age; school fears, unwittingly encouraged by some educational systems, are seen with some frequency in children. Those who believe neuroses are learned behaviors explain them in terms of classical or operant conditioning, social learning, and modeling.

Neuroses are treated primarily by psychodynamic or behavioral therapy. Medication, however, may also be used to alleviate some symptoms or prepare patients for more extensive psychological help.

The effectiveness of treatment has been questioned, but several studies show that competent medical, behavioral, and dynamic therapies bring about significant improvement or recovery in a very high proportion of all patients.

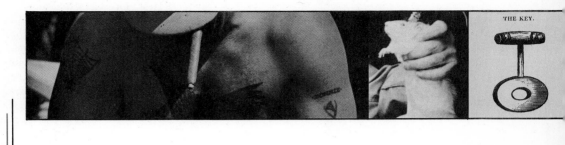

THE KEY.

Psychosomatic Disorders

Today we know that any physical disease can have psychological roots, and we no longer accept the ancient distinction between the psyche (the mind) and the body. We see the human organism as an integrated unit in which mind and body work together in a single living system. Disease therefore can have both physical and psychological causes, and the psychological component can be of greater or lesser importance. Those diseases that frequently have a high psychological component we call **psychosomatic.** They may still sometimes be purely physical in origin, but more often they are due to the interaction of physical and emotional (psychological) variables. High blood pressure, for example, can be just physically caused by arterial damage; it can also be affected by the person's life situation and particularly by stress and diet.

Unlike the symptoms of hysterical, hypochondriacal, or anxiety neuroses, which are vague and usually not associated with enduring physical damage, psychosomatic illnesses are specific and result in actual body changes. An ulcer is literally a wound in the stomach wall; anorexia (not eating) results in drastic weight loss and sometimes death from malnutrition. For a long time, diseases in this category—asthma, ulcers, skin disorders, high blood pressure, migraine headaches—were given the label **psychophysiologic.** But clinicians continue to employ the traditional term psychosomatic, and we will use both interchangeably here.

In this chapter we will look at the categories of psychosomatic illness and at theories of causation; then we will examine the more common conditions in detail to evaluate the evidence for the various theories. We will also take a look at biofeedback, a new treatment technique that is proving effective for certain kinds of psychosomatic illnesses and that uses the patient's mind to control body functions thought to be uncontrollable.

CATEGORIES OF PSYCHOSOMATIC DISORDERS

Psychosomatic illnesses tend to involve organ units such as the gastrointestinal, endocrine, genitourinary, or cardiovascular systems. Below we will briefly summarize possible psychosomatic illnesses by organ system; later in the chapter we will examine in detail some of the more common ones: peptic ulcers, bronchial asthma, essential hypertension, migraine, skin disorders, and eating disorders. (The genitourinary disorders are discussed in Chapters 12 and 13.)

The gastrointestinal system

Peptic ulcer	A wound or lesion on the wall of the stomach or duodenum.
Colitis	Inflammation of the colon (the large intestine), resulting in diarrhea, pain, constipation, and sometimes bleeding and anemia.
Gastritis	Inflammation of the stomach causing pain, gas, nausea, and other discomfort.
Constipation	Lack of regular bowel movements.
Diarrhea	Frequent and loose bowel movements.
Heartburn	Burning feeling in the stomach or esophagus.

The respiratory system

Bronchial asthma	Attacks of difficult breathing with spasms of coughing and wheezing.
Hyperventilation	Attacks of overly deep breathing resulting in dizziness or fainting.
Chronic hiccups	Diaphragmatic spasms that may result in vomiting, insomnia, and fatigue.

The cardiovascular system

Hypertension	High blood pressure leading to eventual heart, kidney, or blood vessel damage.
Tachycardia	Irregular and rapid heart rate (above 100 beats per minute).
Migraine	Severe headaches usually preceded by warning symptoms and accompanied by vomiting.
Raynaud's disease	Spasms of the small blood vessels, especially in the fingers, leading to coldness and numbness.
Angina pectoris	Sudden intense chest pain caused by temporary inability of the blood vessels to supply sufficient oxygenated blood to the heart muscles.
Myocardial infarction	Sudden damage to the heart muscle due to failure of a coronary blood vessel, frequently resulting in death (medical term for a heart attack).

The endocrine system

Hyperthyroidism	Too much thyroid hormone, often resulting in overactivity, nervousness, and weight loss.
Hypothyroidism	Insufficient thyroid hormone, often causing sluggishness, obesity, and fatigue.
Diabetes mellitus	Inability to metabolize sugars; indicated by symptoms including excessive thirst, weakness, and weight loss.

The skin

Hives (urticaria)	Usually raised, weltlike, itchy lesions that erupt in batches.
Eczema	A term for any kind of dermatitis (skin disease) in which symptoms include redness, crusting, oozing, and scaling.
Psoriasis	A chronic skin disease frequently marked by shiny, scalelike patches.
Pruritis	Itching, usually marked at night and often involving the legs and genital organs.

The genitourinary system

Impotence	Male inability to achieve or sustain erection.
Frigidity	Female inability to be sexually aroused or achieve orgasm.
Dysmenorrhea	General term for irregular or painful menstruation.
Dyspareunia	Pain during coitus, often due to vaginal spasm.
Urinary disorders	Bedwetting, painful urination, excessively frequent or involuntary urination.

The musculoskeletal system

Cramps, pain	Muscular tension and pain in the neck, low back, shoulder, legs, and head.
Arthritis	A general term indicating a number of different conditions that may cause swollen and painful joints.

Other

	Allergies, eating disorders such as bulimia (overeating) and anorexia nervosa (inadequate eating), and sleep disorders

CAUSES OF PSYCHOSOMATIC DISORDERS

It seems that a number of factors often combine to bring about psychomatic illnesses. There may be organic predispositions, but many of these conditions may be more dependent upon the nature of the stress to which an individual is subjected and life circumstances. Cultural, environmental, and learning variables may also play a role; the function of personality traits is less obvious. Often one particular approach fits a specific ailment quite well but does not account for others. We have, as in the case of the causes of neurosis, no satisfactory comprehensive explanation. What we do have is a number of theories from different viewpoints—medical, psychological, social—each of which broadens our knowledge.

The stress theory

In 1936 a Canadian scientist, Hans Selye (1975), injected extracts of cattle ovaries into rats during some hormonal experiments. The rats underwent several drastic physical changes, including an increase in adrenal gland activity. Selye saw this as an *alarm reaction* and demonstrated it to be part of an overall response to stress. Whenever an organism is subjected to any stress—a foreign chemical, a microorganism, or a psychological challenge—the body responds by a call to arms, biologically mobilizing itself for defense.

Following an increase in the production of adrenalin, accelerated heart rate and respiration, and many other changes, the body enters a *resistance stage* fully equipped to deal with the threat. But if the resistance stage continues, either because the threat is chronic or the body responds as if the threat were still present, the organism eventually becomes exhausted, impaired by the effects of its own defensive resources. In other words, the increased adrenal production, the changes in the lymphatic structure, spleen, muscles, and other organs eventually prove damaging to the body itself. In Selye's rats, one of the long-

Figure 6.1. As a group, gastrointestinal disorders such as colitis, constipation, and peptic ulcers, may be the most common of all psychosomatic conditions. (Photo: Scribe)

range consequences of their continued preparation to resist attack was bleeding ulcers.

The stress theory, developed by Selye and his followers over the last generation, that biochemical changes brought on by stress are eventually self-damaging, has received wide acceptance. It is thought that emotional, environmental, and other personal stresses cumulatively leave biochemical scars that eventually result in ulcers, hypertension, asthma, and other psychosomatic diseases (Gottschalk, 1975).

The specific reaction hypothesis

Since each human being is in some ways different from every other, the idea that people have their own special pattern of physical response to challenge has been put forward as another explanation for psychosomatic disorders. In one person, for example, threat may produce rapid heartbeat; in another, it may produce diarrhea. These individual differences in response to stress have been explained in several ways: some theorists ascribe them to body type; others, to learning or conditioning.

CONSTITUTION Some theorists suggest that *body type* predisposes a person to particular stress responses. Endomorphic (well rounded and usually overweight) people, for example, are believed to be more likely to develop gastrointestinal symptoms. Others argue that people have "organ weaknesses" due to heredity, earlier physical disease, malnutrition, or possibly intrauterine (before birth) conditions. But whichever position they hold, advocates of the constitutional explanation emphasize that individuals are born with or physically acquire certain bodily organs more likely than others consistently to react to and eventually be impaired by stress (Rees, 1976).

LEARNING Whenever a person is emotionally aroused, a number of familiar autonomic changes take place: Heartbeat and respiration speed up, intestinal mobility is altered, muscles are tensed, and so on. Those who take the learning position contend that a single reinforced response tends to be *selected out* of the constellation of emotional reactions. For example, children who respond emotionally to the threat of having to attend school may have their stomach discomfort rewarded, out of their entire group of complaints, by being permitted to stay home. An autonomic response is thus learned on the basis of operant reinforcement. Lachman (1972) sees a second step as necessary to complete psychosomatic reinforcement learning:

The concept of vicious-circle effects is also necessary to understand certain psychosomatic phenomena. Once initiated, a psychosomatic event may produce stimuli that lead to implicit reactions, which rearouse or intensify the psychosomatic event, and so on. For example, the noxious stimulation from a gastric ulcer may elicit implicit reactions including facilitated stomach-acid secretion, which intensifies that ulcerous condition, which leads to further emotional reaction and further irritation of the ulcer.

Simply put this means having an ulcer may make a person worry more, which may cause even more acid to be secreted, worsening the ulcer, causing more worry, and so forth.

CLASSICAL CONDITIONING   In the classical conditioning explanation, previously neutral stimuli may be conditioned to elicit autonomic responses that later result in psychosomatic disorders. For example, one patient recalled: "When I was seven I had to take a painful series of allergy shots. Ever since then whenever I see a certain shade of green wall paint in a room, it instantly takes me back to that doctor's office and my heart starts to race, I get a deep stabbing pain in my chest and I have passed out." Patients with asthma, ulcers, and migraines are particularly liable to experience discomfort in certain situations. They may or may not be aware that their symptoms have been classically conditioned or even generalized so that seemingly neutral stimuli (an odor, food, or person) can precipitate a psychosomatic episode.

EVALUATION   Specific reaction hypotheses, though they seem logical, have not received conclusive experimental support. Vaillant and McArthur (1972), for example, followed 199 male liberal arts college students for thirty years, beginning in 1940. Periodically over the course of three decades each man was psychologically and medically examined and questioned in detail concerning his physical health, problems, and symptoms. Some consistencies in health and related behaviors (such as marital adjustment) were found, but overall Vaillant and McArthur were unable to find clearcut organ vulnerabilities: "Where in the body a man would experience stress in adult life could rarely have been predicted from examination of the men at (age) 19." No specific body type was correlated with ulcers or any other psychosomatic complaint. In addition, as each man grew older, the symptoms he reported for stress usually *changed* (Table 6.1). The authors concluded that the organ in which stress is experienced, and which may eventually become psychosomatically damaged, appeared to vary with time, age, and the circumstances of stress.

Although this study casts doubt on the consistency of stress symptoms, it does not entirely rule out the possibility of organic weaknesses. It may be that under ordinary

	TABLE 6.1 PERCENTAGE OF MEN REPORTING SAME STRESS SYMPTOMS AT DIFFERENT AGES	
Symptom	Ages 19, 33, 47	Ages 33, 47
Insomnia	6	18
Headache	1	5
Constipation	1	1
Diarrhea	1	4
Indigestion	2	10
Sweating	5	14
Palpitations	1	1
Number of subjects	(147)	(147)

Source: *Vaillant and McArthur, 1972.*

pressures any number of physical reactions could occur; only a high degree of stress might be sufficient to bring out specific psychosomatic predispositions. We will see later in this chapter that, for illnesses such as ulcers, there does seem to be an innate biological contribution.

Dynamic theories

Most dynamic theorists can trace their explanations of psychosomatic disorders to Sigmund Freud, who believed that psychophysiologic symptoms were "organ neuroses." The symptoms symbolically expressed the patient's hidden emotional needs (see Table 6.2). The wheezing and coughing of asthma, for example, was seen as a "repressed cry for help." The patient wanted to be an infant again and was metaphorically looking for mother. The diarrhea of colitis was symbolic infantile compliance. The patient was showing his parents—that is, society at large—that he was a good boy at heart, moving his bowels as he was supposed to.

Psychoanalyst Flanders Dunbar (1947) suggested that psychosomatic conditions were related not so much to repressed frustrations as to personality characteristics. Ulcers, for

TABLE 6.2

PERSONALITY AND PSYCHOSOMATIC DISORDERS

Disorder	Personality traits
Asthma	Overdependent, infantile, wants to be cared for, ambivalent feelings toward self and others
Backache	Sexual conflicts, repressed desire to run away
Colitis	Comforming and obsessive, depressed, conflicted, stingy
Heart disease	Hurried, competitive, impatient, success-oriented
Hives	Craving for affection, guilt-ridden, self-punishing
Hypertension	High achievement needs, repressed anger, conforming
Migraine	Perfectionistic, rigid, competitive, envious
Ulcer	Dependency needs, repressed hostility, affectional frustrations, ambitious, driving

Sources: *Alexander et al., 1968; Friedman and Rosenman, 1975; Gottschalk, 1975.*

example, were seen as the outcome of a driving, ambitious personality. Perfectionism and rigidity led to migraine headaches; guilt, to eczema.

Franz Alexander (1968) explained how personality traits gave rise to particular psychosomatic symptoms by using the concept of regression. According to Alexander, adult emotions stir up childhood organ fixations. A child deprived of sufficient mothering (nursing) during the oral stage fixates his or her need on the gastrointestinal system. The stomach, craving mother's milk, expectantly pours out digestive acids. When affectional needs are aroused during adulthood—and they are eas-

ily triggered in such a deprived personality—the stomach once again overproduces acid. But now the eventual result is an ulcer.

Efforts to validate the relationship of personality traits and psychophysiologic symptoms experimentally have not been very successful. Peters and Stern (1971), for instance, worked with highly suggestible hypnotized subjects who were capable of mimicking physical symptoms. They taught these people to feel hostility and helplessness, personality traits supposedly typical of several psychosomatic skin diseases. Despite the fact that the experimental subjects followed instructions well, they did not show the skin changes characteristic of hives or Raynaud's disease.

Another attempt to correlate personality with illness was more successful. Friedman and Rosenman (1975) studied heart disease and reported two distinct character types, which they called A and B. Type A people are hurried, impatient, competitive, easily irritated, extra-busy, and have a compelling sense of time urgency. Type B people are relaxed, easygoing, and more interested in living well than successfully. When both groups were matched for diet, age, smoking, and other health-related variables, type A people had significantly more coronary disease and heart attacks. This study does not validate the entire concept of psychosomatic illnesses being characteristic of certain personality types; it supports only the notion that some more competitive, hurried people are more likely to have heart problems.

The environmental-cultural theory

Hypertension among black American men is at least double that found in white men. Obesity is two to three times as common in women from lower socioeconomic backgrounds than in middle-class females (Kiritz and Moos, 1974). In a study of cultural differences in response to pain, Zborowski (1952) found distinctive ethnic components. Patients of Jewish origin were anxious about the symptomatic meaning of their pain and its significance for their health. Those of Italian origin were primarily concerned with the pain itself and how it curtailed their work or leisure activity. Patients described as "old American" tried to be impersonal about their discomfort. When they reported pain to the doctor they tended to do so in an objective manner that avoided complaining. These and many other similar findings demonstrate that a diversity of cultural and environmental factors, such as education, group attitudes, diet, and income, probably play a role in psychosomatic conditions.

It is suspected, for example, that so much hypertension among American black men may be partly dietary (excessive salt intake) and partly the result of economic inequity (lack of job opportunities and related stresses). It

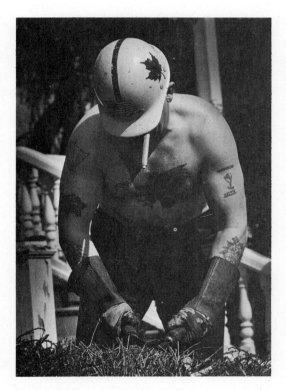

Figure 6.2. Some psychosomatic illnesses seem to be related to socioeconomic status and life styles. Hypertension and peptic ulcers may be partially the result of diet, smoking, and alcohol consumption. (Photo: Alan Carey/Kingston Freeman)

seems likely too that acquired cultural styles of handling pain or stress can be an important determiner of symptoms. Women in lower-income and educational groups appear to have learned to respond to stress by overeating. The result is a very high incidence of obesity. Among middle-class women, where a premium is put on slimness, stress more often causes undereating, and much greater frequency of anorexia nervosa.

Perhaps the most important variable underlying cultural and environmental differences in psychosomatic diseases is in both the number and type of life challenges. We have already pointed out in Chapter 3 how life change is correlated with illness. The greater the life stress (death of a spouse, being fired), the greater the chance of a mental or physical disorder.

In a Swedish study of 32 pairs of identical male twins, Liljefors and Rahe (1970) found such life stresses clearly correlated with coronary heart disease. Despite their genetic similarity and many environmental constancies, when one of the twin pair had a higher life stress score he also had a greater rate of coronary illness. In a subsequent study, Arthur (1974) explained the biochemical mechanics of stress. Careful physiological measurements showed that stressful environmental events (as could be predicted from the Selye theory) led to increases in serum cholesterol and uric acid, and other chemical alterations that have a potentially negative effect on physical well-being.

In the United States, people with limited educational and economic backgrounds seem both to have a much higher incidence of major stresses and psychosomatic illnesses (Table 6.3). The lower-class person's life has been described as almost constantly besieged by job difficulties or unemployment, pressured living and housing conditions, educational failure, family discontent and hostility, and a host of other life stresses. The accompanying disproportionately large number of health complaints, most of which fit the psychosomatic classification, are seen by observers as cause and effect. The reasoning is that the lower the

TABLE 6.3
SOCIAL CLASS AND LIFE STRESS

	Annual family income	
Life stress	Under $8,000	Over $15,000
Death	6%	4%
Unemployment	28	9
Arrest	16	6
Divorce-separation	2	2
Total life stresses	52	22

Sources: *Figures are percentage estimates per family unit derived from 1974–1977 Bureau of the Census, Department of Health, Education, and Welfare, Department of Labor, and Federal Bureau of Investigation statistics.*

socioeconomic level, the more the stresses and consequently the greater the number of health problems (Deutscher, Thompson, 1968).

Before we conclude that socioeconomic class and psychosomatic disorder are causally related, the view of the Dohrenwends (1972) should be considered. They argue that people with lower-class backgrounds and more stress and disease could simply be "losers." Their research raises the possibility that illness and environmental stress do not fit a neat causal model, since both could be a "function of something analogous to accident proneness." It may be that some people, because of their limited resourcefulness or other basic incapacity, simultaneously drift socially downward, pile up traumatic life experiences, and suffer psychosomatic illnesses.

COMMON DISORDERS

In this section we will examine in detail a few of the more common psychosomatic conditions in terms of symptoms, causes, and treatment.

Peptic ulcers

Peptic ulcers are craterlike lesions (sores) in the wall of the stomach or duodenum. They are caused by digestive juices such as hydrochloric acid and pepsin, which normally break down food, eating away at the stomach lining itself. Most ulcers seem to be the result of an oversecretion of digestive juices, but a failure in the protective chemistry of stomach tissue may also play a role. The major symptom of ulcer is pain several hours after eating.

Ulcers are common; nearly 10 percent of the adult population has some symptoms of the disorder. Men outnumber women, although in recent years the number of female ulcer patients has consistently increased. Some believe this a result of the growing degree to which women are assuming vocational and personal responsibilities. But it could also be due simply to dietary changes, since the number of women who drink substantially and smoke has greatly increased in the last two decades (Mausner, 1974).

The role of stress in ulcers has had some confirmation in both animal and human studies. Rats and monkeys put in extreme conflict situations, subjected to unavoidable electric shocks or stressed by overactivity, have often developed ulcers as a result (Pare, 1977). In humans, increases in secretion of HCl (hydrochloric acid) has been shown in people undergoing interviews, medical and other examinations, and similar emotion-arousing and stressful situations (Wastell, 1972).

Genetic factors also seem important. Studies have shown that the frequency of ulcers among parents and siblings of duodenal ulcer patients is two to four times greater than expected on the basis of chance alone (Silen, 1970). Together with this data, evidence found earlier by Mirsky (1958) strongly suggests that ulcers may be linked to inherent predisposition. Mirsky discovered significant quantitative differences in the pepsin levels of newborn infants. Further investigation revealed that babies with high levels of secretion were most often related to adults with ulcer histories. Such findings may demonstrate that some individuals innately overproduce digestive juices and are therefore possibly more prone to peptic ulcers.

Hypotheses of an "ulcer personality" have

DIATHESIS AND STRESS

Whether we are discussing psychosomatic disorders or depression or schizophrenia, we will find the concepts of diathesis and stress useful. Diathesis comes from the Greek and means arrangement or disposition. It indicates that a person may be physically or psychologically so structured that he or she is more vulnerable to certain traits, disorders, or diseases. Ulcer patients may be more disposed to their condition since they could have inherited a gastrointestinal structure that overproduces digestive chemicals. When an ulcer diathesis is coupled with chronic conflict, anxiety, dietary inadequacies, or other stresses, a peptic lesion may be the result. In contrast, the same stresses in an individual with low diathesis may not result in an ulcer. A few psychosomatic illnesses, such as peptic ulcers, clearly seem to be the result of a diathesis-stress relationship.

not had much experimental support, although clinicians continue to affirm the frequency of such people in their practices. The psychoanalytic version of the ulcer type is a person, usually male, who is fundamentally dependent. Such people may seem externally aggressive, but underneath they long for a mother. The more general sociocultural view is that of a driving, ambitious, competitive executive who is continually faced with crucial decisions. Both personality types have been subjected to experimental scrutiny for well over a generation, and results have not been supportive. In his careful review of all the important investigations, Baron (in Wastell, 1972) concluded that despite entrenched beliefs to the contrary, ulcer patients do not fit a particular personality stereotype. The personal traits of ulcer patients are as varied as those for the rest of the population except perhaps that they tend to be slightly more anxious.

The role of diet in relation to ulcers has been validated. Many ordinary substances such as alcohol, cigarettes, spices, caffeine, aspirin, and everyday foods stimulate HCl secretion. Physiological measurements and X ray and other medical studies have vividly demonstrated the dramatic changes in gastric secretion following the ingestion of a highly irritating substance such as alcohol. But many dietary beliefs have also been discounted. For a long time, for example, physicians advised ulcer-prone people to avoid red meat and eat only veal or chicken. These and other older views concerning ulcer-inducing diets have not been confirmed (Beeson, 1977).

The accumulated evidence today suggests that perhaps the best way of describing the cause of ulcers is in terms of a number of factors. Diet, genetic predisposition, anxiety, and many other variables may in *combination* bring about a peptic ulcer.

In most instances, the treatment of ulcers is primarily medical. Physicians advise dietary restrictions and usually prohibit alcohol, fried foods, and other gastric irritants. Patients may also be given medication to help regulate gastric acidity and an eating schedule requiring small, bland meals every few hours. Along with reassurance, such treatment is usually sufficient for most ulcer patients. Occasionally psychotherapy is also called for and helpful. In the last section of this chapter we will discuss the possible uses of biofeedback as an ulcer therapy.

Bronchial asthma

Bronchial asthma is a respiratory disease resulting from the lungs and airways becoming blocked by mucous membrane thickening and other restrictive changes. Most patients breathe almost normally until an attack occurs. Then the rapidly accelerating respiratory blockages, usually heralded by a feeling of tightness in the chest, leave the patient wheezing and coughing. Attacks may last a few minutes or days, and be minor or severe enough to cause a convulsive struggle to breathe so that emergency medical care is necessary. Almost 5 percent of children are asthmatic, but since symptoms usually improve with age, the condition is not too common among adults (Beeson, 1977).

About half of all bronchial asthma is *extrinsic,* traceable to specific allergens. Attacks are precipitated by pollen, dust, animal odors, or sometimes consuming a particular food. *Intrinsic* asthma is due to a respiratory infection such as a cold or bronchitis. A small proportion of asthmatic attacks—and realistic estimates have varied from 5 to 20 percent—seem to be set off by emotional factors. Sights such as a dog fight, or experiences of shock, surprise, sexual arousal, and tension have all been reported to trigger asthma in susceptible individuals.

Dividing asthma patients into categories based on whether attacks are related to specific allergens or emotional factors is not easy. Many asthma patients whose conditions seem to have clear allergic or infective roots also report attacks caused by strong emotions and other psychological events. In addition, among many asthmatic people the number of stimuli that are provocative may expand or shift so that new triggers may be added or old ones dropped.

The range and shifting of stimuli triggering respiratory seizures suggests the strong possibility of classical conditioning as a cause. This is sometimes verified by patients' reporting a formerly neutral odor or event associated with an attack later becoming a stimulus for further seizures:

When I was called to write on the board, chalk dust used to trigger my attacks. I didn't figure it out for a while. . . . Then later on, just seeing a blackboard, even from in back of the room, brought on an attack.

Experimental attempts to condition asthmatic reactions to neutral stimuli have not been successful. What has been demonstrated, however, is that some asthmatic patients are extremely suggestible. This may help account for the range of physical and psychological stimuli that often acquire trigger properties (Phillip et al., 1972).

Luparello et al. (1971), for example, chose forty asthmatic patients with allergic histories and an equal number of normal control subjects. All were told that air pollution was being studied and that they had to inhale several different concentrations of known irritants. In reality, without any subject knowing it, all the inhalants were harmless, nonallergenic saline solutions. After inhaling the solutions, none of the healthy control subjects showed any respiratory symptoms. But a third of the asthma patients had respiratory difficulties, and twelve went on to have asthmatic attacks. To check that it was suggestion and not the saline which activated the asthmatic seizure, the affected subjects were later presented with the *same* solutions. This time they were told the solutions were medicinal. Several subjects now responded to the inhalant with respiratory improvement.

Another psychological component that has been implicated in asthma is family interaction, particularly the relationship between mother and child. The mothers of asthmatic children have been seen as excessively controlling, as attempting to prevent their children's growth and independence. This observation has had a very limited kind of verification from the frequent observation that when asthmatic children are removed from their homes, their symptoms almost always improve. Of course this improvement might also be traced to being removed from hidden allergens or other extrinsic triggers.

To evaluate the role of the mother, family, and home, Purcell et al. (1969) designed a complex experiment in which asthmatic children would stay in their own homes, but without their parents. Thirteen families in which emotional factors seemed to play a leading role in attacks were selected. Another group of families in which children's attacks did not seem related to emotional circumstances was also chosen. Every family member but the asthmatic child moved out of the home for two weeks and a housekeeper was employed to care for the child. During the separation, the asthmatic children for whom emotional factors were low showed no important changes in their disease. The children for whom emotional factors were rated high demonstrated remarkable improvement. But when the two-week experimental separation was over and the parents returned, the improved children returned to their old pattern.

Although this research suggests that the home life of some asthmatic children may play a role in their disease, it does not necessarily confirm the causal role of mothers or parents. It could be, for example, that asthma which has an allergic or infectious cause may just be perpetuated by family attitudes. Perhaps the overprotective mother, rather than somehow causing the asthma, just manages to maintain it. A child who is ill in such a home might be given extra care, attention, and other reinforcers whenever he or she has an attack. As a consequence, the overly affectionate

Figure 6.3. Dynamic theorists contend that bronchial asthma is the result of dependent, clinging children, longing for their mothers. There has not been much experimental data to validate this position. (Photo: Scribe)

mother unwittingly uses operant learning to encourage the continuation of asthmatic symptoms.

How important is personality in asthma? Dynamic theorists have attributed asthma to the relationship between an overly fond mother and clinging child, and there are still occasional individual reports that seem to confirm such an outlook. Kaminski (1975) reported on a 17-year-old with very strong maternal needs, metaphorically crying for his lost mother. But the overall evidence has not been supportive. Jones et al. (1976), in their evaluation of the asthmatic character, were unable to find a distinctive personality. Asthma, like peptic ulcer, seems to occur in all sorts of people with widely differing personalities and family backgrounds.

Asthmatic attacks are medically treated with epinephrine and other medications intended to restore breathing or prevent future episodes. Long-range treatment requires protection from allergens and the prevention of respiratory infections. Whenever emotional factors play a role in bronchial asthma, counseling, psychotherapy, or behavior therapy may also be useful. A number of clinicians have used systematic desensitization and other learning procedures intended to help patients respond less intensively to triggers and generally become more relaxed. One method is to have patients visualize trigger situations and their own reaction while actually being safe and relaxed in the therapist's office. For some patients, these exercises help them to decrease medication and reduce the severity of attacks (Phillip et al., 1972).

Essential hypertension

Blood pressure is a measure of the force produced in the arteries as the heart pumps blood through them. The systolic pressure results from the heart muscle's contraction; the diastolic occurs during the heart's momentary resting phase. Measured in terms of millimeters of mercury (Hg), blood pressures in excess of 150 systolic and 90 diastolic (150/90 mm Hg) are considered the beginnings of hyperten-

SLEEP DISORDERS

Sleep disorders are common, with insomnia being the most frequent. Although medical problems account for many different types of sleep disturbances, psychological factors also play a large part. Depression, apprehension, and many other anxious emotions are often at the root of sleeping difficulties. The following are the major sleep conditions:

Name	Definition	Treatment
Insomnia	Great difficulty falling asleep or staying asleep	Psychotherapy and/or sleep-inducing medication
Narcolepsy	Recurrent, uncontrollable brief episodes of sleep, often with temporary paralysis and hallucinations	Psychotherapy and stimulant drugs like amphetamines
Hypersomnia	Greatly increased duration of normal sleep, often with depression and confusion on awakening	Treatment usually directed at underlying cause
Klein-Levin syndrome	Periodic episodes of hypersomnia, (several times a year) beginning in adolescence and often associated with bulimia (excessive eating)	Eventual recovery without treatment
Night terror	Extreme panic during sleep, shouting, confusion, and activity far exceeding ordinary nightmare	Psycotherapy and sometimes medication
Pickwickian syndrome	Hypersomnia associated with obesity and labored breathing	Management of obesity and other underlying problems

vated by an accelerated heartbeat or by an increase in the resistance of the blood vessels. Because of age, diet, or possibly emotional factors, the arteries may become narrowed, clogged, lose their elasticity, or otherwise force the heart to work harder to push blood through.

Hypertension is common; about 10 percent of the adult population is affected. Slightly more women than men have elevated pressures, but for black male Americans it is at least twice as high as among white men. In many cases, a physical cause for the hypertension can be identified. Frequently a diet high in salt, excessive smoking, or kidney, arterial or other pathology is responsible. But in many instances, perhaps in as many as half of all cases, no physical cause is evident. The hypertension is assumed to be *essential,* a medical term meaning cause unknown.

Blood pressure is easily measured by a usually no distinctive symptoms clearly indicate moderate pressure increases, hypertension is often well advanced before it makes itself known by signs such as dizziness, headaches, fatigue, and the like. Serious hypertension, being related as it is to heart, blood vessel, and other organic pathology, forecasts a very shortened life expectancy. Untreated hypertensive patients live ten to twenty years less than those with normal blood pressure.

Of all the organ systems, the cardiovascular is the most reactive to stress. Even a slight disruption of a person's anticipated routine— a mild shock, momentary fright, or emotional arousal—brings about an increase in heart rate, tightening of some blood vessels, and an increase in blood pressure. When the interruption passes, the cardiovascular system returns to normal. But if the tension or emotion is prolonged, the increased blood pressure may continue. A psychodynamic version of this the-

Figure 6.4. This hypertensive patient has been trained in relaxation techniques and taught to monitor her own blood pressure. (Photo: Scribe)

sis is that hypertension is the result of defensiveness, repressed anxiety, or anger (Wennerholm, 1976). The hidden anger view, which is perhaps the most popular, is that the person, inhibited by the superego or social restrictions from expressing rage, is chronically hostile. His or her enduring emotions continuously provoke cardiovascular changes leading to hypertension (Alexander et al., 1968).

The hypothesis of chronic repressed anger causing hypertension is difficult to investigate experimentally. A trait that is repressed can by definition not be overtly measured by any psychometric technique. In recognition of these difficulties, the work of Harburg et al. (1973) suggests that confirmation may come indirectly from the much higher rate of hypertension for black as compared to white males. Black males are assumed to have to endure much more social frustration and anger-arousing restrictions, and thus are far more likely to have to repress hostile emotions.

In a series of studies, Hokanson et al. (1971) has attempted a laboratory evaluation of the anger-hypertension view. Generally subjects have been provoked and then either permitted or not permitted to vent their anger. Those who had to rein in hostile responses usually continued to have higher blood pressures. In one such situation, two subjects were confined

to a room with a panel of buttons to press, one of which gave the *other* subject a shock. Without the experimental subject knowing it, his partner was actually a confederate in the experiment and instructed to shock the innocent subject. In situations where the unknowing experimentee was allowed to "get back" at his tormenter by shocking him, his blood pressure usually decreased. In those situations where the subject was prohibited from shocking back, blood pressure often remained high.

The Hokanson and Harburg efforts are instructive, but at best they offer only indirect evidence for the repressed anger thesis. We are not able at this point to confirm the psychodynamic view that repressed anger is at the core of essential hypertension. Some scientists even question the meaningfulness of the entire concept; they believe repression is an unproved assumption and think the entire hypothesis is too vague to be experimentally evaluated.

Environmental anxiety and stress have often been cited as factors in hypertension. It has been reported that people in high-stress occupations such as air traffic controllers, police, and firefighters often have higher blood pressures. In specific prolonged stress situations such as marital separation, court trials, and unemployment, blood pressure has frequently also been shown to be high (Thiel, 1973). In a very careful evaluation of the multiple family, economic, and social stresses of unemployment, Kasl and Cobb (1970) compared men whose plant was closing to workers who were similar in age and health but in secure jobs. The unemployed workers were followed for over two years, beginning with the anticipation of the loss of their job, unemployment, looking for work, and adjusting to a new situation. At nearly every point, blood pressure checks showed the unemployed group nearly continuously and significantly higher than the employed men.

Genetic and biological factors could also play a role in hypertension. There seems to be a slight tendency for blood pressure levels for parents, children, and siblings to resemble one another. There is also a moderate correla-

CAUSE AND CAUTION

Psychological factors may play a part in all physical diseases. Whenever people are ill, their attitude (optimistic, motivated, or gloomy) can help influence the course of the illness. We know too that the person who is mentally sound not only has a better chance of recovering from illness but of staying healthy in the first place.

But because psychological factors play a role in all disorders does not mean that they are causally linked to every physical disease. Sometimes emotional roots are attributed to all kinds of illnesses on the basis of the scantiest evidence. This is particularly true for ailments such as cancer, diabetes, arthritis, and many others whose causes are not yet fully understood. Cancer patients, for example, have been reported to be more likely to suppress their anger, and have more psychologically critical incidents in their lives (Greer and Morris, 1975; Sebastian and Smith, 1976). Kaestner et al. (1977), working with rats, showed that the amount of insulin they secreted could be modified by simple classical conditioning procedures, and by implication suggested that human diabetes may be a learned response. Before any of these research findings lead us to conclude that cancer or diabetes are psychologically caused, we need to remember these cautions:

Correlation is not cause. Demonstrating that anger suppression is statistically related to tissue malignancy does not in any way establish a causal linkage.

Animal experiments often provide excellent leads for further study, but the results of such research cannot be treated as proof of what occurs in human beings.

Psychological tests, psychometric evaluations of personality or emotions, are at best fairly rough measurements and of limited use in predicting behavior or describing life situations.

Psychological experimentation is complex and subtle, so that false leads are common and substantial findings elusive.

Because of experimental limitations, results based on one or two investigations have to be viewed as tentative. As of now, for instance, there is no verification that cancer really is associated with the suppression of anger, and none whatsoever that the two are causally linked. Research pointing toward physical diseases should serve as a stimulus for thought and further scientific exploration. But until there is extensive corroboration, all preliminary findings must be regarded with caution.

---

tion between elevated heart rate in children and later hypertension. It has been observed that the heart rate of black American newborns is frequently higher, so that perhaps this could account for the later disproportionate incidence of essential hypertension in this group. But it has also been suggested that both the heart rate of infants and later increased blood pressure could be related to maternal and family patterns that include smoking, high salt intake, diets rich in saturated fats, and other nutritional variables (Rushmer, 1976).

Essential hypertension is medically treated with tranquilizing drugs or medication specifically aimed at altering cardiovascular physiology. When emotional factors are thought to play a role, psychotherapy is very helpful. Biofeedback techniques seem particularly promising in treating essential hypertension, as we will see in the last section of this chapter.

Migraine headaches

Migraines are classified as cardiovascular disorders (Figure 6.5) because they are begun by dilation of the cranial arteries and other circu-

Figure 6.5. This nineteenth-century caricature by Charles Aubry shows the entire family trying to cope with mother's headache. (Photo: National Library of Medicine, Bethesda, Md., 20014)

latory disturbances within the head. For many people the attack of pain is severe and lasts for a few hours or even longer. The migraine is usually preceded by symptoms such as flashes of light, depression, irritability, numbness, or tingling. The pain may cover the entire head or be limited to one side, and attacks may occur as frequently as several times a week or only a few times a year. During the attack many patients vomit, are sensitive to light, and want to lie quietly in a darkened room.

Migraines involve a number of factors. There seems to be some genetic contribution, since such headaches are found with much greater than chance frequency in many families. More conclusive proof has come from sibling studies. The concordance rates for iden-

tical twins has been reported as much as 50 percent or even higher. That is, when one monozygotic twin had the migraines, the chances were 50 percent or better the other would also. Sometimes a specific allergen such as pollen, odor, food, or a circulatory or structural defect can be found to account for the headaches. On the other hand, there are few psychological constancies. Several decades of research have failed to agree on a personality type or the traits related to migraine disorders (Cumings, 1970).

Since migraines are often triggered by strong emotion, fatigue, or conflict, many clinicians assume a diathesis-stress mechanism. Often, for example, patients are able to specify the conditions under which their attacks occur:

I get a headache only twice a year and then it's whenever I have to sit in the meeting with my department head and justify my accounts.

I get a headache just before menstruation. I don't always feel tense but if I feel tense and am about to menstruate, then for sure I'll get a terrific migraine.

The treatment of migraines is both medical and psychological. Aspirin and codeine sometimes relieve milder attacks, but often potent chemicals like ergot are required to constrict blood vessels. Psychotherapy and behavior therapy procedures have also been reported effective, as has biofeedback training.

Skin disorders

Rashes, hives, acne, and many other types of dermatitis (any skin disease) are often clearly the result of specific allergens or toxins. Poison ivy, some industrial chemicals, as well as a large number of bacteria, fungi, and other microorganisms, may all cause skin conditions. But the skin is also responsive to emotion. Many people blush, "turn red," or blanch when frightened or embarrassed. Severe skin reactions to psychological difficulties may sometimes end in a dermatitis, as the case of Kevin demonstrates.

Kevin, an 18-year-old college freshman, came to the infirmary complaining of a rash on his arms, trunk, and thighs. He said the rash started two weeks after school began and occasionally itched. The rash consisted of pinkish lesions with a raised border and resembled tinea corporis (ringworm of the body). But skin scrapings and microscopic examination failed to reveal any fungal or bacterial cause. Careful examination also ruled out an allergic reaction or any other known skin disease.

An hour-long interview with Kevin revealed that he had been unhappy and frightened since he came to college. He wanted to do well and

prove his independence, but he was also very lonely and fearful of failure although he tried very hard to repress all his anxieties. . . .

Kevin was recommended to the university counseling center and after a month of twice-weekly sessions was much more relaxed and confident of his abilities. At the same time, his rash almost entirely cleared up.

Psychodynamic writers have suggested a number of emotional correlates for dermatitis. Skin reactions may result from resentment, exhibitionistic needs, or sexual inhibition or frustration. Acne, for example, was once blamed on masturbation and now occasionally is attributed to lack of appropriate sexual outlets. The evidence for all these conclusions is scanty and inconsistent; we are not yet able clearly to understand the way in which psychological components might be involved in various skin disorders (Musaph, 1974). Occasionally too, therapists learn not to jump too quickly to the conclusion that a skin condition is psychosomatic:

The patient was an educated middle-aged man who appeared at the clinic complaining of a rash on his legs. The rash began at mid-thigh, was prominent under the knees and stopped at about the level of his socks. The dermatitis began three weeks before, about the time the client separated from his wife. The patient was convinced that the rash was related to his separation and came to the clinic to get help for what he described as "repressed sexual emotions."

After four weeks of therapy the patient's adjustment to his separation improved but his rash was worse. On a hunch, the clinic director sent the patient to an allergist. After careful questioning by the doctor the patient was asked to bring in all clothing he had purchased in the weeks preceding his rash. The patient brought in one pair of jeans purchased just after his separation. The label on the jeans showed they were treated with a chemical intended to repel stains and dirt. Since the chemi-

cal could have caused the rash, the patient was asked not to wear the pants. Within two weeks the rash had entirely cleared up.

The treatment of skin disorders varies with the cause. It is usually best to evaluate the patient's customs and habits carefully to ferret out possible allergens and toxins as well as emotional difficulties. When psychological factors clearly seem to play a role, psychotherapy is frequently helpful. On the other hand, some skin reactions such as eczema are difficult to analyze and often resist treatment.

Eating disorders

Overeating and eventual obesity is very common. At least 10 percent of all adults and children in the United States are overweight. In the great majority of cases, the extra weight is due simply to eating too much (Stunkard, 1974). The opposite condition, **anorexia nervosa,** severe undereating to the point that the victim looks almost like a skeleton, is relatively rare. But in one comprehensive survey, Crisp et al. (1976) found anorexia in as many as one in every two hundred adolescent girls in England. Among boys, the condition is much less common. Both serious overeating, called **bulimia,** and anorexia usually begin in late childhood, though the roots can often be traced to infantile food refusal or overindulgence.

Eating disorders are complex and may be primary or secondary. If they are primary, it means that they alone are the main disturbance. If they are secondary, it means the excessive appetite or food refusal accompanies another, more prominent disorder. Thus anorexia and bulimia may be symptomatic of conditions like schizophrenia, depression, or mental retardation. When that is the situation, treating the more important underlying cause frequently solves the eating difficulty. In either case, the weight gain or loss may be so excessive as to be life threatening. Anorexic patients especially may diet to the point where hospitalization is necessary.

OBESITY Obesity can often be traced to a number of interrelating factors. For some peo-

ple, heredity plays a role: some innate metabolic and body types are more likely to be overweight than others. For others, psychological factors such as loneliness, boredom, and affectional deprivation are stimulants to overeating. In fact, very often people themselves recognize that they eat too much or too often to compensate for emotional dissatisfactions in their lives.

Socioeconomic and cultural variables play a role in obesity. Among some ethnic groups, being overweight is fairly common and admired. At lower income levels it has been estimated to be as much as five times more frequent than among the total population (Figure 6.6). People with limited finances and inadequate education may often be heavier for a number of reasons: they may buy cheaper, more fat-producing foods (such as carbohydrates), or they may have to endure more stress and tensions that could motivate them to eat more (Stunkard, 1974).

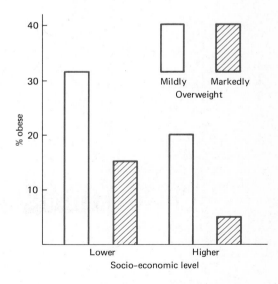

Figure 6.6. Obesity and socioeconomic status. Women from lower socioeconomic backgrounds are more frequently obese than those from higher social and income levels. This difference may reflect learned cultural patterns of eating and the economics of food purchasing, as well as psychological factors. (Sources: Leon, Roth, 1977; Stunkard, 1975.)

Two experiments were conducted in which anorexic patients revealed their attitudes concerning weight and body dimensions. In the first experiment six recovered anorexic patients were given false information, either that they were losing or gaining weight. In contrast to control subjects, anorexic patients who thought they were losing weight quickly reacted with a weight gain and vice versa.

In the second experiment, fourteen current anorexic patients were asked to gauge the width of their body at the level of the face, bust, waist, and hips. In comparison with normal controls, anorexic patients consistently overestimated their body widths.

George Russell and the other authors of these studies (1975) believe their results demonstrate that anorexic people overreact in food intake and also have false perceptions of their body size. They see themselves as much heavier than they actually are and overrespond to this perception by excessive decreases in eating.

ANOREXIA NERVOSA Refusing to eat usually begins in adolescence with an overconcern with being slim and beautiful. Sometimes it is the result of a childlike rebellion against parental eating prescriptions or a refusal to grow up. Often anxiety about responsibilities, sexual involvement, and other uncertainties concerning adulthood seem to trigger anorexic episodes. Several of these factors are revealed in the following case.

Donna, a 22-year-old woman, was brought to the hospital by her parents. At the time of admission this 5-foot 4-inch woman weighed 52 pounds and looked like a skeleton with a thin coat of skin stretched over her. Since the malnutrition had continued for over seventeen months, there was danger of serious liver and other organic damage, requiring the patient to be admitted to the intensive care unit.

Five months after hospitalization, medical, and psychological treatment, the patient's weight was 101 pounds and she was judged to be in good health. Donna worked in a factory and was an inhibited and shy woman who had been lonely and fearful most of her life. About two years before admission she had acquired her first boyfriend. Some months after the relationship began, she had intercourse with her boyfriend and felt guilty about it. Her sexual anxieties began centering on the feared possibility of pregnancy. To avoid this, she reasoned that if she ate only for herself and not "for two," as she heard some expectant mothers say, she would not be pregnant. In addition, she believed she was "too fat" anyway; she wanted to be slim "like a model" to appeal to a "nicer class" of men.

At first Donna skipped breakfast and lunch and ate only a modest supper. After several months she was still dissatisfied with "fat" on her thighs and buttocks and started a meat, apple, and water diet. This resulted in her being too weak to work in the factory. She stayed home and was taken care of by her parents, a reward that further reinforced her anorexia. For several months before hospitalization the patient ate only apples and drank only water, bringing her weight to less than half what it was when she started her restricted food intake almost two years before.

Medical procedures and psychotherapy may prove useful in eating problems, but both anorexia and obesity have responded particularly well to behavior therapies. Musante (1974), for example, combined weekly group therapy meetings with learning procedures to teach appropriate eating behaviors and extinguish inappropriate ones. He used relaxation procedures, conditioning, and other behavior training techniques. Maxmen et al. (1974) used simple reinforcement for alleviating anorexia. Patients were hospitalized and assigned daily weight gains (usually a few ounces). They were fed on a frequent predetermined schedule and

ical approaches. Peptic ulcers, hypertension, asthma, and most other psychophysiologic illnesses often require specific and immediate medical help and psychotherapeutic follow-up. In addition, tranquilizers such as Valium are often prescribed to help alleviate some of the anxiety and tension that could be contributing to the malady. Recently, biofeedback training

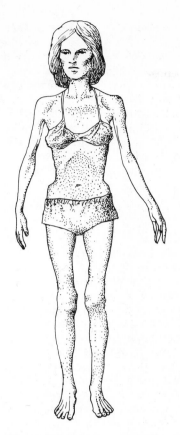

Figure 6.7. A young woman suffering from anorexia nervosa.

weighed daily. Whenever the weight criteria were met, they were reinforced by praise from the medical staff. Psychological issues, emotions, or motivations were not discussed until the reinforcement procedure was successful and the patient had regained a good deal of weight. As is frequently the case, both behavior therapies were successful in bringing about normal weight.

THE USE OF BIOFEEDBACK TRAINING

Good treatment of psychosomatic conditions usually combines medical and psycholog-

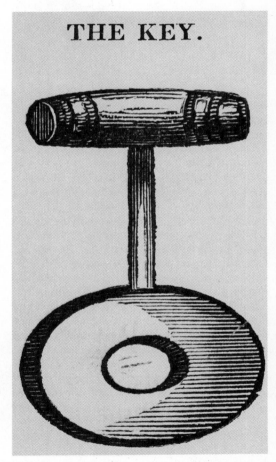

Figure 6.8. During the nineteenth century and the early part of the twentieth, anorexia patients who refused to eat were forcibly fed with the key. Today patients who refuse food are treated with medication and counseling or behavior techniques. (Photo: National Library of Medicine, Bethesda, Md. 20014)

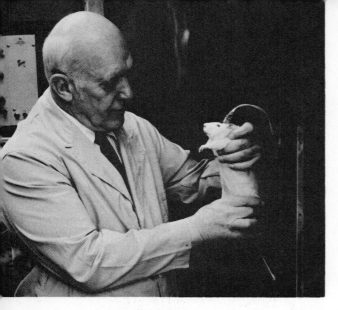

Figure 6.9. Dr. Neal Miller, one of the pioneer investigators of biofeedback training, has shown that humans and animals can influence some autonomic physical processes when they are given appropriate information. (Photo: The Rockefeller University, Ingbert Grüttner)

(BFT) has been used since it seems uniquely suited for psychosomatic disorders.

Self-control of involuntary bodily processes had been explored by a number of scientists when in 1965 Barbara Brown (1977) discovered that brain-wave patterns could be altered. Subjects were put on an EEG (electroencephalograph), an instrument that records the electrical activity of the brain. Normal thought results in an electric pattern called a beta wave. Alpha waves are fairly uncommon and occur only when the person is distinctly relaxed and peaceful. Neither brain wave, nor for that matter any brain electrical activity, it was thought, could be voluntarily or consciously controlled. Dr. Brown suspected, however, that if subjects could know what sort of electrical activity was going on, they might be partially able to regulate it.

In one of the first biofeedback experiments, subjects were attached to an EEG rigged so that a blue light went on whenever there was alpha wave activity. The result was that the more alpha the person "saw," the more he or she was able to produce. Subjects were in-

structed simply to concentrate on keeping the blue light lit. As a consequence, they consciously controlled a bodily activity believed inaccessible to voluntary regulation.

As a treatment BFT, involves two major steps. First a base rate for each subject must be established; second, patients need feedback. They have to know how "successful" they are in controlling their bodies. This information is usually provided by a visual or auditory signal. The way in which this works can be illustrated from the report of a hypertensive patient:

First I went a few times and just sat quietly for about a half hour, rigged up to the apparatus. Then after they had my base rate blood pressure, in that situation, I was told my objective would be to bring my pressure down to 170/100. I was not to try to relax or feel calm or anything, but to act normal and think about keeping my pressure lower. Whenever I met the criterion a green light stayed on. My job was to keep the green light on. . . . Later on they did it a little differently. After I had made some progress they played music. So long as my blood pressure stayed under 160/90 the music played. When it went above that, the music stopped. My job was to keep the music on.

Biofeedback training has been used to treat many types of psychosomatic complaints (Table 6.4), and the results have often been impressive. Some researchers, however, believe the effects of BFT are of insufficient intensity or duration. Blood pressure may be reduced or the frequency of migraines diminished, but they question whether substantial changes have actually occurred in the psychosomatic process. Biofeedback techniques are new, and our information is incomplete. They do seem to have considerable potential both in explaining and treating psychosomatic conditions, but we just do not yet know how good they will prove to be (Barber et al., 1976).

TABLE 6.4
BIOFEEDBACK TREATMENT OF PSYCHOSOMATIC CONDITIONS

Hypertension

Patients taught to lower systolic pressure through auditory and visual feedback	Benson et al., 1971
Diastolic blood pressure decreased in patients by relaxation, pleasant thoughts, and visual feedback	Schwartz and Shapiro, 1973

Headaches

Patients with tension headaches taught to reduce muscle tension by music being interrupted whenever muscular activity exceeded criterion	Epstein et al., 1975
Migraines decreased by training blood vessel constriction/dilation monitored by finger temperature method	Turin and Johnson, 1976

Asthma

Severely asthmatic children trained to lower their respiratory resistance by self-monitoring procedure	Feldman, 1976

Heart rate

Patients with tachycardia taught to decrease heart rate using direct information about heart activity	Engel and Bleeker, 1975

Peptic ulcer

Ulcer patients trained to alter stomach pH (measure of acidity) through visual feedback	Wegan, 1974

SUMMARY

Physical illnesses that frequently have a high psychogenic component are called psychosomatic. Such diseases usually result in actual physical damage and involve single organ units such as the gastrointestinal, respiratory, or cardiovascular systems.

Stress theory suggests that psychosomatic ailments could be due to the body's own defensive responses. Those who hold the specific reaction hypotheses contend there are innate, acquired, or learned predispositions, but research evidence questions the generality of this conclusion. Dynamic theorists believe personality traits or emotional interactions are symbolically related to psychophysiologic symptoms, but there is only limited support for this contention. Environmental and cultural factors such as diet, education, income, and group attitudes may have some influence on psychosomatic illnesses.

Peptic ulcers seem related to stress, but inherent vulnerability also seems to play a role. Bronchial asthma could be linked to mother-child relationships, the suggestibility of patients, or related learning variables. Essential hypertension has been tied to repressed emotions, but confirming evidence is scanty. Stress and genetic patterns may play important, interacting roles. Perhaps too, a driven personality may be more prone to coronary and cardiovascular disease. Migraine headaches and skin disorders also seem to have emotional components, but specific personality or dynamic patterns have not been consistently evident. Eating difficulties resulting in obesity or anorexia nervosa seem linked to attitudes and habits partly the product of socioeconomic status. Sometimes emotional conflicts or psychological needs also seem to play a part.

The treatment of psychosomatic disorders is primarily medical. When appropriate, psychotherapeutic techniques, including counseling and behavior methods, may also be useful. Biofeedback training has sometimes proved especially worthwhile in controlling some psychosomatic conditions such as asthma and high blood pressure.

7

The Diagnosis of Schizophrenia

All the conditions described as neuroses are typified by anxiety and adjustment failures (Chapter 4). Schizophrenia, affective disorders, and most organic syndromes are called **psychoses.** These *major* mental disabilities are all characterized by serious malfunctions in emotion, thinking, and the ability to understand reality. That is, all psychotic individuals may act withdrawn, be hallucinated or delusional, and appear disoriented and confused. When emotional symptoms stand out, such as extreme exaggerations of mood, the condition is likely to be defined as an affective psychosis (see Chapter 9). Organic psychoses (Chapter 15) are marked by memory and intellectual deficits. When cognitive (thinking) disturbances predominate, the diagnosis is schizophrenia.

Schizophrenia itself is not one disorder with a clear set of symptoms. There are several different types, and the abnormal behaviors schizophrenic persons display can vary a good deal. One patient may be extremely aloof and refuse to speak, standing rigidly in a corner. Another may seem sociable, be an interesting conversationalist, but reveal false ideas of persecution and importance. Because of this breadth of symptoms, it is difficult to describe a "typical" patient. We will therefore cover the range of maladaptive schizophrenic behaviors and the various types. It is important, however, to recognize that a core of symptoms is found in almost every schizophrenic individual. The signs may not always be obvious, but most show hallucinations and/or delusions, flattened emotionality, and an inability to interact or communicate with other people.

It is also important to correct some misconceptions. The uninformed often believe all schizophrenic persons have to be locked away or that they cut out paper dolls or pose like Napoleon. Although some patients need to be institutionalized and may act bizarrely, most need little or no hospitalization. For many patients, symptoms may in fact be so mild that they can continue to function and carry out routine responsibilities. Schizophrenia is also *erroneously* thought to mean split personality. The patient supposedly assumes the identity of John Jones one moment, Sam Smith the next, Bill Brown later on, and then perhaps goes back to being John again. There is such a condition, but it is *not* schizophrenia: It is called multiple personality, and it is very, very rare (see Chapter 4).

The term schizophrenia was introduced at the beginning of this century by Paul Eugen Bleuler, the eminent Swiss psychiatrist. He coined the word to suggest the "split-mindedness" he believed characteristic of this psychosis. He wanted the diagnostic label to indicate that person's thoughts, actions, and emotions are internally divided and also split off from reality. The result of this division is that the schizophrenic person lives in a milieu created largely by his or her feelings and fantasies.

The psychotic division may express itself in different ways, and so schizophrenics have been typed into categories: paranoid; catatonic; hebrephrenic; schizo-affective; simple; acute or chronic; process or reactive. The number and kind of these diagnostic terms have changed over the years, reflecting the fact that schizophrenia is a complex and shifting disorder. Some mental health professionals now dispute the label itself and hold that it is not an illness at all, but an expression of a form of social disapproval.

The disorders called paranoid states (not paranoid schizophrenia) are also the subject of debate within the mental health community. Paranoid persons are not schizophrenic and except for their delusional symptoms, may seem normal and function well.

Schizophrenia and paranoia have long been known as mental illnesses. In this chapter we will examine the body of evidence that has accumulated over the years and the current state of our knowledge. We will begin with some universally recognized symptoms.

SCHIZOPHRENIC SYMPTOMS

The form schizophrenic symptoms take depends to a considerable degree on individual background. Those who are technologically oriented tend to use electronic explanations for hallucinations or delusions. Those inclined toward religion, mysticism, or the like may talk about God, witches, or other supernatural phenomena. Thus, although there are fairly reliable signs that distinctively suggest schizophrenia, the actual *content of symptoms* depends a good deal on the character and life situation of each person.

And just as schizophrenic symptoms vary in content, they tend to cluster together in distinctive ways. Persons with a number of schizophrenic signs plus persecutory delusions are likely to be typed paranoid. Another person with several similar schizophrenic behaviors but who is also emotionally flat and withdrawn may be called a simple schizophrenic. We will discuss these classifications later in the chapter; here we will describe the symptoms common to all types of schizophrenia and comment on their frequency. Note, however, that most patients show only a few schizophrenic signs. It is very unlikely that a mentally disordered person will have all or even most of the characteristics discussed.

Disordered thinking

Disordered thinking is believed to be at the core of schizophrenia and its most distinctive symptom. Patients seem to be out of touch with reality, to be living in a world of their own. Perhaps the major reason for this cognitive failure is that schizophrenics no longer seem to be able to sort out relevant from irrelevant information, reason correctly, or distinguish between the imaginary and the real. In many ways the schizophrenic's thinking processes turn inward, focusing on internal needs, perceptions, and conflicts. This kind of thinking may be described as **autistic** because of its almost exclusive concentration on such inner processes as imagination and motivation.

In addition to being autistic, schizophrenic

Figure 7.1. Schizophrenic patients, particularly those in hospitals, typically look withdrawn, distant, and confused. Many also have odd expressions and neglect their personal appearance. (Photo: Smith, Kline and French Laboratories, by G. William Holland)

thinking is often called **prelogical.** The intellectual processes seem primitive, incomplete, often resembling those of a young child. For example, schizophrenics may use erroneous logic. A patient who thought he was dead argued, "Only the good are dead. I am good. Therefore I am dead." Or patients may seem unable to pick correctly among a number of related associations. In answer to the question what is the name of the president of the United States, one patient answered "White House," while another said "George Washington."

Still another way in which schizophrenic patients manifest primitive thinking is in *rigidity* and *concreteness.* Just like some very young children, schizophrenic patients can be very inflexible. They are unable to think abstractly, to use analogies or conceptualizations:

DOCTOR: Here's a proverb. "A stitch in time saves nine." What does that mean?
PATIENT: A stitch in time. Right? That's a magazine, right?
DOCTOR: This is a proverb. What does it mean? "A stitch in time saves nine."
PATIENT: In time. You put nine stitches. You're fixing it.

DELUSIONS The failures in thinking lead to **delusions,** false and irrational beliefs. Of all these mistaken notions, delusions of persecution are among the most common. The person falsely believes he or she is being plotted against, cheated, hunted, poisoned, or otherwise abused. An unhappily married schizophrenic husband saw his wife put salt on his hamburger, became convinced it was poison, and refused to eat. A young woman believed her employer was "gassing" her through the ventilation system and reported her convictions to the police. In countless other such instances, those with delusions of persecution write letters to the authorities, sue their neighbors, or on occasion even act violently, in order to rectify imaginary grievances.

Persecutory delusions are sometimes accompanied by feelings of grandiosity. The person believes he or she is gifted with a very special talent, possessed of some powerful knowledge or secret, or is for some other reason a very important person:

I'll tell you why they are out to get me . . . Because I can make the fusion bomb . . . I have always had an intuitive ability with the sciences. I can make anything I set my mind to . . . I do not plan to sell it. I will give it away . . . All those nations, you know, the little countries being picked on by Russia, when they come to me, I will give it to them. I have a great heart. A heart so big. I could be making a fortune. I know it. I'm just too good. I know it.

Persecutory, grandiose, and other delusions often have a religious content. Some people believe they are prophetically gifted and communicate directly with God. Or they may assert that other people are trying to tempt them away from "holy purity," as one patient put it, by using the "tricks of harlotry of the Philistines." Some schizophrenic persons spend inordinate amounts of time praying; others try to convert fellow patients, nurses, and doctors; and a few write long religious poems and tracts. Figure 7.2 shows a drawing made by an individual who believed he was hand-picked to draw up a plan for humankind.

Delusions of *control* and *exposure* are particularly suggestive of schizophrenic psychosis. That is, many delusional preoccupations, such as those of a religious or persecutory nature, may accompany many different kinds of mental disorders. But the false conviction that our thoughts and actions are either being controlled by others or known to everyone are limited almost exclusively to schizophrenia. In delusions of control, the person believes that by electronic technology, hypnotism, or some supernatural means, his or her ideas and behavior are being manipulated by someone else:

You see I'm wired up. It is my hand, but not my command . . . You understand me now. They pull all the strings on me . . . Yes, even what I say now. It is not me talking. They put the words in my mouth. They make my jaw move. My hands touch here or there. Not me. You understand.

Do you know what is possession, Doctor? It takes over your soul. Your body, it is not yours. You have to say what he wants . . . You do!! Where you move and sit and what you eat. Not yourself! He doesn't like this. You cannot eat it. He breathes for you and he moves for you.
No. Now, thank God, I am not possessed. But I cannot tell you when it will happen. He moves in and out and I can't stop him . . . No, not medicine, not the pills. They can't stop him! He takes hold of you when he wants to. That's all.

Delusions of exposure are similar to and sometimes overlap feelings of control. The exposed person believes he or she is helpless, open, and vulnerable. There is no way to hide. Every thought and action, no matter how intimate, is known and recorded. Some patients believe others can read their secrets in their eyes. Others are convinced that every aspect of their lives is being broadcast on the radio or shown nightly on television.

Delusions of exposure, control, and persecution have been described as an *inability to establish boundaries*. Like a very young infant, the schizophrenic is unable to define himself. He does not recognize whether thoughts, feelings, or actions come from inside or outside. The result is that nearly any personal feeling may be attributed to someone else, and nearly any external event believed to be an intimate experience (Blatt and Wild, 1975).

The delusions discussed above are those

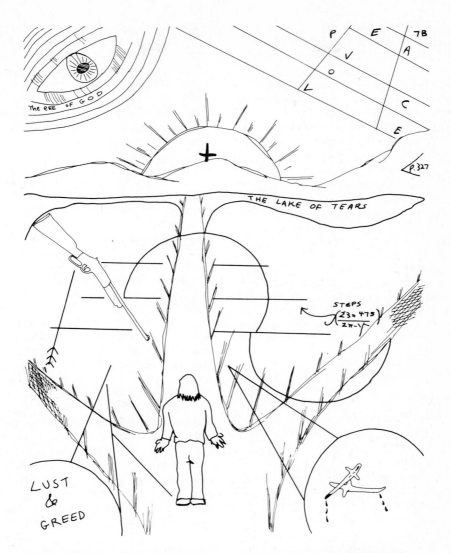

Figure 7.2. This is part of the "blueprint" drawn by a grandiose paranoid schizophrenic patient to bring "peace and love" to the universe. Like many paranoid patients, this man's drawing gives considerable evidence of his hostility (Photo: Scribe)

most frequently found among schizophrenic individuals. Some less common false beliefs are these:

REFERENCE: The belief that nearly all events, that others' every conversation or act, involve the patient.

IDENTITY: The delusion that the patient is someone else, such as an individual of the opposite sex, a child, or a famous person.

SIN AND GUILT: The belief that one has committed great crime, been unfaithful or sexually deviant, or otherwise wicked.

HYPOCHONDRIA: The delusion of an illness or

physical problem, usually with bizarre symptoms: "My insides in my stomach, are turning to dust and it's leaking out all over me."

UNREALITY: The idea that self, others, or the world are not real or that something very important such as houses, gravity, or all women are suddenly no longer in existence.

HALLUCINATIONS Delusional thinking is often associated with **hallucinations,** false perceptions. Of all the different kinds of erroneous perceptions, auditory hallucinations are the most frequent. People believe they hear commands, cursing, whispering, or other noises, and frequently refer to these hallucinations as "voices." The voices may be positive, amusing, and even flattering, but they are more commonly obscene, accusatory, or otherwise unpleasant or frightening:

He talks to me. Not nice you know. Very nasty. He tells me secrets and he tells me what I have to do . . . I'm ashamed to say it. I can't tell you . . . It's not nice. Dirty. He's very nasty.

Sometimes people can be seen talking back to their auditory hallucinations. Others may try not to hear the disturbing sounds. They plug up their ears, hum or shout, cover their heads, or otherwise attempt to block out the hallucination. One patient held his breath whenever voices ordered him around or put "evil thoughts" in his head. During group therapy sessions, this patient would suddenly audibly hold his breath, tremble, and turn red and blue till he started breathing again minutes later.

In addition to auditory misperceptions, patients may also have other hallucinations:

VISUAL: Falsely seeing animals, people, events, etc. These hallucinations are often frightening, supernatural, religious or sexual.

TACTILE: Patients hallucinate being stabbed, pinched, tickled, touched, abused, or having bugs crawling on their body.

LILLIPUTIANS: Seeing the self or others as exceptionally small and helpless.

OLFACTORY: Perceiving false smells. Patients may hallucinate the smell of smoke, or poison, or "lust," or ordinary food and other aromas.

GUSTATORY: Taste hallucination; familiar food is perceived as strange, poisoned, or otherwise out of the ordinary.

SOME CAUTIONS Delusions and hallucinations are often the clearest evidence of schizophrenia. Sometimes they are also dramatic, complex, or markedly bizarre. But people do not readily reveal their disturbed thinking. Typically, patients newly admitted to the hospital, confused and at the height of their disorder, talk fairly freely about their false ideas and perceptions. But very quickly new patients learn from older ones; "Don't tell them that or they'll think you're crazy." Patients may also be embarrassed about the content of their hallucinations and delusions. The violence, sexuality, religiosity, and other deviation of their thinking is unacceptable to themselves and they do not want to share it with anyone else. Finally, many schizophrenic individuals recognize that their hallucinations and delusions are not "normal" experiences and therefore, perhaps, should not be revealed.

Because people tend to hide hallucinations and delusions, and for similar reasons also downplay other psychiatric symptoms, even hospitalized patients may not seem obviously psychotic. The schizophrenic patient may just seem a little distant, inadequately groomed, and perhaps a bit incoherent or difficult to understand. Beginning clinicians are unlikely to see any of the more dramatic or classical signs of schizophrenia, and when they inquire about hallucinations, the patient is likely to shake his head. "No, I don't hear anything odd. I feel good. There's nothing bothering me." Psychotic patients, just like people who are not mentally ill, often try to put their best foot forward, attempting to appear as well adjusted as possible. It requires an experienced mental health professional, and a good working rela-

LYCANTHROPY

Lycanthropy, the false belief that one is a wolf, is a very rare but classic delusion which has become the focus of many mythological tales. Twenty-five hundred years ago, for example, according to the Old Testament, the Babylonian king Nebuchadnezzar suffered from this delusion. Extremely few instances of lycanthropy are seen today, but University of Kentucky doctors recently reported two cases. In addition to the more usual psychotic behaviors, these patients were so convinced that one often slept in a cemetery and howled at the moon. The other chased rabbits and ate them. *Source: Family/Today's Health,* October 1976, p. 30.

tionship with a patient, to elicit many of the more revealing psychotic symptoms.

Flattened emotions

The emotions of schizophrenic patients are usually described as *flat* or *inappropriate*. The patient who is flat seems distant, unresponsive, and shallow. In ordinary conversation we expect the face of the person we are talking to, to register the meaning of our words. People smile, look interested, or frown, showing that they are in contact with us. In contrast, an emotionally flat patient has a masklike face. He or she may understand what we are saying but appear withdrawn and disinterested. This

distance is even more apparent when the affectively flat person talks. The speech may be halting, the voice a monotone, and the features so motionless that he or she looks like a robot.

Schizophrenic persons may also act in emotionally inappropriate ways. They may laugh when they should be sad or be grief-stricken about apparent trivialities. This inappropriateness is demonstrated by a patient who loudly and laughingly told a nurse about a suicide in her family. Talking about events that would depress other people made this patient laugh and joke instead. Other schizophrenic emotions are sometimes described as *disharmonious.* Patients may both laugh and cry, or be very depressed and seemingly elated, either simultaneously or in a very short period of time. During group therapy one such patient could become instantly depressed and crying, but then within a few seconds laugh merrily.

Although flatness and inappropriateness are the most common emotions seen, a few schizophrenic patients also experience *intensified* feelings. Patients may seem unusually happy and lighthearted or very sad and fearful. Beginning professionals, expecting all their patients to be affectively neutral or irrelevant, are sometimes surprised at the depth of genuine fear found in some schizophrenics. Often the extreme fear is associated with terrifying delusions or perceptual distortions. One patient, for example, was convinced that gravity did not work for her. She was terrified that she might float off into space and "burn into a cinder in the atmosphere." To prevent this, she would hold on to tables, beds, and doors with all the strength she could muster, trembling at the prospect of having to let go. Another patient, a former college student, became more and more anxious and depressed about going to class lest he be called on to give an answer. Ultimately his despondency was so great that he was unable to leave his dormitory room.

Another emotion that is seen in a few schizophrenics has been called an *exquisite sensitivity*. Some people are apparently very "tuned in" to both their own and others' feelings. Sometimes this sensitivity manifests itself as a very keen and bold insight. Such patients have an almost uncanny knack for sensing or guessing what their doctor or another patient is thinking. Or this hypersensitivity may leave the patient unusually vulnerable to the ordinary stresses of life. Some writers even hypothesize that all schizophrenic individuals are born unusually open and unguarded. Thus they are almost defenseless and are forced to turn their emotions and thinking inward so that they appear cognitively and emotionally withdrawn to the rest of us. Melissa may have been such a person:

Melissa, age 16, committed suicide by taking an overdose of medication. Her last year had

been a difficult one for her, filled with emotional turmoil and parental violence.

Melissa was described by her friends as quiet, withdrawn, sweet, shy, very alert, and extremely sensitive. Despite her timidity she had many boyfriends, probably since she was considered sexually available. She herself told her friends that sex was a loving thing and she could not deny anyone who desired her. Melissa was also very friendly with younger children and would spend hours reading to them and playing with them. A girlfriend described this activity as the result of Melissa's trying to escape back to childhood. She believed Melissa too naive and trusting to deal with other teenagers.

After Melissa's death a notebook was found with highly imaginative, although quite confused, drawings and essays. One theme frequently repeated was that of a Tarzan-like figure who would take her away and live with her in a wilderness free of all lies, hurt, and pain.

Melissa's mother considered her lazy, a daydreamer, confused, immature, too imaginative, irresponsible, and "a slut." Before her suicide Melissa had been beaten by her mother and accused of being a "harlot, tramp, and bitch." Unable, apparently, to defend herself in any aggressive way, Melissa resorted to medications to shut out the hurt caused by her mother's punishment.

Communication difficulties

Schizophrenics' disabled thinking and handicapped emotion are often evident in their writing and language. At one extreme, patients may be so withdrawn that they are mute or use only a few words or hand signals to express their desires. *Mutism* and *signaling* are often most apparent in psychotic children. They may reject all language—or because schizophrenia coincided with their physical and intellectual growth, normal language acquisition may have been prevented (see also Chapter 13).

Some patients seem to be using language, although they are not actually communicating. Such persons may repeat the last word or phrase spoken by another, a behavior called **echolalia.** Other psychotics may **verbigerate,** meaninglessly repeat words and sentences. Occasionally echolalia or verbigeration is repetitive and/or explosive. The words are reiterated and burst out rapidly.

At the opposite end are psychotic personalities who become verbal exhibitionists. They speak in grandiose, pompous phrases:

I sir, my dear learned Doctor, wish only to convey to you, to the utmost of my very humble abilities, to you a distinguished man of letters and sciences, that your green pills, sir, are disturbing the deepest bowels of my digestion.

The pressure to communicate, plus the autistic quality of much of their thinking, leads many patients to make up new words or *neologisms,* or condense several thoughts and ideas into *symbols.* The following excerpts demonstrate neologism and symbolism.

I say to him that he tells me I conlift (neologism apparently conveying wish to love and stay together). Nobody cares much. Never together, only partling (another neologism). Conflict. That is it. Forever I say. That's the right way. He makes himself clear but I don't.

My side is rubber-rubber citymeal. I can't sleep you know, rubber-rubber. They got to cut it out of me. I can't take that. That all tendial and such.

DOCTOR: In your note to me you said that the red leaves are shaking loose. What does that mean?
PATIENT: Up there are the leaves . . . they cover . . . remember Adam and Eve? And God commanded them, "Be modest, wear those leaves."
DOCTOR: Yes, go on.
PATIENT: And I read the leaves. I know the sex that will happen. I read (red) it in the future.
DOCTOR: Why are they shaking loose?
PATIENT: Because I need a fair shake. My wife is down on me. I drink so I got fired.

I need a break. Have you seen that sign, J O B, just one break.
DOCTOR: So you think everything's going to be good in the future, sex, work, your life.
PATIENT: Yes, I think so, I see it happening. The leaf is shaking loose. You know I'm getting free. I am leaving my roots behind. You know, getting loose from the past.

When all else fails, patients trying to communicate may fill in the gaps in their thinking and language with words seemingly drawn at random, from nowhere. Words and terms seem almost haphazardly thrown together in a **word salad.** Or words may be used simply because they rhyme with a previous word; these are so-called clang or rhyme associations:

Depart from the train, barbells, I said . . . Two pounds, cherries, throw a mother song. Like it is, time, quarter, disco in Manhattan. I, that I, want to go. Yes I can take the train. Dumbell. Trust me. Two pounds. I can not quarter.

DOCTOR: Then you did what? I'm sorry, can you tell me again?
PATIENT: I lit a fit. Sit man, sit. A bike to get them there where it hit. Bit and tit. Bit the tit. Like I said, I know this person, right?
DOCTOR: Right.
PATIENT: Right to bite, man. Bite tight, right? Out of sight. Doctor, that is docked her, fur. Fur what? It can wait man. I tell you, Doctor.

It should be evident from these examples that often the seemingly incoherent, nonsensical speech and writing of schizophrenic patients conveys meaning. Messages that are outwardly random, rhyming collections of words or symbols may be saying something significant and important. R. D. Laing (1969), has argued that schizophrenia is a valid way of adjusting to a disordered society. Consistent with this hypothesis, Laing believes that schizophrenic language legitimately conveys personal feelings, thoughts, and perceptions. If we, in the so-called sane world, listen carefully and enter at least partly into the psychotic patient's frame of reference, his communications begin to make sense. Most clinicians agree with Laing that schizophrenic speech deserves careful listening. Often, behind the seeming illogic and incoherence, there is meaning. The person is trying to convey to us, in his or her own altered way, thoughts, fears, experiences, and hopes (Brown, 1973).

Disorientation

Schizophrenic patients are sometimes disoriented. They may be confused and not know where, or who, they are. Such disorientation to place, person, or time is seen mainly during the early and acute stages of psychosis and is often accompanied by fright or even panic. Suddenly all seems strange, unknown, and unreal to the person and he or she becomes plainly scared:

I could not put anything in its place.
I did not know whether it was night or day
or who you were or even I was . . . The most
scary thing, strangely to say too, was that I
did not know where I was. Was this back in
my room at school . . . No it wasn't . . . I
thought maybe there was this somebody, maybe
it was me and I was talking with this man.
He was a tribal chief or something. I was going
to be initiated in this tribe. I felt lost, alone.
I was crazy scared.

Some disoriented patients respond to their bewilderment by withdrawing. They may act **stuporous,** meaning that they seem unaware of, and unresponsive to, their surroundings. When spoken to or asked a question, they either ignore the speaker or answer with a barely audible word or shrug. The world seems too demanding, too complex and incomprehensible, so such persons cling to themselves, seemingly ignoring or not caring what happens around them. We know from the reports of recovered stuporous patients, however, that

while they seem oblivious, much of what does happen is understood and remembered.

Disturbed motor behavior

The movements, posture, and motor activities of many schizophrenics appear odd or disturbed. Sometimes they have peculiar mannerisms, grimaces, twitches, tics, or facial expressions. Or they may hold their arms, eyes, or head at an odd angle. Sometimes they may pick at themselves, incessantly pull their hair, or pinch or scratch endlessly until they have numerous sores.

Schizophrenic patients may assume and remain in certain favorite body positions. They may lie curled up in a fetal position on a bench or stand rigidly in the corner of a room, a condition called **catalepsy.** Patients in such cataleptic postures often show *cerea flexibilitas,* waxy flexibility, so that limbs placed in a particular position tend to remain there. A doctor illustrating this quality may take the arms of a cataleptic patient and move them up and out. Once set, this awkward position is likely to be maintained for as long as the muscles endure the strain (Figure 7.3).

Figure 7.3. Catatonic patients may maintain a position for many days or weeks. Generally patients will interrupt their pose to eat and toilet themselves, though occasionally even vital functions are ignored. (Photo: Smith, Kline and French Laboratories, by G. William Holland)

Other peculiarities of motor behavior occasionally seen in schizophrenic patients include the following:

CATAPLEXY: Loss of muscle tone. Patients seem without any control over their body and act limp.

ECHOPRAXIA: Imitating another's movements. Schizophrenic persons may try to walk or otherwise act like someone else.

AUTOMATISM: Movements seem slow, very labored and mechanical, like those of a robot.

NEGATIVISM: Cataleptic patients' tendency to resist movement—refusing to shake hands or get up from a chair.

HYPOACTIVITY AND HYPERACTIVITY: Too little or too much movement. A few schizophrenic patients become underactive, doing little or nothing; others may be overactive to the point of talking and running around almost out of control.

Somatic complaints

Schizophrenic patients may have real physical illnesses and/or delusional medical problems. Generally, psychotic persons experience the same sicknesses as normal people. But they may also be erroneously convinced they are ailing. One patient complained of pain in his lower abdomen so insistently that an appendectomy was performed. The operation revealed normal intestines, and it was later learned that the patient talked of pain only because of a delusional belief about a "fertilized egg" lying in his stomach.

Occasionally, schizophrenic persons have disturbed ideas about their health and body functions. One patient refused mashed potatoes, puddings, and all such "pasty" mixtures because he was convinced they would "gum up" his "insides." Another patient did not drink water, consuming only soft drinks, contending that his bones were "rusting" and water was the cause. In rare cases delusions or other distorted thinking lead to self-mutilation. Patients may cut off a finger or damage the face or genitalia. Those with religious preoccupations sometimes try to burn or crucify

themselves or copy the physical stigmata attributed to Jesus. Suicide also occurs among schizophrenic individuals, but it is not common. Rarest of all are instances of sudden schizophrenic death. It has been reported that patients intent on death, or convinced of its imminence, may apparently become so detached and alienated that they actually hasten their own demise.

Cyclical fluctuations in symptoms

There is considerable inconsistency and variability in schizophrenic behavior. Hallucinations, motor disturbances, and other symptoms may last for months or years, and delusions for a lifetime. Yet from one day or week to the next the intensity of abnormal symptoms may increase or diminish. On some days even those patients usually most disturbed may seem relaxed and cooperative. Hospital staff members often describe patients with diminished symptoms as having a good day or "in contact."

In addition to short-term fluctuations, there are also long-term cycles in schizophrenia. Depending upon age, diagnosis, and many other personal and social factors, first-time discharged schizophrenic people have roughly a 50 percent chance of being rehospitalized (Mosher, 1972). Although most first schizophrenic admissions are sufficiently recovered to be released within a year, many will have a return of serious symptoms. If we look at those patients who are rehospitalized, we see a pattern of long periods of well-being alternating with episodes of exacerbation (return of symptoms). For years patients seem to be functioning well, with the psychosis in remission, meaning that they are without marked signs of abnormality. They may be employed, married, and acting like responsible members of the community. Then, slowly or suddenly depending on individual circumstances, familiar schizophrenic signs reemerge and intensify. Hospitalization is once again necessary. Figure 7.4 shows a fairly typical schizophrenic life history. The important point to remember is that although many schizophrenics sooner

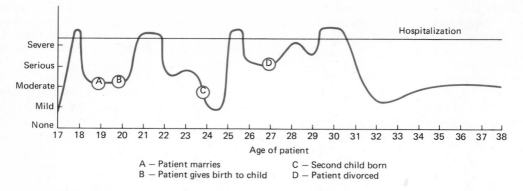

A — Patient marries   C — Second child born
B — Patient gives birth to child   D — Patient divorced

Figure 7.4. This chart describes the intensity of schizophrenic symptoms experienced by a woman over twenty years of her life. On four occasions she needed to be hospitalized. Most of the time, however, with the help of psychotherapy and medication, this patient has lived a relatively normal existence. She has held responsible jobs, married, had children, and taken care of her family.

or later experience an exacerbation, during long periods of remission they can be functioning members of society.

SCHIZOPHRENIC TYPES

The complete array of schizophrenic symptoms is never present with equal intensity in any person. Some people seem primarily cognitively disordered; others may act mainly withdrawn. Nearly all have some delusional experiences, but relatively few show such signs of communication failure as neologisms or word salads. When diagnoses are made, schizophrenic patients are "typed" according to the constellation of symptoms they display. For example, someone with several psychotic signs and prominent persecutory delusions is likely to be categorized as schizophrenia: paranoid type. Another patient with similar indicators but whose emotional ups and downs are outstanding may be diagnosed schizophrenia: schizo-affective type.

Descriptions of the types of schizophrenia have ranged from the original three introduced by Kraeplin at the beginning of this century (paranoid, catatonic, and hebephrenic) to several dozen listed in some psychiatric texts. The DSM III suggests five types. Why such

disagreement about the varieties of schizophrenia? A major reason is that schizophrenia is a multifaceted, often changing disorder manifesting itself in varying ways. Symptoms in the same person may well change or be perceived differently by one or another clinician. Another reason for the disagreement reflects the controversy concerning the entire concept of schizophrenia. Many argue that schizophrenia is not a single disorder but only a contrived term describing a variety of symptoms that may not have much to do with one another.

Although hospital procedures usually require exact classifications, in practice most clinicians are impatient with attempts to draw fine distinctions. Whether a patient is typed paranoid or hebephrenic does not make a great difference in treatment, has some bearing on prognosis, but usually tells nothing about causes. Further, longitudinal studies show that as the years go by patients are often classified differently. Even the same patient, seen simultaneously by several doctors, may be variously diagnosed. On the positive side, type descriptions are of value in communicating the cluster of symptoms found in a specific patient. Accurate subclassification helps prepare the nurse or therapist to better understand and cope with the behavior of the psychotic person.

SCHIZOPHRENIA AROUND THE WORLD

Research under the direction of the World Health Organization (Tsuang, 1976) in many nations around the world, including the United States, India, Denmark, USSR, Nigeria, and Colombia, shows that the incidence of schizophrenia is about 1 percent. Wherever adequate health care services are available, roughly one of every hundred people in the population may be diagnosed as schizophrenic during life. The most common diagnosis in nearly all nations will be paranoid schizophrenia. There are also a number of consistent symptoms that suggest psychosis. The most frequent and revealing universal signs of schizophrenia are auditory hallucinations, flatness of affect, delusions of control and/or exposure, and poor orientation and withdrawal from social contact.

Paranoid schizophrenia

The paranoid type of schizophrenia is the most common variety seen in hospitals. About one-third to half of all patients are diagnosed in this category, with the other types accounting for less than 10 percent each. The primary symptom in paranoid schizophrenia is a *delusion of persecution*, often associated with supporting hallucinations. The patient falsely believes he or she is being threatened, poisoned, hated, or violated, and may have erroneous perceptions that back up his invalid claims. Paranoid patients may also show any or all of the following characteristics: grandiosity (exaggerated feelings of self-importance), hostility (intense, though frequently hidden, feelings of rage and anger), and conspiracy (schemes or plans to organize and combat some alleged evil).

Paranoid schizophrenia is often a chronic disorder. Patients may not come to the attention of a psychiatrist or hospital till they are well into adulthood, but it is likely that they have been suspicious, jealous, irritable, and conniving since childhood:

Mr. K. V. was hospitalized after throwing green paint on his neighbors' laundry, hanging outdoors. This action had been preceded by months of angry and accusatory notes. The patient believed his neighbors were "smut merchants" and put "unnatural" thoughts in his head. The patient was described by his wife as conscientious, conservative, and cool toward people. He worked as a bookkeeper and was known to be very suspicious and demanding concerning any expenses. Mr. K. V.'s mother described him as a quiet child who kept to himself, was frightened of people, and had a "nasty streak in him."

Paranoid schizophrenic patients usually appear well in a hospital setting. Unlike some other schizophrenic types, they are groomed, seem interested in their activities, and are friendly and relevant. They present a façade of "sanity" because their motor, affective, and communicative abilities are largely unimpaired. They have usually led a close to adequate life before hospitalization, have a job and family, and are established in the community. Their persecutory and hostile ideas are not evident unless one is able to induce them to talk freely. Further, as long as a conversation remains away from the delusional area, the patient can appear like any normal person, talking about sports or the weather. Because paranoid patients can appear to be adequately adjusted, they are sometimes able to convince friends, lawyers, or legislators that they should not be hospitalized. Here is a letter written to a state senator:

I ask your assistance in obtaining my release from this institution. I am not insane, psychotic, schizophrenic, or anything else. I am a normal human being with the ordinary share of problems that everyone has nowadays. I need to return to work so I can support my family and become a taxpayer again. I am in this hospital only through the connivance of my wife and doctor. My doctor is not a very forceful person but my wife is. She has convinced him that I am insane and this is ridiculous. We have had a few husband and wife problems, but who hasn't. If she wants out of this marriage then she can have it. Putting me in this hospital, and swearing all those falsehoods is not the way to do it. Our problems can be settled in a court of law and keeping me here is not the way to do it.

This patient was a literate, intelligent man who dressed neatly and talked appropriately, usually convincing visitors of the justice of his cause. The truth was that he had a long history of violent behavior centered about his wife's alleged infidelity. Finally his delusions led him to attempt to kill his wife and children, an act prevented only through the accidental intervention of a neighbor.

Most paranoid schizophrenic people are not intact enough to execute violent plans or formulate reasonable-sounding letters. They are, after all, not only paranoid but also schizophrenic. There is too much associated schizoid pathology, particularly autistic and prelogical thinking, to permit effective action or the construction of impressive delusions. When one listens carefully, the irrationality of their thinking becomes evident:

I will name you their high-placed people and you will see that it is them who are running the country . . . You see they say who is going to be president, run the banks, and what you teach in the schools. They are the ones behind the throne of power, and putting all that sex and violence in the movies . . . I know it because I have studied it for fourteen years and I am gifted with this brain that you cannot fool . . . I read it in their hands. They are out to grab, you see . . . They are out to make slaves of us all and I am one of the few people today that see what is happening . . . So we have to get smart. Get them before they get us. Just look at their hands, you'll see it if you study it like me.

Catatonic schizophrenia

The catatonic type of schizophrenia manifests itself in either or both of two ways. Most of

the time the majority of catatonic patients act *withdrawn*. They are mute, stuporous, or otherwise seem to block out the world. When withdrawal is extreme, catatonic persons are cataleptic and exhibit negativism or waxy flexibility. A less often encountered subtype of catatonia is the opposite of withdrawal. The motor behavior of the catatonic *excited* type seems unrestrained and uninhibited, sometimes to the point of violence. Such hyperactive patients may babble or shout incoherently and senselessly dash around. Catatonic withdrawal can last for weeks, or even months, but the excited phase usually passes quickly, often in a few hours.

Why are two such very different seeming sorts of behavior, excitement and withdrawal, both called catatonic? The reason is that both motor disturbances often appear in the same person. The withdrawn state is far more prominent, but an excitement phase can be entered suddenly and unexpectedly—as in the case of the service station owner.

The patient is an automobile service station owner, aged 36 and recently divorced. He was admitted after relatives found him sitting in a stupor in his closed gas station late on a Sunday evening. Shortly after admission the client recovered from his stupor, and except for some emotional flatness and mild suggestions of hallucinations, seemed appropriate and cooperative.

The patient spent a good deal of time decorating his room and was particularly busy cutting pictures of the queen of England from magazines, framing them, and hanging them in his room. He stated that he carried on an active correspondence with the queen and that the two were considering plans for marriage.

Three weeks after admission the client was found stuporous and cataleptic, sitting on the floor in a corner of his room and refusing to move. If left in his spot, his arms and legs could be placed in any position and the posture maintained until muscular fatigue involuntarily forced their repositioning. At first the patient refused food or toileting, but with effort these resistances were largely overcome. After eleven days of catatonic withdrawal, crashing sounds were heard from the patient's room. He had ripped up his mattress and managed to tear the sink from the wall. When the aides reached him he was smashing the sink against the wooden door of his room, shattering it with each blow. Four aides were needed to subdue him.

Hebephrenic schizophrenia

Hebephrenic patients come close to the common stereotype of insanity. This type of schizophrenia is characterized by grossly disordered thinking, emotions, and motor behavior. Patients are likely to have fragmentary (as opposed to well-organized) delusions and/or hallucinations. Their emotions are typically shallow, inappropriate, and changeable, so that giggling, crying, and anger may follow each other in rapid or alternating succession. In addition, patients often adopt peculiar mannerisms and use neologisms and word salads. Sometimes they also tease, flirt, or act as if they were very beautiful or important people. For early twentieth-century psychiatrists, all these behaviors were evidence of regression to childhood; hence the term *hebephrenia* (Greek, young mind). Current psychiatric practice advocates calling this type of psychosis *disorganized* schizophrenia. The following is a description of a hebephrenic patient in group therapy:

Mrs. S entered the room with a flourish, imitating the sound of trumpets, "Ta ta, ta ta, I have arrived." She is 43, very thin, and poorly groomed; her dress and appearance are haggard and disheveled. Nevertheless, she is often flirtatious and conducts herself as if she were extremely attractive.

During group the patient giggled a great deal. She particularly seemed amused by another patient with a slight lisp. She would look at him, cover her mouth and part of her face with her hands, and seem to giggle almost uncontrollably. Later in therapy the client seemed morose and was observed crying intermittently. Several times during the session the patient made relevant comments. But she also seemed to get lost, with phrases like "Take my auto-

graph," "lands stick till dawn," "menpill till its right."

As the meeting ended, the client seemed both moody and amused. She giggled but sometimes appeared to scowl. Finally she spent the last few minutes tearing at the hem of her dress and pulling out threads.

Schizo-affective schizophrenia

In this type of mental disorder, patients with schizophrenic symptoms also show marked exaggerations of emotion. Their thinking, communication, and other behaviors appear schizophrenic, but their emotions resemble those characteristic of manic-depressive psychoses (Figure 7.5). Patients in this category are subtyped schizo-affective, manic or schizo-affective, depressed. An example of each follows.

The patient was accompanied by his mother and admitted to the hospital voluntarily. He said that he felt unable to cope with his own "energy state" and that his "creativity" confused him. The patient talked continuously, his speech had an explosive quality, and it was sprinkled with irrelevant phrases. He spoke of contact with "liberating energies," and "mind trips to paradise." Throughout the admission procedure, the patient seemed enthusiastic and elated.

Mr. E. E. is 32 and a picture of confusion and despair. He complains of noises in his head and crampy feelings throughout his body. He says he has difficulty sleeping and resting and feels "grounded." He wants to get "back in the right slot," but is miserable and pessimistic about his future. When asked to describe what he meant by "grounded," the patient began to cry.

What distinguishes schizo-affective disorder from manic-depressive psychoses is primarily the presence of *clear schizophrenic symptoms*. And although schizophrenic emotions are exaggerated, they seem to lack the depth or profoundity seen in true affective psychoses. One clinician has suggested that whereas manic

Figure 7.5. The patient, a young schizo-affective man with artistic ability, drew this picture of a scene that "once used to bother me." The hallucination usually started with smiling faces that soon became saber-toothed tigers tearing at his flesh.

and depressive emotions are deep and intense, schizo-affective feelings are more like caricatures.

Simple schizophrenia

Simple schizophrenics lack obvious psychotic symptoms. Instead, they are seclusive and withdrawn individuals who since childhood have been considered quiet and a little peculiar. As adults their outstanding symptoms are apathy and disinterest. Simple schizophrenics retreat from life, are uncomfortable with others or the demands of relatives, friends, or employers. Such persons may perform adequately in school and even hold a job that is routine and does not require much interaction with people. Before his hospitalization for a heart attack, one simple schizophrenic person held a job as a changemaker in a subway toll booth for twenty-four years. This position enabled the man to sit alone, separated by a thick, barely transparent glass partition, silently issuing tokens for money pushed through a narrow slot.

Simple schizophrenic people are sometimes delusional or have indications of psychosis, but all the signs are very subtle. From the patients' own point of view, they just want to live their own lives and not be intruded upon. Because dramatic schizophrenic symptoms are absent and such patients shun others, few are hospitalized. On the other hand, their social isolation and consequent ineptness force many down the socioeconomic scale until they become dependent on welfare. A fair proportion of recluses, drifters, prostitutes, vagrants, and others in similar alienated life styles are likely to be simple schizophrenics.

The latest official compilation of nomenclature, the DSM III, no longer lists simple schizophrenia. But it has been a recognized diagnostic entity for well over half a century, and many practitioners continue to insist that the term accurately describes a recognizable variety of schizophrenia. The reasoning behind DSM III was that if simple patients have other schizophrenic features they ought to be given a different type description. But if the only signs are apathy and withdrawal, then we are not witnessing a psychosis at all but a personality disorder (see Chapter 11).

Other descriptive categories

ACUTE AND CHRONIC   Good clinical practice requires that each type of schizophrenia be described as acute, subacute, subchronic, and chronic. Patients newly hospitalized, experiencing a symptom peak and without a previous pathological history, will be described as acute (for example, paranoid schizophrenia, acute).

PROCESS AND REACTIVE SCHIZOPHRENIA

Reactive	Process
Relatively normal childhood and adolescence and adequate parents	Difficult childhood characterized by ill health, loneliness, family problems, and poor parental attitudes
Adolescent adjustment satisfactory, with no more than usual frictions or uncertainties	Awkward adolescence, lack of friends, mediocre performance in school, increasing withdrawal, narrowing of interests and emotions
Onset of schizophrenic symptoms rapid and related to serious stress such as marital failure	Psychotic symptoms develop gradually, usually without a significant event connected with their appearance
Causes are thought primarily psychological and environmental	Cause is thought primarily biological
Hallucinations and delusions; disjointed and poorly organized; attempt made to remain rational and stay in contact	Hallucinations and delusions; usually long standing and well worked out; personal behavior and motor habits very peculiar and distinctively psychotic
Chance of improvement or recovery usually good to excellent	Chance of improvement or recovery usually fair

Based on Arieti, 1974; DeWolfe, 1974; Strauss, 1973.

Another patient with schizophrenic signs, even if they are fairly moderate, but with a long history of psychoses, is likely to be diagnosed as chronic. As with other psychological or medical disorders, acute patients may seem more noticeably ill than chronic ones, but they usually have a much better chance of recovery.

PROCESS AND REACTIVE Many clinicians believe that schizophrenia can be differentiated as *process* or *reactive,* terms somewhat resembling chronic and acute. Process and reactive schizophrenia cut across all types, so that either may be paranoid, catatonic, or any other variety. Process schizophrenic symptoms become evident during childhood and increase continuously until the behavior is so disordered that hospitalization may be necessary during early adulthood. The reactive schizophrenic is a relatively normal person who de-

velops symptoms fairly suddenly, usually in response to significant stress such as marital failure, unemployment, or ill health.

The reactive-process distinction is not official psychiatric terminology, nor is the difference always clear. Some seemingly reactive patients without prior mental health histories on close examination turn out to have had several earlier abnormal episodes. In other instances, some adolescents who act withdrawn, seem to have peculiar thoughts and to be following a schizophrenic developmental pattern never actually manifest a disturbance serious enough to be diagnosed psychotic. The process-reactive dimension may represent an adjustment continuum rather than polar opposites.

With the caution in mind that viewing a particular patient as a process or reactive type may be a loosely fitting generalization, clini-

DANGER—PARANOIA

People with paranoia, both paranoid states and paranoid schizophrenia, are often disconcerting or frightening. Each year government officials and well-known entertainers receive thousands of letters with grandiose ideas or hostile threats. Normal people living or working with someone who is paranoid may become the target for pathological suspicion, jealousy, or bitter hatred. But are paranoid individuals *really* dangerous?

After being denied a promotion, a 42-year-old man burst into his company office, wildly firing a shotgun. He intended to "get" those who had "connived" against him. He killed two people and held seven others hostage for 37 hours.

The jealous, arrogant, and conspiratorial demands of a 33-year-old man finally became so oppressive that his wife left him. The divorce brought about the total collapse of the man's

cians sometimes make this distinction, for it may influence their treatment plans.

PARANOID STATES

Paranoid states are rare conditions, seen in less than a fraction of 1 percent of hospitalized patients. They are characterized by an intricate, complex, and well worked out delusional system. The person has a set of beliefs that, once the initial delusional premise is accepted, seems coherent and logical. Such paranoid people are *not* schizophrenic, for they show none of the intellectual, emotional, orientational, or other disturbances seen in that psychosis. Many professionals even object to classifying paranoid states as a psychosis. Except for the single erroneous conviction, and the accompa-

nying arrogance and hostility, the person with paranoia is normal.

Since the 1900s scientists and doctors have debated about paranoid states. Distinctions have been proposed differentiating pure paranoia, paranoid states, involutional paranoia, induced paranoia, and monomania (single madness). All these distinctions may have some diagnostic validity, but given their infrequency, careful delineation seems unnecessary. The one distinction we would like to emphasize is that between paranoid schizophrenia and paranoid states. The paranoid schizophrenic is psychotic, likely hallucinated, and emotionally disordered. The person diagnosed as paranoid is *not* psychotic. Except for the deluded idea, he or she is relatively well adjusted.

All that was said for the paranoid schizophrenic in terms of ability to impress others

exaggerated ideas of self-worth, and he committed suicide.

A young woman, convinced she was acting as the conscience of the people of the United States, attempted to assassinate the president.

A 28-year-old man stabbed a woman who barely knew him. He contended that she secretly communicated her love to him but then unjustly turned him down because she fell in love with someone else.

Assaults by paranoid patients and arrest records are considerably above those of the rest of the population (Zitrin, 1976), but most paranoid people are *not* physically violent. Behavior cannot be predicted with certainty, but estimates suggest that perhaps about 10 percent of persons with marked paranoia make suicidal

and/or homicidal attempts (Lefkowitz, 1975; Shneidman, 1976; Wilber, 1975).

More dangerous than personally violent paranoid individuals are those whose delusional schemes are turned against entire groups of people. Such paranoids often select a particular ethnic or religious group and make accusations that sound almost plausible. Or their paranoia may convince them that every teacher, politician, police officer, scientist, or other authority with whom they disagree is a hidden Communist, sexual deviant, Fascist, spy, or subversive. Occasionally the pretensions of genius, violent hatreds, and religious or ideological convictions of a paranoid strike a responsive chord in large masses of followers. At best, such people become the leaders of harmless cults. At worst, as history proves, paranoid leaders may be propelled to positions of great power where their hatred and persecutory passions prove tragic for many millions of innocent people.

---

with delusional thinking is far more true for paranoia. The schizophrenic suffers from the disadvantage of having trouble understanding reality and is sometimes burdened with other psychotic symptoms, making some potential sympathizers reject him or her as a lunatic. But the person with paranoia appears, and likely is, technically sane. For the average mental health professional, individuals with paranoia usually represent a considerable challenge. Many are so convincing that even therapists may begin to believe their story; it takes considerable skill to detect paranoid thinking and grapple with it in therapy, as the case of Mrs. A. T. demonstrates.

Mrs. A. T. went to a psychiatrist complaining of anxiety. After some weeks in therapy it became apparent that she was likely paranoiac instead. She was convinced that her husband,

a medical doctor, was having affairs with some of his patients.

Mrs. A. T. was a bright, attractive, and fashionably dressed 52-year-old woman. She was oriented, realistic, and appropriate in all ways except for her paranoia and condescending manner. Interestingly, what seemed to disturb her most of all was not her husband's supposed infidelity, but the fact that he was so clever she could not "get any evidence on him."

Mrs. A. T. found many "clues" that indicated her husband was allegedly cheating. Some of these that the patient cited were:

A. *Husband dressing better than usual.*
B. *Cut his office practice by two half days and announced he was going to the "Y" or to play golf.*
C. *Showed more interest in the patients—she interpreted this as trying to cover up.*

D. *Took large doses of tetracycline for two weeks. Patient interpreted this as medication for gonorrhea while the doctor said it was for ordinary prostatitis.*

E. *Accepted chairmanship of a medical committee which sometimes took him on trips out of town. Patient alleged he was with mistresses.*

In order to confirm her convictions, the patient several times confronted her husband. He always denied any infidelity and tried to be reassuring, telling his wife it was only middle-age jealousy. The patient had also hired detectives to follow her husband and listen to his office and telephone conversations. All the results were negative. Nevertheless, the patient remained firmly convinced. She was now contemplating hiring a prostitute to pose as a patient. The prostitute was supposed to seduce the doctor. Mrs. A. T., however, was unsure about how to find a prostitute for her plan.

Sexual and jealous motives are common among paranoid people. They carefully watch their spouses, friends, or even strangers for any hint of sexual impropriety or, like Mrs. A. T., build up a totally imaginary case. Other paranoids may imagine that a famous person or a doctor or minister is in love with them and makes it known in hidden ways—"by the ways his eyes open when he sees me." Occasionally such patients even falsely believe that their imaginary love affair has been consummated and supply a host of intimate details that makes the alleged romance sound very real.

Another favorite preoccupation in many paranoid states is litigation. Based on imaginary or grossly exaggerated wrongs, paranoid individuals spend their time suing, requesting police assistance, and demanding that one or another person be arrested. A paranoid who is intelligent, free of psychotic symptoms, and highly motivated can stir up a host of police and judicial procedures and cause considerable anxiety or harm to guiltless victims.

SCHIZOPHRENIA: REALITY OR DELUSION?

Does the condition we call schizophrenia actually exist? Or does the term, supposedly describing a cluster of disordered behaviors, reflect nothing more than bias and erroneous convictions? For centuries, schizophrenia has been the focus of controversy, possibly because it is the key mental disorder. If and when we are able to understand schizophrenia, we may have opened the door to the comprehension of all psychiatric illnesses.

Two thousand years ago, the Greek physician Soranus described withdrawal, grandiosity, and people who believed they were gods. Over the centuries, such observations were lost and recovered countless times. By the 1800s, along with the vigorous revival of scientific thought, the classification of mental disorder began anew. Catatonia, paranoia, and several other syndromes were detailed, and Emil Kraeplin showed they could be grouped together and called dementia praecox. A few years later, Bleuler rejected this label and devised the term schizophrenia. Today, psychiatrist Thomas Szasz (1974) stands at the head of a large group of critics who declare schizophrenia does not exist. Psychosis is a myth, even a fraud, perpetuated largely by the mental health professions to justify their own existence. An experiment conducted in the early 1970s by D. L. Rosenhan is often cited as evidence that mental illness is more of a cultural bias than a reality:

D. L. Rosenhan (1973) sent eight normal people faking mental illness to twelve different mental hospitals. The group included psychologists, a pediatrician, and several other accomplished and well-adjusted men and women. All the pseudo-patients went to hospital admission offices and complained of hearing "voices" that said such things as "hollow" and "thud." Except for the fake symptoms, and hiding their identity and professions, patients described their actual childhood, marriages and life his-

tories. In all instances the case histories were normal—free of serious pathological problems. Once in the wards the patients acted normally, but it took them an average of almost three weeks to be discharged. In no case were patients sent home as faking or sane. Nearly all were discharged as schizophrenia—in remission. While in the hospital, some patients were mistreated, most were ignored and nearly all felt dehumanized. The label schizophrenia became a stigma resulting in their being viewed as inferiors.

Based on this study and follow-up efforts, Rosenhan questioned the concept of schizophrenia and insanity. By virtue of a psychiatric label, all the patient's behaviors are shorn of credibility. A wish to go home, sleep in a quieter room, or make notes on his or her experiences are seen as evidence of emotional turmoil or defective thinking. That is, once we *label* someone mentally ill, we falsely see everything he or she says or does as evidence of the supposed illness. Most significant of all, for Rosenhan and other critics, is the idea that apparently no one is capable of detecting sanity even when confronted with it. Despite some of the fake patients being interviewed by highly qualified psychiatrists in excellent hospitals, none was diagnosed as normal.

In medicine, diagnostic labels describe genuine, unitary diseases. Each diagnosis, whether hepatitis or chicken pox, conveys accurate information concerning causes, prognosis, and effective treatment. In psychodiagnosis many authorities assert that labels tell nothing about cause or cure, for what has been named is not a disease entity. Szasz, for instance argues that psychiatric classification is nothing more than a collection of "stigmatizing labels" (1974).

The attack on the concept of schizophrenia and medical nomenclature has generated a vigorous defense. It is granted that psychological diagnoses are often inexact and that the Rosenhan patients successfully deceived their psychiatrists. But just because a malingering patient fools a doctor into believing he has had a heart attack does not discredit the physician or make all cardiac problems unreal. More to the point, Millon (1975) argues that Rosenhan did not successfully test his hypothesis that normal people could not be differentiated from psychotic ones. In order to verify whether sanity or insanity could be detected, Rosenhan should have had several control groups participate in the investigation. Psychotic patients should have been trained to simulate sanity. Perhaps both sane and insane subjects should have been instructed to talk their way into a hospital, even without feigning symptoms of psychoses. But as the study now stands, Millon believes it so deficient in experimental controls and flawed in design that it proves nothing.

Another criticism of the Rosenhan position comes from Kety (1975). First it is pointed out that the stigma attached to mental illness long predates the term or the medical model. Labeling someone schizophrenic is not the root cause of cruel attitudes or harsh treatment. Such feelings have a long and unfortunate history which the medical approach has actually done much to alleviate. More to the point, experimental and clinical experience continuously provides evidence of the accuracy and meaning of the diagnosis of schizophrenia. Kety surveyed 5,500 adults adopted as children, of whom 33 had been hospitalized as schizophrenic. For each diagnosed patient, a total of 365 adopted and biological relatives were carefully interviewed. After omitting revealing clues from each interview, the transcripts were given to several professionals for diagnosis. Two clear findings emerged. First, the different judges showed a high degree of agreement on diagnoses and classification. Second, and this is important for our later discussion of causes, the incidence of schizophrenia was strongly related to the degree of biological kinship. The authors of this study concluded it was not difficult "to recognize independently and reliably the syndrome that Kraeplin described eighty years ago, although there may be disagreement on the . . . degree of incapacity. . . . If schizophrenia is a myth, it is a myth with a strong genetic component!"

A TREATISE ON INSANITY

The mental disorder we now call schizophrenia has been recognized for centuries. The first scientific treatise on insanity, written by Dr. Jean

Esquirol in Paris in 1838, illustrated and described a patient so clearly that we have no trouble today making a diagnosis of paranoid schizophrenia. (Text and engraving, courtesy Wyeth Laboratories, Philadelphia)

"L. is fifty-seven years of age, a laundress, and has been very devout from infancy. Menstruation commences at the age of fifteen years. At the age of seventeen she is married, and becomes the mother of fifteen children. When forty-six years of age she loses her husband and one of her children which expires in her arms; since which period there have been anomalies with respect to menstruation. Near this time she indulges in religious scruples; accuses herself of having partaken of the sacrament unworthily, takes an exaggerated view of religious exercises, neglects her occupations, and passes her time in the church. There is insomnia. She groans and stands in fear of hell. Fifty-two years of age. Cessation of the menses. Her fears are converted into religious terror, and she believes herself to be in the power of the devil. Fifty-four years

SUMMARY

Schizophrenia is a psychosis characterized by a wide variety of symptoms. The behaviors themselves often take different forms depending upon the patient's background and personality. The following are the most common symptoms: Disordered thinking—loss of contact with reality, autistic and pre-logical reasoning, rigidity, concreteness, false beliefs and perceptions, and, particularly, delusions of control and auditory hallucinations. Flattened emotions—flat, inappropriate, disharmonious, or extra-sensitive feelings and emotions. Communication difficulties—mutism, signaling, echolalia, verbigeration, neologisms, and the use of symbols instead of words. Disorientation—confusion about place, time, or identity. Disturbed motor behavior—catalepsy, cataplexy, echopraxia, automatism, negativism, and extremely little or exaggerated motor behavior. Somatic complaints—possibly realistic as well as bizarre and delusional physical maladies.

Most schizophrenic patients have only a few symptoms, may try to hide them, and may experience periods of remission and exacerbation. Depending upon which symptoms are most prominent, patients are categorized as to type. In paranoid schizophrenia, delusions

of age; fever and delirium. She throws herself from the window and is sent to the Hôtel-Dieu, from whence after five months she is transferred to the Salpêtrière. Extreme emaciation, skin sunburnt, earthy, and complexion sallow. Expression of countenance restless. The whole body is in a sort of vacillation and continual balancing. She is constantly walking about, seeking to do mischief, to strike, to kill.

'For a million of years I have been the wife of the devil. I know that I am with him for he lodges with me, and ceases not to say to me that he is the father of my children. I suffer from uterine pains. My body is a sac made of the skin of the devil and is full of toads, serpents, and other unclean beasts which spring from devils. I have no occasion to eat (though she eats largely). All that is given me is poison. I should long since have been dead were I not the devil. For more than twenty years I have had no alvine evacuation. I have committed every kind of crime, have slain and robbed. The devil is continually telling me to slay and even to strangle my children. In one minute I commit more crimes than all rogues have committed in a hundred years. Hence I am not sorry to wear a strait waistcoat, for without this precaution I should be dangerous. In giving myself away to the devil, I have been constrained to devote my children to him. But in return, I have required the devil to bring low him that sits on high, to slay God, and the Virgin. When I was accustomed to receive the sacrament, I treated with contempt the good God of the Church. I no longer believe in him; it is no longer necessary for me to do so. It is no longer necessary to make confession; the devil forbids.'

L. remains aside, avoids her companions, fears lest she shall do them harm, talks to herself, sees the devil on every side, and often disputes with him. This unhappy being presents an example of demonomania complicated with dementia and fury. The strangest illusions and hallucinations maintain her delirium and provoke acts of the blindest fury."
Translated from the French of E. Esquirol, by E. K. Hunt, M.D. (in Mental Maladies, A Treatise on Insanity, *1845).*

of persecution are usually the most noticeable symptom. The catatonic type is typified by motor withdrawal. In hebephrenia grossly disturbed thinking and behavior is common. When there is marked emotional fluctuation, the disorder is likely to be called schizo-affective. Simple schizophrenia is evidenced mainly by social withdrawal. Each condition may be acute or chronic, part of a lifelong developmental process, or a reactive psychosis triggered by stress.

Paranoid states are rare syndromes in which an otherwise intact person has an elaborate, seemingly logical delusional system. Delusions frequently have a sexual, jealous, or political conspiracy content. Most paranoid people are not dangerous although a few may prove violent.

The meaningfulness of the diagnosis of schizophrenia is contested. The term seems to embrace a broad variety of symptoms for which there are often very different causes and outcomes. The label may also be used too loosely to include any behaviors we have been falsely led to believe indicate psychosis. In defense of the diagnosis it is conceded that the term is often employed inaccurately. But both the clinical history of the disorder and biological research reveal that schizophrenia is a valid mental illness.

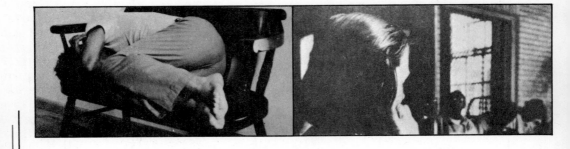

8

The Causes and Treatment of Schizophrenia

Schizophrenia is a complex disorder characterized by different behaviors and often by varied histories and outcomes. In the previous chapter we described the symptoms and types of schizophrenia and talked about the debate concerning this diagnosis. In this chapter we will look at the possible causes of schizophrenia. As before, because we are looking at a puzzling and controversial disorder, several different explanations and viewpoints will be presented.

Etiological explanations of schizophrenia have been essentially psychosocial or biological. The biological search for cause has concentrated on heredity and on the biochemical mechanisms that account for the disrupted thinking and emotion of this psychosis. Psychosocial explanations have emphasized the role of the parents or society either as models or sources of stress resulting in schizophrenia. We will examine each position and suggest our view of the etiological dimensions.

BIOLOGICAL EXPLANATIONS

Because schizophrenia occurs often in families and because of the successes attained with medication, the biological search for the causes of this disorder has focused on genetics and on the chemical mechanisms that control thinking and emotion.

Heredity

Schizophrenia has long been recognized to occur in families with more than accidental frequency. But is the familial appearance of schizophrenia proof of a hereditary linkage or is it the result of shared psychological and social circumstances? The heredity argument is very old, but it has been given increasing scientific validation by research efforts dating back to the beginning of this century.

Much of the evidence for a genetic basis for schizophrenia comes from studies of identi-

TABLE 8.1

CONCORDANCE RATES FOR SCHIZOPHRENIA

Year	Country	Investigator	Number in study	Dizygotic concordance rate	Number in study	Monozygotic concordance rate
1928	Germany	Luxenberger	33	0%	17	67%
1934	U.S.A.	Rosanoff	101	10	41	62
1946	U.S.A.	Kallman	517	10	174	86
1953	England	Slater	112	9	37	65
1961	Japan	Inouye	17	12	55	60
1968	Finland	Tienari	21	10	16	6
1972	U.S.A.	Allen, Cohen	113	6	81	27

cal and fraternal twins. Both share the same environment, but only the former have the same genetic makeups. The result is that whatever traits are uniquely shared by identical twins are likely to be inherent. Table 8.1 shows the result of several major investigations of the degree to which schizophrenia is shared by twins. Almost without exception, the concordance for schizophrenia is much greater for identical than for fraternal twins. The rate in identical twins has been reported as low as 6 percent and as high as 80 percent. Because many earlier studies suffered methodological errors, their reported rates of concordance may have been overestimated. A compilation of rates found by more careful investigators suggests a monozygotic schizophrenic concordance rate averaging about 40 percent.

It is sometimes argued that comparing mono and dizygotic twins does not really rule out the effects of environment. Identicals, for example, may be far more likely to be treated alike than fraternals. Several studies of identical twins, however, were able to evaluate the effect of different environments. In one such investigation, Inouye (1972) studied identical twins separated from infancy and raised apart. These individuals had the same concordance for schizophrenia as those raised together by the same parents.

Another focus of genetic research has traced the frequency of schizophrenia among parents, children, and other close relatives. Karlsson (1973) carefully examined family pedigrees in Iceland and found that the closer the kinship, the more likely the presence of schizophrenia or other psychotic disorders (see Table 8.2). An individual with a schizophrenic sibling, for example, is five times more likely to manifest this psychosis than someone without such a relative. In a much more controlled investigation, Heston (1970) selected 47 children born to schizophrenic mothers who were permanently separated from them during their first month of life. Fifty other adopted children whose original mothers were not schizophrenic were matched with the experi-

TABLE 8.2

RATE OF PSYCHOSIS IN RELATIVES OF SCHIZOPHRENICS

Relative	Number investigated	Comparative rate of disorder Schizophrenia	Other psychosis
Parents	641	3.8	3.5
Siblings	1,208	5.0	3.9
Children	128	4.4	5.1
Grandparents	233	2.1	2.6
Uncles-aunts	709	2.9	2.4
Nephews-nieces	562	4.1	2.7
First cousins	1,068	1.6	1.3

mental group as control subjects. When the children had become adults, they were interviewed and psychologically evaluated for schizophrenia. Heston found 5 of his experimental group to be schizophrenic and none in the control group, a highly significant statistical difference.

A similar approach has been taken by Kety and Rosenthal et al. (1975), who for over two decades have been observing the family occurrence of schizophrenia in Denmark. In this continuing investigation researchers have the advantage of working within a small, relatively homogeneous, nation that keeps complete records of every citizen's birth, location, jobs, and major illnesses in its *Folkeregister*. Initially, the investigators selected from a list of all children adopted in Denmark over a twenty-three year span those who subse-

quently became schizophrenic. For a control they matched children, also adopted, who never became mentally ill. In almost all cases the adopted children were less than a month old when they were separated from their parents; most never even saw or knew their real mothers. In comparisons for schizophrenia between legal and biological relatives, this psychosis was found to be at least four times as high in the latter. The authors cautiously concluded that their data are "compatible," with the hypothesis that schizophrenia is genetically transmitted.

Unlike most of the twin studies, the adoption investigations eliminate the confusing effects of parental child-rearing practices. If schizophrenia is caused by a disturbed mother psychologically imparting her psychosis, the schizophrenic correlation should also exist be-

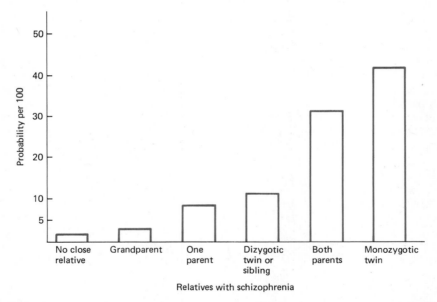

Figure 8.1. The probability of schizophrenia. The large number of genetic studies of schizophrenia in many nations permits us to approximate the probability of any one person developing this disorder. People without close schizophrenic relatives have only about a one in a hundred chance of this psychosis; someone with an identical schizophrenic twin has better than a 40 percent probability. Statistics such as these have only limited usefulness for individuals, since personal and environmental factors may be more important than genetics. (Based on Fieve, Brill, and Rosenthal, 1975; McClearn and DeFries, 1973)

Laing on the Genetics of Schizophrenia - "Worthless!"

R. D. Laing believes schizophrenia to be a valid strategy invented by the person to cope with confusion and stress. Laing leads many psychiatrists and psychologists who are critical of the organic view of schizophrenia (Wahl, 1976). In his biographical book on Laing, Evans (1976) quotes him as saying that he has gone over the genetic work in detail and that it is scientifically less than worthless:

It's a disgrace. In fact all the major published statistics so far on monozygotic twins and twin family research are, I would say, scientifically inconclusive . . . not a single one of the major studies . . . offers scientific evidence to confirm a so-called genetic theory of schizophrenia. (p. 27)

Laing's criticism of the research on the genetics of schizophrenia is based on the conflict among, and weaknesses in, some of the twin and family heredity studies.

Several of the studies have been vague and imprecise in their definition of schizophrenia, which may itself not be a unitary disorder. This can sometimes result in labeling a research subject psychotic when it is convenient to do so.

When identical twins are reared together, psychological and environmental influences are sufficient to account for any joint patholo-gies. Further, even when they are reared apart, birth or prenatal conditions, such as oxygen deprivation, and not faulty genes, could have contributed to the likelihood of psychosis.

If schizophrenia is genetic then why do different studies report such varying rates of concordance? Why also do some twins in apparently ordinary environments become schizophrenic, while others in similar situations do not? The evidence for the genetic transmission of schizophrenia is not conclusive. But it is also far too extensive to be dismissed. Study after study has confirmed that schizophrenia, in at least some form, is in the broadest sense hereditary. The genes determining the hereditary contribution are likely to be complex, so that what is transmitted may not be a specific mental disorder but a *vulnerability* to pathology. The person with a genetic likelihood of schizophrenia may simply "inherit" an intellectual and emotional structure less capable of dealing with family or environmental stress and thus be more likely to develop behaviors such as withdrawal, hallucinations, and other defensive symptoms. Further, the degree of vulnerability may vary from mild to severe. Thus, for some people, little stress may be necessary to produce symptoms, whereas others may prove resistant to even considerable conflict and disorder.

tween children and adoptive mothers. But if schizophrenia is genetic, then the unknown and unseen biological parent, and other relatives as well, should be psychotic. Since the latter proves to be the case, it suggests a significant hereditary contribution to schizophrenia (Figure 8.1).

Equally as interesting as the genetic results of several of the twin and adopted child studies are some other findings that may help clarify the role of heredity. As part of their overall investigation of concordance, Allen and Pollin (1972) evaluated pairs of twins of which only one was schizophrenic. They found the psychotic twin was usually distinguishable from earliest childhood. He or she was not only markedly sensitive, shy, and generally neurotic, but also much less physically hardy. The schizophrenic twin was almost invariably lighter at birth, far more likely to have had breathing difficulties at delivery, and generally weaker and sicklier throughout childhood. This study raises the interesting possibility that some sort of prenatal or birth disadvantage, a physical but *nongenetic* factor, made one twin more likely to develop schizophrenia than the other.

Other investigators have also been impressed with how often the more physically disadvantaged twin is the one who is schizophrenic. Campion and Tucker (1973), after reviewing the genetic studies of schizophrenia, suggest that

care must be taken in the interpretation of twin studies. Birth complications and resultant neurological damage may account for schizophrenia just as much as defective genes. "Part of what is widely taken as genetic may, in fact be due to intrauterine insufficiency, perinatal hypoxia, or birth trauma." (p. 463)

Heston (1970) and Stephens and Atkinson (1975) have provided similarly revealing data. Along with showing a direct mother-child schizophrenic linkage, they noticed that often other relatives also had major disabilities. These psychological and social disorders included neurosis, behavior problems, addictions, and criminality. What this suggests is that psychotic mothers may not so much specifically impart schizophrenia as transmit or bring about some constitutional vulnerability. They give birth to a child neurologically, biochemically, or otherwise less psychologically and physically fit to deal with the environment in a competent way.

Biochemistry

The search for the biological and chemical causes of schizophrenia poses a number of problems. Like other investigations of cause, biochemical searches cannot necessarily assume that schizophrenia is a single entity. The causes of sudden and dramatic catatonic symptoms may be different from those of slowly developing paranoid delusions, though both are called schizophrenia. Perhaps even more important, biochemical hypotheses have to distinguish between cause and effect. Are the toxins, hormones, or other chemicals found in the blood or brain of schizophrenics causing the psychotic symptoms? Or could the distinctive biochemistry of schizophrenic patients be due to hospital diets, years of confinement, prolonged periods of stress, or the many drugs they have taken?

For years, investigations of the metabolic

and neurological functioning of schizophrenics annually brought a new explanation. A unique chemical was found in the brain tissue or urine of psychotic patients; or a distinctive substance was withdrawn from the blood of schizophrenics, injected into normals, and psychotic symptoms produced. Some of the major hypotheses (Mosher and Gunderson, 1973) have been these, identified by the chemical thought to be the causative agent:

EPINEPHRINE This hormone, secreted by the adrenal glands, generally acts as a powerful stimulant and is released when the body experiences stress. The hypothesis was that psychological stress caused an overproduction of epinephrine which in the brain was converted to a form that resembles mescaline, a known hallucinogenic drug. The mescaline-like form of epinephrine supposedly interfered with neural transmission and gave rise to psychotic symptoms.

TARAXEIN A protein said to have been discovered only in the blood of schizophrenic patients, taraxein was described as a toxin that interferes with the functioning of the limbic system of the brain and thereby leads to an inability to experience pleasure or pain. In addition, normal volunteers given taraxein derived from the blood of schizophrenics were reported to have manifested psychotic symptoms.

SEROTONIN A naturally occurring chemical found in many body tissues, serotonin acts as a vasoconstrictor and plays a role in neural transmission. It was noted that serotonin was chemically similar to LSD, a synthetic drug that can induce potent psychotic symptoms. Wooley (1962, pp. 183–184) held that schizophrenia begins with a failure to form enough serotonin in the brain; the result is shyness and depression, usually forerunners of the disease. When emotional strain increases, the control mechanism governing the level of serotinin in the brain fails; production then increases sharply, or the rate of destruction may decrease. This coincides with an agitated phase. Later production may again decrease, and the patient may seem normal.

THE DOPAMINE HYPOTHESIS The biochemi-

THE AMPHETAMINE PSYCHOSIS: A MODEL

Amphetamines are drugs often prescribed for weight reduction and frequently used illegally. Heavy and prolonged use often results in psychotic symptoms including hallucinations, paranoid delusions, peculiar motor behavior, and disordered speech.

Study of the action of amphetamines shows that they tend to both release and block the reuptake of dopamine and other neural transmitters from peripheral and central nerve terminals. Further, amphetamines disrupt the normal feedback mechanisms, resulting in a host of symptoms clearly similar to paranoid psychoses. Just as in actual psychosis, amphetamine disturbances are relieved by administration of antipsychotic drugs. The medications seem to act as antagonists against amphetamine, restabilizing the role of dopamine and correcting the neural transmission process.

Amphetamine-induced psychoses have served as a model for many investigators. The hope is that reproducing and treating an induced psychosis in the laboratory will help unravel the biology of actual schizophrenia (Groves, Rebes, 1976).

Photo: Smith, Kline and French Laboratories, by G. William Holland.

cal research has often been ingenious, but so far none of the hypotheses have been unequivocally supported. Many of the findings have been found to be artifacts of diet or treatment or correlated only with specific schizophrenic symptoms such as hallucinations. As a result, attention now has shifted to understanding what makes antipsychotic drugs work. Why, for example, do psychotic symptoms subside when patients are given thorazine, a very common psychiatric medication.

The search for an understanding of the chemical effectivenss of antipsychotic drugs has led to the **dopamine hypothesis.** Dopamine is one of several chemicals involved in neural transmission. (All the neural transmitters, as a class, are called the catecholamines). Careful biochemical studies of schizophrenics have shown that patients often have an unusually high level of a dopamine derivative called DMPEA. DMPEA, like some other neural

chemicals, has potential hallucinogenic properties and simulates psychosis when injected into an individual. It is not clear whether schizophrenics overproduce DMPEA or whether other antagonistic chemicals normally in the brain have failed. In either case, schizophrenic patients seem to manifest the symptoms associated with excessive dopamine. The final argument for the dopamine hypothesis is that drugs like thorazine can be shown to block dopamine receptors. They seem to work because they "neutralize" the hallucinogenic effects of DMPEA (Matthysse and Kety, 1975).

Whether dopamine or another of the neural transmitters will prove responsible for schizophrenia is still questionable. At the same time that evidence mounts for some sort of biochemical disorder in the brain and the neural transmission process, other data fail to be supportive (Meltzer, 1976). Wyatt and

Schwartz (1975), for instance, analyzed post-mortem brain specimens of nine schizophrenic and nine control patients for dopamine activity and found no significant difference. Before a causal role can be assigned to dopamine, its character and function need to be much more clearly demonstrated.

PSYCHOSOCIAL EXPLANATIONS

Psychosocial explanations of schizophrenia have centered on such factors as the effects of disordered family interaction patterns, faulty learning, and the effects of social class and of rapid social change. Psychodynamic theorists, following their orientation, have focused on the events of childhood and on disruptions in normal psychosexual development.

Family patterns

For many psychologists, the evidence for a biological explanation of schizophrenia is inconclusive, whereas that pointing to the family is persuasive. But this is not because investigations of the role of mother, father, family communication, or child-rearing practices have necessarily been precise or definitive; many psychologists are partial to psychological explanations because they tie in with their clinical experience. Silvano Arieti (1974) has remarked, for example, that he has yet to find "even a single case that did not come from a very disturbed (family) environment. . . ."

Those who favor the family explanation emphasize the critical importance of the first year or two of life. Erikson (1963), like other psychoanalysts, is convinced that during the year following birth children learn "basic trust." The child needs to be fed, touched, played with, and held in a warm, affectionate way in order to develop a secure personality core. The youngster whose early life is deprived, who is neglected or abused, supposedly grows up suspicious, insecure, and vulnerable to psychoses.

MATERNAL DEPRIVATION Research probing the importance of care during the first year

of life began over a generation ago. Spitz (1946) compared infants raised in an orphanage with those living in an institutional nursery. Both groups were physically well cared for, but those in the orphanage were seldom held, caressed, or played with by an overburdened staff. The nursery children interacted with their own mothers nearly every day. The result reported was that although the orphanage children were often physically and emotionally disabled, the nursery children remained well. The studies that followed this one often took a partisan position in favor of "mothering." All sorts of evils, not only psychosis, were attributed to maternal deprivation. Summarizing several studies, Bowlby (1952) wrote for the World Health Organization that

. . . when deprived of maternal care, the child's development is almost always retarded—physically, intellectually, and socially—and . . . symptoms of physical and mental illness may appear. (p. 15)

Additional evidence came from laboratory research. Human isolation experiments in which adults were kept in a dark, soundproof room deprived of all sensory input showed that psychotic symptoms such as hallucinations and depression become evident relatively quickly (Kammerman, 1977). Another confirming cue came from animal studies. (Figure 8.2). Baby monkeys denied maternal care, for example, develop slowly, huddle fearfully in their cages, and otherwise seem to resemble psychotic children (Harlow, 1973).

But the case for the damaging effects of isolation and maternal neglect has not always been confirmed. Other investigations have found infants and children surprisingly hardy and resistant to a painful milieu. Koluchova (1976), for example, carefully studied twin boys who had been subjected to severe deprivation. From infancy till 7 years of age they had been isolated, locked away, and mistreated so that when they were discovered they could barely walk, were frightened of familiar objects, and failed to understand the meaning or function of pictures. Their IQ was in the

Figure 8.2. Monkeys kept from their mothers and isolated from other monkeys as well develop slowly, seem retarded, and act frightened and withdrawn, very much like psychotic people. By implication, such animal research seems to support the harmful effects of maternal (or other human) deprivation for children. (Photo: Scribe)

forties and they were seriously malnourished. Nevertheless, ten years later, after living in normal homes and attending school, the twins were fully recovered. "The boys are sociable, happy and have firm emotional bonds with their foster family . . ." (p. 188).

Today, those who argue for the destructiveness of maternal deprivation need to settle for less than certainty. Research has continued to support the potential harmful effects of minimal human contacts; children who grow up isolated either because of inadequate parents or in negligent institutions are frequently, but not always, poorly socialized and emotionally distant. Sometimes their intelligence and adjustment may also be impaired. But schiz-

ophrenia and psychosis are *not* usual outcomes (Rutter, 1972; Van Den Berg, 1972).

SCHIZOPHRENOGENIC PARENTS Another family variable that has received a great deal of attention is **schizophrenogenic parents,** that is, parents *not* themselves clinically psychotic, but whose behavior generates schizophrenia in their children. The schizophrenogenic mother has been a particularly intense object of study. Such women have been characterized as seductive yet rejecting, overprotective yet insensitive, seemingly good-humored and affectionate but actually demanding, puritanical, and controlling. The picture of the supposed schizophrenogenic father that has emerged is less clear, but generally he has been found to tend toward being callous and contemptuous of his family and/or weak, passive, and ineffectual. He may also, like the mother, be at least psychologically if not actually seductive toward the opposite-sexed child (Cheek, 1965; Higgins, 1968; Lamb, 1976).

The interaction of both parents and children, the entire family pattern, has also come under scrutiny. To many clinicians, it appears that some families are more likely to produce schizophrenic children. But in a review of more than eighty family studies spanning several decades, Jacobs (1975) and Reiss (1976) actually discerned only a few reliable trends. Although the particular family constellation likely to result in schizophrenic children cannot be pinpointed, there are some suggestive tendencies, particularly in *communication.* Families more likely to encourage schizophrenia:

Express more negative affect, jealousy, and suspiciousness
Fail to complete thoughts or allow others to finish sentences
Have a high frequency of disagreement and accusations
Express bigotry and rigid standards
Make many verbal responses that are inept or irrelevant

Many of these communication deficiencies can be detected in the following conversation. The talk was recorded while the parents were waiting for their hospitalized 19-year-old schizophrenic daughter to finish saying goodbye to fellow patients and return home with them.

FATHER: Are we going to take her home and eat supper first. I got to go out to Billy since he—

MOTHER: Well, never mind Billy, I'm not going if that's what you mean.

FATHER: It's too late now. What's she doing up there anyway?

MOTHER: They never tell you anything. You don't ask. You just sit.

FATHER: Well you said you wanted to eat supper, so I—

MOTHER: Well never you mind. I don't need supper. What is it you want anyway?

FATHER: I'm trying to tell you that I want Billy. You're such a busybody. You ought to know.

MOTHER: Don't you start that. I got to go shopping.

FATHER: I don't know what you mean. I just want to tell you—

MOTHER: Will you please shut up! I'm trying to finish this puzzle.

FATHER: Even if you are college, it don't make you nothing.

MOTHER: It says something of value, four letters down.

FATHER: I don't give a damm. I want to eat first.

MOTHER: Value could mean money. Or is it something dear.

FATHER: Value means something rare. It is rare. That's four letters.

MOTHER: Rare is like meat. You don't say rare when you say it is expensive. Besides you spend too much. Yesterday—

FATHER: I don't give a damm. Where the hell is Doreen?

MOTHER: She's your daughter. She's just—— ignorant, like you.

FATHER: I'm calling Billy and tell him about supper if it's now.

MOTHER: You're acting so stupid, finish this puzzle and I'll go up and look for her. Why don't you ever do something?

FATHER: We should eat supper out.

MOTHER: Why do they paint these rooms this dirty green?

FATHER: Shut up, I can't—

MOTHER: Here she comes. Smile! Hello, baby doll, hello.

In addition to the disturbed pattern of communication often evident in families producing psychotic children, many also tend to be distinguished by one or more of the following (Alexander, 1973; Beels, 1975; Crago, 1972; Riskin, 1972):

Chronic marital conflict, with children often forced to take sides

At least one parent with marked adjustment problems or alcohol or drug addiction

One or both parents with a history of job instability, legal entanglements, or other social failures

THE DOUBLE BIND   Viewing the entire family situation as a whole, a few writers have concentrated on the *contradictions* supposedly imparted by parents of schizophrenic persons. In many instances, parents actively place children in situations where they have to choose between mother or father. They may have to take sides in a marital dispute or follow one set of instructions by the mother and another by the father. Or the children may be confused because parents seem to both love and reject them. The children are placed in a **double bind:** If they do what they are supposed to do, they are at the same time doing what they are not supposed to do.

The double bind hypothesis as an explanation for schizophrenia has intrigued many psychologists, but it has received only limited research support. In one attempt to replicate the double-bind family pattern, Kim Smith (1976) devised an experiment in which 156 women college students played the role of daughter. They were read a letter by an experimenter posing as a mother. The letter would contain contradictory material; it might, for example, criticize the daughter for gaining too much weight but at the same time say the mother was going to show her love by sending the daughter a box of her favorite cookies. Subjects were then asked questions such as "Is mother really saying that she wants you to look ugly?" to see if they understood the letter. If they did not give the correct response, they were punished.

In the Smith experiment, subjects were not only fed contradictory messages but were also given false information and punished in almost irrational ways. The result of this complex double bind was that subjects experienced a significant increase in anxiety, and many found it impossible to adapt to the situation.

Such research, however, is not proof of the function of the double bind in causing schizophrenia. Nevertheless, based on their own observation, many clinicians believe that at least something like a double bind characterizes many schizophrenogenic homes. In his book *Knots* (1970), R. D. Laing, for example, gives many poetic illustrations of the double bind family situation. The parent says "love me," yet when the child comes to hug his mother she pushes him away and tells him to act grown up. The child cannot win, for either one or both parents continually give contradictory messages and feelings. After reading *Knots,* one patient wrote:

Mother loves me, she wants me close
Mother hates touch
She loves me, I touch her
She touches me, she hates me
I love her, I want to touch her,
To touch her, I must hate her
I touch her, I love her
I hate her, I touch her
I hate her, I love her,
She hates me, she loves me
I hate, I love, I am loved, I am
    hated. Hate, love.

Social learning theories

Many learning theorists give genetics at least a partial role in schizophrenia. Wolpe (1973), for example, while arguing that psychosis is

learned, agrees that biological factors may play a triggering role. But for Ullman and Krasner (1975), schizophrenia is exclusively the result of *social learning*. The key is that schizophrenics have been extinguished from attending to relevant stimuli and rewarded for psychotic activities. For example, a child may approach a parent with an ordinary question (What's for lunch?) or make a comment on the weather. When such responses are ignored, not reinforced, their frequency gradually declines. As social responses decline, the child may find that only the most demanding or unusual behaviors are attended to. Or he or she may be thrown more and more upon fantasy, imagination, and other internal cues.

As time goes by a vicious cycle may start. The more "crazy" the behaviors, the more likely they will be reinforced. This is particularly the case when schizophrenic individuals are brought to a psychiatrist or hospital. Not only does the institution and treatment reward crazy behavior by attending to it, but the very process of therapy stimulates additional psychotic activities. Thus, for Ullman and Krasner schizophrenia consists of several behaviors, each of which is present only because it has been reinforced. Schizophrenia may therefore be divided into four major components: (1) disorganized thinking, (2) apathy, (3) social withdrawal, and (4) bizarre verbalizations. When we conceive of schizophrenia in terms of these behavioral categories, the social learning explanation is supported in two ways. First, we see that schizophrenia is not a total, all-enveloping condition. In every schizophrenic there are a few psychotic and many nonpsychotic activities. The patient's conversation with a psychiatrist may be bizarre, filled with clang associations or neologisms. But when he talks to a friend about baseball, his speech is relevant and appropriate. Or although thinking about motives or family may be very disorganized, he or she is nevertheless able to answer a great many questions on an intelligence test. In short, the person who has learned enough psychotic behaviors, even if they constitute only a small part of all his or her activities, is diagnosed schizophrenic.

THE CAUSES OF PARANOIA

Paranoia, *not* paranoid schizophrenia, seems to be solely the result of psychological determinants; there is little evidence suggesting biological causes. Paranoid people seem to come almost exclusively from homes characterized by suspicion, meanness, bigotry, punitiveness, and cold, authoritarian parents. Children from such backgrounds feel devalued and learn to think in absolutes. You are either friend or enemy; something is absolutely right or wrong; there are no gradations of meaning or feeling; and no human failing is forgivable.

The paranoid emerging from such a background is a hostile, frightened, wary individual who needs a "cause." A commitment will let him or her feel important, provide a vehicle for hatreds, and solve self-doubts: "Now I am somebody, powerful, important and informed." The action paranoids take against those they hate depends upon how much encouragement and opportunity society provides as well as upon their own inclinations toward aggression and violence.

The second support for the social learning position comes from the fact that psychotic behavior can be unlearned or new behavior substituted.

Meichenbaum and Cameron (1973) set out to correct the rigid and disorganized thinking of schizophrenic patients. In one study patients needed to give a correct interpretation of an abstract proverb. Whenever an appropriate interpretation was forthcoming, the patients received a social reinforcement such as a smile or an encouraging "good." After suitable training, schizophrenic patients were able to give appropriate and correct responses just about as well as normals.

In another study, subjects were taught to *teach themselves*. In order to remember a series of numbers or interpret ink blots, they needed to know how to approach a problem, make relevant responses, and maintain their attention. Not only did the patients meet all the experimental goals and give correct answers, but they also learned "self-control strategies." The patients learned to monitor their own disordered responses and produce correct ones instead.

Other studies have demonstrated corrective changes in the remaining areas spelled out by Ullman and Krasner, but is this proof that schizophrenia is learned? It could, but it need not necessarily be the case. A child born with a cleft palate may have impaired speech that can be corrected with training. But the fact that speech was remedied is not proof that the initial deficiency was learned.

In support of the learning position, the fact that most schizophrenic patients come from disordered families suggests that learning processes such as operant conditioning, modeling, and the like may explain at least some of their abnormal behavior. Schulsinger (1976), for example, applied S. A. Mednick's learning model to understand the behavior of over three hundred children, divided between offspring of normal and schizophrenic mothers. The children from schizophrenic backgrounds appeared to be learning avoidance responses. They were diminishing their anxiety by switching from the thought or experience that was stressful to an irrelevant stimulus. They were, in short, being reinforced for thinking and acting "out of contact," in the manner we have come to call schizophrenic.

Social class and social change

The frequency of schizophrenia appears to be somewhat higher among lower socioeconomic groups and ethnic minorities. This can be seen with almost dramatic intensity by comparing so-called inner-city residents with those in the suburbs. In many studies the incidence of schizophrenia, in the poverty core of urban areas, as well as most other physical and psychological disorders, is greater by as much as

50 percent or more (Littlestone, 1976; Kohn, 1976; World Health Organization, 1976).

The usual explanation for these findings has been in terms of change or stress. People living an economically or socially disadvantaged existence may well be subjected to more uncertainty, frustration, and despair. The process of moving up the socioeconomic ladder for those motivated to obtain an education, material goods, and psychological status often necessitates rapid changes in habits and life styles. Such mobility accentuates differences between parents and children, bringing yet another source of anxiety into an already difficult existence (Birtchnell, 1971). How this causes schizophrenia has been suggested by Kohn (1973). He argues that the conditions of life experienced by people of lower social position tend to impair their ability to deal resourcefully with the problematic and the stressful. Such impairment does not in itself result in schizophrenia. But together with a genetic vulnerability and the experience of great stress, such impairment could well be disabling. Since *both* genetic vulnerability and stress may occur disproportionately at lower social class levels, people in these segments of society may be much more likely to be schizophrenic. Other writers have suggested that biology, though not genetics, combines with the stresses of low socioeconomic status to produce schizophrenia. In simple terms, people who are poor tend to be less well nourished, and their medical care both before and after birth fairly inadequate.

But the causal role of social class in accounting for schizophrenia can also be questioned. It is possible that people who are less well endowed physically are *both* more likely to drift down the socioeconomic scale *and* more prone to develop schizophrenia. Another possibility is that people from poorer backgrounds who are psychotic are simply more visible. In the United States, disadvantaged people are more likely to seek admission to public hospitals than those from middle-class backgrounds. The latter tend to seek outpatient care from private physicians. In addition, the

Figure 8.3. People from lower socioeconomic backgrounds appear to have a higher incidence of schizophrenia and constitute a disproportionately large segment of hospital patients. While this may be partially due to the stresses that poverty and low social status entails, it may also be attributable to a number of biological factors. Poor people tend to have fewer options when they are ill and their consequent reliance on public facilities may simply make them more visible than those who are from middle-class backgrounds. (Photo: Scribe)

pathologies of the poor are easier to recognize and count because they must register for unemployment benefits or be investigated by welfare officials (Siassi, 1976; Udell, 1976).

The belief that psychosis is the outcome of rapid social change or destabilized patterns of living has also been disputed. During the last several decades women have experienced new opportunities and challenges; many have shifted from dependent to independent roles, from home to school or career, fairly rapidly. The U.S. Census projection for the 1980s, com-

DIATHESIS-STRESS AND HIGH RISK

The diathesis-stress hypothesis contends that there is hereditary *diathesis* (meaning predisposition) toward schizophrenia, but that the psychosis will only appear if sufficient *stress* is encountered. For example, a child with minimal genetic predisposition, a low diathesis, subjected to serious infantile deprivation or an intensely schizophrenogenic parent may develop schizophrenia. But a child with high diathesis, raised in an unusually peaceful and loving milieu, despite his high inborn tendencies, may never show clinically detectable schizophrenia.

Many attempts to verify this hypothesis have

centered on children at "high risk" for schizophrenia, those whose parents are psychotic. The progress of such high risk children has been followed in their own homes and in adoptive surroundings. Studies are continuing, but already it appears that current findings partially support the diathesis view. Those high risk children who in their own or in adopted home manifest schizophrenia seem to come from families with pronounced genetic psychotic histories or family circumstances that are distinctively stressful.

Source: Fieve et al., 1975; Rosenthal, 1974.

---

pared to the 1970s, shows, for example, that the proportion of employed women among some age groups has nearly doubled. But despite a history of social discrimination and the new avenues for mobility, the frequency of schizophrenia among women today is not much different from the past (Dohrenwend, 1975).

If we take genetic and biological factors in consideration and try to filter out the effects of visibility, schizophrenia may not be as distinctively related to socioeconomic class or change as was once suspected. After a careful examination of the research on social causes since the 1900s, Dohrenwend and Dohrenwend comment (1974): Data on the "true" prevalence of psychopathology and its distribution in populations around the world has accumulated since the early twentieth century. These data suggest that some currently popular hypotheses about relations between social factors and psychopathology are questionable.

The results of these studies give pause, for example, to speculations about an increase in psychopathology as a function of the stresses and strains of modern society, and about an excess of psychopathology among women as a function of their changing role in modern society. (p. 446)

Psychodynamic theories

Psychoanalysts, existential psychologists, and many other psychodynamic therapists attempt to explain schizophrenia in terms of their orientation. Some of these views are supported by considerable research evidence, but in the main most rely heavily on clinical experience. A small sampling of some of these theoretical positions follows.

THE FREUDIAN VIEW For Freud (1924) and most of his followers, schizophrenia was a *regression to primary narcissism*. Schizophrenics are like infants who cannot distinguish between what happens inside their bodies and outside them, between themselves and other people. The only interest and concern of infants, and by extension schizophrenics, is in themselves and their experiences. Convention and reality are not understood and are rejected. This regressive process begins when the ego is overwhelmed by id impulses. Intensely primitive feelings of lust and aggression force the ego to retreat to ever-earlier stages of psychosexual development. When one sees severely schizophrenic patients babbling like babies and even playing with their own feces, a hypothesis of regression seems tenable.

Schizophrenia begins with regression. At first such people become infantile; they act withdrawn and passive, and their thinking and communications exhibit all the apparent illogic and confusion of a baby (Figure 8.4). Then an attempt is made at *restitution:* They try to continue to function, or at least to substitute some acceptable version of reality. The result is neologisms, hallucinations, delusions, and all other such inventions designed to create a new framework for living. Schizophrenics attempt to rebuild their existence, but they do so according to their own standards, which may depart considerably from those of the rest of us.

Freud's description of how paranoid disorders originate illustrates his theory. Psychoanalysis of paranoid patients convinced Freud that underlying nearly every case of paranoia was a repressed homosexual urge. The individual was faced with a powerful id impulse erotically attracting him or her to members of the same sex. These homosexual wishes were unacceptable and aroused profound anxiety. The result was the regressive process leading to schizophrenia. As the person rebuilt reality, he or she dealt with the "love" for the same sex by turning it to hate. Using the defense mechanism of reaction formation, desire is turned into its opposite. "I do not love him, I hate him." "She does not love me, she hates me." The other possibility is that the homosexual impulse is avoided by using the defense mechanism of "It is not my own mind that stimulates me to homosexuality." "They are beaming wicked messages into my brain." "My neighbor is forcing me to do things I don't want to do by the way he fixes his eyes on me."

THE NEO-FREUDIAN VIEW Analysts such as Harry Stack Sullivan (1953) and Karen Horney (1950) have recast the Freudian position and emphasized the interpersonal process and the role of anxiety. According to their view, schizophrenia is a disordered way of relating to and dealing with others that derives from the person's anxiety.

Anxiety arises in childhood when children are excessively punished, rejected, or ridiculed by abusive parents. Anxiety is a motivator, so it is almost a reflex for children to attempt to avoid it. Very quickly they learn to soothe the unpleasant stirrings of fear either by stay-ing away from people and/or by controlling their own awareness. If they have nothing to do with others, if they withdraw, then others cannot cause them pain. Even more effective, if they are able to change their own consciousness, mentally experiencing only what they want to experience, then almost nothing can cause psychological discomfort. For Sullivan, this kind of total, anxiety-motivated retreat was most clearly seen in catatonic schizophrenia. For him catatonia was the initial psychosis from which all other forms followed as the person developed new methods for dealing with fear.

The views of Ronald Laing (1967) are very much in the contemporary psychoanalytic mold. For Laing, the core of schizophrenia lies in the interaction of the child with the parents. Fathers and mothers who hate, love, tease, tempt, punish, and provoke their children force them to live with contradiction, stress, and ambiguity. Laing speaks, for example, of the process of *mystification,* a conflicted and confusing interaction parents impose on their children that makes the children distrust the validity of their own perceptions and actions. To survive in such a milieu, the growing child devises strategies that enable him or her to exist amid the turmoil and pain of what Laing calls the "family politics."

Laing sees schizophrenic symptoms as attempts to integrate self-doubts and anxieties.

Figure 8.4. Schizophrenic patients sometimes lie curled up in a fetal position for days or weeks. Some psychoanalysts contend this lends support to their view that schizophrenia is an infantile regression. (Photo: Scribe)

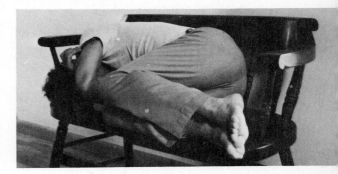

Thus "madness," the seeming retreat from normal life, is part of a personal journey toward fullfillment. Schizophrenic behaviors are a growth process; our attempts to medicate or talk them away interfere with the evolution necessary to attain wholeness. Laing calls for guides, not therapists, who will enter the schizophrenic's world, go "down" with him to the point of utter insanity, and then assist in the struggle to give birth to a new personality.

China and Europe

Psychiatrists in the Peoples Republic of China apparently view schizophrenia as a biochemical and genetic disorder that is also greatly influenced by life experiences. Conflict with other people, dissatisfactions with work, or other sources of stress and fear are seen as key causal components. The result is disordered thinking necessitating both medical treatment and study of the works of Mao Tsetung. Patients attend talk and reading sessions with other patients and professionals. Their task is to understand their illness and learn the political ideology of former Chairman Mao, or "correct thought" (Walls et al., 1975).

Among many European psychiatrists, and to an extent in the United States, existential philosophers such as Soren Kierkegaard and Jean-Paul Sartre have been very influential. For them, disorder is the result of the loneliness and futility people experience in contemporary society. In a complex, rootless, and superficial world, all people are alienated at least to some degree; they live estranged from themselves and wander from one meaningless relationship to another. The mentally ill are even more greatly troubled than normal people by their feeling of *nothingness*, their lack of purpose and identity. Failing to relate meaningfully to themselves, they can neither satisfy their need to become, to self-actualize in Abraham Maslow's (1971) terms, nor establish satisfying relations with others. Alienated individuals, unable to achieve success in the quest for meaning, experience *ontological anxiety* at its deepest and profoundest level. They are nothing, there is nowhere to go and nothing to hope for. They succumb to nothingness and

disorder, confusion, despair, and fantasy—or what we would call schizophrenia.

THE SOCIAL LABELING VIEW   To those who like Szasz (Chapter 7) dispute whether schizophrenia even exists, the term itself is the result of an attempt to impose the medical practice of labeling distinctive disease processes on a variety of behaviors that have neither a common origin nor a common outcome. Taking this view a step further, Thomas J. Scheff (1970) holds that schizophrenia is not a neutral, value-free, scientifically precise term. It is rather the leading edge of an ideology embedded in the historical and cultural present of the white middle class of Western societies. The concept of illness and its associated vocabulary—symptoms, therapies, patients—legitimatize the prevailing public order at the expense of other possible worlds.

For Scheff, the "symptoms" of schizophrenia are simply socially disapproved behaviors. Since we cannot call a hallucination criminal and have given up the practice of labeling it witchcraft, we categorize it as mental illness. Once we dispose of behaviors we do not tolerate by calling them "sick," we initiate a self-perpetuating process of labeling and reinforcement. The person labeled schizophrenic is impressed by his or her new identity. After all, haven't bright and prestigious doctors decided "what I am?" And he or she is rewarded for willingness to carry the new label. Hospitalization and psychotherapy reinforce patients' dependency, withdrawal, and acceptance of themselves as mentally sick. The social labeling view sees the cause of schizophrenia in intolerance. So long as people are unwilling to let other people live as they see fit, so long as society insists on punishing people who "march to a different tune," we will have schizophrenia.

Resolution?

It is not likely that we will be able to resolve different theoretical positions until we know much more about the etiology of schizophrenia and can state with certainty just which behaviors are properly diagnosed as psychotic. We do know that some hypotheses, such as the

Freudian idea that homosexual impulses underlie paranoia, have not received much research support. But it is also evident that several theorists have described the schizophrenic process with great insight and sensitivity. Though psychiatrists such as Laing and Sullivan may doubt that there is a biological basis for schizophrenia, their psychological description of its development need not totally conflict with organic views. Schizophrenia may be a many-faceted disorder, explicable in terms of biology, family, and social experience.

Perhaps the explanation that may eventually satisfactorily account for schizophrenia will center about the concept of vulnerability. In their review of the six major causal models, Joseph Zubin and Bonnie Spring (1977) contend that current approaches have reached an explanatory plateau. Despite continuing research and scholarly effort, it seems that schizophrenia cannot be completely understood in terms of learning, neurochemistry, or any of the other present causal descriptions. Instead, whether or not a person manifests schizophrenia may depend on a combination of the intensity of stressors and the personal level of psychobiological tolerance. Some people with an innate or acquired low stress threshold—that is, a greater vulnerability—may become schizophrenic fairly easily. They may have schizoid reactions to even relatively minor traumas, such as ordinary frictions in the family or common social hardships. Other people who have little vulnerability may endure all sorts of chronic emotional, environmental, and physical crises and remain free of psychosis. Such a vulnerability hypothesis may enable us to link the several different causal models of schizophrenia into a comprehensive and useful tool for understanding this complex phenomenon.

TREATMENT

Chemotherapy

By the end of the 1950s the number of hospitalized schizophrenic patients numbered almost 500,000. During the 1980s, despite large increases in the population of the United States, estimates are for fewer than 200,000 schizophrenic patients. In good part this radical decrease in hospitalized patients is due to a shift in treatment philosophy; people are no longer institutionalized as often or as long as they were a few years ago. But another important reason for the decrease is the use of medication that effectively helps control schizophrenia. Notice that we do not say cure: at present, chemical therapy seems mainly to diminish anxiety and confusion, facilitate thinking, and moderate several other psychotic symptoms.

The most commonly used antischizophrenic drug is thorazine, which has been called the single most effective treatment technique available (Mosher, 1972). Thorazine is one of a group of chemicals called the phenothiazines. This class of drugs seems to help regulate the neurotransmitters in the brain, particularly dopamine, thereby reducing the disruptive effect of excessive amounts of this chemical. Other medications frequently used with schizophrenic patients include anti-anxiety drugs such as Valium, antidepressants such as Tofranil, and a unique drug effective in both reducing maniclike symptoms and enhancing reality contact, Haldol. In all, the psychiatric drugs have been remarkably useful in alleviating symptoms, enabling patients to participate in psychological therapy and resume jobs, schooling, or other functions. Estimates suggest that more than half of all schizophrenic patients will experience significant improvement with chemotherapy (Salzinger, 1976).

Hospitalization

Only a small portion of actively schizophrenic individuals need to be hospitalized. Today, only one of every six patients who can be diagnosed schizophrenic is institutionalized (Figure 8.5). Many other individuals, even if their symptoms are serious, can frequently be maintained outside a hospital, so long as they continue to take their prescribed medication.

A decision to hospitalize should be made when symptoms are extremely disruptive or dangerous, when chemotherapy appears inef-

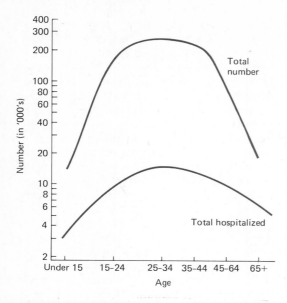

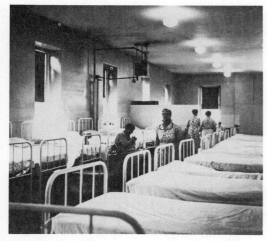

Figure 8.5. This is an estimate of the total number of schizophrenia patients, both in and out of hospitals, receiving care in the United States in 1985. Of a total of 1.2 million patients, the majority are under 40 years of age and only about one-sixth (200,000) are likely to be hospitalized (from Kramer, M., U.S. Dept. HEW). (Photo: Smith, Kline and French Laboratories, by G. William Holland)

fective, or when prolonged diagnostic study or complicated treatment procedures need to be worked out. But this is not always the case. Many patients are hospitalized because they are old and unwanted, out of work, lacking in resources, or deliberately escaping from responsibility. Thus hospitalized patients tend to include a disproportionately large share of people with little motivation or energy, as well as those with the most severe and debilitating behaviors. Despite such disadvantages, over two-thirds of first hospital admissions can count on being discharged within a few months (Bland, 1976).

Many of the better hospitals today have **milieu therapy** programs in which an entire ward, or the whole facility, are looked upon as a therapeutic community. Patients are encouraged to help govern the ward and plan their own activities. Every staff member is trained to act as a therapist, and the atmosphere is designed to stimulate motivation and growth. In some situations this approach has been extended out of the hospital to the family. **Family therapy** is directed at husbands or parents or at marital, child-rearing, or other adjustment difficulties that contributed to the schizophrenic episode.

Community care

Hospitals have been increasingly recognized as poor places to get well. Although many facilities offer conscientious care and provide competent staff, it is difficult to get away from the apathetic, impersonal climate of large institutions. As a result, community-based programs have become very popular. Some of these are "day" hospitals where patients go only for treatment; they live and sleep at home. More popular are the small houses where twenty or thirty patients live with psychiatric aides and a visiting doctor. Medication, therapy, and other treatment is the same as at the hospital, but patients feel much more like individual human beings and are more stimulated to improve. Sometimes such facilities are reserved for patients who have made a good hospital recovery and are almost but not quite ready to return to the community. A facility used for this purpose is often called a **halfway house.**

Many community residences are much more than miniature hospitals, and some have

WHO WILL RECOVER

Forecasting who will recover is a very uncertain task, for like other human beings, schizophrenic patients are unpredictable. As a whole, with good treatment, the majority can expect a degree of improvement sufficient to enable many of them to return to work or school, reestablish their marriages, or take care of other responsibilities. But those most likely to recover, with rates ranging up to 80 percent or more, tend to have several of the following characteristics (May, 1976; Mosher, 1972):

No previous record of mental hospitalization
Adequate prior work, family, or social
   adjustment

Reactive rather than process schizophrenia
Access to good treatment and care facilities

One of the most important contributors to recovery, in addition to good medical and psychological treatment, is that patients are no longer inevitably put behind locked doors and largely forgotten. In that kind of atmosphere, the hospital, rather than encouraging improvement, actually causes deterioration. Today most clinicians, recognizing the debilitating effects of confinement, urge community care and early discharge, and otherwise do their best to avoid long hospitalization.

---

quite innovative programs. One of the best known is Kingsley Hall in London, started by R. D. Laing a decade before his influential book on the personality of schizophrenic people (1969). At Kingsley Hall, patients and staff, who are mainly nonprofessionals, are seen as equals, people who may need one another. All live together and share food, financial, and housekeeping responsibilities in commune fashion. If necessary, the staff member and patient "go down" together into madness. They descend even if it means bottle feeding, encouraging kicks and screams, or experiencing the most bizarre hallucinations.

In the two decades since the founding of Kingsley Hall, many imitations have disappeared. Normal people often find the constant attention, demands, or extreme behaviors of schizophrenics too hard to endure. But modified versions of therapy communes like Soteria, a twelve-room house in the San Francisco area, have survived (Mosher, Menn, Matthews, 1975).

At Soteria the emphasis is on personal interaction, group discussion and decision; more conventional psychotherapy, including the use of medication, is used if necessary. The Soteria group has evaluated its results against those of standard hospital practice. In a continuing study, Soteria patients and first-admission schizophrenics both showed good reduction in symptoms after six months and a year of treat-

ment. The Soteria people, however, appeared far more socially competent. They were much more capable in areas like finding a job, establishing friendships, and learning new skills. It may be fair to conclude that although small residential community programs may not do everything that early enthusiasts claimed, they can make a valuable contribution to the treatment of psychoses.

Many community residences also function as **aftercare** units, increasingly recognized as an important part of any kind of treatment (Figure 8.6). Patients who receive follow-up care after leaving the hospital or any kind of treatment have a better chance of staying well and getting better. It is now common for therapists to continue to see their patients perhaps once or twice a month for a year or more after discharge.

Psychodynamic treatments

Treatment of schizophrenia using individual therapist-patient approaches are rare. With few exceptions, most of the founders of various psychodynamic techniques did not intend them to treat psychoses. But group techniques based on analysis, Gestalt, transactional, or similar orientations have been quite effective and become widespread. Group methods permit patients who have usually been through many of the same experiences to assist one

Figure 8.6. A small community treatment center. Sixteen patients live in this nine-room house in a residential neighborhood and cooperate in all housekeeping chores. A psychiatric social worker administers the facility, and other professionals visit for group therapy and medication. Patients usually stay three to six months before being discharged or referred elsehwere for more intensive treatment. (Photo: Scribe)

another in a realistic way. They also enable one therapist to serve a fairly large group of patients, an important consideration because of continuing staff shortages.

Behavior therapy has also been extensively used with schizophrenic patients. Symptoms can be reduced, anxieties relieved, communication encouraged, and even delusions modified by techniques such as desensitization, a token economy, and reinforcement. But as O'Leary and Wilson point out (1975), although behavior therapy has increased work performance, decreased apathy, and reduced bizarre behavior

when judged by discharge data and recidivism rates, . . . behavioral approaches have been much less encouraging. This is because most of the programs have not aimed at discharging patients on a long-term basis, an outcome

which requires considerably greater effort and extensive community intervention. (p. 428)

It may be unfair to single out behavior therapy for not bringing about more lasting or total changes in schizophrenic patients. At present, all therapeutic approaches have relatively limited goals. Their primary aim is to enable the patient to resume functioning. A total reversal of lifelong schizophrenic adjustment patterns is not likely, no matter what treatment techniques are employed.

Ancillary treatments

Music, art, vocational, and other work therapies can be valuable in enabling a patient to make contact again with the real world. Often the patient who is mute, withdrawn, or even stuporous may nevertheless respond to music or dance and in this way slowly be drawn back to reality. Ancillary modes of treatment are usually at their best when coordinated with other treatment techniques. But although this is the recommended procedure in some institutions, because of lack of personnel or effective planning patients sometimes get little more in the way of treatment than several hours of weaving rugs or making ceramic pots. Little as this may be, if it involves patients in worthwhile interactions with teachers and other people, it may still be beneficial.

The future

This history of the treatment of schizophrenia has had many dark moments. Even in modern times, treatments have been not only ineffective but destructive as well. During the 1950s, for example, brain surgery was hailed as a cure for psychosis, and tens of thousands of patients were lobotomized. **Lobotomy,** severing the front lobes of the brain, is now very rare and used only in selected instances. Still other techniques have come and gone: carbon dioxide inhalation, insulin coma treatment, whirlpool baths and other hydrotherapies that kept patients clean but did little else.

This history of highly touted but ineffective treatments for schizophrenia makes most

WHAT IS SCHIZOPHRENIA?

Is schizophrenia a unitary disorder?

Probably not. We believe schizophrenia is a reality and not just a stigmatizing label to help society rid itself of nonconformists. But the symptoms we presently group together as schizophrenia may actually comprise two or three different disorders. There is evidence, for example, that schizophrenia may be divided into process/reactive, or paranoid versus nonparanoid disturbances. Future refinements seem likely to lead to greater precision in diagnosing the several behaviors we now loosely call schizophrenia.

Is schizophrenia hereditary?

It is probable that some forms of schizophrenia are hereditary, and that others which seem genetic are due to neurological damage inflicted before or shortly after birth. But the genetics of schizophrenia are complex, so that psychotic parents will not necessarily have schizophrenic children.

What is the role of the family and environment?

A disordered family or severely stressful environment may be sufficient to bring about schizophrenic symptoms even in a presumably biologically intact person. But it seems that in many instances schizophrenia is the result of an interaction between a physically vulnerable individual and stressful experiences.

What is the future of treatment?

The old mental hospital with its locked doors and impersonal staff will play less and less of a role. Day hospitals, community residential facilities, and the like will become the major resource for treating patients who require extensive care. It also seems likely that more specific medication and refinements in behavioral and psychological therapies will enable nearly all patients to experience considerable improvement or recovery.

---

professionals skeptical of all new and unproved methods. It is now recognized that by *suggestion* alone, nearly all new treatments appear effective for a while. Recently multi- and megavitamin techniques have been tried, but there is as yet no conclusive proof that they work (Ross, 1974). New drugs have also been introduced, but again the results are not yet definitively known. Psychological methods too usually require lengthy periods of evaluation. Hunterkopf (1975), for instance, has been training patients to use client-centered counseling with one another and seems to be obtaining encouraging results. There are also developments in behavior techniques and in group and ancillary approaches that may someday contribute substantially to the treatment of schizophrenia. For now, however, we will have to keep looking and testing.

SUMMARY

Schizophrenia is a complex disorder and has resulted in a number of different biological and psychosocial causal explanations. Genetic studies with twins and families have shown that schizophrenia may have a substantial hereditary component. The genetic data are disputed, however, with many contending that at best what is transmitted is more accurately described as a vulnerability to psychosis. Biochemical research has attempted to isolate the neurological substances triggering schizophrenia. A number of different chemicals such as epinephrine, taraxein, and serotonin have been suspected, but confirmation has been lacking. Most recently, the neural transmitters like dopamine have been considered as possibly playing a critical part in schizophrenia.

Those who argue for a psychological etiology suggest that the family is the source of schizophrenia. They have singled out variables such as maternal deprivation, schizophrenogenic parents, faulty and double bind communications. Behavior advocates state schizophrenic behavior is learned and often the result of the extinction of normal responses and the reinforcement of psychotic behavior.

Since schizophrenia frequently appears to be greater among inner-city and lower socioeconomic people, the social view has contended that this psychosis is largely a result of societal stress and inequity.

For some psychoanalysts schizophrenia results when id impulses overwhelm ego resources and severe regression results. For other analysts, schizophrenia is a defensive strategy, a way of attempting to cope with confusing parental and social demands. The most controversial approach suggests that schizophrenia is not a mental illness but simply an unconventional life style labeled insane by an intolerant society. Ultimately schizophrenia may prove a multi-faceted disorder, the result of the interaction of biological, psychological, and social factors.

In terms of treatment most schizophrenic patients are given medication and usually respond quite well, often being enabled to resume their lives and responsibilities. Formerly, hospitalization was believed necessary, but today only a small proportion of patients are confined. In addition, because large institutions have many disadvantages, there is an increasing tendency to use very small, community-based, treatment units. The psychodynamic treatment of schizophrenia is uncommon, but group treatment based on analytic, transactional, or similar orientations is frequent. Behavior therapy has also been used fairly extensively, but its effectiveness, like all other psychological approaches, has been limited. Music, art, and other ancillary treatments are often useful in enabling a patient to reestablish contact. In the future it is likely that treatment will be more community based and employ medical as well as psychological techniques.

9

Depression and Suicide:
The Mood Disorders

Disorders of mood or feeling (affect) are described as manic or depressive. Manic people are characterized by hyperactivity, overtalkativeness, and exaggerated ideas of success and well-being. Depressive patients often show feelings of worthlessness, slow, labored movements, and excessive pessimism and unhappiness. Both mania and depression may be either quite mild or so severe that hospital care is necessary. In this chapter we will cover the varieties of mood disturbances and also describe a frequently related behavior—suicide.

MOOD DISORDERS

Depression or mania, or both, may occur just once or repeatedly in the same person. There are, in fact, at least three common variations:

1. Single or recurrent manic episodes
2. Single or recurrent depressive episodes

3. Single or recurrent periods of mania and depression

Mood (or affect) disorders with only one emotional swing, up or down, may be called **unipolar**. But when a person is successively both manic and depressive, the condition is described as **bipolar.** Thus, a person who has a history of several depressions would be diagnosed as having recurrent unipolar depression. An individual who has been depressed and is now manic would be diagnosed as bipolar manic.

The description of mood or affective psychoses was first proposed by Kraeplin in 1896. He hypothesized that mania and depression are opposing signs indicating the same pathology, just as chills and fever both point to pneumonia. Kraeplin coined the phrase **manic-depressive psychosis,** a term still used synonymously with affective or mood disorder.

Like other psychopathological symptoms,

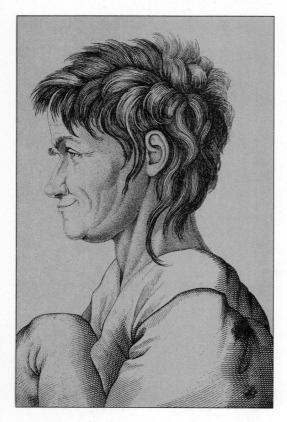

Figure 9.1. This engraving is from the first scientific treatise on mental illness by Esquirol, published in Paris in 1838. The patient's expression and behaviors can be seen in many manic patients today. (Photo: Wyeth Laboratories, Philadelphia)

many depressive and manic signs may appear as part of or secondary to other mental conditions. When affective symptoms coexist with schizophrenia, the disorder is diagnosed as schizo-affective psychosis (see Chapter 7). When neurotic and depressive symptoms are mixed, neurotic reactive depression may be the appropriate diagnosis (see Chapter 4). A diagnosis of manic or depressive psychosis is made only when affective symptoms are *primary*—that is, predominate in curtailing the effective functioning of an individual. More specifically, a clinician looks for the following criteria in order to establish the presence of a mood psychosis:

1. The emotional disturbance is severe and primary.
2. There is at least some minimal indication of psychotic thinking, such as delusions, hallucinations, or disorientation.
3. Affect seriously disrupts adjustment and function.

Affective psychoses are particularly serious because suicide is a possibility for all depressive patients and even some manic ones. Perhaps about one-fourth of markedly depressed persons actually make suicidal gestures. But nearly all affective conditions are relatively *short-lived* and respond to treatment within a few weeks or at most several months. Schizophrenic hospitalizations, in contrast, usually last months and years.

The incidence of untreated mood recovery is also high. Seventy to 90 percent of emotionally disordered men and women improve by themselves or with a minimum of psychological help. Thus a caring husband or wife, or an alert family physician is often able to give sufficient reassurance to permit a depressed individual to "hold on" for a month or two till remission occurs spontaneously. It must be pointed out, however, that although this is a common practice, it is *not* recommended. Mental health professionals consider all depressed patients suicide risks, so that anyone with depression should be urged to seek professional help.

A final distinctive attribute of nearly all affective conditions is that most are *recurrent*. Repeated depressive and/or manic episodes are common. But in between such "attacks," most people function perfectly well. Unlike many schizophrenics, who often manifest some degree of disordered thinking even when their more extreme symptoms are in remission, affective psychotics are essentially normal between attacks.

MANIA AND DEPRESSION: SYMPTOMS AND DIAGNOSIS

Mania

Relatively few affective patients have a history of only manic episodes. Those who do sometimes have a background of being extremely energetic, busy, and emotionally high for most of their lives. Such superficially radiant and active individuals can be very successful. Their outgoing personality is best described as **hypomanic** (mild, nonpsychotic mania), a trait that often propels them into positions of wealth or authority.

In psychotic mania, the person is ceaselessly busy, inconclusively jumping from one conversational topic or activity to another. Movements and speech seem pushed or forced, and the person is impatient with energy. He or she demands attention, performs, puns and jokes, and treats interruptions or frustration with hostility or even extreme anger. Delusions of wealth or power and sometimes hallucinations and confusion are evident, but these thinking failures are typically not as deep or severe as they are in schizophrenia.

The most extreme form of this affective psychosis is **delirious mania,** a very rare occurrence. Gradually or suddenly the manic person becomes even more energized, constantly and purposelessly running about busy and preoccupied. He or she seems totally out of contact with reality and unrestrained: there may be wild shouting, loss of bowel and bladder control, and even attacks on other people. The following transcription of a brief conversation with a hospitalized 42-year-old college professor who wrote thousands of dollars of worthless checks that he gave away illustrates the behavior of the manic person. The professor spoke with force and energy:

I'll tell you why I wrote the checks . . . Share all, the point is share and share alike. Give if you have. The banks ought to give it all away. All, all away. . . . Sharing yourself, you know. After, I'm going to San Diego. I have secrets. The elixir of life which I will tell you about, or sell you, whichever comes first. Its just organic vitamins, ah ha, but which? My cousin is a psychiatrist and makes buckets of money because he knows how. Do you? The situation and the conditions need a lot of improving. I'm writing to the governor's commission on mental health and telling all; an expose. (Sings) "If you got love, you've got it all." I

don't remember the words. Life is glorious. I'm a poet, Life is a climb up, so don't clam up; enjoy, breathe deep and live. . . . My mother was a great lady. Definitely English royalty, the real thing in my veins. When I get to London I will look up my peerage. I have a recipe for them, Kidney pie, organic, that will sweep the British Isles, bring peace to Ireland. I'm writing you a check right now.

Depression

Depression, in all forms, is both the most frequent psychological disorder and the one most often unrecognized. A good estimate based on sampling studies suggests that 10 percent of adult Americans, with women considerably outnumbering men, suffer from some sort of

Figure 9.2. Most manic patients appear extra energetic, talkative, and euphoric but are *not* hostile or violent. In rare instances, however, mania can result in unrestrained and even dangerous behavior. When medication fails to control such extremes, patients may have to be forcibly restrained. (Photo: Smith, Kline and French Laboratories, by G. William Holland)

depression. Depression also tends to recur, so that the majority of persons have from two to six episodes during their lifetimes. But although as many as 15 million Americans may be depressed, annually only a few hundred thousand are known to be treated by mental health specialists: perhaps 200,000 receive outpatient care and 125,000 are hospitalized (Beck et al., 1977; Levitt and Lubin, 1975). Several hundred thousand more may get help from family doctors or counselors, but the vast majority do not seem to be receiving any professional assistance at all. Research in other nations such as England and Japan reveals similar statistics, so that depression could well be the foremost mental health problem worldwide.

So much depression goes undetected because it is frequently hidden. Classic depressive signs such as pessimism and feelings of worthlessness may masquerade as aggressiveness or stoical courage. Cultural, age, and educational factors also play a role. Among children and adolescents, depression often manifests itself as antisocial behavior. Children who "act out" may be motivated by hostility, but they may also be driven by despair. In the aged, depression frequently appears as withdrawal and hypochondriacal complaints. Among lower socioeconomic groups, depression is commonly marked by insomnia, digestive problems, nervousness, and other physical aches and illnesses (Lesse, 1977), as the case of the factory worker illustrates.

The patient is a 37-year-old factory worker who has been unemployed for three months. He complained of feeling restless, jumpy, and nervous. He thought he might have something wrong with his glands, since he also perspired a great deal. . . . In appearance he looked pale, fatigued, and apprehensive. His facial expression was downcast, his shoulders were hunched, and his movements were slowed and retarded. In the waiting room he was observed sitting with his hands in his pockets and staring vacantly at the floor. . . .

The patient was reassured that a thorough medical examination was negative. He smiled weakly, apparently relieved to learn he was physically well. . . . Questions about his unemployment, financial condition, and his wife's supporting the family gradually led to more and more evident signs of depression. . . . The patient felt worthless, physically weak, and unmasculine, "a poor example" for his children, "nothing but a failure" and too "old and too dumb" to "ever make anything" of himself. Along with his self-descriptions, the patient became morose and tearful and then started crying bitterly when he admitted contemplating suicide.

Many depressions, perhaps the majority, seem to be in response to external events. The precipitants that most frequently trigger depression include these:

Marital discord, separation, or divorce
Serious physical ill health
Loss of employment, business, or social
   standing
Death of an important person
Failure to meet role demands (act like a
   "mother" or "man")

Because depression may present itself in several different forms and vary in intensity from mild melancholy to severe and suicidal misery, there is some question as to whether the term actually describes a unitary disorder. Often too, there is considerable clinical disagreement. Studies of the reliability of the diagnosis have revealed only a fair to moderate likelihood that two practitioners will reach the same conclusion. One psychiatrist may believe the condition to be a neurotic depression, another may argue for affective psychosis, and a third may insist it is within the limits of normal grief. To help alleviate some of these problems, several different classificatory schemes have been proposed to help describe depression: endogenous-exogenous, psychotic-neurotic, unipolar-bipolar, agitated, involutional. None, however, is universally accepted as definitive (Kendell, 1976; Kerry and Orme, 1975).

THE FREQUENCY OF DEPRESSION

This sixteenth-century engraving by Dürer allegorically presents an artist's view of depression. (Courtesy National Library of Medicine, Bethesda, Md.)

The frequency of depression and its often hidden character is illustrated by a family physician's analysis of the histories of 538 patients. Though these patients complained of physical ailments, 214 or 40 percent were diagnosed as having evident psychiatric problems. Of the total number psychiatrically identified, two-thirds were classified as depressed. (Looked at another way, 23 percent of the 538 "physical" patients were found to have depression.) Of the 129 depressed patients, 78 had complained only of abdominal pains, headache, or other somatic distress or just came for a medical checkup; 51 talked of nervousness, fatigue, and frank feelings of depression. In 76 of the 129 depressed patients, a precipitating cause could be identified. Eleven of the depressed patients were considering suicide, and six had actually made attempts (Justin, 1975).

The family physician, clergyman, school counselor, or lawyer is the nonfamily member most likely to encounter the depressed person who is unaware of his or her condition or unwilling to seek psychiatric help. Such professionals can, however, be trained to recognize depressive symptoms and refer clients for ap-

ENDOGENOUS-EXOGENOUS Depressions that seem to be a response to an outside event—an observable loss such as death of a family member or financial ruin, are called **exogenous,** a term equivalent to reactive. The term **endogenous,** meaning originating within the body, is used to describe depressions that are supposedly the result of internal physiological malfunction. Several investigators have reported endogenous depressions, those without an evident external trigger, to be more likely to involve physical symptoms, to be deeper and generally more serious. Critics have pointed out, however, that the exogenous-endogenous distinction can be quite erroneous. For example, a depression may still be *endogenous* even if a stressful event has preceded it. The stressor could be coincidence or could have acted

as a catalyst to actualize a depressive vulnerability. Or an exogenous depression may be as profound and pervasive as an endogenous one if a personal catastrophe has initiated it.

PSYCHOTIC-NEUROTIC At one time it was believed that neurotic depressions were always reactive (exogenous) and psychotic depressions always endogenous. Today it is recognized that both types may be reactive. Psychotic depression is now diagnosed largely on the basis of such characteristic symptoms as delusions, confusion, or other cognitive disturbances. But neurotic/psychotic depressions may still be difficult to separate. Sometimes there is a gradation of irrationality: Physical complaints, for instance, may range from the merely exaggerated to the frankly delusional. The result is that many practitioners and the

DSM-III now just use the diagnosis depression, without making a psychotic/neurotic distinction.

UNIPOLAR-BIPOLAR   Unipolar depressives have no history of mania, and their emotions may or may not be tied to an external event. That is, unipolar depressions can be endogenous or exogenous. In contrast, bipolar depression is commonly believed to be the result of an internal biochemical or psychological fluctuation sometimes resulting in mania, other times bringing about depression. Bipolar depressions are theoretically shorter, closer to psychosis, and found in several generations of a family. In practice, however, unipolar and bipolar depressions are often indistinguishable.

AGITATED DEPRESSION   The usual picture of the depressed person is of someone who wearily and sadly drags himself or herself through the day. This is an accurate portrayal for the great majority of seriously depressed patients. A few, however, become stuporous and need to be fed, clothed, and cared for. Equally few evidence their despair by going to the opposite extreme, restlessly and vocally lamenting and complaining. Such *agitated* persons may pace back and forth excitedly, moaning and crying, beating their breasts and wringing their hands. One woman hospitalized three times for depression became well known to the doctors and nurses. She was usually very agitated, excitable, and demanding; she would order any nearby staff member to "kneel down with me, pray with me, Oh dear God, please, please, please make it better." In rare instances depressed patients, like some very few manic persons, appear to lose control over themselves entirely and run about purposelessly shouting and crying and sometimes even attacking others.

INVOLUTIONAL MELANCHOLIA   **Involutional melancholia** is a psychotic type of mood disorder usually marked by guilt, somatic delusions, and some agitated depression. Traditionally, this diagnosis has been given to women in their late forties to late fifties because it was theorized that involution (return to nonfunction) of the uterus and ovaries—that is, menopause—was responsible.

Figure 9.3. The agitated depressive often becomes extremely vocal, loudly weeping and lamenting. This patient is crying and pulling her hair. (Photo: Smith, Kline and French Laboratories, by G. William Holland)

But since investigations have revealed that specifically female endocrine changes may not be involved, the term is now used for both men and women who are depressed in late middle age. Technically the diagnosis should be applied only if the depression is a single and apparently nonrecurrent event, but this rule is not always followed.

Depressive episodes are typically sudden in onset. About 70 to 80 percent of patients have little warning of their rapidly declining emotional tone. Melancholic patients, however, usually feel progressively more anxious, apprehensive, and tense for many months before the full onset of their pathology. As a result, involutional melancholia usually follows menopause, or in the case of men retirement, by a year or more. The typical irrational feelings of guilt also tend to build up slowly. Patients at first may feel they did not give their chil-

Figure 9.4. Grief is a normal and expected response to loss. But if the grieving person begins to lose the ability to function and signs of increasing mental and emotional turmoil appear, depression may be suspected. (Photo: Scribe)

dren as much attention as they needed, a thought that eventually becomes delusional. They falsely believe they caused their daughter's divorce or son's alcoholism because of something they did or said during childhood.

Today, most theorists believe involutional melancholia to be largely exogenous. The later period of life is one in which children leave home, employment comes to an end, sexual capabilities or interests may decrease, and physical health often declines. These and many other major adjustive challenges confront men as well as women (Figure 9.4). As a result, both sexes are thought to be especially vulnerable to unipolar depressive experiences during their fifties and sixties (see the case of Mrs. O. P., for example).

Mrs. O. P., aged 51, was admitted on the recommendation of her family doctor, who had tried to treat her for the past six months. During admission she was agitated and tearful,

loudly lamenting, "I knew it would always come to this. I'm crazy. Oh my God. I've been such a bitch. . . . Oh, Harry, dear God, forgive me. I'm being punished now."

Mrs. O. P. believed she had caused her husband's heart attack because she was a "nag." She was also preoccupied about her own supposed chest pains, severely depressed, and convinced that she was at last being punished by being put in an "insane asylum" for her transgressions. (In actuality the clinic was an outpatient treatment center where patients stayed only during the day and returned home nightly.)

Manic-depressive psychosis

Bipolar or **manic-depressive** patients make up about one-fifth of those suffering serious affective psychoses and have *both* emotional lows and highs. They may be alternately depressed and then manic with no "normal" time in between, or periods of ordinary feeling may last for hours, months, or years. Some patients alternate manic and depressive episodes, while others have several depressive and then several manic periods in a varied, seemingly random order. In rare instances, emotional switches occur so often that it is difficult to know when one mood ends and the other starts. Such patients may have both manic and depressive symptoms simultaneously and be called *mixed* manic-depressive.

Carlson and Goodwin (1973) did a longitudinal analysis of twenty manic-depressive patients in their manic phase and found several consistencies: Each manic episode lasted an average of four weeks, and patients had a mean of 4.4 manic and 2.2 depressive episodes over an average of 12.3 years.

In all twenty persons studied, the *initial phase* of mania was characterized by increased psychomotor activity, euphoria, and irritability. They also became grandiose, overconfident, and expansive; many showed increases in sexuality, smoking, letter-writing, and telephone use. An *intermediate phase* followed, typified by even greater pressured speech, dysphoria, hostility, flight of ideas, some disorganized thinking, and depression. The *end stage*

AFFECTIVE SYMPTOMS

	Mania	Depression
Emotional	Elation Euphoria (exaggerated feelings of happiness and well-being) Irritability and aggressiveness Increased sexual feelings Fluctuating emotionality	Feelings of inadequacy, fear, and hopelessness Dysphoria (exaggerated feelings of sadness and pessimism) Loss of interest in other people, current happenings, and sex Decreased motivation Emotional fluctuations
Cognitive	Flight of ideas (continuous and inconclusive jumping from one topic to another) Tendency to grandiose delusions and sometimes hallucinations and other disordered thinking	Poor concentration Delusions of guilt, worthlessness, somatic disabilities, hallucinations, and other disordered thinking Suicidal ideas Indecisiveness
Physical	Talkativeness and rapid/pressured speech Hyperactivity (constant motion and distractibility) Decreased sleep Singing, dancing, joking	Loss of appetite and weight Slow speech and movements Worried and grim facial expression Sighing, moaning and crying Fatigue and some physical aches and complaints

Only a few of these affective symptoms are present in most patients. Nevertheless, they are typically so pronounced that the diagnosis of mania or depression is unmistakable.

Source: *Beck, 1974; Taylor and Abrams, 1973; Woodruff et al., 1974*

---

was seen in fourteen subjects and was marked by frenzied activity, panic, delusions, some ideas of reference and hallucinations, and clear depression. The severity of each person's manic or depressive phase was not related to recovery or recurrence. All twenty patients studied were treated and were free of symptoms when discharged and followed up within a year.

CAUSES OF MANIA AND DEPRESSION

The causes of affective psychoses, like those of other psychopathologies, are not yet known. Psychodynamic, behavioral or learning, medical, and social explanations, however, all offer clues, and it now seems that the mood psy-

choses, like schizophrenia, are a complex of many overlapping pathologies. Each disturbance may be the result of a differently weighted combination of individual predispositions and external stresses and circumstances.

Behavioral, psychodynamic, and cognitive explanations seem most adequate in accounting for depressions triggered by an evident external loss. The causes of endogenous depressions remain uninterpreted, and manic behavior, if it is described at all, seems to be mentioned as an afterthought. Psychological explanations, therefore, appear applicable to only a limited range of affective disorders.

Psychodynamic Explanations

There are many different psychodynamic explanations for affective psychoses. Existential psychologists see depression as the result of individuals being confronted with their ultimate powerlessness. Many humanistic writers speak of dependence and independence. They hypothesize that depression often follows the loss of friend, job, or good health because it forces the individual into an independence he or she cannot handle. The lost person or situation helped prop up a false self-image; when it was removed, the fractured self crumbled, leaving only desperate emotions.

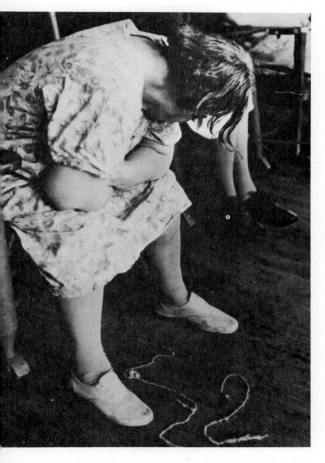

Figure 9.5. The psychoanalytic hypothesis that depression is anger turned inward often seems clinically apparent, but experimental evidence is incomplete. This depressed patient seemed to be angrily tearing apart the piece of twine on the floor. (Photo: Smith, Kline and French Laboratories, by G. William Holland)

SELF-PUNISHMENT The classic psychodynamic position was set forth by Sigmund Freud in his 1917 paper, "Mourning and Melancholia," in which he differentiated between grief, a healthy and conscious response to loss, and depression. The latter was postulated to be the result of unconscious ambiguous and hostile feelings once focused on the lost person and now turned against the self. The loss that brought on the depression was most often that of a loved person, but it could also be loss of an inanimate object (such as a watch), a personal failure such as bankruptcy, or even a symbolic event.

The psychoanalytic formulation sees depression as a form of *self-punishment*. The woman who is deeply melancholic supposedly because she has lost her husband is really angry at herself for previous and hidden aggressive feelings toward her spouse. The symptoms of depression and of manic reactions as well are the way the person punishes herself or himself for imagined guilt.

The Freudian view that depression is anger turned inward has remained alive for three-quarters of a century because many practitioners believe that therapy often reveals the hostility underlying mood disorders (Figure 9.5). Affective patients often seem to recognize and admit that their negative feelings toward the departed person are playing a role in their own despair.

Experimental evidence has been both supportive and critical. Hauri (1976) compared the dreams of recovered depressed subjects to those of normal adults. Dreams were evaluated by independent raters uninformed about the backgrounds of their subjects. Both groups were awakened at intervals, and the formerly depressed were found to have more dreams filled with self-punitive rage. Atkinson and Polivy (1976) offered support from another direction when they showed that subjects experimentally provoked to anger and then prohibited from expressing it were more likely to be depressed. But the verification offered by these studies is at best incomplete. An attempt by Cochrane (1975) to obtain more direct evidence was entirely critical. He evaluated the emotions of 124 women and 76 male psychiatric patients on the Object Relations Test, a scale particularly sensitive to negative feelings. Four different measures of hostility and aggression were used, and none meaningfully differentiated depressed from other abnormal patients. In Cochrane's view, his results cast doubt on the idea that anger turned inward plays a determining role in depression.

COGNITIVE DISTORTION   A more contemporary dynamic position sees depression as the outcome of a cognitive (thinking) distortion. Depressed persons are seen as emerging from family backgrounds that predispose them to think of life in negative, defeatist ways. They have been emotionally stunted by parental rejection, punitiveness, and demand so that they feel inadequate and expect only the worst (Beck, 1974). Congruent with this thesis is the learned helplessness model proposed by Seligman (1975), which we examined in Chapter 5.

Additional support for the cognitive model comes from earlier work by Rotter (1966) on what he called the *locus of control*. Rotter found that many people could be described as tending to believe either that they did or did not have control over what happened in their lives. "Internals" believed that events depended mostly on their own resourcefulness and activity; "externals" were of the opinion that what occurred was the result of luck, fate, or the attitudes and conduct of other people. Subsequent research has shown that those who believe the locus of control is external are much more prone to depression. Using Seligman's formulation, "externals" respond to the world as if they had been conditioned to endure and accept whatever happens to them; their cognitive scheme tells them that effort is hopeless.

Investigations originating from a number of directions have given some support to the cognitive-helpless position (Mendels, 1976; Minkoff, 1973; O'Leary and O'Leary et al., 1977; Seligman, 1975). It has been found that depressed patients much more often come from childhood homes broken by death or divorce—an atmosphere nourishing feelings of helplessness—and that affective patients in general tend to come from competitive and achievement-oriented backgrounds where their efforts were often made to seem incompetent and useless. In addition, the findings are that experimental subjects unable to control stressful events frequently show signs of depression and that psychological tests measuring helplessness as a personality trait correlate well with tests evaluating depressive emotions.

Like psychoanalysts, some advocates of the cognitive approach believe mania to be a variant of depression. The person who has a *negative frame of reference,* who expects no good to come out of any new situation, may be primed to respond with either despair or hyperactivity. Both behaviors are seen as ways of attempting to cope with challenges that are fundamentally viewed as overwhelming (Beck, 1974; Mendels, 1976).

Behavioral explanations

Heretical as it may sound, perhaps one of the first behavioral or learning explanations of affective disorders was given by Sigmund Freud. In his paper "Fragment of an Analysis of a Case of Hysteria" (1948), Freud held that children in their greed for love do not enjoy having to share the affection of parents with brothers and sisters. Soon they notice that all the parents' affection is lavished on them whenever they arouse the parents' anxiety by falling ill. They have now discovered a means of enticing love from the parents.

When such a child has grown to be a woman, she may find all the demands she used to make in her childhood countered because of her marriage to an inconsiderate husband. In that case, ill health will procure the care she longs for; it will force her husband to show her consideration. It will compel him to treat her with solicitude if she recovers, for otherwise there may be a relapse. Her state of ill health will have every appearance of being objective and involuntary; she will not need to feel any conscious self-reproach at making such successful use of a means she learned in childhood was effective.

Freud theorized that sick behavior, whether hysterical complaints or depressive symptoms, was in part maintained because it was rewarded. Contemporary behaviorists believe depression is a function of a reduction in reinforcement for normal behavior and an increase in reward for distorted emotions. We include this excerpt from Freud not only because it shows a surprising awareness of the role of learning, but because it illustrates how much we need to be aware that behavioral, psychoanalytic, and other explanations overlap. The distinctions emphasized by labels such as "behaviorist," "dynamic," or "humanist" are often far less important than the *similar insights* emerging from all these approaches.

For the behavior psychologist, the cause of depression centers about the *rate of reinforcement*. The social rewards individuals receive are dependent upon their personal skills and appeal, socioeconomic status, and the number of "attached" persons with whom they interact. When there is a change in any one of these sources of reinforcement, such as a friend dying or deprivation of a skill or financial standing, the amount and frequency of reinforcement may be reduced. Once reinforcement diminishes, dependent behavior also decreases. What is more, the new lower response level may now be reinforced by social rewards such as sympathy. For example, a person suffering a loss may appear less outgoing, talkative, and interested; he or she may sit quietly and avoid company. This new behavior is reinforced by the affectionate attention and ministrations of others. In fact, a vicious cycle is easily created since a progressive reduction in the amount of reinforcement for normal feelings is almost matched by an increase in the quantity of reward for emotionally abnormal symptoms (Lewinsohn, 1976).

Werner and Rehm (1975) tested the hypothesis that depression is a reflection of rate of reinforcement. Ninety-six normal female college students were carefully evaluated to determine their affective state. Next, they were assigned equally either to a high- or a low-reinforcement group. Subjects believed they were taking part in an intelligence study in which they would be required to make associations to stimulus words. Whenever they gave an allegedly correct response (to words like *needle* or *dog*), a light flashed to indicate accuracy. The low-reinforcement group was arbitrarily rewarded only 20 percent of the time; the high group was reinforced for 80 percent of responses. The results were revealing. The low-reinforcement group showed distinctly more depressive behavior as measured by a psychological test, self-ratings, and behavioral indices of response speed. Subjects who were initially a little depressed often tended to underestimate the amount of reinforcement (number of times they were told they were correct) and also became more markedly depressed.

Werner and Rehm believe their investigation supports the belief that depression could be related to rate of reinforcement. They point out, however, that depression may be a multidimensional phenomenon, with level of reinforcement accounting for only part of a very complex condition. What appeared most interesting was the tendency for subjects who were already a little depressed to understate how often they were correct. This finding is consistent with the view of those taking a cognitive approach. One background cause of depression may be the inclination of some people to be pessimistic, to see things far more negatively than they are in reality.

In addition to reinforcement explanations, other behavioral hypotheses have been proposed. It is postulated, for instance, that the behavior seen in depression and mania—hand wringing, pacing, compulsive talking, and lamenting—are social stratagems for avoiding responsibilities, decisions, or dealing with others. Still another possibility is that depressed or manic conduct is the result of modeling. The person may have learned through the example of parents, friends, or the entertainment media to act manic or depressed in response to certain stimuli (Eastman, 1976).

Medical explanations

HEREDITY Along with differentiating manic-depressive psychosis in his 1896 text, Emil Kraeplin insisted that the illness had little to do with external events. Based on his years of observation, he was certain that this psychosis was innate and probably hereditary. Since Kraeplin's time, many different studies of twins have helped support the hereditary argument. Research in the United States, England, and other nations has shown that if one identical twin is affectively disordered, the chances are 60 percent the other will be also. In contrast, fraternal twins, who presumably have the same psychosocial environment but are less genetically alike, have a concordance rate for affective disturbances of about 20 percent (see Figure 9.6).

The genetic position is further strengthened if we separate affective disorders into types. Both unipolar and bipolar illnesses seem to have distinctive lines of transmission, as

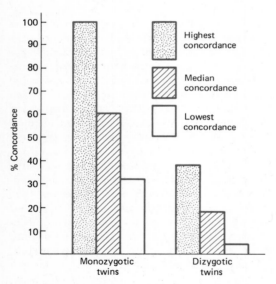

Figure 9.6. A dozen different studies of identical and fraternal twins in the United States and Europe have carefully evaluated the concordance for mood disorders in twins. Over the course of half a century, the investigations have reported different results. The lowest, median, and highest concordance rates that have been found in this research are shown in the graph. It is apparent that all have consistently pointed out the likelihood of a significant genetic contribution to affective disorders. *Sources:* Allen et al., 1972; McLearn and DeFries, 1973; Woofruff et al., 1974)

do endogenous and exogenous ones. Exogenous depressions reveal inconsistent hereditary patterns, but in the case of endogenous disturbances, the closer the kinship the greater the chance that relatives of bipolar patients will have bipolar psychoses. The same is true for unipolar patients. Further, when a very close relative like an identical twin becomes ill, say with a bipolar mania, the sibling tends to have the same emotional disorder at the same time (Goetzl et al., 1974; James and Chapman 1975; Woodruff, 1974).

But impressive as these statistics are, they do not prove that heredity is the only cause of mood disorders. If there were a simple, single genetic determinant, then identical twins might show a concordance of 100 percent instead of the range of from 30 to 90 percent now reported. It is likely, and this was suggested earlier when the genetics of schizophrenia were considered, that the heredity of affective illnesses may be complex. The responsible gene or gene cluster may have less than 100 percent **penetrance,** or ability to actually make the characteristic appear. What may be inherited could be varying degrees of vulnerability—tendency to manic and/or depressive behavior awaiting sufficient stress in order to be brought out.

BIOCHEMISTRY Biochemical explanations focus on biological deficiencies or chemical irregularities that may account for severe variations in mood. One hypothesis is that affective fluctuations may be the result of a malfunctioning hypothalamus, the part of the brain that helps to regulate emotions. Since the hypothalamus is also involved in maintaining endocrine function, perhaps some affective conditions that seem to be related to glandular irregularities (like involutional melancholia) might be understood in this way (Mendels, 1976).

Another biochemical hypothesis sees affective psychoses as the result of a disturbance in the very delicate electrical balance between nerve cell excitation and inhibition. Perhaps in manic individuals the excitation threshold is too low or in depressive persons electrical transmission is slowed. There is little direct evidence for these views, but several EEG studies have shown distinctive electrical patterns for manic-depressive patients (Scott and Schwartz, 1975).

The most promising line of research has concentrated on the role of catecholamine and indolamine, two groups of chemicals that serve as neural transmitters and are also implicated in schizophrenia. According to this view, depression is caused by too little and mania by too much of these amines. One specific chemical in these amine groups, norepinephrine, has been singled out. Excessive levels of norepinephrine may overstimulate nerve fibers and therefore result in mania; depression could be accounted for by the opposite process. This contention has been supported both by diagnostic and treatment studies. Measurements of the level of catecholamines in spinal fluid, urine, and blood have frequently shown correlations between these amines and emotional tone. More important perhaps, treatment agents such as electric shock, chemical mood stabilizers, and lithium in particular, seem to have a measurable corrective effect on the presence of the catecholamines and indolamines (Fieve, 1975; Jain and Jain, 1973).

Figure 9.7. Many instances of depression and mania seem unrelated to either external precipitants or internal psychological events. Along with increasing biological evidence, this observation seems to support the biochemical view of affective disturbances. (Photo: Scribe)

Social explanations

It is clear that social crises can precipitate depressive and sometimes manic episodes. Unemployment, arrest, family disruptions, personal conflicts, and many other environmental and psychological events may contribute to affective disorders. Since several of these problems are found in greater number in people of lower financial and social status, the incidence of mood disorders could be expected to be higher in these groups. This expectation has had some confirmation in investigations reporting bipolar illnesses to be more typical of middle-class persons and unipolar depression to be more characteristic of lower-class persons. But these findings are inconsistent and disputed. At the present time, the only uncontested epidemiological characteristic is that affectively disturbed women considerably outnumber men. Otherwise, mood illness seems to be almost equally distributed among all social groups in the United States, and in most nations around the world (Chopra, 1975; Schuyler, 1974).

Only a limited number of psychosocial factors have been found to be reliably related to affective impairments. Two of particular interest are *achievement needs* and *maternal separation*.

HIGH ACHIEVEMENT NEEDS People with high intellectual and social aspirations have been reported to be slightly more prone to develop mood disorders. Such individuals often have elevated expectations of success, are extra vigorous in its pursuit, and conversely feel "crushed" when they fail. It is possible, however, that rather than the emotional disability following high achievement needs, these drives were the result of an innate heightened emotional tone in the first place (Woodruff et al., 1971).

MATERNAL SEPARATION Adults who as children have had their mothers taken away by death or divorce seem more disposed to depression. Studies by a number of investigators suggest that the absence of a mother, or an adequate substitute, may leave a child emotionally vulnerable to serious despondency (Beck, 1974). Given what we have already learned (Chapters 2, 5, 8) about the importance of childhood deprivation in mental health and pathology, this conclusion is not surprising (Roberts, 1974). What is of special interest, however, is that maternal separation may bring about unipolar depression in the mother.

Mothers may be separated from their children by divorce, institutionalization, or, most commonly, employment. Even though they have to work in order to support their children, many employed mothers report a measure of guilt, and some despair at having to leave their children with a babysitter or by themselves. In a study of the actual frequency of depression in mothers of pre-school children, Richman (1976) found this emotion the most common problem in otherwise psychologically healthy women.

In the following case, depression in the mother is due to a legally forced separation from her children. Like many other parents whose children are taken away for foster placement or by a divorced spouse, serious depression quickly follows.

Ms. S.D., age 27, was separated from her common-law husband and living with her two young children and boyfriend. Because of a history of marijuana arrests, when she was found to be illegally collecting double welfare payments the court declared her "unfit," and her children were placed in foster homes. Soon

after the children were removed, the client became increasingly morose and abusive. She fought violently with her boyfriend, made offensive phone calls to court and welfare officials, and hired "five fat lawyers to get my kids back." She carved the initials of each child on both arms and made a suicidal gesture by taking an overdose of aspirin. Through her parole officer, Ms. S.D. became an outpatient in a local mental health center. By this time she was dysphoric, felt hopeless, was withdrawn, falsely believed her boyfriend wrote letters about her to the police, and had lost fifteen pounds. She was diagnosed as psychotically depressed and was placed on medication and psychotherapy. Consideration was also given to the possibility of helping her regain custody of her children.

TREATMENT

Treatment for affective disturbances is often challenged by the urgent need for immediate relief. Patients who are severely depressed are suicide risks and may also be self-destructive in other ways. As a result, medication is often the first form of treatment offered, and psychodynamic or behavioral therapies are instituted when the most acute symptoms have passed. All the treatment procedures will be described in detail in Chapters 17 and 18. At this point we will discuss some techniques more specifically suitable for mood disturbances.

Psychodynamic therapies

The insight approach is used sparingly by dynamic therapists. Most feel their first job is to be supportive and reassuring. They want to make their depressed or manic patient less anxious and feel relaxed and comfortable. Once patients have regained some emotional stability then slowly the roots of the psychosis can be explored.

DR. You've said a good deal about your older sister, how she made you feel so helpless and angry. I'm wondering if this anger, this helpless feeling is not somehow related to what you have just said about your wife.

PATIENT You mean when she acts so caring. You know, takes charge. Well, maybe. I know I don't like it.

DR. Does this reawaken those feelings you had about your sister?

PATIENT You mean that's how I get to feel so depressed? Yes, I think that could be it. The more she takes care of me, the more I resent it. I just resent that in her. I hate it. She and that whole situation depress the hell out of me. That's why, too, I think, about my job. That's why when I lost my job, it was not losing the job. It was her taking charge of me then. That's it, then. Don't you think?

DR. It could well be. The job could have served as a catalyst but I think we are getting closer to the roots of your depressed feelings when we talk about your childhood family relations and your relations now with your wife.

Behavioral methods

Transactional, client-centered, analytic, and other dynamic therapists have long recognized that depressed patients have a uniquely bleak view of themselves and the world. As a result, many even fail to understand situations or events that might offset their mood. Such patients need to gain insight and understanding so that they can see how much their own expectations falsely color their emotions. Interestingly, behavior therapists, whose views are supposedly contrary to those of psychodynamic practitioners, are increasingly concentrating on the distorted attitudes of depressed patients. Many behaviorists are talking about teaching depressed (and manic) patients how to perceive and respond more realistically and how to achieve greater control of their own emotion-based behaviors (Davidson, 1976).

Such an approach was worked out by Carilyn Fuchs and Lynn Rehm (1977). Fuchs and Rehm contended that many of the symptoms observed in depression result from impairment in self-control. Although normal persons are deliberately able to ignore negative events, depressed persons are unwillingly pulled to focus on them. Second, depressed persons set unrealistic, high, and unattainable goals. Finally, normal persons often give themselves internal or explicit "rewards" for meeting certain goals. Depressive patients are less likely to be self-reinforcing and far more likely to be self-punitive.

Thirty-six depressed women volunteers were chosen for this study. One-third were told they needed to wait about eight weeks before therapy sessions began. Another third met together and group discussion and interactions were encouraged—but no behavior methods were taught. The experimental group was instructed in techniques intended to help these people regain self-control of the processes hypothesized to lead to depression. Experimental subjects were instructed in self-observation and self-control procedures and taught the principles of reinforcement. They kept written logs of their behavior and were taught to shift from a negative focus to a more positive one, and also to set realistic and attainable goals. The women were urged and encouraged to schedule pleasant events and self-rewards and further reinforced by a point schedule for positive behaviors.

The results reported by the investigators seem to affirm their thesis. Although not all subjects completed their assignments, compared to the two control groups, volunteers in the experimental unit showed very significant improvement. Pencil and paper psychological tests and behavioral ratings revealed the mood of the women instructed in self-control to be much better at the end of two months of supervised learning. The recovery was also reported to be maintained in an evaluation six weeks after the teaching sessions ended. These findings led the authors to believe that learning treatment methods might be useful and practical in alleviating most mood disorders.

ELECTRIC SHOCK: TREATMENT OR TORTURE?

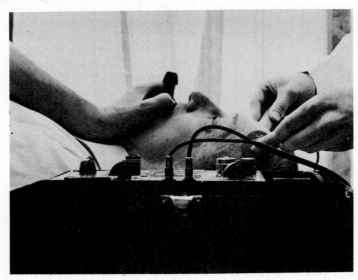

Photo: Smith, Kline and French Laboratories, by G. William Holland.

Electroconvulsive therapy (ECT) has been found to be singularly effective in the treatment of most depressions and sometimes in mania. Studies show that nine out of ten patients have their depression rapidly improved or lifted following treatment (McCabe, 1976; Mendels, 1976). But although ECT is extremely helpful in affective psychoses, its use is very controversial.

Procedure: Early in the morning, before breakfast, patients are administered relaxant medication and then lie down on a surgical table. They are given a hard pad to bite on to prevent their injuring the tongue, and electrodes are held

Medical techniques

If psychiatric medication can be said to have dramatically altered the treatment of schizophrenia, then it is fair to state that chemotherapy has revolutionized the care of affective disorders. In the last decade several new drugs have almost totally replaced all other modes of therapy in clinics, hospitals, and private practice. Nevertheless, although medication is now almost universally the first order of treatment, psychological approaches are still recommended by many practitioners. Often behavioral or dynamic techniques provide a good follow-up to chemotherapy. Some clients have to be helped to work out new response patterns; others may require counseling in order to resolve the personal and emotional tangles created by their affective disorder.

Each of the different types of mood disorder is handled best by particular drugs or combinations of drugs. The common unipolar depressions are effectively treated with the so-called tricyclic group, which consists of medications like imipramine and amitriptyline. These drugs fit in well with the catecholamine hypothesis, that depression is the result of certain neurological amine deficiencies. The tricyclics have been found to act directly on the amines in the brain and stabilize synaptic activity (Frazier, 1976).

Another chemical agent that works both as a treatment and preventive is lithium. A relatively old and neglected chemical, lithium

to each temple. Next, 70 to 130 volts of alternating current are applied for a fraction of a second. The first electrical surge causes immediate loss of consciousness, so that ECT is *painless.* Following the shock, the limbs and body move spasmodically in a convulsive manner for about a minute. Several minutes later, patients regain consciousness, feeling a little confused. ECT is usually given two to five times weekly for a total of five to twenty sessions.

Effects: ECT has some undesirable effects. Many patients are frightened of the confusion following treatment; others are fearful of permanent memory or intellectual impairment. There *is* some partial amnesia, but most memory is restored in a few days or weeks. In rare instances it may take several months for full memory recovery. Many patients complain of headaches, nausea, and excessive appetite as a result of ECT, but more serious side effects are rare.

Controversy: The entertainment media have depicted ECT as a horrifying experience used as punishment by sadistic doctors. Some social scientists have attempted to show that ECT is used "against" poorer or less educated people. These contentions have not been supported by evidence (D'Agostino, 1975; Woodruff et al.,

1974). Because of the adverse publicity, many patients are dreadfully afraid of ECT. It is their fear, and not the treatment, which is painful. Reports from a few patients of outrageous abuses of this treatment could be true, but they could also be delusional or hallucinatory. ECT has been used to treat neurotic and schizophrenic patients, but such applications have proven futile. Often such patients, whose psychoses do not improve or worsen as a result of ECT, become extremely critical of the procedure.

Result: Because of patients' fears, however unjustified, most psychiatrists and hospitals, fearing lawsuits, are now reluctant to use ECT even when it is known that the procedure would be uniquely helpful. The result is that ECT is now used less and less. Though in competent hands it is a worthwhile, safe, and painless therapy, some possible early abuses of the technique and public misconceptions have effectively nullified its potential. Probably an equal contributor to the decline of ECT is the growing diversity of medications now available to treat mood disorders. In many instances, drugs can just as effectively and quickly relieve the conditions formerly treated by electric shock.

---

has recently been rediscovered and proved practical in treating mania and hypomania, and to a lesser extent, depression. It may also serve as a prophylactic. Several studies have shown that bipolar I (episodes of depression and severe mania) and bipolar II patients (depression and hypomanic episodes) may have their mood swings prevented by maintenance dosages of lithium (Fieve et al., 1976).

Still other drugs and medical techniques are also worthwhile in affective disorders. The MAO (monoamine oxidase) inhibitors were beneficial for a decade before the newer tricyclics were introduced. Sometimes the antischizophrenic group of medications such as thorazine and other tranquilizing agents may also be employed. If drug therapy is not feasible,

the once-common method of electroconvulsive therapy may prove practical. The most recent evidence suggests that electric shock may work in ways similar to the tricyclics, that is, correctively altering the function of the amines in neurological conduction (see box, Electric Shock: Treatment or Torture?).

In all, the medical techniques available provide psychiatrists with a choice of procedures that, appropriately employed, have brought about very great improvement or total recovery in close to 100 percent of patients. The impressive potency of present medications has also given support to those who argue that most affective disorders are biochemically rooted (Aden, 1976; Fieve, 1975; Marini et al., 1976; Neis et al., 1977).

SUICIDE

Each year in the United States, about 25,000 people reportedly commit suicide. The actual number who intentionally kill themselves may be two or three times that total, since many choose means such as one-car collisions, which are listed as accidents. Estimates and surveys also show that there are at least ten attempts for every successful act, so that the number of potential suicides can be expanded to include hundreds of thousands of people annually. If we also include as suicidal those who have seriously contemplated it, concretely planning how they might kill themselves, then many millions of Americans can be counted as possible risks for at least some period in their lives. In other words, the people who die represent only the small proportion we know about and see (Shneidman, 1976).

Suicide can be viewed as part of a continuum of self-destructive behavior. At one extreme of the continuum are those determined to kill themselves, who use certain methods like putting a gun to their head. A little further along the continuum are those who are not so sure they want to die. They swallow eleven sleeping pills and leave to chance or fate whether or not they will survive. Quite low on the continuum of self-destruction are the people who deliberately smoke or drink to excess, continually violate their medically prescribed low-salt or low-fat diets, drive recklessly, or otherwise consciously or unconsciously inch ever closer to death. Like most actual suicides, these individuals are not sure they want to die; they gamble with their lives, perhaps to satisfy some self-destructive urge or attitude.

Three times as many men as women commit suicide, but the number of women who *attempt* to kill themselves is considerably greater. This difference is probably accounted for by the fact that men tend to choose more violent and hence more lethal means (such as guns), whereas women choose gentler and more ambivalent methods such as drug overdoses. Suicide is also clearly related to age, in that the frequency rises in almost linear

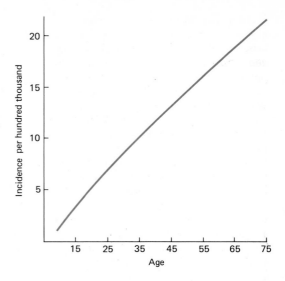

Figure 9.8. Suicide and age. This smoothed curve shows that in the United States and most of the world, suicide increases with age. This is probably because as adults get older, conditions associated with suicide, such as family loss and ill health, become more likely. (Choron, 1972; World Health Organization, 1978)

fashion from early adolescence onward (Figure 9.8). This progression is probably a result of the fact that many of the correlates and precipitants of suicide, such as ill health, marital crises, and financial and mental health problems, tend to increase with age.

Fallacies about suicide abound (see box, Suicide: Fallacy and Fact). Many can be traced to spurious and ill-considered statistical comparisons. Some of these popular ideas are that suicides rates are supposedly unusually high for college students, black men, and psychiatrists. Or it is alleged that suicide rates are very low in Catholic countries like Ireland or during wartime. All these purported findings have been presented as evidence of powerful psychological and social forces. But we should be careful to view these conclusions with skepticism. Accurate suicide figures are difficult to gather, frequently inconsistent, and the numbers in question are almost always small (Brooke, 1974; Roberts, 1975; Seiden, 1970).

For example, it has been reported that suicide is third as a cause of death for college students and that their rate is almost 40 percent greater than for individuals of the same age not in college. Before one looks for profound reasons to explain these figures, a glance at the actual numbers will be instructive. First, college students, being young, do not die of heart disease or cancer in any great numbers, so that accidents and suicide become leading causes of death. Second, their suicide rate is less than .00008 percent, so that for 9 million students, there are about 700 suicides yearly. The reported contrast is that the suicide total is roughly 500 for 10 million noncollege young men and women. The difference in the actual number of reported suicides between college and noncollege people, then, is about 200 out of a total population of 20 million. Such a tiny difference, even if we could be certain of its accuracy, does not seem to justify any far-reaching conclusions about the supposed hazards and stresses of college life (Roberts, 1975).

Prediction

A great deal of research and clinical effort has been directed at understanding the antecedents of suicide. What kinds of people try and what sorts of situations trigger suicide? Demographic (social statistical) studies have shown the "average" suicidal person is a white male, middle-aged, Protestant, and the father of two children. Such information is of little value. For one, it narrows down suicide potentials to 30 million inhabitants of the United States. More important, it diverts us from understanding that suicide is found among all peoples, young and old, rich and poor, with and without previous psychiatric histories.

Suicide prediction studies have also been plagued by disagreements and questionable statistics. Some authorities have contended that nearly 100 percent of suicidal persons are mentally ill; others suggest only a minority are truly disturbed. Even more important is the disagreement over what constitutes suicide. Is an alcoholic who dejectedly leaves a

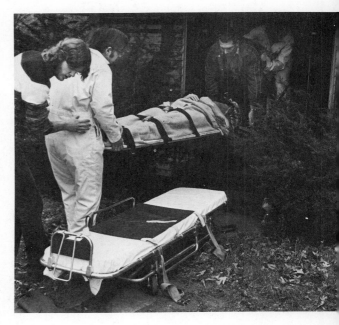

Figure 9.9. Since most suicidal attempts are "gambles with death," expert rescue training, as seen here, can save the majority of potential victims. (Photo: Alan Carey/Kingston Freeman)

bar after a lonely night and then has a fatal car crash a suicide? Are the suicide counts in religiously observant areas and nations accurate? Or do officials in such places often tend to charitably call suicides natural or accidental deaths? For all these reasons, our predictive efforts are uncertain. All we do know is that a few predisposing factors are sometimes, but only sometimes, of value in warning of the possibility of suicide: a history of depression, drug dependency, paranoia, life crises.

SUICIDE TRIGGERS Suicidal persons often have a history of primary or secondary depression. In fact, some studies suggest that as many as one-fourth of depressed patients attempt suicide and that nearly all contemplate it. Further, people who have been seriously depressed and then seem suddenly recovered are often in a most vulnerable stage. Such seeming recoveries, particularly when they are without the help of professional care, are frequently

SUICIDE: FALLACY AND FACT

Fallacy	Fact
People who talk about suicide rarely actually do it.	Talking about suicide is an important warning sign. Most people who threaten suicide may not make successful attempts, but all should be considered serious risks and urged to seek professional help.
The industrialized nations have a much higher suicide rate than more tranquil rural societies in Africa and Asia.	Suicide statistics are *notoriously unreliable.* In many cases, the number of suicides reported depends more on the accuracy and dedication of those in charge of collecting such statistics than on the number of persons who actually kill themselves. The result is that the most literate and well-governed nations tend to have relatively high reported suicide rates. In actuality, the frequency of suicide in most large countries of the world probably differs very little.
Doctors have the highest suicide rate.	Suicide statistics comparing different professions and socioeconomic classes often depend on the thoroughness of the investigation of the death or the literacy of the victim. The death of a professional is more likely to be carefully examined, and such people also more frequently leave a note. A construction worker who deliberately falls from a scaffold is likely to be listed an accident. Overall there are differences in the incidence of suicide in various vocational groups. But the inequalities are not great and are frequently inconsistent, so that drawing any substantial conclusions from them would probably be erroneous.
Suicidal people clearly want to die, so it is no use stopping them.	Only a few people who attempt suicide are unequivocally determined to die. Most are "gambling with death," testing whether they have taken enough medication or anticipating that someone will intervene and pull them from the ledge. For most people, suicidal attempts are cries for help rather than outright efforts at self-destruction.
Once a person has attempted suicide, he or she is suicidal forever.	Most people who are suicidal may make more than one attempt, but usually only for limited periods in their lives. The suicidal person whose life circumstances change, who is given worthwhile therapeutic help, or who has a "hopeless" outlook favorably altered can recover fully from suicidal impulses.
Everyone who tries suicide is mentally ill.	Depression, schizophrenia, and other mental illnesses occur with a fair degree of frequency among suicide victims. But many others, probably the majority, are relatively normal people without marked psychopathology. Their only distinguishing characteristic is, perhaps, that they feel life especially futile, empty, and hopeless.

(Brooke, 1974; Kraft and Babigian, 1976; Roberts, 1975; Schneidman, 1976)

the result of people being relieved because they have secretly reached a "solution." They are content and no longer feel despondent since they have decided to kill themselves:

R. T. W., a clergyman aged 51, was in a serious automobile accident that resulted in the death of his wife. For several weeks following the accident he was hospitalized for his injuries. He was also depressed and talked about "joining" his deceased spouse. The depression and feelings of hopelessness persisted after his physical recovery, so the clergyman's married daughter invited him to stay with her family. After two months in this setting, R. T. W. seemed to get better and reassured his daughter that he was "over it." He moved back into his own house and two days later hanged himself.

In addition to depression, other mental health problems may lead to suicide. Patients who have become dependent on alcohol or drugs have an elevated risk, particularly during periods of voluntary or forced abstinence. Compulsory withdrawal, for instance, accounts for many jail suicides. Persons who are frightened by their own homosexual impulses, who experience a so-called homosexual panic (Chapter 12), are sometimes catapulted into self-destructive behavior (Woodruff, Clayton, and Guze, 1972). Many schizophrenic patients, particularly paranoid persons, may be driven to end their lives by delusional or hallucinatory experiences. One study of 250 patients with mood disorders, 170 schizophrenics, and 109 controls, followed for nearly forty years, showed suicide rates of 14 percent for the affective psychoses and 4 percent for schizophrenia. None of the control group attempted suicide (Winokur and Tsuang, 1975).

Another finding is that a few suicidal people seem to come from situations in which they have closely experienced death. The most obvious manifestation of this is a history of previous suicidal efforts. Though past attempts may have been half-hearted and more dramatic than lethal, such a background is a very serious indication of possible future effort. Other suicidal persons do not have a personal history of attempts, but death has been common in their immediate families. Lester and Beck (1976), for instance, found that in their sample of attempted suicides, many had lost one or both parents during childhood. Such people, and those who have lost spouses, siblings, or close friends, sometimes seem preoccupied with dying and perhaps are more vulnerable.

Environmental and personal circumstances may also help in predicting suicide. The same crises that initiate depressions (marital breakup, ill health, and so on) can also trigger suicide. In addition, aging and living alone, particularly for middle-aged men, are situations frequently correlated with self-destructive attempts.

COMMUNICATION The majority of suicidal persons communicate their attitude. They let others know they are tired of living and are contemplating death. Many do so directly and bluntly; others hint or joke about their intention. Rosenbaum and Beebe (1975) believe that intention can be read by three kinds of moods evident in a psychiatric interview. First, many patients show hopeless resignation. Life is no use, all is over, so it is best just to reconcile oneself to the end. Second, some patients evidence a hollow euphoria following depression. Like most suicidal persons, they have exhausted themselves trying to decide whether or not to go ahead with a suicidal plan. Now they have finally concluded they need to end it all and are relieved and "happy" about their decision. A third clinical warning sign is psychomotor retardation. Clients take a very long time to answer questions, and their movements are slow and labored. They are communicating that life is an impossibly difficult effort.

Many suicidal people often communicate their intentions verbally; they talk about what they plan to do. Hudgens et al. (1972) investigated 87 suicidal psychiatric patients for more than a decade to ascertain specifically how they made their plans known. They found that

Figure 9.10. Most suicidal people talk about their plans, warn of their intent, or threaten self-destruction. A middle-aged and depressed businessman who commuted to a nearby city every day continually warned his wife, "One of these days I'm taking a one-way trip." A month after his threats began he committed suicide at work. (Photo, Scribe)

at least two-thirds clearly indicated their objective in one or more of six ways:

1. Actual previous attempts
2. Statements that they wanted to die
3. Statements that they would be better off dead
4. Assertions that their family would be better off if they were dead
5. Avowals that they intended to kill themselves
6. References to methods of self-destruction

Note, however, that about a third of the potential suicides kept their plans to themselves and could not easily be spotted as dangerous. The prediction of suicide is still an uncertain clinical art.

Causes

Suicide seems almost to defy explanation, since it appears absolutely contrary to every deep-rooted human urge to endure, to live on. We will present several social and psychological insights, but we recognize that poetic and philosophical explanations may even have greater validity. We will also limit ourselves to suicide that is the outcome of adjustive crises rather than an ideological act. Since the beginning of recorded history, men and women, rightly or wrongly convinced of the value of their goals, have sacrificed their lives to further a cause. Here we will offer some explanations of suicide that are motivated by more personal fears, stresses, and challenges.

BIOCHEMICAL EXPLANATIONS Since suicide is often linked with depression, it could be that the same biochemistry which accounts for the dysphoric mood might also explain suicide. But studies of suicidal persons reveal that many are not clinically depressed, nor do they evidence any catecholamine alterations. Further, despite some dramatic instances to the contrary, suicide does not "run in families." Only a few studies have shown individual chemical aberrations. Murphy (1972), for example, reported a good correlation between suicides and elevated urinary 17-hydroxycorticoid levels. But corroborative evidence for this and other chemical hypotheses has not come along, making it doubtful that biological factors play a role in self-destruction.

PSYCHODYNAMIC EXPLANATIONS Freud believed that suicide, like depression, was the outcome of guilt and aggressive feelings turned in upon the self. One psychoanalytic version suggests that those who kill themselves actually commit murder. They have "incorporated" the ego or identity of another (their spouse or parent) and by killing themselves are disposing of the person against whom their rage is focused. Another version argued by later psychoanalysts was that suicide represented the triumph of the death wish (Thanatos) over the opposing life force (Eros). For normal people, the two supposed inborn drives are in rough balance, with Eros usually having the edge. But when significant props supporting the life force are eroded (ill health, loss of a loved one) Eros is weakened, allowing Thanatos to triumph (Menninger, 1938).

Other psychodynamic writers, taking a cue from the psychoanalytic position, have also emphasized feelings behind suicide similar to aggression. The self-destructive man or woman is seen as a person who is expressing intense hatred. They are unleashing their deepest motives for revenge and control. Such persons destroy themselves, but with their act they want to center their hostility on another, hurting and manipulating that person for the rest of his or her life (Alvarez, 1972). These feelings were very evident in part of a note left by a young man who committed suicide:

. . . I would have murdered you for what you have done to me. But that would have been too easy for you. . . . Now live with this, what you have made me do. Live with this guilt [my suicide] gnawing everlasting at your brain and your vitals. . . . You will never have a night without thinking of me in this horror for what you, you and only you have made me do!

Aaron Beck (1977) and several of his co-workers consider *hopelessness* the catalytic agent behind most suicides. Using psychometric tests such as the Beck Depression Inventory (BDI), the Generalized Expectancy Scale, (GES) and the Suicidal Intent Scale, Beck probed suicidal motives. Surprisingly, he reports that high scores on hopelessness, as measured by the GES, rather than elevated depression scores (BDI), are primarily correlated with suicidal intent. Beck grants that the suicidal person is depressed, but more important is the fact that his expectations are consistently negative. He systematically misconstrues experiences and anticipates only the bleakest, most pessimistic outcome. It is the attitude of hopelessness more than depression that ultimately impels the attempt to end life.

Shneidman (1976) sees suicide as a plea for help. The suicidal person has come to the end of his or her resources and needs the support of others. This viewpoint seems supported by the fact that the vast majority of those who attempt suicide do not succeed. Their effort is perhaps more of a demonstration of their desperate need for assistance than it is an outright act of self-destruction.

Undoubtedly, drives such as aggression or desperation do play a role in suicidal behavior. Judged both from the notes victims leave behind and interviews with unsuccessful persons, hostility, revenge, hopelessness, and many other such feelings trigger suicidal attempts. And although these self-reports cannot always be relied upon, they may still give us a rough idea of the kinds of attitudes that seem to activate suicidal intention.

Bancroft et al. (1976) interviewed 89 women and 39 men immediately after their recovery from an overdose of medication. To begin with, less than half stated that they clearly wanted to die. Most were apparently toying with the idea of suicide and leaving the final decision to chance or fate. In terms of their motives for taking the overdose, 33 percent said they were seeking help, 42 percent said they were escaping from a hopeless situation, 52 percent stated they were seeking relief from a terrible state of mind, from depression, and 19 percent were trying to get at or manipulate someone. It is important to notice that many patients had several reasons for suicide and thus the statistics add to more than 100 percent. It is also revealing that no single motive accounted for everyone's behavior. Suicide may be the outcome of any number of profound human needs.

CULTURAL AND SOCIAL EXPLANATIONS There appear to be sizable differences in suicide rates among countries. Nations such as Mexico (Figure 9.11) have a frequency of 2 per 100,000, whereas the United States has five times and Austria over twelve times that number. It is tempting to suggest that the varied life styles of these nations account for these different rates. Cultural factors such as religion, the availability of weapons, and attitudes about violence and aggression may play a role. But we need to be very careful before deducing possible explanations.

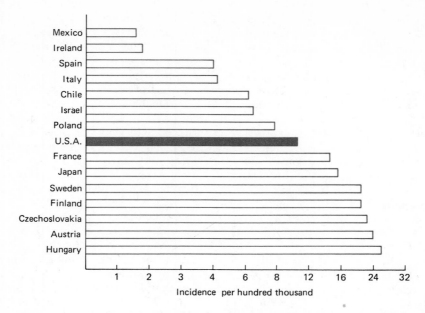

Figure 9.11. Suicide rates in different nations. These differences cannot be attributed to cultural factors alone. Many nations, particularly those less technologically advanced, find it difficult to gather accurate statistics. Another factor partly accounting for discrepancies is the unequal proportion of older people in each country. It is likely that the true incidence of suicide is not as different from one country to the next as it appears. (Alvarez, 1972; Brooke, 1974; Roberts, 1975; Shneidman, 1975; WHO, 1974, 1978).

We have already noted that suicide statistics are often inaccurate, so that generalizations based on such data can be very fallible. Further, it is important to consider the demographic characteristics of each society. West Berlin, for example, has close to the highest suicide frequency in the world. Is this because the citizens of this long-divided former capital city are a special focus of political rivalries? Before we become too involved with the ideological tensions supposedly responsible for Berlin's high suicide rate, we should also be aware that this city has an extremely large number of older citizens. Since suicide increases markedly with age, it is to be expected that any city or nation with a disproportion of older people will have a similarly elevated suicide rate. When comparing suicide rates for different nations, one must be certain to take all possible relevant factors, such as age and economic conditions, into account.

For a long time it was popular to relate suicide to homicide. Following the psychoanalytic precept that suicide is aggressive behavior, it was theorized that homicide and suicide would be inversely related. When aggression could be released against others, there would be little need for suicide. But when it is restrained, when society strongly prohibits extrapunitive behavior, then aggression is allegedly turned inward and results in suicide. Some evidence for this thesis was produced: Japan, for example, has a relatively high suicide rate and a low frequency of homicide. In contrast, Mexico with supposedly very little suicide, has a fairly high incidence of homicide. But careful evaluations of this theory have not confirmed the initial suspicion. Although

Increasingly the news media report men and women incurably and painfully ill who wish to end their own lives or succeed in doing so. On occasion too, eminent and successful people declare that when life has become meaningless or unbearable, they will not hesitate to speed their own death. Thomas Szasz (1974), the iconoclastic psychiatrist, some of whose views were discussed earlier in the chapters on schizophrenia, has written:

Suicide is a fundamental human right. This does not mean that it is morally desirable. It only means that society does not have the moral right to interfere, by force, with a person's decision to commit this act. (p. 75)

Szasz calls suicide "death control" and emphasizes that this act simply enables a person to determine when and how he or she will die rather than leaving it to chance. But at the same time that the "right" to suicide is being affirmed, self-destruction is still illegal and opposed by nearly all religious faiths. The large majority of physicians and all health practitioners also feel bound by the ethical commitments of their profession to make every effort to preserve and maintain life. Many point out that since suicide is nearly always a "gamble" with death, most rescued victims are glad to be alive.

At the present moment several states, the first of which was California in 1977, have adopted legislation permitting dying patients to request their doctors *not* to use extraordinary means to keep them alive. But no state or nation permits suicide. Should suicide continue to be prohibited, or should it be, as Szasz argues, respected as a fundamental human right?

aggressive motives doubtlessly play a role in homicide, and to an extent in suicide, both forms of destruction do not seem related in an inverse or any other way (Alvarez, 1972; Roberts, 1975).

For Emil Durkheim, the nineteenth century French sociologist, suicide was not so much an individual act as it was a response to a disintegrating society (Aron, 1977). Durkheim coined the term **anomie,** to describe a society that is disintegrating because of economic crises, revolutionary unrest, value conflicts, or other massive discontent. This anomic, cultural instability was postulated by Durkheim to deprive individuals of meaningful social support and thereby weaken their ability and will to survive. Durkheim's ideas have endured for a long time, but are they accurate? Does social disorder and deterioration bring about an increase in suicide rates?

The popular notion is that during social, moral, or financial crises people are more likely to commit suicide. But the cartoon notion of stockbrokers jumping off Wall Street skyscrapers during the Great Depression of the 1930s is not very accurate. Social disgrace, failure, or rejection may lead to suicide, but economic or political upheavals and other forms of social instability do not appear to affect suicide rates in a consistent way (Roberts, 1975; Shneidman, 1976).

BEHAVIORAL EXPLANATIONS From the behaviorist perspective, suicide is the result of a cognitive shift in anticipated reinforcements. The person sees no further rewards in living and visualizes death as reinforcing. It will result in the attention, sympathy, revenge, and other reinforcements he or she wants. In a paradoxical way, the person is reinforced before the actual behavior is performed. This anticipated reinforcement could help explain the calm and satisfaction seen in many suicidal persons shortly before their attempt.

Viewing suicide as operant behavior, Bostock and Williams (1974) successfully "retrained" a young woman whose repeated attempts were reinforced by the reactions her efforts were generating in others. The behavior therapists began a program of desensitization with the patient so that previous fears and tensions would become defused. More important, they strictly controlled the patient's environment so that she was reinforced not for threatened or potential self-destructive behavior but only for adaptive responses. In the hospital, for example, she was rewarded for helping others but not for being morose or isolating herself.

Treatment and prevention

TREATMENT   The treatment of suicide has to be directed both at the immediate crisis and at the long-range problems. The immediate situation is often handled best by establishing a *lifeline* and by an *ecological group* approach (Rosenbaum and Beebe, 1975). Creating a lifeline means finding the one or more person(s) interested in keeping the suicidal patient alive. This may be a relative, friend, or professional counselor but he, she, or they must be identified and fully available. The patient must know the lifeline is there, accessible and ready to help whenever needed.

The patient's ecological group (parents, spouse, friends, or children) must be informed and enlisted to participate in the client's rehabilitation. They have to learn to give support and reassurance, solve mutual problems, and be alert to suicide signals:

The patient, a 22-year-old divorced woman lived alone in an apartment several miles from the home of her parents. Following the daugh-

Figure 9.12. The suicidal patient needs a lifeline—a person who will be immediately available to give support and counsel. (Photo: Scribe)

ter's attempted suicide with an overdose of barbiturates, the parents were alerted by the attending social worker to participate in the therapy. As a result, father, mother, and daughter discussed and worked on their differences concerning independence, sexual standards, and mutual needs. Five weeks after the first suicide attempt, the visiting father noticed the patient taking a careful inventory of all her possessions. The patient's counselor was notified, and she was persuaded to come for an interview. This contact revealed the patient was again seriously contemplating suicide and was making careful preparations.

The ecological group does more than just talk with and watch the patient. They are also the people from whom the suicidal individual obtains new motivation to live. With the help of a therapist, the group helps the patient find alternatives to self-destruction. Patients who have attempted suicide need to learn that there are other ways to extricate themselves or attain some of their objectives.

Once the immediacy of the suicidal impulse is relieved, the counselor can begin to work out the underlying causes. Suicide, after all, is actually only a single symptom of an entire pathological complex. It is almost always rooted in depression, alcoholism, psychosis, or some other tangle of despair, hostility, and maladaptive emotions. Very often fairly extensive psychological and medical therapy is necessary to help the suicidal individual recover from the disturbed emotions or attitudes that propelled him or her toward self-destruction.

PREVENTION   In most large cities of the United States and around the world, suicide prevention centers (SPC) have sprung up to handle the hundreds of thousands of potential victims every year. Most SPCs have a hot-line telephone service so that clients can reach a trained worker any time of day or night. The immediate task for the SPC attendant who receives a phone call is to encourage the client to keep talking. The caller must be assisted to communicate and a confidential, trusting relationship established. Next, the likelihood or immediacy of the threat is evaluated. Many prevention clinics have a psychometric rating scale to evaluate the seriousness of self-destructive impulses. Such checklists contain the kinds of information we have mentioned as correlating with suicide. For example, if the person calling in revealed the following information about himself or herself, the potential would be considered extremely high:

Previous attempts
Currently depressed
Middle-aged male living alone
Wants to die and has contemplated methods

About half of the callers at most centers are the clients themselves; the other half are friends, relatives, clergy, or counselors. In good SPCs, once the call is received and the client evaluated, he or she is put in touch with competent professionals. On occasion, an SPC worker may be forced by a client's unwillingness to talk to anyone else to try to persuade the client to hesitate. In such instances it has often been found worthwhile to talk of *alternatives*. Getting the dangerously suicidal person to consider other possibilities may be enough to help prevent an immediate attempt and allow time for more professional assistance to be mobilized. Here is a transcript of part of a call to a center:

CLIENT: It's no use. Leave me alone.
I don't even know why I called. . . .
SPC: There are a lot of other things to do besides slashing your wrists. I mean you did say you gave thought to just dropping out, that is, running away, just assuming another identity.
CLIENT: But that's crazy. That's nothing. That's a dead end.
SPC: Well, maybe it is. But look, this is a time to think of all sorts of crazy things. I mean if you were able to do anything at all. What else could you possibly, conceivably think of? I mean anything. Anything at all.
CLIENT: I could put an ad in the paper and say I was a drunk and I was desperate and I wanted to marry an 18-year-old girl and start over again.
SPC: Well, don't you think you might get answers?
CLIENT: I might but they would be just as lonely and hopeless as me. Who else would want anyone like me?

Suicide prevention centers seem to work: Most people who call do not kill themselves and very many enter treatment programs that help improve their overall adjustment. But SPCs have also been criticized for being too passive and dealing only with the more verbal, less intent individuals. Studies have shown, for example, that nine out of ten actual suicides never contact an SPC and that the presence of such a facility has no effect on a community's suicide statistics. In fact, Lester (1972) argues that such centers may sometimes even have a negative effect. By their very existence, they could suggest the possibility of suicide to some vulnerable people. In answer to these challenges nearly every SPC can mobilize hundreds of testimonials from callers explaining how their own lives were saved by the timely presence of such facilities. More important, many SPCs are now making efforts to enlarge their role. They are trying to continue the communication established with callers and to reach out to the chronically ill, the aged, and the isolated, who may be especially prone to suicide (Roberts, 1975; Shneidman, 1976).

SUMMARY

Disorders of mood are characterized by depressive or manic symptoms or both. Manic symptoms include elation, euphoria, irritability, talkativeness, and hyperactivity. Depression is signaled by behaviors like feelings of hopelessness, dysphoria, slow movements and speech, and suicidal ideas. In both conditions, the person may be somewhat delusional or even hallucinated. Mania may range from delirious mania to hypomania. Depression may be further described as neurotic or psychotic, endogenous or exogenous, unipolar or bipolar, stuporous or agitated. Involutional melancholia is a form of depression originally described as limited to women but now applied to both sexes.

There are various causal explanations for affective disorders. The thesis of most psychodynamic clinicians centers about the notion that depression is anger turned inward, though there is only partial experimental support for this position. Newer dynamic views emphasize cognitive aspects and postulate that depressed patients have learned a negative view of the world or been taught to feel helpless. Mania is often believed to be a reverse form of depression resulting from essentially the same roots. Behaviorists see depression as a consequence of decreasing reinforcement for normal affect and increasing reward for abnormal emotion. Affective disorders could also be the result of modeling or be social strategems intended to manipulate others. The medical model sees affective disorders as having a large genetic component and explicable in terms of neurochemistry. What seems most likely is that aberrations in the neural transmitters may account for mood extremes. This hypothesis is supported by the fact that chemotherapeutic agents seem to help restore normal function. Social components may also help to account for mood disturbances. Environmental crises may trigger manic or depressive periods, and both conditions could be related to achievement needs and maternal separation.

Mania and depression can be treated with dynamic and behavioral therapies and usually respond very quickly to chemotherapy and electric shock. In fact, chemical agents have been found to work so well in treatment and prevention that psychotherapy is often used as a follow-up rather than a primary therapy.

The number of people actually recorded as suicides is low, but far more make active attempts every year. Because it is difficult to collect accurate statistics, and for other reasons as well, erroneous ideas about suicide abound. One of the leading false notions is that people who talk about suicide never attempt it.

Suicidal persons often have a history of depression or other mental disorder, although more than half of all suicides are functionally normal. Most who attempt suicide communicate their intention by attitude, conversation, or emotions. Those most likely to kill themselves are older, have a history of previous attempts, and say that they want to die.

Suicide has been explained dynamically as aggression turned inward, as the outcome of wishes of hostility and revenge or a feeling of hopelessness. Suicide also seems related to cultural norms and life styles, since despite some likely errors, cross-cultural rate comparisons reveal large discrepancies. Behaviorists have attempted to explain suicide in terms of modeling or operant conditioning. There is also a medical explanation based on biochemical factors.

The treatment of suicide must be a two-phase program. Something must be done to cope with the immediate crisis—the attempt—and then other strategies must be used to work on the underlying depression or other adjustment problems. Suicide prevention centers (SPCs) can also play a role in helping deter potential suicides.

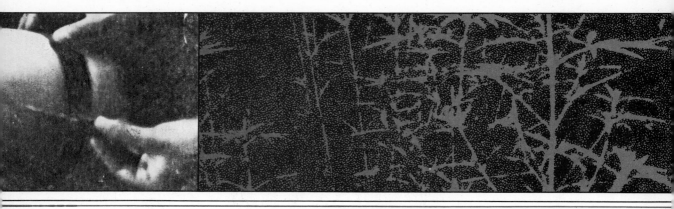

]]] DEVIANT AND ALTERNATIV

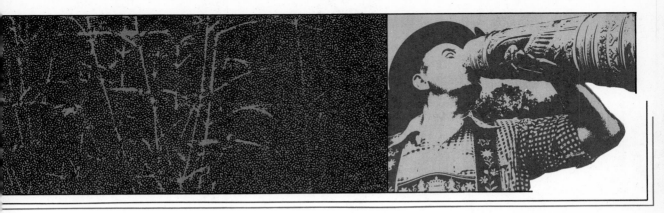

10 Drug Use Disorders

11 Deviant Behaviors: Personality Disorders, Crime, Gambling, Sexual Aberrations

BEHAVIORS

12 Sexual Alternatives and Dysfunctions

Drug Use Disorders

Until relatively recently, drug abuse, or use, was considered a moral or legal problem. The person who drank too much or enjoyed a prohibited chemical was held to be lacking in character or respect for the law. In the last several decades, however, drug use has increasingly been viewed as a mental health issue. Those who are unable to control their drug use are thought of not as morally weak, but as psychologically ill.

Because drug use has long been conceived as a matter for legislation, varying standards, incomplete scientific information, and personal customs have brought about a mass of conflicting legal and social practices. Heroin, for example, is now illegal. But at the beginning of this century, its parent, opium, was freely available in patent medicines sold in every drugstore. Alcohol, though it is fairly toxic and addictive, has taken the opposite route. Once illegal, it is now freely available

throughout the United States and most of the world. To point up the paradoxical nature of drug regulations even further, the possession of small amounts of a relatively harmless chemical like marijuana is a felony in some parts of the United States; in others, it has been "decriminalized." In our discussion we will recognize the inconsistent attitudes that frequently characterize social policies concerning drug use. But our main focus will be on the causes and treatment of drug use disorders. To achieve this end, our first task is to agree on several definitions.

A large variety of terms has been proposed to distinguish various degrees of usage and to separate legal from illegal drug consumption. In order to avoid a complex terminology, we will confine ourselves to three phrases to describe the consumption of what may loosely be considered **psychoactive** or **mind-altering chemicals.** These are substances obtained by medical prescription, legally purchased, or illegally procured. They include alcohol, barbiturates, marijuana, amphetamines, and other substances that help the user feel relaxed, stimulated, aware, or pleasureable or otherwise seem to change or enlarge mood or perception.

Recreational drug use is the occasional and limited intake of a substance. The person who drinks a glass or two of wine with some meals or on weekends smokes some marijuana falls into this classification. **Drug abuse** indicates excessive consumption of a drug. The individual who frequently drinks "too much" or uses barbiturates almost every night is a drug abuser. **Drug dependence** means addiction; the user is physically and/or psychologically "hooked." He or she actively seeks and needs the drug.

Drugs like heroin create physical dependence because they seem to alter the biochemical equilibrium of the body. When the drug is withdrawn, the body signals its physiological need by symptoms ranging from perspiration to convulsions. Drugs like cocaine may not stimulate a biological need, but they often create a psychological craving. The user seems to become emotionally dependent upon the drug and begins to use it habitually in much the same way as does a physically dependent individual. The distinction between physical and psychological dependence is questionable, since probably all drug use is partly motivated by both. Some chemicals may be more physically addictive and others less, but in clinical practice, addictions, from whatever source, are resistant to treatment. We will *not* attempt to separate the two but instead will point out the general dependency potential for each drug.

There is a fourth term we should know, tolerance and reverse tolerance. Many drugs eventually seem to "lose" their potency; larger and larger amounts are needed in order to feel their effects. This is called **tolerance. Reverse tolerance** occurs when a chemical seems to "sensitize" a person so that in subsequent administrations smaller amounts achieve the original effects.

These terms will be useful in recognizing where a particular person fits on the continuum of drug use, although the differentiation is not always objectively clear. A smoker who consumes a pack of cigarettes daily may consider himself or herself a recreational user. But since from the point of view of physical health a pack a day is excessive, such a smoker could be called a drug abuser. Judged by even stricter criteria, it might be argued that this same smoker is dependent because the daily intake of nicotine has characteristics that suggest addiction. In other words, the dividing lines between recreational use, abuse, and dependency are often thin and uncertain. Further, many drug users tend to fluctuate, moving back and forth between periods of recreational use, abuse, and even dependency.

We will also have to look at the several drug use patterns separately. Heroin addiction, cocaine abuse, and alcoholism are all drug use disorders, but the life circumstances and personality of consumers of each are likely to be quite different. Heroin addicts frequently come from socioeconomically depressed backgrounds, and drug dependency dominates their lives. Alcoholics, in contrast, come from all social strata and often deny they are drug-dependent. Those who favor cocaine and some other supposedly less addictive substances are frequently educated and affluent and see themselves as trendsetters. In other words, the psychiatric classification **drug use disorder** is an umbrella term for a group of people whose character and background are distinctly varied. For this reason, we will describe the major drugs separately and point out the problems and issues typical for each one.

ALCOHOL

Human beings have been familiar with alcohol for at least several hundred thousand years. Archeological evidence suggests that even Stone Age cultures understood how to make alcohol from fruit juices, grains, or honey. In many instances wine and spirits were considered medicinal or part of religious ceremony. But even among many early peoples, such as the Sumerian, Hebrew, Greek, and Roman civ-

Figure 10.1. A beer festival. The use of alcohol is thousands of years old and rooted in cultural and religious traditions. (Photo: R. R. Haines/Kingston Freeman)

ilizations, alcoholic beverages were also secularized—that is, used for entertainment and recreational purposes. Just as alcohol has been known since the most ancient of times, so has drunkenness. The Old Testament repeatedly warns against inebriation and counsels moderation. Attempts were apparently made in ancient Egypt to forbid alcohol or at least restrict its use to the most "trusted" classes. Muslim peoples, following the injunctions set forth in the Koran, and Asian cultures guided by Buddha eventually forbade alcohol. In the Western world the Protestant Reformation brought Christian denominations also opposed to intoxicants. In the United States, the reaction against alcohol was climaxed by Prohibition, the nationwide ban imposed by the Eighteenth Amendment to the Constitution in 1920.

Prohibition was the result of several decades of vigorous campaigning led by women's and church groups such as the Anti-Saloon League and the Woman's Christian Temperance Union. But Prohibition lasted only thirteen years; it was repealed by the Twenty-first Amendment in 1933. Although many issues motivated repeal, perhaps the most powerful argument was that Prohibition did not work. With or without the law, alcoholism remained a serious problem. Even worse, a massive criminal apparatus sprang up to supply alcohol to millions of citizens who indicated they would rather be lawbreakers than do without whisky and beer. Thousands of police officers, judges, and district attorneys were bribed to "look away" so that illegal bars could operate in almost every town and village of the United States. From the point of view of law enforcement officials, the clergy, social scientists, and ordinary citizens, legal prohibition as a means of solving a social-psychological problem simply did not work.

Today alcohol abuse and dependency is by far the most serious drug problem in the United States and probably worldwide. The amount of personal and social damage done through alcohol excess is greater by a considerable margin than the ill effects of *all other drugs combined* (Chafetz, 1976; Gibbins et al., 1976; Hollis and Slater, 1974):

1. Well over 100 million Americans drink alcohol; of these, a minimum of 5 million to

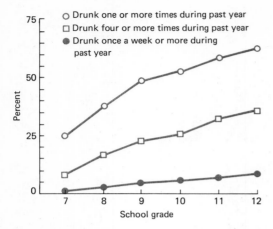

Figure 10.2. Percentage of American teenage drinkers who report getting drunk or very high. (Courtesy: National Institute on Alcohol Abuse and Alcoholism, 1974)

as many as 15 million are addicted. In children aged 12 to 17, 5 percent are estimated to get "drunk" at least once a week.

2. About half the people killed annually in automobile accidents (30,000) are the casualties of intoxicated drivers. Another 20,000 alcoholics die annually from liver and other alcohol-induced ailments. Alcoholism also accounts for half of all first mental hospital admissions.

3. In several nationwide polls conducted throughout the decade, the Gallup organization has found one in six adults in the United States stating that alcohol had been a serious "cause of trouble" in the family.

4. In over half of all murders (about 12,000 persons annually) the killer and/or victim have been drinking substantially. Alcohol also plays a prominent role in at least one-third of all cases of rape and in nearly half of all assaults, so that the total victim count is in the hundreds of thousands.

5. Although exact figures are difficult to compile, excessive drinking is a frequent concomitant of child abuse, a major cause of family disruption and divorce, and a leading factor in unemployment. The National Institute on Alcohol Abuse and Alcoholism (part of the U.S. Department of Health, Education and Welfare) estimates the economic cost of misuse of alcohol at $25 billion a year.

We do not cite these findings to sound horrified warnings of the terrors of demon alcohol or to advocate a return to Prohibition. The consumption of wine, beer and other beverages is a practice founded in religious, dietary, recreational, and other cultural practices. Controlled drinking is widely accepted, considered pleasureable, and encouraged as a means of relaxation and establishing friendship. There is also some evidence that modest adult drinking may contribute to general health and longevity. But we have mentioned all the negative effects of alcohol because its potential for abuse is often overlooked. Heroin, amphetamines, and even marijuana command the attention of the news media and their dangers are vividly portrayed. In reality, though it is a common and accepted drug, alcohol is a highly toxic and addictive substance and the cause of one of the leading mental health problems.

The effects of alcohol

The effects of consuming alcohol are very rapid; within minutes after it enters the body, the bloodstream has carried the chemical to the brain. On the other hand, since the alcohol has to enter the bloodstream through the walls of the stomach and small intestine, a full meal immediately before drinking, several glasses of milk, or the like moderate the absorption rate and the intoxicating effects.

The actual psychological results of alcohol are somewhat varied and contradictory. Medically, alcohol is a **sedative,** an anesthetic that suppresses neurological function. It decreases steadiness, reaction time, and motor and perceptual abilities in general. But since alcohol impairs the cortex and other brain areas, it can "feel" like a stimulant. For example, it hinders brain areas that make us aware of fatigue or urge caution, and so drinking makes us feel energetic, emotionally free, and uninhibited, at least for a while.

The discrepancy between actual ability and

personal conviction induced by alcohol can be most clearly seen in the sexual area. Because of the disinhibiting results of drinking, men and women may believe themselves erotically stimulated and aroused; but when actual performance is required both may find their bodies distinctly unresponsive. In fact, many men have their first experience of impotence following attempted intercourse after considerable drinking (Chapter 12). A more dangerous contradiction occurs when the inebriated drinker is convinced he or she is fit to drive (Figure 10.3). Because critical areas of the brain have been sedated, he or she feels sharp, alert, and competent. In fact, vision, coordination and motor skills may be so impaired that the person cannot even walk a straight line.

When enough alcohol is consumed, the sedative effects become more and more obvious. With about five to ten shots of whiskey or most

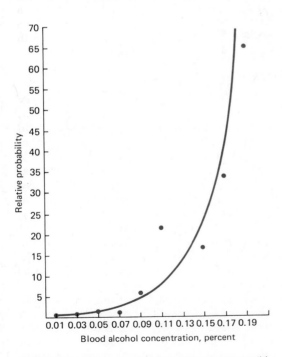

Figure 10.3. Relative probability of being responsible for a fatal crash and blood alcohol concentration. (Courtesy M. W. Perrine and National Institute on Alcohol Abuse and Alcoholism)

of a bottle of wine, nearly all drinkers are intoxicated. Their speech, judgment, and vision are conspicuously disturbed; they stagger and stumble and may lose consciousness. Passing out is actually protective, since drinking much beyond, say, a bottle of wine or ten mixed drinks could result in coma and even death (Figure 10.4).

The long-range effects of alcohol depend on the quantities consumed. Modest recreational use seems to have no ill effects even over the course of a lifetime. But prolonged and heavy use can be damaging. Some of the more prominent psychological and physical results of heavy consumption are shown in the box on Alcohol Pathology.

Alcoholism

There is no single agreed-upon definition of alcoholism. Medical descriptions such as the one suggested by the American College of Physicians tend to emphasize the physical and addictive aspects of heavy drinking. This definition sees alcoholism as a chronic disease characterized by physiological dependence and accompanied by damage to organs such as the liver and brain. Alcoholics Anonymous and various psychiatric and social groups have proposed broader definitions emphasizing psychological and social factors. Alcoholism is believed to be the inability to control drinking, to stop or moderate consumption despite family disruption or loss of employment. A third approach seeks to differentiate degrees and types of alcoholism. For example, the person intoxicated four times a year is labeled an episodic alcoholic; the one inebriated twelve times is called a habitual alcoholic.

JELLINEK'S DESCRIPTION There is also disagreement about the psychiatric meaning of excessive consumption. The traditional and older view is that alcohol misuse is a progressive mental illness. People who are alcoholic are sick, suffering from a disordered personality that prompts them to drink more and more. Jellinek (1960) gave the classical description of this view. He saw alcoholism as the result of a maladjusted or defective person-

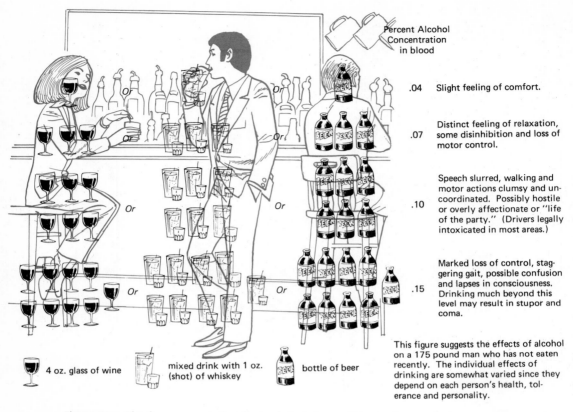

Percent Alcohol Concentration in blood

.04   Slight feeling of comfort.

.07   Distinct feeling of relaxation, some disinhibition and loss of motor control.

.10   Speech slurred, walking and motor actions clumsy and un-coordinated. Possibly hostile or overly affectionate or "life of the party." (Drivers legally intoxicated in most areas.)

.15   Marked loss of control, stag-gering gait, possible confusion and lapses in consciousness. Drinking much beyond this level may result in stupor and coma.

This figure suggests the effects of alcohol on a 175 pound man who has not eaten recently. The individual effects of drinking are somewhat varied since they depend on each person's health, tol-erance and personality.

4 oz. glass of wine   mixed drink with 1 oz. (shot) of whiskey   bottle of beer

Figure 10.4. This figure suggests the effects of alcohol on a 175-pound man who has not eaten recently. The individual effects of drinking are somewhat varied, since they depend on each person's health, tolerance, and personality.

ality: Potential alcoholics are people whose anxieties and tensions are greater than those of most others and who have not learned to handle their problems in an effective manner. When such individuals are introduced to social drinking, they quickly find alcohol an almost magical source of comfort. In this way, addiction begins. During this stage, the *prealcoholic level,* the drinker, prompted by the relief experienced, moves slowly (over the course of a year or two) to almost daily use of alcohol in order to feel good and competent. The next phase is the *prodromal* level. Consumption is now marked by such serious signs as secret drinking, guilt feelings, and occasional blackouts.

After several years, the *crucial phase* begins. The person has now almost completely lost control of the addiction. There are alcoholic binges lasting weeks or months interrupted by guilt-inspired periods of abstention. Daily drinking, often beginning in the mornings, is now a well-established pattern; family breakups and loss of employment threaten or have become actualities. The last or *chronic* level is indicated when alcohol totally dominates the person's life. Now there is a reverse tolerance, so that relatively small amounts of alcohol are sufficient to produce inebriation and even stupor. At this stage too, many of the serious consequences, such as the DTs and

ALCOHOL PATHOLOGY

Blackouts: Short periods of amnesia usually limited to the time during which the person has been drinking. The result is that the "morning after," the drinker does not recall what he or she did or whom they were with the evening before. Blackouts are common among heavy drinkers, and are regarded as indication of possible addiction. Blackouts are frequently accompanied by feelings of guilt, the drinker fearing he or she acted injudiciously while inebriated.

Drug synergism: Though not strictly a long-range effect of drinking, drug synergism is a hazard often encountered by many alcohol abusers. Many drugs which at moderate doses might not in themselves be injurious become dangerous when combined with alcohol. Central nervous system depressants like sleeping pills and some allergy medications and most tranquilizers have their effects *multiplied* when combined with alcohol. The use of several drugs, particularly barbiturates, along with alcohol sometimes results in stupor, coma, and death.

Cirrhosis of the liver: This condition is a consequence of the toxic effects of alcohol itself as well as the serious malnutrition common in very many heavy drinkers. The symptoms include loss of appetite, weakness, abdominal pain, and jaundice. In advanced cases less than 30 percent of patients live for more than a year.

Delirium tremens (DTs): Withdrawal symptoms usually beginning a few days after drinking stops. The abstinent drinker begins to shake and tremble, perspire profusely, and soon becomes restless and irritable. Confusion and memory losses are common, but most terrifying are the sudden vivid and frightening visual hallucinations alcoholics call "snakes." Rats, snakes, and the like are seen crawling and attacking, or bloody hands and knives threatening and stabbing. High fevers and convulsions (rum fits) may also occur. After several days the attack subsides, inducing many badly frightened alcoholics to refrain from drinking at least temporarily.

Alcohol paranoia: Chronic alcoholics frequently become quite paranoid, with a favorite delusion being that their spouse is unfaithful. The extreme jealousy engendered by such false beliefs often leads to considerable violence directed against the suspected partner or against the self. Homicide and/or suicide could even be the result.

Korsakoff's psychosis: This is the result of usually at least ten to twenty years of very heavy drinking and nutritional deficiency. The symptoms are similar to other organic brain syndromes that stem from cortical damage. They include memory loss, disorientation, and many sensory-motor impairments. A particular distinguishing feature of this psychosis is the tendency for alcoholics to make up imaginary experiences to fill in blanks in their defective memory. This fabricated recollection is called confabulation. Wernicke's disease, which manifests itself primarily in neurological deficits, often accompanies Korsakoff's psychosis.

Korsakoff's psychosis, become clearly manifest.

CURRENT VIEWS Current observation has cast doubt on the view that alcoholics uniformly fit a particular personality pattern or even follow a distinctive addiction sequence. The traits that lead to alcohol abuse and addiction are quite variable, and the lines separating the recreational drinker from those who abuse alcohol or become dependent on it are shifting and indefinite. Some of the more important research findings that have emerged include the following (Chafetz, 1976; Pattison, 1977; Seixas, 1977):

1. Ten to 15 million individuals drink heavily enough to possibly be called alcoholic, but most "stabilize" their addiction. They drink substantially almost every day, but by largely limiting periods of inebriation to weekends or evenings manage to keep families and jobs relatively intact.

2. About a third of all alcoholics are able to stop entirely or return to being occasional recreational drinkers without professional help. Consequently, it cannot be said that alcoholism is necessarily progressive or irreversible.

3. The differences between drinkers classified as recreational, abusive, and addicted are often vague and may depend as much on social circumstances as on the amount consumed. For example, a prosperous steelworker and an unemployed laborer may both be heavy consumers. The former may be considered a "two-fisted" drinker; the latter is likely to be called an alcoholic.

4. Many of the damaging consequences associated with consumption, such as automobile accidents, criminal violence, and assaults, may as often be the result of recreational drinking as of alcohol abuse or dependence.

5. Multiple drug use is increasingly common, so that even relatively light drinking coupled with other drugs may signal abuse or addiction. Alcohol dependency is often coupled with other psychiatric problems, particularly depression, so that treatment needs to be directed at far more than just excessive drinking.

6. Some recreational alcohol users are "spree" drinkers; although their consumption is controlled most of the time, occasionally they appear to have all the behavioral signs and symptoms of alcoholism.

7. Alcoholism often (but not always) develops slowly, beginning in late adolescence and clearly manifesting itself during early middle age. But though alcoholism may worsen over the years, the Skid Row alcoholic, long used to depict the supposed evil end results of drinking, is actually rare. Not more than about 1 percent of all heavy drinkers, about 100,000 individuals, drift down the social scale to become derelicts. In addition, many of these Skid Row alcoholics are not just addicted but are schizophrenic or otherwise psychotic.

8. Men were once believed to outnumber women alcoholics by as much as five to one. Recent statistics show that while women addicts are still more hidden, the number of men and women alcoholics is not vastly different.

So although there is no doubt that alcohol is a potent and addictive drug, alcoholics are not stamped out of the same mold and the dependency is not necessarily progressive. In our estimate, therefore, the usual figure of up to 20 million American alcoholics is much too large. It includes far too many people who are essentially recreational users with only infrequent forays into excessive consumption. It also includes many admittedly consistent and heavy drinkers who nevertheless manage to control their lives so that personal, social, or occupational damage is minimal.

If we limit our definition of alcoholism to people who habitually and uncontrollably drink excessively to the point where they seriously damage their own and other persons' lives, then it is likely that only about 5 percent of all adolescent and adult drinkers could be called alcoholic. But even this strict and demanding definition still leaves us with a large alcoholic population in the United States, making this addiction account for a great proportion of all those who could be considered mentally ill (Figure 10.5).

The causes of alcoholism

MEDICAL EXPLANATIONS Proponents of the medical view have suggested that alcoholism might be the result of biological error. One version of this hypothesis holds that some people metabolically need alcohol in order to compensate for their own body's inability to manufacture or absorb certain nutritive substances. In another version, alcoholism is explained as the result of the brain falsely signaling that alcohol is chemically required. Such hypotheses have been based on laboratory research primarily with animals; the evidence for a biochemical explanation of alcoholism in human beings is weak (Israel et al., 1971; Pattison et al., 1977).

More convincing data has bolstered the genetic explanation. It has long been observed

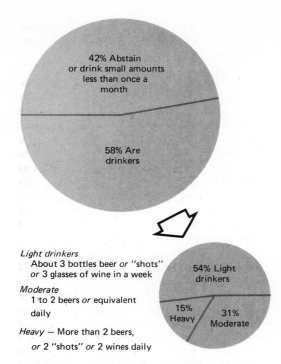

Figure 10.5. Adult drinking patterns in the United States. (Harris, 1974)

Light drinkers
About 3 bottles beer or "shots" or 3 glasses of wine in a week

Moderate
1 to 2 beers or equivalent daily

Heavy — More than 2 beers, or 2 "shots" or 2 wines daily

that alcoholics frequently come from families in which at least one parent is also a heavy drinker. This could also, of course, be the result of environmental influences. But Goodwin (1976), in a number of different studies, compared children taken away from alcoholic parents during their infant months to those reared in alcoholic homes. In one investigation Goodwin was able to contrast boys placed in normal adopted homes with brothers who remained with their alcoholic families. The results strongly supported the genetic hypothesis, since about one in four of the men from alcoholic parents, whether or not living at home, became alcoholic themselves.

Several studies with many thousands of subjects in the Scandinavian countries, which have the advantage of a relatively uniform population and excellent statistical records, have revealed similar results. Whenever there is an alcoholic father, the chances are about

25 percent that a male child will also be alcoholic. Among twins, the concordance for alcoholism may be over 50 percent higher for identicals than for fraternals. In all, although these data are not conclusive, they make a persuasive case for the likelihood of at least some genetic components contributing to alcoholism (McClearn and DeFries, 1973).

PSYCHODYNAMIC EXPLANATIONS Since Freud, psychodynamic writers have attempted to account for alcoholism in terms of a number of largely unconscious motives. The traditional psychoanalytic position is that excessive drinking traces back to the oral period in childhood. The alcoholic is an orally dependent person who seeks to gratify a wish for maternal love and support by drinking. Through alcohol, he or she replicates that fantasized feeling of total warmth, care, and satisfaction denied at the mother's breast. One early analyst, Alfred Adler (1941), objected to this hypothesis and proposed an almost opposite view. He stated that alcohol addiction was the result of excessive coddling and overindulgence which led to an inability to face life and cope with challenge. Such children reach adulthood knowing only how to escape responsibility and soon become alcoholics in order to avoid having to face reality on their own.

Among adolescents and young adults, alcohol abuse and other drug involvement is sometimes traced to motives like rebellion and conformity. Adolescents wanting to demonstrate their independence from and disregard of parental and societal restrictions drink or use other drugs to emphasize their autonomy. Related to this is peer pressure. Many younger drug consumers may be initiated into the drug world or become confirmed users because their friends are involved and they want the acceptance of people their own age. In addition to both these motives, like adults, younger people may drift into alcoholism or drug abuse because it seems to offer a refuge—an escape from depression, failure, conflict, or any number of the challenging problems of living (Abel, 1976; Grinspoon and Hedblom, 1975; Hardy and Cull, 1975; National Institute of Alcohol Abuse and Alcoholism, 1978).

Other psychodynamic writers have seen alcoholism (and other drug addictions) as hidden suicidal behavior. Menninger (1965), for instance, thought that powerful feelings of rage and aggression, turned partly toward one's parent and partly toward the self, often culminated in alcoholism. The excessive drinking became a way both of punishing the parents

Figure 10.6. There are at least 5 million alcoholics and many millions more who seriously abuse the drug. Though excessive alcohol consumption is personally and socially damaging, very few alcoholics become skid row derelicts. In fact, many derelicts have other psychiatric problems, which may have helped cause their decline. (Photo: Scribe)

and of destroying oneself. One indication of the validity of this view for Menninger is the frequency with which alcohol produces barroom brawls and is also a prominent correlate of homicide and suicide. In an eight-year study of homicide in Memphis, Tennessee, Hollis and Slater (1974), for example, found that 74 percent of the victims and 86 percent of the offenders had been drinking. Still other psychodynamic authorities contend that alcohol is used in an attempt to relieve fear and guilt, particularly sexual anxiety. It is pointed out that in psychotherapy alcoholics often reveal themselves to be frightened and ashamed of their own libidinal impulses, which may be quite ordinary or homosexual, promiscuous, or otherwise unconventional.

For many different psychodynamic orientations, alcoholism is seen not as a disease but as a *symptom.* Depression, anxiety, mania, and other maladaptive emotions and behaviors often prompt heavy drinking. In fact, the maladjusted person may be using alcohol in a sort of primitive way—almost like a psychiatrist prescribes drugs. In other words, alcohol may be employed to alleviate some personal distress. But since it is powerfully addictive, it may ultimately become more of a problem than the underlying mental health concerns that prompted its use.

Some psychodynamic writers have attempted to identify an **alcoholic personality.** Certain traits have been pinpointed as likely to lead to excessive drinking: feelings of inadequacy, hypersensitivity, hostility, and impulsivity (Garitano, 1974). In one of the best studies advocating this view, Jones (1968) followed several hundred children for a period of over thirty years. Those men in their forties who were alcoholic were, according to Jones, almost certainly extroverted, concerned about masculinity, and rebellious as young children. Based on such evidence and on clinical observation, it appears reasonable to believe that certain personality types are more likely than others to become alcohol-addicted. But the findings of a great many studies have not been very consistent.

Schuckit (1975) studied young Navy men

and found that although many drank heavily, most did not become addicted. More important, those who became alcoholic could not be predicted, since their clinical histories and personal backgrounds were quite different. Another study by Zeichner et al. (1977) comparing the personal and social behavior of addicts also concluded that it was difficult to discern any clear-cut character patterns. In addition, finding that addicted people have unique personality traits is not a valid indication that these distinctive traits produced the addiction; they could be the result of the addiction and the life style it imposes. Zimering and Calhoun (1976) concluded that perhaps a number of different personality predispositions could trigger addiction, but the traits alone are not sufficient. In their opinion, what is needed to produce alcholism is a combination of personal traits or vulnerabilities together with sufficient environmental stress.

There may or may not be a specific alcoholic personality, but perhaps there is a broader possibility—a set of traits and attitudes that incline an individual to some kind of drug abuse. Obviously more is needed for addiction than a set of personality inclinations; environmental stresses, customs, and opportunities play a role in recreational as well as addictive drug use. And anyone—old or young, male or female, from any socioeconomic or ethnic background—may be addicted. But many clinicians believe that a distinct type of individual is more likely to become addicted, that there is an **addictive personality.** These people have a low stress tolerance; they are unable to handle even the ordinary challenges of living and tend to evade responsibility. They also seem to have a low self-image. They may act self-important and confident but are generally internally weak. Many also seem to have a tendency toward depression and are believed to be somewhat psychopathic, sharing some of the impulsivity, tendency toward denial, rationalization, and impoverished interpersonal relationships often found in this personality disorder (see Chapter 11).

BEHAVIORAL EXPLANATIONS Behavioral and learning psychologists assert that despite decades of research, both psychodynamic and medical approaches have failed to identify any consistent traits or neurophysiological defects to account for alcoholism. From the behavioral perspective, the only characteristic alcoholic addicts share in common is that they drink excessively; they apparently have *learned* to drink far more than they should (Miller, 1976).

Consuming alcohol is almost immediately reinforcing because the alcohol quickly anesthetizes tension and fear and makes the drinker feel relaxed. Several animal studies have verified that when rats or primates are stressed by electric shocks or isolation, they rapidly develop a preference for alcohol over other liquids. In an investigation with habitually drinking males, the men were assigned to talk with strange women whom they knew would later rate them on a number of personal qualities. Given a pretext for drinking wine, the men in this mildly stressful rating situation drank significantly more than a control group in a nonevaluative situation (Higgins and Marlatt, 1975).

But granted that alcohol is a reinforcer, why does drinking persist—especially since addiction is "punished" by hangovers and financial and marital difficulties? For learning proponents, the answer lies in several related determinants.

First, the **gradient of reinforcement** explains why the drinker's immediate feeling of relaxation is more important than punishment the next day. It is a well-established learning principle that the more distant the reinforcement or consequence, the less effect it has on behavior. Whatever behavior is reinforced *now* is strengthened, even if it is punished later on. Second, as drinking continues, both tolerance and physical dependence develop. The drinker needs to consume more in order to feel good. Even more critical, dependence introduces a new set of reinforcers. The alcoholic (and the heroin addict) experiences unpleasant withdrawal effects during periods of abstinence. He or she now *needs* to drink to avoid the aversive consequences of not drinking. Third, alcohol is believed to be reinforced by a host of social and psychological

THE ADDICTIVE PERSONALITY

Mr. A. R. is a 48-year-old delicatessen owner. He began his business twenty years before and to everyone's surprise it succeeded. This was because both Mr. A. R.'s wife and relatives had always thought of him as an irresponsible and impulsive individual who was not likely to be able to handle suppliers, customers, ordering, stocking, and so on. But another side of Mr. A. R.'s personality was revealed by his store. He was able to be charming with customers and aggressive with suppliers. Admittedly he also manipulated and cheated a good deal, always rationalizing his practices as "good business sense."

Mr. A. R. came from a disordered family. His mother had left his father when he was 7 and placed him in the care of her own parents. These foster parents were stern people, and drank heavily.

At 19 A. R. graduated from high school and was already known as a heavy beer drinker. His consumption progressed, and when he was 22 he experienced his first blackout. . . . Be-

cause Mr. A. R. was unable to handle even minor stresses and frustrations, he drifted from one job to another for several years until he got married. After marriage he worked for his father-in-law as a salesman in the family clothing store. Despite his lack of success, the father-in-law, anxious to keep him employed, accepted his drinking, bragging, excuses, and undependability. During several periods of abstinence from alcohol, Mr. A. R. quickly shifted his drug dependence to Valium and other tranquilizers. He admitted to a psychologist he saw for a brief period that he had always had some drug to "rely on." During the last few years, the client had begun serious drinking in the morning and continued to sneak drinks while in his store. Several times he had become so intoxicated that he passed out in the store's bathroom. . . . Mr. A. R. had been persuaded to attend a few AA meetings but rejected them because of their "tub thumping religion" and also because he insisted he was not an alcoholic.

rewards. Being in a bar means acceptance, fellowship, and admiration from fellow drinkers. Alcohol also allows the expression of behavior which may be gratifying but which has been psychologically suppressed. While intoxicated, the person feels free to be aggressive, sexual, or assertive. Finally, drinking is learned in a family and cultural context. For learning advocates, genetic explanations that show how often alcoholism appears in family and cultural groups are evidence of modeling. Individuals pattern their own actions and conduct on the parental and peer examples presented to them. For Ullman and Krasner (1975), such modeling identification with friends and relatives may be all the explanation needed for how alcohol (and other drug) addiction is learned.

SOCIAL EXPLANATIONS Because alcohol consumption follows some distinct ethnic and cultural patterns, a number of social factors may also play a role in alcoholism. In North America, Black, Indian, Irish, and Eastern European males have somewhat higher rates of alcohol-related problems. In contrast, Americans of Chinese, Jewish, and Italian backgrounds seem to have relatively low rates of alcoholism. Occupation also appears to be significant. Alcoholism rates are high for musicians, longshoremen, and waiters and lower for postal workers, carpenters, and accountants (Brod, 1975; DeLint and Schmidt, 1971). The meaning of these differences is difficult to interpret, since the ethnic discrepancies seem to have little to do with country of origin. For example, in many African nations alcoholism rates are very low, whereas Italy is very high in per capita consumption of alcohol and associated problems (Table 10.1). Another factor is that in the United States, as generation succeeds generation and background factors fade, differences in drinking behaviors also grow less prominent.

One set of explanations for the relative differences in the frequency of excessive use may lie in the way in which alcohol is treated in

TABLE 10.1

APPARENT CONSUMPTION, IN 20 COUNTRIES, OF EACH MAJOR BEVERAGE CLASS, AND OF ABSOLUTE ALCOHOL FROM EACH CLASS, IN U.S. GALLONS PER PERSON IN THE DRINKING-AGE POPULATION* (LISTED IN DESCENDING ORDER OF TOTAL)

Country	Distilled Spirits	Wine	Beer	TOTAL Absolute Alcohol
1. France	2.35	43.03	20.10†	6.53
2. Italy	[1.11]‡	41.29	3.54	4.01
3. Switzerland	1.53	13.61	29.73†	3.39
4. West Germany	[2.35]	4.04	44.65	3.26
5. Australia	0.54	2.58	42.86	2.89
6. Belgium	0.67	3.14	42.07†	2.87
7. U.S.A.	2.56	1.84	25.95	2.61
8. New Zealand	0.79	0.98	39.28	2.58
9. Czechoslovakia	[0.83]	[3.51]	[30.91]	2.45
10. Canada	[1.86]	[1.12]	[25.47]	2.20
11. Denmark	0.78	1.53	29.03	1.94
12. United Kingdom	0.51	1.08	31.77	1.90
13. Sweden	2.13	1.77	15.57	1.74
14. Japan	[1.10]	[5.10]	8.22	1.53
15. The Netherlands	[1.38]	[0.86]	[15.38]	1.53
16. Ireland	0.70	0.56	22.26	1.49
17. Norway	1.20	0.70	10.82	1.13
18. Finland	1.33	1.06	6.85	1.03
19. Iceland	2.11	0.62	4.26	0.96
20. Israel	0.89	1.66	3.58	0.82

* Age 15+
† Includes cider.
‡ Bracketed data converted from source terms.
Source: *National Institute on Alcohol Abuse and Alcoholism, 1974.*

particular groups. Supposedly, peoples low in alcohol abuse have *not* forbidden their children to drink and also see alcohol more as a festive food. But such explanations seem at best only partly correct. Among some native American groups such as Eskimos, alcohol is not forbidden and is treated festively, yet Eskimos have a very high rate of alcoholism (Brod, 1975). What seems important in determining group differences in alcohol abuse appears to have more to do with social stress than with specific life styles. Although the evidence is incomplete, social explanations of alcoholism indicate that addiction appears greatest among these groups (Gibbons et al., 1976; Worich and Schaller, 1977):

1. Socioeconomic and ethnic groups subjected to the most deprivation, particularly unemployment
2. Cultural groups whose previous traditions, family ties, and values have been disrupted or are in the process of rapid change
3. Peoples who have fairly high rates of so-

cially induced stress disorders such as depression and psychosomatic and other maladies closely related to anxiety and tension

Treatment

The effective treatment of alcoholism has been a challenge for all the therapeutic approaches we have mentioned in preceding chapters. Leaving aside the approximately one-third of alcoholics who seem to recover largely on their own, most other heavy drinkers have been resistant to nearly all techniques. Typically, alcohol (and heroin) addicts seem at first to respond well to treatment. But within a few months or a year after therapy, many have relapsed and resumed their old habits. This does not mean that addiction is incurable, but it does point to the fact that long-term and follow-up therapeutic efforts are needed if a drug-dependent person is to be successfully rehabilitated.

DETOXIFICATION   Often the first step in the treatment of alcohol and other addictions is helping the person physically withdraw from the drug. This is usually best accomplished in a hospital or clinic designed for this purpose, and hundreds of such facilities are now located throughout the United States and Canada. In these centers, alcoholics are medicated to help relieve withdrawal symptoms such as hallucinations, tremors, and anxiety, and treated to improve their nutrition and general health. In the best of such detoxification programs, psychological and social rehabilitative efforts are phased into the physical treatment program, and the addiction viewed as part of an overall adjustment failure.

DYNAMIC PSYCHOTHERAPIES   Those who follow psychoanalytic and client-centered approaches usually insist that alcoholism is a symptom. The focus of these therapies has been the personality as a whole. Possibly because such an orientation is very demanding of time and self-discipline, alcoholics do not often seek or submit to dynamic psychotherapy. One exception has been transactional analysis, practitioners of which have reported a good deal of success with alcoholics.

Transactional analysis describes alcoholism as a game and identifies some of the players as the patsy (the person who gives money and/or sympathy) and the persecutor (the person who scolds and nags). In group and individual therapy sessions, alcoholics learn how they continue to play the game, following the script, in an effort to avoid intimacy. They endlessly repeat the cycle of drinking, pleading, aggression, and guilt, never finding out who others are or who they are either. TA sessions confront alcoholics with their avoidance and help them construct more valid life styles (Kovel, 1976).

ALCOHOLICS ANONYMOUS   Founded in 1935 by alcoholics, AA was possibly the first national, and subsequently worldwide, organization attempting to help addicts. AA meetings are held several times a week; through a combination of persuasion, religious conviction, friendship, and some psychotherapeutic techniques, the organization assists drinkers to remain abstinent. Perhaps most important, in an approach similar to the lifeline concept mentioned earlier for suicide, members learn to call others in the group when their resolution wavers. AA is guided by several fundamental beliefs, a sample of which demonstrates the direction of the organization:

We admit we are powerless over alcohol, that we are alcoholics and will always be alcoholics. Our goal each day is not to drink even one drink, to remain totally sober today.

We turn our lives over to God and ask His help to overcome our shortcomings.

We will continue to take inventory of our lives, admit when we are wrong and make amends to all those we have harmed.

Affiliate organizations such as Al-Anon and Al-Teen have been formed to enlist the aid of those who are closest to alcoholics. Through these groups, the spouses or children of drinkers learn to relieve some of their own conflicts and anxieties and also how to help a drinking husband, wife, or parent remain abstinent.

CAN ALCOHOLICS DRINK NORMALLY?

Alcoholism has long been regarded as an "incurable disease" that is swiftly reactivated if a reformed alcoholic takes even a single drink. Alcoholics Anonymous, for instance, holds the view that the only way for an alcoholic to remain sober is to never ever again drink.

The need for total abstention has been called into question by a number of studies. In one, over a thousand alcoholics, half of whom were unemployed or separated from their families, were in a number of different psychotherapeutic programs whose goals were not total abstinence. Follow-up surveys one year later showed the majority were able to become acceptable "social" drinkers. In another, behavior therapy techniques were used with alcoholics in a barroom setting to teach them moderate drinking styles. Allowable drinking goals were set, and clients were reinforced for acceptable behaviors. This study demonstrated that alcoholics could learn normal drinking behaviors through reward, rather than just through aversive—that is, punishment—procedures. Research has also shown that former alcoholics given alcoholic drinks do not automatically "fall off the wagon." Some abstinent alcoholics were given alcoholic beverages disguised as soft drinks; others were aware they were consuming alcohol. Yet none of the reformed subjects were prompted to once again become active alcoholics.

The research suggesting that alcoholics can become normal recreational drinkers is persuasive but not conclusive. In many studies, the number of alcoholics examined is small and the sample quite limited. In addition, follow-up has not been sufficient. The drinking habits of alcoholics who supposedly become moderate drinkers need to be examined over the course of several years to ascertain the durability of the reform. Whether or not alcoholics can become social drinkers is not yet settled. At this point, though, it seems possible that with adequate treatment and follow-up care, perhaps at least some alcoholics could learn more moderate drinking behaviors.

Sources: National Institute on Alcohol Abuse and Alcoholism, 1978; Pattison, 1976; Strickler et al., 1976)

Alcoholics Anonymous continues to attract members and report substantial results. Although chapters differ somewhat in their makeup, orientation, and effectiveness, nearly all are usually optimistic about the proportion of members who recover. But the value of AA has been questioned. The organization is criticized for its religious emphasis, for its failure to adopt updated reporting and therapy procedures, and for its lack of effort to reach out and bring in those who are not likely to seek help on their own. Because it does not actively reach out, the organization may get only the most well-motivated alcoholics, those who are already well on the way toward abstinence. Overall, although assessments of AA have brought several weaknesses to light, the organization probably continues to be helpful to many alcoholics who can benefit from this approach (Bebbington, 1976).

BEHAVIOR THERAPIES Many different learning techniques have been tried to help relieve alcoholism. The most direct approach is to attempt to make drinking itself a punishing experience. Such aversive conditioning procedures usually employ chemicals antagonistic to alcohol. For many patients, the administration of disulfiram (trade name: Antabuse) is sometimes effective. The alcoholic is given the drug several times a week for several months. If alcohol is consumed during treatment, the drug interaction rapidly causes nausea, cramping, and other unpleasant gastrointestinal symptoms.

Other aversive procedures have made use of electric shock. Addicts are informed of the procedure, permitted to drink, and then shocked by a supervisor. In a refinement of this method, addicts are taught to punish their own drinking by using a portable shock apparatus on themselves. Since alcoholics may simply learn not to take the Antabuse or not to shock themselves, attempts have been made to make punishment more of an unavoidable psychological experience. Some addicts have been taught to associate well-inculcated, imaginary painful consequences with drinking. But in general, these conditioning procedures have been effective with only a small proportion of alcohol addicts (O'Leary and Wilson, 1975).

An entirely different approach has been not to punish drinking, but to reinforce abstinent behavior. The reasoning is that if responses essentially incompatible with drinking could be strengthened, imbibing alcohol would decline. In one such investigation, a complex social and psychological reinforcement program was developed. Alcoholics were helped to obtain good jobs. Through counseling, marital and family relations were made enjoyable and the camaraderie of the bar replaced with sober, supportive friends. In other words, the addict was lifted out of the drinking life style and all its reinforcers and introduced to a whole new set of rewards. Now reinforced for remaining sober, most of the subjects reportedly recovered (O'Leary and Wilson, 1975). Another nonpunitive behavioral approach was attempted by Watson et al. (1977), who focused on altering the motivation underlying drinking by means of biofeedback training. The idea was that since anxiety often causes drinking, perhaps consumption could be reduced if anxiety were alleviated. Watson taught patients to produce alpha wave patterns, signaling feelings of relaxation. The experiment showed that some patients were capable of bringing about limited modifications in anxiety and consumption.

COMMUNITY TREATMENTS   The breadth of the alcohol addiction problem, its immense personal and financial costs as well as its social roots, is increasingly being recognized. As a result, halfway houses, storefront clinics, and more formal treatment facilities are becoming common (Chapter 17). Such facilities offer more than just individual therapy. Since alcohol and other drug addiction is a psychological *and* socioeconomic dilemma, community ac-

tion is needed to secure adequate housing, medical care, nutrition, and—perhaps most important of all—employment. Alcoholism remains difficult to treat, with most therapies reporting some success with about half of all patients. But community-based multidimensional treatment programs, which make use of a number of different therapeutic techniques appear to have considerable promise for the future (Pattison et al., 1977; Seixas, 1977).

HEROIN

Heroin is produced by heating morphine, the chief active ingredient of opium, which comes from a plant called the opium poppy. Heroin is usually sold as a powder and diluted with sugar or quinine. Though prices and proportions vary, a typical heroin "bag" illegally purchased on the street contains roughly 10 mg of heroin mixed with about 90 mg of adulterants and costs about $10. Heroin is sometimes sniffed—that is, the powder is inhaled; or it is diluted in liquid and injected into the skin (skin popping). For maximum effect, however, nearly all serious users mainline; they inject the heroin directly into the veins of their arms and legs, under the tongue, or into other fairly inconspicuous areas (Figure 10.7).

Heroin and opium are **narcotics,** a class of drugs that relieve pain and induce a feeling of calm and pleasure. Throughout the nineteenth century in the United States, narcotics were widely and freely available. Although physicians dispensed opiates directly to patients or wrote prescriptions for them, they could also be obtained without medical supervision. Drug and grocery stores sold dozens of patent medicines, the main ingredient of which was an opiate.

The use and availability of narcotics can be judged from an 1885 survey of the state of Iowa, which then had a population of nearly 2 million. Three thousand stores directly sold opium under such names as Mrs. Winslow's Soothing Syrup, Dover's Powder, and McMunn's Elixir of Opium. Throughout North America it is conservatively estimated that 4

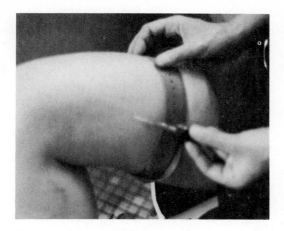

Figure 10.7. Heroin addicts inject the drug directly into their veins, often using homemade syringes. Inconspicuous veins in the thigh, back of the neck, or under the tongue are frequently favored in order to help avoid detection. (Photo: Scribe)

million adults and hundreds of thousands of children were regular users of opium, and a large proportion of them were clearly addicted. Usually the opium was drunk daily as a syrup. Sometimes it was smoked, and some heavy users also "mainlined."

Opium was a staple for physicians because it seemed to relieve arthritis, tuberculosis, cancer, and countless other maladies for which there was no cure or treatment. Many nineteenth-century physicians even used opium to cure alcoholism, a switch in addictions that frequently worked. But what has been called a century of "opium paradise" came to an end in 1914 with the Harrison Narcotic Act, which forbade the importation and the free use of narcotics.

The prohibition of opium was somewhat similar to the prohibition of alcohol a decade later. The overwhelming majority of the citizenry did not object to the drug, and in the case of opium large numbers of physicians and scientists testified to its relative harmlessness and benefit. Unlike alcohol, opium did little physical damage and rarely induced violence. The ban on opium was widely ignored until the 1920s, when stricter and stricter punish-

ments were legislated for violators. By the 1930s, the restrictions on narcotic traffic were effective enough to end the use of opium by ordinary citizens and limit it to only about a million or so of the most adventurous, those with professional access (like physicians), or those whose poverty and alienation made them critical of many social restraints.

Today the addict population fluctuates with the availability of supply as well as with fad and fashion. By 1980, estimates suggest there will be close to three-quarters of a million addicts. Since addicts tend to cluster in cities, most are found in places like New York City (about 100,000), Los Angeles (75,000), Chicago (50,000), and Dallas and Atlanta (10,000). About half of all those developing a narcotic dependency are from minority groups. Men outnumber women, and contrary to most impressions only about a fourth of all addicts support their habits through crime. Even those who use criminal means to obtain money or drugs are largely nonviolent. Prostitution, shoplifting, forgery, and "dealing" drugs are much more common than armed robbery or mugging (O'Donnel, 1972).

Despite the restrictions and punitive laws, heroin smuggling and marketing remain big business. In 1976, a congressional committee headed by Senator Birch Bayh estimated the profit from annual heroin sales in the United States at more than $10 billion. Gross sales are greater than 34 of the 50 largest industrial companies in the world—double those of Eastman Kodak, triple those of Lockheed Aircraft, and seven times those of Campbell Soup. A large portion of the money involved also finds its way into the pockets of police and law officials, who are bribed to facilitate the heroin traffic (Platt and Labate, 1976; Worick, 1977).

The drug and the user

Heroin addiction may begin as early as 10 or 12 years of age, but more typically starts during late adolescence. Some addicts have used other drugs and progressed to heroin, but for most, other drugs have been incidental. There are no "recreational" heroin consumers.

Judged by the past, if opiates were again legal it might be possible for some people to consume heroin occasionally without developing true dependency. But under present circumstances, very few people just sometimes inject or sniff the drug without developing an addiction. This is not to say that a single or even half a dozen experiences inevitably result in being "hooked." But the evidence shows that the pattern is for addiction to develop after toying and experimenting with heroin for a month or two. An important reason for the addictive propensity of heroin is its extreme tolerance effect when injected. Opium that is drunk, as was the case with nineteenth-century patent medicines, had a somewhat different mode of action and did not appear to have the same tolerance results. But the rapidly increasing need for heroin quickly motivates the user to try larger and larger quantities in order to experience the same "high." The addict may begin with a $10 a day habit and within a few months require $100.

When heroin is injected, it produces a "rush," a good, warm, almost euphoric feeling that some liken to a sexual orgasm. This is soon followed by lethargy and sleepiness. Some six to twelve hours after the injection, the heroin has begun to wear off and withdrawal symptoms begin. The eyes tear, the nose runs, the addict yawns and may fall into a fitful sleep. After awakening and during the next few days more unpleasant symptoms appear: vomiting, chills, restlessness, and abdominal cramps. This is an uncomfortable period but by no means the horrible experience sometimes depicted in the entertainment media. In fact, many addicts liken withdrawal to no more than a few days of being ill with the flu (Hardy and Cull 1975; Platt and Labate, 1976)

Heroin addiction appears in all socioeconomic groups, including medical professionals who have access to it. But it is more commonly found among socially disadvantaged people and in crowded, deteriorating inner city areas. In other words, in most instances heroin addiction appears to be a sociocultural phenomenon. The addict is likely to be a person from

Figure 10.8. Experimentation with and abuse of drugs sometimes begins very early. Children as young as 10 or 12 may be driven by curiosity, rebellion, peer pressure, adult models, or any number of needs to smoke marijuana, drink alcohol, consume pills, and even try heroin. (Photo: Scribe)

a poor and disrupted family whose schooling has been inadequate or incomplete. Most are not psychiatrically ill, but they are often lacking in adaptive skills. They seem to find it difficult to cope with frustration, tend to be rebellious and manipulative, and are clinically close to the description of the addictive personality (see Box, p. 208) (Kurtine et al., 1975; Koslowsky et al., 1975).

The "ghetto" heroin addict may, in a manner of speaking, be a special variation of the addictive personality in general. Collum and Pike (1976) believe such drug-dependent persons emerge from a background characterized by hopelessness, confusion, and conflict. They do not know who they are or what they can do; they are "borderline" personalities who have little sense of identity. When such individuals come into contact with the drug culture, which is part of almost every depressed city neighborhood, they are given a sense of identity and a set of values. Their life takes on meaning, even if it is a negative and self-destructive one centered about obtaining heroin. Like Leroy, they now have a purpose: to obtain money, avoid the police, and "shoot up."

Leroy began using heroin when he was 14. He came from a family kept together by his mother and grandmother, both of whom worked long hours to maintain five children. Leroy's father had died when he was 6, and he had little memory of him except that he used to drink heavily. Leroy's mother also drank excessively but nevertheless managed to hold a job in a dry cleaning plant. Leroy's grandmother was very religious and attempted to impose her faith on the children. Two of Leroy's siblings were churchgoers, but Leroy was rebellious and resentful. There were frequent fights at home about Leroy's apparent disobedience and his tendency to stay out late or sometimes all night. Leroy also had significant school problems. Although he was intellectually capable, he read poorly and was often truant.

Together with a friend, Leroy persuaded an older known neighborhood heroin addict to let him shoot up. Leroy's first experiences were unpleasant, but within a week or so he had become accustomed to the needle and technique and began to enjoy the feeling. His friend became frightened and stopped using heroin, but Leroy became useful to the neighborhood users by acting as a lookout and messenger. For this he was rewarded with an occasional fix. By the time he turned 15, Leroy had developed a firm habit and was shooting two to three $10 bags every day. Since he now needed money to buy his own dope, Leroy became a "booster," shoplifting from stores and stealing equipment from his school. Leroy's grandmother became aware of his addiction and cajoled and intimidated him to begin a treatment program available in the neighborhood. At the clinic, Leroy seemed to respond positively for two months but then relapsed and resumed his addiction.

Over the next five years, Leroy became a confirmed addict and supported his habit by dealing in several drugs as well as by shoplifting.

He was arrested three times, including one offense for carrying a revolver. He was jailed only once, for six months, and also had two lengthy periods when he was heroin-free. At 19 Leroy had resumed his habit, which he sometimes alternated with alcohol dependence when heroin was not available. At 20 Leroy was found dead in an abandoned building in his neighborhood. The autopsy reported septicemia (blood poisoning), likely due to a contaminated needle.

Mortality among addicts is high. Perhaps one or two out of every hundred die every year from drug-related causes. One major contributor to the fatality rate is erroneously called "overdose." Supposedly the addict, not really having any way of knowing what is in the bag of heroin, obtains too large an amount of the narcotic. In actuality, this is very rarely the case. Most addicts die of sensitivity reactions to heroin adulterants like quinine or from tetanus, hepatitis, or other infections because of unsterile instruments. Occasionally too, a supplier may deliberately add a poison like strychnine to a bag in order to get rid of a troublesome customer. Serious fights among addicts, or involving dealers, are also common, so that homicide (and suicide) is not infrequent among heroin-dependent individuals. The chances of legal entanglements for addicts are very high. Sooner or later most addicts are arrested and incarcerated, or at least accumulate a police record (Platt and Labote, 1977).

Causes

BIOLOGICAL EXPLANATIONS The focus in biological explanations has been on the chemistry of addiction. Perhaps enzyme, metabolic, or other biochemical aberrations can account for drug dependence. One such avenue of research has shown that in rats specific nerve cells in the brain seem to serve as special receptor sites for opiates. The narcotic drug molecules become bound to these sites, fitting in like a key in a lock. All that is needed is a chance for the brain to be exposed to the opiate, and a vital biological call for these drugs

DOES THE BRAIN MANUFACTURE ITS OWN HEROIN?

Scientists working with the National Institutes of Mental Health, the Salk Institute, and other research facilities have recently identified a number of opiatelike chemicals within the brain. The actions of these agents resemble those of narcotics, and they have been called *endorphin* (internal morphine) and *enkephalin*. The discovery of endorphin and enkephalin has suggested several possibilities:

1. Perhaps the body both manufactures its own opiates and has specialized nerve cell receptors for these chemicals. The reason that heroin fits the neurochemistry of the brain like a key in a lock is that its molecular structure is identical to those of endorphin and enkephalin.

2. Endorphin and enkephalin may act as modulators that regulate and subdue perceptual information and signals carried by neurotransmitters. Deficiencies in these narcoticlike chemicals could cause mental confusion and intensified feelings of pain and emotion, resulting ultimately in mental illness. It is interesting to note that the limbic system of the brain, identified as the center of emotion, has an unusually high concentration of opiate receptors.

3. Acupuncture, the Chinese anesthesia, may work because the needles prompt nerve cells to produce more endorphin and enkephalin, thus blocking the signaling and perception of pain.

---

will follow. In this way, addiction is seen as almost the inevitable result of physiological opportunity, with personality having relatively little to do with it (Platt and Labate, 1976).

BEHAVIORAL EXPLANATIONS   Behavior theorists invoke social learning explanations and particularly point to modeling. In poverty areas the addict seems to have successfuly escaped from the frustrating routines of deprivation and the dealer appears as an enviable and affluent personality. Both are people to look up to and emulate. Many inner-city and middle-class drug users also seem to be presented with parental addictive models. Several investigations have revealed that up to half of the families of addicts contained a parent who used alcohol or other drugs excessively. Needless to say, a third factor, once heroin addiction is established, is the avoidance of withdrawal symptoms as a prominent source of reinforcement (O'Leary and Wilson, 1975).

PSYCHODYNAMIC EXPLANATIONS   Like alcoholism, heroin addiction is not absolutely correlated with any one special type of personality. People with many different character traits may become heroin-dependent, and the addiction is also sometimes secondary to other psychiatric disorders. From the psychody-

namic perspective, however, heroin users are thought to share some very special personality trends. Some analysts, noting the apparent frequency of depression, aggression, and suicide among addicts, believe that these are essentially self-destructive individuals whose drug habits are a not so hidden means of doing away with themselves. Other psychodynamic writers have focused on the "addictive personality." They point out that just like alcoholics and other drug abusers, heroin addicts have low stress tolerance and lack of ordinary psychological resourcefulness. Instead of coping, they deny and rationalize, and escape into the anesthetized fantasy world provided by drugs.

What still needs to be explained, however, is why so many heroin addicts come from socioeconomically marginal circumstances, why they seem to be alienated and part of a very special subculture. Possibly the frequency with which heroin users are antisocial is the selective result of the fact that opiates are illegal. One has to break the law to consume heroin and not feel intimidated by the possibility of grave punishment. As a result, those who are drawn to this narcotic must have more than the usual addictive personality deficiencies. They also need to be individuals who have not been adequately socialized, or who feel so disenfranchised from the majority culture that moral and legal restraints have lost their meaning.

Thus heroin addicts are both the same as and different from alcoholics. Like the alcoholics, for a combination of biological, motivational, and learned reasons they have a drug habit. But whereas most alcoholics are more or less average, law-abiding citizens, heroin addicts tend to be indifferent to social values and punishment, to reject cultural conventions and restraints (Gibbins et al., 1976; Hardy and Cull, 1975).

Treatment

A first treatment step for most heroin addicts is detoxification. The heroin user is built up physically and with the help of medication brought through the withdrawal period. The psychological efforts that follow, however, are frequently disappointing. Given the rebellious and antisocial character of many heroin users, it is not surprising that psychotherapy is difficult. Both dynamic and behavior treatment methods have had very limited success. In fact, even severe punishment such as incarceration has failed, since nine out of ten addicts return to their habits even after being jailed as long as five to fifteen years (Hersen and Eisler, 1977; Stachnik, 1972).

The techniques that have had more success are polar opposites, and advocates of each are in disagreement with the other. These are the methadone and Synanon-type programs.

SUBSTITUTION Methadone is a synthetic narcotic that was clinically introduced in 1965. It has many of the same effects as heroin, but it is taken orally and lasts twenty-four hours or more, eliminating the need for a "fix" two or three times a day. Methadone is legal and is dispensed to enrolled addicts at medical facilities in every city and most larger towns. The advantage of methadone is that since the drug is legal, cheap, and readily available, it permits addicts to attend school or work and live relatively normal lives. The entire day need no longer center on getting the money

to maintain the drug dependency; the addict can come out of the drug subculture and back into society.

Many methadone facilities also aid addicts by gradually administering less and less of the narcotic until they are drug-free. Together with counseling, educational, vocational, and psychological assistance, the treatment sometimes results in recovery. An additional benefit of methadone derives from the fact that many addicts often end their dependency on their own as they reach their late thirties. Methadone can keep users free of heroin until their own maturity stops their addiction entirely. Estimates are that methadone is helping as many as 200,000 addicts stay away from heroin and that perhaps two-thirds of these, despite relapses, sooner or later "kick" their addiction (Handal and Lander, 1976; Worick and Schaller, 1977).

Similar programs in Great Britain provide addicts with heroin under controlled medical supervision and seem to have resulted in keeping illegal addiction to a minimum. In the United States, experimental efforts using heroin or other opiates have also shown some possibilities. As a whole, however, drug substitution or medically supervised narcotics administration programs have not lived up to their promise to end addiction and have been seriously criticized for perpetuating dependence instead of treating it (Blumberg, 1976; Savage et al., 1976).

Those opposed to substitution techniques point out that switching from illegal to legal drug consumption solves few personality or adjustment difficulties. Addicts still have a drug-oriented approach to life, are still evasive and defensive, and look to drugs for magical answers to complex human and social problems. In addition, many methadone users "cheat"; they combine methadone with alcohol or heroin, smuggle the legal drug into street use, and depend on methadone during periods when their normal heroin supply is unavailable. Perhaps the most compelling argument of those opposed to methadone is the historical fact that heroin was introduced at the begin-

SHOULD HEROIN BE LEGAL?

Yes:

Many if not most of the psychological, physical, and social ills of heroin—the drug subculture, crime, and corruption of officials—are the result of the drug being illegal. Studies of the effects of morphine, heroin, and other opiates show that they do not stimulate aggressive or violent behavior and are generally less damaging to the liver, brain, and body than alcohol.

If heroin were legal it would be safe, medically pure, and cheap. For example, the United States now produces 50 million doses of morphine every year which are inexpensive and meet the highest pharmaceutical standards set for injectable products. In the nineteenth century, millions used morphine regularly and there was little personal or social damage.

Another argument for legalization is that prohibition backfires. It not only spawns a vast criminal network, but excites the curiosity and rebelliousness of adolescents. Perhaps worst of all, it lulls society into thinking that drug problems will be cured simply by increasing penalties or hiring more police. Short of the kind of authoritarian police found in dictatorships, law enforcement cannot stop drug use.

The real causes of drug abuse are psychological and social: economic deprivation, unemployment, hopelessness, and a myriad of other problems that motivate people to escape rather than face life. We should be addressing ourselves to these issues and not be diverted by thinking tougher laws will stop addiction.

Drugs should be legal and backed by excellent educational and rehabilitative efforts to prevent and treat abuse.

No:

Drug use may stem from personal and social difficulties, but it is utopian to hope to remove all inequities in life. There will always be people who for any number of reasons will want to experience the relief or thrill of drugs, and we should limit their possibilities as much as possible.

Heroin itself is rapidly and powerfully addictive, much more so than alcohol. Consequently, even normal people without psychological problems are likely to become dependent. Now we have several hundred thousand addicts, but if heroin were freely available millions would become habitual users. Alcohol provides an example. It is legal, and though not as addictive as heroin, has still resulted in at least 5 million alcoholics who do immense damage to themselves, their families, and society. If heroin and alcohol were both legal, we might have a nation in which one-fourth of the population was so sedated and dependent that the rest would have to support them completely.

It is erroneous to assume that the law cannot stop heroin traffic. A thorough and disciplined police force, together with severe punishment, including the death sentence, has ended heroin use in countries like China.

---

ning of this century as a means of combatting widespread morphine addiction. There were even licensed medical clinics designed to administer the new opiate, and heroin then, like methadone now, was hailed as an agent that would eventually block an addict's craving and end dependency.

SELF-HELP   A totally contrary approach is taken by Synanon and other communal self-help groups. Founded in 1958 by a former alcoholic, Synanon embodies several of the practices of AA. As in AA, members are forbidden any drug use and must give up their drug-abus-ing friends and subculture. Synanon members also live together, share work and expenses, and participate in intensive group encounters. During these sessions members discuss their former life style and motivations and are helped to examine their defenses. Such encounters are often brutal and direct, with members verbally attacking one another to expose rationalizations and pretensions. Despite the rigor of the programs, many members of such groups become strongly attached to one another and proud of their new identity and ability to abstain from heroin.

There are many therapeutic communities (Daytop Village, Phoenix House, Chabad House) whose programs are variations of that initiated by Synanon. Most claim a high degree of effectiveness for those who complete the program. But since it takes a great deal of motivation to remain with these groups, many addicts drop out and resume their dependency. Research evidence suggests that a third to half of all the graduates of such treatment programs remain drug-free. Many of these, however, maintain their improvement only by continuing in the treatment facility as staff members or moving with other graduates to a follow-up community (Platt and Labate, 1977).

OTHER DRUGS

The variety of drugs obtained from plants, manufactured in laboratories, or diverted from medicine or commerce that may be legally or illegally used numbers in the hundreds. Mescaline, peyote, hashish, glue, nitrous oxide, nail polish remover, Quaalude, and nutmeg are only a few of the products that have enjoyed some popularity among drug users. We cannot cover all the chemicals that may be employed or the variety of motivations that foster experimentation or addiction. We will, however, briefly describe some of the more common drugs: cocaine, marijuana, LSD, amphetamines, and barbiturates.

Cocaine

Cocaine is a stimulant that gives an energetic feeling of well-being and permits users to believe that their sexual, creative, and affectional powers have been enhanced. The drug is derived from the South American coca plant and was, like opiates, a major ingredient of tonics and elixirs until the 1914 Harrison Act. Now it is usually refined to a fine powder and very small amounts are inhaled or "snorted." Because of the problems involved in its manufacture and importation, it is extremely expensive. An evening's use employing only a fraction of an ounce costs several hundred dollars.

The National Institute of Drug Abuse in Washington, D.C., estimates that about 8 million Americans have tried cocaine, but only a few hundred thousand seem to use it with any regularity. Though cocaine is not clearly physically addictive, some frequent users do seem to develop dependency and resemble alcohol or heroin addicts. But the majority of cocaine users employ the drug only occasionally and often make the event a social one marked by special food, wine, music, drug paraphernalia, and the like.

Sigmund Freud experimented with cocaine as a medical anesthetic and in the process briefly became an advocate. At first Freud thought the drug assisted his insight and productivity. Soon, however, he found that cocaine only made him falsely believe he was extra-aware or creative. In fact, Freud's experience so convinced him of the delusional and hazardous effects of drugs in general that many years later, when sedatives were prescribed to ease the pain of his cancer, he refused to take them lest they muddle his thoughts and feelings.

A few cocaine users are from relatively impoverished backgrounds and seem to develop a subculture which resembles that of the heroin addict. Most, however, are middle class or more affluent and contend that cocaine is harmless. They call for "decriminalization." But research evidence suggests that prolonged use can lead to chronic insomnia, severe anxiety, and hallucinations (Grinspoon and Bakalar, 1977).

Marijuana and LSD

Marijuana and LSD are psychedelic or hallucinogenic drugs, meaning they heighten emotion, perception, and feeling and lead to hallucinatory experiences. Marijuana use almost rivals alcohol, since at least about 40 million Americans have smoked it. LSD is far less popular; recent figures suggest that even occasional users number no more than several thousand.

COMMON DRUGS

	Classification	Potential for dependence	Effects
LEGAL			
Alcohol (whisky, wine, beer)	Sedative	High	Small amounts induce relaxation, drowsiness, and disinhibition. Larger quantities bring about loss of motor control, exaggerated emotions, and unconsciousness.
Caffeine (colas, coffee, tea)	Stimulant	Moderate	Small amounts produce alertness and give a "lift." Larger amounts may cause anxiety, palpitations, and restlessness.
Nicotine (cigars, cigarettes)	Stimulant	High	Small amounts seem to have a calming effect. In large doses may produce irritability, nervousness, and depression.
PRESCRIPTION			
Barbiturates (Nembutal, Seconal)	Sedative	Moderate to high	Induce relaxation, sleep, or coma depending on the amount taken.
Psychiatric medications (Miltown, Valium, Quaalude, Noctec, Thorazine)	Considered sedatives, anti-anxiety, or tranquilizing medications	Moderate	In small doses have desired effects and help relieve neurotic and psychotic symptoms. Large quantities can induce neurological symptoms, emotional disturbances, and coma.
Amphetamines (Benzedrine, Dexedrine)	Stimulant	Moderate	Depending on amount and frequency of use, feeling of energy, enthusiasm, or irritability and psychosis.
Methadone	Narcotic	High	Effects essentially the same as for heroin.
ILLEGAL			
Heroin	Narcotic	High	In small doses gives a feeling of well-being and relaxation. Larger amounts cause loss of motor control, physical and emotional symptoms, and coma.
Marijuana	Psychedelic	Low to moderate	Gives a feeling of relaxation, friendliness, heightened awareness, sensuality, or anxiety and suspicion, depending on amounts consumed.
Mescaline LSD	Hallucinogens	Low to moderate	In smaller amounts intensify perceptual experiences. Larger quantities can produce hallucinations and psychotic behavior.
Cocaine	Stimulant	Low to moderate	A feeling of energy and sensuality is stimulated by low doses. Larger amounts cause irritability and psychotic reactions.

Many of the results of drug use are unpredictable and potentially dangerous since they depend only partially on the amount consumed. The individual's personality, health, and environmental circumstances play a substantial role in determining reactions to drugs.

Sources: *Leavitt, 1974; Physician's Desk Reference, 1979; Worick, 1977.*

Marijuana is a very mild hallucinogen and is derived from the cannabis sativa plant (Figure 10.9). Many users believe it arouses and heightens sensations and leads to a greater appreciation of music, food, and sex, and a congenial atmosphere. It is rarely addictive and its occasional consumption has been shown benign enough for the American Medical Association, the American Bar Association, and a presidential commission to call for its decriminalization. In fact, a large number of states including Mississippi, New York, and California, have already removed most criminal sanctions for personal use.

Marijuana, however, is not entirely without hazards. Excessive consumption sometimes leads to temporary paranoid or psychotic episodes. Heavy users also seem to show impaired coordination, perception, and motor ability. A study reported by the National Institute of Drug Abuse of 300 fatal automobile accidents in Boston showed that 30 percent of the drivers were under the influence of alcohol and 16 percent appeared to have smoked significant amounts of marijuana (Abel, 1976).

LSD (lysergic acid diethylamide) is a synthetic chemical popularized in the United States in the 1950s. It is a powerful psychedelic that leads to vivid sensory and cognitive hallucinatory experiences. It is not especially addictive, but "bad trips"—frightening and destructive fantasies—are not uncommon. On occasion, LSD has also triggered serious and enduring psychoses. Probably because the unpredictable nature and potential dangers of LSD have become apparent even to its advocates, the chemical is no longer very popular. On the other hand, the medical potential of LSD to help alleviate pain or psychological distress is still being investigated (Gibbins et al., 1976).

Amphetamines

Dexadrine, benzadrine, and methedrine are amphetamines, powerful synthetic stimulants medically prescribed to assist dieters or relieve depression or hyperactivity. Nonmedically, they are employed to temporarily increase energy, elevate mood and perception, and allow the user to feel extra strong and alert. Tens of millions of Americans, including athletes, truck drivers, entertainers, adolescents, and men and women in every walk of life have used amphetamines legally or illegally. Among those who take amphetamines excessively, tolerance may develop very rapidly: "speed freaks" may progress from 20 mg a day to well over 1000 mg within a few weeks.

Amphetamines are moderately addictive; withdrawal symptoms for most users are limited to feelings of fatigue and some depression. Those who are heavily addicted, however, particularly if they "mainline" the drug, often experience a painful "crash." By injecting amphetamines they boost themselves higher and higher into an exaggerated, energetic period of hyperactivity lasting several days, followed by a perilous physical and psychological collapse. Amphetamine use, sometimes even in relatively moderate doses, stimulates psychoses. Such **amphetamine psychoses,** with their paranoid delusions and hallucinations, so closely resemble schizophrenia that the drug has been used in many experimental in-

Figure 10.9. Marijuana is often grown in home gardens. Although its personal use has been decriminalized in many areas, growing or sale is still illegal. (Photo: Town of Saugerties Police Department and Glendale Studio, Saugerties, N.Y.)

vestigations of this disorder (Grinspoon and Hedblom, 1975).

Barbiturates

Barbiturate drugs such as Butisol, Donnatal, Nembutal, and Seconal are sedatives medically prescribed to induce sleep or muscle, intestinal, and general relaxation. Every year, tens of millions of people use these medications and obtain relief. But perhaps about a million or more become addicted. In moderate doses, the barbiturates have desirable sedative effects; when taken to excess, the results resemble alcoholic intoxication. The person stumbles and staggers, speech is sluggish, and thinking and judgment are impaired. Withdrawal symptoms are also common in those who have accustomed themselves to over 400 mg daily.

Those addicted to barbiturates are sometimes adolescents whose initial contact with the drug is through an illegal dealer. More often, however, adults are introduced to the barbiturates by their physicians. Because of the tolerance effects of the barbiturates, the person soon needs more and more and begins devising strategies for obtaining an additional supply. Forging prescriptions, going to a number of different physicians, hoarding the drug, or ultimately resorting to illegal purchases are typical patterns. Like alcoholics, many barbiturate-dependent individuals consume the drug daily, but many others are the equivalent of "spree" drinkers, taking large barbiturate doses only once in a while. Many others combine their barbiturate intake with other drugs, particularly those intended to give them a "lift," so that they feel as if they are going up and down through drugs.

Barbiturates are powerful and highly addictive; dosage "mistakes" ending in coma and death are common. Used with alcohol they are dangerous in the extreme, since the two chemicals together multiply each other's effects. Barbiturate users seem to be aware of these dangers and yet continue to take the drug in fairly large amounts, lending some validity to the hypothesis that they are suicidal personalities unconsciously toying with their own destruction. Other hypotheses intended to explain barbiturate use runs parallel to those we have already described for alcohol and heroin abuse. That is, although barbiturate addiction seems to occur in all people for a number of reasons explicable in terms of biology, motivation, and learning, many addicts clinically resemble the addictive personality. An additional feature of barbiturate dependence is that whereas women are usually less frequently alcohol- or heroin-dependent, they seem to be overrepresented among barbiturate addicts. Many of the women addicts, and often the men as well, seem to have some associated medical or psychological problems that appear related to their need for the drug. Anxiety, depression, and psychosomatic concerns may be especially common (Lech, Friedman, and Hans, 1975; Gibbins et al., 1976).

Causes and treatment

The causes for and treatment of those abusing or addicted to the "other" drugs is essentially the same as those given earlier for alcohol and heroin. In fact, many of those who use drugs excessively readily switch from heroin to alcohol to amphetamines, depending on what is available and what seems to promise a desirable experience. But although a great deal of drug abuse and dependence may be accounted for in psychological, biological, and social terms, it must be recognized that the consumption of drugs is much more than a mental health issue.

A great deal of recreational drug use, even of illegal drugs, may not necessarily indicate psychiatric problems. For many years before marijuana was decriminalized in several regions of the United States, "pot" smokers were by definition assumed to be maladjusted individuals. We now know that for the last decade millions of marijuana smokers were perhaps a little daring but otherwise more or less like everyone else. They were just as rational, confused or adjusted, trustworthy or untrustworthy as the rest of the population (Abel, 1976). In other words, we need to be careful *not* to assume that anyone who uses drugs, even in minimal and controlled ways, is necessarily mentally disordered. More important is the fact that billions of people all over the world are addicted to licit and illicit drugs, including alcohol, narcotics, coffee, and cigarettes. Drug use, abuse, and addiction are multidimensional problems with profound cultural and historical as well as personal roots. Such a complex phenomenon needs to be understood and explained in terms of the entire structure and function of human society.

SUMMARY

People unable to control their drug consumption are usually considered psychiatrically ill. Standards for legal and illegal drugs have changed and are often inconsistent and conflicting. Whatever the drug, its use may be described as recreational, abusive, or addictive, depending on the amount consumed and the personal and social consequences. Drugs themselves have differing addictive potentials and tolerance effects.

Alcohol is the most commonly used and abused drug. In moderation it may be harmless, but its excessive use results in more personal, social, and economic damage than all other drugs combined. Alcohol is a sedative, depressing inhibitory, motor control, and similar areas of the brain. Excessive consumption can cause blackouts, DTs, paranoia, Korsakoff's psychosis, and many other conditions. There are at least 5 million and possibly as many as 20 million alcoholics, who come from all social classes and who have many different consumption styles and histories.

Alcoholism could be due to biochemical deficits, but there is better evidence for at least a minimal genetic component. Psychodynamic theorists have postulated that it is due to needs such as dependency, conformity, and aggression. Theorists have described both alcoholic and addictive personalities typified by traits such as depression, feelings of inadequacy, low stress tolerance, impulsivity, and irresponsibility. Learning advocates see alcoholism as

the result of the reinforcing effects of drinking and social learning variables, particularly modeling. Sociological explanations note cultural differences and point to socioeconomic variables such as unemployment.

Alcohol dependency has not been responsive to most dynamic therapies. Good treatment frequently starts with detoxification and may then be phased into counseling or other therapy programs. No special form of treatment has had consistently productive results, but AA and a number of behavioral approaches are often fairly effective.

Heroin, a narcotic, is illegal and is used by about three-quarters of a million addicts. Although the chemical itself is fairly benign, its impure street form and expense have led to a destructive subculture and generated criminality, smuggling, and corruption. Addiction usually starts during adolescence, is rapid, and is not typically associated with other significant drug use. It is found among people of all social levels but is more commonly seen in socioeconomically deprived groups. Addiction may be partly the result of the neurophysiological properties of narcotics, but is better explained in psychological and social terms. Many addicts often share the characteristics of the addictive personality and tend to be antisocial. Modeling and other learning factors also seem to play a role. Heroin dependency is very difficult to treat; both dynamic and learning approaches have met with little success. Methadone, Synanon programs and other drug substitution or group communal approaches often report good long-term results.

Several hundred chemicals are used and misused to alter emotion or perception or for other psychological purposes. Cocaine has been tried by millions, but partly as a result of its expense is regularly used by only few. It is a stimulant that provides an energetic feeling of well-being, and although it is not entirely harmless, it is not usually addictive. Marijuana is smoked recreationally by tens of millions and as such is relatively harmless. It is a mild hallucinogen but may sometimes encourage paranoia and also, like alcohol, result in impaired motor control. It is not ordinarily addictive and its personal use has been decriminalized in a number of areas. LSD is a very potent hallucinogen that can lead to psychoses. Possibly because of its hazards, it is no longer employed with any frequency. Amphetamines (stimulants) and barbiturates (sedatives) are prescribed medications used by millions. They are also procured illegally and abused, with some people becoming dependent, particularly on barbiturates. Though their modes of action are different, both are potentially very hazardous: excessive amphe- tamine intake is associated with psychosis and barbiturate consumption with death. The causes of cocaine, amphetamine, and other drug use and the appropriate treatments re- semble those described for alcohol and heroin. Not all drug use, however, is psychiatrically abnormal. In fact, even drug misuse is more than just a mental health issue. The use of mind-altering chemicals has complex histori- cal and cultural roots and needs to be under- stood in terms of the entire structure and func- tion of human society.

Deviant Behaviors: Personality Disorders, Crime, Gambling, Sexual Aberrations

In this chapter we will cover a number of different disturbances that were once called **character disorders.** The original psychiatric reasoning was that neuroses and psychoses were the result of a failure in intellect or emotion. In contrast, personal peculiarities, criminal, and other deviant behaviors were thought to be the product of a defect in morality or character. Today we know that such a distinction is inaccurate since all behavior arises from an interaction of personality, biology, and environment.

Although we no longer use the phrase character disorder or subscribe to what it implies, the abnormal conditions described in this chapter do have some common characteristics. First, people who are diagnosed as personality disordered or sexually deviant are ordinarily *not* hallucinated, exceedingly anxious, or burdened by any of the other common symptoms

of mental disability. But they are all more or less *adjustively deficient.* Their behavior is socially and/or personally inadequate, inappropriate, or even harmful. For this reason, some current writers, looking for a more accurate label, have used the phrase *nonpsychotic personality disturbances* (McCall, 1977) to describe them.

A second characteristic of many nonpsychotic personality disturbances is that they are lifelong traits and have no definite point of onset. The beginning of a neurotic or psychotic episode can frequently be pinpointed. But "character" disorders develop slowly and gradually, like normal traits and dispositions. Just as one person is friendly and generous from childhood, another may have a long history of suspiciousness or antisocial behavior. Also as a result of their being an integral part of personality, most of the disorders discussed

225

in this section are frequently more difficult to treat than most other psychological abnormalities.

PERSONALITY DISORDERS

The phrase **personality disorder** covers a good deal of mental health territory. We shall use it very much as suggested in the current DSM III to refer to a number of personality distortions or exaggerations. These disorders may be relatively benign, as in the case of an excessively withdrawn or dependent individual. Or they may be psychologically and socially quite dangerous, as in the case of the antisocial character.

Another difference among the personality disorders is that many, but not all, are **borderline adjustments.** Most people with difficult personalities are able to meet the usual demands of life, although they do so in a minimal way. That is, they go through school, work, and establish families—but their achievements are limited and precarious. They are too defensive, unstable, or egotistical to cope effectively with all the challenges of living.

When an individual with a personality disorder is threatened by unemployment, family conflict, or any other stress, the borderline adjustment patterns are very likely to fail. The schizoid personality may become schizophrenic and the labile individual depressed or otherwise affectively disturbed. In other words, *personality disorders can indicate a heightened vulnerability to mental disorder.*

We will first briefly summarize the more common disorders and then consider the antisocial personality in detail.

PARANOID PERSONALITY: A personality characterized by suspiciousness, envy, and a tendency to blame others. Such people are usually mistrustful, rigid, and demanding and get along poorly with family and friends.

SCHIZOID PERSONALITY: The schizoid is typified by detachment, isolation, and apparent lack of interest in other people. Although schizoid individuals are *not* psychotic, they may be inclined to daydream and fantasize.

COMPULSIVE PERSONALITY: Compulsives are inhibited, conforming, and overly conscientious. They are very concerned with being correct and acting appropriately and find it difficult to relax.

HISTRIONIC PERSONALITY: This behavior pattern is characterized by self-dramatization. Such people tend to be vain, seductive, and attention-seeking, exaggerating their feelings and emotions to impress others.

NARCISSISTIC PERSONALITY: A personality characterized by excessive self-concern, egotism, and selfishness. These people often pay close attention to their own feelings and can be highly critical of the behavior of others.

DEPENDENT PERSONALITY: A personality marked by excessive reliance on others. These individuals are lacking in resourcefulness and judgment and become dependent on others to make decisions, point out directions, and be generally supportive.

AVOIDANT PERSONALITY: People who are evasive and fail to face challenge are called avoidant. Instead of coping with problems, they rationalize, overlook, turn away, or use any number of other intellectual or behaviorally defensive strategies.

LABILE PERSONALITY: This behavior pattern is marked by unstable, varying, and somewhat exaggerated emotions. Although *not* manic-depressive, these individuals unpredictably fluctuate between periods when they are relatively happy and enthusiastic and times when they are dejected and feel useless.

AGGRESSIVE PERSONALITY: People in this category are forceful, demanding, and overly assertive. When their aggressiveness culminates in gross outbursts of rage, with physical and/or verbal assault, such people are said to have an *explosive personality.*

Causes and treatment

Because the traits marking personality disorders develop like normal characteristics, there has been no special research into causes. Like the normal personality, the disordered character probably evolves through some combination of biological, psychological, and social circumstances. Personality disorders are seldom treated. People who are labile, histrionic, and so on, and are *mislabeled* neurotic by their friends, are rarely motivated to get professional help. There is a danger, too, in insisting that all personality disorders need treatment. This threatens to make conformity to social standards an inordinately significant criterion for mental health, an error discussed earlier. But the scant attention paid to all the more minor personality disorders is more than compensated by the effort that has been expended to understand antisocial individuals.

THE ANTISOCIAL PERSONALITY

The antisocial personality, also called a **sociopath,** or **psychopath,** has been recognized at least as long as the specialty of psychiatry itself. Two hundred years ago Phillipe Pinel called it *manie sans delire,* an insanity without the symptoms of madness. Pinel believed that psychopaths' total lack of concern for others marked them as insane, yet they showed none of the traditional signs of mental disorder. The antisocial personality was, and still is, callous, untruthful, and irresponsible, but also fully oriented and emotionally relevant and appropriate.

The number of sociopaths is not large; they probably constitute less than 1 percent of the total population (Cleckley, 1976). But they more than make up for their small number by the amount of disruption and distress they inflict on other people. Antisocial personalities seem incapable of feeling any loyalty or affection for anyone or anything. They are apparently lacking in remorse or conscience and tend to be impulsive and almost fearless. Their primary motives seem to be to seek pleasure or excitement, to do whatever is necessary to stimulate and reward themselves. As a result of these traits, psychopaths are very often in trouble with their friends and family or with the law.

The antisocial personality may or may not be violent. Those from a violent family and cultural background tend to be fairly aggressive and assaultive. Their behavior is most likely to be criminal and involve physical attack as well as weapons. Others from "gentler" socioeconomic circumstances tend to limit their activities to white collar crimes.

Antisocial people have been a puzzle for psychiatry and the social sciences for a long time. To begin with, they seem almost totally immune to treatment or even severe punishment. That is, even when they appear to be benefiting from psychotherapy they may actually be fooling the doctor. While seemingly making great progress, they continue to steal, sell drugs, or the like. Or despite the fact that they have spent numerous difficult years in prison, they return to crime the moment after discharge. Equally confusing is the fact that many, but not all, psychopathic individuals can *seem* so friendly, intelligent, and sincere. They readily impress others with their veneer of good nature and kindness. They seem so insightful, so understanding, and quickly win the confidence of social workers, the court, and other officials. They talk about their own disordered home lives and claim that discrimination, fear, and poverty gave them no alternative but to turn to crime. They assert how deeply sorry they are for all the misery they have caused and vow that this or that religious faith or method of therapy has enabled them to see the light. Prison records are filled with instances of antisocial personalities that seemed to have been totally changed. Not till after they were discharged and quickly resumed their antisocial activities was it apparent that their "conversion" was nothing more than a clever psychopathic manipulation.

The following are two excerpts from the case histories of antisocial personalities. The first is a more typical instance of a violent criminal; and the second is a white collar criminal.

Al is 34 and has spent a total of fourteen years in prison, beginning when he was 15 years old. He is a tall, neatly dressed, nice-looking individual who seems intelligent and friendly. He has been arrested nine times for offenses including selling narcotics, breaking and entering, sexual molestation, armed robbery, and manslaughter. Al has always managed to obtain light sentences or speedy paroles since he impresses people with his truthfulness and innocence or with the depth of his remorse. He frequently brings up his past as the product of a broken home, inadequate schooling and housing as the causes of his crimes. His last offense, shooting a police officer, was presented as a case of self-defense. Al argued that he was poor, jobless, and had found the pistol, which he was about to turn in to the police. He also claimed he was being harassed by the officer because "they won't give an ex-con a decent break." To his counselor, however, Al confidentially admitted that, as was the case for many of his other crimes, he shot the officer for the thrill and excitement.

Dr. K is a 53-year-old physician who was relieved of his license to practice because he was found billing state agencies for hundreds of thousands of dollars for medical services never performed. An investigation into his background brought out a number of facts: He had been suspended from medical school for stealing copies of examinations but had apparently been readmitted because of family connections. He had previously been investigated for administering hormonal extracts from goat glands supposedly because they restored youth. For many years Dr. K, though not a surgical specialist, had been known as the "appendix doctor." Over the course of seventeen years he persuaded thousands of patients to have their appendixes removed needlessly at exhorbitant fees. Most recently he was found to have made up imaginary patients and treatments and submitted claim forms for payment.

The state attorneys attempted to send Dr. K to prison. They were unsuccessful largely because Dr. K is a distinguished-looking man who won the sympathy of the jury. He and his attorneys convinced the jurors that Dr. K was a dedicated physician, totally immersed in

medicine. He had paid no attention to billing, which had resulted in many unfortunate mistakes.

Even though antisocial people are little concerned about law or ethics, their orientation does not always culminate in violent or white-collar crime. Sociopathic qualities appear in varying degrees. There are many people who are callous, self-interested, and unmoved by moral considerations. But they are not so extremely antisocial that they become criminal. Instead, they are likely to be exploitative, manipulative, and Machiavellian; they try to get away with as much as they can, short of actual illegal activities. Often such people seem to be faithful workers and manage to ingratiate themselves so that they rise to positions of political or administrative power. At other times they unscrupulously take advantage of friendship in order to gain some financial, sexual, or personal advantage.

Before describing the causes of antisocial behavior it is important to distinguish a similar yet different individual, the **dyssocial personality.** The dyssocial person is intellectually and emotionally normal, but he or she has *learned* a criminal life style. Such people have grown up with friends or parents who view illegal activity simply as another way of earning a living. Unlike psychopaths, they are sympathetic and loyal and can be fearful or loving just like any other normal human being. Many have families, raise children, attend church, and aside from their extralegal vocation are conventional members of the community.

Dyssocial criminals may use weapons and be dangerous, but most tend to be prostitutes, professional burglars, pickpockets, swindlers, or other nonviolent and skilled criminals. Many are also connected with organized criminal groups. Overall, however, despite entertainment media portrayals to the contrary, dyssocial and organized criminal activities play only a relatively small part in the overall American crime problem (Sagarin, Montanino, 1977; Sutherland, Cressey, 1974).

Causes

BIOLOGICAL EXPLANATIONS Since biblical times, the notion has been popular that some people are born evil, without feelings of conscience and disposed toward antisocial behavior. In the eighteenth century the phrenologists proposed that antisocial personalities were the result of the underdevelopment of the moral faculties of the brain. Contemporary hypotheses with a similar focus have postulated electrochemical differences between normal and psychopathic brains. EEG tracings in psychopaths seem to indicate the presence of unusual slow wave activity, a finding much more typical for children than for adults. This brain-wave "immaturity," some believe, prevents psychopaths from learning normal fear responses. The result is an apparent lack of self-control or remorse. Still other EEG research has shown a tendency for sociopaths to manifest a relatively high number of brief and sudden bursts of cortical activity called **positive spikes.** Such spikes, it has been postulated, could trigger uncontrolled, impulsive, and irresponsible acts.

It is quite possible that cortical abnormalities, whether due to heredity or early brain damage, may eventually account for both the apparent fearlessness and also the excitement-seeking behavior of antisocial people. At the moment, however, both slow waves and positive spikes are also found in normal people. Conversely, many psychopathic persons do not manifest either of these traits or any other discernible EEG abnormality. As a result, we are not yet able to explain psychopathic conduct in terms of the function or malfunction of the brain (Hare, 1976).

If the brain cannot explain psychopathy, then perhaps hormonal factors may be responsible. **Testosterone**, a male sex hormone, has been found to be related to aggressiveness in rats and chimpanzees. Animals given high testosterone doses typically become violent and domineering, often changing from a subservient role to become the leader of the pack. Among human beings, elevated testosterone has sometimes been found among psychopaths and criminals. Ehrenkranz et al. (1974), using precise radioimmunoassay techniques, found plasma testosterone concentrations significantly higher among imprisoned chronically aggressive males compared to felons who were relatively nonaggressive. These researchers hypothesize that high testosterone may lead to a strong physique and assertive behavior, which facilitates dominance, aggression, and disregard for others. But as with EEG activity, the evidence for a hormonal or biochemical explanation is not definitive. High concentrations of plasma testosterone are found in nonaggressive men, and many psychopaths do not have particularly elevated levels. Much more work needs to be done before the biochemistry of antisocial behavior is clear (Everett, 1977).

A different biological approach has concentrated on the genetics of psychopathy. For a while it was believed that sociopaths and criminals showed an XYY chromosomal abnormality. Every human cell is equipped with a chromosome pair that determines gender. Women have two female (X) chromosomes; males normally carry one female (X) and one male (Y) chromosome. Occasionally, however, male cells have been found to carry an extra male chromosome. Instead of the man being a normal XY, he is an XYY. This discovery was hailed as a breakthrough in the 1960s as investigators reported finding the XYY error as much as ten times as often in criminals. The hypothesis was that those men given a "double dose of masculinity" were more likely to be aggressive and rebel against convention. In addition to the logical deficiencies of this argument (maleness does not necessarily equal aggressiveness), subsequent research has not confirmed these ideas. Among violent criminals, the XYY pattern is actually found in less than one in every fifty, and normal men too may have an XYY chromosomal pattern (Jarvik and Klodin, 1976).

Another line of genetic research has tried to show that antisocial traits are directly transmitted. Twin studies conducted over the last several decades have hinted that perhaps psychopathy is more likely to be shared by identical than fraternal twins. These experiments have been based on very small numbers and have not controlled for the fact that the environment of identicals is far more similar than that of fraternals. More promising leads have come from adoption research. Crowe (1974), for example, followed the offspring of women criminal offenders given up for adoption during infancy. He reasoned that since several of the mothers and/or fathers were psychopathic, if their children manifested similar antisocial attributes genetics might well be held responsible. The children of the offenders were matched with normal youngsters and their behavior compared eighteen years later. According to Crowe, the offenders' offspring, though separated from their biological antisocial parents, showed a higher rate of sociopathic activity than the normal group. Perhaps at this point there is some possibility that biological factors, some of which could be hereditary, might partially account for antisocial personality disorders.

Figure 11.1. Instead of enjoying a warm paternal relationship, the antisocial personality frequently comes from a disordered family with fathers and/or mothers who have served as psychopathic models. (Photo: Scribe)

FAMILY EXPLANATIONS   Broken homes, parental neglect, abuse, and lack of proper emotional and physical care have all been held responsible for antisocial personalities. The data are incomplete and the correlations weak, but some of the more suggestive findings are summarized below (Cleckley, 1976; Hare, 1976). Antisocial personalities often seem to emerge from background characterized by:

A father who exhibits antisocial trends
Discipline which was markedly inconsistent or totally absent
Lack of parental affection and frequent violent punishment
Institutionalization during childhood, or youth characterized by other social and psychological deprivation and isolation

In addition to these findings, sociopathic individuals often have a revealing childhood. Based on decades of careful investigation with over 600 clinic cases, Robbins (1966) found the most likely candidate for a later diagnosis of antisocial personality is a boy with a history of truancy, staying out late, rebelliousness, lying, irresponsibility, sexual aggressiveness, assertiveness, and theft.

We need to caution again that the correlation between the development of antisocial character and family background is imperfect. Very many children emerge relatively intact from apparently unwholesome and inadequate circumstances (Jackson, 1976).

PSYCHODYNAMIC EXPLANATIONS   Classical Freudian theorists argue that the antisocial personality has an underdeveloped superego. Supposedly the superego matures as the child identifies with and internalizes parental values. The child who is abused or unloved rejects the parents and refuses their values, and by extension all social rules. Such a person grows up with a stunted superego, a conscience that is unable to discriminate right from wrong (Freud, 1959).

Current psychodynamic theorists argue that psychopaths may be deficient in their ability to perceive and experience emotion. This could be the result of a constitutional defect, but it may also evolve as a protective mechanism against overwhelmingly difficult parents or environmental circumstances. The child in an extremely hostile, punitive parental or institutional climate needs to *immunize* himself against fear, anxiety, and affection. In order to ensure his sanity, his very survival, he has to deaden himself, shut out all feelings and sensitivities. Hare (1976) has given some support to this view by reporting that psychopaths do seem to operate at low levels of arousal. In experimental investigations they appear much less avoidant of painful stimuli than normal subjects. But emotional immunization, deadening, also means that ordinary pleasures are not enough. To feel alive, the antisocial personality needs a much greater intensity of experience. As a result, the psychopath seems to become almost insatiably hungry for stimulation. Combine the two, emotional deadening and a constant need for intense arousal, and the final product could be the callous, thrill-seeking psychopath.

LEARNING EXPLANATIONS Hans Eysenck (1976) has proposed that antisocial personalities are constitutionally less capable of experiencing fear or anxiety; punishment or the threat of pain or imprisonment is simply not very frightening or effective as a deterrent. Several investigations seem to lend some support to this conclusion. In experimental situations in which electric shocks have been threatened or given, psychopathic volunteers have shown themselves to be far less reactive than normal subjects (Hare, 1976). The supposition is therefore that since antisocial people are not very fearful, they do not learn to suppress undesirable responses.

Social learning approaches have explained sociopathic behavior in terms of the parental role model. In a large number of instances, antisocial people come from homes where the father especially, and/or sometimes the mother, is directly criminal, violent, or otherwise displays antisocial traits. In such a family, children may be severely beaten—supposedly to teach them to "stay out of trouble." In reality, the punitive parent provides a model for the very behavior he or she is allegedly trying to suppress. Instead of making the

children more sociable, he or she is stimulating rebellion and aggressiveness.

Bandura (1973), an advocate of the social learning position, has also pointed out the role played by individual subcultures and the entertainment media. A child growing up in a culture that is aggressive and disdainful of law and ethical considerations is likely to adopt such values. Television and films also play a large part in teaching antisocial conduct. Literally hundreds of careful studies show that for many people, the constant assault, exploitation, sadism, and murder presented as entertainment both deaden feeling and compassion and ignite antisocial impulses (Liebert et al., 1973).

Treatment

Since most antisocial personalities are not overtly criminal and their self-centered qualities may have culminated in personal, business, or political success, few psychopaths voluntarily seek treatment. Psychotherapy is also complicated by at least two other obstacles. Nearly all antisocial people are comfortable with themselves; they like the way they are. Neurotic and psychotic patients want help to relieve their misery. Psychopathic patients may have been "caught" and object to their punishment, but they feel little anxiety. Fear and similar stressful emotions are excellent motivators for therapy, but antisocial personalities seldom have such feelings. A second obstacle to therapy is that most antisocial personalities who come to the attention of psychiatrists and psychologists are in conflict with the law and have been persuaded or forced into treatment. They are unwilling patients and view therapy as punishment. Superficially they may comply with the treatment procedure, and they may even delude their own therapist into thinking they have made progress. But all clients forced into psychotherapy, whether antisocial personalities or not, are likely to be difficult and resistant.

MEDICAL THERAPIES Medical treatment procedures, drugs, and even surgery have been attempted with antisocial personalites, but there is little reported consistent success. Occasionally when antisocial behavior is traceable to a brain lesion or other organic syndrome, medication may be helpful. Otherwise, currently available drugs have not proved useful.

PSYCHODYNAMIC THERAPIES Psychodynamic approaches, given all the obstacles involved in the treatment of psychotherapy, have also not been very successful. But there are some exceptions for both young and older antisocial individuals. Children who are 12, 13, and 14 may just be beginning to solidify antisocial behavior patterns and may respond to appropriate psychotherapeutic efforts. Older psychopathic individuals, those in their later thirties, tend to "burn out." Antisocial tendencies seem to diminish with age, so that people who resist therapy in their twenties may react more positively when they are 40.

Occasionally a very skilled and patient psychotherapist reports a measure of success with seemingly hardened antisocial individuals. By being willing to battle with rationalizations and manipulations, such professionals are sometimes able to reach "core" feelings that are amenable to change. Another approach has been taken by transactional analysts, who try to point out to the antisocial person that his or her behavior is self-defeating. Many TA therapists have worked well with prisoners by showing them their life style results in deprivation, in not getting what they want (Kovel, 1976).

BEHAVIOR THERAPY Behavioral approaches have sometimes resulted in more optimistic reports of the treatability of psychopathy. Some learning therapists have limited themselves to teaching specific skills using various reinforcement procedures. Antisocial personalities have reportedly been taught to attend more fully to the needs of others and to use verbal arguments rather than physical aggression to settle differences. More comprehensive efforts have also been made to modify family interactions by teaching parents to use reinforcement rather than punishment to motivate their children. A promising approach in this direction is a technique called **behavior contracting,** a means of formally scheduling the exchange of reinforcements between two or more people.

One way in which behavioral contracting may work was reported by Stuart and Tripodi (1973). They selected 79 delinquent youths, many of whom seemed psychopathic. The children and families were patiently taught to keep records and revise their life styles to minimize violence and aggression. Clear-cut contractual arrangements such as the following were made:

Condition	Reinforcement
Child is 20 minutes late	Must come in half-hour earlier following day
Child completes school work successfully	Two hours added to recreational period

After the contract period, the children in the investigation were compared with others who were similar but not in treatment. Although the contract period lasted only a few months at most, it succeeded in bringing about some favorable alterations in family interactions, and better school attendance and grades. Contracting procedures have also been tried with prisoners, with privileges being exchanged for socially responsible behavior. Although such learning therapy procedures often seem to work well in institutions, the evidence is that there is little carryover. Once antisocial prisoners are released, most seem to revert to their old patterns (Hersen and Eisler, 1977).

It is important to note that while many people oppose behavioral treatment in general, its use in prisons has proved particularly controversial. It is argued that inmates rewarded with tokens or other reinforcers for following orders or promised sentence reductions for participating in medical or psychological treatments are actually under duress. Under such circumstances, prisoners have been subjected to electric shocks for wrong answers or been given hormones and other chemicals to alleviate antisocial behavior. Those who object to such procedures state that learning therapy is authoritarian and inhumane, since prisoners volunteer only because their liberty is at stake. It is also claimed that since behavior modification usually does not really reform felons, such procedures simply use prisoners as guinea pigs. Those in favor of behavioral treatment in prisons say their methods have already accomplished more than the usual dynamic psychotherapies. Others hold that prisoners have caused serious harm to others and society; if they are made uncomfortable by some learning methods, it is part of the price they have to pay for rehabilitation.

THE CRIMINAL PERSONALITY

Even though criminal behavior is not necessarily a sign of mental disorder, the immensity of the problem has demanded the help of mental health professionals. The United States has the highest crime rate of all the advanced industrialized nations of the world. Each year there are 9 million burglaries, 4 million assaults, 175,000 rapes, and over 20,000 homicides. In terms of victims, this means that if present rates continue, over a lifetime a man has one chance in a hundred of being murdered and a woman one chance in twenty of being raped (Galliher and McCartney, 1977).

Some criminal behavior is found with greater frequency in crowded cities and among some ethnic groups, but it is also increasingly seen among all members of society. Juveniles, people under 18, continue to contribute a disproportionate amount of felony, accounting for half of all serious crimes. In fact, for several years one out of every fifteen juveniles has had an arrest record. The victims of criminals, despite popular misconceptions, tend to be from the *same* ethnic and economic background. Simply put, poor people are usually robbed by other poor people, the victims of black violence are usually other black persons, and homicide is committed by people who know each other. Nearly two-thirds of all murders occur among spouses, friends, or relatives.

Criminal behavior is the outcome of a multiplicity of causes including, poverty, frustration, alienation, faulty parental or environmental models, opportunity, the inducements to violence offered by the entertainment media, the availability of weapons, and the likelihood that criminals will either not be caught or seriously punished. Only a small number of criminals, less than 5 percent, are motivated by psychotic, neurotic, or other mental disturbances. But antisocial personalities contribute a good deal to the crime rate, with most estimates suggesting that about a third of all violators are psychopathic. Dyssocial personalities may account for an additional 5 to 10 percent of all criminals.

Most criminals are neither apprehended or jailed. Of those who are incarcerated, the great majority are repeaters. The **recidivism** rate for robbery, rape, and assault is 75 percent and for murder it is over 60 percent. Given the extremely high crime rate and the failure of many present techniques, mental health professionals and other social scientists have called for major reforms in the criminal justice system. Such recommendations include these:

Figure 11.2. The United States has the highest crime rate of all industrially advanced nations. Each year there are 5.5 million arrests and almost three times as many reported crimes. (Photo: Bob Haines/Kingston Freeman)

1. Trained and skilled police and legal authorities should concentrate on violent crimes rather than expending effort on "victimless" offenses such as gambling, alcoholism, and marijuana.

2. There should be swift and fair trials and significant punishment; in particular, "plea bargaining"—willingly pleading guilty to a much lesser offense to speed the judicial process—should be eliminated.

3. Individualized prison sentences and rehabilitation efforts would ensure that an inmate is not only punished for his behavior but also learns skills which will enable him to become a contributing member of society.

4. There should be psychotherapy for eligible prisoners including medical, psychodynamic, and behavior therapies.

5. Work plans where prisoners earn money to repay their victims and can also accumulate privileges such as conjugal visits, furloughs, and the like should be established.

6. There should be social reform to correct some of the causes of crime, such as unemployment, violence in the entertainment media, and pathological family interactions.

The crime problem in the United States is onerous and complex, and no single or easy solution is available in a democratic society that values personal freedom and liberty. Significant progress will probably be made only when mental health professionals and other scientists, political leaders, police, and legal authorities work together step by step to address the causes of crime and devise effective procedures (Department of Justice, Law Enforcement Assistance Administration, 1973, 1978; Lipton and Wilks, 1975; Lunde, 1976; National Institute of Mental Health, 1973, 1978; Sagarin and Montanino, 1977; Sutherland and Cressey, 1974).

COMPULSIVE GAMBLING

According to the Survey Research Center of the University of Michigan, two-thirds of adult Americans identify themselves as at least occasional bettors. These 100 million people have

Figure 11.3. The occasional poker player limits his bets to a dime or a quarter. In contrast, the compulsive gambler is addicted and has little control over how much he risks. (Photo: Scribe)

available lotteries, horse racing, card games, and numerous other legal ways of risking money in almost every part of the United States. But it matters little whether or not an area has legal gambling, for every city and town has illicit numbers games, sports betting, and dice games for any person wanting to play. For most bettors gambling is an entertainment, a mildly exciting pastime. But it is estimated that for 1 to 2 million men and for a few hundred thousand women, gambling is a compulsive, pathological addiction (Eadington, 1976; *Time Magazine,* December 6, 1976).

Compulsive, addicted, or pathological gamblers (the terms are used interchangeably) are described here because many are, or are similar to, antisocial personalities. They seem to resist convention, have few if any allegiances, and seek excitement. They feel "alive" when they are playing and find ordinary routines or commitments boring. In some ways too, gamblers are like drug addicts; they are hooked and almost driven to satisfy their craving. On the other hand, some gamblers appear to be essentially normal people who for any number of environmental or psychological reasons have become involved in a life style that perpetuates itself. They want to stop but, surrounded by gambling companions, temptations, debts, and the promise of winning the big one, find it difficult to break out of the vicious cycle that has become their daily existence (Kolb, 1978).

Addicted gamblers usually begin fairly early, during adolescence. They have periods when they stop, but during their adult years gambling more and more dominates their lives. Eventually many steal, cheat, embezzle, or use other illegal means to raise money to pay off exorbitant debts to loan sharks, or place huge bets in order to try to recoup losses. In one of the few actual research studies of compulsive gamblers, Livingston (1974) described his sample as rebellious, impatient with ordinary jobs or entertainment, and heavily motivated to seek excitement and impress others. At the same time, also like the classic psychopathic character, several of the subjects were outwardly friendly, sociable, and well rationalized. They knew how to present themselves in the best light and could manipulate the feelings and opinions of others.

Not all pathologically addicted gamblers are antisocial and not all risk their money on cards or dice. Compulsive gamblers may be fairly affluent and "play" the stock or commodities markets or have other expensive tastes. Most often, however, gamblers are from middle-class or more modest socioeconomic backgrounds, as this case illustrates.

Where I grew up, you played the numbers just like you bought milk every day. You went to the man, you told your number, three digits. That night you looked in the paper for the last three numbers of that day's total on the stock market. If you hit you got paid off three hundred to one. You bet a half and you win maybe $150. . . . I started playing heavy when I was 15. I started to play dollars and five dollars. . . . I wanted money and I wanted it bad and quick. . . . It was hope, you know. A way out . . . clothes, good things. . . . After I got married I cut down. I love Joyce. I didn't want to hurt her. . . . Then I started again . . . big, this time. I was losing much more than winning, naturally, any gambler knows that. . . . When I was really heavy into it I was betting

maybe a thousand a week, cards, numbers, OTB. Wherever the action was. My wife and I were making four hundred a week and the rest was borrowing, or winnings. . . . I felt bad . . . I hated myself . . . I kept promising Joyce . . . I couldn't stop. I was waiting for the big payoff. . . . After a year I was forty thousand in the hole. I had to split. Flee for my life. . . . There was no way me and Joyce could make that back and I won't steal. I am a compulsive gambler but I am not a thief.

The psychodynamic view frequently depicts compulsive gamblers as masochistic individuals determined to punish themselves, or symbolically aggressing against their families. Learning explanations center about the concept of partial reinforcement. Any behavior, whether it is a rat pushing a food-release lever or a person playing a slot machine, persists if it is reinforced. But if the behavior is reinforced only once in a while, if the food is delivered or the slot machine "pays off" only after a *variable* number of attempts, the behavior is far more likely to continue. Gambling is a variable reinforcement situation and thus highly persistent. In personal terms, it does not matter that you keep on losing; the fact that you win once in a while powerfully prompts you to keep going.

Of all the addictive behaviors, gambling is still least investigated or understood. Research into causes and treatment attempts are minimal, although the condition is being increasingly recognized as a psychological disorder. Gamblers Anonymous, modeled after AA, has reported some modest success, but like AA it too seems to reach only a very small number of gamblers already motivated to change (Eadington, 1976).

SEXUAL ABERRATIONS

A generation ago, nearly all sexual behavior outside proper marital intercourse was likely to be considered deviant. Today, when many different sexual life styles are recognized, the label deviance, or **paraphilia,** according to DSM-III, is for the most part limited to behav-

Many antisocial personalities, lacking feelings of conscience and undeterred by punishment, commit serious crimes. Some rapists and exhibitionists come from such disordered backgrounds that they are almost unable to develop normal sexual behaviors. Occasionally homicide is the outcome of delusional or hallucinatory thinking. Should all these people be held legally accountable for their conduct?

In 1843 in England Daniel McNaghten committed homicide believing he was commanded by the voice of God. After much debate, the English courts established a precedent by ruling that McNaghten was suffering from a mental disease, a defect of reason such that he could not distinguish right from wrong. The McNaghten Rule was amplified in the last decade by the recommendations of the American Law Institute (ALI): A person is not responsible for criminal conduct if such actions are the result of mental disease that substantially impairs the capacity to understand and conform to the law.

Despite repeated judicial attempts at clarification, in nearly every case psychiatrists and psychologists disagree. One testifies the accused is, or was, mentally deranged and not responsible; another contends that the person on trial is perfectly capable of making valid decisions. Although lawyers and expert witnesses argue in terms of whether the accused is or is not mentally ill, there is a more fundamental question. *Should a diagnosis of antisocial personality, sexual deviation, schizophrenia or any other mental condition defined in the DSM excuse illegal, criminal behavior? No:*

Many mental health and legal professionals argue that with rare exceptions, criminals, including murderers who are clearly psychotic, nevertheless know their act is wrong. In 1977, for instance, New York City was terrorized by a gunman who over the course of a year killed several young women. Though he hallucinated being ordered to carry out the homicides through someone called "Sam" and was diag-

ior that is nonconsensual and possibly harmful. Some deviations such as voyeurism are perhaps only mildly injurious; others such as rape can be traumatic. It should also be noted that sexual deviations may accompany other serious mental disorders. Some schizophrenic patients, for example, may also be sexually exhibitionistic. In such instances, these people are properly diagnosed and treated for schizophrenia; the exhibitionism is only a secondary symptom of the underlying psychoses. In this section we will deal with **primary sexual deviations**—that is, deviations in sexual interest, outlet, or object in an otherwise "normal" personality.

Exhibitionism

Exhibitionists are almost always men, usually in their thirties or older, and are the most common type of sexual offender. Chances are that sooner or later most women will have an encounter with an exhibitionist, a "flasher"

who quickly displays his penis, perhaps makes some sexual comment or gesture, and then flees. A few exhibitionists are psychotic, mentally retarded, or antisocial personalities. The great majority, however, are ordinary people without major psychiatric problems except that they are sexually quite inhibited and passive. They tend to come from puritanical backgrounds, feel great guilt about sexual needs, and though often married have difficult sexual relationships with their wives. Most are actually shy and harmless. (Bullough, 1976; McCreary, 1975).

John L sat in his parked car near a girls' high school. He exhibited his penis and made masturbatory motions as girls walked by. Like most exhibitionists, he waited for a shock reaction, a startled scream, from his victims. . . . After his arrest John was found to be a clergyman, 42 years old, married, and the father of three children. He admitted to almost fifteen years of exhibitionism and expressed his relief

nosed paranoid schizophrenic, he still knew his acts were wrong. He described, for instance, how he ran from the scene of every crime and took other precautions not to be caught. Thomas Szasz is especially critical of the "excuse" of insanity. He has written that formerly Americans charged with murder were considered innocent until proved guilty; "now they are considered insane until proven sane." He also has little use for psychiatric testimony, calling it "mendacity masquerading as medicine" (Szasz, 1974, p. 44). In short, critics of the insanity plea contend that a case can be made for any criminal being rationally or emotionally defective, thereby automatically excusing everyone from every wrongdoing. Every person should receive a fair trial and be judged guilty or innocent based on evidence and not on emotions, thinking, background, or personality.

Yes:

Those upholding the view that a mental condition may excuse personal responsibility assert that often behavior is not a matter of choice. Isenberg (1975) says that acts motivated by neurosis or psychosis may be "compulsively performed" against the person's "will." A hallucinated psychotic, for example, may be driven by what lawyers call an *irresistible impulse* to act. Similarly, a child who has grown up with nothing but deviant models may not understand conventional rules. The case is cited of a 17-year-old boy who was arrested for burglarizing a bakery. He was ill-fed and undereducated, the product of a broken home and a socioeconomic environment where struggle and violence were the daily fare. Are we to blame a child for stealing when callous, negligent, and discriminatory social attitudes have never given him a fair chance to learn appropriate conduct? People cannot be blamed for what they cannot help (Floud, 1975).

---

at finally being caught so that his guilty torment would end. In therapy he revealed a sexually inhibited and punitive background that made it almost impossible for him to have satisfactory relations with his wife. Attempts at intercourse were few and often failed. John recognized that displaying his penis was in a sense an assertion of his masculine capability, a demonstration that he was, after all, a real man.

Voyeurism

The "peeping Tom" is usually a young male secretly watching a woman in bathroom or sexual activities. Most voyeurs are not satisfied by viewing a sexually explicit movie or topless dancer but require the intrusive risk of secret observation. A few voyeurs are also exhibitionists. Some, for example, tap on the window through which they have been secretly watching in order to have the victim see the voyeur masturbating. Voyeurs, like exhibitionists, are generally timid, sexually inadequate, and not violent (Bullough, 1976).

Fetishism

Fetishists are almost always adult males. They obtain pleasure by viewing, fondling, sniffing, biting, or otherwise manipulating an object or sometimes a part of the body. The fetishistic item may be obviously sex-related, such as a woman's scalp or pubic hair, panties, and brassieres or be such seemingly nonerotic materials as a rubber raincoat or tennis sneakers.

Most fetishists are sexually fearful and incompetent individuals who buy the item they desire in stores or from prostitutes. A few steal their objects from such places as public laundries. Rarest of all are the violent fetishists who attack a woman in order to cut off a lock of hair or tear a piece from a blouse (Lester, 1975).

Figure 11.4. The voyeur is not satisfied with pornographic pictures. He needs to feel the risk of secretly peeking at unsuspecting victims. (Photo: Scribe)

Erotomania

Strictly speaking, erotomania (also called de Clerambault's syndrome), a pathological preoccupation with sexual thoughts or fantasies, is usually thought of as a neurotic symptom. Increasingly, however, the term has been used to designate the false belief that a person of high status is one's lover. As such it is almost like a fetish, since sexuality is diverted by a substitute, a fantasy, instead of a personal interaction (Hollender and Callahan, 1975).

Erotomania may occur in adolescents or adults and in either sex but is primarily found among women. Such women, though not neurotic, often seem to have a history of social and adjustment difficulties and feel themselves to be unattractive. Typically the erotomania

develops slowly but is persistent. Eventually the false belief is shared with others and realistic-sounding details are manufactured so that the supposed love affair sounds very believable. Doctors, ministers, attorneys, and other relatively prestigious figures are frequently the target of the erotic fantasy.

Miss L.L., a senior, told her roommate that she was having an affair with her English professor. To lend credibility to her story, the student supplied details of the romance, including motels supposedly used under false names, parking spots, sexual techniques, and the like. In actuality, the only extra contact she had with the professor was several office visits to discuss her short stories, which occasionally resulted in the two of them drinking coffee together in the student lounge. One of the students to whom Miss L.L. told her story wrote an anonymous letter to the professor's wife including all the alleged details. The couple recognized the delusional quality of the "charges" and insisted Miss L.L. see a psychotherapist. After several weeks of treatment, Miss L.L. revealed that her stories were total fabrications.

Sadism and masochism

Sadists (after the French writer François de Sade, 1740–1814) obtain pleasure by inflicting pain on their partners. Masochists (after the Austrian novelist Leopold von Sacher-Masoch, 1836–1895) are gratified by being mistreated and abused. In their true form, both conditions may result in the serious, often criminal infliction of pain and are quite rare. But sadistic elements do appear with some frequency in rapists who brutally beat their victims.

In milder, consensual forms sadomasochism is a little more common, but may not really be considered a deviation. In this playacting variety, sometimes called "bondage and discipline," men and women enjoy being ordered about, chastised, and humiliated, or being the person who does the commandeering. Elaborate costuming frequently accompanies such activities and masochistic men often dress as women. Some prostitutes specialize

CAUTION—DEVIATION OR FUN AND GAMES

The person who intrusively exhibits his genitalia is an exhibitionist and the one who fixates on panties a fetishist. But these deviations should *not* be confused with the variety of ways in which healthy couples may stimulate each other. Some adults find it arousing to dress provocatively. Prior to intercourse the woman may wear black stockings or the man unbutton his shirt to show a hairy chest. Some couples fantasize sadism and masochism and playact tying each other up or spanking. There are many imaginative and even unusual activities that may precede and lead to intercourse. When such interactions are *voluntary* and *pleasurable* they are not considered sexual deviations.

in "humiliating" masochistic men and charge high fees for leading their clients around on a dog chain, urinating on them, or beating them with a whip (Lester, 1975).

Zoophilia

Zoophilia or bestiality is intercourse with animals and is rare today. Although such activity has usually been vigorously condemned by secular and religious law, in former times when most people lived on farms it was more frequent and often of no more significance than masturbation (Bullough, 1976).

Obscene communication disorders

The obscene phone caller or letter writer is, like an exhibitionist, intent on shocking the victim. Like exhibitionists too, nearly all are men and relatively timid. They need the anonymity of a telephone call or letter to express their sexual frustrations and fantasies. Obscene communications are extremely common and vary from the man who mutters obscenities or threats to the clever individual posing as an interviewer. One patient specialized in telephoning new mothers whose names he obtained from the newspapers. Posing as a health official, he made detailed inquiries about breast feeding, changes in vaginal size, and physical changes allegedly related to recent motherhood.

Pedophilia

Pedophilia is sexual desire for children. The need may be heterosexual or homosexual and may take any number of forms ranging from exhibitionism to rape. Many instances of pedophilia are limited to a few occasions with an adult friend or relative, typically male, fondling a child. When an uncle or a neighbor is discovered in such activity, psychological help is usually more appropriate than prosecution. There are also more dangerous pedophiliac persons who may entice and even abduct children in order to force sexual acts. While these latter may do very great harm and should be apprehended, sometimes an innocent man is charged on the basis of misunderstood affection or because of the fantasy of a child (Walters, 1975).

Incest

Intercourse between close family members is reported in the experience of about one in every hundred people. It is commonly limited to one or two episodes, but may also continue for years. Brothers and sisters, as part of experimenting with their own sexuality, are the most likely to have incestuous contact. Such relationships are rarely disclosed and most times not permanently damaging. Though much less frequent, father-daughter incest is more likely to be pathological, since such intercourse is usually compelled by the father. Mother-son incest is extremely rare. Parent-child incest is frequently associated with other adult pathology such as schizophrenia, alcoholism, or child abuse. It may also occur in seemingly adjusted families, where it seems related to the father's inability to establish a satisfactory sexual relationship with his wife or other adult partners (Jones, 1977).

When incest and other sexual crimes are

prosecuted, the word *sodomy* is frequently used. Sodomy is not a psychiatric phrase; it is a legal term referring to *any* sort of sexual contact, like homosexuality or mouth-genital intercourse, that may be considered a misdemeanor or felony in a particular jurisdiction.

Rape

Forcible rape occurs in prisons among men but is far more commonly directed against women. During the last decade the incidence has increased steadily; there are now an estimated 175,000 cases of rape annually. Unlike the stereotype, the victim is not necessarily an attractive woman but may be a child, aged, or otherwise not what is usually portrayed as sexually desirable (Brownmiller, 1975). Many rapists are armed with a knife or gun and threaten their victims' lives. A fourth or more of all rapes are carried out by two or more men together. In some cases, victim and rapist are acquainted. Although nearly all rapists are repeaters and are violent, frequently beating their victims as well as forcing sexual intercourse, homicide occurs in only about 1 or 2 percent of all attacks.

Rape is a violent assault—a crime that often leaves deep emotional and physical scars. Many women are afraid to tell others for fear they may be blamed. Often treatment by police and medical officials is insensitive and imposes additional stress or even suggests the victim is at fault. Helped to recognize these hazards by women's and mental health groups, many hospitals and police jurisdictions have set up special rape units staffed with women and trained professionals to help the victim readjust and get vital information about the attacker. Eventually, psychologically healthy women are able to overcome the trauma and put the incident in perspective so that it does not interfere with their social and sexual function. Women with preexisting emotional difficulties or victims of especially brutal crimes may need extensive psychiatric treatment.

Rapists may be any age, educated or unskilled, but the majority are married, in their twenties, and come from lower socioeconomic backgrounds. For many, violence has been a large part of their upbringing—they seldom got what they wanted without aggression and fighting. For such people rape is not so much a sexual act as it is an aggressive explosion, forcibly taking what is desired. Many of these rapists can also be described as antisocial personalities, people who have never experienced any of the affectional feelings ordinarily accompanying intercourse. Rapists who feel sexually incompetent and doubt their masculinity carry out sexual fantasies through assault. Such attackers sometimes make unusual demands and believe they can entice their victims to enjoy the trauma. They are often borderline psychotics whose behavior ranges from timid to frankly homicidal.

These brief descriptions by no means cover all the types of personalities who may be rapists. As a group, rapists are callous and erratic, but it is a mistake to believe they have a particular personality that can be typed, understood, and reasoned with. As a result, the advice in books and courses on how to dissuade a rapist is often not very useful and sometimes dangerous. Armed rapists are especially difficult to try to resist. Although it can be worthwhile to learn how to respond in a threatened rape situation, emphasis should also be placed on techniques and strategies intended to *avoid* the likelihood of assault (Hilberman, 1976; Lester, 1975; Ruff et al., 1976; Sutherland and Cressey, 1974; Wilson, 1977). A few of the rules formulated by the cooperative effort of a group of concerned women and the police resulted in the following recommendations:

1. Never hitchhike or pick up hitchhikers.
2. Never go with a bar "pickup" or other new acquaintance to his car or home or bring him to your home.
3. Do not open your door to a delivery man, repairman, and so on, unless you are completely certain of your safety.
4. If someone is following or annoying you, do not try to handle the situation alone, but seek help immediately.
5. Avoid entering elevators with any suspicious man or pair of men.
6. Do not falsely signal sexual interest or intent, even to acquaintances.

The causes of deviation

Explanations of sexual deviations depend to an extent on the specific behavior. The personality, background, and conduct of exhibitionists, for instance, are fairly different from those of rapists. But rather than elaborating possible causes for each, we have chosen to discuss them together. There are enough common roots for many of the sexual aberrations to justify such an approach.

It is important, too, to recall that sexual deviations may be *secondary* to other mental disorders. Many rapists are antisocial personalities. Mental retardation or even schizophrenia sometimes motivate voyeurism or exhibitionism. Heavy drinking is sometimes the stimulus for pedophilia or incest. In many instances, sexual deviation is the outcome of a more primary disorder that has made it difficult for the individual to understand and exercise normal restraints.

MEDICAL EXPLANATIONS A generation ago it was widely believed that deviants were oversexed. Castration or equivalent medical procedures were often suggested or carried out. Today it is recognized that rather than having an above-average libido, most deviant individuals are sexually inadequate. The most serious sexual offenders, rapists, seem not so much to be satisfying an intense sexual urge as an aggressive need. Recognizing the sexual incompetence of most offenders, medical researchers have shifted to exploring the biology of aggression.

A typical study investigating the biological causes of sexual deviation was carried out by Rada, Laws, and Kellner (1976). Using prisoners, they investigated the plasma testosterone (a male sex hormone) level in 52 rapists and 12 child molesters. Testosterone is correlated with aggressiveness in many animals, and it seemed reasonable to suspect that some human sexual deviants, particularly violent ones, might have higher concentrations. In this study, the rapists and molesters generally had the same hormone levels as matched controls. But when rapists were ranked according to the amount of aggression accompanying their attacks, the most violent were found to have significantly high concentrations of testosterone. It is possible, therefore, that rape, and by implication other extremely aggressive sexual deviations, might in some small measure be partly accounted for by biochemical factors.

PSYCHODYNAMIC EXPLANATIONS For psychoanalysts, much of the behavior of sexual deviants is symbolic. The brassiere fetishist is asking to be an infant again, to be nursed and mothered. The voyeur may be verifying the reality of his own existence by metaphorically watching his creation. The exhibitionist raised by a dominating mother and made to doubt his masculinity is vividly showing that he is a man.

Psychodynamic theorists also see defensive elements in a good deal of sexually deviant behavior. Salzman (1972) says that problems in interpersonal functioning involving intimacy or the capacity to love and trust "are always present" in deviants. The deviant is afraid or unable to establish a personal and satisfying relationship. Thus he defensively puts distance between himself and women. He secretly watches them or "falls in love" with

Figure 11.5. Animal studies such as with these monkeys suggest aggression is linked to testosterone. Human research, however, has not confirmed the role of biochemistry in criminal or sexual deviation. (Photo: Biology Department, State University of New York, New Paltz)

a remote object or treats them as things, objects to be used and discarded.

Still other psychodynamic views note the frequency with which sexual deviation is associated with puritanical sex-negative attitudes. Most sexual offenders come not from liberal or permissive homes, but from those in which sex was considered indecent, filthy, something to be hidden and ashamed of. Many were punished for normal curiosity and most were grossly uninformed of the ordinary facts of reproduction. These sexual offenders believe sex is disgusting and sinful and feel great guilt about their own biological drives. The end result is that they need to punish themselves and/or their partners. A good deal of sexually deviant behavior, particularly masochism, rape, sadism, and obscene phone calls, may be rooted in such negative and punitive attitudes (Beach, 1977; Lester, 1975).

LEARNING EXPLANATIONS   Many if not all sexual deviations seem to be extreme exaggerations of normal sexual behavior. There are, as an illustration, voyeuristic elements in every adult; the peeping Tom seems simply to have taken these impulses a few steps further. From the learning point of view, voyeurism, pedophilia, and other deviations may be explicable in terms of opportunity and reinforcement. The person lacking opportunities for ordinary sexual outlets may have deviant tendencies reinforced. In this way a person whose social awkwardness, guilt, or shyness make it difficult to establish an adult relationship leading to intercourse may stumble upon a child whom he is not afraid to manipulate.

Many of the sexual deviations may be explained as a result of classical or operant conditioning, generalization, and many of the other principles accounting for human learning. The following case illustrates how a fetish seems to have been learned. (For those who are psychodynamically inclined, it also lends itself to the hypotheses discussed previously. Note, for instance, the history of maternal neglect.)

I consider myself a lactation freak. . . . I trace it to when I was 7. My parents split and my mother, my sister, and me moved into the upper half of a house we rented. My sister slept in my mother's room and I had my own. My mother worked and we were alone most of the day. I missed her, but there was nothing I could do. Pretty soon I discovered that by standing on my dresser I could see our neighbors' bedroom and watch them. I saw them undressing a few times but it didn't interest me. Then once I saw her nursing. Sitting in a chair and putting the baby on one breast, then the other. . . . That was exciting. Her breasts looked so big . . . it seemed so pleasurable. I would sometimes see her in the afternoon, but mainly I caught her at night. It was very good. Then I think I forgot about that till I was 11 and our neighbor had given birth again and was nursing again. Now I watched her with real excitement. . . . I was also going over to their house to play with their son, he was younger than me but we had some fun. . . . I would see her, very big breasts, bulging out against her housedress. Sometimes you would see like a little moist spot on her dress. That was very exciting.

By this time I would masturbate when I was watching her nurse. I would come maybe two or three times. . . . I got especially fascinated by her bra. It was a nursing bra. You know you can keep it on but a flap lowers to expose the nipple. I would see how big her breasts were. They would strain against the bra. And the bra would be wet, you know, and smell milky and cheesy. About that time I started going to their bathroom and looking in the dirty laundry hamper. I would take her bra and I would smell it. And I would masturbate with it. Once I stole one. I was very scared but I kept it at home in a plastic bag. I would smell it and touch it for weeks, till it was impossibly dirty and ragged. . . . The highlight was once when I was over there she hugged me. I think I had brought her a drawing I made in school. I said it was for the baby's room. She hugged me to her breasts. I felt overwhelmed. I remember the softness and I felt they were wet and smelled of milk right through her dress. . . . I'm not sure this really did happen. Sometimes now I think I dreamt it when I was a kid, and came to believe it was real.

Anyway I'm hung up on nursing breasts and

bras wet and dirty with milk. . . . A few times I've peeked into houses where I knew there was a nursing mother. . . . I've gone through dirty laundry baskets in laundromats looking for soiled bras. They don't even have to be lactation bras. Just as long as they smell human, womanly. . . . I've put an ad in an underground newspaper for nursing mothers but it wasn't very real, or very exciting. . . . I'm married but my wife knows nothing. She's a prude anyway and we don't have much of a sex life. Or maybe I can't really get into it with her. . . .

As we have noted so often before, and as this case illustrates, sexual deviations may well be the outcome of a multiplicity of causes. Learning, psychodynamic, and medical explanations may all partly explain sexual deviation as they do other mental disorders.

Treatment

The traditional "treatment" for deviates, exhibitionists, rapists, voyeurs, and all others whose behavior violates sexual-social norms has been imprisonment. Although incarceration is still often necessary and appropriate, today medical and psychological treatment is also advocated. In fact, some deviates whose behavior is essentially harmless, such as fetishists, may be given a choice of avoiding imprisonment by electing psychotherapy.

The prognosis for sexual offenders varies from very good to poor. When the disorders are primary, exhibitionists and voyeurs have an excellent chance for recovery. Studies have shown that for many exhibitionists simply being arrested, without punishment or treatment, usually suffices to end the behavior. On the other hand, the success of treatment for sadists is questionable and rapists have a good likelihood of repeating their behavior. Many rapists are antisocial and are little deterred either by imprisonment or psychotherapy (Jones et al., 1977; Lester, 1975; Sagarin and Montanino, 1977; Walters, 1975).

The actual therapy for sexual offenses varies with the assumed causes. Many medically inclined practitioners still advocate castration or biochemical treatments. Rapists, pedophiles, and others have been given estrogens (female hormones) or anti-androgens to lower the level of their male sex hormones. Results are sometimes reported as encouraging, but there is question as to whether biochemistry, the associated imprisonment, the fear of treatment, or some other related factors are bringing about improvements (Bancroft et al., 1974).

Psychodynamic practitioners believe sexual deviations are only one of many related symptoms of personality insufficiency. For psychoanalysts, deviations are fixations at immature levels of psychosexual development. For Rogerians and transactional analysts, deviations demonstrate the client's inability to form adult, heterosexual relationships. As a result, psychodynamic treatment focuses on the patient's total adjustment. Through individual or group therapy, the person is helped to understand his motives, overcome defensive blocks, and grow into close, loving, and mature heterosexual interactions (Kovel, 1976).

In contrast to psychodynamic approaches behaviorists set considerations of motivation,

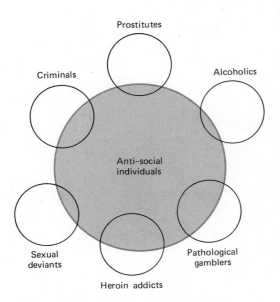

Figure 11.6. The antisocial personality. This diagram suggests the approximate proportion of antisocial individuals in several pathological life styles.

PORNOGRAPHY AND SEXUAL DEVIATION

Do sexually explicit motion pictures, magazines, and books cause sexual deviations? Are exhibitionists, voyeurs, rapists, and the like created or encouraged by such materials? The answer is not simple. It is possible that sexual entertainment which is distinctly violent may trigger aggressive attitudes. Just as violent television programs have been implicated in the growth of juvenile crime, the exploitative and disordered sexual models presented in films may incite similar behavior in some undersocialized young men, the group from whom most rapists are drawn (Goldstein et al., 1973; Liebert et al., 1973).

But most pornographic materials are not violent. They usually consist of pictures or descriptions of men and women engaged in varied types of sexual activities. A decade ago a special investigatory commission was appointed by the Congress and the President of the United States and directed to explore the effects of pornography. This group consisted of scientists, clergy, psychologists, attorneys, and many other professionals and distinguished citizens. They carefully sifted hundred of studies and other available evidence as well as conducting investigations on their own involving thousands of children and adults. After several years of concentrated effort, the group issued the *Report of the Commission on Obscenity and Pornography* (U.S. Government Printing Office, Washington D.C., 1970), in which it concluded:

> In sum, empirical research designed to clarify the question has found no evidence to date that exposure to explicit sexual materials plays a significant role in the causation of delinquent or criminal behavior among youth and adults. The Commission cannot conclude that exposure to erotic materials is a factor in the causation of sex crime or sex delinquency.

internal defenses, and conflicts aside. They are interested in the deviant behavior per se and ways of modifying it. The techniques used vary, but all center about unlearning deviant responses and replacing them with accepted heterosexual ones. A first step in many such programs is desensitization to the opposite sex. Many sexual deviants are afraid of or avoid women and thus have no opportunity to have heterosexual behavior reinforced. It becomes important to desensitize them, to teach them to minimize their heterosexual fear responses. Some therapists also teach their clients assertive behavior, how to be "normally" aggressive so that they will be able to make a sexual approach to members of the opposite sex.

Another step in many learning therapies is associating aversive stimuli such as electric shocks or nauseating medications with undesired behaviors. Fetishists may be shocked after presentation of their fetish object. Exhibitionists are allowed to exhibit but have aversive stimuli associated with their genital display. A sophisticated version of such treatment utilizes a penile plethysmograph. This is a narrow cuff or tubing placed under the head of the penis that gauges blood volume—that is, measures erection. Rigged with a plethysmograph, pedophiles may then be shown pictures of children in different stages of dress. If they become aroused, as measured by the plethysmograph, electric shocks may follow. When they no longer become erect, shock ceases. Such aversive procedures are controversial, especially since they sometimes result in only superficial success. A patient may "learn" not to have measurable penile erections but still be aroused by deviant stimuli (O'Leary and Wilson, 1975; Wickramasekera, 1976).

The success of both behavior and psychodynamic treatments is limited. Based on their likelihood of recovery with even minimal intervention, exhibitionists and the like make good patients. Rapists usually have only a fair prognosis, and not much more progress is likely to be made till a great deal more is learned in general about the nature of aggression and violence.

SUMMARY

People with personality disorders have a lifelong history of adjustive deficiency, although they are not psychotic. Under conditions of severe stress they may become schizophrenic or affectively or otherwise mentally disordered. The personality disorders are classified according to the most prominent trait as paranoid, schizoid, compulsive, histrionic, narcissistic, dependent, avoidant, labile, and aggressive. These conditions arise from the same combination of psychological and environmental circumstances giving rise to normal personalities and are seldom the focus of psychotherapy.

The antisocial personality has little respect for convention, is extremely self-centered, and seems to be without feelings of conscience or affection. Most are not directly criminal, but many are violent and make a considerable contribution to social disorder. Dyssocial personalities earn their living through illegal means but are otherwise normal. Antisocial behavior may be biologically explained, but it is more probable that parental abuse, faulty learning, deficient models, and other psychological fac-

tors account for it. Although attempts to devise medical and psychological treatments continue, antisocial individuals are usually very resistant to change.

The United States has the highest crime rate of all advanced nations. Antisocial personalities account for a substantial proportion, but other factors play a prominent role: poverty, the availability of weapons, the model provided by the entertainment media, and the likelihood that criminals will neither be caught nor punished. Effective strategies for combating crime need to address the causes as well as devise effective punishment and treatment.

Two million Americans are compulsive gamblers, addicted to games of chance to the point where many may bankrupt themselves or steal. Some pathological gamblers are antisocial, but most are ordinary citizens who have grown up in a family or environment that encourages gambling. Psychodynamic theorists may see gamblers as self-punitive; behavioral explanations emphasize the importance of variable reinforcement.

Sexual deviations are behaviors that are nonconsensual and often harmful to the victim. They include exhibitionism, voyeurism, fetishism, erotomania, sadism, masochism, obscene communication disorders, incest, and rape. Many deviants are fearful and sexually incompetent people who have unsatisfactory heterosexual relations. They come from all socioeconomic strata, though rapists tend to be poorly educated and from groups low in social status. Medical hypotheses suggest that sexual deviation may be explained biochemically, but psychodynamic theorists believe it to be the result of defective family interactions. Behaviorists explain deviation through classical or operant conditioning or other modes of learning. Treatment follows explanation, so that many medical practitioners continue to advocate hormone treatment. Psychodynamic practitioners use individual and group therapy, and behavior specialists make use of techniques like desensitization and aversive conditioning. The prognosis for most sexual deviations is good although some, like rape, are resistant to treatment.

12

Sexual Alternatives and Dysfunctions

In this chapter, we will discuss consensual sexual behavior that is considered unconventional. Though such behavior is voluntary and not forced, possibly no area within mental health is as controversial. For nearly two thousand years the Judeo-Christian tradition has insisted that sexual contact be restricted to men and women, within marriage. All other sexual behavior has been forbidden. The Old Testament is crystal clear: "If a man also lie with mankind, as he lieth with a woman, both of them have committed an abomination: they shall surely be put to death" (Leviticus: 20, 13). Thousands of years later, in the 1800s the otherwise perceptive French psychiatric pioneer Esquirol turned his attention to masturbation and helped propagate the myth that it caused insanity, TB, and mental retardation. In the 1920s Sigmund Freud called oral-genital contacts infantile perversions, unable to foresee that a generation later counselors would be recommending these techniques as therapy.

The condemnation of different forms of sexual behavior is not ancient history. In 1976 Pope Paul VI issued a 5000-word "Declaration on Certain Questions Concerning Sexual Ethics." Like similar rules within the Jewish and Protestant faiths, the Declaration strongly condemned homosexuality, masturbation, and pre- and extramarital sexuality as intrinsically wrong and disordered.

Alternate or unconventional sexual forms are also forbidden by many legal codes. Most nations around the world have laws prohibiting homosexuality and many types of voluntary heterosexual conduct. In the United States, the majority of states classify homosexuality, premarital intercourse, and the like as a misdeameanor or felony. About twenty states (including Connecticut, Ohio, Colorado, Oregon, and Hawaii) have passed "consenting adult" laws stating that private, voluntary sexual activities will not be prohibited or prosecuted. But thirty states still have punitive statutes, and instances of homosexuals being sent to prison are not unusual. Since many areas also have laws against oral-genital contact, people are occasionally punished for this as well. In a recent publicized case, a married couple took pictures of themselves, for their own amusement, during coitus. Inadvertently the pictures came to the attention of the authorities. Since the photos showed **cunnilingus** (mouth to vagina) and **fellatio** (mouth to penis), the couple was tried and sentenced to five years' imprisonment (Gagnon, 1977).

In this chapter we will look at alternative sexual behavior, such as homosexuality, transvestism, transsexualism, and other sexual styles, from the mental health point of view. We realize that sometimes what psychologists and psychiatrists may consider normal or healthy may be seen as disordered or illegal by other groups within society. While we and most professionals recognize the validity of conflicting viewpoints, it is important to stress the increasing acceptance of responsible adult sexual behavior, even if it is different. Our purpose here is not to make value judgments but to report what has been learned about alternate sexual behaviors.

In the second part of this chapter we will discuss dysfunctions, the inability to enjoy healthy and pleasurable sexual activities. Most, if not nearly all, instances of impotence, vaginismus, and other dysfunctions are the outcome of sexual anxiety, repression, and negative attitudes toward sex that have long characterized much of the history of the human race.

HOMOSEXUALITY

Homosexuality, physical sexual intimacy between members of the same sex, was considered a mental disorder and listed in every edition of the Diagnostic and Statistical Manual until recently. The latest DSM no longer includes homosexuality, and mental health professionals now believe it is not necessarily a mental disability. The change in the classification of homosexuality came about primarily for two reasons. First, the majority of adults have had at least some homosexual experience. Second, most people who are mainly or exclusively homosexual are not psychiatrically distinctive in any other way. The incidence of anxiety, personality disturbances, psychoses, and other abnormal symptoms are probably more or less the same for the homosexual as for the heterosexual community (Hooker, 1975; Weinberg and Williams, 1975).

The homosexual-heterosexual continuum

Two out of every three men and women have had at least some homosexual experience. For most, the contact will have been limited to one or two occasions during adolescence. Quite a few however, about a third, have had a homosexual partner after their teenage years. For very few, about 4 percent, erotic experiences are exclusively homosexual; heterosexual contacts have never been consummated or attempted. If we count sexual fantasies as legitimate expressions of interest, then homosexuality can be said to be universal. Nearly all men and women have imagined becoming sexually involved with members of their own gender. In fact, therapists are often confronted with patients who, unaware of the "normalcy" of homosexual fantasies, are extremely upset by them (Beach, 1977; Gagnon, 1977; Tripp, 1975). (Homosexual fantasies or attractions in persons who think of themselves as exclusively heterosexual often trigger a severe anxiety attack called a **homosexual panic.**)

The statistics we have reported say very clearly that homosexuality and heterosexuality are not qualitatively distinct. There is a *continuum* of sexual behavior, and whether the object of affection is a man or a woman seems to depend on many different environmental and personal circumstances. Given the usual social conditions, with considerable opportunity and encouragement for heterosexual behavior, people are significantly heterosexual. In situations where the opposite sex is absent, such as in boarding schools, prisons, and other gender-segregated institutions, the incidence of homosexuality is very high. Among long-term prisoners, for example, studies show that 80 percent may have homosexual relations. To confirm how much sexual activity is influenced by opportunity, Sagarin (1976) investigated male inmates. In most cases although homosexuality persisted throughout imprisonment, upon release nearly all men returned to heterosexual activities. Sagarin interpreted his findings as proof of the "malleability of human sexual orientations."

It will help our discussion to include the seven-point homosexual-heterosexual scale proposed by a pioneer sex researcher, Alfred Kinsey (1948, 1953) over three decades ago:

1. Exclusively heterosexual
2. Predominantly heterosexual—few and incidental homosexual experiences
3. Primarily heterosexual—several homosexual contacts
4. Almost equally heterosexual and homosexual
5. Primarily homosexual—several heterosexual experiences
6. Predominantly homosexual—few and incidental heterosexual contacts
7. Exclusively homosexual

The homosexual-heterosexual scale permits us to correct a number of erroneous beliefs about how people actually behave. Although it is hazardous to generalize, current data based on the work of Hite (1976), Kinsey (1948, 1953), Morin (1977), Tripp (1975), Weinberg and Williams (1975), and Wilson (1977) give a picture of behavior distinctly different from that portrayed by stereotypes.

Nearly 10 percent of married men and women secretly continue some homosexual activities ("closet" homosexuals).

Although some predominantly or exclusively homosexual adult men may be effeminate or women masculine, most are not particularly distinguishable from the rest of the population.

The obvious homosexual who dramatizes his (or her) same-sex preference with exaggerated "gay" mannerisms is usually an adolescent, and the flaunting behavior is a transitory phenomenon.

Homosexual men, considerably more so than women, may be very active during adolescence and the early adult years. "Cruising" to pick up other homosexual men in bars, movies, and other public places for quick liaisons or "one night stands" is not unusual. During later adulthood, however, there is increasing evidence that both men and women tend to settle into stable, long-term marriage-type relationships with a single partner.

Although some vocations have continued to

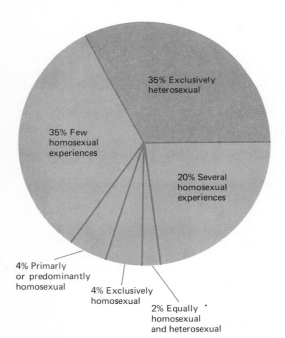

Figure 12.1. Adult sexual behaviors. Although precise figures are difficult to obtain, it is apparent that approximately two-thirds of adults have had at least some homosexual experience. The estimated frequencies are derived from careful research reported by Bullough, 1976; Gagnon, 1977; Hite, 1976; Kinsey et al., 1948, 1953; Tripp, 1975; Weinberg and Williams; 1975.

35% Exclusively heterosexual

35% Few homosexual experiences

20% Several homosexual experiences

4% Primarly or predominantly homosexual

4% Exclusively homosexual

2% Equally homosexual and heterosexual

attract homosexual people (hairdressing, restaurant operation, dance, and interior decorating), gay men and women are found at all social, educational, and occupational levels.

The evidence concerning psychiatric problems among homosexual people is incomplete. It is clear that the childhood or adolescent discovery of homosexual interests can be painful. Social disapproval and punishment of homosexuality often makes young people who are attracted to the same sex feel isolated, guilty, fearful, and depressed. In extreme instances such anxiety has even led to adolescent suicide.

During adulthood, after the homosexual man or woman has "come out"—that is, accepted his or her homosexuality—many continue to report less self-confident and satisfying lives, conditions probably due to social prejudices. Overall, however, in studies involving over a thousand subjects the incidence of serious psychiatric problems was about the same for homosexual as for heterosexual people.

The gay community

About 4 percent of the adult population are exclusively homosexual and another 6 percent have a significant amount of homosexual activity in their lives. This means that between 5 and 12 million Americans consider themselves to some extent homosexual. With such a huge population, and given the punitive and restrictive laws that sometimes send homosexual men to prison, it is not surprising that activist groups have become prominent. (Legal authorities typically overlook female homosexuality; lesbian women are very seldom arrested for homosexual activities even when they congregate in bars, dance together, or otherwise demonstrate their sexual preference.)

Beginning in the politically turbulent 1960s, a number of homosexual organizations campaigned for an end to legal restrictions. Largely through such pressure, as well as the help of other concerned groups and citizens, consenting adult laws are becoming increasingly common. But although such statutes "decriminalize" private, voluntary adult sexual contact, they do not prohibit job discrimination. In many areas homosexual individuals are barred by law from jobs as vastly different as barber or elementary school teacher, and they may even be denied housing and some government services. Much antihomosexual legislation is based on the notion that homosexual people cannot be trusted. As school teachers particularly, they are accused of seducing children or providing models for deviant behavior. The evidence, however, is that homosexual males are, if anything, less often child molesters than heterosexual men. This has caused some militant homosexual organizations to suggest that the safest thing for schoolchildren would be to bar heterosexuals from being elementary teachers (Beach, 1977; Tripp, 1975).

Since the number of gay people is in the millions, they are a sizable minority. Like other special interest or cultural groups, they have their own magazines, newspapers, resorts, housing areas, life styles, and entertainment. In any sizable town there are bars, baths, clubs, and social organizations for homosexual men and women. Because gay people often feel discriminated against and even feared by the "straight" world, these gathering places are thought of as "safe," as havens where homosexuals can relax.

Causes

PSYCHODYNAMIC EXPLANATIONS The "causes" of homosexuality are believed by many contemporary writers to be no different from those of heterosexuality. Both are considered meaningful life styles differing only in the sex chosen for intimacy and affection. For many psychoanalytic writers, however, homosexuality is still viewed as a neurotic aberration, as the outcome of having had a psychologically seductive mother. In more metaphorical terms, the child is said to have an unresolved Oedipal conflict. His wish is to possess his mother, a desire that ultimately results in "castration fear." The child is afraid that should he actually touch his mother, or by extension any woman, his jealous father will mutilate him (Alexander, 1975). Other psychodynamic theorists have emphasized the role of the father in homosexuality. The family that typically generates male homosexual behavior is believed to be characterized by a strong, domineering woman and a weak, passive father. The child identifies with his mother, even introjecting her sexual values—a desire for a strong, capable man. The father himself is so weak and ineffectual that the boy has little opportunity to learn masculine roles (Tripp, 1975).

Both hypotheses are based on research evidence that has shown some consistency for two decades. Since the 1960s, Bieber (1976) has evaluated the family background of male homosexual individuals. In some instances he relied on descriptions of patients furnished by psychoanalysts. In other cases the backgrounds of homosexual men were obtained by direct interviews or through neutral observations. Bieber concluded that a sizable proportion of homosexual men came from homes in which mothers were possessive and seductive and fathers were distant or cold. There was evidence too that boys who later became homosexual at least partly lived up to the stereotype of being less inclined toward rough and tumble play and other aggressive activity.

Lesbianism is little discussed by psychodynamic writers, possibly because of the social and masculine bias that has in general overlooked the sexuality of women. The few psychoanalytic references made to lesbianism are frequently variations on the theme of "penis envy." Women are believed to feel incomplete because they are denied a penis, and supposedly compensate by adopting the interests, habits, and sexual preferences of a man. A related sociological view contends that women who resist sex-stereotyping, refusing to limit themselves to being a housewife or secretary, overidentify with men. As executives they become more aggressive, as scientists more achievement-oriented, and in addition reject their feminine sexuality. There is little evidence to support either psychodynamic or soci-

ological conclusions (Katchadourian, 1974; Wilson, 1977).

What can we conclude about the family constellation affecting sexual orientation? The evidence is incomplete. Although the theory of the weak father and dominating mother has often been supported, homosexual males have been found to come from homes in which fathers played a very important role. In some instances, they have had the close, affectionate relationship supposedly so productive of heterosexual development. At this point it seems that the strong mother hypothesis may account for some proportion of male homosexuality. It may fit those men who are described as **heterophobic**—afraid of sexual relationships with women. Such men, rather than being stimulated to heterosexuality by their overattentive mothers, seem to become frightened of it. During adolescence and adulthood they limit their woman companions to those who are married, much older, or otherwise clearly sexually unavailable. The result may be that, like incarcerated prisoners, their only opportunities for sexual contact are with other men (Gagnon, 1977; Weinberg and Williams, 1975).

BIOLOGICAL EXPLANATIONS Homosexual behavior occurs among most mammals, particularly male members of the species. Occasionally a dog, bull, chimpanzee or other familiar animal seems even to prefer homosexual activities exclusively. The incidence of homosexuality may also be somewhat higher for human identical than for fraternal twins. These observations have led to speculation that homosexuality may have a biological cause. Since both male (androgens) and female (estrogens) sex hormones are present in men and women, perhaps some delicate imbalance leads to homosexuality. But though careful research has continued for several decades, consistent biochemical causes for adult homosexual or heterosexual behavior have not been found.

There is still one other biological possibility. Animal studies have shown that if androgen or estrogen levels are temporarily altered very early in life, later sexual activity and preference may be affected. Infant male rats provided with high estrogen concentrations, for example, develop distinctly feminine characteristics and behaviors. Since we cannot ethically interfere with the hormonal chemistry of children, evidence from human subjects has had to be indirect. At the present moment, the possibility remains open that differences in androgen-estrogen balance before puberty might have some critical effect on later sexual orientation (Beach, 1977; Sherfey, 1973; Tourney et al., 1975).

LEARNING EXPLANATIONS Learning explanations present a number of related possibilities. First, early homosexual experience is reported by most gay men and women. Contrary to social biases, in nearly all instances such experiences are voluntary and with like-aged companions. Seduction of an innocent youth by an experienced homosexual is as infrequent as heterosexual seduction. From the learning point of view, the positive reinforcement provided by early adolescent homosexual relations should lead to the continuation of this behavior. But in fact, less than 10 percent become predominantly homosexual. Further, some homosexual men and women have not had adolescent homosexual relations. Obviously something more than just a few adolescent adventures is necessary to produce homosexuality. What is likely is that early homosexual experiences become important determiners of a lifelong orientation when there is some preceding emotional, intellectual, or other psychological preference. This becomes very clear when we recall that most homosexual men and women also have heterosexual involvements during youth. Many report they found such contacts pleasing but felt most comfortable, "true" to themselves, in a homosexual relationship (Bullough, 1976; Jones et al., 1977).

Sex stereotyping may play a role in the learning of homosexual responses. Although rigid gender expectations are changing, many people still characterize interests and activities as either masculine or feminine. Football, beer, hunting, and fixing cars are believed masculine; cooking, reading, and gossiping supposedly are feminine. Evans (1969) inter-

viewed 43 homosexual men, and under the pretext of studying cardiovascular disease asked them detailed questions about their childhoods. He found that many were frail, fearful of fighting, seldom played baseball, and frequently played games with girls. Evans believed these "feminine" activities and later homosexuality were both the direct result of a domineering mother, a woman who fits the classic psychoanalytic picture. But an equally valid case can be made for an explanation in terms of sex-stereotyping.

The girl who likes to climb trees may be falsely labeled masculine and the boy who plays "house" erroneously called feminine because of the way many people ignorantly and rigidly classify behavior. Children consistently made to feel like a member of the opposite sex may themselves ultimately believe they should in fact be the other gender. *Self-identity comes in large part from the perception of others.* People who consistently treat a boy like a "sissy" or a girl like a "tomboy" in effect convince these children that they are, respectively, inordinately feminine or masculine. In societies less insistent on dogmatic gender distinctions, such as in many Pacific Island cultures, there is also a great deal less exclusive homosexual behavior (Warren, 1977).

In some homosexual histories, heterosexual attempts have been aversively conditioned. Experiences with the opposite sex were unrewarding, unpleasant, or even painful. Sometimes in early heterosexual contact a boy or girl becomes overwhelmed with anxiety and guilt and generalizes these feelings to all heterosexual encounters. Or first heterosexual attempts may be unsuccessful. The boy could be impotent and be ridiculed or the girl fearful of penetration and feel humiliated. In a few extreme instances, new sexual experiences can be traumatic, as in the case of an adolescent who is raped or forced into incestuous contact. All such negative events may aversively condition heterosexuality. Eventually such heterophobic people may find relations with their own sex or some deviant mode of expression positively reinforcing (Sherfey, 1973; Wilson, 1977).

Do we need to explain homosexuality?

Many of the groups (Mattachine Society, Gay Activist Alliance) that have worked to secure equal rights for homosexual people object to the search for an explanation of homosexuality. It is argued that homosexuality is very much a matter of personal inclination and is no more in need of an explanation than is the selection of a particular person for one's husband or wife. Discussing the causes of homosexuality sounds too much like probing for the causes of schizophrenia or some other mental illness.

In our view, homosexuality is not a mental or physical disease; it is a common and natural phenomenon found throughout the world. The United States and many other nations have been punitive toward homosexuality, but other countries, both technologically advanced and undeveloped, have neither punished homosexuality nor regarded it as a perversion. In many rural African societies homosexual men and women are accepted as ordinary members of the community. England, Denmark, and several other European nations long ago repealed legal and discriminatory restrictions.

It appears to us also that people are neither irreversibly nor basically homo- or heterosexual as much as they are fundamentally *sexual*. Although some biological variables may eventually be found to play a role in sexual orientation, learning is probably more critical. In short, we believe the causes of homosexuality can be described and so can the causes of heterosexuality. Given physiological and anatomical cues and coordinated psychosocial experiences, most people are fundamentally heterosexual. Given a similar biology and some slightly different experiences, many people develop interests in homosexual relationships. In parallel ways too, just as some homosexual behavior is the result of maladaptive family situations or adversive experiences, some heterosexuality may also be forced by psychologically unhealthy parental or environmental influences. Hetero- and homosexuality are acquired, and *both* in different degrees may be the outcome of relatively good or poor learning experiences.

Treatment

A generation ago, when there was almost unanimous agreement that homosexuality was a mental disease, many anxious and desperate homosexual people sought treatment. Despite the fact that many patients were intensely motivated to become heterosexual, treatment efforts were generally not successful. Whether the therapy involved years of psychoanalysis, heterosexual surrogates, conditioning procedures, medication, or hormones, all ultimately proved ineffective. Since homosexuality is a sexual orientation rooted in a lifelong complex of individual inclinations and experiences, it is just as resistant to change

Figure 12.2. Although the appearance of some people suggests they might possibly be gay, most homosexual men and women are indistinguishable from the rest of the population. (Photo: Scribe)

FIGURES AND FALLACIES

In his book, *What We Say/What We Do* (1973), Irwin Deutscher has carefully demonstrated how often sexual activities are misrepresented. Even in carefully constructed scientific interviews, respondents, wishing to appear more liberal or more conventional, consciously or unconsciously tailor the truth. In fact, social scientists themselves may let their biases distort investigations (Morin, 1977). In addition, over the last quarter century, possibly beginning with the introduction of the birth control pill, there have been and continue to be vast changes in sexual behavior. To cite just two examples: (1) In the 1950s, college dormitories were strictly sex-segregated. Today not only do most college dormitories house men and women, but in many universities unmarried couples living together in their own apartment are commonplace. (2) Thirty years ago, the Kinsey studies found roughly a third of married men and women with extramarital experience. Current figures suggest the number has doubled and that millions of couples now have some sort of "free" marital arrangement (Gagnon, 1977).

It should also be noted that changes in sexual mores have not been universal. More traditional standards are still adhered to by people who are older and who have strong religious affiliations. Differences in education, income, social status, and many other cultural variables also play a role in determining the variety and frequency of sexual activity.

Given the heterogeneity of sexual standards and the likelihood of some dishonesty in disclosing experiences, *all* statistical descriptions are at best rough generalizations or at worst gross inaccuracies. As an instance, the classic and otherwise excellent Kinsey studies reported 18 percent of males had as much hetero- as homosexual experience for a significant period of their lives. Though this figure is still widely quoted, every subsequent study demonstrates that the incidence of true bisexuality is quite low, somewhere in the range of about 2 to 4 percent.

We are aware of the difficulty of obtaining accurate and applicable statistical information. We have attempted, therefore, to evaluate dozens of studies, weighing information obtained from one against the other in order to report meaningful numbers. Nevertheless, we need to caution that the statistics reported and the result of all surveys in areas as sensitive and changing as sexual behavior should be regarded, at best, as educated estimates.

---

as is heterosexuality (Hooker and Chance, 1975).

Today, when homosexuality is recognized as an alternate life style, treatment is no longer deemed appropriate. Men and women who are occasionally or exclusively homosexual may, of course, have psychiatric problems, but treatment for their homosexuality itself is seldom believed desirable. There are two exceptions. Sometimes it is difficult for a person to accept his or her homosexuality. Because of inhibitions and sexual fears, such people are ashamed of their homosexual feelings or the feelings arouse intense anxiety. In such instances it may be necessary for a therapist to help the person change or to understand and accept the legitimacy of his or her orientation. A second occasion when treatment may be relevant is when homosexuality is the outcome of pathology (Phillips et al., 1976).

Stanley Conrad and John Wincze (1976) worked with four young homosexual men who wanted to increase their heterosexual responsiveness. In order to move toward bisexuality the subjects underwent several dozen orgasmic reconditioning (ORC) sessions. In these sessions sexual arousal was associated with visual or fantasized erotic heterosexual situations. One of the subjects also elected to have homosexual stimuli aversively coupled with electric shocks in an effort to reduce the pleasure associated with the same sex. At the end of therapy, although objective measures were inconclusive, all subjects reported an increase in bisexuality and sexual adjustment in general.

253

TRANSVESTISM AND TRANSSEXUALISM

Although transvestism and transsexualism outwardly resemble homosexuality, they are actually quite distinct. **Transvestites** are people, usually men, who find it stimulating to wear the clothing of the opposite sex. **Transsexuals** are those who so closely identify with the opposite sex that they seek medical help to change their gender. Both transvestites and transsexuals are ordinarily heterosexual. They are also usually free of psychiatric symptoms, and their behavior is consensual. For these reasons, we discuss these orientations as sexual alternatives rather than deviations.

Transvestism

Transvestism is in some ways like fetishism (Chapter 11). There is a sexual fascination with particular items of female clothing. Nearly all transvestites enjoy dressing like a woman in every detail, including lingerie, hose, earrings, makeup, and so on. While costumed they may watch themselves in a mirror, try to be admired by others or otherwise affirm their cross-dressing. The dressing is also often a preliminary to masturbation or ordinary heterosexual coitus.

Transvestites should *not* be confused with homosexuals who enjoy being "in drag." Such homosexual men, and occasionally women, dress and act like a member of the opposite sex. Often this occurs during adolescence as an experiment with, or attempt to define, sexual orientation. At other times such dressing is done for no more substantial reason than novelty or excitement. Interestingly too, whereas homosexual men in drag try to pass as women, transvestites continue to look like men dressed as women. It is an important source of satisfaction for the transvesite to obviously be a man wearing woman's clothing. In contrast, a few male homosexual individuals become so expert at playing women that their imitative abilities become a means of earning a living as an entertainer (Jones, 1977; McCary, 1973).

Figure 12.3. The transvestite man does not try to pass as a woman. He is aroused by obviously being a man dressed in women's clothing. (Photo: Scribe)

Transvestism is relatively rare and little studied. It is known that nearly all are men and that the preference is usually traceable to childhood or adolescent experiences or conditioning. Most are married men and although some keep their interest hidden from their wives, many spouses cooperate in their husbands' preferences.

Transsexualism

Transexuals are extremely rare; there are no more than a few thousand in the United States, and men outnumber women roughly three to one. The transsexual is usually and suitably described as an individual who feels trapped in the physical body of the wrong sex. This person is now a man but believes he is in reality, or ought to be, a woman—or vice versa.

Sexual identification, learning which gender one belongs to, is probably established during the first two years of life. The boy whose parents treat him like a girl or is, through any other psychological or environmental circumstances, convinced he is female may be rudely surprised at age 3 to be told he is actually male. Most transsexuals recall with some clarity that their longing to be of the opposite sex, their belief that their own physical gender was wrong, started in earliest childhood. Nearly all transsexuals are heterosexual and most marry, though they continue to believe they are in the wrong body. In former times many transsexuals hid their convictions and put up with their frustration. At most, a man might take a very "feminine" occupation or a woman a very "masculine" one, positions that allowed some switch in the usually rigid gender roles:

Roberta was an auto mechanic. She dressed in overalls, kept her hair short, walked, talked and "cussed" like any of the other garage workers. She was one of the best and strongest employees and could be counted on to do any work no matter how heavy or difficult. She smoked constantly and was assumed by customers to be a man. Roberta did not hide the fact that she was female and was in fact married and a mother.

Today, many transsexuals seek medical help to switch identities. Men have their genitals removed and an artificial vagina fashioned. Women have breast tissue reduced and may attempt to have a penislike appendage constructed. In addition, appropriate hormone therapy for both gives men and women some of the body lines, textures, and hair distribution of the sex they desire. Gender-change surgery permits some minimal sexual function, but reproduction is impossible. More important for transsexuals, however, it permits them to feel that at last they are in the correct body. After gender surgery many transsexual people separate from their previous spouses and establish a relationship with the sex that is now newly opposite their own (Green, 1974; McCary, 1973; Wilson, 1977).

HETEROSEXUAL ALTERNATIVES

Nonconforming sexual life styles are not limited to homosexuality. Many different heterosexual behavior patterns are socially disapproved, often in violation of criminal codes, and occasionally still viewed with suspicion by a few people in mental health professions.

Some common alternatives

ORAL SEX   Oral-genital contacts were once considered abnormal by many psychiatrists and social scientists. In fact, cunnilingus and fellatio are specifically prohibited by some religions and still considered felonious acts, "crimes against nature," in many states. Nevertheless, recent studies show that well over half of all married partners and probably more than 90 percent of all younger couples have oral-genital contacts. Cross-cultural research and investigations with other mammalian species show that oral-genital contacts, rather than being unusual, are actually the norm. Cunnilingus and fellatio occur with frequency throughout the world. The result of these findings is that oral-genital contact as part of a consenting relationship is no longer viewed as abnormal by psychologists, psychiatrists, or most informed adults (Yankelovich, 1974; Wilson, 1977).

PROMISCUITY   In the past, considerable psychiatric effort was directed at defining the allowable number of partners for, and frequency of, sexual intercourse. The person who had more than five or six partners a year was likely to be considered promiscuous. Such a woman, or one who actively desired intercourse twice or more daily, was likely to be labeled as suffering from **nymphomania. Satyriasis** was the designation applied to a man thought to be "oversexed." Today such labels have largely dropped out of contemporary psychiatric practice.

An extreme number of different sexual partners and a very high, perhaps exaggerated, demand for intercourse could be symptomatic of adjustment difficulties, physical malfunction, or even serious mental disorder. But it does not necessarily follow that everyone who is sexually active is necessarily abnormal. Many people who have potent sexual needs feel uninhibited enough to satisfy them. Though their behavior may not be socially approved, they may still be psychologically and biologically healthy (Bullough, 1976; Anderson, 1976).

FREE MARRIAGE   It is estimated that 2 to 4 million couples, legally married or just living together, have an "open" relationship. That is, up to 5 percent of all couples have jointly agreed to allow sexual relations with other people. For most couples, this means that they occasionally "date" others and develop a sexual-affectional relationship. Sometimes the outside person or persons are brought into the original partnership. Such "threesomes" or "foursomes" may follow any number of different paths. The outside person may be only an occasional visitor or may become at least temporarily an integrated member of the household. Sometimes, when one of the partners is bisexual, a homosexual-heterosexual relationship may evolve. Since women are less hesitant to recognize their bisexuality, "threesomes" with two bisexual women and a "straight" male are a frequent pattern.

Some free partnerships limit their extramarital sexual activities to "swapping" arrangements. Couples exchange partners for sexual purposes. Sometimes such switching is the outcome of ordinary friendship; more often, it is a contact made through a "swingers' "

bar, magazine, or resort. There are a great many correspondence magazines filled with advertisements for couples who want to meet, and every larger city has at least a tavern or club where partners interested in meeting other free couples congregate. Most "swinging" takes place in people's homes. Free couples are invited to parties given by other swinging partners. Ten, twenty, or thirty people may be present at such a party, which appears at first like any other social gathering. Eventually, however, as the evening wears on, couples or groups of men and women seem to disappear into bedrooms for sexual activities (Gilmartin, 1975).

People who participate in various free marriage or partnership arrangements were by former definition almost automatically considered abnormal. This was particularly true for women, since the extramarital affairs of men were judged by the "double standard." Sexual promiscuity and adventurousness were considered acceptable for males but condemned for females. Even now, some psychologists, clergy, and other authorities consider consenting extramarital sexual activities undesirable and unhealthy. The "swinging" mentality is called immature and superficial. The need for more than a single lifelong sexual partner is considered evidence of hidden sexual failure or emotional deficiency. Free marriage or couple agreements may, as is the case with promiscuity, signal a failing partnership or serious maladjustment. But the evidence is that most men and women with open sexual life styles may be more daring but are otherwise as emotionally, sexually, and psychologically healthy as other people (Smith and Smith, 1974; Libby and Whitehurst, 1977).

Alternative life styles and anxiety

Contemporary psychologists and other mental health experts have removed the label of mental disorder from alternative sexual behaviors. There is also some increase in public acceptance and a lessening of discriminatory barriers. But many homosexuals are still afraid to tell their parents of their preference. Some unmarried couples living together or married couples with a sexually open partnership are fearful their employers will find out. A good deal of social and legal disapproval remains, so that it is common for people whose affectional and sexual relationships are other than conventional to feel somewhat pressured and anxious. Such anxiety often makes alternative living more difficult and complex than it might otherwise be.

In order that we may fairly judge the worth of different orientations, Carl Rogers, the distinguished American psychologist and the founder of client-centered psychotherapy, has called for the removal of all social and legal barriers. Rogers asserts that we ought to encourage, not discourage, every adult consensual alternative. He points out that when more than half of all conventional marriages fail, it is high time to explore other options. Perhaps free or open marriage, communal living, or some other form of partnership will prove superior to ordinary matrimony. Maybe some new arrangement will provide a healthier and happier life for adults and a situation in which children can grow and maximize their human potential. Or perhaps alternate living patterns will fail, reaffirming the worth of traditional marriage. The point Rogers makes is that we will never know what is best until we stop calling anything but the most conventional sexual and marital arrangements wrong. We need to give people the opportunity to explore alternatives without making them feel guilty and anxious:

To me it seems high time that here too we begin to move into the twentieth century. It is high time that we recognize and respect the fact that quiet revolutionary as well as evolutionary experiments are a fortunate, not an unfortunate, aspect of our cultural life. Can we accept the fact that here too the name of the game is change, and that we are desperately in need of just such a revolution in the area of living partnerships and family life as has taken place in industry, agriculture, flight, space, and all the other aspects of life? (1972, p. 315)

Prostitution

Prostitution is described here as an alternative sexual life style, although it is not entirely consensual. The money exchanged detracts from the client-prostitute relationship being a totally voluntary act. Nevertheless, the stereotyped notion that prostitutes are helpless prisoners of pimps or organized crime has little foundation in fact. The great majority of prostitutes freely enter the profession and feel little compulsion other than financial pressures (Winick and Kinsie, 1971).

Nearly all prostitutes are women catering to men, but there are male prostitutes with homosexual men as clients. Most prostitutes are in their twenties, although a minority of considerably younger or older people may also be involved. Throughout the world prostitutes can be found in every city and many smaller towns. Some nations have legalized prostitution, but in the United States, with the exception of Nevada, it is a criminal offense. Despite punitive laws and occasional police and political efforts to "crack down on vice," prostitution continues to flourish. There may be as many as 500,000 professionals in North America, though not all of them are active at the same time (James, 1977).

Prostitutes tend to fall into occupational life styles, that is, habitual ways of earning a living. Generally the more resourceful, intelligent, and attractive women are higher on the occupational ladder. But there is also some shifting, so that a woman who thinks of herself as a high-status call girl may on occasion operate out of a bar, or even make a street pickup. Streetwalkers may eventually gather enough steady clients so that they can operate in their own apartments like call girls. The following are a few of the different occupational life styles of prostitutes, beginning with the least prestigious.

STREETWALKER: These prostitutes walk favored streets, usually in the entertainment areas of larger cities, to solicit customers.
BAR GIRL: Many bar girls only encourage customers to buy drinks, but others are prosti-

tutes who operate out of bars or even expensive restaurants.

MASSEUSE: Most masseuses are, of course, highly trained and are distinctly not prostitutes. But in many cities prostitutes work in "massage parlors" or "encounter" or "model" studios. Their income is heavily dependent on the "tips" customers give for sexual services.

HOUSE PROSTITUTE: The "house girl" works with several other women in an apartment under the direction of a madam. In return for the madam organizing activities, the house prostitute shares her earnings.

CALL GIRL: The call girl is the prostitute with the most prestige. Streetwalkers charge $20 or $30 for a fast session; a call girl earns $50 to $100 for a leisurely hour or two. Call girls have their own apartments and consider themselves successful, attractive businesswomen. They depend upon other girls or customers for referrals and are sometimes selective about whom they will accept.

MOTIVATIONS The motivations to become a prostitute are minimally sexual and maximally economic. For most women, prostitution represents an opportunity to earn $20,000 to $40,000 a year. Many prostitutes, very likely about three-fourths, are from depressed socioeconomic groups and/or ethnic minorities. For them, being a "hooker" may seem the only way to pull themselves out of poverty and frustration.

The decision to become a prostitute is not simply a matter of deciding to walk the streets. What usually happens is that inducement is provided through example. Sometimes a pimp or procurer urges a girl to try the life. *Pimps,* incidentally, are essentially "kept men" supported by prostitutes because they provide some measure of affection and security. Some are abusive, but this is not as common as depicted in the entertainment media. Pimps are not procurers. *Procurers* are people like taxicab drivers or bartenders who in exchange for a fee steer customers to the girls. The major role in introducing some women to prostitu-

Figure 12.4. The primary motivation for prostitution seems to be financial, so that the number of women involved increases during periods of unemployment and economic distress. (Photo: Scribe)

tion is played by other women who are already working. A large proportion of prostitutes enter, or more accurately drift into, the profession through an acquaintance "in the life" (Stein, 1974).

I started through Laura. I was seventeen. I was tired of school and at home. I wanted out. I used to write to her and she told me she was going to be an actress. . . . When I visited her she told what she was doing. . . . It didn't shock me. I wasn't uptight about sex. I just didn't want to have to get involved with men I didn't like. . . . But I thought about it. . . . I decided once I'd like to try a date. . . . After all I was giving it away free at home. . . . She told me she would set me up with somebody nice. . . . I stayed with her Saturday and she fixed me up with two guys. They were a little older but they were nice. I made $80 that night and I gave her half. . . . That's how I got started. . . . I'd go in to see her every once in a while at first. . . . Then later I got *set up in my own place. . . . I made a down payment and I got referrals from other girls. . . . Now I'm making close to a thousand a week, every week, tax free.*

But economic motives alone do not lead to prostitution; there are a number of other inducements. A few prostitutes, perhaps about 5 percent, are heroin addicts who find the occupation a means of raising the large amounts of money needed to supply their own (or sometimes a boyfriend's) habit. A much smaller percentage are mentally retarded, schizophrenic, or otherwise seriously disturbed. The largest portion, and some estimates by social scientists such as James (1977) and Winick and Kinsie (1971) suggest it is possibly half of all prostitutes, have a history of extensive promiscuity and sexual maladjustment. This conclusion is largely based on personal disclosures and is frequently attributed by the women to sexual exploitation during childhood by an older male acquaintance or even a relative. One needs, however, to evaluate such stories carefully, since subjective recollections are often embroidered to suit the interviewer or to rationalize present behavior.

Another background circumstance and motive that appears very often in the histories of prostitutes is a disordered family life. Many report abuse, neglect, alcoholism, marital discord, divorce, and other persistent difficulties with parents or siblings. Sometimes this also takes the form of parents who are overly restrictive and punitive. The end result is that many prostitutes report rebelling against their families, running away, or otherwise trying to be free of them as early as possible.

Finally, not all motives for prostitution are negative. Some women are intrigued with the notion of sexual freedom, the supposed adventure and glamour of prostitution, or even the possibility of fulfilling lesbian desires. Many, probably most, prostitutes sooner or later have other women as lovers, so that lesbianism plays a role in the maintenance of prostitution as a way of life. The high incidence of lesbianism among prostitutes has led some psychoanalytic writers to speculate that prostitutes basically hate men. By making their male lovers pay, they are supposedly getting revenge on their father or another man who has psychologically or physically misused them.

Just as there is misinformation about prostitutes there are also many false beliefs about their customers. First of all, for most men contact with a prostitute is infrequent, limited to perhaps a half-dozen experiences in a lifetime. But a small percentage of men, less than one or two of every hundred, depend on prostitutes as a steady source of sexual outlet. These men are by and large middle-class, middle-aged, and essentially normal. They seek out prostitutes because they want a variety of sexual experiences, are alone in a strange city, have some special needs (such as fellatio) not provided by their wives, or like the adventure. A very small proportion seem to rely on prostitutes because they feel disfranchised. They are physically handicapped, aged, considered ugly, or otherwise not accepted by women. The only way they can experience heterosexual contact is by paying for it.

Although not too much is known about them, a good deal of what we have said for female prostitutes holds true for males who cater to other men. Male "hookers" are by and large homosexual, although a few are heterosexual. Perhaps the major difference between male and female prostitutes is that the number of men engaged in the profession is very small and very transitory. Most male prostitutes remain in the profession only for short periods of time (Anderson, 1976; Gagnon, 1977).

MILITANCY Like homosexuals, in the last few years many women who are prostitutes have organized and asked that their life styles be decriminalized. Organizations like COYOTE (Cast Out Your Old Tired Ethics) have pointed out that prostitutes are basically normal women voluntarily providing a needed service to normal men, and neither should be liable to imprisonment. Some members of women's groups have supported such efforts, contending that prostitution should be considered a legitimate and dignified profession, a position it historically occupied in many Euro-

ALTERNATIVE LIFE STYLES: PRO AND CON

Woman Social Worker

My husband and I were married twelve years before we got into sexual freedom. At a special club or a party if we meet a couple and are turned on to each other, we make love. After twelve years of marriage we wanted a little variety. . . . But we didn't sneak around like other people. We were always close and very open and admitted it. We have a very good marriage, happy children, and we deeply love each other. But we've always been a very libidinous pair I guess. We've always enjoyed sex in a very physical way and felt we wanted more. . . . Freedom has added to our relationship in every way, not taken anything away. Sometimes after we've made love to another couple we are fantastically turned on to each other and can't wait to get home. It's beautiful. It's only a small part of our lives, maybe once a month. . . . Some of the people we've been to bed with remain friends and we continue to see each other. Sometimes sex isn't even part of it. We've become good friends with Pat and Clark. We'll go camping together and

of course with all the children there is absolutely no hanky panky. We're straighter than straight. . . . The one thing I want to say, besides that I think a little sexual freedom is the most natural and best thing in the world, is that it is not a bunch of bodies groping at each other in the dark. We make love and have very good feelings for each other. These are complete experiences. They are a sharing with other people you include in your life for a while. It's ridiculous to think sex can't be good unless you're deeply in love.

Clergyman-Psychologist

I'm trained in two professions and believe I know enough about morality, ethics, and normality to see that both sexual freedom and homosexuality are wrong. I am not for restrictive laws either, but I am perhaps old-fashioned. These people need treatment, not imprisonment. The Judeo-Christian view is that marriage is a growing partnership. Good sex comes only from a deeply loving relationship. Casual sex erodes and cheapens one of the most profound bonds that unites men and women and forms

---

pean socieites. Others, however, have opposed the efforts to legalize prostitution; they insist that prostitution is the "end product of sexist exploitation and of a sick society."

Many police and legislators also oppose the legalization of prostitution and often contend that it is associated with or breeds crime. It is true that sometimes men are assaulted and robbed by women (or men) who pose as prostitutes in order to trap their victims. On occasion too, disputes between prostitutes and their customers end in violence. Prostitutes may also be arrested for offenses such as the sale of drugs, shoplifting, and other nonsexual charges. On the whole, however, prostitution remains a "victimless crime." The great majority of prostitutes are not violent, are not associated with organized crime or criminal in any other way. Most regard themselves as "working girls" who give their customers as much service and attention as they are willing to purchase (James, 1977; Sutherland and Cressey, 1974).

SEXUAL DYSFUNCTIONS

Disorders of sexual function, the inability to have satisfactory sexual relations, are extremely common. In fact, most men and women sooner or later have some period in their lives when it is obvious that something is sexually wrong (Figure 12.5). They seem to lose interest in sex, feel incompetent or incapable of experiencing pleasure. Erotic interactions are anxious or even depressing instead of stimulating, satisfying, and affectionate. The following are the most frequently encountered types of sexual dysfunction:

INHIBITED SEXUAL DESIRE: This is impairment in the ability to feel excitement or desire. Such men or women may contend that they are not interested in sex. It has little meaning or pleasure for them, but they "put up with it" to accommodate their partners.

INHIBITED ORGASM: Those with orgasm inhibitions feel diminished pleasure in sexual

the very basis of society, the family. . . . Group sex, with men and women together having sex with one another, is nothing more than a pack of animals; it is dehumanizing. . . . As for homosexuality, of course it is an illness. The love of man for women is normal but that of man for man is perversion. . . . We also need to realize that regardless of what they say, homosexuals, by their very example if not by seduction entrap the young and innocent. . . . They want the stamp of approval for their conduct which in their innermost heart of hearts, their God-given conscience, they know is morally corrupt. . . . When I see pictures of them in the newspapers, "marrying," kissing each other, it is disgusting. Normal people are sickened by such sights.

A Homosexual Man

I've known I've been gay since I was 11, but I got married and raised a family anyway. I always maintained homosexual contact even in the fourteen years I was married. But it was only very occasional. . . . I "came out" two years ago when I moved in with Jack. We are

lovers and my family has come to accept it. . . . My kids are straight and my wife is also heterosexual. . . . It's been hardest on her and I am sorry about that. But my children have accepted it well. . . . I believe my homosexuality started because I was always fascinated by male bodies. I guess I was built that way or learned the fascination early. . . . I'm not obviously gay. I look and dress and act like any other 46-year-old man. . . . I'm still a lawyer and I help support my family and the whole middle-class routine. . . . In this state I commit a felony every time Jack and I make love. That is ridiculous, isn't it? . . . Homosexuals have been around since the dawn of civilization. It is a perfectly natural activity, and all of us have some bisexuality in us. You know that when men or women are locked away in prisons or exclusive schools nearly all of them take lovers. It is as natural as heterosex. We have no more right to persecute homosexuals than we do heterosexuals.

---

climax. Orgasms may be subdued, require unusual efforts to achieve, or be lacking altogether.

PREMATURE ORGASM. This is the almost immediate climax at the start of sexual excitation or at the beginning of actual coitus. A few women climax quickly and then lose interest. Much more common is the man who after minimal foreplay discharges sperm *(premature ejaculation)*, loses his erection, and is unwilling to continue with intercourse.

IMPOTENCE: Impotence is the inability of the man to attain or sustain an erection. There are degrees of impotence: some men attain a weak, partial erection that makes careful coitus possible. Others become erect only under special circumstances (with a girlfriend but not with a wife), or are totally impotent, unable to have an erection even in masturbation.

DYSPAREUNIA: This condition, found mainly in women, results in the person feeling consid-

erable genital discomfort during coitus.

FRIGIDITY: This old term, no longer in favor, refers to the woman's inability to be sexually aroused or to experience orgasm. Inhibited sexual desire or inhibited orgasm are the terms currently preferred.

VAGINISMUS: Spasms of the entry muscles of the vagina may cause a tight closure, thereby obstructing penetration by the erect penis.

Causes

A good understanding of the causes of sexual dysfunction requires some appreciation of male and female genital anatomy and physiology. In the 1960s William Masters, a gynecologist, and Virginia Johnson, a psychologist, measurably advanced sexology by their pioneering efforts at explanation and treatment. Breaking through inhibitory barriers that had restrained even scientific investigation, they recorded and photographed coitus, masturba-

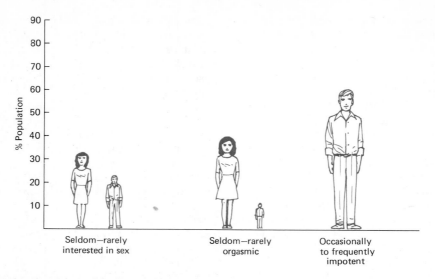

Figure 12.5. Sexual dysfunctions are common and involve tens of millions of adults, although few obtain treatment. Estimates based on Levine and Yost, 1976; MacVaugh, 1977; Masters and Johnson, 1970; Milne and Hardy, 1975.

tion, and other sexual activities. Using cameras as well as internal measuring instruments, they evaluated the changes that took place in the vagina, clitoris, and penis as well as in other body organs for thousands of subjects. After learning what actually happened during sexual arousal and climax, they devised

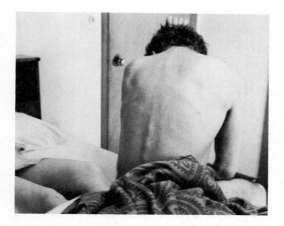

Figure 12.6. Impotence is very common, with two-thirds of all men having occasional to frequent episodes. (Photo: Scribe)

what were then considered daring and direct treatment programs. Therapists instructed dysfunctional clients in what physically and realistically needed to be done in order to overcome problems such as impotence and inhibited desire. The sexual treatment techniques will be covered in Chapter 18; at this point we will briefly review some of the Masters and Johnson (1970) and subsequent findings (Leiblum et al., 1976; Macvaugh, 1977; Milne and Hardy, 1975).

The erotic response cycle

The physical and psychological objective of coitus is orgasm, an intensely pleasurable feeling accompanied by the ejaculation of sperm in the male and vaginal-uterine changes conducive to reproduction in the female. In both sexes, the erotic response cycle is fairly similar and consists of four phases which are the same whether the activity is masturbatory, homosexual, or heterosexual.

1. *Excitement.* Different stimuli initiate sexual excitement (kissing, pictures, genital manipulation): the heart beats faster, breasts enlarge, breathing becomes more rapid, and so on. The increased genital blood supply re-

sults in a firm, erect penis and an enlarged, lubricated vaginal opening.

2. *Plateau.* During this phase, the male and female genitalia are continuously stimulated by friction. For men the neurological center of sensation is the glans (head) of the penis; for women it is the clitoris. Contrary to previous belief, Masters and Johnson found that the clitoris, an almost hypersensitive organ, usually and preferably was stimulated indirectly. The clitoris is covered by a "hood," an extension of the labial folds. As the penis thrusts in and out of the vagina the inner labia are moved back and forth, causing the clitoris to rub against its own hood.

3. *Orgasm.* Continued genital friction of intercourse or masturbation results in a climactic rush of good feeling. Women may experience an initial spasm of pleasure, followed by a number of contractions seconds apart. In men, the penis spurts forth sperm and continues to throb for a minute or so. In both sexes pulse, blood pressure, and the like reach a peak; there is often muscular contraction of the buttocks, arms, and hands so that the partner may be tightly gripped. Frequently a "sex flush"—a heated, perspired vasodilative reaction—covers the entire body.

4. *Resolution.* The fourth phase results in the body returning to its ordinary function and shape. During this phase men enter a *refractory* period, a stage lasting a few minutes to several hours when they are unable to be physically aroused again. Many women, however, do not have a refractory period and may be stimulated to successive orgasms.

Misconceptions

The Masters and Johnson work and later research have cleared up a great many erroneous assumptions concerning sexuality. Sigmund Freud insisted there were two kinds of female orgasms—clitoral and vaginal. He believed that vaginal orgasms occurred as a result of intercourse and were superior and mature. Clitoral climaxes were the result of stimulation through masturbation. Freud did not know that coitus results in clitoral stimulation. Whether it is excited by a finger or penile thrusts, the clitoris remains the center for female sexual sensation. The vagina is poorly supplied with nerve endings, so that just rubbing the vaginal walls alone, without involving the clitoris (which is difficult to do), seldom leads to orgasm. All orgasms are clitoral.

We are now also more informed about the penis. Although the size of the flaccid penis varies a good bit, most are roughly about 15 cm when erect. Penis size has nothing to do with sexual satisfaction or orgasmic capacity in either male or female. And although the vaginal opening, the size of the major and minor labia, and the clitoris tend to vary, their dimensions are also unrelated to sexual competence or pleasure.

A final important contribution of up-to-date sex research shows that the male orgasmic experience should not and cannot be a model for all women. Nearly all men have an almost explosive orgasmic discharge. They reach a peak of excitement, climax, and then enter their resolution phase and refractory period. Women may have the same kind of orgasm, a series of wavelike periods of resolution and climaxes, or a relatively prolonged orgasmic feeling. The patterns are quite individual and even vary for the same woman from one occasion to the next. The point is that the male climax is not the only or the normal orgasm which must be attained by all women, or even by all men (Figure 12.7).

Causes of sexual dysfunctions

MEDICAL EXPLANATIONS Few cases of sexual dysfunction are medical in origin. Older men may take longer to become erect and climax and older women may not lubricate well, but in healthy people age is not a barrier to sexual satisfaction. Dyspareunia is sometimes the result of infection or lesions, and impotence can occasionally be traced to diabetes, prostate disease, or neurological defect. Drugs, alcohol, and even some prescription medications may impair sexual ability. As a result, all sexual dysfunctions must be medically evaluated to rule out physical disease, although in the great majority of cases the disability will be found to have psychological causes.

Men, much more often than women, are

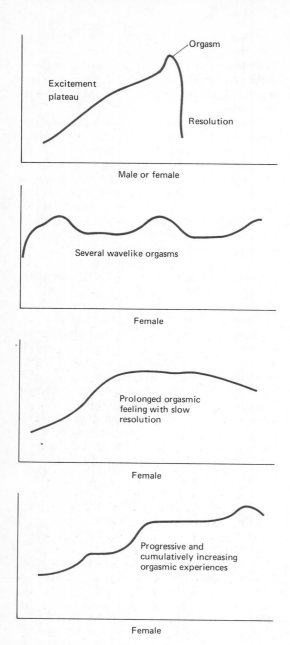

Figure 12.7. Nearly all men have an explosive climax following the excitement and plateau phases of intercourse. The orgasmic experiences of some women are similar to those of men. For many women, however, orgasms can follow a number of different patterns, some of which are schematically suggested here.

fearful that their reputation, their masculinity and status, depend upon sexual performance. As sexual excitement mounts, their anxiety also increases, resulting either in premature ejaculation or, much more frequently, impotence. The autonomic responses accompanying anxiety are actually neurologically incompatible with erection, so that fear is an effective physiological block to sexual arousal. Frequently, episodes of impotence begin a vicious cycle. The man is afraid he will not be potent. His fear reduces his erectile capability, and this in turn triggers even greater anxiety.

LEARNING EXPLANATIONS In our society sexual education is fragmentary, often superficial, and sometimes totally wrong. Inadequate learning ranges from the woman who has been taught that erotic enjoyment is unladylike to the man who believes it proper to crudely and directly manipulate the clitoris. In addition, many adolescents are indoctrinated with a "sex tease" attitude. The object is to entice and provoke the opposite sex in order to gain control. Men and women exploit and manipulate each other, using their sexuality as a weapon to wrest concessions:

I was married for 7 years and my husband told me over and over again that I was frigid. . . . Sometimes I would even fake having an orgasm, but it is true that I usually felt nothing. . . . He had a lot to do with it. He came on like an animal. No tenderness, no affection, just pawing and grabbing. I suppose though my mother was mainly responsible. . . . When I was nine she found me in bed with my pillow between my thighs. . . . I had discovered that pressing it like that between my legs felt good. She caught on; I guess I was masturbating. She said that what I was doing was disgusting. I must never touch myself down there. I would be punished by God. . . . I heard that message a few other times. . . . I did learn about reproduction in high school. I knew the facts but nothing about sex really. . . . I guess I felt all along it was sort of disgusting. I could never masturbate. I heard friends talk about it and I would feel a chill, a revulsion. . . . I did

Some cases of sexual dysfunction can be traced to serious misunderstandings about or even neurotic phobias concerning venereal diseases. Such people may be sexually unresponsive because they are extremely anxious that all coitus or every casual sexual contact will result in venereal disease. Sex therapy and good sex education can easily clear up common misapprehensions (Conn, 1978; Conn and Conn, 1978; U.S. Department of Health, Education, and Welfare, National Center For Health Statistics, 1979).

Misconceptions

Venereal diseases are like other infectious maladies; one needs to be in contact with a sick person in order to become ill. The common cold is spread by inhaling virus-laden microscopic particles sneezed or exhaled by an infected person. Venereal diseases are transmitted by coming into intimate contact with disease microorganisms in the genital area (or occasionally anus or mouth) of an infected person. Prostitutes are not a major source of venereal diseases. Public health surveys show that only a small number of prostitutes are infected at any one time and that as a whole they probably account for less than 5 percent of all venereal illnesses. Venereal bacteria have not become so powerful or exotic that antibiotics are useless. Medication dosages have increased, but they are still sufficient to cure nearly all venereal diseases.

Common venereal diseases

Syphilis. No longer common, new syphilis cases number about 100,000 annually. The disease is caused by a corkscrew-shaped bacteria, the Treponema pallidum, which produces an ulceration on the genitals, mouth, or wherever body contact was made with an active infection. If left untreated, the microorganism may over the course of several years damage the brain, heart, eyes, and other vital organs. About 5 percent of untreated syphilitic patients manifest organic psychotic symptoms an average of ten to thirty years after infection. Syphilis can be cured by penicillin or a substitute.

Gonorrhea. There are over 2 million cases of this bacterial infection every year. Within a few days after infection, it causes urethral pain and discharge in males. Women usually remain symptom-free for months, but may eventually become aware of pelvic infection or arthritic symptoms. Gonorrhea is curable with antibiotic therapy.

Trichomonas Vaginalis. This protozoan infection is estimated to involve as many as 3 or 4 million men and women. In women it causes an uncomfortable vaginal discharge; infected males are symptom-free. The disease can be cured with metronidazole.

Herpes Genitalis. This viral infection causes lesions similar to cold sores to break out on the penis or in the vagina. Once infected, most people have frequent reoccurences, but over the course of time the discomfort usually lessens. Herpes may be the fastest-growing venereal disease; new cases now number over 300,000 annually. If a woman in labor has an active herpes lesion, her baby may become infected. Because in infants herpes can do serious brain damage, infected women who are about to give birth are frequently advised to deliver through Cesarean section.

---

learn to tease. . . . You made believe you were willing but you never did it. . . . Sex is what you offered to get a husband. It wasn't something for you to enjoy really. I guess my mother's lesson really worked.

Difficult early sexual experiences may also lead to dysfunction. For example, premature ejaculation is often found in men whose first erotic encounters were hurried, secretive, and fearful. Sitting in a parked car or hiding in the bushes near school conditioned them to respond rapidly. Dyspareunia and vaginismus are also sometimes traceable to initial sexual encounters that were insensitive and pressured. A man insisted on intercourse, on penetrating, although the woman was hesitant, unaroused, and unlubricated. Rape, incest, and other severe traumas may, of course, also lead to profound sexual as well as psychological disturbance.

PSYCHODYNAMIC CAUSES Sexual malfunction may reflect relationship and motivational difficulties. Partners who are hostile, resentful, competitive, unaffectionate, or bored with each other often express their negative feelings by being sexually unresponsive. Sexual relations may also mirror social changes. Women have been increasingly encouraged toward independence and equality. Wives may no longer wish to play traditional feminine roles; husbands may feel threatened by a woman who is moving away from sex-stereotyped positions. Often such unresolved conflicts result in sexual dysfunctions.

Sometimes the dysfunction is traceable to at least partially hidden motivational preferences. A partner may have strong homosexual or bisexual needs. Sometimes special gratifications may be desired. A husband may be interested in provocative attire, or a wife may want a free marriage. Perhaps all partnership conflicts could be summarized by the suggestion that the real failure is in *communication*. Most men and women have emerged from an atmosphere of sexual confusion and repression; they are ashamed of their needs and distrustful of their feelings. Adequate sexual function requires two cooperative people, and many American adults are too afraid of rejection to even begin to try to share their anxieties and desires.

Treatment

Though sexual dysfunction is very common, involving tens of millions, relatively few people seek treatment (Figure 12.5). A great many men and women accept their own lack of responsiveness, their feelings of disinterest or disgust as "normal." Others refrain from treatment because they are ashamed or believe their condition hopeless. In actuality, problems of sexual function are quite responsive to therapy.

Psychodynamic, medical, and behavior therapies all play a role in helping those with impairments. Mikhail (1976) combined medical and psychodynamic techniques: he treated vaginismus by prescribing a tranquilizing drug, Valium, and individual interviews. During the first several meetings patients were encouraged to tell all. After several such individual sessions, the partners were brought in and the couples counseled together. Therapy focused on the physical symptom itself plus the background and relationship between the partners. After four to six months, the vaginismus was reported relieved for all, and half of the women became orgasmic for the first time.

Behavior therapies have also played a prominent role in the treatment of sexual dysfunction. Sexual inhibitions and anxiety have been decreased through desensitization procedures. By reinforcement and more complex social learning methods, couples have acquired skills that are arousing and pleasing. Therapists also combine encounter techniques with behavior methods. In these situations, several couples together discuss their sexual disabilities and try to understand their causes. They also encourage each other to overcome inhibitory obstacles. The group encounters are supplemented by instruction in specific techniques (Horn, 1975).

But though traditional psychotherapies have successfully treated dysfunction, all have been heavily influenced, and perhaps eclipsed, by the sex therapy initiated by Masters and Johnson, (1970, 1976). Along with other professionals, they have developed practical methods that address themselves specifically to the physical sexual problem. After a fundamental education in the physiology of sex, plus a medical screening, they teach partners how to respond to their own bodies and also how to please each other. These techniques will be discussed in detail in Chapter 18.

SUMMARY

Unconventional but voluntary adult sexual behavior is still often condemned and may even be considered criminal. Until recently homo-

Figure 12.8. The pioneering, realistic research and therapy efforts of William Masters and Virginia Johnson have significantly improved the understanding and treatment of sexual dysfunction. (Photo: Scott F. Johnson)

sexuality was believed to be a mental illness; now most psychiatrists see it as an alternate life style. It is very common; two-thirds of adults have had some experience, and about 10 percent are predominantly or exclusively homosexual. A small proportion of homosexual men appear to come from mother-dominated homes. For most, however, homosexuality (like heterosexuality) seems to be the outcome of biology, learning, opportunity, and conditioning. Though homosexual people may feel the effects of social discrimination, as a group they are about as psychiatrically healthy as the rest of the population.

Transvestism is found almost exclusively in men and is characterized by an erotic interest in dressing like a woman. Transsexualism is the desire to be of the opposite sex; many such people seek sex-change surgery. Both transsexual and transvestite men and women are heterosexual.

Unconventional heterosexual activities are often considered immoral or illegal, though contemporary mental health professionals no longer view them as pathological. Oral-genital relations are very common, and 2 to 4 million couples have free marriage arrangements.

Some couples agree to extramarital relationships, some exchange spouses, and others experiment with group sexual or living arrangements. Carl Rogers believes different partnership arrangements should be encouraged so that their ability for increasing human potential can be evaluated.

There are about half a million prostitutes, nearly all women, who seem drawn toward this life style by primarily economic motives. Prostitutes often come from poor family backgrounds and may have some sexual maladjustments. Nevertheless, both prostitutes and their customers (who are ordinary middle-class men) are not characterized by serious psychiatric problems as a group.

Disorders of sexual function are common, with the number of possible patients in the tens of millions. Conditions such as impaired orgasm, inhibited desire, or impotence are rarely medically caused. In the great majority of cases sexual dysfunction is due to factors such as ignorance, interpersonal conflict, negative attitudes, repression, and performance anxiety. Though relatively few people seek treatment, those who do have an excellent chance of being helped.

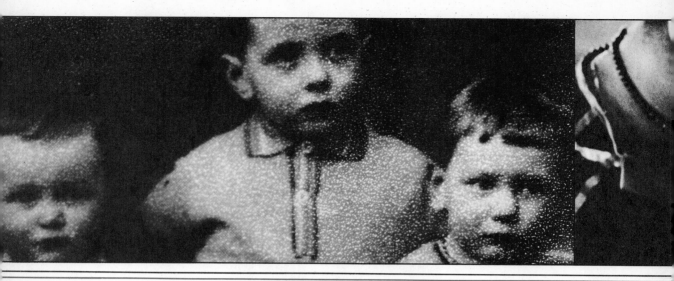

IV CHILDHOOD AND

13 Disorders of Childhood and Adolescence

DEVELOPMENTAL DISORDERS

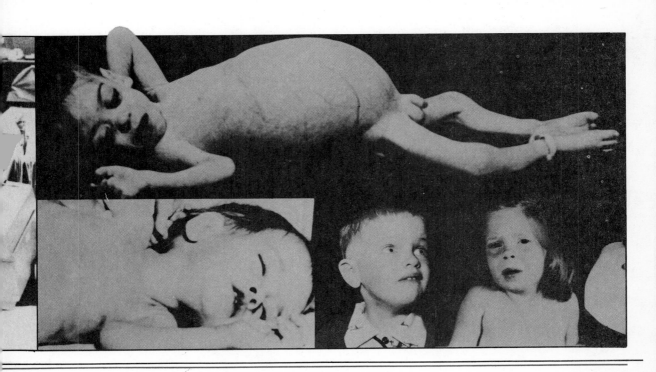

14 Mental Retardation

Disorders of Childhood and Adolescence

Children and adolescents may have any of the mental disorders found among adults. Depression, neuroses, psychoses, even sexual deviations and addictions may be present during the early years of life. But the symptoms that typically characterize abnormalities during childhood usually differ from those seen in adults. In children, depression commonly manifests itself in terms of aggressiveness. Schizophrenia, neuroses, or other serious psychopathologies may make themselves known through inattentiveness, misbehavior, withdrawal, or rebelliousness. Of course, most of the time these behaviors are nothing more than what they seem; the point we are making is that although children also have psychiatric disorders, the symptoms they display are often unique to childhood (Pearce, 1977).

Because we cannot review all the special symptoms found in children for every mental disorder, we will concentrate on those condi-

tions limited to, or clearly arising during, childhood: autism, conduct disorders, delinquency, hyperactivity, learning disabilities.

PSYCHOSIS AND AUTISM

Psychotic children are often exceedingly fearful and confused about their own identity, have impaired language abilities, display odd movements, and have difficulty interacting with others. Unlike adult patients, however, delusions and/or hallucinations are rare.

The diagnosis of childhood psychosis, or schizophrenia, is ordinarily reserved for youngsters between 6 years of age and adolescence. Before that time, many of the same symptoms are diagnosed as **infantile autism.** Why call the young child autistic and the older one psychotic? The answer lies in an unresolved controversy that began a generation ago. Many clinicians insist that particular serious mental symptoms during early childhood indicate a disorder whose origins and outcomes are different from schizophrenia or adult psychoses. Others contend that schizophrenic conduct simply changes with age; a 4-year-old with robotlike movements is just as schizophrenic as a 40-year-old with catatonic postures. In practice, it is difficult to differentiate autism from schizophrenia. As a result, most practitioners (and the DSM III) reserve the label autistic for very young psychotic children (Davids, 1975).

Autism is evident almost from birth. Whereas normal infants respond positively to attentive adults, autistic children withdraw. Instead of smiling as their mother approaches, they may ignore her or even scream when picked up or held. But perhaps the most important autistic sign is *language failure*. While some language irregularity is normal, the autistic child's failure is extreme. When speech develops, it is repetitious, **echolalic** (automatic, like repetition of words spoken by others), and concrete. The child also appears not to understand concepts like "mine" and "yours" and often describes himself in the third person. Instead of "I want this," he states, "Billy wants this."

Autistic youngsters, like slightly older psychotic children, have eccentric motor mannerisms. They may walk on their toes, twirl, bang their heads, act stiffly or mechanically, or hold themselves and rock for hours. Such children are frequently captivated by repetitious events. They may endlessly switch a light on and off or continually flush the toilet. Some observers believe this repetitive behavior is an attempt to "gain environmental control," since psychotic children and adults are often extremely threatened by something new or not understood in their surroundings.

Childhood psychoses are frequently the subject of magazine stories and motion picture and television dramas. But despite this popularity, childhood schizophrenia and infantile autism are *rare*. An excellent study in Denmark, England, and the United States involving a million children showed that psychoses occurred on the average in only about one of every three thousand youngsters (Wing et al., 1976). Another investigator (Rimland, 1971) who has carefully differentiated between what he believes to be true autism and general childhood psychoses finds an even smaller number of autistic children. He evaluated 2,218 psychotic children and found that only about 10 percent met his criteria for autism. For him, the incidence of infantile autism would be one in twenty thousand children. We point out the *infrequency* of childhood psychotic conditions to place them in perspective. It is necessary to know how rare these impairments are in order to avoid the common error of falsely designating as autistic every child who is anxious, lonely, or imaginative (Figure 13.1).

Causes

Explanations of childhood psychoses are similar or identical to those for schizophrenia

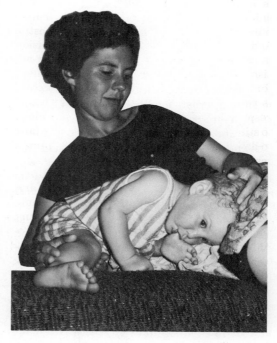

Figure 13.1. Infantile autism is rare; most children who are a little anxious, withdrawn, or imaginative are not autistic. (Photo: Scribe)

given earlier. But there are also some points of departure. First, those investigators who believe autism is distinct from all other childhood psychoses also believe it necessitates a separate explanation. Second, for adult schizophrenia there is still considerable debate concerning the relative weight of biological and psychological factors. For autism, opinions seem to have shifted: Whether justified or not, in the last decade psychological hypotheses in terms of parental mistreatment seem to have given way to those focused on biochemical and neurological deficits.

PSYCHOSOCIAL EXPLANATIONS The traditional explanation for autism and childhood psychoses is a cold, rejecting mother and/or an indifferent, deprived environment. Bruno Bettelheim (1974), a prominent psychotherapist and writer, is perhaps the most well known advocate of this viewpoint. His work in rehabilitating many hundreds of disturbed children has led him to conclude that autism is a defense against unloving parents. The child's seeming apathy, echolalia, and peculiar movements are a way of shutting out a hostile and threatening world. A similar conclusion is reached by behavior theorists; they see autism as the result of inadequate reinforcement for appropriate behaviors. The neglected child is rarely rewarded for smiling, vocalizing, or responding relevantly. He or she is left alone to stimulate himself and as a consequence fails to develop language and other mature human responses (Lovaas and Bucher, 1974).

Many of the families of autistic and psychotic children appear to have a negligent and sometimes even abusive attitude. At the same time, some of them argue that their seeming callousness is the *result* of their child's psychosis, and not the cause. They *were* loving, but their child's continual rejection and bizarre behavior made them act distant. Supporting this contention is the fact that many parents are even unusually warm, patient, and attentive in response to autism—yet the disorder is not alleviated. Overall, current objective investigations show few consistent differences between the parents of psychotic and normal children (Byassee and Murrell, 1975).

BIOLOGICAL EXPLANATIONS The symptoms of autism and childhood psychosis often appear to be present from birth. Almost from the day he or she is born, the autistic or psychotic child stiffens, screams, and resists when held. Further, the characteristics of early psychosis—disturbed perception, impaired language, inadequate sensorimotor integration, and uneven intellectual development—seem to have a "neurological" quality. The signs of autism and childhood psychoses are often indistinguishable from those clearly due to brain damage resulting from infection or injury.

More direct evidence of the possible biological origins of early psychoses comes from biochemical and genetic studies. Results have been scattered, but some researchers have found differences between normal and autistic children in brain wave activity, EEG patterns, amino acid structure, catecholamine chemistry, and serotonin levels (Campbell et al., 1974; Johnson et al., 1974; Ritvo, 1976). Genetic findings, although not definitive, have hinted at a hereditary, or at least a congenital, contribution. First, there is a tendency for psychotic children to be born of psychotic parents. Second, though the numbers are contested, Rimland (1971) has reported the incidence of infantile autism in identical twins at almost 100 percent. If one twin was autistic, it was virtually certain the other would be also.

RESOLUTION In a critical review of autism, Ornitz and Ritvo (1976) categorically state: "No known factors in the psychological environment of a child can cause autism" (1976, p. 618). Although most mental health scientists now lean toward biological explanations, few would go as far as to suggest that psychological factors do not play any role at all. The explanation of childhood psychoses may, like those of most other conditions, involve a complex of factors (Piggott and Simson, 1975; Ritvo, 1976): (1) Though they appear similar, autism and other early psychoses may be distinctive clinical entities and could therefore have different roots. (2) Some childhood psychoses may be biological and some psychosocial in origin. But it is likely too that the diathesis-stress model accounts for many instances of childhood psychoses, just as it does for adult disorders.

Treatment

Despite the increasing preference for a biological explanation of childhood psychoses, drugs have proved to be of very limited usefulness. Another direction has been taken by Delacato (1974), who has treated brain-damaged children by **patterning.** Through exercises and planned repeated movements, Delacato tries to teach the physiological and psychological responses that have failed to develop, supposedly because of the psychotic child's defective nervous system. Both Delacato's theory and treatment are controversial and results are not widely accepted.

Figure 13.2. The divorced mother who remarries confronts the child with two crises. The divorce itself may be traumatic, and then there is the additional stress of adjusting to a new parent. (Photo: Scribe)

Psychological therapies owe much to Bruno Bettelheim (1974), who originated techniques now used throughout the world. At his Orthogenic School in Chicago, psychotic children are exposed to a "round the clock" therapeutic milieu. In an atmosphere of love and concern, youngsters are helped to understand reality and to develop the human responses supposedly cut off by a previously hostile environment. Behavior therapists have used operant conditioning to reorient psychotic children. When a child speaks correctly or makes some other designated response, he or she is rewarded with a candy, token, or privilege. A wrong response may result in withdrawal of the reward, a stern "No!" or a slap (Reichle et al., 1976).

Comprehensive behavior programs and the Bettelheim orthogenic approach involve a continual one-to-one therapist-child relationship for most of an entire day. Both treatment procedures rely on a concerned adult who actively teaches and models socially appropriate behavior. But although such diligent, long-term treatment efforts are often encouraging, the prognosis for psychotic children is only fair. Considerably less than half of all such youngsters make a significant recovery (Ritvo, 1976).

CONDUCT DISORDERS, RUNAWAYS, AND DELINQUENCY

Conduct disorders in children can be viewed as a continuum of maladaptive behaviors. The mildest form is seen in the child who is somewhat aggressive and resistant to school. The most severe form is manifested by youngsters who commit major crimes. This is *not* to argue that the child who is an uncooperative student in school will necessarily become a delinquent; some disorders, such as those resulting from the trauma of divorce, are only temporary. Increasingly, however, the various forms of disordered conduct are seen as congruent pathologies sharing many of the same kinds of causes (Schooler, 1973; Sandhu, 1977). Here we will discuss three conduct disturbances, each dif-

CHILD ABUSE, DIVORCE

Two of the more frequent and especially difficult sources of stress for children are child abuse and divorce.

Parents who are child abusers, who beat their children severely, may have psychiatric disorders ranging from psychoses to alcoholism. Most, however, are relatively normal but were reared by violent fathers and/or mothers and have mistaken notions of discipline (Spinetta, 1972). Some children seem "invulnerable" to abuse and despite painful punishment or neglect emerge relatively unscathed; most, however, are not so fortunate. The violence of their parents contributes to maladjustment in general, and often prompts truancy, learning problems, aggressiveness, and delinquency (Roberts, 1974).

Divorce is usually not as traumatic as child abuse, though it is far more common. Wallerstein and Kelly (1975) studied 34 normal preschool children of divorced parents after the initial separation and again a year later. Three patterns of response emerged. The group aged 2 to 3 showed symptoms like regression, aggressiveness, and greater demand for attention and affection. The 4-year-olds were depressed and many felt responsibility, believing they drove the father away. Those aged 5 and 6 seemed best able to handle the divorce, though some seemed anxious, used denial, and acted confused. One year later, half of the children appeared to have successfully overcome the effects of the divorce. But the other half were described as psychologically "deteriorated" and manifested a number of persistent psychosexual, developmental, and adaptive difficulties.

ferent from but overlapping the others: Aggression, running away, and delinquency.

Aggression

Undersocialized aggressive reaction is characterized by the DSM III as a persistent pattern of disrespect for the feelings and well-being of others. Such children are hostile, bullying, verbally and physically abusive, destructive, and readily lie and cheat. Though most are young, between 9 and 15, they may use drugs, smoke, drink, and be sexually experienced. Some stealing and other minor crimes frequently accompany this behavior. The milder forms of this reaction usually disappear as the child gets older; the more severe forms continue into adult life, warranting the diagnosis of antisocial personality disorder (Chapter 11).

Running away

Runaway boys or girls usually believe, or contend, that they are fleeing from an intolerable situation. Most describe their parents as repressive, physically or sexually abusive, continually fighting, addicted, or psychiatrically ill. A few girls run away because they are pregnant, and some boys leave after committing a serious antisocial act (like setting a fire). Many runaway adolescents are aggressive and undersocialized, with prominent rebellious and hostile traits. A few others, however, are relatively ordinary children who feel overwhelmed by an unbearable home or institutional environment and see no way out except to escape physically. A small minority run away because they want excitement or because of the inducements of friends.

Each year well over a million children between 12 and 16 years of age run away from home. Nine out of ten eventually return, at least for a while. In most larger cities facilities now exist to house, counsel, and reunite such children with their parents. But lacking funds and personnel, such centers can only encourage parent and child to meet; they cannot even begin to address the serious family problems that motivated the running away. The result is that most runaways are repeaters. The exact numbers have not been determined, but approximately half of all runaways become involved with prostitution, drugs, delinquent,

DOES TELEVISION TRIGGER VIOLENCE?

On June 4, 1977, in Florida, Ronald Zamora, age 15, shot and killed Mrs. Elinor Haggart, 82 years old, while burglarizing her home. Although the child confessed to the murder, his attorney sought acquittal. His argument: Zamora was influenced by the continual succession of violent television programs he watched. He did not realize he was taking a life, believing he was merely acting out scripts he had seen day in and day out since earliest childhood. Raised on a steady diet of violence and murder in cartoons and dramas, pulling the trigger became as common to Ronald Zamora as killing a fly.

According to the Nielsen Index, the average child will have watched 18,000 TV murders by

the time he is 18 years old—compared to 11,000 hours spent in school (*Time,* October 10, 1977). Does such viewing help shape a child's behavior? The television industry argues that its programs are harmless. But scientists who have conducted hundreds of careful investigations conclude that television does trigger aggressive and criminal behavior. Just as television is a good teacher of arithmetic or language skills and shapes the consumer habits of millions, it is also an effective model for crime. In a report prepared by dozens of investigators, the Surgeon General of the United States concluded in 1972 that television could clearly be linked to delinquency. In a much stronger statement, the American Medical Association declared: "TV violence is a risk factor threatening the health and welfare of young Americans,

and adult criminal behavior (Schooler, 1973; Trohonowicz, 1978).

Delinquency

In Chapter 11 we mentioned the complexity and unprecedented extent of the crime problem in the United States. When one considers only the more major offenses, *close to half of all felonies* are committed by persons under age 18 (Figure 13.4). In other words, although adolescents account for only about one-seventh of the population, they commit a vastly disproportionate amount of crime. Adolescent criminals, like older offenders, are primarily male; females account for only about 10 to 15 percent of serious teenage crime.

It is important to separate serious juvenile crime from that which is either trivial or better described as mischief or vandalism. Unfortunately many researchers and law and correctional officials do not distinguish between such typical adolescent offenses as running away, sexual indiscretions, truancy, and possessing marijuana and really dangerous offenses such as rape, assault, robbery, and hom-

Figure 13.3. Fifty years ago children were raised to be seen and not heard. A controversial and unresolved question is whether the greater degree of freedom given children today is partly responsible for the increase in conduct and delinquency problems (Photo: Scribe)

indeed our future society." A few of the specific effects of TV violence that have been uncovered by research include the following (Cater and Strickland, 1975; Rothenberg, 1975; Thomas and Drabman, 1975):

1. Millions of marginally adjusted, vulnerable children who might not ordinarily act out their antisocial needs are shown the way by television—it is the final inducement.
2. Most people have inhibitory barriers that restrain them from committing violent acts. After watching violence-loaded programs, many of these barriers are eroded, so that people act more aggressively for several hours.
3. Hitting a person on the head is a felonious assault that may result in skull fracture, brain

injury, paralysis, and death. Nearly all children, who see such assaults continually on television falsely believe they cause only a very temporary and harmless loss of consciousness.
4. Children who rank violent television programs among their favorites commonly believe that physical force, brutality, and homicide are a "normal and acceptable" part of life.
5. Interviews with adolescents and many young adults who have committed serious crimes typically reveal that they consciously and unconsciously model their behavior on violent heroes, most of whom are "good guys" in police dramas.

icide. As a result, many juveniles convicted for possessing a few "joints" or apprehended for running away may find themselves incar-

cerated with violent adolescent criminals. Being institutionalized with major offenders is almost calculated to *teach* the youngster with

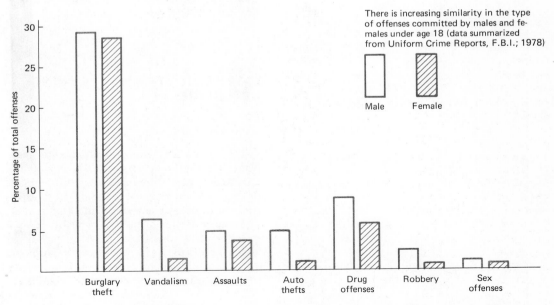

There is increasing similarity in the type of offenses committed by males and females under age 18 (data summarized from Uniform Crime Reports, F.B.I.; 1978)

Male   Female

Figure 13.4. Juvenile crime. There is increasing similarity in the types of offenses committed by males and females under age 18. Data summarized from *Uniform Crime Reports,* F.B.I.; 1978.

what are still relatively minor conduct problems to become an adult criminal.

Causes

The causes of conduct disorders, running away, and juvenile crime parallel those involved in adult criminality and revolve primarily about the family and environmental setting. Despite considerable controversy, it is apparent that *most* delinquent and seriously behavior-disordered children come from a disadvantaged milieu. More often than not they have grown up in single-parent homes characterized by violence or addiction and surrounded by poverty and unemployment. Often too, these conditions motivate children to seek shelter in gangs, which in turn impose a new norm of rebellious, antisocial, or criminal conduct. The result is that much juvenile delinquency is gang or *group delinquency;* the child's needs are met by peers, and aggressiveness is supported by their example and encouragement (Galliher, 1977; Sandhu, 1977; Trohanowicz, 1978).

Only a small proportion of adolescent criminals are psychiatrically abnormal. About 10 percent may be neurotic, psychotic, or mentally retarded. In rare instances too, there seems to be a biological contribution to antisocial behavior. A very few disordered children appear to fit the picture of a muscular, physically domineering, biologically aggressive personality.

Treatment

The treatment of conduct-disordered, runaway, and delinquent children requires careful diagnosis. Just what are the problems and behaviors that require remediation? Typically, as a start, nearly all such children need careful tutoring. Their education is frequently so deficient that no matter what other rehabilitation program is contemplated, they will continue to feel inadequate unless they catch up scholastically.

What also needs to be understood is that only some youngsters have actually committed serious crimes; others may have been aggressive and destructive, but committed only minor offenses. Those who need to be imprisoned for major crimes require effective punishment and rehabilitation. Considering the present high **recidivism** (return to prison) rates of over 80 percent, it does not seem that penal institutions are meeting their goals (Feldman, 1977; Pepinsky, 1976).

Psychotherapy may be helpful for delinquents and for minor offenders. Such treatment can be especially worthwhile if parents willingly participate. An interesting behavior therapy approach that utilized the entire family was demonstrated by Alexander and Parsons (1973). They noted that the families of delinquents had far fewer verbal interactions than normal parents and children. The goal was to increase the quantity and quality of family talk and communication. To reach this objective, the families were trained to listen, to reach solutions through verbal negotiations, and to reward one another for talking. Though this was a simple behavioral approach, follow-up evaluations over a year later showed a sizable decrease in delinquent behavior.

HYPERACTIVITY AND LEARNING DISABILITIES

Hyperactivity

The **hyperactive** (or hyperkinetic) child seems constantly on the move. He or she may talk incessantly, jump from one activity to another, wriggle and squirm, and be poorly coordinated, unusually assertive, and emotionally unstable. Such children are typically 2 to 7 years old and constitute about one of every fifteen pupils in the earliest grades. Numbering over 2 million children, with the majority boys, hyperactive students are a significant challenge for educators and mental health specialists (Safer, 1976).

Hyperactive children are ordinarily just as

HOMOCIDAL DELINQUENTS

Children who commit murderous assaults on other children, adults, or older people account for a small but increasing amount of homicide. Often the attack is part of a gang activity: an entire group of delinquents assault a rival gang member, or fatally injure a victim of robbery or rape. But the homicide may also be the result of an individual attack, and there is apparently almost no lower age limit. Kay Tooley (1975) studied "small assassins," youngsters who murdered. Two of her subjects were 6 years of age and had killed younger siblings. Both children seemed to understand the extreme violence of their act and were described as cool, canny, and self-sufficient. Their histories included such previous attempts as setting fire to the baby's crib and experiments with drowning the younger sibling—attempts, incidentally, the mothers had shrugged off as mischief.

The motivation of children and adolescents who commit murder has been tied to the anonymity of an increasingly mass society, alienation growing out of poverty, and the aggressiveness and a lack of sensitivity toward life continually encouraged by a violent entertainment media. Doubtless these and other factors play a role, and it may require major social changes to alleviate criminal behavior in children (Feldman, 1977; Pepinsky, 1977; Trohanowicz, 1978).

---

intelligent as other youngsters but do have far more school problems. In addition to behavior and discipline conflicts, such children commonly read poorly and have meager arithmetic or other literacy skills. Some of this may be due to their short attention span and impulsiveness. Teachers find it difficult to work with a child who seems uncontrolled and who also disturbs the rest of the class. As a result, hyperactive youngsters are often academically deficient and placed in special classes.

By the age of 10 or 11, and especially by puberty, *even without treatment,* hyperactivity substantially diminishes. For many children too, academic skills improve and they catch up with their peers. But there are also some long-range consequences. Many studies have found that a large portion of children judged hyperactive continue to have serious academic, social, and psychological problems in high school and beyond. Two long-term investigations that illustrate this are those by Huessy and Cohen (1976), who reevaluated children diagnosed seven years previously, and Borland and Heckman (1976), who did a twenty-five-year follow-up. The results showed that about half of the children judged severely hyperactive continued to show some related signs of disorder. Their symptoms included emotional problems, aggressiveness, delinquency, and academic and vocational failure.

Causes and treatment

Hyperactivity is *not* always a singular and distinctive clinical entity; often it is a secondary symptom of retardation, antisocial personality traits, or childhood psychoses. When hyperactivity is secondary, its causes are interwoven with the roots of the dominant disorder. In this section we will consider only those cases of hyperactivity that stand alone, that are not just symptoms of another mental abnormality. We are, in short, talking about *primary* hyperactivity such as that displayed by Clinton.

Clinton, age 7, was removed from an ordinary classroom because he was a "conduct" and "learning" problem. His mother reported that since he was 2 he had always been "on the go" and "into everything." He was born about two months prematurely and was considerably underweight but did not require an incubator. His early years were marked by family instability and hardship, since the father left shortly after Clint was born. At home and in nursery school the child was a whirlwind of activity. He talked continuously, accompanied his play by loud sound effects, nagged adults for attention or to become involved in his activities, climbed over furniture, and in a new environment pushed and pulled every switch and poked into every drawer and closet. In school he bounced in his seat, fidgeted, played jokes, and was easily offended but also quickly recovered. Clint's IQ scores were normal, but he did much better on the verbal parts of the intelligence test than on the performance areas. He was able to define words, reason, and remember, but had difficulty putting blocks into geometric patterns, assembling puzzles, and doing other tasks requiring eye-hand coordination. The psychologist diagnosed hyperactivity due to minimal brain dysfunction.

The most popular explanation for hyperactivity is in terms of subtle brain disability. Many young hyperactive children often show EEG abnormalities and may not be physically well coordinated. They also seem to be deficient in perceptual-motor skills, so that they write or read awkwardly, reverse words or letters, or have peculiar ways of spelling. All these failings suggest a neurological deficit. But even the most careful physiological evaluation of the brain does not reveal a lesion or pathology. As a result, many specialists attribute hyperactivity to **minimal brain dysfunction (MBD).** The supposition is that the brain impairment may be too slight to be detected by present methods but is real enough to manifest itself in disturbed language, motor, and intellectual behavior.

A recent hypothesis attributes the brain disability to a failure in catecholamine biochemistry, particularly to dopamine malfunction. Animal experiments and human electrochemical studies have suggested the possibility of a complex dopamine insufficiency that often gradually improves with age. Perhaps, however, the best evidence for some kind of biochemical failure comes from the fact that hyperactivity responds very well to medication (Ross and Ross, 1976).

Surprisingly, central nervous system stimulants such as amphetamines (Ritalin, Benzedrine), which ordinarily energize normal people, have a quieting effect on hyperactive children. Generally about two-thirds of hyperactive children seem to have their impulsivity and restlessness decreased and show a consequent improvement in ability to pay attention,

learn, and respond to discipline. Since caffeine is a stimulant, some pediatricians who have prescribed daily coffee drinking instead of amphetamines report successful results.

But though medication has proved quite helpful, there is considerable concern about the tendency to overuse cerebral stimulants and particularly to medicate any child who is a school problem. Loney and Ordona (1976), for instance, point out that medication tends to be administered without asking several critical questions. Can the child's behavior validly be described as primary hyperactivity? Is the label and medication hiding other problems? Are other treatment possibilities available? Can we be certain that the drug and not the extra clinical attention produced the improvement? Very often there is a *placebo effect*. The very fact that something is being done suggests both to the child and to the teacher that improvement will follow.

Many parent and professional groups have opposed the notion of minimal brain dysfunction and particularly the use of drugs because of their side effects and potential for abuse (Table 13.1). Much of the opposition has centered around the findings reported by Benjamin Feingold, who put forth the theory that

TABLE 13.1
DRUG TREATMENTS FOR HYPERACTIVITY: SIDE EFFECTS

Side effect	Number of children	Percent of sample (N = 135)
Appetite reduction (weight loss)	59	44%
Sleep disturbance	43	32
Vomiting, nausea	18	13
Headache, dizziness	17	13
Stomachache, cramps	12	9
No side effects	42	31

Source: *Loney and Ordona, 1976.*

EYE-HAND COORDINATION

Instructions: Fill in the correct symbol. Do as many as you can in the time allowed.

Tests similar to this are a part of the performance portion of the Wechsler series of IQ tests. Children who are diagnosed hyperactive or MBD are usually less able to copy the figures as accurately or rapidly as normal children. In fact, in many tasks calling for eye-hand coordination or motor skills, hyperactive children who are otherwise intellectually capable do poorly.

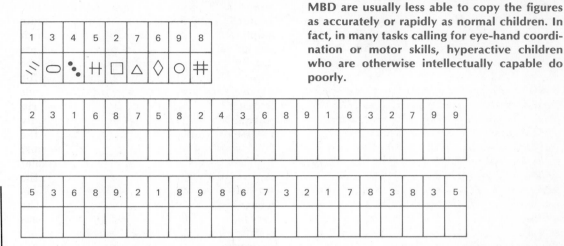

common food additives, dyes, preservatives, and many other chemicals are responsible for hyperactivity. This view is not widely accepted, but several animal and preliminary human studies have seemed to verify his conclusions. It is particularly interesting to note that nitrites and nitrates, commonly found in sandwich meats, have consistently been named as contributing to hyperactivity. This finding coincides with the observation that hyperactivity is much more common in children from socioeconomically impoverished backgrounds, children who eat far more of these treated meat products than middle-class youngsters. For Feingold and many educators and parents, the conclusive proof comes when hyperactive children who have had chemical food additives eliminated from their diets show remarkable improvement in behavior. Such reports are dramatic but need considerable experimental verification before the role of food additives in hyperactivity is validated (Ross and Ross, 1976; Smith, 1976).

For many behaviorally and psychodynamically oriented observers, hyperactivity and MBD are a myth. MBD particularly is criti-cized as a concept that cannot be logically evaluated. The false reasoning is that a child with certain hyperactive symptoms must be brain-injured, but if the brain injury cannot be neurologically demonstrated, then it "proves" the damage is minimal. For psychodynamic writers, hyperactivity is an indiscriminate term that hides a vast array of social and psychological causes for learning and behavior problems in school. Behaviorally inclined psychologists consider hyperactivity a vague generalization that obscures the responses which need to be targeted for change: Productive responses need to be specified and reinforced, and destructive responses need to be eliminated (Halpern and Kissel, 1976; Schrag and Divoky, 1975). The following cases illustrate dynamic and behavioral approaches:

Nine-year-old Molly had been increasingly hyperactive since the age of 5, and medication had not relieved her symptoms. A social work investigation showed she had a younger brother, age 4, and both parents were college graduates. The parents agreed to group counseling with other fathers and mothers, and the child began play therapy. Over the course of months it was revealed that Molly's hyperactivity was both a defense and an attention-getting device resulting from her jealousy of her younger brother. Molly was depressed and angry and discharged much of her feeling by jumping from one activity to another. Treatment of the whole family proved very effective.

A behavior program was designed for a special class of twelve hyperactive children. The children were placed in groups of three. Whenever a child was not hyperactive, the teacher rewarded him or her with a token. Tokens could be exchanged for candy and toys, but needed to be pooled by each group of three. Rewards were shared equally. In this way each child was reinforced for not being hyperactive both by the token itself and by the encouragement and approval of two other children. That is, material rewards were coupled with social rewards. After four months, nearly all the children showed significant decreases in hyperactivity.

Learning disabilities

The concept of specific **learning disabilities (LD)** is preferred by many to the notion of hyperactivity or MBD. According to this view, LD may result from any number of physical or psychological impairments or simply reflect normal differences in learning styles (Figure 13.5). Children do not all develop at the same rate, and even within themselves skills progress unevenly.

There are many different types of LD, of which there are three major varieties. Reading disabilities, sometimes called **dyslexia,** are indicated by signs like failing to recognize certain letters or reading words backward (*saw* for *was*). Language and writing problems result in the child being unable to use or write certain sounds. A third common failure is in concepts and abstractions. Children do not understand how to categorize, confuse before and after, or are unable to grasp notions of time and space.

Although there are probably over 6 million

children with one or a combination of learning disabilities, only about a third are hyperactive. Hyperactivity does not have to accompany LD, nor does LD necessarily lead to hyperactivity (Jenkins, 1973; Myers and Hammill, 1976). The latest revision of the DSM suggests a nomenclature that separates hyperactivity and learning problems into different specific diagnoses. Some of the classifications included in the DSM III are these:

Attention deficit disorders
    Attention deficit disorder without
    hyperactivity
    Attention deficit disorder with
    hyperactivity
Specific developmental disorders
    Specific reading disorder
    Specific arithmetical disorder
    Developmental language disorder
    Developmental articulation disorder
    Coordination disorder

Figure 13.5. Children learn at different rates and may require individual attention. What is sometimes assumed to be a learning disability is often only an individual, and normal, variation in development. (Photo: Alan Carey/Kingston Freeman)

OTHER DISORDERS

The description of children's disorders would not be complete without mentioning several others, all of which are important to the mental health of children.

Epilepsy

Epilepsy is the name given to several different convulsive disorders, all of which result in momentary loss of consciousness and/or muscle control. In a few epileptics there is a discernible brain damage due to tumor, infection, or birth injury. In some others, the epilepsy seems to be inherited or congenital and the central nervous system seems intact. Whatever the cause, epilepsy can usually be detected from EEG tracings; electroencephalograph recordings clearly show irregular brain waves during epileptic seizures (Figure 13.6).

Of the different types of epileptic seizures, **grand mal** is the most common. Youngsters frequently, but not always, get a warning that a grand mal is coming. The sign may be a feeling of pressure in the stomach, seeming to smell a strong odor, trembling of part of the body, or a sudden shift in mood. Often this **aura** (warning) gives the person enough time to lie down before the convulsion begins. The grand mal usually starts with the person emitting a cry, losing consciousness, collapsing, and becoming rigid. The jaws clamp shut, arms are held stiffly at the sides, hands clench into fists, legs are fully extended, eyes are open and pupils dilated. For about 10 to 40 seconds breathing stops and the victim may turn slightly "blue." Following this rigid state there is sudden muscular relaxation alternating with rigidity. Several times a second the person has spasms of relaxation and rigidity, so that the body seems to jerk and quiver. Gradually the interval between each spasm grows longer, the convulsions stop, and the epileptic person regains consciousness. The whole episode has lasted only a minute or two, but many epileptics are left feeling sore, exhausted, or disoriented. Those who have fallen as the attack

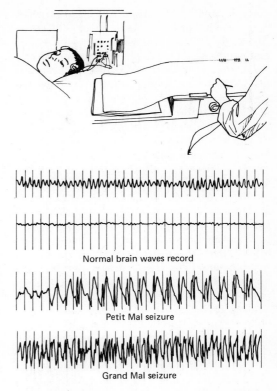

Figure 13.6. The encephalograph records the delicate electrical discharges, or wave patterns, of the brain. This figure shows a comparison of normal and epileptic EEG tracings.

began have also sustained some physical injury.

Many grand mals are preceded by **focal** or **jacksonian seizures,** although these attacks may occur alone. Jacksonian episodes usually begin with a feeling of numbness or tingling in hands and feet or a twitching of an arm, lips, or jaw. At the same time, the person may seem dazed as the feelings or trembling gradually spread throughout the entire body. **Petit mal,** a third variety of seizures, occur without warning and may last as little as a second, or at most half a minute. These episodes can be so fleeting that most observers do not know they have seen a neurological malady and the person may be equally unaware. Usually petit mal momentarily "freezes" the child in whatever activity or movement he or she is engaged. He stops, stares without really seeing, and perhaps in a sudden rhythmic forced way seems to scratch himself, tap his foot, or flutter his eyelids. Such "spells" are found almost exclusively in children and adolescents.

Psychomotor epilepsy, like petit mal, may also be difficult to recognize. For a minute or two the person loses contact with reality and suffers some decrease in voluntary motor control. These epileptics usually do not collapse, but they may perform purposeless movements, or lose their balance, stagger, and make sounds that are not understandable. Some people appear to be quite normal during the attack and simply seem to be doing some routine or task over and over. A very few may seem to act bizarrely—they suddenly spit, or try to undress. Rarest of all are aggressive or violent psychomotor seizures. There are reported instances in which patients with psychomotor epilepsy have supposedly committed complex crimes such as robbery or homicide, but these claims have not always been verified.

The number of epileptic children and adults in the United States is estimated at more than 2 million. For nearly all, seizures have begun in childhood and continue for life, although they frequently become less severe. Without treatment, their frequency may range from several dozen attacks daily, as is sometimes the case in petit mal, to an occasional episode every few months. Most patients also have more than one type of attack, with eight out of ten having at least an occasional grand mal seizure.

There is a great deal of superstition and other misunderstanding concerning epilepsy. Some parents still erroneously forbid their children active games, falsely believing this may provoke an attack. Some misinformed or frightened employers will not hire epileptics, and even those who have been seizure-free for years may be denied driving permits. Needless to say, epileptic individuals are not specially gifted or psychic; most people with epilepsy are essentially normal (Reitan and Davison, 1974).

Our emphasis on the psychological normality of most epileptic individuals should not let us overlook the fact that this neurological condition may be associated with educational and conduct problems. In a study of 200 epileptic children, Whitehouse (1976) reported that 70 percent had poor attention spans, difficulty with reading or with mathematics, or were generally slow. They were also occasionally behavior problems; hyperactivity, irritability, and temper outbursts were common complaints. But Whitehouse noted that these difficulties could be due to neurological impairment or the result of a child trying to cope with a dozen or more petit mal seizures every day. When lapses of consciousness are unrecognized, the child is continually confronted with complex, almost unsolvable adjustment demands. Often simply becoming aware that a youngster has epilepsy and instituting proper treatment makes an immediate and dramatic difference in conduct and academic performance, as the case of Tommy shows.

Tommy was 7 years old and in the second grade when his teacher referred him to the visiting school psychologist. The teacher thought Tommy was capable, but his performance and behavior in class were poor. He seemed very slow to learn, and was inattentive and moody. He got along poorly with the other children and frequently fought with them because they supposedly made fun of him. The teacher also noted that Tommy did a lot of "daydreaming." He would often be seen staring intently at the floor, or looking at his hands in a blank expressionless way while he played with his fingers.

The psychologist noticed several episodes of staring and suspected petit mal seizures. He referred Tommy to a neurologist who confirmed epilepsy and prescribed anticonvulsive medication. Following treatment, Tommy's seizures were controlled and his performance, attitude, and conduct greatly improved. He became a good student and was well liked by the other children.

The treatment of epilepsy requires a combination of medical, psychological, and educational help. Most seizures can be controlled or even eliminated by careful drug regimes including Dilantin, Mysoline, Zarontin, and phenobarbitals. Along with medication, parent and child counseling and special educational help is sufficient, in the great majority of cases, to permit the seizure-prone child to live a normal life (Reitan and Davison, 1974).

Masturbation

Parents, much more than children, are often extremely concerned when they learn that their child is masturbating or attempting sexual relations with other children. Many parents respond to such knowledge with severe punishment, outraged expressions of disgust, or warnings that the child will become a "pervert" or "insane." Such treatment is, of course, almost guaranteed to cause future sexual difficulties. Dr. Mary Calderone (1974), long a leader in sex education and head of the Sex Information and Education Council of the United States (SIECUS), points out that erotic expression should be accepted as the norm *throughout life*. From infancy until old age, human beings are sexual and express their needs. The role of the parent and therapist is to ensure that children act appropriately, are informed, and feel comfortable about their sexuality. Masturbation can be an introduction to healthy adult sexual function and thus should be an anxiety-free source of pleasure in the context of responsible personality development.

Gilles de la Tourette's syndrome

This relatively rare tic disorder usually begins in early childhood. Patients may grimace, blink their eyes, turn and jerk their heads, grunt or make noises, or have any number of other tics and twitches. In some people the entire body is involved, so that there are movements of the arms, hands, or trunk. The disorder is usually progressive; eventually patients become echolalic and **coprolalic,** meaning that they compulsively utter obscenities. Many patients can minimize or eliminate their

symptoms for brief periods, such as while singing or acting. Generally, the tics are distressing to children, parents, and friends. Before there was effective treatment, many became extremely withdrawn and may even have been erroneously diagnosed as schizophrenic. In actuality, Tourette patients are *not* psychotic, nor is there consistent evidence of preceding neurotic or adjustive difficulties. Simple tics are frequent during childhood and are usually quite minor and transitory. These should *not* be mislabeled Gilles de la Tourette's syndrome.

There is little research on the causes of Tourette's disorder, but the symptom patterns plus its responsiveness to specific medication suggest the possibility of a neurological or biochemical cause. Most patients have their symptoms controlled by haloperidol and are able to live normally. Recently, Tourette patients have started groups to enable them to socialize and help one another, as well as make the public aware of the disorder (Fernando, 1976).

Enuresis and encopresis

Bedwetting or **enuresis** is very common, with estimates suggesting that as many as 3 million children between 3 and 16 years of age wet several times a week (Schopler and Reichler, 1976). Enuresis is occasionally due to organic factors, but usually is the result of inadequate learning or of psychological problems. The birth of a new baby, parental divorce, beginning school, educational pressure, or any number of other stresses can precipitate bouts of bedwetting. If inadequately treated, punished, or otherwise unwisely handled by parents, it is likely to persist. In most instances psychological reassurance and behavior therapy techniques are successful in alleviating enuresis. One popular conditioning procedure makes use of a wired mattress pad that rings a bell when it is wet with the first drops of urine. Eventually this teaches the child to wake up before urinating. The technique seems to work very well if it is coupled with counseling intended to relieve the causes of the bedwetting.

Encopresis is failure to control bowel movements during later childhood. The condition often points to fear, jealousy, depression, or anger. Behavioral techniques that succeed in curbing bedwetting frequently fail in encopresis. Careful attention needs to be paid to the roots of the problem, often necessitating a combination of medical and psychological treatment.

Fear and food

Children who are struggling with their parents may manifest their feelings in a number of different ways:

SEPARATION ANXIETY This condition is most clearly seen from 6 months to 1 year of age. When the mother (or her equivalent) leaves, the child may cry desperately or extreme anxiety may be manifested by a fearful withdrawal. Similar reactions can occur later in childhood when the youngster needs to be left with a babysitter or hospitalized. Well-adjusted children may manifest separation anxiety, but it is more common in neglected, fearful, and conflicted youngsters. Separation anxiety needs to be treated with a good deal of warmth, reassurance, and support. For example, when children have tonsillectomies it is now recommended that a parent or other close person stay with the hyperanxious child for most of the hospitalization.

FOOD NEGATIVISM Refusing to eat or extreme pickiness is often the result of a power struggle with the parent. Parent counseling is usually effective. **Pica,** compulsively eating inedible substances such as crayon, paint, or dirt, is another food problem. Pica may be minor and of no significance, but it can also indicate serious childhood pathology, malnutrition, or parental abuse.

NIGHTMARES AND NIGHT ANXIETY ATTACKS Nightmares and anxiety attacks may cause the child to become insomniac, or wake up agitated and screaming. These reactions are usually found in children who are generally anxious or frightened about family events such as divorce, moving, or starting school. Psychotherapy may be necessary, but often parental love and patience are sufficient.

SUMMARY

Children and adolescents may have any of the mental disorders found among adults, though their symptoms may differ. Childhood psychoses and infantile autism are rare conditions and sometimes evident shortly after birth. Both are probably similar to schizophrenia in terms of causes, although they do not respond well to medication or other psychotherapies.

Conduct disorders range from mild rebelliousness to serious criminality. Children who are markedly hostile are said to have an undersocialized aggressive reaction. Runaways may be suffering from conduct disorders or be ordinary boys and girls; most are fleeing undesirable home situations. Juvenile delinquents commit half of all serious crimes and have a very high recidivism rate. The causes of conduct disorders revolve primarily about the family and environment, though individual psychological and biological factors may sometimes play a part. Treatment should include appropriate remedial, psychotherapeutic, and legal efforts.

Hyperactive children are restless and energetic and often have difficulty in school. Many professionals believe the condition is caused by minimal brain dysfunction, but there is also evidence for possible dietary and psychological causes. A great many hyperactive children seem to be helped by stimulant drugs, although the technique is controversial. Behavior and dynamic therapies are often successful. Currently, the preference is to diagnose hyperactive behavior in terms of attention deficits and specific developmental disorders.

Epilepsy is a convulsive disorder resulting in momentary loss of consciousness and/or muscle control. Seizures are classified as grand or petit mal, jacksonian or psychomotor. Epilepsy may be caused by brain injury or may be hereditary. Epileptic children are as capable as others, but many have some adjustment or learning problems. Seizures generally respond well to medication.

Masturbation is almost universal, especially during adolescence. Though it is normal, some anxious children need reassurance and guidance. Gilles de la Tourette's syndrome is an uncommon chronic tic disorder that may be neurological in origin and that responds well to haloperidol. Conditions such as separation anxiety, nightmares, eating problems, enuresis and encopresis often result from fear and stress. Most are relieved when parents provide a more supportive milieu.

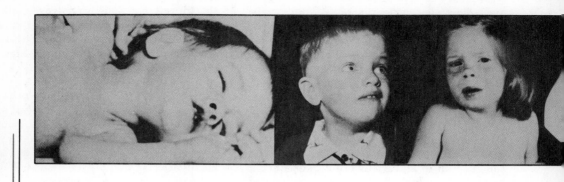

14

Mental Retardation

The *Manual on Terminology and Classification* of the American Association on Mental Deficiency (AAMD, 1973) defines **mentally retarded persons** as significantly subaverage in general intellectual function and adaptive behavior since earliest childhood. Mental retardation is thus defined as consisting of *both* intellectual and social impairment. To meet the first criterion, IQ (intelligence quotient) as measured by a standardized test needs to be two standard deviations below average. The second criterion, adaptive deficiency, is evaluated by comparing the person's living and social skills with those of others in his or her age group. The AAMD definition requires that retardation be apparent during childhood. With very few exceptions, intellectual and adaptive deficiencies that appear later in life suggest psychosis, brain damage, or other pathology, but *not* mental deficiency. In this chapter we will describe the different degrees and types of retardation and examine their causes and treatment.

INTELLIGENCE

In order to understand retardation, we need first to clarify the meaning of *intelligence*. As we presently understand it, intelligence describes a combination of several abilities. Psychologists are not fully agreed on just which aptitudes comprise intelligence, but most point to skills such as the following (Brody, 1976; Jerison, 1973):

Ability to solve problems
Learning skills
Memory and concentration
Numerical ability
Reasoning and judgment
Verbal and perceptual comprehension

Flexibility and adaptability
Perceptual organization and spatial reasoning
Abstract thinking and originality

Those who are brighter usually possess a greater degree of nearly all these abilities. In contrast, the retarded individual is typically very low in every one of these aptitudes.

In addition to being aware that intelligence is composed of many related aptitudes, it is believed that it is also the result of both neurological and environmental circumstances. All of us may be born with many different potentials. Depending upon the biochemistry and organizational complexity of our cerebral cortex, we are probably given a greater or lesser capacity to reason, learn, and remember. (Incidentally, brain size has practically no relationship to intelligence. Human brains are between 1000 and 2000 cubic centimeters, and both geniuses and mental retardates are found along most size dimensions.)

Evidence for the innateness of intelligence, like the hereditability of schizophrenia, comes largely from studies of identical twins. For over half a century, dozens of investigations of identical twins reared together and apart have shown a high intelligence correlation. Typically, the IQs of twins raised together have correlated about .8; raised apart, about .7. When kinship is studied, the closer the biological correspondence, the higher the IQ correlation. The measured intelligence of parents and children usually correlates at about .50, while for foster parents and their charges it is only about .20 (Cancro, 1971; Slater, 1971; Baroff, 1974) (see Figure 14.1). The position that intelligence is in large part genetic has sparked a great deal of controversy. This is primarily because some social scientists, like Jensen (1974), have suggested that since intelligence is presumably hereditary and there are reports of ethnic IQ differences, some groups are innately intellectually ahead of others. At-

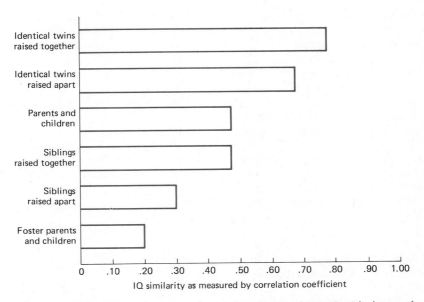

IQ similarity as measured by correlation coefficient

Figure 14.1. The chart is a summary of several studies correlating IQ with degree of kinship. It can be seen that the closer the biological relationship, the higher the IQ correlation. Data reported in McLearn & DeFries (1973) and based on studies including Freeman, 1928; Leahy, 1935; Newman, 1937; Blewett, 1954; Shields, 1962; Erlenmeyer-Kimling, 1962; Vandenberg, 1968; and Wilson, 1972.

THE PROBLEMS OF INTELLIGENCE TESTING

Much of the controversy swirling about the nature of intelligence centers on IQ tests. Some critics believe IQ testing results in so many misevaluations and false labels that they would prefer to do away with all such testing. But although IQ tests are fallible, at the moment we have no other way of making reliable judgments about intellectual potential. Such evaluations are often necessary to help make school placements, design learning environments, and arrive at other educational and social decisions. If some of the problems of IQ tests are kept in mind, it is less likely that we will become overreliant on them.

1. The best-known IQ tests are the Wechsler series (Wechsler Adult Intelligence Scale—WAIS, Wechsler Intelligence Scale for Children—WISC) and the Stanford-Binet. The Wechslers measure verbal, performance, and full-scale IQ. Usually the verbal and performance results are quite close, but those who have special talents (or weaknesses) in either direction—for example, in eye-hand coordination or abstract reasoning—may do better in one of the two IQ ranges. The Stanford-Binet yields a single IQ score and may be used to measure the abilities of children as young as 2 years of age. (At this early period in life, however, IQ scores are frequently difficult to evaluate and may also be quite unreliable.)

2. Both the Stanford-Binet and Wechslers are individually administered tests that yield precise-sounding scores. Because they, and all IQ examinations, produce exact numbers like 42 or 78, they falsely imply a high degree of mathematical accuracy. In reality Stanford-Binet, WAIS, WISC, and other individually given tests yield IQ scores that are fairly rough estimates. Upon retesting, scores may be as much as 5 to 10 points higher or lower. Lower reliability and validity can be also expected from group tests. These examinations, designed to be administered to large groups of people at the same time, are much weaker than good individually based intelligence assessments. IQs derived from group evaluations are often as much as 10 to 15 points in error. Because trained personnel are often not available to use a Wechsler or Stanford-Binet, many school systems depend on group testing and are unaware of their considerable degree of error.

3. Most IQ tests were standardized on white, middle-class children with adequate school experiences. When such examinations are given to children from other ethnic or cultural backgrounds, or to children with limited educational opportunity, the scores may be falsely low. The result is that sometimes children from lower socioeconomic backgrounds may be mislabeled retarded.

4. Because IQ tests are fallible, careful procedures must be followed to reach a diagnosis of mental retardation. In many instances, legal requirements stipulate at least two separate, individually administered intelligence examinations given by licensed professionals plus an evaluation of *social adaptivity*. One form often used to evaluate social adaptiveness is the Vineland Social Maturity Scale. This rating of developmental progress, originated by Doll (1953), measures social and maturational skills and results in a social quotient analogous to IQ.

---

tempts at **compensatory education,** special academic programs for the disadvantaged, are a waste of time. Intelligence is supposedly set at birth and can be little altered even by the best educational efforts.

The Jensen view and the conclusion that intelligence is genetic sparked intense and acrimonious debate during the late 1960s and early 1970s. Books and articles for and against the genetic postion mushroomed. Campus protests, lawsuits, charges and countercharges multiplied. Unfortunately, what was overlooked was that *even if intelligence might be partly hereditary, it does not follow that there are valid biological group differences.* In fact, careful measurements of the IQ of many different socioeconomic and ethnic groups suggest virtually *no meaningful intellectual inequalities* (Block and Dworkin, 1974; Brody, 1976).

The twin studies on which most of the evidence for IQ genetics is based have also been criticized for procedural errors. Kamin (1974) has reviewed the major investigations and found many of them seriously lacking in experimental objectivity and scientific rigor. In one comparison of the IQs of twins, the investigator subjectively "readjusted" test scores to suit his hypothesis. In another, twins allegedly reared separately were actually adopted by relatives, raised in nearly identical families, and actually lived next door to each other.

The most well publicized instances of possible research errors that Kamin has pointed to are in the work of Cryril Burt. In study after study spanning several decades, Burt, a British psychologist, consistently reported very high IQ similarities for twins. In one such project (1966), for example, the correlation for more than fifty pairs of identical twins raised together was announced to be .9; for those raised apart it was better than .8. Burt's work on IQ and in education was so impressive that he became the first psychologist to be knighted by the Queen of England. But from Kamin's point of view, Burt's work reveals methodological errors, self-serving biases, omissions of vital information, and statistical coincidences that are totally implausible. Some of Burt's citations, such as the names of co-workers and references, were apparently fictitious. Kamin suggests the possibility of scientific fraud (*The New York Times,* November 28, 1976, p. 26).

Despite the error and controversy, there is a core of data on the similarity of intellectual functioning in twins and relatives that still points to the probability of some innate factors. It is likely too that the transmission of intelligence involves several genes and is complex. Just as there are many fairly separate abilities that together seem to constitute what we call intelligence, there may be many different gene combinations involved. The part played by innate factors may also vary from individual to individual. For one person, inherited potential may be important; for another,

environment may be critical. Overall, the heritability of IQ is perhaps best thought of as providing each newborn with a wide range of intellectual potentials. A beneficial physical, educational, and psychological environment may maximize the inborn potential; an inadequate milieu may seriously handicap it (Brody, 1976).

LEVELS OF RETARDATION

Several different classification schemes are presently in use for diagnosing mental retardation. The oldest is rooted in the medical model and emphasizes causes. Descriptive labels are derived from the assumed cause of the disorder and the often distinctive physical appearance. For example, the child who because of hormonal pathology grows exceedingly rapidly, has a protruding jaw, eyes widely set apart, and a long head is likely to be diagnosed as having cerebral gigantism. Another person with a chromosomal anomaly who has a supposedly mongoloid appearance (slanted eyes, flattened facial profile, short stature) is diagnosed as having Down's syndrome.

But diagnoses of retardation based on overt physical features or attempts to classify deficiencies based on underlying cause tell us almost nothing about the abilities an individual possesses. One person diagnosed as having Down's syndrome may be able to speak fairly well and take care of his or her own hygiene meticulously. Another who looks very much like the first may be so incapacitated that he or she knows only a few words and is dependent on others for personal care. In order to make clear the degree of intellectual impairment involved, the AAMD now labels retardation according to IQ. We will follow this classificatory scheme to describe the retarded in terms of the extent of intellectual deficit, which can vary from mild to profound (Table 14.1). Later on, when discussing the causes of mental deficiency, we will find the medical diagnostic terms useful.

At this point it is appropriate also to point

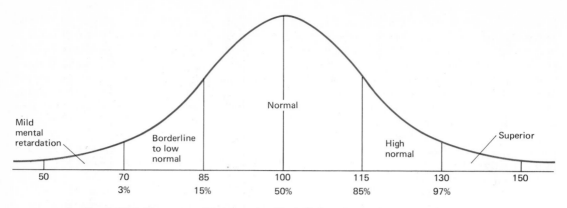

Figure 14.2. IQ scores and their meaning. The bell-shaped curve can be used to illustrate the distribution of intelligence. IQ scores are plotted along the baseline; below them are shown the cumulative percentage of people in each intellectual category. Notice that the mildly mentally retarded (50–70 IQ) simply represent a downward continuation of the curve.

out another practice that has changed in recent years. The terms **mental retardation, subnormality,** and **deficiency** are now used synonymously. Formerly, retardation and subnormality indicated that there was *no* evidence of brain damage; the label deficiency was used when intellectual disability was due to brain pathology. These distinctions have fallen into disuse and the three terms are now interchangeable.

There are four levels of mental retardation: mild, moderate, severe, and profound. Together these four groups constitute about 3 percent of the American population, a propor-

tion that is more or less true for most industrially advanced nations. Three percent of the American population means that in 1980 there will be more than 6.5 million mentally retarded people in this country, a very substantial figure. Of these, the mildly retarded are by far the largest group. Table 14.1 shows the numbers in each category, along with their IQ levels.

Mild retardation

The mildly retarded have an IQ score of between 50 and 70 and make up the very largest

---

TABLE 14.1
LEVELS OF MENTAL RETARDATION

IQ	Classification	(Description)	Number	Percent
50–69	Mild	Educable	5,600,000	85%
35–49	Moderate	Trainable	650,000	10
20–34	Severe	Custodial	200,000	3
under 20	Profound	Life dependent	100,000	2

Sources: *American Association on Mental Deficiency, President's Committee on Mental Retardation (1970); World Health Organization (1976).*

group, about 85 percent. Nearly all appear physically normal, and examination of their brains reveals no damage. They do not have the facial characteristics and physical handicaps typically seen in those with lower IQs, and they speak and understand well enough to hold an ordinary conversation.

With special education the more capable in this category can learn sixth-grade reading, writing, and arithmetic, a level of literacy sufficient to read easy magazine stories, go shopping, and fill out some employment applications. But despite their potential, most are inadequately literate, unemployed, and dependent on financial or other governmental assistance. The few who do receive special tutoring and training typically become self-sufficient and responsible members of society (Robinson and Robinson, 1976). The case of Timothy is an example.

Timothy R is 17 and a special class student. On the Wechsler Adult Intelligence Scale, his full-scale IQ was 62; on the Stanford-Binet his IQ was 67. On the Vineland Social Maturity Scale, Timothy's social age was equivalent to that of a 10-year-old. Timothy was seen by the school psychologist following a long period of frequent absences and apparent decline in motivation and attentiveness in class.

Timothy is the oldest child in his family and has two brothers, two sisters, and one stepsister. His father left home five years ago, and for the last three years the mother has been living with a man in his sixties who has fathered the stepsister. A social worker who visited the home stated that the parents seem to be of marginal intelligence and are living on welfare and the stepfather's disability pension. Timothy's sisters are of normal intelligence, but one of his brothers is borderline and the other mildly retarded. The home itself, a three-bedroom apartment in a public low-rent housing complex, is very crowded but fairly neat.

Timothy is considered one of the better special class students in that his literacy is quite good. Discussing his frequent absences and decline in interest, Timothy related that he had

been having "bad fights" with his stepfather. He accused the stepfather of making fun of him and his friends and of picking on his mother. The result was that Timothy frequently left the apartment upset and angry and instead of going to school went to a nearby shopping area, where he met older friends who were unemployed and did little more than "hang around."

The school psychologist recommended social work intervention in the family to help overcome some of the current frictions and counseling for Timothy. The long-range plan was to send Timothy to a vocational center where he could receive training in automobile maintenance. Timothy was very interested in cars and looked forward to learning how to dispense gasoline, wash and polish cars, and change tires and batteries. If he is motivated and the job market remains good, he should eventually be employable in a garage doing simple maintenance chores.

Moderate retardation

About 10 percent of all the retarded, nearly three-quarters of a million Americans, have an IQ between 35 and 50 and are called moderately retarded. Unlike the mildly retarded, most—though not all—of the moderately afflicted have the appearance of abnormality. Frequently they are shorter than average, disproportionately built and have an oddly shaped body or face. Eyes or ears may seem out of place and the head too small or large. Typically there are also sensory and motor defects such as hearing or visual losses, limb paralysis, and convulsive seizures, all likely due to brain damage. Those at the higher end of the scale can learn to read a few words, write their names, add (but usually not multiply or divide), and talk poorly, with many errors of articulation, vocabulary, and grammar. Those at the lower end are illiterate and talk very poorly, but usually manage to communicate. The entire group learns very, very slowly, can be highly distractible and forgetful, and usually appears awkward and clumsy.

Figure 14.3. People with Down's syndrome are usually moderately retarded. Though commonly used to illustrate mental deficiency, persons with Down's make up only a very small proportion of all those who are intellectually subnormal. (Photos: Scribe and Ulster County Association for Retarded Children, Kingston, N.Y.)

Some 10 to 20 percent of the moderately retarded are institutionalized. The rest also require at least some degree of supervision, since even with the best educational efforts almost none can become employable or socially independent. With very careful and patient training, however, most can become good workers in sheltered workshops and learn enough simple cleaning and cooking skills to be useful in a household. Marlene is a case in point.

Marlene is 14 years old and has been diagnosed as having Down's Syndrome. Her IQ score on the Wechsler Intelligence Scale for Children was 32 and on the Stanford-Binet, 39. On the Vineland Social Maturity Scale her social age was equivalent to that of a child of 5. Although Marlene has been in special classes for the retarded, she can only identify a few letters, cannot do any arithmetic, and is unable to write her name. Her speech is defective and often ungrammatical, but she can conduct a simple conversation.

Marlene's parents are both high school

teachers. Marlene's mother married late and had her first child when she was 37. Another child was born when the mother was 39, and Marlene was born when the mother was 43. Both older children are bright and in college. The parents consulted a psychologist because, now 58 and 66, they were concerned about their retarded daughter's future. They reported that Marlene helped with the housecleaning, bedmaking, and cooking and like many Down's children was easygoing, good-natured, friendly, and affectionate. Nevertheless, she required a considerable amount of supervision and definitely would never be able to live by herself.

The parents felt some guilt about their daughter and needed to understand that eventual institutionalization or residential placement was a necessity which would benefit both the child and her family. A program was worked out whereby Marlene would initially spend just weekends and then gradually more and more time at a nearby residential school for the retarded. In this way, Marlene could gradually adjust to the new environment and not feel "deserted," which was one of the mother's chief concerns.

Severe retardation

The severely retarded are a very small group whose IQ ranges between 20 and 35. Usually they suffer from serious physical handicaps and have misshapen limbs, heads, and bodies. They are likely to have impaired vision and/ or hearing, suffer from seizures, and have defects in important internal organs such as the heart and lungs. With unusually patient and skillful effort the severely retarded may learn to communicate a little, and to dress and toilet themselves. Most are institutionalized and often because of neglect are mute, not toilet-trained, and appear emotionally isolated.

Profound retardation

Approximately 2 percent of the retarded have an IQ under 20 and are classified as profoundly

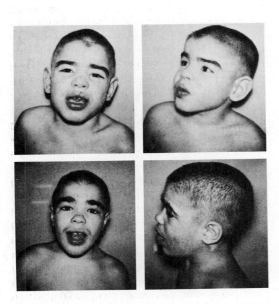

Figure 14.4. Severe forms of retardation are uncommon and constitute only about 3 percent of all mental deficiencies. Mucopolysaccharidosis, also called Hunter's syndrome, is a severe retardation transmitted through a recessive gene. (Photo: D. S. S. Gellis, Tufts-New England Medical Center, and the Atlas of Mental Retardation Syndromes. U.S. Department of Health, Education and Welfare, Developmental Disabilities Office)

retarded. Nearly all are institutionalized and extremely disabled. Many are deaf or blind, nearly totally paralyzed, and bedridden. They also have grotesque distortions of the body, face, and head. Frequently they cannot even indicate simple needs and are totally dependent on others to feed and toilet them and keep them alive. Thus they are often called "life-dependent." The profoundly retarded generally have very short life spans, so that adults in this category are extremely rare.

Other classifications

The mildly retarded are usually physically normal but low in intelligence. The moderate, severe, and profoundly retarded are both very low in intelligence and usually physically abnormal. Many authorities therefore distinguish between the mildly retarded and the more seriously impaired (Chiva, 1973).

It is argued that the mildly retarded simply represent a downward extension of normal intellectual function. In a simpler society than our own, one that does not require such a high degree of literacy, judgment, and planning, the mildly retarded might not even be considered defective. Tarjan and Wright (1973) and others argue that only IQs under the 50s should be considered retarded. Those whose IQ is just under 70 are falsely labeled by advanced technological societies which have rigidly standardized educational systems that will not or cannot accommodate those with significant but normal variations in learning ability. From this point of view, the number of retarded should not be calculated at 3 percent of the American population but at 1 percent or less, or only 2.2 million.

The more serious forms of retardation, it is contended, are not really intellectual deficiencies as much as they are general physical deficiencies. With few exceptions, the more seriously retarded suffer impairments of internal and sensory organs, and skeletal and central nervous systems. The distinction between the two types of retardation is upheld by labeling the mildly retarded as *primary, familial,* or *endogenous* (meaning due to inherent deficit). The moderate, severe, and profound levels of retardation are labeled *secondary, pathological,* or *exogenous* (due to external damage).

ADJUSTMENT PROBLEMS

The mentally retarded may have psychological problems just like any one else. In fact, their intellectual and social disabilities may sometimes make them more vulnerable to neurotic and psychotic symptoms. Much more common, however, are problems in motivation and behavior.

Low motivation   For many retarded people, a self-perpetuating cycle of failure begins very early in life. Continual frustration and defeat lead to low self-esteem, which leads to low motivation and failure again. Skilled teachers of the intellectually deficient recognize this cycle and break it by arranging their teaching so that the retarded can succeed. Such positive learning experiences gradually build up self-confidence and new motivation.

Another personality problem contributing to low motivation is the high degree of dependence developed by most institutionalized individuals and even some who live at home. The lives of many of the mentally deficient are closely regulated. They are told when to sleep, what to wear and eat, whom to befriend, what to learn, and what not to do. They make few individual decisions; almost always, a parent, social worker, or teacher decides what is best. In such situations, initiative and drive are quickly replaced by dependency. Whether the retarded person is in an institution or the child of overprotective parents, when put into a job or classroom, such a dependent person acts passive and confused. He or she expects complete direction, care, and guidance.

Behavior   The retarded frequently have poor judgment and often find it difficult to anticipate results. If they come from families that are not able to offer adequate guidance because of poverty, low educational level, or social isolation, conduct problems such as fighting, truancy, running away, temper tantrums, and negativism are frequent. On the other hand, the incidence of serious delinquency is not much different for the mentally deficient (Jenkins, 1973; Trohanowicz, 1978).

The old stereotype of the retarded characterized them as overly fertile and "immoral" (Goddard, 1912). Such stereotyping is unjustified, but because most retarded individuals are sexually uninformed, the incidence of unwanted pregnancy is sometimes high. In addition, homosexuality and sexual anxiety are frequent in institutions. Recognizing the sexual fears and lack of information of people with low intellectual skills, several agencies, like planned parenthood groups, have developed special programs. When retarded clients are informed and counseled, their sexual behavior is as responsible as that of people with normal intelligence (Balthazzar and Stevens, 1974; Philips, Irving, and Williams, 1975).

Figure 14.5. Among the moderately and severely retarded, the frequency of psychosis is fairly high. Often their intellectual and physical handicaps have isolated them from others and led to psychotic thinking and emotion. (Photo: Smith, Kline and French Laboratories, G. William Holland)

CAUSES

The causes of mental retardation are as numerous as the diseases, toxins, injuries, or conditions that limit or impair the healthy development of a person. To make some sense out of all the possible explanations, the American Association on Mental Deficiency has arranged all known causes into eight different groups. We have further reduced the possible causes into four broad categories: biosocial limitations, genetic pathologies, diseases and injuries, and congenital conditions.

Biosocial limitations

Although it is apparent that the mildly retarded are usually physically normal people with lower intellectual ability, just saying they have less intelligence is not sufficient explanation. Closer examination of individuals diagnosed as mildly subnormal reveals a number of possible *interacting* factors (Karrer, 1976):

1. Most of the mildly retarded come from parents who are themselves mildly deficient or borderline.
2. Most of the mildly retarded come from homes characterized by poverty and/or limited cultural and educational exposure.
3. Many of the mildly subnormal have a history of poor care during infancy and childhood, possible malnourishment, and environmental hardship.
4. A few of the mildly defective come from distinctly pathological homes where there is mental illness, physical abuse, or addiction.

When we look at all the biological and social circumstances responsible for mild subnormality, we are left with a constellation of factors likely to operate differently in varying situations. Some of the mildly defective may be limited primarily because they inherited less potential. Many others classified as mildly retarded, and estimates range from 5 to as much as 40 percent, may have been born with adequate potential only to have it restricted by educational or nutritional deprivation as well as limited family care and other social burdens (Hurley, 1969; Hutt and Gibby, 1976; Prescott and Read, 1975). A case such as Missy's illustrates the point.

Missy was 4 years old when a social service agency had her legally removed from her home. She was being raised by her mother and the mother's occasional boyfriend, both of whom were alcoholics. The biological father had left before Missy was born, but visited once in a while. He testified that Missy was completely neglected. The mother often left Missy alone for as much as a whole day, and even when she was home she sometimes neglected to feed or change her. As she got older, Missy became very demanding and cried a great deal, which confused and frightened the mother. The mother liked her daughter and did not abuse her. But her ignorance of how to deal with her and her frequent alcoholic bouts meant that Missy received very little care or guidance.

When Missy was placed in a foster home she was totally unfamiliar with any children's rhymes, stories, or nursery tales. She had never been read a story, never owned a picture book, or had any toys other than two stuffed animals. Her mother did not have a television set, so watching programs was at first a very frightening experience for her. At the time of her placement the Stanford-Binet test revealed an IQ of 64, indicating mild mental retardation. One and a half years later, after participating in a healthy foster home, Missy's IQ was measured by a school psychologist as 91, within normal limits. It is safe to guess that had Missy remained in her mother's home she might well have eventually attended special classes for the retarded and remained functionally deficient all her life.

Genetic Pathology

Presumably heredity plays an important but ambiguous role in those who are physically normal but mildly retarded. The contribution of genetics is much clearer in several types of retardation directly traceable to heredity pathology. In these conditions there are not only signs of mental retardation, invariably moderate or lower, but also accompanying neurological and physical defects. These retardations, though transmitted along family lines, often appear so erratically that both parents, normal themselves, are unaware they are carrying a faulty gene (Figure 14.6).

Possibly the best known retardation due to transmission of a faulty gene or gene combination is **phenylketonuria** (PKU). PKU is transmitted by an autosomal (non-sex-linked) recessive gene and is a rare disorder occurring only about once in every 15,000 births (Figure 14.7). It appears in all ethnic groups, but is seen with greatest frequency in parents who are both of northern European origin, blond and fair skinned. The gene grouping in PKU results in the child being unable to metabolize some proteins properly, causing the elevation of phenylalanines in the blood. This in turn triggers chemicals destructive to brain tissue. Without treatment, most PKU infants eventually become moderately to severely retarded. Since the 1950s infants have been screened for the possible presence of phenylalanines in their blood or urine with simple tests. The con-

dition is now almost always detected very early and treated by a special diet, so that most susceptible children escape serious retardation.

Other retardations attributable to genetic pathology, and also quite rare, are **Tay-Sachs** and **Niemann-Pick** diseases (Figure 14.7). These are actually two of a related group of genetically transmitted disorders in which the child's growth is impaired by faulty fat metabolism. Because of metabolic and associated chemical failures, body fats are erroneously accumulated in nerve cells and internal body organs, causing their gradual destruction. The outcome is an increasing number of serious physical and intellectual impairments as the child grows older, with death as a frequent outcome.

Down's syndrome, formerly called mongolism or mongoloid idiocy, is the result of a form of genetic pathology, but it is *not* inherited. The parents have an apparently normal complement of chromosomes, but some disturbance in the mother's reproductive function produces an extra chromosome or related aberration in the child. The result is the typical Down's person (Figure 14.3), who is usually moderately mentally retarded, although occasionally intelligence reaches into the low end of the mildly impaired range. About 4,500 children with Down's syndrome are born every year, actually only a very small number, but it makes them *the single largest identifiable group among the moderately retarded.* Older mothers are considerably more likely to have a Down's child. For a young mother the incidence of this retardation is 1 in 2000 births, whereas for mothers over 40 years old it rises to 1 in 50. It has been argued that since older mothers usually have older husbands it may be the father's chromosomal contribution combining with the mother's that produces Down's, but the data are not sufficient to warrant conclusive statements.

Disease and malfunction

Before discussing disease and other sources of brain injury, we need to emphasize that men-

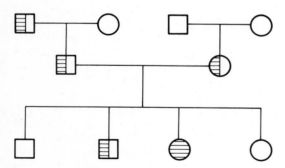

Figure 14.6. Genetic pathology. This is a typical pedigree for recessive inheritance. When an apparently normal female carrying a recessive gene for one of the disorders causing mental retardation ⊕ has children with a male also carrying the recessive gene ▤ , the probability is that one-fourth of their children will show the mental retardation ⊖ . In this pedigree genes from both the father and mother are necessary because a recessive gene manifests itself only when paired in an individual.

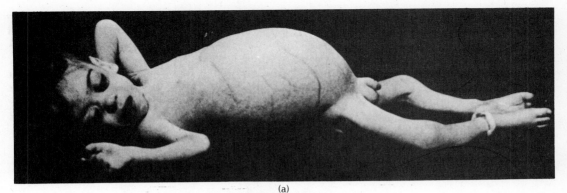

(a)

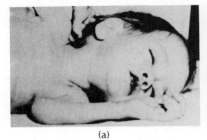

(a)

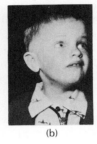

(b)

Figure 14.7. Both PKU (b) and Niemann-Pick's (a) disease are rare, genetically transmitted disorders. In both conditions failures in the body's metabolic processes may result in severe physical and intellectual damage. PKU can be detected and largely prevented, but Niemann-Pick's is usually fatal. (Photos: Dr. S. S. Gellis, Tufts-New England Medical Center, and the Atlas of Mental Retardation Syndromes, U.S. Department of Health, Education and Welfare, Developmental Disabilities Office)

tal retardation occurs only *when the brain is damaged very early in life*. The person with a normal IQ who at the age of 37 loses brain tissue because of an accident may have several intellectual faculties impaired. He or she may find it difficult or impossible to read, talk, or do arithmetic. Judgment, memory, learning ability, and/or concentration may be handicapped, but he or she will *not* be mentally retarded. Past early childhood, intellectual impairments attributable to brain damage in a previously normal person are described as aphasias, agnosias and the like, indicating a specific loss of ability (Chapter 15). To result in mental retardation, the brain injury must occur before birth or during infancy, when the entire range of intelligence is likely to be equally affected.

INFECTIOUS DISEASES Any disease that involves the central nervous system can harm the brain and produce mental deficiency. Encephalitis, infection of the brain, is one. It is not a common disorder, but occasional outbreaks do occur in the United States. The en-

cephalitis virus may be spread by mosquitoes, or the illness may occur as a complication of measles or even the common cold. Most recently, the microorganism responsible for the ordinary cold sore has been implicated in retardation. Cold sores are caused by the herpes virus and usually appear on the lips. But this infection may also be located on other parts of the body, including the genital area. The mother with herpes sores in the vagina or cervix can transmit the infection to her child during birth. In infants this viral infection is frequently very serious and causes extensive neurological and intellectual damage.

So far we have been discussing the intellectual handicap that may result when the brain cells of an infant or child are destroyed by infection. Brain injury may also occur to the unborn child; several diseases in the mother herself may harm her child in utero. The best-documented maternal infection destructive to the fetus is rubella, commonly called German measles. In the winter and spring of 1964, the United States had an epidemic of rubella.

THE IDIOT SAVANT

Occasionally newspapers or television report someone mentally retarded who nevertheless has remarkable skill in a special area. Such people are exceedingly rare in actuality. Called an Idiot Savant, meaning "wise" idiot, such a person could have an IQ of 25 or 40 but be talented in arithmetic or spelling or have the kind of memory able to recall hundreds of telephone numbers. Exceedingly rare as these feats are, rarer still are the very few reported "idiots" who have outstanding musical, painting, or other artistic ability. One explanation of the idiot savant is that following birth, and frequently during the first year or two of infancy, a disease or injury brought about a highly inconsistent degree of brain damage. The damage was sufficient to lower intellectual function, but some areas were spared, accounting for one residual good ability.

Among the several million who contracted the disease were a hundred thousand or more women in the first trimester (first three months) of pregnancy. In 1964 there was still debate as to whether rubella, in the first trimester when the fetal organs are being formed, actually caused mental retardation. Studies in both Europe and Australia, some dating as far back as World War I, had pointed to a probable link. Nevertheless, many physicians rejected these findings and the women were frequently reassured that rubella would not harm the fetus. By the end of 1964, when rubella babies were being born, the destructive effect of the German measles virus was obvious. The rubella child usually has serious heart defects, impaired hearing and vision, and frequently spastic paralysis of various limbs. In addition, IQ measures reveal that most are moderately retarded. Following the 1964 epidemic, which resulted in the birth of 50,000 rubella children, crash efforts were made to produce a vaccine. Since then, immunization against rubella has become possible, and most young women are now protected.

MALFUNCTION The malady producing mental retardation can also be the result of a breakdown in the body's own regulatory system. In erythroblastosis, a mother whose blood is Rh− and who is carrying an Rh+ infant may develop antibodies against her own child. The mechanism is as follows: If sufficient quantities of the fetus's Rh+ red blood corpuscles pass to the mother, this alerts her body's defensive antibodies. In subsequent pregnancies these antibodies may accumulate, and large numbers may cross the placenta and attack the blood structure of the baby; the eventual result for the child may be anemia, liver destruction, and damage to the basal ganglia of the brain. One extreme outcome of this is a disease called **kernicterus,** a life-threatening condition with severe to profound mental retardation.

We have described the mechanism involved in erythroblastosis, also called Rh incompatibility, because there are millions of Rh− mothers with Rh+ children. But it should be emphasized that in the majority of such incompatibilities there is no blood cell crossover, and the birth is normal. That is, in most instances the placenta separating the mother from her unborn child remains intact and effectively separates the two blood streams. In addition, today when an obstetrician detects the possibility of Rh incompatibility, remedial measures are available which can prevent damage and retardation.

Toxins and trauma

Although the brain is well protected by surrounding tissue, fluid, and the skull, it can be injured by any number of toxic substances. Barbiturates (sleeping pills), carbon monoxide, lead, heroin, and hundreds of other chemicals and medications may harm the brain of a child or fetus. Similar impairments may occur as a result of hard blows on the head, tumors, radiation, and other direct trauma to cortical tissue. Generally, the brain damage due to a toxin or other trauma does not lead to an easily labeled type of mental retardation. But there is one exception, and that is **hydrocephalus**.

A number of different injuries to the head, spinal cord, or brain itself may interfere with the normal circulation of cerebrospinal fluid. When the absorption, formation, or circulation of the fluid is hindered, it may build up in the skull, forcing an increase in the size of the cranium. The hydrocephalic individual typically has a greatly enlarged and mis-shapen head and suffers from distortion of the facial features. When the damage from hydro-cephalus occurs very early, before or shortly after birth, and when treatment is lacking or ineffective, the child may be moderately to pro-foundly subnormal and have a wide number of physical and sensory defects (Figure 14.8).

Birth itself may traumatize the brain. In the past, the improper use of forceps (instru-ments to grasp the child during delivery) some-times injured the baby's skull and brain. Equally destructive was the practice of heavily sedating the mother during delivery. This sometimes resulted in a child being born deeply anesthetized and not breathing. An-oxia, deprivation of oxygen, is extremely dan-gerous to cortical tissue. After not much more than a minute without oxygen, millions of sen-sitive neural cells may die. The child born not breathing who takes several minutes to revive is very likely to be substantially handicapped.

Most susceptible to brain injury are the in-fants who are born prematurely. **Prematurity** usually means an infant born less than seven months after conception and weighing less than about 5 pounds. Over 300,000 such babies are born each year. The majority of them, be-cause of good care, thrive and are healthy and normal. Quite a few, however, because of their incomplete development, have problems breathing, eating, and sustaining other life functions. They are also more susceptible to disease, toxins, and other hazards. As a result, estimates suggest, 10 to 20 percent may be neurologically damaged and evidence some de-gree of mental retardation.

A condition often associated with prematur-ity is **cerebral palsy,** although it may also be caused by disease, toxin, or anything else

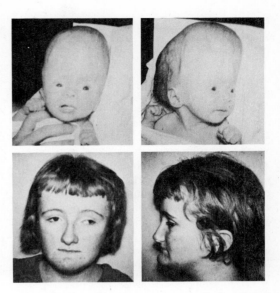

Figure 14.8. Hydrocephalus is the result of an injury or disease that has impaired the normal circulation of fluid in the skull. Not all those with hydrocephalus are retarded. (Photos: Dr. S. S. Gellis, Tufts-New England Medical Center, and the Atlas of Mental Retardation Syn-dromes, U.S. Department of Health, Education and Wel-fare, Developmental Disabilities Office)

that injures the brain. There are approxi-mately 250,000 persons with cerebral palsy, 100,000 of them with associated mental defi-ciency. But although less than half of all cere-bral palsy patients are retarded, many face the danger of false labeling. Because of their difficult speech and body impairments, many CP patients are mistakenly considered re-tarded, treated as such, and as a result often have their real abilities decline.

CP patients may have an arm or leg rigidly contracted (spastic paralysis), move or wave a limb in a constant purposeless way (atheto-sis), and/or stumble, sway, or stagger when they walk (ataxia). Their speech may be thick, slurred, and barely understandable; they may move and twist their arms, head, or body try-ing to produce a word. The seriousness of CP symptoms depends upon the amount of brain damage. Some who are minimally handicap-ped can lead independent lives; at the other extreme, some may have to be strapped into a wheelchair and their every need cared for (Figure 14.9).

Congenital conditions

The word *congenital* means present at birth. We use it here to describe those deficiencies that are present at birth but whose cause is variable or unknown. Three such disorders are **microcephaly** (small head), **macrocephaly** (large head), and **Apert's syndrome**. In microcephaly, brain size may or may not be significantly diminished. In macrocephaly, the brain is unusually big and heavy, producing an enlarged skull. (The big head in hydrocephalus is due to internal fluid pressure enlarging the skull.) In Apert's syndrome, the head is elongated, the body is shortened, and

toes and fingers are thickly webbed—so called mitten hands.

All of these disorders are puzzling. Sometimes the mother's history suggests an injury and on rare occasions a genetic pattern is found, but most of the time the causes are unknown. All three retardations are uncommon, with macrocephaly being the rarest of all. The

Figure 14.10. People with microcephaly are usually mildly to moderately retarded, although some have been reported to have normal intelligence. (Photo: Scribe and Ulster County Association for Retarded Children, Kingston, N.Y.)

Figure 14.9. Cerebral palsy is often associated with prematurity or brain injury at birth. Less than half of all cerebral palsy patients are retarded, though the severity of their physical symptoms may cause them to be falsely labeled deficient. The woman pictured is seriously handicapped, but she is very intelligent and has a responsible job. (Photo: Scribe)

CAUSES AND TYPES OF MENTAL RETARDATION

Cause	Physical type	Explanation	Degree of retardation
Biosocial limitation	Those retarded because of limited biological endowment and/or environmental deprivation are usually physically normal		Mild
Genetic pathology	Mucopolysaccharidosis	Due to transmission of recessive gene	Severe
	Niemann-Pick		Severe
	PKU		Moderate
	Tay-Sachs		Severe
	Down's syndrome	Nonhereditary chromosomal abnormality	Moderate
Disease and malfunction	Rubella	Maternal German measles	Moderate
	Kernicterus	Mother-child blood incompatibility	Severe
Toxin and trauma	Cerebral palsy	Central nervous system damage close to time of birth	None to profound
	Hydrocephalus		
Congenital condition	Apert's syndrome	Causes variable or unknown	Moderate
	Cerebral gigantism		Moderate
	Macrocephaly		Severe
	Microcephaly		None to severe

degree of physical and intellectual disability associated with them is quite variable. Mostly there is moderate or greater retardation, but in a few instances IQs close to normal have been reported (Figure 14.10).

TREATMENT AND PREVENTION

A peek into a textbook on mental retardation a generation ago would have yielded little more in the way of treatment recommendations than sterilization and confinement. Even today, there is still a good deal of unwarranted pessimism about the intellectually deficient, although enough is now known about retardation to help improve the intellectual and social capabilities of many millions of children and adults.

Education

The public schools could reach more than 90 percent of mentally subnormal children and are thus the most valuable resource for upgrading their level of function. Most school systems now have special education classes for the retarded, headed by specifically trained teachers. In the best of these classrooms the most advanced learning techniques, old-fashioned drill, and patient individual attention are combined to enable mildly retarded individuals to achieve substantial literacy. It may take a mildly retarded child until 14, 15, or even older to reach sixth-grade literacy, but with persistent help it can be done. In addition, many schools now teach social skills such as shopping, dating, child care, and sex education.

A current trend in some facilities is **mainstreaming,** placing certain retarded children in *regular* classrooms. This is because some special education classrooms may be inadequate or even injurious. Children who are only mildly deficient, the so-called **educable mentally retarded (EMR),** may be particularly discouraged by such segregated classrooms. Budoff and Gottlieb (1976) studied 31 EMR children in special education classes and mainstreamed in regular rooms. After a year of schooling, the mainstreamed students were more self-controlled, learned more, and had better attitudes and judgment. Mainstreaming may in the future replace the traditional special education classroom for the more capable mentally retarded.

Training and sheltered workshops

The rehabilitation agency and sheltered workshop play a special role in preparing retarded clients for employment. In these facilities they can get psychological counseling as well as vocational and social assistance, all intended to foster their independence. The sheltered workshop is also a place of employment for less capable clients. Work is geared to the level of function of each client and frequently involves packaging, sorting, sewing, cleaning, and domestic activities. Although the workers are too slow to meet industrial standards, many are able to produce enough to earn from $20 to $50 a week or more.

Medical treatment and psychotherapy

Retarded people may be helped by psychiatric and neurologic medications. The moderate, severe, and profoundly defective frequently suffer from seizures which, in addition to their retardation, makes learning and socializing difficult. Anticonvulsive medication such as Dilantin is usually successful in curbing such symptoms and thus indirectly helps the adjustment of these patients. Psychotherapeutic drugs such as Valium or Thorazine may also be used to reduce anxiety or help stabilize emotions and mood. A fearful, defensive, or resistive retarded student often becomes much more cooperative and motivated when appropriate psychiatric drugs are prescribed.

Medical therapies—that is, surgery, drugs, and other physical remedies—are not dependent upon verbal interaction with the patient. The psychological therapies, particularly the counseling approaches are heavily verbal.

Consequently, the psychodynamic therapist is immediately confronted with the retarded person's low verbal productivity. The greater the level of retardation, the less the ability to reason and to understand human interactions. Nevertheless, these deficiencies do not automatically rule out all psychological treatment approaches. Since most defective patients are only mildly impaired, nearly all can be reached if the therapist modifies the verbal approach. In addition, some forms of psychological treatment (finger painting, play therapy, and so on) are only minimally dependent on words and are therefore feasible for even the most seriously retarded.

One of the least verbally dependent psychotherapeutic techniques is behavior therapy. Behavioral techniques are widely used in many institutions, workshops, and schools. Even with severely deficient patients, this therapy has proved successful in reducing fear, defensive symptoms, and behavior problems.

For a few retarded children and adults, about one in ten, institutionalization may be necessary. When behavior or adjustment problems are severe or no other facilities exist to house and care for an intellectually deficient person, the only alternative may be a special hospital or school. The best of such facilities are like halfway houses and try to integrate the retarded person into the community.

Prevention

Every year approximately 125,000 children born in the United States will be mentally retarded. For many of them our present knowledge and skills are sufficient to prevent the retardation altogether or significantly limit its handicapping effect. One type of effort should be general and directed at society as a whole; other types should be specific and focused on particular individuals.

The general effort to prevent mental deficiency requires combined governmental, scientific, and social action at all levels of society. Particular attention needs to be given to the poorest 10 percent of the nation's families, which now account for such a disproportionate

TWO BEHAVIOR MODIFICATION PROGRAMS

Goal: Teach two severely retarded and withdrawn 10-year-old girls beginning social and verbal skills.

Technique: Sit girls facing one another on floor about 3 feet apart for two 30-minute sessions daily. Show them how to roll a ball between them. For each correct response, reinforce with candy or praise. After this task is learned, teach children to pass doll, say "please" and "thank you," and add other responses.

Results: After eight weeks of training, social and verbal responses increased from a beginning average of one per thirty seconds to over five for the same time period.

Goal: Rid moderately retarded of undesired behaviors such as head banging and screaming.

Technique: Study stimuli to behavior and remove (for example, long periods of inactivity frequently led to screaming). Make patients aware of and teach to participate in elimination of behavior; keep charts for each patient showing frequency and duration of undesired behavior. Keep goals small and attainable (for example, if period before breakfast is free of undesired behavior, reward with token). In rare instances punish undesired behavior with aversive stimuli (for example, a firm "no" when undesired behavior occurs).

Results Over a three-week period undesired behavior greatly reduced or eliminated for all five patients.

---

share of retarded people. These families have to be helped to obtain good nutrition, education, housing, medical, and psychological care. The chain of physical and psychological impoverishment and marginal living needs to be interrupted so that whatever intellectual potentials do exist are maximized. At the same time, the entire population can benefit from birth screening (for example, to detect and treat PKU), immunization against damaging diseases, the elimination of hazardous substances, realistic sex and birth control education, and all the other precautions and remedial measures we mentioned earlier.

The more specific preventive methods focus on individual prenatal counseling. Such guidance is useful for all mothers, but it is particularly necessary for mildly retarded adults. Good counseling can help them understand their responsibilities and carry out sound birth and child-rearing practices. For intellectually normal parents who have had or suspect they might have a defective child, genetic guidance is essential. By evaluating the parents' health and their backgrounds, counselors can usually predict the likelihood of a defective birth.

When the woman seeking genetic advice is already pregnant, amniocentesis or fetogra-

Figure 14.11. Proper nutrition, education, maternal care, and genetic counseling could probably help prevent a good proportion of the 125,000 new instances of mental retardation recorded every year. (Photo: Scribe and Ulster County Association for Mental Retardation, Kingston, N.Y.)

phy may be recommended. **Amniocentesis** is a safe and simple procedure in which physicians use a long needle inserted into the mother's uterus to withdraw 10 to 20 ml of amniotic fluid (the liquid surrounding the fetus) at the end of the first trimester of pregnancy. Culture of the cells in the fluid allows the detection of several dozen different types of retardation, including Down's syndrome and Tay-Sachs disease. **Fetography** is a radiographic technique that can outline the shape of the fetus as early as the first trimester. Among the more serious forms of retardation that can be detected by this method is hydrocephaly. Both amniocentesis and fetography permit parents and physicians to anticipate retardation and take whatever measures, including therapeutic abortion, may be effective or necessary.

SUMMARY

The mentally retarded, the intellectually and socially below normal, constitute 3 percent of the population of the United States. One criterion by which retardation is determined is level of intelligence, usually measured by an IQ test. Intelligence may be determined by the structure and function of the brain and be genetically transmitted, though learning and other environmental factors probably modify it significantly. The tests currently used to measure intelligence are imperfect, so that IQ scores are often only an approximate index of intellectual potential.

There are four levels of deficiency: mild, moderate, severe, and profound. More than eight out of ten of the subnormal are mildly retarded. This group is usually physically normal and can be minimally literate and employable. The lower levels of retardation are ordinarily illiterate, have difficulty communicating, are physically impaired, and have a distinctive appearance. The nature of their deficiency and appearance are used to classify and label the more seriously retarded. Because of their intellectual deficits, retarded persons have particular adjustment problems, including low motivation and behavioral difficulties.

Most of the mildly retarded are deficient because they have a lesser intellectual endowment. Some may have had the potential for good intelligence but function at a lower level because of malnutrition, poor education, and inadequate family care or social environment.

Genetic abnormality resulting in brain damage accounts for a large proportion of those moderately and seriously retarded. Conditions such as PKU and Tay-Sachs disease are caused by a recessive gene. Down's syndrome is due to a nonhereditary chromosomal defect and seems to be related to the age of the mother. Another common cause of mental retardation may be disease. Illnesses such as encephalitis in the child or rubella in the mother during early pregnancy frequently result in brain pathology and deficiency. Brain damage and subsequent mental subnormality may also be due to the body's own malfunction, as in the case of mothers whose blood type is RH− and the child's RH+, an incompatibility that sometimes causes the mother's body mechanisms to destroy the child's blood. Toxins and accidents can injure the central nervous system and result in hydrocephalus, cerebral palsy, and many other abnormalities. When the causes of mental retardation are not known, the condition can be described as congenital, meaning present at birth.

Treatment for the retarded includes special education, medical and psychological therapy, and rehabilitation and job training. Most retarded people can be helped; very few actually require institutionalization. Preventive efforts include individual social counseling as well as major social changes. During pregnancy, amniocentesis and fetography allow some serious forms of retardation to be detected.

15 Organic Disorders

ORGANIC AND ADJUSTMENT

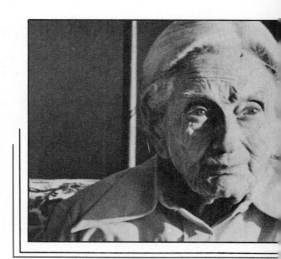

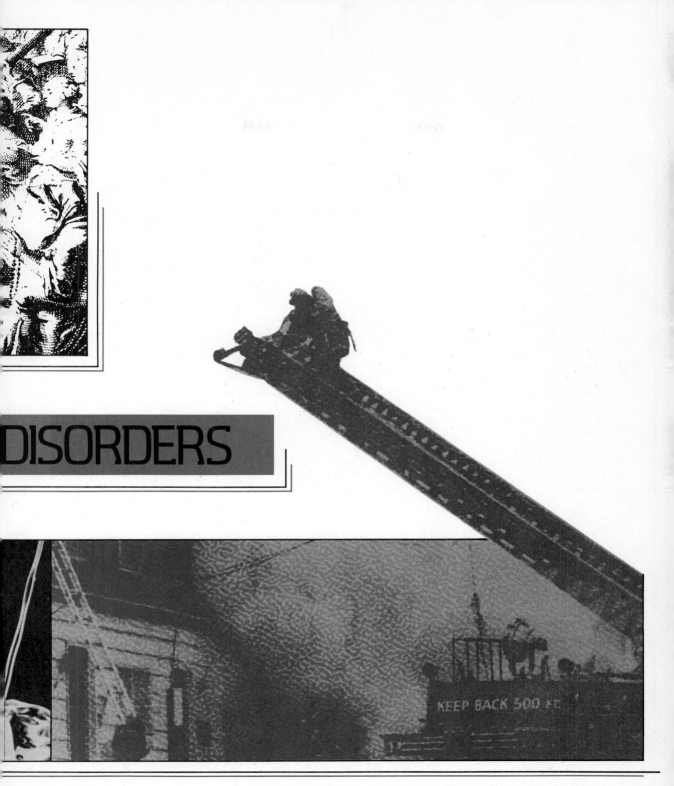

DISORDERS

16 Adjustment Reactions: Trauma and Age

Organic Disorders

The brain, a 3-pound network of neural cells, is the most complex and fundamental human organ. It is at the core of all our behavior. The central role of the brain makes it reasonable to look to it to explain abnormal as well as normal conduct. In fact, many who share the organic view of mental illness argue that some form of brain disturbance has to be responsible for all psychological abnormality. They contend that sooner or later increasing scientific precision will permit us to specify the neurological cause of every mental disorder.

At present, the belief that brain damage is, or should be, the explanation for all mental disorders has not been substantiated. Common abnormalities such as alcoholism and neuroses have not been traceable to specific defects in brain structure or function. It is possible that eventually some psychoses, perhaps schizophrenia, will be shown to be the result of

neurological impairment. But for now, we consider brain injury a cause for mental disorder only when *there is solid evidence of actual impairment* (Figure 15.1). In this chapter we will describe a number of different psychological abnormalities that are clearly the result of brain damage, so called organic disorders. We begin by listing the general symptoms of brain damage, then consider specific causes and conditions and end with a discussion of treatment.

THE PSYCHOLOGICAL SYMPTOMS OF BRAIN DAMAGE

The psychological symptoms of brain damage depend *both* on the areas of the brain that have been injured and on the personality of the person involved. People differ in the way in which they respond to brain injury. With similar organic brain damage, one person may

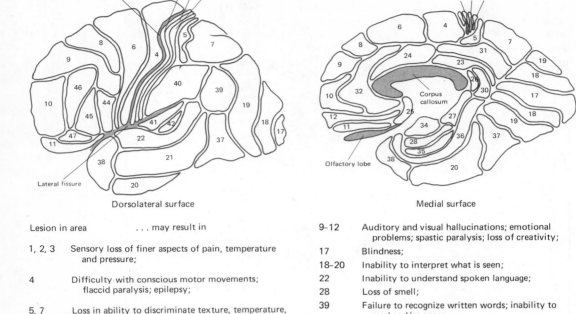

Dorsolateral surface   Medial surface

Lesion in area	... may result in
1, 2, 3	Sensory loss of finer aspects of pain, temperature and pressure;
4	Difficulty with conscious motor movements; flaccid paralysis; epilepsy;
5, 7	Loss in ability to discriminate texture, temperature, and density; losses in awareness of self or body parts, especially if lesion is on dominant side;
6	Disorganized movements of the head, eyes, trunk; flaccid paralysis if area 4 also suffers damage;
8	Difficulty in conscious eye movements;

9–12	Auditory and visual hallucinations; emotional problems; spastic paralysis; loss of creativity;
17	Blindness;
18–20	Inability to interpret what is seen;
22	Inability to understand spoken language;
28	Loss of smell;
39	Failure to recognize written words; inability to read and/or copy;
40	Loss in understanding and speaking language (if dominant side is affected);
41, 42	Inability to locate source of sounds;
43	Loss in taste;
44–47	Loss in ability to speak

Figure 15.1. The damaged brain. Damage to specific brain areas could result in the losses indicated, but the full extent and significance of every loss also depends on each person's overall ability and adjustment. (Source: Roy Hartenstein, *Human Anatomy and Physiology,* D. Van Nostrand, New York, 1976, p. 101.)

become depressed and another aggressive. As a general rule, and there are many exceptions, destruction of brain tissue tends to highlight or exaggerate preexisting personality trends. A person who has always been a little suspicious might become frankly paranoid after organic loss. Another individual who normally was sensitive and methodical may turn out to be extremely rigid and irritable (Horton, 1976).

Emotional disorder

Emotional disorder accompanies nearly all **organic psychosis** (meaning psychosis due to brain injury). Some patients are very **labile,** meaning they shift rapidly from one feeling to another. They are sad for a while, then happy, then morose again. Many others demonstrate **exaggerations of affect;** instead of just being a little blue they become extremely depressed and perhaps weep loudly and lament. Or the opposite may happen; they become **euphoric,** meaning irrationally happy. They feel that everything is just grand, exciting, and marvelous. Such patients may laugh and shout with joy, or engage in wild, exuberant behavior like spending sprees. Occasionally such seemingly uncontrolled affect is one of the earlier signs of brain damage.

NEUROLOGICAL SYMPTOMS OF BRAIN DAMAGE

A diagnosis of brain damage cannot be made on the basis of psychological symptoms alone; a complete neurological evaluation is required. Such an examination might include brain X-rays, checking for signs of motor and sensory loss, spinal fluid examinations, testing reflexes, and electroencephalography (EEG), measurements of the brain's electrical activity. The illustration of the patient shows neurological evidence of a lesion on the right side of the brain.

Some of the symptoms and terms for organic brain damage include the following:

Akinesia: Inability to move a muscle or limb, a paralysis

Ataxia: Inability to coordinate muscles, resulting, for example, in a stumbling gait

Babinski's sign: Improper flexion of the toe or other pathological reflex

Choreiform movements: Jerky, rapid, complex, and involuntary movements

Convulsion: A violent contraction of the muscles and body often resulting in unconsciousness; a seizure

Dysarthria: Slurred speech or other speaking difficulty due to the loss of muscular control in the jaw, tongue, and mouth

Hemianesthesia: Loss of feeling on one side of the body

Hemianopia: Loss of vision for half of the normal visual field

Hemiplegia: Paralysis of one side of the body

Paresthesia: Feeling abnormal sensations in fingers or limbs such as burning, tingling, or pricking

Stereognosis: Loss of the sense of touch

Tic: A spasmodic movement or twitch

Tremor: Trembling, usually of hands or arms

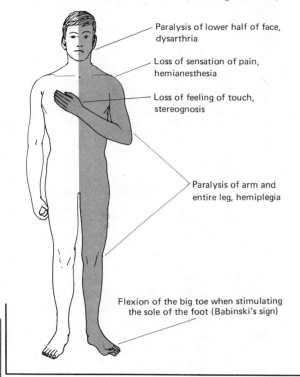

Paralysis of lower half of face, dysarthria

Loss of sensation of pain, hemianesthesia

Loss of feeling of touch, stereognosis

Paralysis of arm and entire leg, hemiplegia

Flexion of the big toe when stimulating the sole of the foot (Babinski's sign)

Still another, and fairly common, emotional effect of brain involvement is *touchiness or irritability.* Such people seem to have a chip on the shoulder, are easily angered, and often seem uncooperative or moody. This irritability is also frequently an early sign of brain malfunction. An older person who has previously been fairly well controlled but who suddenly and without apparent reason becomes unusually "touchy" might be suspected of having organic disorder.

Intellectual disorder

The destruction of brain tissue nearly always causes at least a few intellectual losses. The majority of patients suffer memory defects, specifically in *immediate memory.* They are able to recall distant events but not recent ones. They have no trouble talking about what happened ten or twenty years ago. They gladly reminisce about their high school days or their first job or the games they played as a child. But they cannot remember what they did this morning or even that they left the water running three minutes ago.

In addition to memory defects, most brain-damaged individuals have difficulty focusing their attention. Their minds wander; they are readily distracted and find it very hard to concentrate. They easily become confused and disoriented, failing to understand their surroundings or even themselves. They begin a tale about their schooling, but very quickly all sorts of distantly related, tangential, or unimportant details are introduced. Such excursions into irrelevancy are called **circumstantiality.** It is not uncommon for a patient with both immediate memory losses and a tendency to circumstantiality to be unable to finish a story or conversation.

In a few instances brain injury robs people of intellectual skills such as reading, writing, or doing arithmetic. Usually several skills are lost *together,* with writing the most commonly affected (Duffy and Ulrich, 1976). The medical terms for these dysfunctions are

ACALCULIA: Loss of the ability to do arithmetic

AGNOSIA: Loss of the ability to recognize common sounds, sights, or the passage of time

AGRAPHIA: Inability to write

ALEXIA: Inability to read

APHASIA: Loss of the ability to understand words or language or to respond properly (the term is sometimes used in a general way to describe any intellectual loss—for example, reading aphasia would equal alexia)

APRAXIA: Loss of the ability to carry out skilled motor acts like drawing or using a knife and fork

Thinking disruptions

Most brain-damaged persons have the ability to think disrupted; they are likely to lose some ability to reason and to become very *concrete.* They interpret everything that is said or done in a very solid, specific way. For example, upon admission one patient was asked to fill out a routine hospital form. The clerk pointed the back of her pen to the spaces requiring the patient's name, age, and so on. The person took the pen and tried to complete the form using the back of the pen.

This tendency to think and act very concretely is often called **loss of the abstract attitude.** Organic individuals with this deficit often seem extremely "stupid," unimaginative, and sometimes even retarded. Unable to

think abstractly, a brain-injured lawyer could not answer how an orange and a banana were alike. In response to a psychologist's question about how, "in which way," the two were the same, the lawyer kept insisting they were not the same. "They're different. One is long. The other is round. One is yellow. The other is red."

Related to the deficit in the ability to think abstractly are **rigidity** and **perseveration.** The person who is rigid, possibly in response to his or her own confusion, insists on strict and regular routine. Everything must be done in exactly the same orderly and prescribed way. If, for example, another person is sitting in his TV-watching chair, he does not know what to do. He may stand helplessly at the side of the chair, unable to resolve his dilemma.

Perseveration is doing the same task over and over again. One patient late for breakfast in a hospital was found in his room, continuously tying and retying his shoelaces. Because of their perseverative needs, organically damaged people often find it difficult to shift from one activity to another. When a task is finished, they may start it all over again, unable to readjust and do something new.

In a few instances brain-injured persons may hallucinate or be delusional, although these symptoms are much more common in the functional (nonorganic) psychoses, particularly schizophrenia. Even less common is **delirium.** Delirium is from Latin and literally means "off the track." The delirious patient is hallucinated, excited, deluded, restless, and often panicky. In fact, he or she may be so irrational and unapproachable as to require medical sedation or restraint. Delirium usually follows a sudden brain injury, high fever, or drug abuse, and lasts only a few hours or days.

Decline in social skills

The social skills of nearly all organic patients show at least some decline. In most instances this is the result of a growing inability to judge appropriate from inappropriate behavior or even right from wrong. Consequently, some

PSYCHOLOGICAL TESTING
FOR BRAIN DAMAGE

Possible brain damage may be detected with general psychological tests and with those specially developed to evaluate organicity.

General psychological tests

The Wechsler IQ tests may suggest brain damage if the verbal IQ is much higher than the performance IQ. When subjects do much better on tasks such as defining words or general information than on those necessitating motor skills or coordination, the difference could be due to cortical injury.

The Rorschach may also reveal brain damage. Organic subjects may *perseverate,* giving the same response for each inkblot. Brain-damaged people often have difficulty with Rorschach cards that are colored, rather than just black and white.

Special tests for brain damage

The Bender Visual Motor Gestalt Test requires subjects to copy simple drawings. Brain-damaged patients often draw designs backward or are unable to complete the images.

The Goldstein-Scheerer Tests of Abstract and Concrete Thinking require subjects to sort blocks and different colors and describe the use of common objects (like a cup) in order to evaluate possible thinking impairments due to organic deficit.

In the Minnesota Test for Differential Diagnosis of Aphasia, patients are examined in five different language areas to assess the extent of brain damage and make a prognosis for recovery.

The Wechsler Memory Scale, contains a short series of memory tasks useful for measuring memory, orientation, and possible brain injury, especially in senile and aphasic subjects.

The Pupil Rating Scale for Learning Disabilities is a series of tests measuring a number of educational skills. Because specific learning deficits might be due to brain damage, this test is helpful in evaluating this possibility.

brain-damaged persons become blunt and uninhibited. One of the first symptoms of OBS (organic brain syndrome) for one patient was his increasing use of obscenities in ordinary social conversation. Another patient wrote letters to government officials so filled with four-letter denunciations that the authorities were notified. These judgmental deficiencies are also apparent in the failure of most organic patients to make decisions or plan ahead. They know the car is mechanically defective, yet they start on a 200-mile trip. Or perhaps they go food shopping and bring back 10 pounds of bananas because they were on sale, even though nearly all the bananas will spoil before they can be eaten.

For a few brain-damaged persons, a combination of decline in social skills and disinhibition results in blatant, inappropriate sexual behavior. Both genders may be affected, although men are sometimes more aggressive. One extensively brain-injured 57-year-old woman invited her doctor to "make whoopie" and refused to let go of his tie unless he agreed. A 74-year-old male patient was hospitalized after several incidents involving his stopping women in the street and undressing for them.

A great many organically impaired persons seem to lose interest in their own hygiene or clothing. Some let themselves become very dirty and ungroomed. Others persist in wearing particular clothes even if they are soiled or inappropriate. An inexperienced psychiatric nurse once became upset with one of her organic patients because he insisted on always wearing a disheveled, tattered housecoat. The patient liked his coat and wore it whether he went to occupational therapy, the cafeteria, or a hospital dance.

Acute or chronic

So far we have enumerated the range of symptoms likely to follow brain damage but not mentioned their permanence. Although it would seem that psychoses resulting from actual physical damage to the brain would be permanent, in fact in many instances organic mental disorders are reversible. The majority of psychiatrically hospitalized OBS patients could be discharged as improved or recovered well within one year (Bergin and Garfield, 1971; Iverson and Iverson, 1975).

Whether a person's disorder will be acute or chronic is not easy to predict. But a rough guess can be made by evaluating the extent of neurological tissue destruction and the source of the damage. Acute conditions are usually the result of a toxin, high fever, accident, or other sudden disaster. A great deal of the brain is affected by the initial trauma, but the amount of tissue that is irreversibly lost is not very large. Such conditions are also marked by symptoms suggestive of acuteness. These indicators include delirium, confusion, and sometimes the temporary loss of consciousness.

Chronic disabilities tend to be subtle and insidious. There is a gradual and quiet destruction of millions of brain cells due to a tumor, a progressively malfunctioning artery, or some other extensive pathology. Particular kinds of symptoms also point toward chronicity: the patient's memory is fading, intellectual skills are declining, previous personality weaknesses are accentuated, and the person's entire adjustment is becoming more and more doubtful.

But the permanence or reversibility of all organic psychoses, whatever the causes or symptoms, is not always a certainty. The rule followed in good therapeutic facilities is not to count any one out. No matter how aged the patient or seemingly irreversible the symptoms, he or she is given the best available psychological and medical care. In this way the chronicity of a symptom is never a result of the doctor's or the patient's pessimism or neglect.

CAUSES AND DIAGNOSIS

Organic psychotic patients are diagnosed in terms of the cause of their brain damage. But different events may cause harm to similar or even the same areas of the brain. An infection, stroke, or toxin may each produce equivalent injuries, thereby causing symptoms that are fairly identical. Recall too that the abnormal traits following brain damage are heavily influenced by the preexisting personality. Given these overlapping determinants, it is to be expected that one organic psychosis will have many of the same symptoms as another. In addition, however, distinctive clues sometimes set one diagnosis off from another, and we will point these out as we discuss the various diagnoses (Figure 15.2).

Cerebrovascular psychosis

For most people past middle age, blood vessels in the brain become narrowed and more fragile. When these changes are marked, the condition is called **arteriosclerosis,** meaning a hardening or loss of flexibility of the arterial

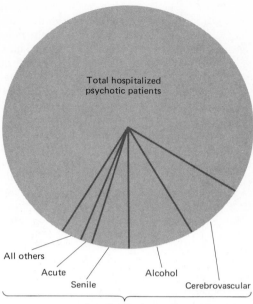

Total hospitalized
psychotic patients

All others

Acute

Senile

Alcohol

Cerebrovascular

Organic psychoses

Figure 15.2. The proportion of all mental illness caused by brain damage is relatively small. Of 25 million people estimated to be mentally disordered, only a million are likely to be diagnosed as OBS. But organic psychoses, when they do occur, tend to be serious and are often chronic. A large number of organic patients are over 60. The result is that one fourth of all *hospitalized* patients are diagnosed organic psychosis. (Sources: National Institute of Mental Health; United States Veterans Administration; U.S. Bureau of the Census, *Statistical Abstract of the United States,* 99th ed., 1978.)

vessels. What happens is that the arteries become thickened, clogged with fatty plaques, and undergo related degenerative changes. Lacking resiliency and increasingly choked, these vessels may break, close, become the site of a blood clot or otherwise have their function crippled. Whatever the cause, when an important artery is lost, hundreds of millions of dependent brain cells are no longer being nourished and sustained.

The artery that is damaged may be minor or major and it may stop working swiftly or gradually (Figure 15.3). When there is a sudden dramatic loss, it is called a **stroke** or a **cerebrovascular accident (CVA).** Each year

in the United States there are several million CVAs and over 200,000 deaths. Most victims are male and older, but women and young adults may be arteriosclerotic and have a stroke.

CVA DAMAGE A cerebrovascular accident is obviously a life-threatening event. When a major brain artery is totally blocked, or a weakened vascular wall tears and there is a massive hemorrhage, large areas of the brain may be damaged. During such an event the person experiences an intense headache, feels confused, and may vomit, have convulsions, and sink into a coma. Shortly thereafter many CVA patients show sensory and motor losses, but only a few develop cerebrovascular psychosis. Nevertheless, because arteriosclerosis is so common, this type of brain abnormality is one of the most frequent forms of organic brain syndrome. Mr. T. G. is a case in point.

Mr. T. G. was a retired 64-year-old lawyer when he had a CVA. The stroke left his right arm and leg paralyzed, he could not read, and he had difficulty pronouncing some multisyllable words. Before his stroke Mr. T. G. had been a fairly quiet person, although he was always demanding as a parent, husband, and employer. Now Mr. T. G. was abusive, paranoid, and hostile. He ordered fellow patients around, and accused the nurses of mistreating him and trying to steal his money. Sometimes he flew into a rage and followed this with crying and withdrawal. During these rages Mr. T. G. would often use obscene language and seemed to derive some pleasure from being able to shock one nurse in particular. When the patient's wife visited him, he sometimes did not recognize her but at other times became extremely apologetic about his appearance. On such occasions he seemed genuinely distressed that he did not properly clothe or groom himself.

The symptoms shown by Mr. T. G. are fairly typical, although "typical" must be used with caution. Many cerebrovascular psychotic patients are emotionally labile, lose some social skills, and have intellectual deficits—though memory is often left intact. What is perhaps

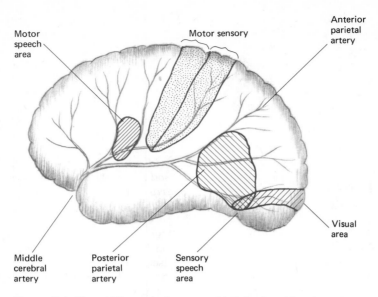

Figure 15.3. The middle cerebral artery and its branches. Mental symptoms following a cerebrovascular attack depend to a considerable extent on which blood vessels have ceased to function. Damage to the anterior parietal artery may result in hemiplegia and disorientation. If the posterior artery is lost, alexia may follow. Damage to the middle cerebral artery may cause memory losses.

particularly identifying is the feeling and expression of remorse. Quite a few cerebrovascular persons are abusive or unkempt but seem genuinely regretful. They seem to be saying that they have no control over their behavior but recognize its impropriety and feel sorry about it.

GRADUAL IMPAIRMENT The brain-damaging effects of arteriosclerosis do not have to be sudden and cataclysmic, as in a major stroke. In about half of all cerebrovascular psychosis there is only a gradual loss of brain tissue. Usually this is because only a small vessel ruptures or an artery's function is only partially lost. In such instances, the pathology tends to be cumulative. After the first hemorrhage another minor arterial branch is afflicted or an already defective vessel loses even more of its ability to sustain brain cells. The result is a quiet, almost insidious progression of physical and mental symptoms.

The psychological signs of gradual cerebrovascular disorder are usually two or three symptoms drawn from the following: headache, memory loss, irritability, emotional excesses, and fatigue. The last sign, fatigue, accompanying several of the others just cited is especially suggestive. A once well-adjusted older person who gradually becomes more and more forgetful, easily upset, and particularly is always tired could be suspected of OBS. These symptoms are, of course, fairly general and might point to any number of other conditions. For this reason too, because early signs of brain damage can be so indistinct, they are overlooked or misdiagnosed:

Mrs. T. R. is 56, overweight, and an elementary school teacher. She has always enjoyed her work and been well liked by her students. She is popular with the other teachers, for she is willing to share her experiences and help others. But after her return from her three-month summer vacation she seemed changed. She acted moody and distant, and her colleagues thought she was depressed about some-

thing that had happened at home. But according to another teacher who knew Mrs. T. R. personally, her home life was satisfactory. She also pointed out that she had noticed Mrs. T. R. becoming very forgetful. The first month of school she had twice failed to turn in her attendance reports and several times forgotten her lunchroom duty. Another teacher said that when she asked Mrs. T. R. a question, Mrs. T. R. first snapped back an irritated, "Why don't you find out for yourself." Then she apologized for her answer and began crying.

In early November Mrs. T. R. came to the principal and requested a leave, stating she felt too tired to continue teaching. She was sent to the school physician for approval of a medical leave. This doctor decided she was having "menopausal" difficulties and prescribed tranquilizers. But since the difficulties got worse, Mrs. T. R.'s husband took her to a medical clinic for thorough examination. There a neurologist diagnosed Mrs. T. R. as having arteriosclerotic disease. X-ray studies of the blood vessels nourishing the brain revealed several that were greatly narrowed. More specifically, the examination indicated that a branch of the middle cerebral artery was virtually closed (Figure 15.3).

CHRONIC OR ACUTE Cerebrovascular psychosis, particularly when it is initiated suddenly because of a CVA, is most often an acute condition. With treatment the majority of patients can look forward to a diminution of both physical and psychological symptoms and substantial recovery. Cerebrovascular patients who do not improve significantly, even after many months of therapy, are likely to remain chronically ill. In addition, since most CVA patients are older, the increasing and overlapping symptoms of senility may contribute to continuing disability.

Psychosis due to infectious or degenerative disease

Any infectious disease, particularly if it brings about a high fever, may cause organic brain symptoms. Generally if the disease is short-lived and does not directly damage a great deal of brain tissue, the neurological symptoms are temporary. Delirium is often the outcome of such an acute episode:

During a two day period of very high fever with viral pneumonia, the patient was delirious. While conscious he mumbled about the "Tarry Tarry" who seemed to be telling him not to get wet. During one episode, when an aide came to turn him in bed, he struck out wildly, yelling phrases like, "stay dry . . . oh God . . . Tarry fire . . . move out . . . dream drip . . ."

A great many diseases, both infectious and degenerative, tend to produce massive and/or continuing neurological damage. We cannot discuss all the many illnesses that result in chronic OBS but will limit ourselves to three: encephalitis, syphilis, and Huntington's chorea.

ENCEPHALITIS This infection of the brain may be due to a direct viral invasion or follow as a complication of measles, mononucleosis, influenza, and many other diseases. In the United States the disease is rare, although there have been some isolated cases, particularly of a variety called equine encephalitis. The name derives from the fact that horses

Figure 15.4. Some organic patients appear to deteriorate. They become distant, confused, and lacking in motivation, and lose interest in their surroundings and in personal hygiene. The same symptoms may also indicate schizophrenia, so that neurological examination is often necessary to establish the diagnosis. (Photo: Smith, Kline and French Laboratories, G. William Holland)

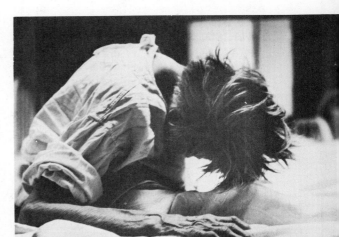

have served as hosts for a virus that is then transmitted to humans by ticks or mosquitoes. Generally children and older people are most likely to suffer the most serious consequences of encephalitis.

The disease usually begins with the patient feeling lethargic and feverish and complaining of headache and stiff neck. Soon more extensive disabling symptoms develop: tremors, convulsions, delirium, and deep sleep. During wakeful moments, the patient is confused, disoriented, hallucinated, agitated, and excited. But for much of the time the person is literally asleep, even comatose; hence the common name for this illness is sleeping sickness. In most cases recovery from encephalitis is complete, and there are no important residual symptoms. But if there is permanent brain damage, in youngsters mental retardation and associated physical disability is a frequent outcome. In older children the psychological aftereffects often result in conduct disorder. The child seems to lose inhibitions and self-control. Such children may become aggressive, impulsive, destructive, and hyperactive. They may assault, lie, steal, commit sexual offenses, and appear totally uncaring about punishment.

Among adults, the chronic effects of encephalitis sometimes resemble the conduct disturbances seen in children. But the destructiveness and antisocial behavior is usually less marked, and most become very remorseful about any disturbance they have caused. There is also a tendency for adults to become depressed and hypochondriacal. They complain of various pains, feelings of tension and restlessness, and justifiably talk about visual discomfort. In some encephalitic individuals there may be some loss of the eye blink reflex, so that they tend to stare.

SYPHILIS After the initial symptoms (chancre, rash) of this venereal disease have subsided, a small percentage of patients suffer neurological consequences. Perhaps about 3 percent of untreated persons manifest organic brain symptoms anywhere from two to as many as forty years after initial infection. In a few other cases the syphilitic microorganism attacks the cardiovascular system, the eyes, or other important organs. But the frequency of neurological involvement and other serious physical damage appears to have decreased over the centuries. Several hundred years ago in Europe, syphilis was apparently a much more virulent illness. At times it was epidemic, disabling, crippling, and killing huge numbers of people. It is hypothesized that the bacteria causing syphilis may have changed or less lethal strains become prominent. In any case, because of the altered potency of the bacteria, and much more important, because of antibiotic therapy, syphilitic psychosis is not common any more (McNeill, 1976). During the 1800s this disease accounted for as many as one-third of all mental patients. Today the average hospital may have only a handful of people diagnosed as mentally disordered due to syphilis (Figure 15.5).

The proper psychiatric term for syphilitic psychosis is **general paresis.** Paresis means paralysis, and the condition is also occasion-

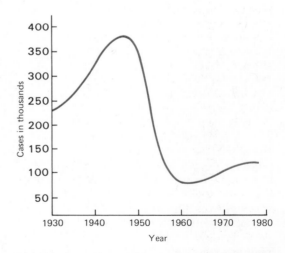

Figure 15.5. The incidence of syphilis. Despite a large increase in the United States population and changing sexual practices, the incidence of syphilis has declined greatly over the last generation. The decrease in syphilis and paresis is due to the advent of antibiotics, better public health measures, and probably the lesser virulence of the syphilis microorganism. (Source: Projection based on U.S. Department of Health, Education and Welfare, National Center for Health Statistics.)

ally referred to as general paralysis. These descriptions suggest the diversity of syphilitic symptoms and physical consequences of this infection. In fact, paresis generally announces itself physically long before psychological signs become obvious. Early signs often are hemiplegia, dysarthria, and loss of muscle control in the face. It is common for paretic persons to have a sagging jaw, difficulty controlling the tongue and lips, and trembling hands and fingers, especially when extended. A classic symptom is hesitant speech. The person has trouble articulating words, and phrases are thick and slurred. Generations of neurologists were taught to look for general paralysis by asking patients to say "Methodist-Episcopal clergyman."

Psychologically, at first paretic patients seem only to have fairly typical organic symptoms such as memory losses and deficiencies in judgment. Later, more characteristic syphilitic indicators may emerge. Patients become euphoric and grandiose. Although they are already neurologically damaged, walk with a shuffle, and have slurred speech, they seem remarkably happy. Their attitude is that everything is wonderful, that they are fine and things "are going to be just marvelous." Here is a description of a syphilitic patient, summarized from a report written at the turn of the century.

. . . *He confided to me that he is President McKinley . . . reincarnated through him, through the special intervention of his deceased mother. (McKinley was assassinated in 1901.) He walks about the asylum wearing a morning coat and dispensing favors, awaiting his return to the White House. . . . When I spoke with him he was jolly, reassuring me that despite the unpleasant conditions of his life and his physical frailty, he would take care of me too. . . . He limps, his jaw sags, and he speaks poorly but he is happy.*

HUNTINGTON'S CHOREA There are several rare degenerative neurological diseases, of which Huntington's chorea is best known. Since it is a clearly hereditary disorder, it ap-

pears in some family histories or communities with surprising frequency, though overall the number of Huntington's cases are very small. Exactly what alterations occur in the brain and nervous system is not clear, but changes in cortical cell structure and convolutions have been noted.

Huntington's patients are normal until early middle age, when symptoms typically begin. Personality difficulties tend to appear first. Patients may seem increasingly moody, withdrawn, and lacking in judgment and generally act strangely. At this stage, if the genetic history is unknown, it is easy to misdiagnose this condition as neurosis or schizophrenia. Soon after the personality changes occur, or sometimes accompanying them, choreic movements begin. There are jerky, irregular twitches of the arms. The face is contorted by grimaces. Speech becomes hesitant and explosive. Soon the entire body is involved, with the trunk stretching spasmodically and the patient swaying and stumbling as he walks. Psychological deficiencies also worsen. In later stages patients show profound deterioration in emotion, intellect, and social skills. Some become euphoric, others paranoid and violent, and a few suicidal. Ten to twenty years after onset, death is the usual outcome. Although there is no cure for Huntington's chorea, many of the symptoms can be moderated by medication and psychotherapy.

Psychosis due to tumors, injuries, and toxins

TUMOR A tumor is an abnormal growth of tissue (neoplasm) that may occur anywhere in the body, including the central nervous system. Because brain tumors account for only a small proportion of all psychotic disorders, their presence may often be overlooked. The early psychological symptoms of brain tumor are indistinct and easily mistaken for other mental disorders. The person complaining of anxiety, forgetfulness, and emotional instability is usually thought of as mildly neurotic. During later stages tumors make their presence known by more conclusive signs: head-ache, nausea, peculiar visual experiences like flashes of light, aphasias, paraesthesias, olfactory hallucinations (smelling something not really present), tremors, and convulsions.

The following patient, a 58-year-old carpenter, had several of the symptoms usually found in temporal lobe tumor. His neoplasm was detected and surgically removed. The tumor proved to be the size of a walnut and of a rapidly growing type called glioblastoma. After surgery, the patient made a satisfactory recovery.

Patient first noticed headaches, slight tremor, and episodes of nausea. For several weeks he attributed these symptoms to "the stomach flu." Very shortly these symptoms were superseded by an increasing difficulty in reading and visual disturbances. Mr. R said he would look at the paper and the words would not make any sense (aphasia). He also had two episodes of hallucination. He saw tiny animals jumping about—a perception that disturbed him since he knew they were not real. . . .

While at work Mr. R had a convulsive seizure and was rushed to the hospital by the community volunteer ambulance squad. Neurological examination revealed the likelihood of a growth in the temporal lobe, and the patient was scheduled for surgery.

INJURIES   Each year there are several hundred thousand head injuries due to automobile accidents, falls, violent assaults, and other mishaps. According to the entertainment media, people can be hit on the head, pass out, quickly recover, and immediately resume their activities. The fact is that any blow on the skull is serious, and a blow hard enough to cause unconsciousness may be very grave, even life-threatening. Fortunately, however, very few head injuries, even if they cause physical disability, result in permanent mental disorder.

We need first to clarify the meaning of psychosis due to head injury. Often neurotic, psychotic, and other abnormal behaviors are erroneously attributed to accidents or other stressful events not actually causing brain damage. During World War I, for example, a good deal of mental disorder was incorrectly explained as "shell shock." Supposedly the brain was hurt by the noise and concussion of exploding artillery. Fires, floods, earthquakes and other disasters can also stimulate abnormal behavior. Someone involved in such a catastrophe may be dazed, have memory losses, be amnesic, and otherwise appear organically deranged. But in the clear absence of head injury, such abnormal reactions must be thought of as the result of overwhelming or sudden stress and not of brain damage. The course and outcome of such stress reactions is very different from that of organic brain syndromes—a discussion we shall leave to Chapter 16.

The skull can be struck a violent blow or crash against a hard object. In such cases the brain may be injured because it is pushed out of its normal position and slams into the hard, bony interior of the skull itself. Or a blow on the head may crush or fracture bone, forcing fragments into the brain. The most destructive injury of all is when the brain is torn by a foreign object, like a bullet, entering the skull. Whatever the source of injury, any significant assault on the brain is usually followed by a

Figure 15.6. Each year automobile accidents cause several thousand cases of permanent mental and/or physical disability due to brain damage. Any blow on the head, particularly if it results in loss of consciousness, can cause serious brain injury. (Photo: R. Haines/Kingston Freeman)

loss of consciousness. The person may pass out for a few seconds or remain comatose for many months. When the injury is mild to moderate, the person is likely to recover within hours, feeling dazed, unable to remember what happened, and perhaps complaining of headache, dizziness, and fatigue. Some also talk incoherently, or carry on conversations as if another person were present or as if they were at work, a symptom called occupational delirium. During the days following the initial recovery from the injury other organic symptoms become apparent: inability to concentrate, irritability, and some emotional apathy or excitement. Patients also tend to complain for long periods afterward that they are no longer able to tolerate noise, bright light, strong smells, alcohol, and many other previously accepted potent sensory stimuli.

The majority of head injuries are *acute*. Within a few weeks or months there is both physical and psychological recovery. The prognosis is, of course, related to the severity of the physical injury. It also depends on the person involved. Those most likely to become *chronically* mentally disordered fall into one or more of the following categories:

1. The amount of brain tissue destroyed is considerable or in critical areas.
2. The person has preexisting major adjustment or social difficulties (alcoholism, antisocial behavior).
3. There are already ongoing organic processes (for example, arteriosclerotic degeneration).
4. There is a history of repeated head injuries (for example, professional boxers).

If six months to a year have gone by and the person has not improved, his or her condition is likely to be diagnosed chronic OBS. By that time abnormal personality changes have usually stabilized and the symptom picture resembles that seen in most other organic disorders. The person is rigid, shows losses in memory and abstract ability, perseverates, and may be hallucinated. The case of Mr. K. N. is a description of the symptoms of a "punch-drunk" fighter. The patient was a professional heavyweight boxer for twenty-four years. He

was not a good defensive fighter and both in training and competitive bouts suffered many hard blows to his skull. He was knocked out while sparring, was unconscious for three hours, and was hospitalized.

Mr. K.N. has a poor memory and is slow to learn. After four months he is still unfamiliar with the hospital routine. His speech is hesitant and slurred, and his walk is uncoordinated, almost staggering. Together with his flattened nose, enlarged ears, and scarred face, he very much resembles the stereotype of a punch-drunk fighter. . . . Although Mr. K.N. is generally mild-mannered, he has a tendency to be moody and suspicious. He also has some auditory hallucinations. He frequently talks about, and back to, the "roar of the crowd." Psychological testing has revealed rigid thinking, language aphasia, and a tendency toward confabulation. . . .

TOXINS Medication, legal and illegal drugs, chemicals, and an almost infinite array of old and new toxins can cause temporary or permanent organic impairment. Alcohol is by far the most frequent offender. About one of every six organic patients is brain damaged because of years of heavy drinking. Barbiturates and several other of the commonly abused drugs discussed in Chapter 10 may cause acute or chronic brain symptoms and result in coma or even death.

Aside from drugs, a number of industrial and commercial chemicals and products are sometimes implicated in neurological symptoms. Lead, gasoline, and carbon monoxide are frequent environmental hazards. Lead has been a particularly elusive culprit because it can enter the body via the mouth or skin without any awareness on the part of the consumer. Once in the body, the metal accumulates and slowly damages the central nervous system and other organs.

Mr. W was admitted to the Veteran's Administration hospital with puzzling symptoms (cramps, fatigue, headache, tremor, and anxiety). Because lead poisoning is rare, no one suspected this etiology. One of the consulting phy-

sicians found the patient was a potter and particularly proud of his custom-crafted dishes. This doctor remembered the historical claim that Rome declined because its educated and wealthy classes ate from lead-impregnated dishes. He had the potter's wife bring samples of all her husband's materials from his workshop. Laboratory analysis found small amounts of lead in one of the glazes. Apparently, over the course of twelve years lead had entered through the potter's skin and accumulated.

Gasoline contains many toxins, including tetraethyl lead, which make it harmful to inhale and extremely dangerous to swallow. Sometimes an attempt to siphon gasoline results in its accidental ingestion. The consumption of even small quantities can lead to substantial neurological damage and subsequent physical and psychological symptoms. Carbon monoxide poisoning is most likely to occur as part of a suicide attempt. Each year, hundreds of people are known to lock themselves in their garage or automobile and try to kill themselves with exhaust fumes. Many of these efforts are lethal; others result in extensive brain damage.

TREATMENT

The treatment of organic psychoses requires close coordination between medicine and psychotherapy. The first essential is diagnosis so that therapy can be directed at the physical cause. Two patients with memory defects and emotional lability may have entirely different conditions. One could have general paresis and recover completely when antibiotics are administered. The other may have advanced arteriosclerosis, and treatment may consist of anticoagulant drugs to prevent blood clots. To ensure an accurate understanding of each brain syndrome, the joint efforts of neurologists, psychologists, and psychiatrists, each using their own special skills, may be required.

Medical therapies

Treatment of organic abnormalities often begins with surgery or medicine. Surgery may be used to remove clots and tumors, repair blood vessels, or remedy the effects of other sources of brain damage. Penicillin and other drugs may control or eliminate infections. In addition to drugs directed at the organic cause, psychiatrists have available a wide spectrum of tranquilizers useful in controlling anxiety, emotional lability, and disordered thinking. Perhaps even more important, recently a new group of drugs that seem to increase alertness, mental activity, and memory has become available. For example, pentylenetetrazol (trade name: Mentalert) helps brain-injured and older patients retain intellectual skills and often reverses a seemingly hopeless spiral of deterioration.

Psychological therapies

Psychotherapists working with organic patients direct their efforts both at the current symptoms and at the preexisting personality. We know that the life problems the person had before the organic disorder play a prominent role in determining subsequent adjustment. Consequently, a good deal of the work of mental health professionals deals with the home situation and previous difficulties. For example, an individual hospitalized with cerebrovascular psychosis may also have a history of family tension and depression. Another patient with a head injury sustained in a fight may have a background of alcoholism. In both cases, most psychotherapists focus as much on the long-standing emotional disorder as on the present organic symptoms, as this dialogue shows:

PATIENT: I get to feeling so low . . . I guess because of my stroke, I can't do a lot of things any more.

DOCTOR: You talked just before about how you felt you were not worth much, feeling a failure, long before your stroke.

PATIENT: Well, yes, but now it sort of proves it.

DOCTOR: I don't agree. I think we've got to find out a little more about you. Why did you have such a low opinion of yourself? What has been depressing you, these last five years, maybe?

PATIENT: You don't think it's just now I feel so bad? Well, maybe you are right. But it is a long story. I don't even know where I could begin.

DOCTOR: O.K. Let's try.

Unlike most other psychotherapists, behaviorally oriented practitioners are relatively little concerned with previous adjustment. They agree that brain damage causes deficits in memory, thinking, emotion, and in the learning process itself. Nevertheless, they contend that whatever areas of the brain have been damaged, organic patients still retain the ability to learn by reinforcement. Behavior that is rewarded persists and that which is

Figure 15.7. The treatment for people with intellectual losses, seizures, and other neurological symptoms is portrayed in this 1737 engraving by Picard. Such patients needed to have their heads stepped on, be stretched, or have people dance upon their chest. Therapy today is both more rational and far more effective. (Photo: National Library of Medicine, Bethesda, Md.)

not rewarded or punished drops out. Organic patients have been taught, or retaught, skills ranging from the simplest to the most complex: proper dress, social conduct, organizing one's day, reading, and conceptual thinking:

Mr. W was 63 years old, in a nursing home after a CVA, and showed only a few mild symptoms of organicity. But he was often quite obscene to the female staff, so that he was threatened with being sent to a mental hospital. A behavioral psychologist carefully observed Mr. W's activities. He found that for most of the day, since Mr. W was a quiet, nonassertive person, he was largely ignored. Toward evening, however, Mr. W frequently went to see a nurse and made obscene suggestions. This was usually followed by the woman acting angry, shocked, amused, or giving Mr. W a "good talking to."

To change Mr. W's behavior, the psychologist suggested a simple shift in reinforcements. At present just about the only time the patient was rewarded by attention was when he made blunt sexual proposals. The staff was instructed to completely ignore Mr. W's obscene comments. Instead, they were to talk with him and otherwise give him attention when he was "well behaved." When the reinforcements for obscenity were discontinued, Mr. W's behavior soon stopped. In addition, the helpful attention he now received during the day increased his overall adjustment as well.

Psychological recovery is also aided by a number of auxiliary treatments. Organic patients frequently lose some visual-motor skills and feel clumsy and useless. Such attitudes can often be reversed by occupational, art, music, dance, and other creative therapies. In such workshop situations patients can explore their remaining potentials, revive old abilities, and once more feel productive. Occasionally, the creative therapies help "open up" a patient. An organic individual previously too inhibited or resistant to talk directly to a therapist or participate in a group can often be brought into treatment through art or music.

Hospitalization

Because most organic patients are older and their symptoms often at least moderately disabling, hospitalization is common. Traditionally such patients are kept apart in their own buildings or wards. Even in the best facilities, where food and treatment are otherwise good, such segregation is demoralizing. Now in more advanced hospitals, the therapeutic value of mixing ages throughout the institution is recognized. Organically impaired patients share living space with younger, physically more capable people. For the older patient this acts as an encouragement to dress properly and use appropriate social skills, and is a general motivational stimulus. Younger patients also benefit. Some are brought out of their own psychotic world by being helpful and concerned about older people who appreciate their interest.

PREVENTION

Much research is still needed to help us understand memory, learning, and all the factors involved in organic disorders. Our knowledge of the brain is quite incomplete, and we also know very little about how nerve cells grow, recover, and transmit and store information. But our understanding of neurology and psychology is good enough at this point to enable us to suggest important preventive measures. Estimates are that at our present level of knowledge, even modest effort would reduce organic disorders by half (Eccles, 1977).

Infectious diseases such as syphilis and encephalitis and others with possible neurological consequences could be eliminated almost entirely. Public health techniques such as diagnostic screening, early detection, and immunization can minimize the reservoir of infective sources and carriers. Other public health measures could reduce exposure to most toxic substances at home and in industry. What is also needed, particularly in regard to commonly abused toxins such as barbiturates and alcohol, is competent and available treatment programs to cure dependence. Automobile, motorcycle, and other highway accidents contribute hundreds of thousands of serious head injuries every year. (Many of these, incidentally, are associated with intoxicated drivers.) What is required here is radical improvement in automobile and highway safety design and vigorous law enforcement to remove irresponsible drivers.

A third major way to reduce organic abnormalities is to encourage good mental and physical health practices. This means, for example, proper diet to decrease the intake of fats and other substances associated with arteriosclerosis and other degenerative changes. This also means making psychotherapeutic facilities easily available so that adjustment problems can be treated early, long before they are compounded by organic deficits.

Figure 15.8. Organic patients are older and often assigned to wards limited to people with similar disorders. The discouraging effects of such segregation have led to mixed wards, so that older patients can associate with younger ones suffering from different conditions. (Photo: Smith, Kline and French Laboratories, G. William Holland)

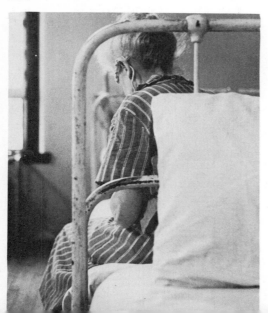

SUMMARY

Brain damage may lead to organic mental disorder. The symptoms resulting from brain injury depend on the extent and/or location of the damage and the person's preexisting personality. Organic brain syndromes differ, but most share these signs: emotional disorder, intellectual losses, thinking deficits, and a decline in social skills.

Organic psychoses are diagnosed according to cause, although the symptoms of different conditions often overlap. The leading cause of organic psychosis is malfunction of the cerebral arteries. A large number of diseases, including encephalitis, syphilis, and Huntington's chorea, may also affect the central nervous system and cause acute or chronic organic brain symptoms. Tumors and most drugs account for a small proportion of OBS, but alcohol and to a lesser extent brain injuries play a significant role in organic psychoses.

The treatment of organic disorders requires coordinated medical and psychological efforts. Surgery, medication, and other remedial techniques may have to be directed at the neurological cause of the disorder. Psychiatric drugs and behavior and other psychotherapies may be needed to reduce symptoms and facilitate adjustment. Many organic patients require hospitalization or similar custodial care. The more advanced hospitals are careful not to segregate OBS patients, since organic wards can accelerate psychological deterioration. Preventive efforts that can greatly reduce the incidence of organic psychoses include these: control of infectious diseases, automobile safety, protection against toxins, and good physical and mental health care.

Adjustment Reactions:
Trauma and Age

Everyone is confronted with adjustive demands throughout life. Most are ordinary and minor, such as passing a test, being interviewed, or meeting a new person. But occasionally there are more serious challenges. Family breakup, legal entanglements, or a disastrous accident may call for all the resources a person can muster to stay psychologically healthy. In this chapter we will describe some of the conditions that can arise in normal people as a result of adjustive challenges such as trauma and aging.

ADULT ADJUSTMENT DISORDERS

The DSM III defines **adjustment disorder** as a maladaptive reaction that is *not* merely a worsening of a preexisting mental disability. In diagnosis, we need to make sure that what looks like an adjustment reaction is not actu-

ally the beginning of a neurosis or psychosis. To be diagnosed as an adjustment reaction, the symptoms should be in response to an identifiably stressful event, relatively short-lived (lasting a few weeks or months), and clear up when the stress ceases.

The stressors leading to adjustment reactions are many and varied. The range includes divorce, death, business failure, unemployment, and graduation from school. (Extraordinary events, such as a fire or criminal assault, are also adjustive challenges, but they call forth more distinctive symptoms and will be described later in the chapter in the section on posttraumatic disorders.) The stressors producing adjustment reactions may vary in intensity, and symptoms may be relatively minor or fairly incapacitating. Although longer and more serious crises usually bring more significant symptoms, people who are more vulnerable, who have difficult family or environmental backgrounds, frequently have serious reactions to even moderate adjustment demands. The symptoms following an adjustment challenge therefore vary from person to person but usually include some combination of the following:

SOMATIC COMPLAINTS: Headaches, diarrhea, loss of appetite, sleeplessness

EMOTIONAL UNEVENNESS: Irritability, suspiciousness, rigidity

DEPRESSION: Tearfulness, worry, tension, anxiety

Although adjustment reactions are common, few adults seek psychiatric help. Most recognize that the symptoms are related to their stress and are aware that they will feel better when the situation is resolved. Others seek help from the family doctor, a clergyman, or a friend. As a result, adult adjustment reactions account for only about 2 percent of all patients seen in mental health facilities. Careful epidemiological studies have also pinpointed the most common source of stress, namely, marital problems, and the most frequent symptom, depression (Freedman et al., 1976; Moos, 1976):

F. J., age 32, was in the process of separating from her husband. After several years of contin-

Figure 16.1. Most people adjust to such life changes as graduation very well. A few, however, find the new challenges and responsibilities stressful, and adjustment symptoms result. (Photo: Scribe)

ual strife, and following the disclosure of her affair with her tennis teacher, the pair had finally resolved to end their marriage. F. J. was a religious woman who had found both her own affair and the termination of her marriage difficult to accept. She was also the daughter of demanding parents who had always made her feel incompetent. Following the separation, F. J. became very confused, had difficulty sleeping and concentrating, and complained of almost constant headaches. Most of all, however, she said she felt useless and worthless and was very pessimistic about her future and that of her two children. In a word, she was depressed. A family doctor treated her with tranquilizing medication and reassured her that she would soon feel better. Four months after the husband moved out, a final divorce decree was granted. A few months after this, F. J. seemed to have reconciled herself to her new situation. She was largely symptom-free and had begun to socialize with her friends.

Not everyone confronted with adjustive stress necessarily develops psychiatric symptoms; most people are able to handle even serious life challenges realistically. But individuals who have been weakened, who perhaps have had an unsatisfying childhood, appear to be more vulnerable. Once again, as is the case with many mental disorders, the person most likely to develop symptoms is the one with a history of family or health problems.

George Vaillant (1974) confirmed the importance of childhood experiences in a thirty-year study of adult male adjustment. In the 1930s he screened college sophomore men and selected 268 who were free from emotional, intellectual, and physical health difficulties. Thirty years later, 94 subjects were arbitrarily chosen for reexamination. Most were still psychologically sound; their marital and job satisfaction was good, and they were mentally healthy. A careful background investigation showed those with good parents, warm mothers and fathers, and beneficial environments consistently adjusted well throughout adolescence and adulthood. Those whose adjustment had failed frequently had had a stressful childhood. Vaillant concluded that at least insofar as life adjustment patterns are concerned, a "continuum" of psychological health exists from earliest childhood into adulthood.

Similar conclusions were reached by Borus (1973), who studied the reentry problems of soldiers. In the early 1970s 3 million Vietnam veterans returned from Southeast Asia to civilian life in the United States. Borus, who investigated a small sample of discharged men shortly after they returned, found that about a third reentered without any real difficulty, but that another third faced adjustment and emotional hurdles. Once again, a background search found that those with the greatest adjustment difficulties were likely to have a history of defensive behavior dating back to childhood. In contrast, soldiers who adjusted most easily appeared to have had an encouraging childhood during which they had learned effective coping behavior.

CHILDBIRTH Special mention needs to be made of childbirth, since it sometimes poses a difficult adjustive challenge for the mother and other family members. It is easy to see how a woman may feel awed, even overwhelmed, with the responsibility for the life and well-being of another human being. Or the mother may be fearful of returning home and caring for her baby and other children in a fair and equitable way. Given all the challenges and demands of motherhood, it is not surprising, *nor* is it abnormal, that many women have a few mild and temporary adjustment symptoms following childbirth. Once in a great while, however, approximately one of every two or three hundred mothers develops a mental disorder called **postpartum** (after birth) **psychosis.**

Nearly all postpartum psychotic women have a previous history of anxiety, conflict, insecurity, and other adjustment difficulties. The psychosis may precede actual birth or follow it, and the usual symptoms include confusion, hallucinations, paranoia, or manic or depressive episodes. Frequently symptoms are severe enough to require hospitalization. On the other hand, the psychosis is usually short-lived; most new mothers recover within a few weeks or months.

POSTTRAUMATIC DISORDERS

So far we have been considering more "usual" stresses such as divorce or childbirth. But occasionally people are subjected to extraordinary adjustive challenges. Their resourcefulness, stability, and competence are severely tested by a fire, a destructive accident, military combat, or a brutal crime like rape. Such **trauma** (pain) can trigger a hidden psychosis or other mental disorder. More commonly, however, such disasters result in most victims manifesting a number of typical posttraumatic symptoms:

1. Numbness: Immediately following the event, many victims act numb, dazed, and helpless. They become detached, emotionally flat and unresponsive. At this stage too many are typically very *suggestible*. Since they are confused and feel strange, they look to others for directions.
2. Disinterest: The feeling of numbness and detachment may persist so that interest is lost in friends, activities, and work. When stress continues, such as in combat situations in wartime, the feeling of disinterest or detachment ("its not really happening to me") may last for months.
3. Recurrence: After the event the original stress is reexperienced in thinking, fantasy, and dreams. Many survivors talk constantly about their trauma or keep reliving it in nightmares.
4. Excessive reactions: For some time after a trauma has ended ordinary problems continue to seem extra-important and emotional responses are exaggerated. People become hyperactive, startle easily, have difficulty concentrating, and are often irritable and moody.

Posttraumatic disorders may immediately follow the disaster, or there may be an incubation of several hours or days. That is, the first numbing response to the catastrophe may last two or three days before the other signs become apparent. It has also been noted that poststress reactions are most severe when they result from direct human mistreatment, in contrast to a flood or airplane crash. Victims

THE ENDOCRINE GLANDS

Adjustment reactions may be mistaken for more chronic pathology; great care, also needs to be taken to be sure that glandular difficulties are not misdiagnosed as adjustment disorders. Bockar (1976) suggests that since normal people frequently have some marital, financial, or employment tension, it is too easy to assume that symptoms such as depression, anxiety, or restlessness are psychologically determined. It is therefore important to rule out other psychiatric and physical causes before reaching diagnosis of adjustment reaction. Particular attention should be paid to the endocrine system. Sometimes what appear to be psychologically derived symptoms are actually the result of hormonal irregularities:

M.C., aged 25, had been increasingly more irritable, restless, emotional, and depressed for well over a year. She seemed an otherwise normal person but was experiencing some problems in her marriage. As a result, the physician she consulted assumed that her symptoms were due to marital friction, although her family difficulties were not really extraordinary. Despite counseling by the doctor and a prescription for Valium, M. C. did not improve. Several months later, on a routine visit to her family doctor, M. C. was noted to have bulging eyes—a possible sign of excessive thyroid activity. Careful diagnostic study revealed a papillary cystadenocarcinoma, a malignant thyroid gland tumor. Surgery was performed, the patient's psychological symptoms disappeared, and she recovered completely.

Here are a few of the possible psychological signs arising from glandular malfunction:

Hyperthyroidism (too much secretion): tension, restlessness, overactivity, emotional lability
Hypothyroidism (too little secretion): apathy, depression, anxiety, irritability
Adrenal hypofunction: fatigue, depression, anxiety
Pituitary hypersecretion: headaches, depression, decreased sex drive, anxiety

Figure 16.2. Following an unusual stress like a fire, many people experience posttraumatic symptoms such as numbness and disinterest. (Photo: Bob Haines/Kingston Freeman)

of a vicious crime or of unjust and inhumane imprisonment may have profound traumatic symptoms.

THE CONCENTRATION CAMP SYNDROME Prisoners of war and concentration camp victims almost always manifest serious and chronic symptoms. Such people have been subjected to physical and psychological abuse for long periods of time. They are also ill with diseases such as tuberculosis and hepatitis. Many such victims demonstrate what has been called a **concentration camp syndrome.** They behave numbly and mechanically and are seemingly without feeling while in prison. But even long after their confinement they may remain overreactive, suspicious, fearful, and especially prone to depression and suicide. The following descriptions of special posttraumatic responses are by an expert in military psychiatry:

The Vietnamese War gave us at least two types of military psychiatric disorders. First there was the typical combat reaction, something they used to call "shell shock" in the first world war, though we now recognize it as a variation of a post-traumatic reaction. Soldiers frequently started by having difficulty sleeping and nightmares. Next restlessness, fear, and depression became evident. Many also act dazed, or numbed, or become hyperactive. They would startle so easily that another soldier coughing would make them duck for cover or grab their rifle.

The second disorder we saw, and the residuals of which are still with us years after the war is over, is simply a concentration camp syndrome. *These soldiers were imprisoned for years and starvation, beatings, and psychological pressure was common. . . . While in the camps many became automatons. They could not accept or believe what was really happening and describe their experiences as something encountered in a nightmare. . . . They survived, and there's not much more many were willing to say about their survival. . . . Still today many of those we have seen remain suspicious, anxiety prone, pessimistic, manipulative, and what's worse impart some of this to their children. They have been emotionally scarred for life.*

THE SURVIVOR SYNDROME

Traumatic symptoms can linger and seem most likely to continue when the event has been especially painful, intense, or catastrophic. The victims of terrorism—hostages in an airplane hijacking or kidnapped children or adults—may continue to feel distress for many years. Even an impersonal disaster may produce chronic anxiety. An example of such enduring symptoms was investigated by Janet Newman (1976) who studied children survivors of the Buffalo Creek disaster. On a Saturday morning in June, an Ohio dam collapsed, sending millions of gallons of water roaring through the Buffalo Creek Valley. The flood swept away cars, trailers, houses, and lives. The immediate effects of the disaster were the usual posttraumatic symptoms. Survivors

acted dazed and confused and for several weeks the event predominated in conversation, thoughts, and dreams. But Newman found that in children particularly, the scenes of cascading water and people helplessly swept away were still fresh in drawings, dreams, and fantasies two years later. Most seemed to have developed a distinctly greater awareness of death and also impressed clinical investigators with their increased vulnerability to future stress. Thus, although it is still true that usually people soon recover from adjustment and stress reactions, an extreme experience may well have long-range effects (Hall, 1976; Horowitz, 1976).

AGE AND SENILITY

Advancing age poses perhaps the most difficult adjustment problem of all normally encountered by most people. Sheehy (1976) has shown that each life stage, each "passage" from one age to another, presents new challenges and new opportunities. But when people advance into their sixties and seventies, demands seem to increase and opportunities to diminish. Failing health, limited financial resources, and increasing loneliness make old age a very difficult adjustment for many. Though the majority of older people meet the stresses of aging well, estimates suggest that in the United States at least 5 million citizens show many distinct signs of **senility,** that is, intellectual and emotional deficits due to aging (Freedman et al., 1976; Kolb, 1978).

The symptoms of senility are traditionally considered organic conditions, since many of the behaviors may be the result of brain damage. But a careful examination of senile patients shows that although some do have clear neurological signs (like memory losses), others seem to have more typical indications of adjustment failure (like depression). Senile disorder is commonly subdivided into several types, mainly as a convenience for labeling and expository purposes. In actual practice, all senile persons do not fit into clearly defined categories. There is also some shift in symptoms as patients get older, are institutionalized, or receive therapeutic help.

SENESCENCE **Senescence** (also called **simple senility**) is the term often used to describe the first noticeable effects of aging. At this level the person is only mildly impaired and is *nonpsychotic*. The most common loss is in immediate memory. Slowly, the ability to retain new events declines; previous, older experiences and recollections become increasingly more important. The failure in immediate memory has corollary effects in several directions. New and recent events tend to be rejected and old experiences relied upon and

Figure 16.3. Advancing age can be a period of loneliness and rejection; such feelings might help explain some of the supposed symptoms of senility. (Photo: Alan Carey/ Kingston Freeman)

pushed forward. The senescent person becomes disinterested in what is happening now, and resists learning and innovation. He or she keeps referring to how things were done in his or her youth and seems intolerant, conservative, rigid, and old-fashioned.

DELIRIOUS-CONFUSED The constellation of symptoms constituting the **delirious-confused senile psychosis** include confusion, restlessness, hallucinations, and incoherence. Such indicators, in addition to the usual signs of senility (memory deficit, poor social skills, and so on), make the older person stand out as clearly psychotic. But the psychosis is inconsistent and disorganized. The delusions are fleeting and the hallucinations are fragmentary. One gets the feeling that these patients are above all just very confused, and there is nothing substantial or consistent about their normal or abnormal thinking.

When the delirium and confusion are extreme, the old term **presbyophrenia** is occasionally still used. The presbyophrenic patient demonstrates the symptoms we have mentioned in an intense, exaggerated way. Thinking is almost bizarrely deranged. He or she is so restless and excited as to seem busy all the time. Such people run around, fuss, move things from here to there, lose things, look for them, and are agitated and annoyed with themselves. Many of these patients do misplace things and do get lost because of their confusion and because of short periods of amnesia (forgetting).

The amnesia seen in presbyophrenia is inconsistent and variable. Like so much of these patients' behaviors, their memory is mixed up and unreliable. Partly to compensate for this undependable memory, many presbyophrenic persons rely on "made up" recollections; they invent answers to suit the occasion. Like most *confabulatory* responses, the false recollections of this 82-year-old man tended to be boastful and extravagant:

PATIENT: I was a surgeon, you know. An oral surgeon.
DOCTOR: Oh. What is that exactly?

PRESENILE DISORDERS

Several infrequent organic disorders found in middle-aged people closely resemble senile psychoses. Two of the better known are Alzheimer's and Pick's diseases. Both occur during the forties or early fifties. They are progressively disabling. Since there is no specific treatment, they usually lead to death within three to six years. The cause of these disorders is not clear. In a few cases the possibility of heredity has been pointed out; in other situations infectious diseases have been suggested. In most instances, however, the explanation for these illnesses is unknown. The physical changes in the brain in Alzheimer's and Pick's diseases closely resemble those of senility and cerebrovascular psychosis. There is shrinkage and atrophy, and senile plaques and arteriosclerotic blood vessels may be found. In addition, in both disorders there are often tell-tale nerve cell changes. In Alzheimer's the delicate threads running in every direction through the

PATIENT: Well, I'll tell you. You know that there are the surgeons for your bones. And for your back and all that. Well it ain't them. I was seventeen when I quit school and went to work. Depression. My father married a girl was half Indian. She was a wild one. The kids today got too much money. Cars and they race them up the road. Bad tires, like they squeal. . . .

DOCTOR: Are you still an oral surgeon?

PATIENT: Always was. You learn something you never forget. I was a major. Had a platoon full of people under me. Sergeant major you know. The big war. . . . Lunch's bad here.

This patient shows his confusion, confabulates, and like many other senile patients is quite circumstantial. He is unable to concentrate and stick to a question or topic. He jumps from one thought to another and lets whatever idea or circumstance occurs distract him. The end result is that most normal listeners give up trying to talk to such people, forcing them into ever greater isolation.

PARANOID Senile psychotic paranoid patients usually have a history of suspiciousness, hostile attitudes, and poor interpersonal relations long preceding their organicity. With age, these character traits become highlighted and persecutory or grandiose ideas begin to form. Often too, there are auditory hallucinations like hearing voices:

Mr. N. N. is 74 years old. He was first diagnosed as having paranoid schizophrenia but then his senile symptoms became obvious (confusion, memory defect, rigidity).

Mr. N. N. believes he is "unofficially" governor of the state and that his votes were "stolen" by "those in mufti." His 60-year-old wife and 54-year-old brother-in-law were the particular objects of his suspicion. Before hospitalization he attempted to beat his wife with his cane. He also stood in the window of his house and shouted obscenities to people walking past. He confided to the psychiatrist that a "little inner voice lets me know what to do and say." But

body of the nerve cell may be damaged. In Pick's there may be a distinctive type of nerve-cell swelling and evidence of frontal lobe degeneration (Hagberg and Ingvar, 1976).

Alzheimer's disease typically begins with vague symptoms such as headaches, dizziness, emotional unevenness, and eventually some confused and restless behavior. The person seems to be mixed up and forgetful, and even does things backward. A dentist with Alzheimer's disorder first became a source of concern for his staff when he started acting forgetful and restless. He ordered X-rays after finishing a patient, refilled a tooth he had just completed a few moments before, wandered from one room to another, fidgeted constantly with his tools, and a few times was unable to assemble some familiar equipment. The early signs of Alzheimer's are followed within a few months by more marked signs such as emotional instability, thinking disturbances, apraxia, agnosia,

aphasia, and other serious language disorders. Many patients manage only to string words together incorrectly, mispronounce, or explosively repeat fragments of the speech of others. Toward the end there is increasing loss of sensory and motor capabilities. The patient is reduced to babbling and purposelessly repeating a few simple acts (like bedmaking) over and over. The malady continues until the patient is grossly disabled and bedridden and then dies.

Pick's disease usually results first in the person suffering some memory defects, feeling tired and indifferent, and seemingly unconcerned about personal hygiene and grooming. As the months go by, the person may also become withdrawn. He or she responds less and less to others and seems particularly disinclined to talk with anyone. As in Alzheimer's disease, patients eventually show severe and even fatal neurological symptoms.

sometimes the voice apparently grew too dominant. He was overheard shouting at the top of his voice to "shut up, you're crowding my head." When he arrived in the hospital, the patient kicked an attendant and told everyone that he would fire them using his "governor's privilege."

DEPRESSED Depressed patients are very clearly senile, but there is also marked depression. In most instances the depression is described as agitated, meaning the patient is actively sad, crying, moaning, wringing his hands, and giving other signs of distress. Sometimes the depression is centered about supposedly bad things the patient did (or falsely believes he or she did). Other times patients are depressed about real or imagined physical disabilities or the prospect of imminent death.

Causes of senility

MEDICAL EXPLANATIONS Senile psychosis is so called because it is an accompaniment of aging (from the Latin *senilis*, meaning aging). As the person grows older, there are a

great many inevitable changes in the body. In the brain the most readily visible change is shrinkage. Because of the wasting and degeneration of cells and the loss of lymphatic fluid, the size and weight of the brain decreases by anywhere from 100 to 300 grams. In addition to shrinkage, the brain undergoes a great many other evolutions as the years go by. Brain cells begin to appear "yellowed," there is a reduction of ribonucleic acid (RNA), electrical patterns are altered, and there is an accumulation of what are called **senile plaques.** These are small areas of destroyed tissue that appear shredded and are scattered throughout the cortex, particularly in the frontal lobe.

Because the various physical indicators of aging all seem to result in incapacitating brain cells, they seem likely to play some role in bringing on the abnormal behaviors we associate with aging. There is evidence, for example, that the number of senile plaques may be related to the severity of psychotic symptoms. On the other hand, autopsies on normal brains have shown senile plaques and other signs of advanced age in patients who were mentally healthy (Rosenfeld, 1976). The aging losses in the structure and function of the brain are nearly always accompanied by arteriosclerotic processes. As in cerebrovascular psychoses, senile individuals have arteries that are narrowed, fragile, and malfunctioning. The combined result makes it almost a certainty that large areas of the brain are impaired. The blood-vessel pathology of arteriosclerosis, together with the degenerative effects of old age, often assure significant neurological and pathological deficit and may account for many senile symptoms.

PSYCHOSOCIAL EXPLANATIONS The tendency toward senile symptoms often seems accelerated by retirement and/or the death of a spouse. While working and married, the older person feels at least minimally competent. Being a husband (or wife), he or she was intimately involved in the life of another person. After the job is over or the spouse has died, such people may feel worthless and inadequate. At this point senile and adjustment symptoms such as depression, loneliness, irritability, self-centeredness, and hypochondria often first become prominent.

Social structure and cultural biases may also contribute to the psychological failings attributed to aging. In the United States, older people are prejudicially regarded as childish and ignorant. Their abilities may be denied and their need to feel useful negated. Their emotional and sexual requirements are similarly ignored or become a source for derogatory jokes. Both individually and as a group, the aged are often resented as a burden and segregated in "homes" or senior citizen communities. Like other groups who suffer discrimination, the aged may react to their outgroup status by becoming defensive, hostile, and alienated.

Leo Rangell (1976) has raised another possibility. Senile signs could be the cumulative result of psychological conflict, pain, and defense. He reports treating a woman in her mid-seventies and discovering that her apparent senility was due not to an organic aging process but to the repression of decades of traumatic life. She had told herself that she did not want to remember any part of a married life of close to fifty years. The volume and intensity of the traumatic memories being repressed, Rangell stated, left her almost no room for normal living: "She had by now assumed the posture, both mentally and physically, of a diffuse cortical atrophy, without evidence, either neurological or radiological, of any organic syndrome nor even convincingly of cerebrovascular disease. She was like a young, acute, traumatic amnesia, except that this was chronic, old, and massive. Her mental state undulated dramatically with the emergence and repression of forbidden thoughts. This poignant clinical experience has made me wonder about the general psychopathology of 'old age.' "

TREATMENT OF ADJUSTMENT REACTIONS

Many adjustment reactions clear up rapidly, even without formal treatment, over the course of a few weeks or months. The person becomes accustomed to the new job, living alone, or changing status from student (or soldier) to independent adult (or civilian). Very often, however, therapeutic counseling and some "tranquilizing" medication is helpful. This is particularly true when present adjustment symptoms are related, as is often the case, to a long history of ineffectively confronting or coping with life challenges.

Posttraumatic disorders

Posttraumatic disorders often call for at least some minimal medical and psychological therapy. In fact, being momentarily trapped in a burning house or being the victim of an assault may trigger chronic and profound mental disorder requiring extensive treatment. Most often, however, a combination of anti-anxiety medication or sedatives, plus reassurance and the passage of time, successfully alleviates symptoms. Behavior therapists sometimes treat a traumatic experience much like a phobia. They may use systematic desensitization and other conditioning techniques to help patients overcome the frightening emotions generated by the accident or catastrophe.

SEX, MEMORY, AND SENILITY

Two of the most common, and apparently false, beliefs about age is that all older people lose both their memories and their interest in sex. Norman West (1975) obtained careful sexual histories from patients aged 68 to 98 in a rural nursing home. As residents of a nursing facility, most had at least some physical impairments. Nevertheless, the great majority of the women and more than half of the men reported high interest in sexual relations. A few of the subjects, in fact, continued to have vigorous intercourse on a regular basis.

The belief that memory necessarily declines

in older people may be as erroneous as the view that sexuality disappears. Kahn, Zarit, Hilbert, and Neiderehe (1975) examined 153 men and women ranging in age from 50 to 91. Only about half complained of significant memory loss. More important, however, testing revealed that the people concerned about memory impairment were often little handicapped in actuality. But they were *depressed*. It was depression, apparently the outcome of a poor adjustment to aging, and not organic deficit that accounted for most of what was falsely perceived as memory loss.

A few decades ago it was widely believed that posttraumatic victims should be medically encouraged to *relive* the disaster. The fact that most are already preoccupied with their trauma, thinking and dreaming about it, is believed to show how the personality itself attempts to overcome the effects of the painful event. Many patients were given sleep-inducing drugs such as sodium pentothal to encourage them to talk a little more freely. Today such drugs are rarely used. Instead, since the value of talking about the disaster, "getting it off your chest," is recognized, people who have undergone similar experiences may join together in a group to discuss their common trauma. In fact, group therapy is generally

recommended as particularly worthwhile both for adjustment and traumatic reactions, because it enables people to work out common fears as well as hopes.

I thought I was going to be just another one of those statistics after I told the police. . . . I was hitchhiking and I was picked up by a man and assaulted. Very vicious and ugly, but the old story. . . . The police treated me very well. A woman was assigned to me and she helped me through the whole routine. After, I was seen by the doctor and he encouraged me to talk it out. I was told I would meet with a group of women who had similar experiences. . . . I think this group was the best part of it. I stayed with them for fourteen weeks. I talked about my own guilt. What did I do to encourage this? And the hate I felt. And how I felt so powerless. It was all a bad dream. . . . They helped me learn to relate to my friends again . . . to trust people and feel good things about sex. . . . Then later I helped others. I had been through it and they needed a person to relate to, you know, that understood. . . . It's not easy but it helps a lot when you can feel the support of other people who understand, and you trust them. . . . You become yourself again.

Figure 16.4. Group therapy is often useful in adjustment and posttraumatic disorders because it enables people with similar experiences to help one another. (Photo: Scribe)

Combat reactions are treated much like other posttraumatic syndromes, but it has been found best for aid to be immediate and close to the scene of military operations. The soldier near his unit seems more motivated to recover and return to help his friends. Prison camp inmates, however, often need many years of physical and psychological help, and even then many will remain emotionally scarred. On the other hand, even survivors of the German concentration camps of a generation ago, an atrocity without parallel, were in most ways eventually able to adjust to ordinary life (Rabinowitz, 1977).

Senility

In senility, adjustment symptoms such as paranoia or hyperemotionality often respond to medication like Thorazine or Valium. For deficiencies in alertness or memory, drugs such as Mentalert are also often worthwhile. In addition, many hospitals and therapists now recognize that senility is *not* hopeless, that older people can benefit from psychological therapy. Both dynamically oriented counseling approaches and behavior techniques show promise in helping senile psychotic patients readjust. (Bergin and Garfield, 1971; Davidson, 1976; Park, 1977). Another important change in the treatment of older patients is the recognition that they frequently do poorly in hospitals. Routinely placing older people with minor adjustment problems or even more significant senile symptoms with organic and psychotic patients can be very destructive. Hospital milieus foster dependence, erode self-image, and often prompt a rapid mental and emotional decline. The following case excerpts are from psychological reports written two weeks and then eight months after a senescent patient was admitted. The intellectual and emotional decline seems to be due to the hospitalization itself.

February 3, 1977: The patient was admitted two weeks ago. She is a short, stocky, alert looking, 67-year-old woman who is slightly depressed. She had been living in Cleveland with her husband till he died four months ago. While her husband was alive he supplemented their income by repairing TV sets and small appliances. After his death, unable to live on Social Security benefits, the patient moved south to live with her daughter. The daughter

felt her mother's presence was disruptive and looked for other living arrangements. Because of her limited income and the lack of other available facilities, the daughter and the family doctor admitted the patient to the hospital.

The patient is of high normal intelligence with some failings in memory, concentration, and emotional steadiness. She is a little depressed but said she is trying to be cheerful and make the best of her situation. For the record, her diagnosis is simple senility.

September 10, 1977: The patient stated she assaulted Mrs. L because she was gossiping about her. She said she could hear Mrs. L say mean and dirty things because they came to her through the electrical wiring. In addition to her hallucinations, the patient is disorganized, slovenly, extremely suspicious, and hostile. According to the ward nurses she appears a little disoriented and confused. She has been unable to find her room and also persists in asking the name of this hospital. Diagnosis: senile psychosis—paranoid type.

Today hospitalization for senile symptoms is avoided unless absolutely necessary; grim "geriatric wards" are a thing of the past in many institutions. Older people who need psychiatric help are frequently sheltered in halfway houses or similar facilities that permit a more normal interaction with younger and healthier people.

In terms of prevention, older men and women are being encouraged to keep working, continue their interests, and otherwise stay in contact and alert. In 1977, for example, federal legislation in the United States largely ended mandatory retirement at age 65 in order to encourage older citizens to stay active. "Senior citizens" clubs and organizations are increasingly playing a role in combating loneliness and social prejudice so that older people can continue to feel accepted and useful.

In his book, *A Good Age*, gerontologist Dr. Alex Comfort (1976) argues: "In our society the elderly are patronized, disrespected, and excluded. Most of the handicaps of oldness are social, conventional and imaginary. The physical changes are trifling by comparison. Older

Figure 16.5. Many of the supposed senile symptoms of aging may be preventable if the person remains motivated and active. Exploring new talents is often a recommended way of staying alert. (Photo: Scribe)

people should reject retirement, reliance on hobbies and leisure pursuits. Work, learn, think, make love, read, have friends, above all stay active!''

SUMMARY

Any number of life challenges may produce adjustive symptoms in some people. These signs include depression and somatic complaints and clear up when the stress ceases. Childbirth is one type of adjustive challenge that infrequently results in temporary psychoses. Most people are able to handle adjustive challenge, but those who fail seem to have had a fairly difficult family background.

Posttraumatic symptoms such as numbness, disinterest, and recurrence may follow a disaster such as a flood or accident. Post-stress symptoms are usually most severe when the trauma is the result of human mistreatment, such as in criminal assault or being a prison camp victim. The symptoms resulting from such traumas, or even sometimes those of an impersonal but severe disaster, may linger for years and leave an individual emotionally scarred.

Advancing age is a complex adjustive challenge and sometimes results in symptoms described as senility. Senile psychosis is often divided into several types, though most patients show mixed symptoms. Senescense indicates only mild impairment, with a few losses in immediate memory as the chief symptom. In delirious-confused types of senility, patients are likely to have memory defects and be restless, confused, hallucinated, and incoherent. In an extreme form, called presbyophrenia, patients seem almost totally disorganized and deranged. Paranoid senile patients frequently have had a previous history of suspiciousness and hostility; these feelings become exaggerated with the brain degeneration of aging. Depressed senile persons are often seriously distressed.

Those offering a medical explanation of senility have demonstrated that in older people there is brain shrinkage, senile plaque formation, and other neurological impairment. Psychosocial explanations point to the fact that the extent of brain pathology is little related to senile symptoms. They suggest that retirement, loneliness, defensiveness, and other adjustment variables may account for the impairments of aging.

Adjustment and posttraumatic reactions ordinarily clear up spontaneously, but medication and counseling—particularly group therapy—may be helpful. People who have had especially severe experiences such as imprisonment or criminal assault may require extensive psychological and medical help, but even then the great majority recover. Senile symptoms respond to medication and psychological therapies. Because hospitalization often results in deterioration, older patients are best housed in halfway houses or similar facilities. Efforts to keep older people employed and motivated are important both as treatment and prevention.

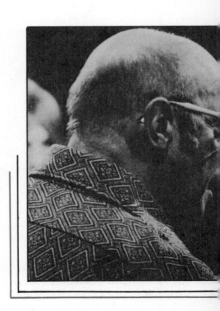

17 Medical, Community, and Behavior Therapies

VI TREATMENT

18 Psychoanalytic, Humanistic, and Related Therapies

Medical, Community, and Behavior Therapies

In this and the following chapter it will be evident that most therapies originate in a viewpoint, a model of human behavior and pathology. By and large, medical therapies are based on the premise of a biochemical explanation for mental disorders; behavioral approaches postulate that symptoms are learned. The various psychodynamic models assume that a disordered family and/or social experience causes abnormality.

Psychiatrists, psychologists, and other mental health professionals often identify with a particular model. In practice, however, most therapists are fairly flexible. If, for instance, their interests or skills do not include medication, they are likely to refer a patient who will benefit from such an approach to another practitioner. Or if they are dynamically inclined but believe some learning techniques will help, behavioral methods may be tried. Most therapists are open minded; they will

look for the type of treatment, or combination of approaches, most beneficial for their patients.

MEDICAL THERAPIES

From the medical point of view, the first step in determining treatment is accurate diagnosis. In physical medicine this means finding the causal roots of the disease. In the mental health sciences, because causes are elusive, diagnosis is based on symptom clusters described in the DSM-III.

The diagnostic process ordinarily begins with an interview. A psychiatrist talks with the person in order to uncover symptoms, feelings, and experiences. Next, a social worker may probe the person's school, family, job, and health history. Finally, the work of the diagnostic team is rounded out by the psychologist, who uses a number of tests to determine intelligence, personality traits, and adjustment. To increase the chances for an accurate diagnosis, all the data will be pooled when the different specialists meet to make treatment plans.

Diagnostic tests

We have already described some of the tests used to evaluate intelligence (Chapter 14) and organic brain syndromes (Chapter 15). Here we will cover some of the tests commonly used to evaluate personality. Despite the precautions taken to assure truthfulness on any one test, clients may still reveal relatively little of themselves or communicate erroneous information. To make up for this, and to compensate for the weaknesses of any one test, psychologists usually depend upon a **battery.** They use a number of different measuring instruments in order to arrive at a diagnostic conclusion. The typical test battery consists of an intelligence test such as the Wechsler Adult Intelligence Scale, an objective test like the MMPI, and a projective instrument such as the Rorschach. In this way, the clinician has approached the person from a number of different angles and obtained enough clues from each evaluation to formulate an overall diagnosis.

THE MMPI The Minnesota Multiphasic Personality Inventory is the best-known *objective* test of personality. It is a pencil and paper examination consisting of several hundred questions that clients must mark True or False, such as

I frequently have headaches.
I wake up fresh and rested most
  mornings.
Little things often annoy me a
  great deal.
Most of the time I feel nervous
  and jumpy.

Answers to the MMPI questions are scored in terms of the degree to which they fit psychiatric categories. Some of the classifications used appear at the bottom of the page.

The MMPI was devised to be an "empirical" examination. Those who constructed it did not assume that if a person said "true" to a question such as "I feel blue," this response must contribute to the D (depression) score. Instead, they gathered the answers to MMPI questions from known diagnostic groups. Preliminary forms of the test were given to schizophrenic, depressed, hypochondriacal, and other already diagnosed individuals. For each psychiatric group, a typical pattern of answers was worked

Score	Name	Description
K	Defensiveness	Persons with high K scores may be defensive, putting their best foot forward or covering up symptoms.
F	Falsification	High F scores can indicate that the testee may have been trying to look worse, exaggerating symptoms.
Hy	Hypochondriasis	Those who score high on Hy have many bodily aches and pains, somatic complaints and fears.
Pt	Psychaesthenia	Pt is an older term suggesting symptoms such as rigidity, self-consciousness, sensitivity, and compulsivity.
D	Depression	Elevated D scores may indicate anxiety, fear, and withdrawal as well as depression.
Pd	Psychopathy	Pd is a measure of rebelliousness, nonconformity, and antisocial traits.
Pa	Paranoia	People with high Pa tend to be suspicious, jealous, and hostile.
Sz	Schizophrenia	High Sz scores suggest the possibility of disordered thinking and emotions.

THE RELIABILITY OF DIAGNOSIS

Several studies have shown that clinicians change their mind about the proper diagnosis, or disagree with one another, in as many as one out of every three cases. The signs of fear that were first assumed to suggest anxiety neurosis are later interpreted as unipolar depression. The hallucinatory perceptions that once suggested schizophrenia are later seen as the result of drug abuse and addiction. Diagnosis is so frequently in error that many question its usefulness in the first place (Blashfield and Draguns, 1976).

Because the present DSM III nomenclature sometimes fails, behavioral, statistical, and functional alternatives have been proposed (Woodruff et al., 1974):

Using *behavioral* labels, patients are diagnosed in terms of specific behaviors. In this way, everyone can understand what is "wrong," and therapy can be targeted to problem areas. For example, instead of saying a person has depression, in behavioral terminology he or she would be described as eating and sleeping irregularly and complaining of gastrointestinal and cardiovascular disturbances. If the *statistical* alternative is used, computer analysis would determine which symptoms actually cluster together most often. Such studies have shown that the distinction between neurotic and psychotic may be erroneous since, for example, anxiety and withdrawal often occur together. In the *functional* or *prognostic* system, all mental disorders are described in terms of the degree to which they disturb present normal function and/or their probable outcome. A serious schizophrenia might be labeled severe-chronic-disorder and a minor neurosis, mild-temporary-disorder.

out. It provided examiners with a basis for comparing and scoring the test responses of undiagnosed individuals. Thus, for example, every time a testee answers a question the same way as a previously diagnosed schizophrenic person, he or she gets one point in schizophrenia. Every time a person answers the same way as a preexamined psychopathic individual, he or she gets a point on the Pd scale. It does not matter what the clinician thinks an answer means; what matters is whether or not it is the same as that given by a known group of previously diagnosed individuals (Anastasi, 1976).

Today the MMPI is often scored and interpreted by computer. An individual clinician reporting test results may be able to base findings on dozens of similar experiences. A psychologist might recall that other people with Sz scores similar to a particular client's frequently required hospitalization. But a computer can "remember" several thousand persons with similar Sz scores and accurately recall which benefited from medication, psychotherapy, or hospitalization. The following is part of a computer MMPI interpretation for a young woman who was hospitalized following a suicide attempt:

The patient's high K score, along with other test indices, indicates she is defensive and lacking insight. People with similar scores frequently believe they understand themselves, though in reality they intellectualize their problems and probably shift the blame to others.

The combination of elevated Pt, D, and Pa scores is seen with greatest frequency in single young women who get along poorly with other people, frequently have personal crises, and often make repeated suicidal gestures. . . . Nearly all such patients are motivated and respond well to psychotherapy.

A small proportion (about 5 percent) of young women with high Pt, D, and Pa later show prominent psychotic signs. Repeated examination or alternative clinical assessments may be advisable to evaluate this possibility.

The MMPI contains a number of so-called validity scales that attempt to evaluate the examinee's test-taking attitude. The F scale, for example, can give some idea as to whether or not the person is trying to look worse or faking mental illness. F items are ones like "I hate my mother." Saying "true" to a few such statements may be "normal," but answering too many in a negative direction suggests that the person is indeed extremely different, or really trying to appear peculiar. The K scale is also an attitudinal subtest and helps measure the degree to which an individual is covering up, trying to present herself or himself in as "average" a manner as possible.

THE RORSCHACH The Rorschach test consists of ten cards, each originally a black and white or colored inkblot. It is a *projective* test, meaning that the person has to "invent" an answer. He or she cannot just say "true" or "false," but must make up a response. The assumption is that since the test permits the person complete freedom, the answers will reveal unconscious, deep-seated attitudes, conflicts, and motivations. (Although many medically and behaviorally inclined clinicians favor objective instruments like the MMPI, psychodynamically oriented practitioners sometimes tend to value projective tests.)

The Rorschach was devised by a Swiss psy-

Figure 17.2. The Rorschach frequently gives some insight into a person's thinking and emotions. Though the reliability and validity of the test is low, experienced examiners may find the results useful. (Photo: Scribe)

chiatrist, Hermann Rorschach, at the beginning of this century. He believed that the way in which patients used parts of the inkblots, as well as what they saw, could differentiate schizophrenia, mania, and other mental conditions. Since that time many different systems for scoring and interpreting the Rorschach cards have been proposed. One of the most widely used requires that clients first be shown all ten cards, one after another. Next, clients are again presented with the cards and asked to locate their response and tell what made it look the way it did. Finally, all the responses are scored for location, determinant, and content. A few of these scoring symbols and their possible meaning are described below (Semeonoff, 1976):

Location (which parts of the inkblot were used)
W The whole blot is used for the response. A large number of W responses may suggest a tendency to overgeneralize or too high a level of aspiration.
D The client used a usual or common detail of the blot for the response.

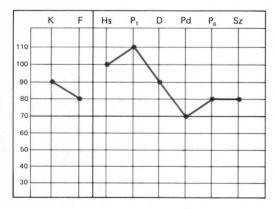

Figure 17.1. MMPI scores are usually "profiled" in a manner similar to that illustrated. The actual MMPI contains four validity and nine clinical scales. This profile, with the concentration of high scores in hyprochondriasis, psychaesthenia, and depression, might suggest a neurotic disorder.

A fair number of D responses may show good commonsense reasoning.

Dd An uncommon area of the blot was used for the perception. High Dd may suggest rigidity or unconventional thinking.

Determinant (what about the blot made it look the way it did)

F The perception was determined by form or shape. Good form responses, when the blot actually looks like what was described, suggest realistic thinking; poor form may indicate disordered thought processes.

M The response involves human movement. The presence of many M percepts suggests emotional well-being; a lack of M may indicate poor interpersonal relations.

C The perception was determined by color. C may indicate emotional health or depression or mania.

Fc Fc is scored when the examinee says the response was determined by the way the inkblot is shaded. Fc may suggest the presence of anxiety.

Content (what is the content of the response)

H Seeing human beings on the inkblots supposedly suggests at least the potential for warm relations with others.

A Animal responses are "normal," although seeing too many animals could indicate immaturity.

AT Anatomy responses (bones, organs, and the like) may suggest anxiety or a tendency to use physical symptoms as a psychological defense.

THE TAT AND BENDER The Thematic Apperception Test is a projective instrument that consists of twenty picture cards. Clients are instructed to make up a complete story to suit each picture. There is no agreed-upon formal scoring technique, so that individual clinicians are free to use their own skill and resourceful-ness in making interpretations. Many clinicians assume that the stories told reflect the client's hidden needs and look for consistent themes from one picture to the next. The following is a story told by a 26-year-old man who was supposed to be married but postponed the wedding because of his depression. He is looking at a picture of a man standing next to a woman who seems to be sleeping on a couch.

Story: This man has had it with her. She's no good. Not to be trusted. She's fooled him for the last time. She's been screwing around like crazy and now she's lying there pretending to be sleeping. Or maybe he's killed her. I don't know which. That's all. (Clinician: Then how does the story end?) He goes out. He leaves her. I guess he goes and gets drunk and has a good time.

Interpretation: Based on this and several other cards in which the client revealed a great deal of hostility toward women, it seems that this is a central theme in his life. He finds it difficult to accept a woman's love or be loving. Possibly these feelings are related to his fear of women and some sexual confusion seen in earlier cards.

The Bender Visual Motor Gestalt Test is sometimes classified as a projective instrument, although it is more properly called *expressive*. Subjects are required to copy simple designs presented to them, and interpretations are made on the basis of the way in which each design is duplicated. The assumption is that subjects reveal their needs and abilities by the way in which they express themselves graphically. There are several different scoring systems, but in one of them sketchy, overlapping pencil lines suggest anxiety. Or the person who reverses the designs and carelessly crowds them together on the paper might be suspected of possible psychosis or brain damage (Semeonoff, 1976).

TESTS: RELIABILITY, VALIDITY, USEFULNESS The reliability and validity of all measuring instruments needs to be known so that we can tell how trustworthy they are. Whether we

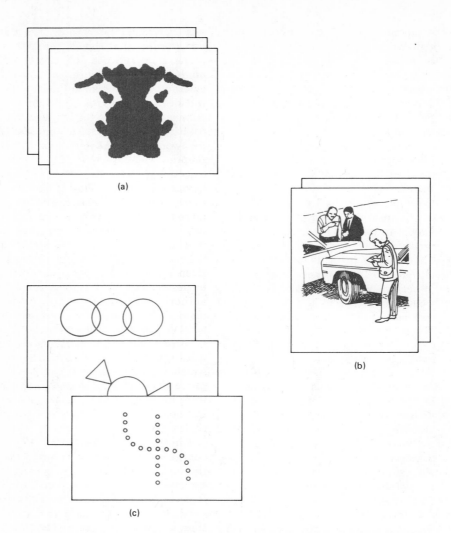

(a)

(b)

(c)

Figure 17.3. The tests illustrated are similar to the Rorschach, TAT, and Bender Gestalt. Projective tests have low validity and reliability, but in expert hands they often contribute important psychological and diagnostic information.

are concerned with a bathroom scale or an IQ test, mathematical techniques are available to ascertain the validity and reliability of both.

Reliability is a measure of consistency. The same test may be given to the same people over a period of time in order to see whether the score remains the same, a technique called test-retest reliability. Or several different peo-

ple may be asked to score a test to find out if all the results agree, a measure of inter-scorer reliability.

Validity deals with the question of meaning; just what is the test actually measuring? If we wanted to find out if a high D score on the MMPI really gauges depression, we might correlate the MMPI results with the ratings psychiatrists give to patients they have individually examined. Such a study would be an assessment of criterion validity. We are checking the meaning of the test score by comparing it with the criterion of personal clinical assessment. Predictive validity forecasts behavior. For example, IQ scores supposedly at least partly predict the school grades a child will receive. If we found IQ totally unrelated to school grades, it would cast grave doubts on the meaning of what was being measured by tests such as the WAIS or Stanford-Binet.

Both reliability and validity are calculated by using correlational techniques that produce a coefficient ranging from a low of 0 (no correlation) to a high of 1 (perfect correlation). Precise scientific instruments such as those found in physics and chemistry often have a reliability and validity of 1, or as close to perfection as possible. Even an ordinary bathroom scale is usually found to have validity and reliability coefficients of about .8 or .9. Psychological tests, however, do not fare very well. Objective personality tests like the MMPI usually have a validity and reliability in the range of .6 to .8. In other words, their consistency is fair to good and their ability to measure what they are supposed to measure is similarly in the medium range. Projective tests are lower, with validity and reliability coefficients in the .3 to .5 area. This means that, mathematically at least, the results of projective measurements are more often misleading than correct.

The modest validity and reliability of psychological measuring instruments means that no single score can be depended upon. This is the major reason why psychologists prefer to give a battery of tests; the tentative results of one may be confirmed or rejected by another. But when the same conclusions are reached using different instruments, the clinician can be more and more certain of the findings. It should also be pointed out that some psychologists are unusually expert with tests like the Rorschach. Though the test may have low validity overall, specialists using personal interpretive skills are often able to obtain worthwhile results (Anastasi, 1976; Andrulis, 1977).

Psychological testing often helps clinicians arrive at a diagnosis and formulate treatment plans. In some instances, test results such as an IQ score may be the deciding factor in whether or not a person is institutionalized. But despite the amount of information some clinicians are able to derive from tests, overall, psychological evaluation techniques are weak. As a result, many mental health workers are skeptical of tests or reluctant to use them. The objection to testing also comes from some behaviorally and psychodynamically oriented therapists. Both want to address themselves more to specific behaviors (or feelings) and are impatient with attempts to categorize individuals. Others are concerned about the way in which tests often tend to stigmatize people. Even though the tests themselves have only modest validity and reliability, the supposed authority surrounding the results tends to make labels (such as retarded or schizophrenic) stubbornly permanent.

HOW USEFUL ARE TESTS? Loro and Woodward (1975) studied 500 patient diagnoses in which tests like the Wechsler Adult Intelligence Scale, MMPI, Rorschach, and Bender were involved. They compared the diagnostic statements made on the basis of testing with the conclusions independently reached by the psychiatric staff by the time patients were discharged. Finding only a 43 percent agreement, the investigators point out that psychological tests were of value in less than half of all cases. It is obvious that a great deal of progress still needs to be made if testing is to make more than a minimal contribution to diagnosis and treatment.

Medication

Since the introduction of **psychotropic** (mind-affecting) drugs in the 1950s, medication has become the chief means of treating psychiatric symptoms. Each year, tens of millions of patients receive prescriptions for Valium, Nembutal, and dozens of other drugs intended to relieve anxiety, induce relaxation, and otherwise help alleviate disturbing symptoms. In fact, psychiatric drug therapy is so common

PSYCHIATRIC MEDICATIONS

Classification	Use and Conditions Treated	Generic name	Trade name example
Analeptic	To increase alertness in older patients (senility, organic brain damage)	pentylenetetrazol	Mentalert
Anti-alcohol	To combat alcoholism	disulfiram	Antabuse
Anticonvulsant	To reduce seizures (epilepsy)	phenytoin	Dilantin
Antidepressant	To relieve depression	amitriptyline	Elavil
		isocarboxazid	Marplan
		imipramine	Tofranil
Antihyperactive	To reduce hyperactivity	methylphenidate	Bitalin
Antimanic	To relieve mania	lithium	Lithane
Narcotic detoxicant	To combat heroin addiction	methadone	Methadone
Sedative	To induce sleep or relaxation (combats anxiety, neuroses, reactive and adjustment disorders)	amobarbital	Amytal
		pentobarbital	Nembutal
		secobarbital	Seconal
		methaqualone	Quaalude
Tranquilizer	To reduce anxiety, promote relaxation, and stabilize thinking and emotions	butyrophenone	Haldol
		chlordiazepoxide*	Librium
		diazepam*	Valium
		piperidine	Mellaril
		piperazine	Stelazine
		phenothiazine	Thorazine
		reserpin	Serpasil
		thioxanthene	Taractan
		meprobamate*	Equanil

Note: The "major" tranquilizers are used for schizophrenia and other psychoses; the "minor" tranquilizers, marked with an asterisk, are more likely to be used for anxiety conditions.

Sources: *Hollister, 1977; Iverson and Iverson, 1975; PDR, 1978.*

that the number of patients receiving medication far outnumbers the total for all other therapies combined (Iverson and Iverson, 1975; Kovel, 1976).

Modern drug therapy began a generation ago with the introduction of chlorpromazine. Clinical trials in mental hospitals led to the observation that administering the drug quickly led to marked reduction in the most disturbing signs of schizophrenia. Patients who were withdrawn, catatonic, or hallucinated resumed many normal behaviors and were able to engage in ordinary social activities. At roughly the same time that chlorpromazine and other "major" tranquilizers were being introduced, the "minor" tranquilizers

were also being developed. Among the first was meprobamate, which was found somewhat effective in treating tension and anxiety. A decade later, antidepressant and mood-stabilizing chemicals made their debut. The tricyclics, for example, proved quite effective as mood elevators and are now widely employed for a variety of depressions. More recently, lithium has been used as a mood stabilizer in manic and bipolar affective conditions, but the final verdict on its effectiveness is not yet in.

We have mentioned only a few of the several hundred drugs now available to treat abnormal symptoms (see box, Psychiatric Medications). The list of psychotropic chemicals is constantly expanding, and encouraging devel-

Figure 17.4. Until the 1960s mental hospitals often had a grim and forbidding atmosphere. Drug therapy, legislative efforts, and the shift to community care have substantially improved the rehabilitative milieu of modern institutions. (Photos: Smith, Kline and French Laboratories, G. William Holland)

opments appear to lie ahead. But psychiatric medications are not without their problems. First of all, there are side effects and complications for nearly all patients. Fisher (1975) surveyed the drugs used by a thousand physicians and found Valium, Librium, Elavil, and Thorazine the ones most commonly prescribed. Nearly all patients suffered some minor side effects such as drowsiness, appetite changes, or constipation. Occasionally, serious complications arose (blurred vision, tremors, jaundice, or coma) so that it is vital for all patients to have their medication carefully supervised.

The second concern is the effectiveness of medication. Does it cure mental illness? The answer to that question would have to be "No." Psychopharmacologic agents do not cure mental disorder in the same sense that penicillin cures strep infections. But volumes of studies have shown that generally medication effectively relieves symptoms. New drugs are usually pretested for potency and safety with animals and then given to clinical groups. Control populations with the same psychiatric condi-

tion are administered placebos, and neither patients nor administering physicians know who is getting the real medication. This "double blind" experimental approach has eliminated far more chemicals than have been retained. The ones that have been kept have had to show that they work and are safe.

A generation ago, three-fourths of hospitalized schizophrenic patients were expected to remain indefinitely. Today, largely because of medication, only 10 to 20 percent are likely to stay hospitalized. Before antidepressants and mood stabilizers, virtually the only medical source of relief was electric shock therapy. Today the great majority of affectively disordered individuals who are medicated are soon able to resume their normal lives. The same is true for many neuroses, posttraumatic and adjustment reactions, organic symptoms, and some sexual and personality disorders. Medication can sufficiently alleviate symptoms so that patients can function and adjust. Perhaps equally noteworthy is the fact that when the major tranquilizers are not adequate to enable a psychotic person to resume independent living, they can at least make him or her *accessible* to individual or group psychotherapy. Psychotropic agents can alleviate the confused and disordered thinking and exaggerated emotions of even the most disturbed patients so that they can participate in psychotherapy or other rehabilitation. In sum, psychiatric medication is not curative, but in the great majority of cases it reduces symptoms to the point where the patient can obtain other help or even resume normal living (Hollister, 1977; Iverson and Iverson, 1975; Kolb, 1977).

Shock, surgery

At the beginning of this century, several reports had pointed out that when psychiatric patients experienced convulsions, their symptoms diminished. As a corollary, it was believed that people who were seizure-prone, such as epileptics, were seldom schizophrenic. As a result of these ideas, psychiatrists sought various means to induce seizures in their patients and finally settled on an injected chemical, metrazol. Metrazol proved unreliable, so attention turned to electricity, which had long held a fascination for physicians and psychiatrists. Since the turn of the century it had been the object of much trial and error research in order to make use of it as a treatment technique (Figure 17.5). Finally, in the 1930s it was found a safer, more dependable procedure for inducing convulsions than any chemical. Gradually **ECT** or **EST** (electroconvulsive or electroshock therapy) was applied for nearly every psychiatric condition. In general, although it proved worthless with schizophrenia and neuroses, it is still used as a harmless and potent means of treating depression (see pp. 180–181) (Berkwitz, 1974).

Psychosurgery operations on the brain date back several thousand years to the early Egyptians and South American Indian peoples. Archeological evidence demonstrates that in both cultures, **trephination,** surgically removing skull bone and brain tissue, may well have been used to alleviate abnormality. In more recent times, in the 1880s a Swiss psychiatrist named Burckhardt operated on the cerebral cortex to treat mental disturbances. But psychosurgery remained infrequent until the 1940s, when relatively safe and swift procedures were devised to sever the frontal lobes from the rest of the brain (**lobotomy**). Using special instruments and entering the brain from a small hole drilled in the temple, or going over the orbit of the eye, beneath the brow, a surgeon could perform a lobotomy in a few minutes. Lobotomies were supposed to help relieve extreme and severe symptoms such as those found only in the most incurably agitated, violent, or bizarrely disturbed patients. Eventually, however, the technique spread, so that people with obsessive-compulsive and other neuroses were also lobotomized. Until lobotomy became unpopular in the 1950s, it is estimated that more than 50,000 patients underwent this surgical procedure.

Figure 17.5. The treatment value of electricity was explored for nearly a century until the usefulness of shock therapy was discovered in the 1930s. This 1904 pictures shows the interior of the electric room in a Massachusetts asylum. (Photo: National Library of Medicine, Bethesda, Md.)

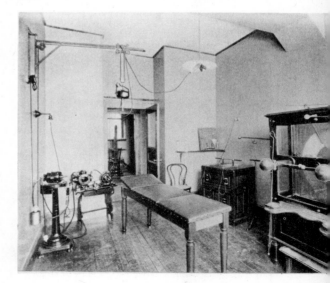

PLACEBO EFFECTS

Louise Ricalla (1975) has investigated people who benefited from a "laying on of hands," men and women who profoundly believed in the religious or mystical power of the "healer" and actually improved mentally and physically after being prayed over and touched. For several years Dr. Linus Pauling, a Nobel chemist, has reported that large doses of vitamin C and other nutrients restore mental health. In fact, this view has led to a specialty called orthomolecular psychiatry. These practitioners use a megavitamin approach, giving the vitamins and other biochemical substances the body supposedly lacks.

Many people who are anxious, confused, or mentally ill have been helped by meditation, prayer, vitamins, acupuncture, and several other unconventional or even peculiar forms of treatment. But is it the treatment or the placebo effect that brings about recovery? Because people are suggestible, a harmless, neutral placebo procedure often works quite well. Patients in pain given placebo pills frequently feel their aches relieved. Those who are worried and anxious feel better if an authority tells them they will be helped by screaming, deep breathing, or almost anything. In addition, many people with mental health problems recover on their own. Nearly half of all neurotic, and an almost similar number of psychotic, patients eventually improve, even without treatment (Lambert, 1976). When people who would get better anyway start therapy, they may falsely give credit to the treatment. They should instead praise their own recuperative powers.

Because of the relatively high rate of spontaneous recovery and the suggestibility of people, almost any kind of therapy, or in fact any sort of intervention, may seem to work—at least for a while. Consequently, we need to view all therapy claims with sound scientific skepticism. Before any type of psychotherapeutic technique is accepted, years of impartial, objective evaluation are necessary. The procedure needs to be tried on hundreds of patients, careful control situations devised, and the results analyzed with thoroughness and rigor. If the strictest and most demanding criteria were applied, it is likely that many past therapies like psychosurgery, as well as many present claims, would be proved invalid (Spitzer and Klein, 1976).

Psychosurgery is rare today because its effectiveness is questionable and also because it is irreversible. Brain tissue that is destroyed will not regenerate; lobotomized patients tend to be irremediably passive, lacking in motivation, and lifeless. In addition, all the benefits psychosurgery was supposed to bestow were actually and safely achieved through the discovery of psychotropic medication (Freedman et al., 1975).

Hospitalization

Well over a hundred years ago, the English philosopher John Stuart Mill wrote in his *Essay on Liberty,*

The only purpose for which power can be rightfully exercised over any member of a civilized community against his will, is to prevent harm to others. His own good, either physical or moral, is not a sufficient warrant. He cannot rightfully be compelled to do or forbear because it will be better for him to do so, because it will make him happier, because, in the opinion of others, to do so would be wise, or even right.

Until very recently, the ideas of John Stuart Mill were largely ignored. Although by the middle of this century hospitals provided a decent environment, most patients were still forcibly detained. Medically oriented professionals were convinced that serious mental disorders necessitated hospital care, whether or not the person gave consent. The public too accepted involuntary institutionalization as "good" for the disordered individuals. The result was that not too long ago the number of people in mental hospitals was beginning to approach the million mark.

The hospital population peaked in the 1950s and then started a decline because of three events. First, newly discovered psychotropic drugs made it possible for thousands of patients to live at home or return to work. The new therapy emptied once massively overcrowded wards. Second, in 1963, President John F. Kennedy announced a nationwide goal and initiated legislation to halve the mental hospital population. He wanted to shift mental health care away from large, impersonal, and isolated hospitals and into the community. Third, and perhaps most important in ending centuries of confinement, a number of courtroom challenges contested the right of a state or a psychiatrist to forcibly detain a person in a hospital. The most far-reaching judicial decision was that of *O'Connor* v. *Donaldson*.

Kenneth Donaldson had been diagnosed as paranoid schizophrenic and on this basis confined to a mental institution for fifteen years. Though he was not considered dangerous, he was repeatedly denied discharge because he supposedly needed to receive treatment. In actuality, Donaldson demonstrated that in all his years of confinement he, like many similar patients, had received little more than two weeks' worth of active therapy. In 1975, Donaldson's case reached the United States Supreme Court. His petition for discharge was upheld, and he was awarded $38,000 in damages for invasion of his civil rights by the doctors and hospital staff.

The *O'Connor* v. *Donaldson* decision, plus the new medication and legislative efforts, have dramatically reduced mental hospital populations. In 1979, less than 175,000 patients were hospitalized, one-fifth of the all-time high, and most of these were voluntary rather than forcible commitments. Further, prompted by the courts and "rights" groups, nearly all institutions are now careful about each patient's civil liberties. Most hospitals have adopted guidelines similar to the following (Kopolow, 1975):

1. The sole ground for involuntary hospitalization is that the person is dangerous.
2. It is the responsibility of the hospital to ensure that all patients continually receive adequate care and treatment.
3. Patients must be fully informed of their rights and of all treatment procedures. With few exceptions, treatment consent must be obtained.

Mental hospitals still exist to care for the few dangerous patients and others who voluntarily admit themselves. In fact, the great majority of mental patients today are voluntary; they have "signed" themselves in and can leave at their own request. In the best hospitals too, treatment is not limited to a single hour per day. The entire staff and the environment have a rehabilitory function. This **milieu therapy** approach enlists nurses, psychologists, and all staff members in the therapeutic effort. Each patient's emotional and interpersonal needs are examined and understood. Interaction with the staff and even physical facilities are consciously designed to facilitate recovery (Figure 17.6).

COMMUNITY THERAPIES

The shift away from hospitals has accented what communities can do to help people recover. Actually, this approach taps an ancient resource, since the treatment potential of a good home and environment was recognized at least several hundred years ago. Currently, the community mental health view has led to a new specialty, **community psychology** (or psychiatry). From this perspective, psychological well-being or illness is the outcome of far more than biochemistry and individual psychodynamics. As demonstrated by numerous studies in the last few decades (Dohrenwend and Dohrenwend, 1974), employment, housing, nutrition, minority status, and other social factors play an important role in adjustment. Community psychology, therefore, is *both* preventive and therapeutic; it seeks to understand and change the social factors involved in mental health and devise relevant individual therapies as well.

Halfway houses and family care

Halfway houses were originally designed to be temporary way-stations. Before being fully discharged, hospitalized patients spent time at a halfway house learning to shop, find employment, and live independently. Today, many halfway houses and similar facilities have almost replaced mental hospitals as treatment centers. Since they are small, personal units, patients avoid the feeling of powerlessness and abandonment so typical in enormous psychiatric institutions.

Halfway residences include simple two-story houses with ten patients or facilities that are imaginative and innovative. The Sane Asylum in San Francisco, for example, is a self-supporting community consisting of several mansions, an apartment complex, a school, and a business. It has 300 residents and offers help to drug addicts, alcoholics, and criminal offenders (Hampden-Turner, 1976).

Although the organization of halfway houses differs, they all share a number of common features. They are small units, located in residential areas, and with few exceptions average only about twenty to forty people. Patients are not confined and often play a part in running the facility. They are encouraged to find work and become part of the community in which they live. Professional help and treatment services are provided, though patients who live in halfway facilities may have been chosen because they are no longer severely impaired. Dennis Rog and Harold Raush (1975) examined twenty-six reports on psychiatric halfway houses in order to evaluate their effectiveness. They found that 55 percent of the residents were employed or had returned to school; 58 percent (including some of the above) soon began to live independently; and in total, 80 percent of those living in half-

Figure 17.6. The modern mental hospital encourages patients to have contact with "normal" people and the community. Here student volunteers are participating with patients in a hospital picnic and games. (Photo: New York State Department of Mental Hygiene, Creedmore State Hospital, N. J. Devine)

way houses were eventually able to be on their own. Only 20 percent needed to be referred to hospitals.

In family care, patients are housed with "normal" families. Originally this meant only a place for patients who were recovered to board. Today, acutely ill patients may be placed with families as a therapeutic measure. Brook and Cortes (1976), for example, studied 220 patients who needed intensive care and were placed in a network of five homes. Family sponsors were paid and selected for their commitment, intelligence, and warmth. The patients included individuals who were schizophrenic, paranoid, suicidal, and otherwise seriously disordered. A careful two-year study of the families and patients showed that not only did patients like family care better, but it was superior to hospitalization in many important dimensions: "Our experience has shown that ten beds in community homes meet the psychiatric intensive care needs of the citizens of southwest Denver. The warm family setting, small number of clients in each home, and familiar neighborhood setting has proved to be an effective treatment model" (p. 197).

Outpatient care

An outpatient is a client who comes to a hospital or clinic for treatment but is not a resident. Therapy may take only an hour, or most of the day, but patients do not live in the facility. They return home. Medical centers have long used this procedure, but the mental health field has only recently subscribed to this concept. The advantages are obvious. In addition to the person being able to continue family living, job responsibilities, and the like, the debilitating and discouraging effects of institutionalization are avoided. Today, outpatient mental health clinics and treatment centers are found in almost every sizable community. In many instances too, former resident mental hospitals have converted both space and professional staffs to outpatient care.

Workshops

Workshops play a pivotal role in the community effort to reestablish mentally disordered people in society. Patients who for years have been hospitalized or struggled with disabling symptoms have usually lost whatever job skills they had in the first place. Even if they are psychologically rehabilitated, they may be unable to live "normally" unless they are able to work. They need to offer employers job skills and/or experience. Workshops are of different types and go under different names from one region to another. The function of all of them, however, is to teach specific skills and good general work habits (punctuality, speed) to mentally or physically impaired clients. The three most common types of workshops are evaluation centers, rehabilitation workshops, and sheltered workshops.

Evaluation facilities use job samples and aptitude tests to explore the abilities and potentials of each client. When a person is found to have distinctive aptitudes for jobs such as bookkeeping or mechanics, he or she may then be sent for further training. **Rehabilitation workshops** are essentially controlled industrial situations. Clients work at jobs such as packaging, power sewing, or typing. From re-

habilitation centers, clients are expected to move on to regular employment. **Sheltered workshops** employ clients not able to meet industrial standards because their speed or quality may be too low. In a sheltered facility such clients work at their own pace and earn accordingly. In most workshops a number of additional psychological and social services are offered, including counseling, educational tutoring, and job placement.

Paraprofessionals

Community programs have discovered the economic need for and therapeutic importance of **paraprofessionals.** These are people with ordinary educational backgrounds who are trained to assist mental health specialists such as psychiatrists and psychologists. The range of paraprofessional activities varies. At a minimum, they may simply be people who are taught to take a case history or provide companionship. At a maximum, a well-trained paraprofessional may counsel clients and provide other therapeutic services. Often paraprofessionals are chosen from the sociocultural group that will be served or are themselves former patients. People who were once diagnosed schizophrenic or drug-addicted are often surprisingly effective with patients who have similar disabilities.

Paraprofessionals are also important for serving minority or disadvantaged groups. In such situations, the psychiatrist, who may be white and middle-class, sometimes has neither the skills, words, nor insights that will enable him or her to establish a satisfactory rapport. But a paraprofessional coming from the group that is to be served knows its language, defenses, and survival techniques. In addition, such people are far less likely to be "judgmental," falsely evaluating clients' behaviors from a conventional perspective (Martinez, 1977):

We didn't get anywhere with Joe till we had him work with one of our paraprofessionals, Mike. What it came down to was that Joe's language and his manner came across to us as threatening. But Mike grew up here. He knew the style and he wasn't intimidated. He saw it as a game. The "dirty dozens" sort of. He is hep, or hip, I guess you might say. Anyway he worked with Joe, he cut through the defenses in a way we never could. He established a relationship and the two of them together got results none of us could foresee.

CAUTION Paraprofessionals should not be confused with the unfortunately large number of people who call themselves therapists but have little or no background or training. Paraprofessionals are specifically educated for the jobs they perform. They limit themselves to their assigned function and do not try to pass themselves off as full-fledged psychotherapists. In contrast, many unscrupulous individuals with inadequate professional training set themselves up in practice. Since in most areas there are *no effective laws* regulating the use of title like psychotherapist, it is difficult to restrain such people. Such unqualified therapists often have some "success," but many have caused their patients great harm. Genuine therapists have earned college degrees from recognized universities and are licensed to practice their specialty (Table 17.1).

Crisis intervention facilities

These facilities, walk-in storefronts or simply a telephone number, are designed to give immediate counsel to people who are in crisis. Frequently they serve potentially suicidal patients, people who are frightened by a drug experience, or a husband, wife, or child in the midst of a violent family dispute. But such centers are also confronted with less dramatic problems such as runaways, friendship quarrels, and requests for assistance for long-standing and chronic conditions.

The effectiveness of crisis intervention centers varies with the population served and the

TABLE 17.1
MENTAL HEALTH PROFESSIONALS

Title	Education	Duties
Psychiatrist	M.D.	Diagnose mental disorders, prescribe medication, and give therapy
Clinical psychologist	M.A. or Ph.D.	Administer psychodiagnostic tests and give therapy
Psychoanalyst	usually M.D. or Ph.D. plus psychoanalytic training	Give psychoanalytic therapy
Psychiatric social worker	M.S.W.	Assemble case histories and give therapy
Psychiatric aide	high school or some college	Assist in patient care and therapy
Music therapist	B.A. or M.A.	Treat patients through musical expression
Rehabilitation counselor	B.A. or M.A.	Help patients adjust socially and/or vocationally

Note: *In addition, many other people, such as speech therapists, teachers, and psychiatric nurses, may help in the treatment of mentally disordered individuals. The duties described also show only a portion of each person's function. In most mental health settings, the responsibilities of each professional broaden to include their own skills and patient needs.*

Figure 17.7. This rehabilitation counselor in a mental health agency is often particularly effective because of his own physical limitations. (Photo: Scribe)

staff available. Many such facilities have been criticized for doing nothing more than delaying action, but this in itself may be a useful function. Yarvis (1975) reviewed several major studies of such centers and concluded that they seemed to function effectively as a first line of defense. His survey showed the centers provided at least three different benefits: One, they diminished the need for hospitalization; two, they often prevented a condition or situation from getting worse; three, they helped people in the community feel safer by possibly reducing the incidence of suicide and violence.

Intervention and advocacy

Community psychologists have described the mental health problem in "system" terms and advocated corrective action (Caplan, 1974). The individual is seen as a participant in various systems—the economy, the schools, the political structure. Treatment, or intervention, therefore ought to take place at the point where the social system or the person generates abnormal behavior. Such corrective effort may be thought of as preventive and can take place at three levels: primary, secondary, and tertiary.

Primary prevention means changing conditions that contribute to abnormality, like unemployment or malnutrition. Just as public health measures ended yellow fever by eradicating disease-bearing mosquitoes, so the social causes of mental disorder need to be similarly attacked. Realistically, however, alleviating the major environmental causes of abnormality is at best a very long-term effort. A more modest version of prevention attempts to work with the *population at risk*. For example, it is difficult to eradicate the maladaptive attitudes and socioeconomic failure that can lead to marital conflict. But children from homes where there is serious disharmony can be helped. Such youngsters, more than ordinarily vulnerable to psychological distress, need to be identified as early as possible. Similarly, treatment should be available for all other high-risk groups, such as children from psychotic or addicted homes, adults who are unemployed, or people who are objects of discrimination.

Early detection and treatment is considered intervention, or *secondary prevention*. This means mass screening for psychological symptoms in the same way there is mass screening for tuberculosis or high blood pressure. Such early detection efforts have a chance of treating potentially serious conditions before they become too disruptive. Secondary prevention also means crisis centers. Such facilities can intervene immediately to help defuse difficulties or initiate treatment quickly to prevent additional complications.

The final level, *tertiary prevention*, aims at continuing services. Patients who have recovered may need vocational retraining or other readjustment help. They may require assistance in learning, or in getting, a job or reintegrating themselves into society. At the same time, it is necessary to educate the com-

Community psychology has been especially critical of conventional mental health services for not reaching minority Americans. Many ethnic groups, particularly black, Indian, Eskimo, and Hispanic people, have received meager psychotherapeutic and preventive assistance (Sue, 1977). Such neglect may be due to lack of facilities or personnel in ethnic communities, discrimination, or the inability of mental health professionals to successfully reach people from different cultural or socioeconomic backgrounds. Two successful efforts to provide full services were reported by Carroo (1975) and Abad et al. (1974).

Agatha Carroo described the goals and methods of BAMHU (Black American Mental Health Unit) in Florida. Working in an area of 15,000 people disrupted and fragmented by urban renewal and highway construction, BAMHU initiated miniclinics and a system of informing and educating area residents. Full assistance in many legal, economic, and other social problems was also offered. The result

was that a community which had lost many of its traditional institutions and was faced with disintegration was revitalized.

Vincente Abad, Juan Ramos, and Elizabeth Boyce created a mental health program in New Haven, Connecticut, they believe could serve as a model elsewhere for Spanish-speaking peoples and other ethnic groups. The program included the following:

1. A bilingual staff
2. Recognition of the unique cultural and linguistic characteristics of the population being served
3. Immediately available walk-in services
4. Development of ties with ethnic and religious groups, faith healers, and local hospitals and organizations
5. In-service training programs for locally recruited paraprofessional workers
6. Additional services such as legal and financial counseling, consultation, transportation to and from the clinic, and home visits

munity so that discriminatory barriers against hiring people who have been mentally ill are removed.

The intervention-prevention approach moves away from the sickness-treatment model of traditional mental health practice. Community psychologists feel that, given the difficulty and complexity of abnormal behavior, it is better to create conditions conducive to health rather than to try to correct disability. As a result, many community mental health approaches take an advocacy position. Advocates work actively for the population at risk for health services and for social improvement as a whole. Advocates may be psychologists, social workers, professionals, or nonprofessionals. They may campaign for funding for mental health facilities or organize a disadvantaged neighborhood to press for drug treatment, jobs, or educational improvement. On a smaller scale, they may critically examine the mental health services delivery system,

the type and quality of care people get. Hirschowitz (1977), for instance, scrutinized several psychiatric agencies and found the pace and quality of patient processing labored, fragmentary, and redundant. Too much of the work that went on was "for the record" rather than for the patient. Such investigations often lead to modifications so that people will be better served by the facilities that are available.

BEHAVIOR THERAPIES

Though many people still erroneously equate behavior therapies with behaviorism, behavioral methods now encompass a range of orientations. Watson undoubtedly laid the foundation, but theory and methods have changed radically. What was once called *behavior modification* has by this time gone beyond simple reward and punishment to become a complex array of techniques for treating human beings.

What has happened is that the original "pure" behavioristic stimulus-response approach has given way to a **social learning** model. This view suggests that behavior is the result of a complex of reinforcers (both obvious and hidden) as well as modeling influences. Further, whereas earlier learning explanations stressed only the impact of the environment in determining behavior, the social learning approach focuses on the interaction between individual and milieu. Thus, a person may learn to behave in a highly anxious manner through modeling and particular reinforcement experiences. But in addition, he or she also structures the environment, alerting other people to continue to reinforce their own fearfulness.

Unifying themes

Today behavior therapies have opened up to include numerous techniques that many of the earliest strict stimulus-response advocates might have rejected. But despite the branching, both in theory and technique, behavioral therapies still share several common assumptions. We will present these unifying themes and then describe a small sample of the many therapies now in use (Lazarus, 1977):

The basis for all behavioral treatments is the idea that abnormal as well as normal behavior is *learned*. This means that nonorganic mental disorders are the result of the way people have learned to cope with their lives and environments.

Treatment is concerned with the *present;* uncovering the historical roots of a problem, insight, or awareness are ordinarily irrelevant.

Therapy *targets* the specific responses, which may be internal or external, that are to be treated. Typically, the behaviors to be altered are described as symptoms.

The techniques used by behavior therapists are usually *experimentally derived* from an understanding of learning and related processes.

Behavioral treatments are *individualized*. For each case, therapists use conditioning, operant, social learning or other behavioral techniques suited to the problem and the person.

Systematic desensitization

One of the earliest behavioral treatment procedures, **systematic desensitization** was introduced by Joseph Wolpe (1973) to help overcome phobias and other fear situations. It involves two steps: construction of a fear hierarchy, and relaxation exercises. First, a scale of anxiety is devised. The patient conceptualizes the *most to least* feared experience. The following hierarchy was built by a claustrophobic person who was unable to travel in cars and airplanes. The hierarchy actually consisted of twenty-two steps, of which we report only a few of the more critical.

1. being alone in my room
5. going into my walk-in closet to pick clothing
12. waiting in the dentist's waiting room
16. riding in an elevator
17. being in a closed public telephone booth
20. riding in an airplane
21. riding in a station wagon
22. riding in a small car

After the phobic hierarchy is clear, the patient learns to relax. A frequent method is to teach the client to lie quietly, breathe deeply, and successively concentrate on tightening and loosening every muscle and limb till there is a total feeling of relaxation. The final step is to countercondition the anxiety-provoking experiences. Patients relax and then vividly imagine the first step in the hierarchy. When patients can both fantasize the first situation and remain calm, they are ready to move to the next hierarchical step. Eventually, over the course of a few weeks, with the help of a therapist patients can imagine the most feared situation and still remain deeply relaxed. They have reconditioned many of the cues that once evoked anxiety to stimulate relaxation responses.

Desensitization works well on a fantasy level, but overcoming anxiety on the therapist's couch does not always transfer easily to real life. For this reason, systematic desensitization is often thought of as the beginning of a treatment process. Having been relieved of some anxiety, patients can now be encouraged by the therapist to confront their actual fear situations, step by step (Hersen and Eisler, 1977).

Cognitive therapy

Originally behavior therapists avoided any sort of human activity that suggested feeling or thinking. A response that could not be described as visible and overt was called "mentalistic" and considered outside the province of the objective psychologist. But as behavior therapists became more deeply involved in the treatment process, it was evident that thinking or cognition often plays a critical role in determining normality and abnormality. Thought and mental processes are now conceived of as internal behaviors, and like more overt responses, also subject to the laws of learning. Beck (1976) explains:

Cognitive therapy assumes that some of the individuals' problems are largely the result of distortions of reality based on erroneous premises. These errors result in defective learning and, ultimately, incorrect thinking. The therapist should help patients unravel their distorted assumption and learn more realistic ways to think.

Cognitive therapy is often effective with psychotic, paranoid, and other people who persistently misinterpret reality. Such patients are first encouraged to reveal the nature of their thoughts and then helped to correct their assumptions and logic. For example, a hospitalized psychotic individual with persecutory delusions perceived the words that others used as having a secret and harmful meaning. "He said, 'How are you,' but I know that what he

really means is 'Hate you.' " This patient was shown how his convictions were based on erroneous learned assumptions. Next he was trained to act "as if" words really meant what they were ordinarily supposed to mean. By cooperating with the therapist—that is, agreeing to interpret words "realistically"—the paranoid patient was able to restructure his own thinking and reduce its delusional content.

Aversive training

Attempts to eliminate behavior by punishing its occurrence are called **aversive training.** The most obvious example is the parent who slaps a toddler's hand and says "No" when the child touches a hot stove. As psychotherapy, aversion has been used to treat disorders as different as alcoholism, sexual deviation, and psychoses. A sex fetishist who was attracted to panties, for instance, was presented the garment and electrically shocked at the same time. Attempts have been made to teach schizophrenic patients to give themselves a shock with a portable apparatus every time they have an auditory hallucination. Aversive procedures using electric shock, however, are no longer in common use, for not only does the procedure raise ethical questions, but its effectiveness is doubtful.

A more acceptable aversive procedure is the time-out technique. This requires that undesirable behavior be followed by a brief period of inactivity or isolation. A school may, for example, set aside a time-out room or area to which a child must go when he or she is aggressive or inattentive. The time-out period must be relatively short and humane if it is to be effective. Along these lines, Murray (1976) recommends three methods for controlling tantrum behaviors in public places for use with retarded and brain-damaged children: As soon as tantrum behavior begins, take the child to a quiet corner for two minutes before resuming normal activities, or take the child to the car and wait outside till the behavior ceases, or place a coat or blanket lightly over the child's head and body till the tantrum subsides.

The **incompatible response** technique involves teaching a behavior that is contrary to, that will conflict with and restrain, the undesired conduct, and is often coupled with aversive training. For example, many retarded and psychotic children exhibit self-injurious behavior. They bang their heads, pull their hair, scratch themselves, and so on. Here is an example of the use of the incompatible response technique with such a child:

The object was to eliminate Astra's head slapping. Using candy and other reinforcers, she was taught to clap her hands in time to rhythmic music. During the same period, whenever head slapping occurred, the child was looked at sternly and told a firm "No." After the clapping had been thoroughly learned and the "Nos" had begun to reduce the frequency of head slapping, the two procedures were combined. Whenever the child started head slapping, she was told "No" and the music played
to which she had learned to clap. The result was that head slapping was eliminated.

Incompatible responses have been tried in more complex behaviors as well. Attempts have been made to teach responses incompatible with anxiety, deviant sexual arousal, and aggression, but the effectiveness of these procedures has been limited (Davidson, 1976).

Self-training

Clinical patients have been taught to alter their behavior using their own internal processes as punishment or reward. Punishment techniques are similar to aversive conditioning. But instead of being given an electric shock, clients learn to imagine a distressing scene. For example, a person who wanted to diet was taught to see himself weighing 310 pounds, clumsy, ill-kempt, and laboring for breath, every time he was tempted to reach

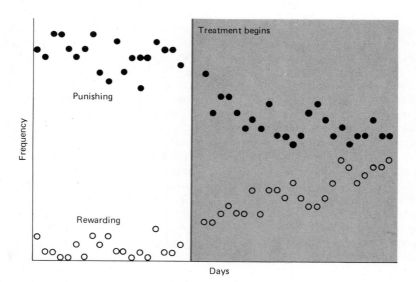

Figure 17.8. An important part of many behavioral treatment programs is charting. Patients keep a before and after record of the target response, the behavior to be changed. In this example, an abusive parent is learning to discipline her child by punishing (● ● ●) less and rewarding (○ ○ ○) more. After the mother began treatment, on the twenty-fifth day her punishments (yelling, slapping) decreased and her rewards (praise, tokens) increased. Charting permits patients to see their progress and acts as an additional reinforcer.

for a forbidden food. This approach has had some success in modifying smoking and alcoholism and in reducing some deviant sexual responses like exhibitionism (Hersen and Eisler, 1977).

An opposite self-training technique makes use of reinforcement. Subjects learn to reward themselves for desired behavior. A woman who was afraid to face her male employer and ask for better working conditions and salary was helped to devise a graded series of challenges, beginning with looking at her boss as he made his rounds and saying "Good morning." As each increasingly fear-producing response was successfully faced, the client reinforced herself by recording her progress and awarding herself praise and points. In addition, the client reported weekly to a therapist who further reinforced her with praise. After four weeks, the client was able to present her request to her employer.

The token economy

Operant conditioning procedures in which people are rewarded for desired behavior by being given a token are called **token economies.** The tokens may be plastic chips or coupons that can later be traded in for more tangible rewards like money, candy, gift items, or special privileges. Token systems have worked well in mental hospitals and other institutions where patients can be reinforced for activities like making beds, tying shoes, combing hair, and brushing teeth. Of course, every patient must be informed of the token system, and it is advisable to have a bulletin board that announces the earnings for each task and the cumulative rewards (Figure 17.9).

An important part of token economies, and of many behavioral techniques generally, is to *stop reinforcing undesired responses.* A teacher who worked with problem children wanted his pupils to be better behaved and more attentive. A study of the situation showed that the teacher was actually reinforcing the very behavior he wanted eliminated. He paid attention to children when they were talking, teasing, or clowning around, but when

Figure 17.9. In order for a token system to work, patients need a careful explanation of the responses expected and the rewards to be earned. Here, in an effort at resocialization patients are being informed in a family like setting of the rewards to be earned by appropriate eating and grooming behavior. (Photo: Scribe)

they studied he usually ignored them. In this situation the teacher was instructed not to reinforce disruptive behavior, thus eventually extinguishing it. Desired responses (reading, hand raising) were reinforced by a token. As a rule, token economies have been shown to be particularly effective with children and have been used to modify some behaviors in areas as different as aggressiveness, autism, phobias, and feeding problems (Lovaas and Bucher, 1974).

Modeling

Social learning theorists have emphasized that a great deal of behavior is learned simply by imitation. Even without deliberately wanting to copy parental example, children learn many of their responses and attitudes from their fathers and mothers. This human tendency to learn by imitation has been used to treat several undesirable behaviors, particularly fear and anxiety. Claustrophobic people, afraid to be in small rooms, have been shown demonstrations and films of people in telephone booths, elevators, and the like. This has often helped them substitute more suitable responses for their phobic behaviors. Similarly, a man afraid of initiating a conversation with a woman was taught by his therapist in a role-playing situation: "Watch, see what I say, what I talk about and do."

Modeling may also be useful for seriously disordered patients. Jaffe and Carlson (1976) worked with chronic psychotic patients who had been hospitalized for over twenty years. The patients chosen had few interpersonal skills and were withdrawn and isolated. One group of seven patients was selected for modeling and two other similar groups as controls. The modeling patients were exposed to games of ring-toss and "coffee breaks" and instructed to imitate the personal interactions of their therapists. Effects of the treatment were assessed by before and after records and psychometric techniques. Compared to the controls, the modeling group had clearly learned several specific social skills.

Effectiveness of behavioral therapies

Behavior therapists specify the symptoms or behaviors to be increased, decreased, or altered. Since these goals are concrete and often limited, the frequency of reported success is high. But critics contend that the behavioral approach frequently does little more than relieve one set of symptoms which are then quickly replaced by another. In fact, even when specific symptoms are relieved, the question of generalization is raised. Are behaviors learned in the therapist's office effectively transferred to everyday life? As an instance, does learning to realistically interpret the therapist's words prevent a paranoid patient from misinterpreting what a spouse or neighbor is saying?

To the criticism of symptom substitution, behavioral therapists respond that typically the symptom *is* the disorder. When the symptom is removed, the person is literally cured. Studies with alcoholics, for example, show that

when drinking is eliminated, the person's entire life changes. They themselves, and those around them, judge they are fully recovered. But what if the symptom is not the disorder? Children who are anxious, jealous, or distressed sometimes manifest their unhappiness by bedwetting. If the enuresis is stopped in such cases, it is possible that another sign of anxiety will rise in its stead. In such instances, O'Leary and Wilson (1976) agree that symptom substitution might be a problem. Overall, however, their survey of research findings convinces them that substitution is the exception. It is surprising how many mental disorders, *whatever their origin,* eventually revolve almost completely around the symptom, be it bedwetting or hallucinations. Remove the symptom and most often, in effect, you are treating the core of the problem.

The question of the generalizability of recovery is equally encouraging. Davidson (1976), for example, working with depressed patients, reported that alleviating specific depressive thoughts and behaviors appeared to permit general and overall mood changes. Patients learning not to feed themselves dysphoric cues and manifest depressive symptoms seem to transfer this learning from a special therapeutic to a broad social setting. Another demonstration of generalization was shown by Cooke and Apolloni (1976), who trained four handicapped children in positive social-emotional responses. Using modeling, praise, and instruction, they taught the children smiling, sharing, physical contact, and complimenting. After learning the behaviors, the children were integrated with untrained children in unsupervised situations. Several weeks of follow-up observation showed that not only did the trained social responses transfer and generalize, but some increased. The children carried their newly learned social skills to other children and even served as positive models while their own friendliness continued to grow.

For some behavior advocates, their approach ushered in a new era that promised the almost complete understanding and perhaps even control of human beings. The remedy for every disorder was either at hand or about to be discovered. At the same time, some critics called the behavioral orientation a fad; others denounced it as dangerous. In our view, the evidence shows that behavior therapies are neither all good nor all bad. It is unlikely that any one process or medication will turn out to be the sole basis for effective treatment. If behavior procedures are viewed dispassionately and objectively, it is apparent that they can make a valid contribution (Hersen and Eisler, 1977).

SUMMARY

Medical therapies begin with diagnosis, which is usually established after the patient has been interviewed and administered a battery of intelligence and personality tests. The MMPI is an objective, empirically derived examination that describes the degree to which patients fit psychiatric symptom categories. It also contains scales that help to evaluate test-taking attitudes. The validity and reliability of the MMPI is fair, so that most scores can help clinicians understand and diagnose a disorder. The Rorschach and TAT are projective tests requiring clients to make up their own responses to inkblots or pictures. Although the Rorschach has a fairly standardized scoring procedure, the TAT is frequently interpreted on an individual basis. Both projective instruments, and the Bender drawing test, have modest reliability and validity. Nevertheless, a few experienced examiners are sometimes able to obtain significant clues from these personality evaluations.

Medication is the most common and widespread form of medical therapy. Over the last few decades, several hundred drugs have been developed that significantly alleviate the symptoms of many neuroses, psychoses, and other mental disorders. But while millions of patients have been considerably benefited, side effects and the potential for abuse require that all medication be judiciously administered and supervised. Psychosurgery was popular in the 1950s but is rarely used today, mainly because

of the nature of its side effects. Electric shock is an effective and safe procedure to alleviate depression, but it too is less frequently employed, largely as a result of unwarranted and unfavorable publicity. In all therapies, the placebo effect needs to be guarded against. It must be certain that the treatment itself, and not the patient's suggestibility or hopeful expectations, is responsible for the recovery.

The number of hospital patients has steadily declined over the last several years. Drug therapy and legal and legislative efforts have limited hospitalization largely to people who are dangerous or who voluntarily institutionalize themselves. The best facilities now emphasize a total treatment approach, milieu therapy, where every aspect of the hospitalization is designed to be rehabilitative. Community facilities such as outpatient clinics, halfway houses, family care units, workshops, and crisis centers, which are smaller and more personal, are replacing large and isolated institutions. In these settings patient motivation is frequently high, and the process of treatment and recovery far more rapid than in hospitals. Paraprofessionals are people specially trained to assist in the treatment of patients. Because some have been patients themselves, and many are from the same culture and community as clients, they can be highly effective members of the mental health team. Paraprofessionals should not be confused with self-appointed therapists.

The shift to community facilities has led to the specialty of community psychology, a discipline that emphasizes prevention in addition to treatment. Prevention can be primary—that is, an attempt to change social conditions such as unemployment which may lead to abnormal behavior. Prevention, or community intervention, can also be secondary or tertiary. This means, respectively, identifying the population at risk for early treatment or providing continuous services for those who have been mentally ill.

Behavior therapy has advanced beyond the stimulus-response approach to include cognitive and other social learning techniques. As a result, many different behavioral treatments are now available, though all tend to be experimentally derived and focus on present behavior. In systematic desensitization, anxiety stimuli are counterconditioned to evoke relaxation responses. Cognitive therapy uses learning techniques to restructure thinking and expectations. Aversive therapy attempts to eliminate behavior by punishing its occurrence. Incompatible response, self-training, and token economy techniques alter behavior through the judicious use of reinforcers. Modeling capitalizes on the human tendency to learn by imitation and example. As a whole, behavioral therapies are neither as totally effective as early advocates claimed nor as superficial or dangerous as many opponents feared. Like other worthwhile treatment techniques, learning-based psychotherapies make a valid contribution to the rehabilitation of many mentally disordered persons.

Psychoanalytic, Humanistic, and Related Therapies

When Sigmund Freud early in this century encouraged his patients to talk, he set the pattern for nearly all future psychological treatment. Today, the psychoanalysis he pioneered and all the psychotherapies derived from it may be called *psychodynamic,* for they assume that internal forces, needs, anxieties, and the like determine behavior. They may also be called *insight* therapies, for they are based on the premise that an understanding of one's own motivations and defenses is essential to recovery. The insight or psychodynamic therapies may themselves be subdivided into psychoanalytic and humanistic categories, as we shall see in this chapter.

PSYCHOANALYSIS

When Freud returned to Vienna after his studies in France, he was taken in by a senior colleague, Josef Breuer. Both believed that ca-

tharsis, telling all, would relieve neurotic symptoms. Soon, however, Freud found that advising patients to get everything off their chests was not enough. Patients were organizing what they were saying. They were being logical and proper.

To counteract the tendency to speak rationally, Freud devised the technique of **free association.** He instructed patients to say absolutely everything that came into their heads: "Speak all, no matter how illogical, disconnected, silly or obscene it may seem." The psychoanalyst's job was to put together the words, stories, symbols, and images revealed by the patient and deduce the struggles and conflicts taking place in the unconscious. In other words, the analyst interpreted or revealed the psychodynamic meaning of what the patient was saying, thinking, or experiencing. The following dialogue between patient and doctor is an example.

PATIENT: Just now while I told you about my wife I got this picture of my boss working on next year's budget. You know deciding who to cut out; the company is in trouble. Silly, isn't it. I know I am not going to get fired. I have a pretty long seniority. That's what they go by. But I can't figure out why this intruded about my telling you about her. You know she's complaining I'm withholding things from her, withholding love from her, I guess and all that.

DOCTOR: Well it is beginning to make sense to me. You remember your Oedipal fantasy you told me about last time.

PATIENT: You mean like I was afraid of my father, I thought he was jealous of the relationship between me and my mother.

DOCTOR: Hm mm.

PATIENT: Now wait. Wait a minute. You mean I was afraid, literally afraid to love my first wife and Alice. I withheld love from her, and I withheld love from Alice. Like I was afraid to love really love my mother because of my father.

DOCTOR: Yes.

PATIENT: So the boss, his budget, that was symbolically my father. My unconscious was telling me this. When I spoke of my wife, lurking there in the background was my inability to love her because of fear of my father's retribution. And my seeing the boss threatening to fire me, that was the symbol.

DOCTOR: Yes, I think so. I believe you have never felt really able, free to love a woman because of this unresolved unconscious Oedipal fear. You might want to give that thought some time.

When free association does not reveal sufficient unconscious material, the analyst looks for other ways to probe behind the patient's repressions and other defenses. Freud believed that during sleep, ego controls were lowered,

so that dreams could be the "royal road to the unconscious." But even in dreams the psyche is still self-protective; dreams are *symbolic representations* of hidden wishes and desires. It is therefore necessary to distinguish the *manifest,* or apparent, content of a dream from its *latent,* or hidden, meaning. For example:

Just as I was waking up, I saw this hand. You know not a whole dream, just a fragment sort of. It was a tough, workman's hand with a leather cuff on the wrist. . . . It was big, like covering up the whole space in my dream. But it was also delicate. Like it was a lady's hand. Thin, very soft. . . .

In order to arrive at the meaning of a dream, patients are required to carefully examine every event and symbol. Frequently they free associate to a specific element to see what that image actually suggests. Asking to free associate about the leather cuff in the dream above,

Figure 18.1. Psychoanalysts believe that dreams symbolically reveal unconscious needs. A patient's repeated dream of jumping in front of a subway was eventually interpreted as revealing a hidden wish to sexually dominate her husband. (Photo: Scribe)

the young man finally recalled a girl who played basketball in his high school and whom he much admired. Ultimately, carefully tracing every possible clue in this dream led to the interpretation that the patient, a man, unconsciously wished to be a woman.

Two other important aspects of psychoanalysis are resistance and transference. **Resistance** refers to the person consciously and unconsciously avoiding material that is threatening or too revealing. The person may show resistance by talking about trivialities, changing the subject when a sensitive area is approached, or forgetting therapy appointments. **Transference** refers to the person's tendency to treat the therapist in the same way as a spouse, parent, or other important personal figure. By carefully noting both the areas of resistance and the feelings transferred, the therapist obtains further clues about what is really important in the person's life and adjustment.

Freud was at first uncomfortable with transference, not wishing to be treated by his women patients as their father, husband, or lover. But on analyzing his own discomfort, he discovered that this apparent "falling in love" with the therapist was neither a true personal affection nor limited to women. Clients of both sexes used the therapist to act out past loves and hatreds. Transference was neither a compliment nor threat to the therapist, but a valued and integral part of treatment.

Psychoanalysis lasts until patients achieve as full an understanding of their own conscious and unconscious processes as possible—usually several years. It is hoped that by being aware of all the needs, desires, and experiences that were once repressed, patients can now make rational choices. Their behavior will no longer be forced by deeply buried motives or distorted by an accumulation of ego defenses. But *insight* is only one of two important goals in contemporary psychoanalysis. In addition to understanding themselves, patients are also encouraged to *work through*, to try new modes of responding. With the assistance of the analyst, patients expand their lives by entering

once forbidden situations and simultaneously giving up nonproductive emotions and responses.

Therapies derived from psychoanalysis

Alfred Adler, Gustav Jung, Otto Rank, and dozens of Freud's other contemporaries introduced numerous modifications to the new system. Over the past half century, however, the great majority of psychoanalytic revisions have fallen into disuse. The classical or strict Freudian psychoanalysis described above is also relatively rare today. What has happened is that the *form* of psychotherapy Freud initiated, patient-therapist dialogue, has become the common property of all therapists. Whether psychoanalytic, humanistic, or in some other orientation, therapist and client talk, probe, and plan together. The substance of Freud's work is spread among many different treatments whose roots can be traced back to psychoanalysis (Nye, 1975).

EGO ANALYSIS Most current psychoanalysts are dissatisfied with what they consider Freud's excessive emphasis on the role of the id and on innate, unalterable drives. They disagree too that the ego acts only as a mediator between the superego and id, and have elevated it to a central position. According to the *ego psychoanalysts,* people such as Erik Erikson, Anna Freud (Sigmund Freud's daughter), and Heinz Hartmann (Rangell, 1975), a great deal of behavior is learned and is not the result of inborn or instinctual energies. Personality development and change continue throughout life; the personality is not fixed after the first seven years of psychosexual development. And many motives—far, far more than Freud believed—are conscious. That is, people are not at the mercy of their unconscious but can make rational decisions. An important aspect of therapy, therefore, is strengthening the ego—that is, encouraging rational, conscious, adaptive responses and adjustment.

INTERACTION ANALYSIS Many therapists, led by Karen Horney and Harry Sullivan, have pointed out that Freud seriously neglected the effect of other people. From the interaction point of view, personality is largely the result of social influences, and maladjustment is essentially an *interpersonal* disturbance. People who are neurotic or otherwise disordered are impaired in their ability to interact with others. Therapy needs to focus on how the person's interaction failures developed and how to correct them. Like ego analysts, interactionists are far less concerned with unconscious mechanisms and dream analysis and far more interested in helping the person devise more effective personal relationships (Friedman, 1975).

TRANSACTIONAL ANALYSIS This therapy was created in the late 1950s by a California psychiatrist, Erik Berne (1972). In many ways, it is an updated parallel of traditional psychoanalysis. Instead of talking about ego, superego and id, transactional therapists use the almost analogous terms adult, parent, and child. Several other TA concepts also seem to have psychoanalytic roots. The transactional notion of a script, for example, is close to the old psychoanalytic word *complex* (as in inferiority complex). A **script** is a life plan, a way of acting and reacting throughout life that meets the person's needs. Four common scripts are (1) I'm OK—You're OK (this is a healthy life script showing self-acceptance and acceptance of others); (2) I'm OK—You're not OK (a life plan typical of suspicious or paranoid people); (3) I'm not OK—You're OK (typical of people who feel inferior or depressed) (4) I'm not OK—You're not OK (this position is found among seriously ill and psychotic patients).

In transactional analysis, therapist and client agree on a **contract,** a behavioral goal the patient wishes to achieve. The therapy itself consists of analyzing the person's life script and the **games** he or she plays. Games are in many ways similar to Freud's ego defenses. They are transactions that help patients avoid intimacy, really facing themselves or others. The alcoholic, for instance, is playing the game of "I'm irresponsible and can't control myself, therefore it's not my fault." In therapy the aim is to give patients the insights and resources that will permit them to stop playing games (drop their defenses) and function as genuine people. Toward this end, treatment can be conceived of as a learning and teaching situation. Patients are taught how their scripts and games are disabling and learn instead to be competent human beings.

Figure 18.2. Charcot at his clinic in Salpetriere, France, a century ago demonstrating hypnotherapy as a treatment for hysteria. Freud studied here and was influenced to try hypnosis at the beginning of his own practice. (Photo: National Library of Medicine, Bethesda, Md.)

GAMES PEOPLE PLAY

Games are manipulations, *defensive maneuvers* intended to control others and provide the player a "payoff." For example a common husband-wife game is, "If it weren't for you." The wife says, to her husband, "If it weren't for you, I would have finished college and have a job now, and be making some money." Analyzing such a case a TA therapist found that it was true that the husband was domineering and did insist his wife stop college after they married. But the wife actually picked him because he was bossy. She did not want to continue college, and she wanted to be dominated. Nevertheless the game of, "If it weren't for you," permits her to blame someone else for her own lack of initiative.

Some common games include these (Berne, 1972):

"Now I've got you, you son of a bitch!" The person allows himself or herself to be taken advantage of, even encourages abuse, until the adversary is out on a limb; then he or she reacts with furious indignation.

"I know I shouldn't be so fussy but I do have very high standards." The man who is actually afraid of women and marriage insists instead that his bachelorhood is a result of his lofty ideals.

"I'm not a well person." This statement becomes an excuse for not doing one's share, for disappointing others, and a rationalization for all sorts of selfish acts.

"Yes, but." I invite your confidence or advice and when you have told all, I find all sorts of weaknesses in what you say and put you down.

"Victim." The alcoholic's wife sometimes helps perpetuate the addiction by continually playing victim. She works to maintain situations in which she can suffer.

"I've got to be in the mood." The person who is irresponsible, egotistical, or being controlling asserts he would like to (go to work, make love, or study his textbook), but it wouldn't work unless he is in a supposedly correct mood.

Hypnotherapy

Hypnosis has been known for many centuries. Until a hundred years ago, however, it was largely regarded as a mystical phenomenon that had no place in science. It was probably the work of Anton Mesmer that caused a modern revival of interest in hypnosis and ultimately led to its use by Freud. Early in his career, Freud studied in Paris with Jean Martin Charcot (1885) and learned that the symptoms of hysteria could be removed through hypnotic suggestion (Figure 18.2). When Freud returned to Vienna, he expanded both his understanding of hysteria and his use of hypnosis. He found that hypnosis could help "open up" patients, prompt them to lower their defenses and reveal many unconscious motives. Ultimately, however, like many present-day therapists, Freud found hypnosis an unreliable technique. For one, only a few patients proved to be really good hypnotic subjects.

More important, neither the hypnotic cooperation elicited from patients nor the relief from symptoms endured very long.

Hypnosis is an altered state of consciousness characterized by extreme suggestibility. Good subjects willingly carry out almost any reasonable suggestion made by the hypnotist. But there are limits. First, there are several different levels or stages of hypnotic trance. Nearly all people can be induced to enter the lightest trance, where they can be persuaded to relax and perhaps even go to sleep. But although most people can be lightly hypnotized, the treatment value of this early stage is minimal. The more advanced trance levels, particularly the deepest stage, can be useful in treatment. During a deep trance, people are capable of several hypnotic phenomena, including these:

AMBULATION: Subjects talk, walk, are fully awake and behave in an ordinary manner, although they are hypnotized.

ANESTHESIA: A few people can be induced to become so insensitive to pain that surgery may be performed.

POSTHYPNOTIC SUGGESTION: Subjects can be given orders to be carried out *after* they have been awakened from the trance.

HALLUCINATION: Subjects can be convinced to see things that are not there (positive hallucination) or not see things that are present (negative hallucination).

RECALL: Some patients seem to be able to recall past and seemingly forgotten events with unusual detail and clarity.

REGRESSION: The ability to seemingly recall or reenact early childhood feelings, experiences, and behaviors.

SOMATIZATION: Using only suggestion, some bodily changes in perspiration, heart rate, and glandular output can be brought about.

Only 5 to 10 percent of all patients are capable of achieving the deepest trance. It also often takes considerable effort to reach the deeper stages, so that many therapists believe their time is better spent trying other treatment methods. When hypnosis is used, it is likely to be employed in cases like traumatic reactions, phobias, psychosomatic illnesses, and breaking habits and minor addictions (Crasilneck and Hall, 1975).

Hypnosis is *not* magic and it cannot regress patients to act exactly the way they did as infants or relive a previous incarnation. Deeply hypnotized subjects are very anxious to please the hypnotist. If they are asked to remember the life they lived in another body two hundred years ago, they cooperatively make up a coherent story. Such tales in no way confirm reincarnation, but they do demonstrate the extreme suggestibility of a few individuals. In addition, though some hypnotized subjects may be helped to do their best in a game or on a test, hypnosis cannot call forth physical or intellectual abilities that are not present in the first place. Hypnosis is a natural, not a supernatural, condition, which in the hands of a competent professional plays a small part in the treatment of mental disorders (Crasilneck and Hall, 1975).

HUMANISTIC THERAPIES

Humanistic therapies have been called the "third force" in psychology. Their approach is contrasted with those of psychoanalytic and behavioral therapies, both of which are said to fail in their recognition of the full potential of each human being. The humanistic therapies suggest too that disordered behavior cannot be corrected just by probing unconscious memories or altering responses. People are seen as possessed of the ability to make rational choices and to heal themselves, though they may need the warmth and encouragement of another human being to do so. Of the several therapies that can be called humanistic, Carl Rogers' client-centered psychotherapy is the most prominent. We will look at it in some detail, and at the existential and gestalt therapies that also center on the person realizing his or her potential.

Client-centered therapy

According to Carl Rogers, in psychoanalysis and behavior therapy the therapist is an expert, an authority who directs the treatment process. In client-centered therapy, leadership falls to the person being treated. So called clients (not patients since they are not considered to be ill) determine the pace, direction, and content of the sessions. The therapist should be like a skilled friend who provides an atmosphere of warmth and trust that encourages growth.

Like other dynamic therapists, client-centered counselors ask their patients to talk openly. But clients need not free associate or in any other way deliberately narrow their verbalizations. What the Rogerian therapist is mainly interested in is helping the person to air feelings. To this end, counselors frequently underline their clients' emotions with a **reflection.** They restate the essential feeling conveyed in the client's discussion (Kovel, 1976), as in the following example:

CLIENT: My husband said, well then, maybe I should go back to school.

But this left me puzzled. Maybe, I thought he is trying to psych me out. He was against it and now he is for it. Confusing, I guess.

THERAPIST: I sense a feeling of anger. You are upset.

CLIENT: Yes I guess I am. It made me mad. What's he trying to do? Yesterday I said to Phyllis (mother-in-law) that maybe she understands him. But I don't! She can read him inside and out for all I care. . . . I wonder if she's back home already and busy with her own husband. It's only four hours.

THERAPIST: You feel some anger here too, maybe jealousy, perhaps.

CLIENT: I am not angry at her. Maybe I am jealous. I have a lot of trouble in that area anyway. It is very easy for me to get jealous. Even if he's out with his kids. I feel lonely, left out.

THERAPIST: You often feel jealous, alone. Maybe you feel sort of sorry for yourself.

CLIENT: I feel miserable. I feel I'm no good. I'm not worthy. I'm a bitch. I'm not anything. Nobody really wants me.

In this treatment segment, the therapist's reflections enabled the client to reveal herself. She was able to produce a highly critical self-perception that lay at the bottom of many of her symptoms and complaints. From the client-centered view, it is this negative self-perception, the distorted, unfavorable view of the self, which needs to be brought out and changed in order for clients to make progress.

Client-centered therapists do not offer interpretations, seldom ask questions, and never provide answers. Instead, counselors supply a setting characterized by three conditions: (1) **genuineness**—therapists are totally honest and open fellow human beings; they do not use manipulations or tricks to produce changes in their clients; (2) **emphatic understanding**—counselors try to enter the client's own frame of reference; their reflections and other statements emphasize understanding of the client's feelings and experiences; (3) **unconditional positive regard**—the therapist fully accepts and values each client as a human being with all the good potential every person possesses.

Rogers believes that therapy provided the setting for an inevitable progression from negative to positive. Clients first have to be helped to rid themselves of all their negative and defensive feelings so that positive, wholesome attitudes can emerge. Each person has an inborn tendency to **self-actualization,** a basic motive to make the most of their good skills and emotions. Once therapy removes the toxic, disabling, self-destructive attitudes, healthy self-actualizing, loving, creative emotions and capabilities follow (Maslow, 1972).

Existential therapy

Existential psychotherapy derives from the philosophy of existentialism. This viewpoint questions traditional values and explanations and sees human beings as confronted by choices. There is no predetermined purpose in life, nor do our experiences necessarily have any meaning. It is up to each person to make decisions, derive goals, and struggle with such basic issues as "What is existence" and "Who am I?" Psychotherapists influenced by existentialism do not attempt to impose any standard psychodynamic view on their patients. No outside explanation is suitable, for every person interprets the world differently. What is important is for the therapist to perceive each patient's **phenomenological reality,** how the client understands and experiences existence.

In this framework, psychotherapy becomes an exploration of potential and future. It is more appropriate for persons in treatment to become aware of what they want to be than to probe their past for what they have been. They are required more to examine conscious choices than to explore unconscious memories and experiences. The emphasis is on the here and now, on what can be done, and not on past grievances or disabilities. In the person's

quest for being, the therapist becomes an equal, a guide. He or she has no shortcuts to resolve anxieties or to derive meaning, but helps move the person forward in his or her own pursuit of identity.

Along with the search for personal meaning, each person must learn to cope with individual responsibility and disorder, to recognize the inevitability of death, uncertainty, and suffering. Such **confrontations** can make people anxious, but this misery is not pathological and is not in need of cure. It is through grappling with limitations and pain and enduring anxieties that people find out who they really are (Enelow, 1977; Kovel, 1976):

Existential therapy is different. You encounter yourself, you encounter nothingness, you see yourself as a nonbeing. Like all my neurotic anxieties, symptoms, defenses, they kept me from seeing myself, my potentials, and who I was. They kept me a nonbeing, a creature acting reflexively, not by choice but by fear. . . . The inevitability of death, the ambiguity and uncertainty. . . . These realities I learned, I accepted them. . . . The emphasis for my therapist was always what is to be done, given the limitations, the necessities, what are my choices. . . . The implication was always there, the meaning of each decision for my own goals, my definition of my self. . . . What I got from existential therapy was, I think, a self-definition. I don't want to say I am happy with the world or what I see. But I have developed a meaning for my own existence. I am a person.

Gestalt therapy

The name Gestalt therapy suggests the early twentieth-century experimental psychology which emphasized the importance of perception. A half-century ago, rebelling against the then prevailing tendency to understand consciousness by analyzing it into its component parts, Gestaltists pointed instead to the importance of the total configuration, or *gestalt*. They asserted that the perceptual whole was not only different from, but far more important than, the sum of its individual parts. This

: : for example, is not just four dots, but appears to most people to be a square. The configuration "square" is much more than can be understood simply by analyzing the separate parts of the gestalt.

Gestalt therapy employs a little of the terminology and a few of the concepts of the old school of experimental psychology, but it would not be accurate to say that the therapy is an outgrowth of the original discipline. Gestalt therapy is very much the creation of Fritz Perls, who was heavily influenced by psychoanalysis, bioenergetics, and client-centered therapy (Rosenblatt, 1975). One of its cardinal rules is to concentrate on the present, the **here and now.** The past and future may be brought into therapy, but what is essential is that the person talk about his or her feelings at this moment. The therapist may say, "When I say that word, 'love,' what do you feel, now." "You are crossing your legs, how does that feel, tell me?" Notice too that not only is living in the now vital, but so is the recognition of feeling rather than thinking. In order to be healthy, people have to learn to feel, to open their awareness to pleasure and to pain.

Gestalt therapists may confront their clients with challenges and emotion-provoking questions and statements. They may also investigate their dreams. But unlike Freudians, their intent is not to uncover hidden wishes as much as it is to ferret out and stimulate feeling. A common therapy technique makes

Figure 18.3. Existential therapists require clients to derive their own goals and assign their own meaning to their lives. (Photo: Scribe)

use of the empty chair. This involves the client switching back and forth between a role being played in the occupied chair and one visualized in the empty one. For example, a neurotic, anxious man came to the third therapy session concerned about the behavior of his woman friend. She seemed to be becoming distant and disinterested, and he was unable to understand his feelings. The therapist then directed him to imagine the woman sitting in the empty chair and started the conversation by saying the woman had just said bluntly, "I'd like to stop seeing you." After some hesitation, the man was caught up in the situation and supplied the dialogue for himself and for the woman. Before too long, he was pouring out his hurt and rage on the empty chair.

Like client-centered and humanistic approaches in general, Gestalt therapy values *awareness, feeling,* and *personal responsibility.* The belief is that when feelings are liberated from repressions and emotional distortions, they are basically positive and wholesome. One of the main goals in therapy is therefore to rid people of their inhibiting pretenses and personality defenses. Hidden in each person is a genuine, feeling human being who can be brought out through the process of therapy.

Gestalt therapy intends to leave people knowing how to continue to be aware and take responsibility for their own actions. Throughout treatment, therapists stress "you." "You, not me, are responsible for yourself." "You, the patient, not me the therapist, must learn to cultivate awareness, so that you will know your feelings." Gestalt therapists also seldom interpret. Unlike analysts, they do not tell patients what their actions mean or what their feelings are. Their intent is to produce a whole person, a self-reliant, aware individual who can guide and shape his or her own life.

BODY THERAPIES

Dissatisfied with what they consider the exclusive emphasis on psychological processes, a number of therapists have broadened treatment to include the body. Malcolm Brown

Figure 18.4. This patient, participating in a body therapy, has torn off her clothing and is writhing on the floor in a painful reenactment of her own birth. (Photo: Scribe)

(1973) calls these approaches **body therapies.** In procedures such as **primal therapy** or **bioenergetics,** therapists insist that patients not only understand but also experience their psychological and physical selves. They need to know how their body has suffered from their psychic impairments and to learn to free the **energies** that have thus been blocked. Bioenergetic therapists usually start sessions with breathing exercises. They want to break through the person's defensive **character armor** and may require clients to assume a "stress position," such as stretching over a stool on the floor. Primal therapists typically begin with a long and intensive daily treatment routine in order to make patients vividly bring into focus their unfulfilled basic infantile needs. In both therapies, the treatment stress that clients undergo is believed to help them liberate hurtful experiences they have repressed or **encapsulated.** In both treatments too, patients soon kick, cry, beat pillows, or scream, literally reliving their earliest traumas, ridding themselves of pain and learning to integrate their feelings.

Many other therapies have also begun to include body techniques. Massage, touch, exercise, screaming, crying, and aggression are believed to have treatment value and are encouraged. But although this approach is popular, its effectiveness is controversial. The exponents of body techniques have done little in terms of objective evaluation of their methods or theories. There is also a distinct placebo effect. People who undergo physical treatment are often convinced that something good must have happened simply because of the drama of their experience. But what little scientific evidence does exist suggests that when professionally conducted with suitable patients, body techniques are probably valid psychotherapeutic procedures (Kovel, 1976; Smith and Glass, 1977: Spitzer and Klein, 1976).

SEX THERAPY

Until the 1940s, sexual dysfunctions were likely to be treated by some form of psychoanalysis or insight therapy. The person with dyspareunia, impotence, or some other coital or orgasmic problem was assumed to have an overall adjustment deficiency that required psychodynamic treatment. By the 1950s, however, a number of new developments began to encourage the direct treatment of sexual difficulties. Behavioral therapists, concentrating on symptoms rather than dynamics or insight, were reporting a good deal of success. The new body therapies were breaking through the "physical" barrier—people could be asked to do things with their bodies. Perhaps most important, the puritanical attitudes prevalent even among professionals were being challenged. A full and healthy sexuality was increasingly seen as a wholesome, positive, and pleasurable life experience (Gagnon, 1977).

Sex therapies today are a combination of dynamic and behavioral techniques and have their foundation in the work of William Masters and Virginia Johnson (1970). Their explorations of how people actually function during intercourse and other sexual experiences quickly led to a number of innovative methods to improve or rehabilitate erotic capability.

(Note that their concern is with "normal" sexuality and dysfunction, not deviant activities like exhibitionism or fetishism. Although people with these sexual aberrations are sometimes helped by Masters-Johnson types of therapy, they usually require a wider range of professional care.) For Masters and Johnson and in most programs derived from their work, *negative and fearful attitudes are at the core of sexual dysfunction*. The man, for a number of historical and personal reasons, is not quite sure his erotic desires are proper and/or he is afraid he will not perform properly. The woman, equally immersed in sexually anxious social and educational beliefs, is convinced she will not or should not be physically responsive.

The first step in sex therapy is usually diagnosis and instruction. Following a complete medical evaluation to rule out physical malfunction, the couple is encouraged to talk about their fears and preferences in an atmosphere resembling client-centered counseling. Therapy is conducted jointly, by a male and a female clinician, and with rare exceptions the patients too are always a male-female partnership. During this beginning phase, the couple is taught the physiology and anatomy of sexual function. Using diagrams, plastic models, and the like, the therapists instruct the couple on the roles of the penis and clitoris, the different types of orgasm, and so on (Chapter 12).

Most sex therapy programs last two weeks. The couple is often requested to move into a hotel, away from home and its usual distractions. During treatment, coitus is also expressly forbidden until the therapists actually sanction intercourse. Needless to say, despite popular misconceptions therapists do *not* have intercourse with clients, nor do they watch them in intimate scenes. Instead, clients are assigned specific tasks, do their "homework" in the privacy of their room, and then report back for more discussion, instruction, and assignments.

After the first few days of assessment and teaching, the couple will be taught massage techniques. The man and woman are told to lie naked and take turns touching and stroking each other's bodies, avoiding the genital areas. Sexual arousal may occur, but must not be consummated. The intent of this so-called **sensate focus** is to break down inhibitory barriers and to become thoroughly familiar with one's own and one's partner's body. The man and woman may then be taught masturbatory techniques. The woman may be instructed to work alone and using a mirror explore her own genitalia and try different means of pleasurable touch and manipulation. At the same time, the man arouses himself so that both eventually can tell each other what they find exciting. After this, the couple can extend massage to include each other's sexual organs. They may use the "hand over" technique, so that the partner will know exactly what to do. The woman, for example, may place her hand over the man's and guide him to give exactly the amount of pressure and stroking she wants on her vagina and clitoris.

These steps, which usually take about a week, are followed by procedures especially designed for whatever problems are faced by the couple. The "impotent" male, for example, may be helped by the woman learning to rhythmically squeeze the penis to facilitate erection. Or the man may be taught to use his fingers or a vibrator to help his "frigid" partner become aroused and lubricated. In addition to learning techniques designed to meet specific sexual dysfunctions, the couple learns to enjoy their own bodies, to stop challenging themselves or their partner to perform, to relax and feel pleasure in their own bodies.

When sexual dysfunction is a "symptom" of a broader relationship difficulty, for example, marital discord, the effectiveness of treatment is very low (Leiblum et al., 1976). Similarly, sexual therapies fail when erotic problems are only one aspect of a schizophrenic or other extensive mental disorder (Gagnon, 1977). But when sexual dysfunction is the major problem and is treated in a comprehensive therapy program, results have been impressive. Follow-up studies on patients completing a Masters-Johnson type of program show 80 percent or more continue good sexual functioning (Macvaugh, 1977; Munjack and Kanno, 1976).

GROUP METHODS

Nearly every theory of and treatment for human behavior has been applied to groups as well as individuals. That is, groups may be psychoanalytic, behavioral, transactional, Gestalt, and so on. Groups vary in size and structure, but most consist of about six to eight clients and one trained professional. Typically they meet for an hour or so once or twice a week, and sessions continue for many months.

One of the pioneers of group methods was Edward Lazell (1921), who in 1920 worked with a group of schizophrenic patients. At the begin-

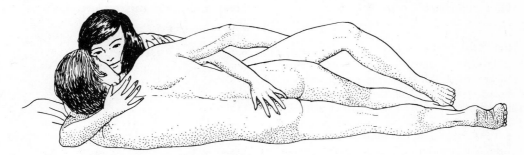

Figure 18.5. During the final phases of sex therapy, specific techniques and coital positions may be suggested. A side-by-side position may be recommended when it is important to maximize the couple's seeing and touching each other. This technique may also result in a tighter fit for the penis in the vagina.

ning treatment consisted primarily of lectures, three a week, for four weeks. Lazell discussed fear of death, masturbation, hallucinations, feelings of inferiority, and a wide range of other psychological topics. Although Lazell lectured, he encouraged open discussion and a cohesive group feeling among his patients. Eventually, nearly all were reported to have made considerable progress because of the group experience. Lazell, incidentally, was viewed as quite unconventional two generations ago. His new methods to draw psychotic patients out of their isolation were strongly disapproved. Among other things, Lazell used music, performed stunts, organized debates, promoted educational and work activities, and sponsored social tea parties mixing patients and normal people.

Another impetus to group treatment resulted from the efforts of social psychologists, who in the 1940s started T-groups (T for training) at the National Training Laboratory in Bethel, Maine. These groups were limited to business executives and designed to help them increase awareness of their own feelings and their influence on others. At about the same time, Carl Rogers at the University of Chicago began training counselors using group methods. He encouraged free and open discussion to increase communication and to stimulate personal growth. From these several seeds, a host of different groups have developed. To sketch a picture of what is available today, we will describe a few current group methods (Goldberg and Goldberg, 1973).

Self-help groups

We call self-help those groups which themselves try to resolve specific problems. Of course, all treatment involves self-help, but self-help group therapy is very highly focused. Alcoholics Anonymous, for example, is set up for the single purpose of helping addicts stop drinking. The problem confronted by Parents Anonymous is to assist themselves to stop mentally and/or physically abusing their children. Any people who share the same disorder or problem may become part of a group

especially designed to help them cope. Self-help groups usually consist only of those who need help. Groups such as AA or Synanon, for instance, seldom include a trained therapist, and their methods may depart considerably from traditional therapy. Child-abusing parents or a group composed of adolescents learning to "live with" epilepsy are occasionally under the guidance of trained mental health workers.

A relatively unique and new self-help group was reported by Comstock and McDermott (1975), who brought together individuals who had attempted suicide. Groups were formed from patients referred from the emergency room of a large hospital. They met once a week for a one- to two-hour session, and most attended for a period of about six weeks. The groups were headed by skilled therapists, but they deliberately tried to avoid immediate problem-solving. Instead, the emphasis was that alternative behavior is possible for those contemplating suicide. A related secondary goal advanced by the therapists was to foster "psychology mindedness" in group members. Every impulsive behavior was identified as such, with the point being made that action without reflection is what accounts for many suicides. Observations over a two-year period convinced the authors that the groups were working well, and they suggest that a similar approach may be suitable for most suicidal patients.

Consciousness-raising groups

Many groups are aimed at making particular people more alert to their position in society. Consciousness-raising groups, for instance, may show women how they have been discriminated against. Such groups often follow a prepared program which suggests questions to be discussed, such as the following:

1. What are some of the ways in which my parents consciously or unconsciously discouraged me from following a career?
2. When did I become aware of my sexuality and what was I taught about it by my mother, my father?

CR, encounter, and like groups are not strictly psychotherapy. People in such groups are *not* mentally disordered and are not in need of treatment. Rather, the aim of these groups is to help normal people increase their awareness and potential. Even individuals who are well adjusted may still be handicapped by social restrictions and personal deficiencies. Consciousness-raising groups grew out of the perceived need to assist women to become more alert to discriminatory pressures and to make them more aware of their own abilities.

Grace Baruch and Rosalind Barnett (1975) describe how women in our society often have their potential restricted by rigid social expectations of what is appropriate for each sex. A forty-year-long intelligence test study showed that the higher the IQ of a male as a youngster, the more he gained as he got older. But the brighter a woman was as a child, the less IQ points she gained as she grew older. Along with this, empirical research demonstrated that the more closely a woman identifies with the traditional role played by her mother, the fewer positive adjustment qualities, like independence and self-esteem, she possesses. Baruch and Barnett believe that most women are not encouraged to be bright or self-confident. The result is that very many highly qualified women suppress their initiative and intelligence. Further, while departing from the commonly assigned sex roles may increase a woman's feeling of self-actualization, it is also likely to be accompanied by guilt, anxiety, and uncertainty. For such women, consciousness-raising and encounter group experiences have served the dual role of helping relieve anxiety and reawakening potential.

---

3. What are some of the words used by men and by society that put down women (the little lady, baby, broad)?

Consciousness-raising groups have enabled many people to recognize that their position in life or their self-image may be more a product of the social structure than of their own capabilities. For this reason, CR groups have proved appealing to minority peoples such as black and Hispanic Americans and also to those whose life styles are often disapproved, such as homosexual men and women. Consciousness-raising groups are not intended to be therapeutic, but by making people more aware of their abilities and roles seem to help improve individual adjustment. In an analysis of CR groups, Warren (1976) has concluded that the CR process makes use of many of the same factors operative in therapy. In both situations too, favorable personal change is the intended outcome.

Encounter and sensitivity groups

Both encounter and sensitivity groups are directed at helping people make more of their lives. The original sensitivity groups usually had awareness as their major goal. They wanted people to become sensitized to their own feelings, their environment, and their effect on others. The more recent encounter groups attach importance to awareness but emphasize growth. Their aim is to stimulate each individual's full potential. Neither encounter nor sensitivity groups are for mentally impaired people, but often neurotic and other maladjusted persons join such groups. Since these groups are "growth" rather than treatment oriented, the abnormal person is not likely to be helped. In some instances, people who are seriously anxious or otherwise disturbed have found their situation worsened by an encounter experience.

The structure of encounter groups (and we include sensitivity and similar units under this heading) varies immensely. Some are influenced by Gestalt therapy and insist on a complete and honest revelation of immediate feelings. "You're lying! Lying! Now how do you feel. Tell me, tell me now, how you feel." Others lean toward the client-centered approach advocated by Carl Rogers. These sessions are far gentler and more supportive. They seek to provide an atmosphere of warmth and acceptance in which people can slowly learn to understand themselves and free some of their inherent abilities. Still others have included some body therapy techniques. Exercises, massage, and touch experiences are part of almost every session. In a very few instances some encounter groups have required nudity in the belief that being unclothed promotes total honesty. In still a few other cases, encounters have not been limited to an hour or two of meetings twice a week, but have been "marathon" sessions. Such long encounter periods may last ten hours or an entire weekend and put participants under a great deal of physical as well as psychological stress.

Given the many different types of encounter and sensitivity groups, it is difficult to generalize about results. Even when encounter groups carry the same label, say a Gestalt orientation, they may still differ because the character of the participants can be all-important. What happens in an encounter session can sometimes be unforeseen or even harmful. In one very careful study of many different groups, a fairly high "casualty" rate was revealed. About one out of ten of the participants suffered serious psychological harm, including psychotic reactions and depressive disorder, as a result of their encounter activity (Lieberman et al., 1973).

Hartley et al. (1976) have examined the types and causes of poor encounter experiences and found leadership to be critical. Without excellent guidance, people may be pushed into situations they cannot handle. They may become seriously upset or anxious when anger and other strong emotions are brought out. Or some inept leader may fail to recognize psychiatric problems and permit such people to participate in the group. To help prevent encounter casualties, the authors recommend that leaders be trained and certified, potential participants screened for psychopathology, and all members have the purposes, techniques, and structure of the encounter clearly explained to them.

GOALS AND METHODS   Most competent groups share several of the following goals and methods (Haas, 1975):

GROWTH: The objective is to become aware of oneself and put into practice one's own capabilities, to self-actualize.

LEADERS AS PARTICIPANTS: The leader guides the group, sets limits, protects members, and so on, and also participates. Instead of remaining aloof professionals, leaders talk about their own feelings and reactions.

FEELING OF INTIMACY: Many people feel alone and alienated. Encounter groups offer warmth, acceptance and support. Participants frequently become like family members, hugging each other, sharing joys and sorrows.

ICE-BREAKERS: Techniques to encourage trust and talking may be employed, such as the trust walk (one person is blindfolded and led around by another), "who am I" (participants use five adjectives to describe who they are), fantasy (participants describe their most longed for experience), and massage (members touch and massage one another's back, stomach, face, and so on).

CONFRONTATION: Members are encouraged to confront one another with their deepest feelings, doubts, and uncertainties. Occasionally confrontations become quite emotional, with members accusing one another, declaring their love or jealousy, and even screaming and crying.

OPEN AND HONEST: O and H have almost become slogans exemplifying the encounter movement. Group members react strongly to lies, covering up, and "phoniness" and insist that every member be open and honest in his or her participation.

GROUP STAGES   A similarity of many encounter and most therapy groups as well is that participants seem to move through three stages. The stages overlap, progress unevenly, and shade into one another, but are usually discernible (Haas, 1975). The first stage can be called *learning trust*. At the beginning, nearly all new participants have the feeling of "What's a nice man (or woman) like me doing in a group like this?" Gradually, as members open up to one another, the feelings of strangeness and suspicion are replaced by con-

PSYCHOTHERAPIES: DIFFERENT ORIENTATIONS, SIMILAR FOUNDATION

The terms used to describe the various forms of psychotherapy often have an unfortunate pejorative sound. The label depicting one's own treatment preference can make it appear that other therapies are in some way defective. For example, calling oneself a humanistic therapist may imply that other techniques are inhumane. Or being client-centered seems to suggest that other practitioners are self-centered. But Gestalt therapists are not the only practitioners who work with the whole person. Neither is psychoanalysis alone in its ability to analyze what is happening in the psyche. The fact is that no one form of psychotherapy can claim to have a monopoly on altruism, ability, or insight. All legitimate therapists are in the broadest sense concerned about behavior, are client-centered, analytic, humane, and interested in their patients as total human beings.

Therapists' orientations help determine the techniques they use. Toward the beginning of therapy it is easy to detect the differences, say, between a client-centered therapist who does a great deal of reflecting and an analyst who interprets dreams. But as therapy continues, as the relationship between counselor and client becomes increasingly intense, good therapists tend to resemble one another. Numerous comparisons of the words spoken and methods used by competent practitioners in the advanced stages of treatment have shown few characteristics that identify them as belonging to one or another theoretical school. What is revealed is that all valid treatments tend to share several essential elements (Enelow, 1977):

A warm and helping relationship: The therapist accepts the client and does not disparage or judge his behavior. Instead, the therapist creates a warm and trusting atmosphere that prompts the patient to speak freely and reveal himself.

Transference: In one way or another, patients begin to transfer both positive and negative feelings, to like and dislike the therapist. Therapists make use of these feelings to understand and point out disordered emotions and behaviors, and also to help motivate their patients to change.

Self-expression: Therapists help patients to express their feelings, fears, and confusions. They want patients to probe their emotions and responses, and perhaps for the first time experience themselves psychologically and physically as they never have before.

Labeling: Therapists label and to an extent explain the process of treatment. Often too, they teach their patients or guide them to an understanding of what has happened in their lives.

New behavior: As treatment progresses patients attempt new behavior. They are encouraged to discard ineffective and maladaptive patterns and replace them with healthier attitudes and responses.

---

fidence. The people in the encounter or therapy group appear increasingly decent and worthy of trust.

The middle stage of encounter is *self-discovery.* With the help of the others in the group, people learn what their assets and shortcomings are, as well as how others perceive them. This is followed by the last stage, the *growth experience.* People, perhaps for the first time, discover emotions like love or experience their own creativity. In everyday terms, growth for some people can mean returning to school, becoming less anxious or defensive, changing jobs, writing poetry, or just taking more time to relax and enjoy friendships:

Through encounter I really discovered my capacity and need for love, emotionally and physically. . . . I had remained a Puritan, a good standard little girl just like my mother, and everybody else taught me. . . . But now I have discovered I am an adult and I have powerful affectional needs and I am an animal and I delight in my biology. . . . There is no more reason for me to be a repressed little girl now than there is for me to kiss my mother good night. I am a passionate woman and did not know that it was this that was burning within me. . . . I need a lot of experience and a lot of depth. . . . Fred told me that he never realized I had it in me. He said we now have such a lusty, free relationship that he smiles from one day to the next just thinking about us.

Family and marital groups

In both marital and family therapy, the emphasis is not so much on individual mental disorder as it is on disturbed interactions among a group of people. Consider, for example, a wife who is anxious and worried, or a child who is disobedient and aggressive. The wife could be diagnosed as having anxiety neurosis and the child as having an unsocialized aggressive reaction. But we would be much further along in our understanding of both if their individual behaviors were seen as part of a disordered family relationship. In this group, the father is a domineering and punitive individual whose constant criticism of his wife makes her feel incompetent and apprehensive. The wife in turn imitates her husband's dictatorial manner and is very severe with their child. In reaction to all the restrictions imposed upon him, the child has become rebellious and particularly disruptive in school, where he feels he can get away with his behavior.

Marriage and family treatment approaches are like group therapy, for much of the focus is on the reciprocal effects of who is doing what to whom. The mother's behavior affects her child, the child has an impact on the father, and all together provoke and control one another's responses. Leon Robinson (1975) describes family and marriage therapy as differing from individual treatment on three dimensions:

1. *Personality development:* In family therapy, personality development is seen more the result of family rules and expectations than of individual needs and potentials. The fam-

ily functions as a system that imposes standards and demands conformity.
2. *Symptom formation:* Symptoms are only minimally the result of intrapsychic processes—that is, conflict within the personality itself. More important in the formation of symptoms is the conflict between individual needs and the demands of the entire group or other family members. A functional or healthy family or marriage encourages individual potential. A dysfunctional, mismanaged marital or family system arrests or impairs independent and mature behavior.
3. *Treatment:* Treating the symptoms of one individual is ineffective, since families and marriages tend to be committed to the continuance of faulty interactions. Treatment must be directed at the whole family, at all group participants, so that they will learn to live harmoniously and productively with one another.

TECHNIQUES In therapy, many counselors spend a good deal of time attempting to encourage communication. Family members need to learn to express their desires and feelings directly. Instead of manipulating each other, instead of "playing games," they have to learn to talk openly:

Whenever I wanted to go out I would put Charlie in the position of asking me to do what I wanted to do all along in the first place. Like I would tell him my girlfriend asked me to go with her to the movies. But I would say I shouldn't go, I couldn't go, I had laundry to do, bake the cookies and so on. So he would say it's all right, Go out. . . . I would get him to almost beg me. . . . Then when I came home late, or a little high or something, I could tell him that I hadn't really wanted to go out. I was only listening to him. . . . Now, of course, we don't play those games. . . . We discuss our needs for a little freedom, private space, very openly.

Encouraging open communication is not easy and has led to several innovative methods.

Dayringer (1976) presents a technique called Fair-Fight-for-Change, which "creatively" utilizes the aggressive impulses that develop in most marriages. During therapy, couples are encouraged to vigorously express themselves, to discharge their assertive and emotional needs. In other words, they learn to fight, but do so following certain guidelines. A first rule is that while criticisms may be angry and aggressive, they should also be constructive. A final rule is that demands should always be negotiable and eventually lead to a contractual agreement reached by both husband and wife. Thus while "fighting" is encouraged, it is guided by a constructive purpose.

Not all marriage and family counselors are primarily concerned with the communication process. Many therapists use traditional approaches that are an outgrowth of their understanding, or model, of human behavior. The following two cases illustrate the work of behaviorally and psychodynamically oriented family therapists.

Felix and Fanny had a great many complaints about their marriage many of which centered about Felix's supposed lack of "warmth" and Fanny's alleged lack of sexual interest. Fanny said Felix seldom kissed her or gave her a hug or pat, and so on. Felix said that Fanny was inhibited "in bed" and much too often refused him intercourse. The therapist set up a complex recordkeeping and mutual reinforcement system. Essentially it required that Felix be awarded points for every affectionate gesture, such as kissing Fanny when he came home. In return, when Felix had accumulated sufficient points he could trade them in for intercourse, at any time. A second part of the program rewarded Felix for the amount of time and type of foreplay preceding intercourse. The longer and more varied the foreplay, the more points Felix earned with which he could "purchase" particularly preferred erotic techniques.

Abe complained that Alice was not a "real" wife. Alice said Abe was demanding, immature, and moody. The therapist, a psychoanalyst, believed the problem centered about Abe's unconscious insistence that his wife play a maternal role. Abe wanted to be mothered, cared for, and pampered. He had never successfully resolved his Oedipal feelings, his affectionate maternal attachments, and was now treating Alice like his mother. Alice in turn had an unconscious need to compete with men, traced to her unhappy experience with her father and brother. Instead of seeing Abe as a partner, she viewed him as a rival and tried to give him as little as possible. From the analyst's point of view, the marital problem could only be solved when both Abe and Alice had worked out their own unconscious motives and personality fixations.

FAMILY THERAPY WITH DISORDERED CHILDREN Family treatment approaches have gained increasing popularity. Of course, all mental disorders are not the outcome of family interactions. Nevertheless, illness in any one family member is likely to affect all the others. For this reason, many therapists now prefer to work with several family members as well as the specifically disordered patient.

Family treatment is particularly important, in fact almost indispensable, in all child therapy, regardless of the cause of the disorder. Children are especially vulnerable to the family milieu and cannot be expected to improve unless positive parental changes occur at home. Most child treatment clinics and therapists require at least one parent be in therapy along with the child. The chances that a child will be treated successfully are vastly improved if the mother and/or father also undergo psychotherapy.

Group psychotherapy

The objective of group therapy is treatment. Consciousness raising, encounter and similar groups may be partly therapeutic, but their direct goal is not to rehabilitate neurotic, psychotic, or other disturbed individuals. Here, we are reserving the term **group therapy** for situations specifically designed to treat those who are mentally ill. The psychotherapeutic group model may be client-centered, psychoanalytic, Gestalt, or follow many other theoretical directions, but the intent is treatment. Rather than again describing the basic premises of these different models, we present excerpts from three different group therapy sessions.

MILLER: No. That's not true. I stay aloof because I want time to think. I need to figure things out.

CHERYL: I think you feel afraid of other people, that's what I think.

MILLER: No. I need time.

THERAPIST: As I sense it, Cheryl, Miller feels he needs now to feel he is on his own. Not obligated sort of.

MILLER: I think that's it. Other people take things out of you. I want to avoid that.

CARL: I feel the same way. I like not having any obligation to anyone. I mean I have said to my sister, "Look they called me schizophrenic in the hospital. So what do you expect. I'm not to be relied on."

ARLETTE: I think you [Carl] feel very depressed. That's what that statement just said to me. You're very unhappy.

CARL: I feel bad. I feel bad. I feel so alone . . . (becomes tearful and stops talking).

The group above was led by a therapist influenced by the client-centered approach. He continually reflected the feelings expressed and as such provided a model for the patients in the group to do the same. As in nearly all groups, the techniques used by the leader are copied by the patients themselves. When they switch roles from patient to therapist, and this back and forth movement is very common,

Figure 18.6. Carl R. Rogers, the founder of client-centered therapy, is seen here leading a treatment group. (Photo: Carl R. Rogers, from the film *The Steel Shutter*)

they often sound very much like the professional psychotherapist.

During the psychoanalytic group session illustrated below, just as in individual sessions, a great deal of attention is paid to the meaning of behavior. Joan *interprets* Sonja's blush as anger. Bill believes that Sonja's slip of the tongue exposes her true but hidden feelings of hostility.

JOAN: May I say, I think I noticed something just now? I mean I think I know what is happening.

THERAPIST: Yes, please go ahead.

JOAN: When you [therapist] mentioned how Sonja handles her libido by regressing, she becomes a baby again, you [Sonja] blushed. Now I think you [Sonja] will argue that it was modesty or something, but I think it's anger. You have a need to strike out. You can't stand to have your defenses probed.

SONJA: That's not true! I feel no affection, I mean I feel *only* affection, for you. Just a slip.

BILL: Was that a slip. Weren't you really telling us how you feel?

ALVIN: Don't pick on her. It's a slip of the tongue. You never make mistakes?

BILL: That's not the point. The point is slips reveal the unconscious, how we really feel. Sonja should face it; she has a lot of the aggressive drive to work through, she is forced to be destructive and hostile. It is not her fault. We're not blaming you. . . .

JOAN: God knows your mother was a bitch. You had to defend yourself to survive. But she's no longer here. You're on your own now and can work through it. You don't have to be that hostile anymore.

THERAPIST: Slips of the tongue do reveal a great deal of our hidden selves. I think, Sonja, you should face some of your hostile feelings. And we need to work more on your tend-

ency to act infantile in the face of sexual arousal. Alvin too, you too, have some needs vis à vis Joan and her defenses that we should explore.

ALVIN: I like her.

RAY: What I think is more like it is you are a frustrated father. You come on very often with a paternal role. . . . I had a dream even, where I saw you giving out lollipops to all of us.

JOAN: Well [Ray] I think that says more about your unconscious than it does about Alvin's. (laughter)

The transactional group below is also interpretive, but the vocabulary differs and members make few if any assumptions about unconscious motivation. In this excerpt Henry begins by restating why he came. Like many TA clients, he made a contract. He wanted to learn to handle his anxiety. The other clients try to persuade him that his anxiety is part of one of the several games he plays to avoid intimacy or coming to grips with himself and the world as it is. The games Henry is told he plays are Salesman and Rescue. The therapist also takes the opportunity to restate what has become an important belief for many TA therapists, and that is the theme of self-responsibility.

HENRY: What I am here for is part of my contract with the group and you [therapist]. I need to learn to handle my fears and my anxiety. I don't need an analysis of my salesman game, thank you. Or my ego states either. I've read the same books you have and I can teach it all to myself if I want to.

MYRA: But aren't they all related. As I see it what you are doing is selling yourself all the time. You are merchandising yourself in little units. And you suit your pattern to fit the customer. Sell a little enthusiasm here. Sell a little hostility there. Now you are selling anxiety. It works great with women. Or does it? Maybe you are continuing to do it just because the anxiety you are selling attracts the wrong kind. The payoff for you is that you get one that will not work out.

MITCH: There is always a payoff. You sell to get what you want. What you want is a woman who will never get really close. That's how you avoid intimacy.

HENRY: Frankly, that's bullshit. I am here for help.

JEAN: He wants to be rescued.

THERAPIST: I think we all know that we are here on our own. Neither I nor anyone else can rescue Henry, nor any one of you. We are responsible to ourselves and for ourselves. We and only we in the long run can help ourselves.

CONNIE: I know that is doctrine, Lord knows we have heard it enough.

HENRY: You don't think she's [the therapist] very sympathetic either.

JEAN: Boy, you are really pulling all the stops trying to get us to rescue you again. No. We are all responsible for ourselves. Here we help each other see the games we are playing. But the rest is up to us.

PSYCHOTHERAPY: RESEARCH AND EFFECTIVENESS

At the turn of the century, the psychiatric establishment denounced Freud's psychoanalysis as not only useless but morally and psychologically dangerous. In 1977 Dorothy Tennov, in a well-documented book of selectively chosen studies, argued that psychotherapy is not only ineffective, but worse yet is a "hazardous cure." No form of psychotherapy (medical, behavioral, insight, or psychodynamic) has ever been totally accepted or proved flawlessly effective. As we saw in previous chapters, whatever the evidence that most therapy does work, there is still debate and division. Many psycho-

dynamic practitioners continue to believe that behavioral treatment is temporary and superficial. Some behavioral therapists assert that insight approaches inculcate a mythology which falsely convinces patients they are better. A few of those who are medically inclined accuse all other therapists of ignoring the central role of biochemistry. They in turn are charged with doing little more than sedating patients till they are passive.

The criticisms directed against one or another form of treatment are often ideological overstatements and far too pessimistic. All legitimate forms of treatment have advantages and weaknesses and are better suited to one or another disorder. Medication, for example, seems to work best with psychotic patients or those who are neurotically anxious. Dynamic therapies such as gestalt, analysis and client-centered treatment may be most helpful in neuroses and adjustment disorders. Behavioral psychotherapies seem applicable in some sexual, neurotic, and anxiety disorders and in the rehabilitation of the mentally retarded. Psychotherapists ordinarily have preferences for one or another form of treatment. But most recognize the advantages and disadvantages of particular approaches and try to pick the therapy most suitable for the particular person. It is our contention that all appropriate psychotherapy can be helpful, and we base this statement on evidence that has accumulated for almost a century. Why then the continuing doubt among some critics? We believe the central problem lies in the fact that good psychotherapy research is difficult to conduct and perfect evidence perhaps impossible to obtain. We will look first at some of the research problems and then report a few of the more significant recent findings on the effectiveness of psychotherapy.

Research design

The worth of psychotherapy cannot be ascertained simply by asking the doctor or the patient if there is improvement. Given the placebo effect, the suggestibility of people, and the tendency for spontaneous recovery, the effectiveness of psychotherapy must be objectively studied. An excellent therapy investigation would include the following:

A CONTROL GROUP: In addition to those treated, a group needs to be left untreated. These controls resemble those treated in motivation, age, sex, length and seriousness of disorder.

RANDOMIZATION: Patients should be randomly assigned to treatment and nontreatment groups, and ideally neither the clients themselves nor the therapist should know who is receiving treatment. This is easily accomplished when the treatment is medical; while one group is given the actual medication, the other can receive a placebo. But this so-called double-blind design is almost impossible to duplicate when the treatment is behavioral or dynamic. In such instances the best that can be done is to tell untreated patients they will be put on a waiting list and obtain therapy some months later.

GOALS: The behavior that is supposed to change should be spelled out. Before, during, and after therapy, changes in the critical traits (such as anxiety, social competence, sexuality) should be evaluated by reliable techniques and objective observers. The patient's or doctor's own report is often too biased to be very dependable.

COMPETENCE: The therapist and the treatment method should meet the highest standards of competence and appropriateness. Then, if treatment fails, neither the inexperience of the clinician nor the unsuitability of the method can be blamed.

FOLLOW-UP: The effects of treatment should be evaluated approximately three and six months after therapy has begun, at the end of treatment, and for several years after. This permits a full statement of the short- and long-range effects of the psychotherapy.

Effectiveness

Currently no study meets all the ideal criteria for good research we have outlined. Mentally disordered patients are not experimental animals, and the treatment of a randomly selected group cannot be postponed for two years or even nine months while they are used as controls. It is difficult to match people or abnormal behaviors exactly, and neither can the precise traits to be changed always be spelled out. But although no one study has been able to conclusively affirm the worth of all psychotherapy, the cumulative evidence is persuasive.

Strupp (1974) reported more than two decades of Menninger Foundation research with forty-two adult hospital and outpatients receiving some form of psychoanalytic treatment. Not all were cured, but eight out of ten recovered or showed substantial improvement. May et al. (1976) studied 228 first-admission psychotic patients for as long as five years. They were treated by one of five different methods: (1) psychotherapy, (2) psychotherapy plus medication, (3) medication, (4) electric shock, and (5) milieu therapy. Every therapy method resulted in significant patient recovery, although some treatments took longer than others. What was perhaps most interesting was that combined treatments—for example, psychotherapy with medication—were often most effective.

Approaching the evaluation of psychotherapy from a different angle, Luborsky et al. (1975) reviewed the majority of recent published investigations. Their survey included the entire range of treatments from behavioral to psychodynamic to medical methods. The authors found that all the therapies work, but *they do not work equally well for all disorders.* For example, behavior rather than client-centered therapy may be most appropriate for phobias. Similarly, the most effective treatment for psychosomatic conditions is probably a combination of dynamic therapy and medication. Luborsky and his colleagues concluded that all psychotherapies do work. But to ensure their maximum effectiveness, patient and disorder should be carefully matched with the appropriate treatment.

Finally, what will likely remain one of the most comprehensive reviews of the effectiveness of psychotherapy has been conducted by Mary Smith and Gene Glass of the University of Colorado (1977). They statistically coded for calculitic analysis thousands of bits of data gleaned from 375 separate investigations of psychotherapy. The treatments ranged from behavioral techniques to nearly the full gamut of insight methods. Among the variables considered and analyzed were these: (1) the experience and training of the therapist, (2) diagnosis of the patient and the length of the disorder, (3) outcome measures based on psychometric tests, rating techniques, and objective evaluations; (4) criteria for improvement, including changes in personality, marital and social adjustment, self-esteem, and physiological indices such as blood pressure; (5) adequacy of experimental design, including presence of control groups, internal validity checks, and follow-up measures. Following the most careful mathematical analysis, in which variables were differently weighted, ranked, and compared, the authors state their data forced them

Figure 18.7. Many hundreds of studies have shown that all competent psychotherapy is effective. Often too, treatment combining medical, psychological, and other therapy is particularly suitable. (Photo: New York State Department of Mental Hygiene, Creedmoor State Hospital, N. J. Devine)

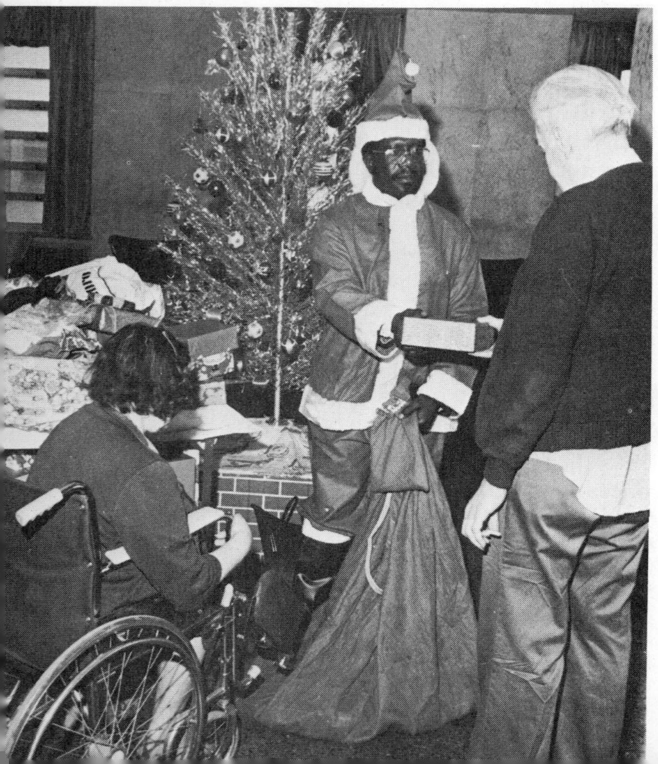

to conclude that therapy works. They chastise the critics of psychotherapy who, they believe, have done little more than base their opinions on personal bias:

Most academics have read little more than Eysenck's tendentious diatribes in which he claimed to prove that 75% of neurotics got better regardless of whether or not they were in therapy—a conclusion based on the interpretation of six controlled studies. The perception that research shows the inefficacy of psychotherapy has become part of conventional wisdom even within the profession.

Based on their analysis, Smith and Glass found that treated clients are far better off than eight out of ten untreated individuals. Further, despite "volumes devoted to the theoretical differences" among the several schools of treatment, "the results of research demonstrate negligible differences in the [beneficial] effects produced by different therapy types." The evidence for the worth of psychotherapy is convincing and conclusive.

SUMMARY

Psychoanalysis was the prototype for the many different forms of psychological treatment used today. In psychoanalysis, patients free associate and therapists help interpret the meaning of their dreams and other behaviors. The goal is to provide insight so that patients can overcome defensive responses and try new behaviors. Ego analysts have modified the Freudian position and contend that a great deal of behavior is learned. They also believe that therapy should strengthen the ego, and encourage rational and conscious solutions to problems. Interaction analysts have revised the classical psychoanalytic viewpoint by emphasizing the importance of personal relationships. Therapy is directed at helping clients establish more satisfying and effective interactions with people. Transactional analysis was originated by Erik Berne, and tends to use contemporary language to convey original Freudian concepts. Patients contract the behaviors they wish to change. The treatment itself consists of analyzing patients' life scripts and the games they play. Clients are given insight into their manipulations so they can construct more genuine life styles. Hypnosis, an altered state of consciousness characterized by extreme suggestibility, is used as another therapeutic technique. Almost 10 percent of patients can enter the deepest hypnotic state and may thus be helped to free associate, or overcome phobias, traumatic reactions, and several other abnormal conditions. Generally, however, hypnosis is of limited usefulness as a treatment technique.

The humanistic treatments, the most well known of which is Carl Rogers' client-centered therapy, emphasize the potential of each person. Client-centered therapists reflect patients' feelings and provide an atmosphere of understanding and unconditional positive regard. In this situation clients progress from negative to positive emotions and are propelled toward growth by the need to self-actualize. Existential therapists try to understand the patient's reality and help him or her become aware of choices. Each client is encouraged to find his or her own purpose and meaning in life. The emphasis in Gestalt therapy is on the here and now, rather than on past determinants of behavior. Patients are helped to be freed of their defenses so they can become whole, feeling, and responsible human beings.

The body therapies, critical of what they believe is an excessive emphasis on psychological insight, attempt to involve the entire physical being in the therapeutic process. The Masters and Johnson sex therapy approach combines many of the features of client-centered, behavioral, and other treatments. Patients are prompted to reveal fearful attitudes and taught the fundamentals of healthy sexual function. Working together, dysfunctional couples learn massage, masturbatory, and other techniques to relax and gratify themselves and each other. When sexual dysfunction is not complicated by marital or other psychological difficulties, more than 80 percent of patients are significantly helped. Group methods have the advantage of permitting patients the benefit of interacting with a number of other people in a similar situation. There are many different types of groups, some of which are only indirectly oriented to treatment itself. Many self-help groups like Alcoholics Anonymous are designed to be therapeutic, but are commonly run by members themselves. Consciousness-raising groups are primarily intended to help alert members to social discrimination and to their own potentials. Encounter and sensitivity groups are aimed at awareness and personal growth. In many of these groups, particularly in encounter situations, it is important for leaders to be trained and competent.

Family and marital therapy, like group treatment, sees mental disorder largely in terms of a disturbed interaction among a group of people. Treating individual symptoms may be ineffective; all relevant family members need to participate in therapy. Group therapy itself, in contrast to encounter or CR groups, is directly intended for the treatment of people with mental disorders. It may be psychoanalytic, behavioral, humanistic, or involve any number of other theoretical and methodological approaches.

The effectiveness of psychotherapy continues to be questioned by a few critics. Ideally, good research would contrast identical groups of patients who have, and have not, received several different forms of treatment. But although such perfect investigations have not been conducted, hundreds of separate research findings have confirmed the worth and effectiveness of psychotherapy. Further, despite the volumes devoted to the theoretical variations among the several schools of treatment, research continually shows negligible differences in the beneficial effects produced by different types of therapy.

GLOSSARY

ABNORMAL. Refers to behavior or emotion that is maladaptive or disordered.

ABREACTION. Expression of pent-up feelings.

ABSTRACT THINKING. Capacity to generalize, conceptualize, and plan logically.

ACALCULIA. Loss of ability to perform mathematical operations.

ACTING-OUT. Expressing anxiety, hostility, or other emotions by overt behavior.

ACUTE. A recent, temporary condition which is often severe.

ADDICTIVE PERSONALITY. A set of traits and attitudes that may incline an individual to some kind of drug abuse.

ADJUSTMENT REACTIONS. Temporary situational personality or mental disorder.

AFFECT. Emotion or feeling.

AFTERCARE. Follow-up care given after the patient has left the hospital.

AGITATED DEPRESSION. Psychotic reaction characterized by depressed mood and hyperactivity.

AGNOSIA. Defective ability to recognize familiar objects or persons.

AGORAPHOBIA. Fear of open places and crowds; most common phobia.

AGRAPHIA. Impaired ability to write words.

AKINESIA. Inability to move a muscle or limb; a paralysis.

AL ANON. Organization affiliated with Alcoholics Anonymous to help relatives cope with alcoholics.

ALCOHOLICS ANONYMOUS. A self-help organization attempting to rehabilitate alcoholics.

ALCOHOLISM. Alcohol addiction.

ALEXIA. Inability to read.

ALPHA WAVES. Brain waves accompanied by feelings of tranquility.

ALZHEIMER'S DISEASE. A disease causing psychosis resembling senility.

AMNESIA. Total or partial loss of memory.

AMNIOCENTESIS. Test of amniotic fluids to detect defects in fetus.

AMPHETAMINE. Drugs that often produce stimulating and energizing effects.

AMPHETAMINE PSYCHOSES. Delusions and hallucinations resembling schizophrenia brought about by amphetamine use.

ANAL STAGE. In psychoanalytic theory, period in which behavior is presumably focused on anal pleasure.

ANIMAL MAGNETISM. Old name for hypnotic-like treatment developed by Anton Mesmer.

ANOMIE. Extreme social disorder and disruption.

ANOREXIA NERVOSA. Severe diminution of appetite resulting in extreme weight loss.

ANOXIA. Lack of sufficient oxygen.

ANTISOCIAL OR PSYCHOPATHIC PERSONALITY. Disorder involving lack of ethical or moral development.

ANXIETY. General feelings of fear, apprehension, and worry.

ANXIETY NEUROSIS. Type of neurosis characterized by chronic anxiety and occasional panic attacks.

APHASIA. Loss of the ability to understand words or language or to respond properly.

APRAXIA. Loss of the ability to carry out skilled motor acts like drawing or using a knife and fork.

ARTERIOSCLEROSIS. A hardening or loss of flexibility of the arterial vessels.

ASSERTIVE TRAINING. Behavior therapy technique for helping individuals become more self-assertive.

ASTHMA. Respiratory disorder which may sometimes be psychosomatic.

ATAXIA. Inability to coordinate muscles resulting, for example, in a stumbling gait.

ATHETOSIS. Recurring involuntary, spasmodic movements of the hands and feet.

AURA. Feeling or sensation preceding an epileptic seizure.

AUTISM. See Infantile Autism.

AUTOMATISM. Slow, labored, and mechanical movements.

AUTONOMIC NERVOUS SYSTEM. The involuntary section of the nervous system that regulates the internal organs. It is divided into the sympathetic and parasympathetic systems.

AVERSIVE CONDITIONING. The use of an unpleasant event, such as shock, to punish unwanted behavior.

AVOIDANT PERSONALITY. Personality characterized by evasiveness and failure to face challenges.

BABINSKI'S SIGN. Improper flexion of the toe or other pathological reflex.

BARBITURATES. Sedatives used to induce sleep or relaxation.

BEHAVIOR CONTRACTING. Behavior modification technique which involves formally scheduling the exchange of reinforcement between two or more people.

BEHAVIOR DISORDERS. Any of a large range of responses that are troublesome for the persons themselves and/or society. These include addictions, anti-social personality, exhibitionism, runaway reaction, and delinquency.

BEHAVIORISM. A model of psychology where observable behavior is the subject matter.

BEHAVIOR THERAPY. Psychological treatment based upon principles of learning.

BESTIALITY. Sexual relations with animals.

BETA WAVES. Brain waves which occur with normal thought processes, problem solving, and tensions.

BIOENERGETICS. A body therapy which makes patients aware of how their bodies have suffered from psychic impairments.

BIOFEEDBACK. Providing persons with immediate information on their physiological functions.

BIPOLAR. Mood (or affect) disorder in which a person is successively manic and depressive.

BIRTH TRAUMA. Anxiety supposedly experienced by an infant at birth.

BISEXUAL. Individual who enjoys sexual relations with members of either sex.

BLACKOUT. Short-term memory loss induced by excessive drinking.

BODY THERAPIES. Psychological therapies that include treatment of the body as well as the mind.

BRAIN WAVES. Electrical potentials of the cerebral cortex measured by the electroencephalograph.

BULEMIA. Overeating, intensive hunger.

CATALEPSY. A condition in which the limbs tend to maintain any position in which they are placed.

CATAPLEXY. Loss of muscle tone. Patients seem

without any control over their body and act limp.

CATATONIC SCHIZOPHRENIA. Type of schizophrenia marked by catalepsy, motor rigidity, or loss of control.

CATECHOLAMINES. All the neurotransmitters, together as a class.

CATHARSIS. Discharge of emotion by talking it out.

CEREA FLEXIBILITAS. Waxy flexibility sometimes seen in catatonic schizophrenia.

CEREBRAL CORTEX. The surface layers of the brain.

CEREBRAL PALSY. Condition characterized by physical and sometimes intellectual loss due to brain damage.

CEREBROVASCULAR ACCIDENT (CVA). A stroke. A blockage or rupture of large blood vessel in brain.

CEREBRUM. Main part of brain; divided into left and right hemispheres.

CHARACTER DISORDER. Behavior which is considered socially or personally inadequate, inappropriate, or harmful. Often used synonymously with personality and behavior disorders.

CHEMOTHERAPY. Treatment by chemicals, that is, medication.

CHLORDIAZEPOXIDE. Type of psychiatric drug.

CHLORPROMAZINE. Psychiatric drug: brand name, Thorazine.

CHOREA. Involuntary spasmodic movements of head and extremities.

CHOREIFORM MOVEMENTS. Jerky, rapid, complex, and involuntary movements.

CHROMOSOME. Bodies in the nucleus of cells that contain genes.

CHRONIC. A relatively permanent pattern or condition.

CIRCUMSTANTIALITY. Mental symptom characterized by irrelevant or trivial details in conversation.

CLANG ASSOCIATIONS. Word uttered on basis of similarity of sounds, that is, rhyme.

CLASSICAL OR RESPONDENT CONDITIONING. Learning by pairing a previously neutral stimulus with a stimulus that elicits the desired response.

CLAUSTROPHOBIA. Extreme fear of small places.

CLIENT-CENTERED PSYCHOTHERAPY. Therapy developed by Carl Rogers which lets patient determine direction of treatment.

CLINICAL PSYCHOLOGIST. Psychologist specializing in diagnosis and treatment of mental disorders.

CLITORIS. The sensitive female organ at the upper end of the vagina.

COCAINE. An illegal stimulant that gives an energetic feeling of well being.

CODEINE. A narcotic derived from opium.

COGNITIVE. Pertaining to thinking.

COITUS. Sexual intercourse.

COLITIS. Inflammation of the colon, which may be psychosomatic.

COMA. Deep, usually prolonged unconsciousness.

COMBAT REACTION. A posttraumatic reaction once referred to as "shell shock."

COMMUNITY PSYCHOLOGY. Speciality focusing on social factors involved in mental health and therapy.

COMPULSION. Irrational, ritualistic act.

COMPULSIVE PERSONALITY. Personality characterized by extreme inhibition, conformity, and conscientiousness.

CONCENTRATION CAMP SYNDROME. A posttraumatic reaction characterized by numbness, suspiciousness, and depression.

CONCORDANCE. In genetic studies, the occurrence of the same disorder in two subjects.

CONCRETE THINKING. Impaired ability to generalize and think abstractly.

CONDITIONING. See Classical conditioning; Operant conditioning.

CONFABULATE. Make up memories to cover gaps in recall.

CONGENITAL. Present at birth but not necessarily hereditary.

CONSCIOUSNESS RAISING. Group technique to make people more alert to their position in society and their potential.

CONVERSION NEUROSIS OR HYSTERIA. See Hysteria.

CONVULSION. Seizure; an involuntary, muscular contraction.

COPROLALIA. Compulsive uttering of obscenities.

CORRELATE. Characteristics that are related so

that changes in one are accompanied by changes in the others.

CRISIS INTERVENTION. Methods for rendering immediate therapeutic assistance.

CUNNILINGUS. Stimulation of the vagina by the mouth.

CYCLOTHYMIC PERSONALITY. Behavior characterized by alternating periods of depression and elation.

DEFENSE MECHANISM. In psychoanalysis, behavior which protects the person from anxiety provoked by sexual and aggressive impulses.

DELIRIUM. Confusion characterized by disorientation, excitement, and often hallucinations.

DELIRIUM TREMENS (DT'S). Delirium provoked by prolonged alcoholism and characterized by anxiety, tremors, and hallucinations.

DELIRIOUS MANIA. Rare, extreme form of mania in which patient seems totally out of contact with reality and unrestrained.

DELUSION. False belief maintained in spite of realistic evidence to the contrary.

DEMENTIA PRAECOX. Old term for schizophrenia.

DEMEROL. A synthetic narcotic.

DEPERSONALIZATION. Loss of sense of personal identity.

DEPRESSION. Emotional state characterized by dejection, feelings of worthlessness, and apprehension.

DEREALIZATION. Believing one's surroundings are unknown and unreal.

DERMATITIS. Inflammation of the skin.

DESENSITIZATION. Behavior technique through which anxiety responses are reduced in intensity by repeated exposure.

DETOXIFICATION. Process of withdrawal from a drug.

DIATHESIS. Hereditary predisposition or vulnerability.

DIAZEPAM. Tranquilizer; brand name Valium.

DILANTIN. Drug used in treatment of epilepsy.

DISORIENTATION. Confusion with respect to time, place, or person.

DISPLACEMENT. An ego-defense mechanism which redirects emotion to less dangerous objects.

DISSOCIATIVE REACTION. Neuroses characterized by amnesia, fugue, and the like.

DISULFIRAM. Drug used in treatment of alcoholism; brand name Antabuse.

DIZYGOTIC OR FRATERNAL TWINS. Twins that develop from two separate eggs.

DOMINANT GENE. A gene whose hereditary characteristics appear in offspring.

DOPAMINE. Chemical involved in neural transmission possibly related to schizophrenia.

DOUBLE BIND. Situation in which subject is forced to choose between conflicting or contradictory demands.

DOUBLE-BLIND. Research method in which one group is given medication and the other a placebo but neither the researchers nor the subjects know which group is receiving medication.

DOWN'S SYNDROME OR MONGOLOIDISM. A type of moderate mental retardation due to chromosomal defect.

DRUG ABUSE. Use of a drug to extent that it interferes with health and/or adjustment.

DRUG ADDICTION. Continual use and complete dependence upon a drug.

DRUG DEPENDENCE. Physiological and/or psychological reliance on a drug.

DSM III. "Diagnostic and Statistical Manual of Mental Disorders" of the American Psychiatric Association. The official, latest list of diagnostic terms and definitions.

DYSARTHRIA. Slurred speech or other speaking difficulty.

DYSFUNCTION. Impairment in the functioning of an organ or system.

DYSLEXIA. Impairment of the ability to read.

DYSPAREUNIA. Painful intercourse in women.

DYSSOCIAL PERSONALITY. An otherwise normal person with a criminal lifestyle.

ECHOLALIA. Automatic repetition of words by individuals of whatever is said to them.

ECHOPRAXIA. Automatic imitation of another person's movements.

ECOLOGICAL GROUP APPROACH. Method of handling suicidal behavior in which the relatives participate in the client's rehabilitation.

EGO. In psychoanalytic theory, the rational part of the mind which mediates between id, superego demands, and reality.

EJACULATION. Male orgasm involving release of sperm.

ELECTRA COMPLEX. In psychoanalytic theory, an excessive emotional attachment of the daughter for the father.

ELECTROENCEPHALOGRAPH (EEG). Instrument for recording brain potentials.

ELECTROSHOCK (EST) OR ELECTROCONVULSIVE THERAPY (ECT). Use of electric shock as treatment, usually for depression.

EMPIRICAL. Based upon experiment and observation rather than on theory.

ENCEPHALITIS. Infection of the brain.

ENCOPRESIS. Failure to control bowel movements.

ENCOUNTER GROUP. Group aimed toward awareness and personal growth.

ENDOCRINE GLANDS. Glands which secrete hormones directly into the blood stream.

ENDOGENOUS. Resulting from internal causes.

ENDORPHIN. Opiate-like chemical produced and found within the brain.

ENURESIS. Bed-wetting.

EPIDEMIOLOGY. Study of the distribution of physical or mental disorders in a population.

EPILEPSY. Group of disorders characterized by momentary lapses in consciousness or convulsions.

EPINEPHRINE. A hormone secreted by the adrenal glands. It acts as a powerful stimulant and is released when the body experiences stress.

EQUANIL. Tranquilizer; generic name meprobamate.

EROTIC. Pertaining to sex.

EROTOMANIA. False belief that a person of high status is one's lover.

ERYTHROBLASTOSIS. A type of blood incompatibility between mother and fetus.

ETIOLOGY. Cause.

EUPHORIA. Exaggerated feeling of well-being and happiness.

EXACERBATION. Return of symptoms.

EXHIBITIONISM. Public exposure of genitals for purpose of sexual pleasure.

EXISTENTIAL. Branch of philosophy concerned with existence. A psychosocial model that views disorder as the result of the loneliness and futility experienced in contemporary society.

EXOGENOUS. Resulting from external causes.

EXORCISM. Techniques practiced in medieval times for casting "evil spirits" out of the mentally ill.

EXTINCTION. Disappearance of conditioned response due to lack of reinforcement.

EXTRAPUNITIVE. Behavior in which aggression is released outward against others.

FAMILY CARE. Treatment where mental patients are housed with normal families.

FAMILY POLITICS. The strategies family members perform to ensure their personal security, even at the expense of other family members.

FEEDBACK. Knowledge of results of one's behavior or responses.

FELLATIO. Manipulation of the penis by the mouth for sexual gratification.

FETISHISM. Sexual gratification from objects.

FETOGRAPHY. A radiographic technique that can outline the shape of the fetus.

FIXATION. Exaggerated attachment to a person or object or developmental arrest at a childhood level.

FLATTENING OF AFFECT. Dulling of emotional responses.

FLIGHT OF IDEAS. Rapid, involuntary jumping from one thought to another.

FLOODING. Deliberate anxiety-eliciting treatment used in phobia therapy.

FRATERNAL TWINS. See Dizygotic.

FREE ASSOCIATION. In therapy, the uninhibited telling of all the memories and thoughts that come to mind.

FREE-FLOATING ANXIETY. Anxiety not traceable to any specific situation or cause.

FREE MARRIAGE. Agreement by married couples to have sexual relations with others.

FRIGIDITY. Former term indicating lack of sexual responsiveness in a woman.

FUGUE. Loss of memory associated with running away.

FUNCTIONAL DISORDER. Disorder arising from psychological as opposed to physical causes.

GALVANIC SKIN RESPONSE (GSR). An electrochemical measure of anxiety derived from palmar sweating.

GANSER'S SYNDROME. Prison neurosis or the

syndrome of approximate answers.

GAY. Slang term for homosexual.

GENERAL-ADAPTATION SYNDROME. Reaction of the individual to excessive stress; consists of the alarm, resistance, and exhaustion stage.

GENERAL PARESIS. Mental disorder due to syphilis of the brain.

GENERALIZATION. Tendency of a response that has been conditioned to one stimulus to be evoked by similar stimulus.

GENES. Ultramicroscopic DNA structures responsible for transmission of hereditary traits.

GENETICS. Science of heredity.

GERIATRICS. Science of the characteristics and disorders of the aged.

GESTALT THERAPY. Type of psychological therapy emphasizing wholeness and the present situation.

GHEEL. Belgium town which has rehabilitated mental patients since the fifteenth century.

GILLES DE LA TOURETTE'S SYNDROME. Rare tic disorder characterized by grimaces, grunts, and body movement.

GLANS PENIS. Head of the penis.

GONORRHEA. Type of venereal disease.

GRAND MAL. Type of epileptic seizure characterized by convulsions.

GRANDIOSITY. Exaggerated feelings of self-importance.

GROUP THERAPY. Treatment of mental illness carried out with a number of people at one time.

HALFWAY HOUSE. A small facility which provides aftercare following institutionalization and eases the individual into the community.

HALLUCINATION. False perception of sights, sounds, and so forth.

HALOPERIDOL (HALDOL). Drug used to control Gilles de la Tourette's syndrome and psychoses.

HARRISON NARCOTIC ACT. 1914 law which forbade the importing or free use of narcotics.

HEBEPHRENIC SCHIZOPHRENIA. A form of schizophrenia characterized by inappropriate responses and highly disorganized thinking.

HEMIANESTHESIA. Loss of feeling on one side of the body.

HEMIANOPIA. Loss of vision for half of the normal visual field.

HEMIPLEGIA. Paralysis of one-half of the body.

HERPES GENITALIS. A viral infection that causes lesions on the penis or in the vagina.

HETEROSEXUALITY. Sexual interest in members of the opposite sex.

HISTRIONIC PERSONALITY. Personality characterized by self-dramatization and attention seeking.

HOMEOSTASIS. Maintaining necessary balance among physiological processes.

HOMOSEXUALITY. Sexual preference for member of one's own sex.

HUMANISTIC. Type of psychotherapy emphasizing personal growth and self-direction.

HUNTINGTON'S CHOREA. Disease of hereditary origin, with mental and physical symptoms.

HYDROCEPHALY. Form of mental retardation marked by abnormally large head.

HYPERKINETIC. Behavior characterized by overactivity, distractibility, and restlessness.

HYPERTENSION. High blood pressure.

HYPNOSIS. Trance-like mental state induced by suggestion.

HYPOCHRONDRIACAL NEUROSIS. Neurosis marked by preoccupation with one's health.

HYPOMANIA. Mildest form of manic reaction.

HYPOTHALAMUS. Structure at the base of the brain important in emotion.

HYSTERIA (Hysterical conversion neuroses). Disorder characterized by physical symptoms without organic cause.

ID. In psychoanalysis the primitive, instinctual drives.

IDENTICAL TWINS. See Monozygotic.

IMIPRAMINE. Drug used in treatment of depression; brand name Tofranil.

IMPOTENCE. Inability of male to achieve erection and/or orgasm.

IMPULSE DISORDERS. Overpowering urge to carry through an act which may harm the person or others.

INADEQUATE PERSONALITY. Disorder characterized by inability to cope with life.

INCEST. Sexual relations between parent and child or among siblings.

INFANTILE AUTISM. Severe psychoses in early

childhood characterized by mutism, withdrawal, and repetitive meaningless acts.

INHIBITED ORGASM. Feeling diminished pleasure in sexual climax or not reaching orgasm.

INSANITY. Legal term for psychoses.

INSIGHT. Understanding of one's own motivation and defense.

INSTRUMENTAL OR OPERANT CONDITIONING. Type of learning in which the subject is reinforced only for making a particular response.

INTRAUTERINE. Before birth or within the uterus.

INVOLUTIONAL MELANCHOLIA. Depression in later middle age; mostly seen in menopausal women.

JACKSONIAN EPILEPSY. Seizure usually restricted to a small group of muscles.

KORSAKOFF'S PSYCHOSIS. Psychosis usually due to chronic alcoholism.

LA BELLE INDIFFERENCE. Attitude of indifference shown in some conversion neuroses.

LABILE. Behavior marked by unstable, varying, and often exaggerated emotions.

LATENT. Inactive or dormant.

LESBIAN. Female homosexual.

LESION. Damaged tissue or area.

LIBIDO. In psychoanalytic terminology, the sexual drives of the id.

LIFE-LINE. Technique employed by self-help groups where members learn to call others in moments of need.

LIMBIC SYSTEM. Structures in brain associated with attention, defense, and emotion.

LITHIUM. Medication used to treat mood disorders.

LOBOTOMY. Surgically severing the front lobes of the brain as treatment.

LOGARRHEA. Excessive, often incoherent speech.

LSD (LYSERGIC ACID DIETHYLAMIDE). Illegal, powerful psychedelic drug that leads to hallucinatory experiences.

LYCANTHROPY. The false belief that one is a wolf.

MACROCEPHALY. Form of mental retardation characterized by abnormally large cranium.

MAINLINING. Injecting heroin directly into veins.

MAINSTREAMING. Integration of retarded children with normal students.

MALINGER. To consciously fake illness or disability.

MANIE SANS DELIRE. Term meaning insanity without the symptoms of madness once used to describe anti-social personality disorders.

MANIC-DEPRESSIVE PSYCHOSES. Psychotic disorders characterized by alternating periods of mania and depression.

MARIJUANA. Mild, illegal drug derived from plant and smoked.

MARPLAN. Drug used in treatment of depression.

MASOCHISM. Condition in which an individual obtains sexual gratification from having pain inflicted.

MASTURBATION. Self-stimulation of genitals for sexual gratification.

MATERNAL DEPRIVATION. Severe lack of care by the mother or the equivalent.

MCNAGHTEN RULE. Rule based on old English decision that a person is not responsible for criminal conduct if such actions are the result of mental disease.

MEDICAL MODEL. View of mental disorders which explains them as the result of physical disease or defect.

MEDICAL STUDENT'S DISEASE. Tendency for students to be suggestible when studying abnormalities.

MELANCHOLIA. Depression.

MENTAL DEFICIENCY. See Mental Retardation.

MENTAL DISORDER. Any abnormal behavior.

MENTAL RETARDATION. Below normal intelligence, and deficiencies in learning and social ability.

MEPROBAMATE. Tranquilizer; brand names Miltown and Equanil.

MESCALINE. An hallucinogenic drug, derived from mushrooms.

MESMERISM. Old theory of "animal magnetism" (hypnosis) by Anton Mesmer.

METHADONE. A synthetic legal narcotic that has many of the same effects as heroin.

MICROCEPHALY. Mental retardation marked by abnormally small head size.

MIGRAINE HEADACHE. Possible psychosomatic disorder characterized by recurrent headaches.

MILIEU THERAPY. Treatment which attempts to make the total environment therapeutic.

MINIMAL BRAIN DYSFUNCTION (MBD). Controversial term referring to mild brain damage supposedly responsible for behavior and learning problems.

MINNESOTA MULTIPHASIC PERSONALITY INVENTORY (MMPI). Objective paper-and-pencil test of psychological well-being.

MODELING. Behavior learned through imitation of another person.

MONGOLISM OR MONGOLOIDISM. See Down's Syndrome.

MONOAMINE OXIDASE (MAO) INHIBITORS. A group of drugs used in the treatment of depression.

MONOZYGOTIC TWINS. Identical twins, developed from one fertilized egg.

MORAL THERAPY. Therapy based on kindness and favorable environment begun during nineteenth century.

MULTIPLE PERSONALITY. Very rare dissociative reaction characterized by independent personalities in the same individual.

MUNCHAUSEN SYNDROME. Disorder where patients tell dramatic stories about their imaginary and dangerous illnesses.

MUTISM. Refusal or inability to speak.

MYSTIFICATION. Confusing explanations that parents impose on their children which makes them distrust the validity of their own actions.

NARCISSISTIC PERSONALITY. Personality characterized by excessive self-concern.

NARCOTICS. A class of drugs which relieve pain and induce a feeling of calm.

NARDIL. Drug used in treatment of depression.

NEGATIVISM. Patient's tendency to resist movements.

NEOLOGISM. A new word often coined by schizophrenic person.

NEOPLASM. Tumor.

NERVOUS BREAKDOWN. A vague phrase used by nonprofessionals to describe any mental disorder whose onset is usually sudden.

NEURASTHENIC NEUROSIS. Disorder characterized by complaints of easy fatigability and lack of enthusiasm.

NEURON. Individual nerve cell.

NEUROSES. Mental disorders with symptoms such as anxiety, feelings of inadequacy, headaches, and fatigue.

NEUROTIC-DEPRESSIVE REACTION. Reaction characterized by dejection and discouragement, possibly prompted by environmental setback.

NEUROTIC PARADOX. Failure of neurotic patterns to extinguish despite their self-defeating nature.

NEUROTRANSMITTERS. Chemical substances which transmit information from one neuron to another.

NIHILISTIC DELUSION. Belief that nothing really exists.

NONDIRECTIVE THERAPY. See Client-centered.

NYMPHOMANIA. Excessive sexual desire in females.

OBJECTIVE TEST. A pencil and paper examination consisting of several hundred true-false questions.

OBSESSION. Persistent idea or thought which individual cannot get rid of.

OBSESSIVE-COMPULSIVE NEUROSES. Disorder characterized by fixed thoughts and rituals.

OEDIPUS COMPLEX. In psychoanalytic theory, belief that boys desire sexual relations with their mother.

ONTOLOGICAL ANXIETY. Existential term indicating succumbing to nothingness, disorder, despair, and fantasy.

OPERANT CONDITIONING. See Instrumental.

OPIATES. Drugs derived from opium including heroin, morphine, and codeine.

ORAL STAGE. Stage of psychosexual development in Freudian theory, in which mouth is primary source of pleasure.

ORGANIC BRAIN SYNDROMES. Mental disorders caused by brain damage.

ORGANIC VIEWPOINT. Concept that all mental disorders have physical basis (see Medical Model).

ORGASM. The climactic rush of good feelings resulting from the continual genital friction of intercourse or masturbation.

OXAZEPAM. Minor tranquilizer; brand name Serax.

PARANOIA. Psychosis characterized by a delusional system.

PARANOID PERSONALITY. Individual showing extreme suspiciousness, jealousy, and the like.

PARAPHILIA. Sexual deviation.

PARAPROFESSIONALS. People with ordinary educational backgrounds who are trained to assist mental health specialists.

PARASYMPATHETIC. A part of the autonomic nervous system which controls heartbeat and digestion and works to conserve bodily resources.

PARESTHESIA. Unusual sensations, such as tingling.

PEDOPHILIA. Sexual deviation in which an adult engages in relations with a child.

PERSEVERATION. Performing the same task over and over again.

PERSONALITY DISORDER. See Character Disorder.

PETIT MAL. Mild form of epileptic seizure usually involving a partial lapse of consciousness.

PHALLIC STAGE. In psychoanalytic theory, the stage during which the genitals become a main source of pleasure.

PHENOMENOLOGICAL. A person's own understanding and experience of reality.

PHENOTHIAZINES. Class of drugs used primarily with psychotic patients.

PHENYLKETONURIA (PKU). Form of mental retardation caused by a recessive gene.

PHOBIC NEUROSIS. Disorder characterized by intense fear of an object or situation.

PHRENOLOGY. An eighteenth-century theory that personality traits are located in specific regions of the brain.

PICA. Compulsive eating of inedible substances.

PICK'S DISEASE. A disorder closely resembling a senile psychosis.

PLACEBO. A harmless substance given in such a way that individuals think they are receiving an active medication.

PLAY THERAPY. The utilization of play as a form of treatment with children.

POLYGENIC. Combined effect of many genes.

POSTPARTUM. After birth.

POSTTRAUMATIC DISORDER. Mental disorder following painful experience.

PREMATURE EJACULATION. Too rapid orgasm in males.

PRENATAL. Before birth.

PRESBYOPHRENIA. A senile psychosis in which there is extreme delirium and confusion.

PRIMARY PREVENTION. Changing social conditions, like unemployment, that contribute to abnormality.

PROCESS-REACTIVE. Description of schizophrenia as based upon gradual versus abrupt onset of symptoms.

PROCHLORPERAZINE. Major tranquilizer; brand name Compazine.

PRODROMAL. Warning beforehand; premonitory conditions.

PROGNOSIS. Prediction as to the probable outcome of a disorder.

PROJECTION. Defense mechanism in which individuals attribute their own unacceptable desires and impulses to others.

PROJECTIVE TECHNIQUE. Psychological tests utilizing unstructured stimuli like ink blots.

PROLIXIN. Major tranquilizer; generic name fluphenazine.

PSYCHEDELIC DRUGS. Drugs, such as LSD and marijuana, which result in hallucinations.

PSYCHOACTIVE CHEMICALS. Substances that seem to change mood, perception, or personality.

PSYCHIATRIST. Medical doctor who specializes in the diagnosis and treatment of mental disorders.

PSYCHOANALYSIS. Theoretical model and therapy developed by Freud.

PSYCHODRAMA. Therapy requiring the acting of various roles.

PSYCHOGENIC. Of psychological origin.

PSYCHOMOTOR EPILEPSY. Seizure in which the individual may involuntarily perform complex actions.

PSYCHOMOTOR RETARDATION. A clinical symptom in which movements are slow and labored.

PSYCHOPATHIC. See Antisocial Personality.

PSYCHOPATHOLOGY. Mental disorder.

PSYCHOPHARMACOLOGICAL DRUGS. Drugs used in treatment of mental disorders.

PSYCHOPHYSIOLOGIC DISORDERS. See Psychosomatic Disorders.

PSYCHOSES. Conditions in which patients' mental or emotional activities are so impaired that they lose touch with reality.

PSYCHOSOMATIC AILMENTS. Physical diseases which may be caused by tension and conflict, such as asthma and ulcers.

PSYCHOTHERAPY. Treatment of mental disorders by psychological methods.

PSYCHOTROPIC. Psychiatric or mind-affecting drugs.

RATIONALIZATION. Defense mechanism in which the individual thinks up "good" reasons to justify behavior or feelings.

REACTION FORMATION. Defense mechanism in which individual does exact opposite of repressed unconscious wishes.

REACTIVE DEPRESSION. Depression prompted by environmental setback.

RECESSIVE GENE. Gene which results in characteristics only if matched by both parents.

RECIDIVISM. A shift back to one's original behavior after treatment or imprisonment.

REFLECTION. In Rogerian therapy, the counselor's method of underlining the client's emotions.

REGRESSION. Defense mechanism in which the individual retreats to the use of less mature responses.

REINFORCEMENT. In classical conditioning, the process of following the conditional stimulus with the unconditioned stimulus; in operant conditioning, the rewarding of selected responses.

RELIABILITY. The extent to which a test is consistent in measuring whatever it does measure.

REMISSION. Improvement or recovery.

REPRESSION. Defense mechanism which forces desires and memories out of consciousness.

RESERPINE. Psychiatric drug; brand name Serpasil.

RITALIN. Drug used to treat childhood hyperactivity.

RORSCHACH. A projective personality test making use of inkblots.

RUM FITS. High fevers and convulsions that accompany withdrawal from alcohol.

RUSH. A euphoric feeling that occurs when heroin is injected.

SADISM. Sexual gratification through inflicting pain on others.

SATYRIASIS. Excessive sexual desires in males.

SCHIZO-AFFECTIVE SCHIZOPHRENIA. Mental disorder showing symptoms both of schizophrenia and mood disturbance.

SCHIZOID PERSONALITY. Personality characterized by shyness and withdrawal.

SCHIZOPHRENIA. Psychosis characterized by withdrawal from reality, emotional distortion, and disturbances in thought and behavior.

SCHIZOPHRENOGENIC. A parent not diagnosed as clinically psychotic, but whose behavior generates schizophrenia in his/her child.

SCREEN MEMORIES. According to Freud, stories that are made up to suit particular psychological needs.

SCRIPT. In transactional analysis a way of acting and reacting throughout life that meets the person's needs.

SECONDARY GAIN. Indirect benefits from neurosis.

SECONDARY PREVENTION. Early detection of mental illness through measures such as mass screening.

SELF-ACTUALIZE. The fulfillment of one's potentialities as a human being.

SENESCENCE. A term used to describe the first, noticeable effects of aging.

SENILE. Pertaining to old age.

SENILE DEMENTIA. A form of psychosis sometimes caused in part by brain changes due to aging.

SERAX. Minor tranquilizer; generic name oxepam.

SEROTONIN. Neurotransmitter linked to the etiology of schizophrenia.

SHAPING. Use of operant reinforcement to build new behavior.

SHELTERED WORKSHOPS. Workshops where mentally and physically handicapped individuals can engage in constructive work.

SHOCK THERAPY. See Electroshock.

SKIN POPPING. Slang term denoting a drug is injected into the skin.

SOCIAL LEARNING. Behavioral theory concerned with the learning of complex responses.

SOCIOPATHIC DISORDER. See Antisocial.

SODOMY. General term for fellatio and other legally forbidden sexual practices.

SOMATIC. Pertaining to the body.

SOMATOFORM. A neurotic disorder characterized by physical symptoms.

SOMNAMBULISM. Sleepwalking.

SPHYGMOMANOMETER. An instrument used to measure blood pressure.

STANFORD-BINET. An individually administered intelligence test.

STELAZINE. Major tranquilizer; generic name trifluperazine.

STEREOGNOSIS. Loss of feeling of touch.

STUPOROUS. Unaware of and unresponsive to surroundings.

SUBLIMATION. Defense mechanism which channels sexual energy to other activities.

SUPEREGO. In psychoanalysis the conscience or ethical or moral part of the personality.

SUPPRESSION. Defense mechanism to deliberately force desires or thoughts out of consciousness.

SWINGER. Term used to denote married persons involved in sexually free relationships.

SYMPATHETIC DIVISION. Part of the autonomic nervous system involved in emergency actions.

SYNANON. Self-help program used to help drug addicts.

SYNDROME. Group of symptoms which occur together and characterize a disorder.

SYSTEMATIC DESENSITIZATION. See Desensitization.

TACHYCARDIA. Rapid pulse or heart rate.

TARAXEIN. A component of blood serum possibly implicated in schizophrenia.

TAT. Thematic Apperception Test; a projective instrument consisting of twenty picture cards from which clients are instructed to make up complete stories.

TERTIARY PREVENTION. Treatment intervention aimed at continuing services like vocational training and readjustment help.

TESTOSTERONE. Male sex hormone.

THIORIDAZINE. Major tranquilizer; brand name Mellaril.

THORAZINE. Most commonly used anti-schizophrenic drug.

THOUGHT DISORDER. Synonym for schizophrenia.

TIC. Twitching or jerking of arms, hands, or facial muscles.

TOFRONIL. Anti-depressant drug.

TOKEN ECONOMIES. Operant conditioning procedures in which persons are rewarded for desired behavior by being given a token.

TOLERANCE. Need for increasing quantities of an addictive drug to maintain its effect.

TRANQUILIZERS. Drugs used to alleviate anxiety tension and mental disorder.

TRANSACTIONAL ANALYSIS. Form of psychological therapy based on interaction of "child," "adult," and "parent" ego states.

TRANSIENT SITUATIONAL DISORDER. Temporary mental disorder due to overwhelming stress, as in combat or catastrophe.

TRANSSEXUAL. Individual who firmly wants to be the opposite sex.

TRANSVESTISM. Sexual gratification derived from wearing the clothes of the opposite sex.

TRAUMA. Physical or psychological injury.

TREPONEMA PALLIDUM. Spirochete which causes syphilis.

TRICHOMONAS VAGINALIS. A venereal infection.

TRICYCLICS. Group of medications used against depression.

UNCONSCIOUS. In Freudian theory, that portion of the psyche storing needs, memories, and desires of which the person is unaware.

UNDOING. Defense mechanism by which the individual responds to "atones" for misdeeds.

UNIPOLAR. Mood (or affect) disorder with only one emotional swing—up or down.

VAGINISMUS. Painful contraction of vagina during intercourse.

VALIDITY. The extent to which a test accurately evaluates what it is supposed to.

VALIUM. A commonly used minor tranquilizer.

VENEREAL DISEASE. Disorders transmitted by sexual contact.

VERBIGERATION. Prolonged repetition of meaningless words and phrases.

VINELAND SOCIAL MATURITY SCALE. Test rating social and maturational skills.

VOYEURISM. Sexual gratification from watching others in intimate behavior.

WORD SALAD. Jumbled or incoherent use of words.

ZOOPHILIA. Sexual intercourse with animals.

ZYGOTE. Fertilized cell formed by union of male sperm and female egg.

BIBLIOGRAPHY

ABAD, V., ET AL. Model for delivery of mental health services to Spanish-speaking minorities. *American Journal of Orthopsychiatry,* 1974, **44,** 585–595.

ABEL, E. L. *The scientific study of marihuana.* Chicago: Nelson-Hall, 1976.

ADEN, G. C. Lithium carbonate versus E.C.T. in the treatment of the manic state of identical twins with bipolar affective disease. *Diseases of the Nervous System,* 1976, **37,** 393–397.

ADLER, A. *The science of living.* New York: Greenberg, 1929.

ADLER, A. The individual psychology of the alcoholic patient. *Journal of Criminal Psychopathology,* 1941, **3,** 74–77.

AGRAS, S., SYLVESTER, D., AND OLIVEAU, D. The epidemiology of common fears and phobias. *Comparative Psychiatry,* 1969, **10,** 151–156.

AKTHAR, S., WIG., N. N., VARMA, V. K., DWARKA, P., AND VERMA, S. K. A phenomenological analysis of symptoms in obsessive compulsive neurosis. *British Journal of Psychiatry,* 1975, **127,** 342–348.

ALEXANDER, G. Homosexuality: The psychoanalytic point of view. *Psychiatric Communications,* 1975, **16,** 19–23.

ALEXANDER, J. F. Defensive and supportive communications in family systems. *Journal of Marriage and the Family,* 1973, **35,** 613–617.

ALEXANDER, J. F., FRENCH, T. M., AND POLLACK, G. H. (EDS). *Psychosomatic specificity: Experimental studies and results* (Vol. I). Chicago: University of Chicago Press, 1968.

ALEXANDER, J. F., AND PARSONS, B. V. Short-term behavioral intervention with delinquent families: Impact on family process and recidivism. *Journal of Abnormal Psychology,* 1973, **81,** 219–226.

ALLEN, M. S., COHEN, S., AND POLLIN, W. Schizophrenia in veteran twins: A diagnostic review. *American Journal of Psychiatry,* 1972, **128,** 939–945.

ALVAREZ, A. *The savage god.* New York: Random House, 1972.

AMERICAN ASSOCIATION ON MENTAL DEFICIENCY. *Manual on terminology and classification in mental retardation.* Washington, D.C.: AAMD, 1973.

AMERICAN PSYCHIATRIC ASSOCIATION. *A psychiatric glossary.* Washington, D.C.: APA, 1975.

AMERICAN PSYCHIATRIC ASSOCIATION. *Diagnostic and statistical manual of mental disorders* (third edition-draft). Washington, D.C.: APA, January, 1978.

ANASTASI, A. *Psychological testing.* New York: Macmillan, 1976.

ANDERSON, W. (ED.) *The modernization of sex.* New York: Harper & Row, 1976.

ANDRULIS, R. S. *Adult assessment.* Springfield, Ill.: Charles C Thomas, 1977.

ARIETI, S. *Interpretation of schizophrenia.* New York: Basic Books, 1974.

ARON, R. *Main currents of sociological thought* (Vol. II). Garden City, N.Y.: Doubleday, 1977.

ARTHUR, R. J., RAHE, R. H., AND RUBIN, R. T. Serum uric acid, cholesterol and cortisol variability during stresses of everyday life. *Psychosomatic Medicine,* 1974, **36,** 259–268.

ATKINSON, C., AND POLIVY, J. Effects of delay, attack and retaliation on state depression and hostility. *Journal of Abnormal Psychology,* 1976, **85,** 570–575.

BALTES, P. B., AND SCHAIE, K. W. Aging and IQ: The myth of the twilight years. *Psychology Today,* March 1974, 35–40.

BALTHAZAR, E. E., AND STEVENS, H. A. *The emotionally disturbed mentally retarded: A historical and contemporary perspective.* Englewood Cliffs, N.J.: Prentice-Hall, 1973.

BANCROFT, J., TENNENT, G., LOUCAS, K., AND CASS, J. The control of deviant sexual behavior by drugs. *British Journal of Psychiatry,* 1974, **125,** 310–315.

BANDURA, A. *Aggression: A social learning approach.* Englewood Cliffs, N.J.: Prentice-Hall, 1973.

BANDURA, A., AND WALTERS, C. *Social learning and personality development.* New York: Rinehart and Winston, 1963.

BARBER, T. X., DICARA, L. V., KAMUKA, J., MILLER,

N. E., SHAPIRO, D., AND STOYVA, J. *Biofeedback and self-control 1975/1976.* Chicago: Aldine, 1976.

BAROFF, G. S. *Mental retardation: Nature, cause and management.* New York: Hemisphere, 1974.

BARTELL, G. D. *Group sex: A scientist's eyewitness report on the American way of swinging.* New York: Wyden, 1971.

BARUCH, G. K., AND BARNETT, R. C. Implications and applications of recent research on feminine development. *Psychiatry,* 1975, **38,** 318–327.

BEACH, F. A. (ED.) *Human sexuality in four perspectives.* Baltimore: Johns Hopkins, 1977.

BEBBINGTON, P. E. The efficacy of Alcoholics Anonymous: The elusiveness of hard data. *British Journal of Psychiatry,* 1976, **128,** 572–580.

BECK, A. T. *Depression: Causes and treatment.* Philadelphia: University of Pennsylvania Press, 1974.

BECK, A. T. *Cognitive therapy and the emotional disorders.* New York: International Universities Press, 1976.

BECK, A. T., BRADY, J. D., AND QUEN, J. M. *The history of depression.* New York: Insight Commun., 1977.

BEELS, C. C. Family and social management of schizophrenia. *Schizophrenia Bulletin,* 1975, **13,** 97–118.

BEESON, P. B., AND MCDERMOTT, W. (EDS.) *Textbook of medicine.* Philadelphia: Saunders, 1977.

BEISER, M. Personal and social factors associated with the remission of psychiatric symptoms. *Archives of General Psychiatry,* 1976, **33,** 941–945.

BEISER, M., BENFARI, R. C., COLLOMB, H., AND RAVEL, J. Measuring psychoneurotic behavior in cross-cultural surveys. *Journal of Nervous and Mental Diseases,* 1976, **163,** 10–23.

BERGIN, A. E., AND GARFIELD, A. L. *Handbook of psychotherapy and behavior change.* New York: Wiley, 1971.

BERKWITZ, N. J. Up-to-date review of theories of shock therapies. *Diseases of the Nervous System,* 1974, **35,** 523–527.

BERNE, E. *What do you say after you say hello.*

New York: Grove, 1972.

BETTELHEIM, B. *A home for the heart.* New York: Knopf, 1974.

BIEBER, I. A discussion of "Homosexuality": The ethical challenge. *Journal of Consulting and Clinical Psychology,* 1976, **44,** 163–166.

BIRTCHNELL, J. Social class, parental social class, and social mobility in psychiatric patients and general population controls. *Psychological Medicine,* 1971, **12,** 209–221.

BLACKWELL, E. *Essays in medical sociology.* London: E. Bell, 1902.

BLANCHARD, E., AND HERSEN, M. Behavioral treatments of hysterical neurosis. *Psychiatry,* 1976, **39,** 112–118.

BLAND, R. C., PARKER, J. H., AND ORN, H. Prognosis in schizophrenia: a ten year follow-up of first admissions. *Archives of General Psychiatry,* 1976, **33,** 949–954.

BLASHFIELD, R. K., AND DRAGUNS, J. G. Evaluative criteria for psychiatric classification. *Journal of Abnormal Psychology,* 1976, **85,** 140–150.

BLATT, S. J., WILD, C. M. *Schizophrenia: A developmental analysis.* New York: Academic Press, 1975.

BLOCK, N. J., AND DWORKIN, G. I.Q, heritability and inequality. *Philosophy and Public Affairs,* 1974, **3,** 604–612.

BLUM, K. (ED.) *Alcohol and opiates: Neurochemical and behavioral mechanisms.* New York: Academic Press, 1977.

BLUMBERG, H. H. British users of opiate-type drugs: A follow-up study. *British Journal of Addiction,* 1976, **71,** 65–77.

BOCKAR, J. A. *Primer for the nonmedical psychotherapist.* New York: Halsted Press, 1976.

BORUS, J. F. Reentry: "Making it" back in the states. *American Journal of Psychiatry,* 1973, **130,** 850–854.

BOSTOCK, T., AND WILLIAMS, C. L. Attempted suicide as operant behavior. *Archives of General Psychiatry,* 1974, **31,** 482–486.

BOWLEY, J. *Maternal care and mental health* (Monograph Series #2). Geneva: WHO, 1952.

BRENNER, M. H. *Mental illness and the economy.* Cambridge, Mass.: Harvard University Press, 1973.

BROD, T. M. Alcoholism as a mental health prob-

lem of native Americans: a review of the literature. *Archives of General Psychiatry,* 1975, **32,** 1385–1391.

BRODY, E. B., AND BRODY, N. *Intelligence: Nature, determinants and consequences.* New York: Basic Books, 1976.

BROOK, B. D., ET AL. Community families. *Hospital and Community Psychiatry,* 1976, **27,** 195–198.

BROOKE, E. M. *Suicide and attempted suicide* (Public Health Paper No. 58). Geneva: WHO, 1974.

BROWN, B. B. *Stress and the art of biofeedback.* New York: Harper & Row, 1977.

BROWN, G., BHROLCHAIN, M. N., AND HARRIS, T. Social class and psychiatric disturbance among women in an urban population. *Psychological Medicine,* 1976, **6,** 225–254.

BROWN, M. A. The new body psychotherapies. *Psychotherapy: Theory, Research, Practice,* 1973, **10,** 98–116.

BROWN, R. Schizophrenia, language and reality. *American Psychologist,* 1973, **28,** 395–403.

BROWNMILLER, S. *Against our will: Men, women and rape.* New York: Simon and Schuster, 1975.

BUDOFF, M., AND GOTTLEIB, J. Special class EMR children mainstreamed: A study of an aptitude (learning potential) times treatment interaction. *American Journal of Mental Deficiency,* 1976, **81,** 1–11.

BULLOUGH, V. L. *Sexual variance in society and history.* New York: Wiley, 1976.

BURT, C. The genetic determination of differences in intelligence: A study of monozygotic twins reared together and apart. *British Journal of Psychology,* 1966, **57,** 137–153.

BUSSE, E. W. Hypochondriasis in the elderly: A reaction to social stress. *Journal of the American Geriatric Society,* 1976, **24,** 145–149.

BYASSEE, J. E., AND MURRELL, S. A. Interaction patterns in families of autistic, disturbed and normal children. *American Journal of Orthopsychiatry,* 1975, **45,** 785–792.

CALDERONE, M. S. Eroticism as a norm. *Family Coordinator,* 1974, **23,** 337–341.

CAMPBELL, M. Blood serotonin in psychotic and brain damaged children. *Journal of Autism and Childhood Schizophrenia*, 1974, **4**, 33–41.

CANCRO, R. (ED.). *Intelligence: Genetic and environmental influences.* New York: Grune and Stratton, 1971.

CAPLAN, G. *Support systems and community mental health.* New York: Behavioral Publishers, 1974.

CARLSON, A., AND GOODWIN, F. K. Stages of mania: longitudinal analysis of the manic episode. *Archives of General Psychiatry*, 1973, **28**, 221–228.

CARR, A. Compulsive neurosis: A review of the literature. *Psychological Bulletin*, 1974, **81**, 311–318.

CARROO, A. E. A black community in limbo. *Psychiatric Annals*, 1975, **5**, 39–45.

CATER, D., AND STRICKLAND, S. *TV violence and the child.* New York: Basic Books, 1975.

CAUDILL, W., AND LIN, T. (EDS.). *Mental health research in Asia and the Pacific.* Honolulu: East-West Center Press, 1969.

CHAFETZ, M. E. *Why drinking can be good for you.* Briarcliff Manor, N.Y.: Stein and Day, 1976.

CHEEK, F. The father of the schizophrenic. *Archives of General Psychiatry*, 1965, **13**, 336–345.

CHERTOK, L. Hysteria, hypnosis and psychopathology. *Medicina Psicosomatica* (Italy), 1974, **19**, 341–351.

CHIVA, M. *Normal and pathological retardates.* Newchatel, Switzerland: Delacaux et Niestle, 1973.

CHOPRA, H. B. Family psychiatric morbidity, parental deprivation and socio-economic status in cases of mania *British Journal of Psychiatry*, 1975, **126**, 191–192.

CHORON, J. *Suicide.* New York: Scribner, 1972.

CLECKLEY, H. *The mask of sanity.* St. Louis: C. V. Mosby, 1976.

COCHRANE, N. Role of aggression in the psychogenesis of depressive illness. *British Journal of Medicine and Psychology*, 1975, **48**, 113–130.

COE, W. C., BASDEN, D., AND GRAHAM, C. Posthypnotic amnesia: Suggestions of an active process in dissociative phenomena. *Journal of Abnormal Psychology*, 1976, **85**, 418–421.

COHEN, D. B. On the etiology of neurosis. *Journal of Abnormal Psychology*, 1974, **83**, 473–479.

COLLUM, J. M., AND PIKE, G. W. The borderline and the addict life-style. *Drug Forum*, 1976, **5**, 39–44.

COMFORT, A. *A good age.* New York: Crown, 1976.

COMMISSION REPORT. *The report of the commission on obscenity and pornography.* New York: Bantam Books, 1970.

COMSTOCK, B. S., AND MCDERMOTT, R. Group therapy for patients who attempt suicide. *International Journal of Group Psychotherapy*, 1975, **25**, 44–49.

CONN, H. F. *Current therapy.* Philadelphia: Saunders, 1978.

CONN, H. F., AND CONN, R. B. (EDS.). *Current diagnosis.* Philadelphia: Saunders, 1978.

CONRAD, S. R., AND WINCZE, J. P. Orgasmic reconditioning: A controlled study of its effects upon the sexual arousal and behavior of adult male homosexuals. *Behavior Therapy*, 1976, **7**, 155–162.

COOKE, T. P., AND APOLLONI, T. Developing positive social-emotional behaviors. *Journal of Applied Behavior Analysis*, 1976, **9**, 65–78.

CRAGO, M. A. Psychopathology in married couples. *Psychological Bulletin*, 1972, **77**, 114–128.

CRASILNECK, H. B., AND HALL, J. A. *Clinical hypnosis.* New York: Grune and Stratton, 1975.

CRISP. A. H., PALMER, R. L., AND KALUCY, R. S. How common is anorexia nervosa? A prevalence study. *British Journal of Psychiatry*, 1976, **128**, 549–554.

CROWE, R. U. An adoption study of the antisocial personality. *Archives of General Psychiatry*, 1974, **31**, 785–791.

CUMMINGS, J. N. *Background to migraine.* New York: Springer-Verlag, 1971.

CURTIS, G., NEESE, R., BUXTON, M., WRIGHT, J., AND LIPPMAN, D. Flooding in vivo as a research tool and treatment method for phobias. *Comparative Psychiatry*, 1976, **17**, 153–160.

D'AGOSTINO, A. M. Depression: Schism in contemporary psychiatry. *American Journal of Psychiatry*, 1975, **132**, 629–632.

DAVIDS, A. Childhood psychosis: The problem

of differential diagnosis. *Journal of Autism and Childhood Schizophrenia,* 1975, **5,** 129–138.

DAVIDSON, P. *The behavioral management of anxiety, depression and pain.* New York: Brunner and Mazel, 1976.

DAVIS, I. P. Advice giving in parent counseling. *Social Casework,* 1975, **56,** 343–347.

DAYRINGER, R. Fair-fight for change. *Journal of Marriage and Family Counseling,* 1976, **2,** 115–130.

DELACATO, C. H. *The ultimate stranger: The autistic child.* Garden City, N.Y.: Doubleday, 1974.

DELINT, J., AND SCHMIDT, W. *Biological basis of alcoholism.* New York: Wiley, 1971.

DEUTSCHER, I. *What we say/what we do: sentiments and acts.* Glenview, Ill.: Scott, Foresman, 1973.

DEUTSCHER, I., AND THOMPSON, E. J. (EDS.). *Among the people: Encounter with the poor.* New York: Basic Books, 1968.

DEWOLFE, A. S. Are there two kinds of thinking in process and reactive schizophrenics? *Journal of Abnormal Psychology,* 1974, **83,** 385–390.

DOHRENWEND, B. P. Key problems in the conceptualization and measurement of psychiatric disorders in general populations. In R. Prince and H. B. M. Murphy (Eds.), *Measuring psychosocial stress.* Baltimore: National Education Press, 1975.

DOHRENWEND, B. P., AND DOHRENWEND, B. S. Social and cultural influence on psychopathology. *Annual Review of Psychology.* Palo Alto: Annual Review, 1974.

DOHRENWEND, B. S., AND DOHRENWEND, B. P. Social class and the relation to remote and recent stressors. In G. L. Roff, et al., *Life history research in psychopathology* (Vol. 2). Minneapolis: University of Minnesota Press, 1972.

DOLL, E. A. *The measurement of social competence.* Minneapolis: Educational Test Bureau, 1953.

DOLLARD, J., AND MILLER, N. E. *Personality and psychotherapy.* New York: McGraw-Hill, 1950.

DUFF, R. J., AND ULRICH, S. R. A comparison of impairment in verbal comprehension, speech, reading and writing in adult aphasics. *Journal of Speech and Hearing Disorders,* 1976, **41,** 110–119.

DUNBAR, F. *Mind and body: Psychosomatic medicine.* New York: Random House, 1947.

EADINGTON, W. R. (ED.). *Gambling and society.* Springfield, Ill.: Charles C Thomas, 1976.

EASTMAN, C. Behavioral formulations of depression. *Psychology Review,* 1976, **83,** 277–291.

EATON, J. W., AND WEIL, R. J. *Culture and mental disorders.* New York: Free Press, 1955.

EAVES, L. J. The structure of genotypic and environmental variation for personality measurements. *British Journal of Social and Clinical Psychology,* 1973, **12,** 275–282.

ECCLES, J. C. *The understanding of the brain.* New York: McGraw-Hill, 1977.

EHRENKRANZ, J., BLISS, E., AND SHEARD, M. H. Plasma testosterone: Correlation with aggressive behavioral social dominance in man. *Psychosomatic Medicine,* 1974, **36,** 469–475.

ENELOW, A. J. *Elements of psychotherapy.* New York: Oxford, 1977.

ERIKSON, E. H. *Childhood and society.* New York: Norton, 1963.

EVANS, R. B. Childhood parental relationships of homosexual men. *Journal of Consulting and Clinical Psychology,* 1969, **33,** 129–135.

EVANS, R. I. *R. D. Laing: The man and his ideas.* New York: Dutton, 1976.

EVERETT, W. The pharmacology of aggressive behavior in animals and men. *Psychopharmacological Bulletin,* 1977, **13,** 121–128.

EYSENCK, H. J. The effects of psychotherapy. *International Journal of Psychiatry,* 1965, **1,** 99–178.

EYSENCK, H. J. The learning theory model of neurosis: a new approach. *Behavior Research and Therapy,* 1976, **14,** 251–267.

FEINBERG, J. *Social philosophy.* Englewood Cliffs, N.J.: Prentice-Hall, 1973.

FELDMAN, M. P. *Criminal behavior.* New York: Wiley, 1977.

FERNANDO, S. J. Six cases of Gilles de la Tourette's syndrome. *British Journal of Psychiatry,*

1976, **128**, 436–441.

FIEVE, R. R. *Moodswing: The third revolution in psychiatry*. New York: Morrow, 1975.

FIEVE, R., BRILL, H., AND ROSENTHAL, D. (EDS.) *Genetics and psychopathology*. Baltimore: Johns Hopkins, 1975.

FIEVE, R. R., KUMBARACI, T., AND DUNNER, D. L. Lithium prophylaxis of depression in bipolar I, bipolar II and unipolar patients. *American Journal of Psychiatry*, 1976, **133**, 925–929.

FISCHER, J., AND GOCHROS, H. L. (EDS.). *Handbook of behavior therapy with sexual problems*. Elmsford, N.Y.: Pergamon, 1976.

FISHER, J. V. Complications of psychoactive drugs as seen by family practitioners. *Psychiatric Forum*, 1976, **5**, 8–23.

FLOUD, J. Sociology and the theory of responsibility: "Social background" as an excuse for crime. *Psychological Medicine*, 1975, **5**, 227–238.

FRANKENA, W. *Ethics*. Englewood Cliffs, N.J.: Prentice-Hall, 1973.

FRAZIER, S. H. Changing patterns in management of depression. *Diseases of the Nervous System*, 1976, **37**, 25–29.

FREEDMAN, A. M., ET AL. *Modern synopsis of comprehensive textbook of psychiatry/II*. Baltimore: Williams and Wilkins, 1976.

FRIEDMAN, L. The struggle in psychotherapy. *The Psychoanalytic Review*, 1975, **62**, 453–462.

FRIEDMAN, S. B., AND ROSENMAN, R. H. *Type A behavior and your heart*. Greenwich, Conn.: Fawcett, 1975.

FREUD, S. Fragment of an analysis of a case of hysteria. In *Collected papers* (Vol. 3). London: Hogarth, 1948.

FREUD, S. Neurosis and psychosis. In *Collected papers* (Vol. II). New York: Basic Books, 1924.

FUCHS, C. Z., AND REHM, L. P. *A self-control behavior therapy program for depression*. University of Pittsburgh, unpublished manuscript, 1977.

GAGNON, J. H. *Human sexualities*. Glenview, Ill.: Scott Foresman, 1977.

GALLAGHER, B. The attitude of psychiatrists towards etiological theories of schizophrenia. *Journal of Clinical Psychology*, 1977, **33**, 99–104.

GALLIHER, J. G., AND MCCARTNEY, J. *Criminology: Power, crime and criminal law*. Homewood, Ill.: Dorsey, 1977.

GARITANO, W. W., AND RONALL, R. E. Concept of life style in the treatment of alcoholism. *International Journal of Addiction*, 1974, **9**, 585–592.

GEER, J. H., DAVISON, G. C., AND GATCHEL, R. I. Reduction of stress in humans through non-veridical perceived control of aversive stimulation. *Journal of Personality and Social Psychology*, 1970, **16**, 731–738.

GIBBINS, R., ISRAEL, Y., KALANT, H., POPHAM, R., SCHMIDT, W., AND SMART, R. *Research advances in alcohol and drug problems*. New York: Wiley, 1976.

GILMARTIN, M. That swinging couple down the block. *Psychology Today*, 1975, **12**, 54–56.

GITTLEMAN-KLEIN, R., AND KLEIN, D. F. School phobias. *Journal of Nervous and Mental Diseases*, 1973, **156**, 199–215.

GODDARD, H. H. *The Kallikak family*. New York: Macmillan, 1912.

GOETZ, U., GREEN, R., WHYBROW, P., AND JACKSON, R. X-linkage revisited: Further family study of manic-depressive illness. *Archives of General Psychiatry*, 1974, **31**, 665–672.

GOLDBERG, C. *The human circle*. Chicago: Nelson-Hall, 1973.

GOLDFRIED, M. R., AND GOLDFRIED, A. P. Importance of hierarchy content in the self-control of anxiety. *Journal of Consulting and Clinical Psychology*, 1977, **45**, 121–128.

GOLDHAMER, H., AND MARSHALL, A. W. *Psychoses and civilization*. New York: Free Press, 1953.

GOLDSTEIN, M. J., KANT, H. S., AND HARTMAN, J. J. *Pornography and sexual deviance*. Berkeley, Calif.: University of California Press, 1973.

GOLDSTEIN, S. E., AND BIRNBOM, F. Hypochondriasis and the elderly. *Journal of the American Geriatric Society*, 1976, **24**, 150–154.

GOODWIN, D. *Is alcoholism hereditary?* New York: Oxford, 1976.

GOTTSCHALK, L. A. Psychosomatic medicine: Past, present and future. *Psychiatry*, 1975, **38**, 334–345.

GREDEN, J. F. Caffeine toxicity mimics neuroses. *Journal of the American Medical Associ-*

ation, 1974, **229,** 1568–1569.

GREEN, R. *Sexual identity conflict in children and adults.* New York: Basic Books, 1974.

GREER, S., AND MORRIS, T. Psychological attributes of women who develop breast cancer: A controlled study. *Journal of Psychosomatic Research,* 1975, **19,** 147–153.

GROVES, P. M., AND REBEC, G. V. Biochemistry and behavior. In *Annual Review of Psychology.* Palo Alto, Calif.: Annual Reviews, 1976.

GRINSPOON, L., AND BAKALAR, J. B. Cocaine: a social history. *Psychology Today,* 1977, **39,** 77–78.

GRINSPOON, L., AND HEDBLOM, P. *The speed culture: Amphetamine use and abuse in America.* Cambridge, Mass.: Harvard University Press, 1975.

HAAS, K. *Growth encounter.* Chicago: Nelson-Hall, 1975.

HAGBERG, B., AND INGVAR, D. H. Cognitive reduction in presenile dementia related to regional abnormalities of the cerebral blood flow. *British Journal of Psychiatry,* 1976, **128,** 209–222.

HALL, R. C., AND MALONE, P. T. Psychiatric effects of prolonged Asian captivity: A two-year follow-up. *American Journal of Psychiatry,* 1976, **133,** 786–790.

HALPERN, J. Protection: A test of the psychoanalytic hypothesis. *Journal of Abnormal Psychology,* 1977, **86,** 536–542.

HALPERN, W. I., AND KISSELL, S. *Human resources for troubled children.* New York: Wiley, 1976.

HAMPDEN-TURNER, C. *Sane asylum: Inside the Delancey Street Foundation.* San Francisco: San Francisco Book Co., 1976.

HANDAL, P., AND LANDER, J. J. Methadone treatment program evaluation and dose response relationships. *International Journal of Addiction,* 1976, **11,** 363–375.

HARBURG, E., ERFUTT, J. C., HAUENSTEIN, L. S., CHAPE, C., SCHULL, W. J., AND SCHORK, M. A. Socio-ecological stress, suppressed hostility, skin color and black-white male blood pressure: Detroit. *Psychosomatic Medicine,* 1973, **35,** 276–277.

HARDY, R. E., AND CULL, G. J. (EDS.). *Fundamentals of juvenile criminal behavior and drug abuse.* Springfield, Ill.: Charles C Thomas, 1975.

HARE, D. R. *Psychopathy: Theory and research.* New York: Wiley, 1976.

HARLOW, H. F. *Learning to love.* San Francisco: Albion, 1973.

HARRIS, L., AND ASSOC., INC. *National Institute on Alcohol Abuse and Alcoholism report: Summary study no. 2355.* Rockville, Md.: NIMH, 1974.

HARTLEY, D., ET AL. Deterioration effects in encounter groups. *American Psychologist,* 1976, **31,** 247–255.

HARTWICH, A. *Aberrations of sexual life.* New York: Capricorn, 1962.

HARTY, M., AND HORWITZ, L. Therapeutic outcome as rated by patients, therapists and judges. *Archives of General Psychiatry,* 1976, **33,** 957–961.

HERSEN, M., AND EISLER, R. M. *Progress in behavior modification.* New York: Academic Press, 1977.

HESTON, L. L. The genetics of schizophrenic and schizoid disease. *Science,* 1970, **167,** 249–256.

HIGGINS, J. The schizophrenogenic mother revisited. *British Journal of Psychiatry and Social Work,* 1968, **9,** 205–208.

HIGGINS, R. L., AND MARLATT, G. A. Fear of interpersonal evaluation as a determinant of alcohol consumption in male social drinkers. *Journal of Abnormal Psychology,* 1975, **84,** 644–652.

HIBERMAN, E. *The rape victim.* New York: Basic Books, 1976.

HIRSCHOWITZ, G. Pace of patient processing in the mental health system. *Community Mental Health,* 1975, **11,** 179–183.

HITE, S. *The Hite report.* New York: Macmillan, 1976.

HOKANSON, J. E., DEGOOD, D. E., FORREST, M. S., AND BRITTAIN, T. M. Availability of avoidance behaviors for modulating vascular-stress responses. *Journal of Personality and Social Psychology,* 1971, **19,** 60–68.

HOLLENDER, M. H., AND CALLAHAN, A. S. Erotomania or de Clerambault syndrome. *Archives of General Psychiatry,* 1975, **32,** 1574–1576.

HOLLINGSHEAD, A. B., AND REDLICH, F. C. *Social*

class and mental illness: A community study. New York: Wiley, 1958.

HOLLISTER, L. E. *Clinical use of psychotherapeutic drugs.* Springfield, Ill.: Charles C Thomas, 1977.

HOLLIS, W. S. On the etiology of criminal homicides: The alcohol factor. *Journal of Police Science and Administration,* 1974, **2,** 50–53.

HOLMES, T. H., AND HOLMES, T. S. How change can make us ill. *Stress,* Blue Cross Association, Chicago, 1974.

HOOKER, E., AND CHANCE, P. Facts that liberated the gay community. *Psychology Today,* 1975, **10,** 52–55.

HORN, P. How to enhance healthy sexuality: Behavior mod in the bedroom. *Psychology Today,* 1975 **10,** 94–95.

HORNEY, K. *Neurosis and human growth.* New York: Norton, 1950.

HOROWITZ, M. *Stress response syndromes.* New York: Aronson, 1976.

HORTON, P. C. Personality disorder and parietal lobe dysfunction. *American Journal of Psychiatry,* 1976, **133,** 782–785.

HUDGENS, R. W., ET AL. The communication of suicidal intent in psychiatric illness: A follow-up. In M. Roff et al. (Eds.), *Life history research in psychopathology* (Vol. 2). Minneapolis: University of Minnesota Press, 1972.

HUESSY, H. R., AND COHEN, A. H. Hyperkinetic behaviors and learning disabilities followed over seven years. *Pediatrics,* 1976, **57,** 4–10.

HUNTERKOPF, E., ET AL. Teaching therapeutic skills to mental patients. *Psychotherapy,* 1975, **12,** 8–12.

HURLEY, R. L. *Poverty and mental retardation: A causal relationship.* New York: Vintage Books, 1969.

HUTT, M. L., AND GIBBY, R. G. *The mentally retarded child: Development, education and treatment.* Boston: Allyn and Bacon, 1976.

INOUYE, E. Monozygotic twins with schizophrenia reared apart in infancy. *Japanese Journal of Human Genetics,* 1972, **16,** 182–190.

ISENBERG, M. Responsibility and the neurotic patient. *American Journal of Psychoanalysis,* 1974, **34,** 43–50.

ISRAEL, Y., and MARDONES, J. *Biological basis of alcoholism.* New York: Wiley, 1971.

IVERSON, S. D., AND IVERSON, L. L. *Behavioral pharmacology.* New York: Oxford, 1975.

JACKSON, B. *In the life: Versions of the criminal experience.* New York: Mentor, 1976.

JACOB, T. Family interaction in disturbed and normal families. A methodological and substantive review. *Psychological Bulletin,* 1975, 33–65.

JAFFE, P. G., AND CARLSON, P. M. Relative efficacy of modeling and instructions in eliciting social behavior from chronic psychiatric patients. *Journal of Consulting and Clinical Psychology,* 1976, **44,** 200–207.

JAIN, M., AND JAIN, K. M. Understanding biochemical pathology of depressive illnesses. *Psychiat. Neurol. Neurochirur.,* 1973, **76,** 286–295.

JAMES, N. M., AND CHAPMAN, C. J. A genetic study of bipolar affective disorder. *British Journal of Psychiatry,* 1975, **126,** 449–456.

JAMES, S. Prostitutes and prostitution. In E. Sagarin and F. Montanino (Eds.), *Deviants: Voluntary actors in a hostile world.* New York: Silver-Burdett, 1977.

JARVIK, L., ET AL. Human aggression and the extra Y chromosome. *American Psychologist,* 1976, **28,** 674–682.

JARVIS, E. (ED.). *Insanity and idiocy in Massachusetts: Report of the Commission on Lunacy, 1855.* Cambridge, Mass.: Harvard University Press, 1971

JELLINEK, E. M. *The disease concept of alcoholism.* New Haven, Conn.: Yale University Press, 1960.

JENKINS, R. L. *Behavior disorders of childhood and adolescence.* Springfield, Ill.: Charles C Thomas, 1973.

JENSEN, A. R. Interaction of level I and level II abilities with race and socioeconomic status. *Journal of Educational Psychology,* 1974, **66,** 99–111.

JERISON, H. J. *Evolution of the brain and intelligence.* New York: Academic Press, 1973.

JOHNSON, R. J., WIERSEMA, V., AND KRAFT, I. A. Hair amino acids in childhood autism. *Journal of Autism and Childhood Schizophrenia,* 1974, **4,** 187–188.

JONES, K., ET AL. *Sex and people*. New York: Harper & Row, 1977.

JONES, M. C. Personality correlates and antecedents of drinking patterns in males. *Journal of Consulting and Clinical Psychology*, 1968, **32**, 2–12.

JONES, R., ET AL. Personality profiles in asthma. *Journal of Clinical Psychology*, 1976, **32**, 285–293.

JUNG, C. G. *Memories, dreams, reflections*. New York: Random House, 1961.

JUSTIN, R. G. Incidence of depression in one family physician's practice. *Journal of Family Practice*, 1976, **3**, 438–439.

KAESTNER, E., MILBURN, P., SZAKMARY, G., VASSELI, J. R., VITIELLO, M., AND WOODS, S. C. Conditioned insulin secretion and meal feeding in rats. *Journal of Comparative Physiology and Psychology*, 1977, **91**, 128–133.

KAHN, R. L., ET AL. Memory complaint and impairment in the aged. *Archives of General Psychiatry*, 1975, **32**, 1569–1573.

KAMIN, L. J. *The science and politics of IQ*. Potomac, Md.: Erlbaum, 1974.

KAMINISKI, Z. Case report: An asthmatic adolescent and his "repressed cry" for his mother. *British Journal of Medicine and Psychology*, 1975, **48**, 185–188.

KAMMERMAN, M. *Sensory isolation and personality change*. Springfield, Ill.: Charles C Thomas, 1977.

KAPLAN, H. I., AND SADDOCK, B. J. Paranoid personality states. *Psychiatry Quarterly*, 1971, **45**, 528–541.

KARLSSON, J. L. An Icelandic family study of schizophrenia. *British Journal of Psychiatry*, 1973, **123**, 549–554.

KARRER, R., (ED.). *Developmental psychophysiology of mental retardation*. Springfield, Ill.: Charles C Thomas, 1976.

KASL, S. V., AND COBB, S. Blood pressure changes in men undergoing job loss: A preliminary report. *Psychosomatic Medicine*, 1970, **6**, 95–106.

KATCHADOURIAN, H. A. *Human sexuality: Sense and nonsense*. San Francisco: Freeman, 1974.

KENDELL, R. E. The classification of depression: A review of contemporary confusion. *British Journal of Psychiatry*, 1976, **129**, 15–28.

KENYON, F. E. Hypochondriacal states. *British Journal of Psychiatry*, 1976, **129**, 1–14.

KERRY, R. J., AND ORME, J. E. Varieties of depression. *Journal of Clinical Psychology*, 1975, **31**, 607–609.

KETY, S. S., AND ROSENTHAL, D. ET AL. Mental illness in the biological and adoptive families of adopted individuals who have become schizophrenic: A preliminary report based on psychiatric interviews. R. Fieve, H. Brill, and D. Rosenthal (Eds.), *Genetics and psychopathology*. Baltimore: Johns Hopkins, 1975.

KÏHLSTROM, J. F., AND EVANS, F. J. Recovery of memory after posthypnotic amnesia. *Journal of Abnormal Psychology*, 1976, **85**, 122–129.

KINSEY, A. C., ET AL. *Sexual behavior in the human male*. Philadelphia: Saunders, 1948.

KINSEY A. C., ET AL. *Sexual behavior in the human female*. Philadelphia: Saunders, 1953.

KIRITZ, S. K., AND MOOS, R. H. Psysiological effects of social environments. *Psychosomatic Medicine*, 1974, **36**, 96–114.

KITTRIE, N. N. *The right to be different*. New York: Penguin Books, 1973.

KLEIN, D. C., AND SELIGMAN, M. E. P. Reversal of performance deficits and perceptual deficits in learned helplessness and depression. *Journal of Abnormal Psychology*, 1976, **85**, 11–26.

KLEIN, N. S. Incidence, prevalence and recognition of depressive illness. *Diseases of the Nervous System*, 1976, **37**, 10–14.

KOHN, M. L. Social class and schizophrenia. *Schizophrenia Bulletin*, 1973, **7**, 60–79.

KOHN, M. L. The interaction of social class and other factors in the etiology of schizophrenia. *Journal of Psychiatry*, 1976, **133**, 177–180.

KOLB, L. *Modern clinical psychiatry*. Philadelphia: Saunders, 1977.

KOLUCHOVA, J. The further development of twins after severe and prolonged deprivation. *Journal of Child Psychology and Psychiatry*, 1976, **17**, 181–188.

KOPOLOW, L. E. A review of major implications of the *O'Connor* v. *Donaldson* decision. *American Journal of Psychiatry*, 1976, **133**, 379–383.

KOSLOWSKY, M., AND LEVETT, C. Intellectual functioning in a sample of institutionalized narcotics addicts. *Journal of Clinical Psychology,* 1975, **31,** 578–582.

KOVEL, J. *A complete guide to therapy.* New York: Crown, 1976.

KRAFT, D. P., AND BABIGIAN, H. M. Suicide by persons with and without psychiatric contacts. *Archives of General Psychiatry,* 1976, **33,** 209–215.

KRAMER, M. *Population changes and schizophrenia.* Washington, D.C.: Division of Biometry and Epidemiology, NIMH, 1976.

KRINGLEN, E. Obsessional neurotics: A long term follow-up. *British Journal of Psychiatry,* 1965, **111,** 709–722.

KURTINES, W., HOGAN, R., AND WEISS, D. Personality dynamics of heroin use. *Journal of Abnormal Psychology,* 1975, **84,** 87–89.

LACHMAN, S. J. *Psychosomatic disorders: A behavioristic interpretation.* New York: Wiley, 1972.

LAING, R. D. *The politics of experience.* New York: Pantheon, 1967.

LAING, R. D. *The divided self.* New York: Pantheon, 1969.

LAING, R. D. *Knots.* New York: Pantheon, 1970.

LAMB, L. E. *The role of the father in child development.* New York: Wiley, 1976.

LAMBERT, M. J. Spontaneous remission in adult neurotic disorders. *Psychological Bulletin,* 1976, **83,** 107–119.

LAZARUS, A. A. Has behavior therapy outlived its usefulness? *American Psychologist,* 1977, **32,** 550–554.

LAZELL, E. W. The group treatment of dementia praecox. *Psychoanalytic Review,* 1921, **8,** 168–178.

LEAA. *Law Enforcement Assistance Administration Annual Statistics.* Washington, D.C.: 1976, 1978.

LEAVITT, F. *Drugs and behavior.* Philadelphia: Saunders, 1974.

LECH, S. V., GARY, D., AND URY, H. K. Characteristics of heavy users of outpatient prescription drugs. *Clinical Toxicology,* 1975, **8,** 599–610.

LEFKOWITZ, M. M. *Growing up to be violent.* Elmsford, N.Y.: Pergamon, 1975.

LEIBLUM, S., ET AL. Group treatment format: Mixed sexual dysfunctions. *Archives of Sexual Behavior,* 1976, **5,** 313–322.

LEON, G. R., AND ROTH, L. Obesity: Psychological causes, correlations and speculations. *Psychological Bulletin,* 1977, **84,** 117–139.

LESSE, S. Masked depression and depressive equivalents. *Psychopharmacology Bulletin,* 1977, **13,** 112–118.

LESTER, D. The myth of suicide prevention. *Comparative Psychiatry,* 1972, **13,** 555–560.

LESTER, D. *Unusual sexual behavior.* Springfield, Ill.: Charles C Thomas, 1975.

LESTER, D., AND BECK, A. Early loss as a possible sensitizer to later loss in attempted suicides. *Psychological Reports,* 1976, **22,** 121–124.

LEVINE, S. B., AND YOST, M. A. Frequency of sexual dysfunction in a general gynecological clinic. *Archives of Sexual Behavior,* 1976, **5,** 229–238.

LEVITT, E. C., AND LUBIN, B. *Depression: Concepts, controversies, and some new facts.* New York: Springer-Verlag, 1975.

LEWINSOHN, P. H. A behavioral approach to depression. In R. J. Friedman and M. M. Katz (Eds.), *The psychology of depression.* Washington, D.C.: Winston-Wiley, 1976.

LIBBY, W. R., AND WHITEHURST, R. N. (EDS.). *Marriage and alternatives.* Glenview, Ill.: Scott Foresman, 1977.

LIEBERMAN, M. A., ET AL. *Encounter groups.* New York: Basic Books, 1973.

LIEBERT, R. M., NEALE, J. M., AND DAVIDSON, E. S. *The early window: Effects of television on children and youth.* Elmsford, N.Y.: Pergamon, 1973.

LILJEFORS, I., AND RAHE, R. H. An identical twin study of psychosocial factors in coronary heart disease in Sweden. *Psychosomatic Medicine,* 1970, **32,** 523–542.

LIPTON, M., AND WILKS, J. *The effectiveness of correctional treatment.* New York: Praeger, 1975.

LITTLESTONE, R., ET AL. *Schizophrenia: Implications of research findings for treatment and teaching.* New York: Basic Books, 1976.

LIVINGSTON, J. Compulsive gamblers: A culture of losers. *Psychology Today,* March, 1974, 51–55.

LONEY, J., AND ORDONA, T. T. Using cerebral stimulants to treat minimal brain dysfunction.

American Journal of Orthopsychiatry, 1975, **45**, 564–572.

LORO, B., AND WOODWARD, A. J. The dependence of psychiatric diagnosis on psychological assessment. *Journal of Clinical Psychology,* 1975, **31**, 635–639.

LOVAAS, O. I., AND BUCHER, B. D. (EDS.). *Perspectives in behavior modification with deviant children.* Englewood Cliffs, N.J.: Prentice-Hall, 1974.

LUBORSKY, L. Comparative studies of psychotherapies. *Archives of General Psychiatry,* 1975, **32**, 995–1008.

LUNDE, D. T. *Murder and madness.* San Francisco: San Francisco Pubisher, 1976.

LUPARELLO, T. J., ET AL. Psychologic factors and bronchial asthma. *New York Journal of Medicine,* 1971, **71**, 2161–2165.

MACVAUGH, G. S. *Frigidity: Everything you should know about its cure.* Elmsford, N.Y.: Pergamon, 1977.

MADDI, S. R. The existential neurosis. *Journal of Abnormal Psychology,* 1967, **72**, 311–325.

MADSEN, W. *The American alcoholic.* Springfield, Ill.: Charles C Thomas, 1977.

MALAN, D. H., ET AL. Psychodynamic change in untreated neurotic patients: II Apparently genuine improvements. *Archives of General Psychiatry,* 1975, **32**, 110–126.

MALINOWSKI, B. *Sex and repression in savage society.* New York: Humanities Press, 1927.

MARINI, J. L., ET AL. An evaluation of the double-blind design in a study comparing lithium carbonate with placebo. *Acta Psychiatrica Scandinavia,* 1976, **53**, 343–354.

MARKS, I., AND LADER, M. Anxiety states: A review. *Journal of Nervous and Mental Disorders,* 1973, **156**, 3–18.

MARTIN, B. *Anxiety and neurotic disorders.* New York: Wiley, 1976.

MARTINEZ, J. L., JR. (ED.). *Chicano psychology.* New York: Academic Press, 1977.

MASLOW, A. H. *The farther reaches of human nature.* New York: Viking, 1972.

MASTERS, W. H., AND JOHNSON, V. E. *Human sexual inadequacy.* Boston: Little, Brown, 1970.

MASTERS, W. H., AND JOHNSON, V. E. Principles of the new sex therapy. *American Journal of Psychiatry,* 1976, **133**, 548–554.

MATTHYSSE, S. (ED.). *Catecholamines and schizophrenia.* Elmsford, N.Y.: Pergamon, 1975.

MAUSNER, J. S., AND BAHN, A. K. *Epidemiology: An introductory text.* Philadelphia: Saunders, 1974.

MAXMEN, J. S., ET AL. Anorexia nervosa: Practical management in a general hospital. *Journal of the American Medical Association,* 1974, **229**, 801–803.

MAY, P. R., ET AL. Schizophrenia: A follow-up study of results of treatment. *Archives of General Psychiatry,* 1976, **33**, 481–486.

MCCABE, M. S. ECT treatment of mania: A controlled study. *American Journal of Psychiatry,* 1976, **133**, 688–691.

MCCALL, R. J. The nonpsychotic personality disturbances: A reevaluation and reclassification. In T. G. Burke, *Contemporary issues in abnormal psychology and mental illness.* Dubuque, Iowa: Kendall Hunt, 1977.

MCCARY, J. L. *Human sexuality.* New York: Van Nostrand, 1973.

MCCLEARN, G. E., AND DEFRIES, J. C. *Introduction to behavioral genetics.* San Francisco: Freeman, 1973.

MCCREARY, C. P. Personality profiles of persons convicted of indecent exposure. *Journal of Clinical Psychology,* 1975, **31**, 260–262.

MCNEILL, W. H. *Plagues and people.* Garden City, N.Y.: Doubleday, 1976.

MEDNICK, S. A. A learning theory approach to research in schizophrenia. *Psychological Bulletin,* 1958, **55**, 316–325.

MEDVEDEV, R. *A question of madness.* New York: Random House, 1972.

MEICHENBAUM, D. Ways of modifying what clients say to themselves. *Rational Living,* 1972, **7**, 23–27.

MELTZER, H. Y. Biochemical studies in schizophrenia. *Schizophrenia Bulletin,* 1976, **2**, 10–18.

MENDELS, J. *Concepts of depression.* New York: Wiley, 1976.

MENNINGER, K. A. *Man against himself.* New York: Harcourt Brace, 1938.

MENNINGER, K. A. *The human mind.* New York: Knopf, 1965.

MIKHAIL, A. R. Treatment of vaginismus by i.v. diazepam in abreaction interviews. *Acta Psychiatrica Scandinavia,* 1976, **53,** 328–332.

MILLER, P. M. *Behavioral treatment of alcoholism.* Elmsford, N.Y.: Pergamon, 1976.

MILLON, T. Reflections on Rosenhan's "On being sane in insane places." *Journal of Abnormal Psychology,* 1975, **84,** 456–461.

MILNE, H., AND HARDY, S. J. (EDS.). *Psycho-sexual problems.* Baltimore: University Park Press, 1975.

MINER, G. D. The evidence for genetic components in the neuroses: A review. *Archives of General Psychiatry,* 1973, **29,** 111–118.

MINKOFF, K., ET AL. Hopelessness, depression and attempted suicide. *Journal of Psychiatry,* 1973, **130,** 455–459.

MIRSKY, I. A. Physiologic, psychologic and social determinants in the etiology of duodenal ulcer. *American Journal of Digestive Diseases,* 1958, **3,** 285–314.

MISCHEL, W. Towards a cognitive social learning reconceptualization of personality. *Psychological Review,* 1973, **80,** 252–283.

MOOS, R. H. *Human adaptation: Coping with life stress.* Lexington, Mass.: Heath, 1976.

MORIN, S. F. Heterosexual bias in psychological research on lesbianism and male homosexuality. *American Psychologist,* 1977, **32,** 629–637.

MOSHER, L. R., ET AL. Special report: Schizophrenia 1972. *Schizophrenia Bulletin,* 1973, **7,** 12–52.

MUCHA, F. F., AND REINHARD, R. F. Conversion reactions in student aviators. *American Journal of Psychiatry,* 1970, **127,** 493–497.

MUMJACK, D., AND KANNO, P. An overview of outcome on frigidity: Treatment effects and effectiveness. *Comparative Psychiatry,* 1976, **17,** 401–413.

MURPHY, G. E. Clinical identification of suicidal risks. *Archives of General Psychiatry,* 1972, **27,** 356–359.

MURRAY, M. E. Modified time-out procedures for controlling tantrum behaviors in public places. *Behavior Therapy,* 1976, **7,** 412–413.

MUSANTE, G. J. Obesity: Behavioral treatment program. *American Family Physician,* 1974, **10,** 95–102.

MUSAPH, H. Psychodermatology. *Psychology and Psychosomatics,* 1974, **24,** 79–85.

MYERS, P., AND HAMMILL, D. *Methods for learning disorders.* New York: Wiley, 1976.

National Institute on Alcohol Abuse and Alcoholism. *Special Report.* Washington, D.C., 1978.

National Institute of Mental Health. *Criminal statistics and crime.* Rockville, Md.: Center for studies of crime and delinquency, 1973, 1978.

NEAMAN, J. S. *Suggestion of the devil.* Garden City, N.Y.: Doubleday, 1975.

NEIS, A., ET AL. MAO inhibitors in clinical practice. *Psychopharmacology Bulletin,* 1977, **13,** 54–55.

NEWMAN, C. J. Children of disaster: Clinical observations at Buffalo Creek. *American Journal of Psychiatry,* 1976, **133,** 306–312.

NOYES, R., AND CLANCY, J. Anxiety neurosis: a five year follow-up. *Journal of Nervous and Mental Disorders,* 1976, **162,** 200–205.

NYE, R. D., *Three views of man.* Belmont, Calif.: Wadsworth, 1975.

O'DONNELL, J. A. Lifetime patterns of narcotic addiction. In M. Roff et al. (Eds.), *Life history research in psychopathology.* Minneapolis: University of Minnesota Press, 1972.

O'LEARY, K. D., AND WILSON, G. T. *Behavior therapy.* Englewood Cliffs, N.J.: Prentice-Hall, 1975.

O'LEARY, M., ET AL. Perceived locus of control, experienced control and depression. *Journal of Clinical Psychology,* 1977, **33,** 12–19.

ORNITZ, E., AND RITVO, E. R. The syndrome of autism: A critical review. *American Journal of Psychiatry,* 1976, **133,** 609–621.

PARK, C. C. *You are not alone.* Boston: Little, Brown, 1977.

PATTERSON, C. H. *Humanistic education.* Englewood Cliffs, N.J.: Prentice-Hall, 1973.

PATTISON, E. Nonabstinent drinking goals in the treatment of alcoholism. *Archives of General Psychiatry,* 1976, **33,** 923–930.

PATTISON, E., AND MANSELL, R., ET AL. *Alcohol dependence: Research synthesis and emerging concepts.* New York: Springer-Verlag, 1977.

PARE, W. Organ weights in rats with activity

stress ulcer. *Bulletin of the Psychonomic Society*, 1977, **9**, 11–13.

PAVLOV, I. P. *Conditioned reflexes*. Oxford: Oxford University Press, 1927.

PEARCE, J. Depressive disorder in childhood. *Journal of Child Psychology and Psychiatry*, 1977, **18**, 74–83.

PETERS, J. E., AND STERN, R. M. Specificity of attitude hypothesis in psychosomatic medicine. *Journal of Psychosomatic Research*, 1971, **15**, 129–135.

PEPINSKY, H. E. *Crime and conflict*. New York: Academic Press, 1976.

PERRINE, M. W. *Alcohol and highway safety*. Washington, D.C.: National Institute of Alcohol Abuse and Alcoholism, 1974.

PFLANZ, M. Epidemiological and sociocultural factors in the etiology of duodenal ulcer. *Advances in Psychosomatic Medicine*, 1971, **6**.

PHILLIPS, D., ET AL. Alternative behavioral approaches to the treatment of homosexuality. *Archives of Sexual Behavior*, 1976, **5**, 223–228.

PHILLIPS, L., AND DRAGUNS, J. G. Classification of the behavior disorders. In *Annual Review of Psychology*. Palo Alto, Calif.: Annual Reviews, 1971.

PHILLIPS, L., AND WILLIAMS, N. Psychopathology of mental retardation. *American Journal of Psychiatry*, 1975, **132**, 1265–1271.

PHILLIPS, R. L., ET AL. Suggestion and relaxation in asthmatics. *Journal of Psychosomatic Research*, 1972, **16**, 193–204.

Physicians Desk Reference. Oradell, N.J.: Medical Economics Co., 1979.

PIGGOTT, L. R., AND SIMSON, C. B. Changing diagnosis of childhood psychosis. *Journal of Autism and Childhood Schizophrenia*, 1975, **5**, 239–245.

PLATT, J. J., AND LABATE, C. *Heroin addiction*. New York: Wiley, 1976.

POLLIN, W. G., ET AL. Psychopathology in 15,909 pairs of veteran twins. *American Journal of Psychiatry*, 1969, **126**, 597–609.

PRESCOTT, J. W., ET AL. *Brain function and malnutrition*. New York: Wiley, 1975.

President's Commission on Mental Retardation. *Report of the President's Commission*. Washington, D.C., 1962, 1963, 1973.

PURCELL, K., ET AL. The effect on asthma in children of experimental separation from the family. *Psychosomatic Medicine*, 1969, **31**, 144–164.

RABINOWITZ, D. *New lives: Survivors of the holocaust living in America*. New York: Avon, 1977.

RADA, T. R., ET AL. Plasma testosterone levels in the rapist. *Psychosomatic Medicine*, 1976, **38**, 257–268.

RANGELL, L. Psychoanalysis and the process of change. *International Journal of Psychoanalysis*, 1975, **56**, 88–98.

RANGELL, L. Discussion of the Buffalo Creek disaster. *American Journal of Psychiatry*, 1976, **133**, 313–316.

REES, W. L. Distress and disease. *British Journal of Psychiatry*, 1976, **128**, 3–18.

REICHLE, J., ET AL. Eliminating perseverative speech by positive reinforcement and time-out in a psychotic child. *Journal of Behavior Theory and Experimental Psychiatry*, 1976, **7**, 179–182.

REISS, D. The family and schizophrenia. *American Journal of Psychiatry*, 1976, **133**, 181–186.

REITAN, R. M., AND DAVISON, L. A. *Clinical neuropsychiatry*. New York: Wiley, 1974.

RENNER, K. E. *What's wrong with the mental health movement*. Chicago: Nelson-Hall, 1975.

RICALLA, L. M. Healing by laying on of hands: Myth or fact? *Ethics in Science and Medicine*, 1975, **2**, 167–171.

RICHMAN, N. Depression in mothers of preschool children. *Journal of Child Psychiatry and Psychology*, 1976, **17**, 75–78.

RIMLAND, B. The differentiation of childhood psychoses. *Journal of Autism and Childhood Schizophrenia*, 1971, **1**, 161–174.

RISKIN, J., AND FAUNCE, E. An evaluative review of family interaction research. *Family Process*, 1972, **11**, 365–456.

RITVO, E. R. (ED.). *Autism: Current research and management*. New York: Spectrum, 1976.

ROBBINS, L. N. *Deviant children grown up*. Baltimore: Williams and Wilkins, 1966.

ROBERTS, A. R. (ED.) *Childhood deprivation*. Springfield, Ill.: Charles C Thomas, 1974.

ROBERTS, A. R. *Self-destructive behavior*.

Springfield, Ill.: Charles C Thomas, 1975.

ROBINSON, H., AND ROBINSON, N. M. *The mentally retarded child.* New York: McGraw-Hill, 1976.

ROBINSON, L. R. Basic concepts in family therapy. *American Journal of Psychiatry*, 1975, **132**, 1045–1048.

ROG, D. J., AND RAUSCH, H. L. The psychiatric halfway house: How is it measuring up? *Community Mental Health Journal*, 1975, **11**, 155–162.

ROGERS, C. R. *On becoming a person.* Boston: Houghton Mifflin, 1961.

ROGERS C. R. *Becoming partners: Marriage and its alternatives.* New York: Delacorte, 1972.

ROPER, G., ET AL. An experiment on obsessional checking. *Behavior Research and Therapy*, 1973, **11**, 271–277.

ROSENBAUM, C. P., AND BEEBE, J. E., III. *Psychiatric treatment.* New York: McGraw-Hill, 1975.

ROSENBLATT, D. *Opening doors.* New York: Harper & Row, 1975.

ROSENFELD, A. *Prolongevity.* New York: Knopf, 1976.

ROSENHAN, D. L. On being sane in insane places. *Science*, 1973, **179**, 250–258.

ROSENTHAL, D. *Genetic theory and abnormal behavior.* New York: McGraw-Hill, 1970.

ROSENTHAL, D. Issues in high risk studies of schizophrenia. In D. F. Ricks et al. (Eds.), *Life history research in psychopathology.* Minneapolis: University of Minnesota Press, 1974.

ROSS, D. M., AND ROSS, S. A. *Hyperactivity.* New York: Wiley, 1976.

ROSS, H. M. Orthomolecular psychiatry: Vitamin pills for schizophrenics. *Psychology Today*, 1974, **7**, 83–85.

ROTHCHILD, J., AND WOLF, S. *The children of the counterculture.* Garden City, N.Y.: Doubleday, 1976.

ROTHENBERG, M. B. Effect of television violence on children and youth. *Journal of the American Medical Association*, 1975, **234**, 1043–1046.

ROTTER, J. B. Generalized expectancies for internal versus external control of reinforcement. *Psychological Monographs*, 1966, **80**, 1–28.

RUFF, C. F., ET AL. The intelligence of rapists.

Archives of Sexual Behavior, 1976, **5**, 327–329.

RUPPENTHAL, G. L., ET AL. A ten year perspective of motherless-mother monkey behavior. *Journal of Abnormal Psychology*, 1976, **85**, 341–349.

RUSH, B. *Medical inquiries and observations upon the diseases of the mind.* Philadelphia: Gregg and Elliott, 1835.

RUSHMER, R. F. *Structure and function of the cardiovascular system.* Philadelphia: Saunders, 1976.

RUSSELL, G. F., ET AL. Experimental studies on the nature of the psychological disorder in anorexia nervosa. *Psychoneuroendocrinology*, 1975, **1**, 45–56.

RUTTER, M. *Maternal deprivation reassessed.* Hammondsworth, England: Penguin, 1972.

SAFER, D. J., AND ALLEN, R. P. *Hyperactive children: Diagnosis and management.* Baltimore: University Park Press, 1976.

SAGARIN, E. Prison homosexuality and its effect on post prison sexual behavior. *Psychiatry*, 1976, **39**, 245–257.

SAGARIN, E., AND MONTANINO, F. (EDS.). *Deviants: Voluntary actors in a hostile world.* New York: Silver-Burdett, 1977.

SALZINGER, K. *Schizophrenia: Behavioral aspects.* New York: Wiley, 1976.

SALZMAN, L. Psychodynamic approaches to sex deviations. *New England Journal of Medicine*, 1973, **288**, 345–351.

SANDHU, H. *Juvenile delinquency.* New York: McGraw-Hill, 1977.

SAVAGE, C., ET AL. Methadone/LAAM maintenance: A comparison study. *Comparative Psychiatry*, 1976, **17**, 415–424.

SCHEFF, T. J. Schizophrenia as ideology. *Schizophrenia Bulletin*, 1970, **2**, 15–19.

SCHLESINGER, N., AND ROBBINS, F. Assessment and follow-up in psychoanalysis. *Journal of the American Psychoanalytical Association*, 1974, **22**, 542–567.

SCHOOLER, J. C. *Current issues in adolescent psychiatry.* New York: Bruner/Mazel, 1973.

SCHOPLER, E., AND REICHLER, R. J. (EDS.). *Psychopathology and child development: Research and treatment.* New York: Plenum, 1976.

SCHRAG, R., AND DIVOKY, D. *The myth of the hyperactive child.* New York: Pantheon, 1975.

SCHUCKIT, M. A., AND GUNDERSON, E. K. Alcoholism in young men. *US Naval Health Center Research Reports,* 1975, No. 75–14.

SCHULSINGER, H. A ten year follow-up of children of schizophrenic mothers. *Acta Psychiatrica Scandinavia,* 1976, **53**, 371–386.

SCHUYLER, D. *The depressive spectrum.* New York: Aronson, 1974.

SCOTT, D. F., AND SCHWARTZ, M. S. EEG features of depressive and schizophrenic states. *British Journal of Psychiatry,* 1975, **126**, 408–413.

SEARS, R. R., ET AL. *Patterns of child rearing.* New York: Row, Peterson, 1957.

SEBASTIAN, H., AND SMITH, W. R. Emotional history and pathogenesis of cancer. *Journal of Clinical Psychology,* 1976, **32**, 863–866.

SEIDEN, R. We're driving young blacks to suicide. *Psychology Today,* 1970, **4**, 24–28.

SEIXAS, F. A. *Currents in alcoholism.* New York: Grune and Stratton, 1977.

SELIGMAN, M. E. P. *Helplessness: On depression, development and death.* San Francisco: Freeman, 1975.

SEMEONOFF, B. *Projective techniques.* New York: Wiley, 1976.

SELYE, H. Stress without distress. *Vie Medicine Canada Francias,* 1975, **4**, 964–968.

SHAPIRO, D. Dynamic and holistic ideas of neurosis and psychotherapy. *Psychiatry,* 1975, **33**, 218–226.

SHEDLETSKY, R., AND ENDLER, N. S. Anxiety: The state-trait model and the interaction model. *Journal of Personality,* 1974, **42**, 511–527.

SHEEHY, G. *Passages: Predictable crises of adult life.* New York: Dutton, 1976.

SHERFEY, M. J. *The nature and evolution of female sexuality.* New York: Vintage, 1973.

SHNEIDMAN, E. S. (ED.). *Suicidology: Contemporary developments.* New York: Grune and Stratton, 1976.

SIASSI, I., AND MESSER, S. B. Psychotherapy with patients from lower socioeconomic groups. *American Journal of Psychotherapy,* 1976, **30**, 29–40.

SIEGLER, M., AND OSMOND, H. *Models of madness, models of medicine.* New York: Harper & Row, 1976.

SILEN, W. Peptic ulcer. In M. W. Wintrobe, et al. (Eds.), *Harrison's principles of internal medicine.* New York: McGraw-Hill, 1970.

SKINNER, B. F. *Particulars of my life.* New York: Knopf, 1976.

SLATER, E., AND GLITHERO, E. A follow-up of patients diagnosed as suffering from hysteria. *Journal of Psychosomatic Research,* 1965 **9**, 9–13.

SLATER, E., AND COWIE, V. *The genetics of mental disorders.* New York: Oxford, 1971.

SLATER, E., AND SHIELDS, J. *Genetic aspects of anxiety.* Ashford, Kent, England: Headley, 1969.

SLOAN, R. B., ET AL. *Psychotherapy vs. behavior therapy.* Cambridge, Mass.: Harvard University Press, 1975.

SMITH, J. R., AND SMITH, L. G. *Beyond monogamy.* Baltimore: Johns Hopkins, 1974.

SMITH, K. E. Effect of the double-bind communication on the anxiety of level of normals. *Journal of Abnormal Psychology,* 1976, **85**, 356–363.

SMITH, L. H. *Improving your child's behavior chemistry.* Englewood Cliffs, N.J.: Prentice-Hall, 1976.

SMITH, M. L., AND GLASS, G. V. Meta-analysis of psychotherapy outcome studies. *American Psychologist,* 1977, **32**, 752–760.

SOUTHARD, E. E. Alienists and psychiatrists. *Mental Hygiene,* 1917, **1**, 567–571.

SPIELBERGER, C. D. *Anxiety: current trends in theory and research.* New York: Academic Press, 1972.

SPINETTA, J. J., AND RIGLER, D. The child-abusing parent. *Psychological Bulletin,* 1972, **77**, 296–304.

SPITZ, R. A., AND WOLK, K. M. Anaclitic depression. In A. Freud et al. (Eds.), *The psychoanalytic study of the child* (Vol. II). New York: International Universities Press, 1950.

SPITZER, R. L. More on pseudoscience in science and the case for psychiatric diagnosis. *Archives of General Psychiatry,* 1976, **33**, 459–470.

SPITZER, R. L., AND KLEIN, D. F. (EDS.). *Evaluation of psychological therapies.* Baltimore: Johns Hopkins, 1976.

SROLE, L., ET AL. *Mental health in the metropo-*

lis: The midtown Manhattan study. New York: McGraw-Hill, 1962.

STACHNIK, T. J. The case against criminal penalties for illicit drug use. *American Psychologist,* 1972, **27,** 637–642.

STEFANSSON, J. G., ET AL. Hysterical neurosis, conversion type. *Acta Psychiatrica Scandinavia,* 1976, **53,** 119–138.

STEIN, M. *Lovers, friends and slaves*. New York: Putnam, 1974.

STEPHENS, D. A., et al. Psychiatric morbidity in parents and sibs of schizophrenics and non-schizophrenics. *British Journal of Psychiatry,* 1975, **127,** 97–108.

STRAUSS, M. E. Behavioral differences between acute and chronic schizophrenia. *Psychological Bulletin,* 1973, **79,** 271–279.

STRICKLER, D., ET AL. Moderate drinking as an alternative to alcohol abuse. *Behavior Research Therapy,* 1976, **14,** 279–288.

STRUPP, H. W. Assessment of psychoanalytic therapy. *Psychoanalytic Review,* 1974, **61,** 247–256.

STUNKARD, A. J. Presidential address. *Psychosomatic Medicine,* 1974, **37,** 195–236.

SUE, S. Community mental health services to minorities. *American Psychologist,* 1977, **32,** 616–624.

SULLIVAN, H. S. *The interpersonal theory of psychiatry*. New York: Norton, 1953.

SUTHERLAND, E. H., AND CRESSEY, D. R. *Criminology*. Philadelphia: Lippincott, 1974.

SZASZ, T. S. The myth of mental illness: Three addenda. *Journal of Humanistic Psychology,* 1974, **14,** 11–19.

SZASZ, T. S. *The second sin*. Garden City, N.Y.: Doubleday, 1974.

TARJAN, G., ET AL. Natural history of mental retardation. *American Journal of Mental Deficiency,* 1973, **77,** 369–379.

TAYLOR, M., AND ABRAMS, R. Manic states: A genetic study of early and late onset of affective disorders. *Archives of General Psychiatry,* 1973, **28,** 656–658.

TENNOV, D. *Psychotherapy: The hazardous cure*. Garden City, N.Y.: Anchor Books, 1977.

THIEL, H. G., ET AL. Stress factors and risk of myocardial infarction. *Journal of Psychoso-*

matic Research, 1973, **17,** 43–57.

THOMAS, M. H., AND DRABMAN, R. S. Toleration of real life aggression as a function of exposure to televised violence and age of subject. *Merrill Palmer Quarterly,* 1975, **21,** 227–232.

TOOLEY, K. Small assassins: Clinical notes on a subgroup of murderous children. *Journal of the American Academy of Child Psychiatry,* 1975, **14,** 306–318.

TOURNEY, G., ET AL. Hormonal relationships in homosexual men. *American Journal of Psychiatry,* 1975, **132,** 288–290.

TRIPP, C. A. *The homosexual matrix*. New York: McGraw-Hill, 1975.

TROHANOWICZ, R. C. *Juvenile delinquency: Concepts and controls*. Englewood Cliffs, N.J.: Prentice-Hall, 1978.

TSUANG, M. Schizophrenia around the world. *Comparative Psychiatry,* 1976, **17,** 477–481.

UDELL, B., AND HORNSTRA, R. R. A comparative study of neurotics seen in a community mental health center and in private practice. *Hospital and Community Psychiatry,* 1976, **27,** 269–271.

ULLMANN, L. P., AND KRASNER, L. *A psychological approach to abnormal behavior*. New York: Holt, Rinehart and Winston, 1975.

VAILLANT, G. E. Natural history of male psychological health. *Archives of General Psychiatry,* 1974, **31,** 15–22.

VAN DEN BERG, J. H. *Dubious maternal affection*. Pittsburgh: Duquesne University Press, 1972.

VONNEGUT, M. *The Eden express*. New York: Bantam Books, 1976.

WAHL, O. F. Monozygotic twins discordant for schizophrenia. *Psychological Bulletin,* 1976, **83,** 91–106.

WALLS, P. D., ET AL. Psychiatric training and practice in the Peoples Republic of China. *American Journal of Psychiatry,* 1975, **132,** 121–128.

WALTERS, D. *Physical and sexual abuse of children: Causes and treatment*. Bloomington: Indiana University Press, 1975.

WARREN, L. W. The therapeutic status of consciousness-raising groups. *Professional Psy-*

chologist, 1976, **7,** 132–140.

WARREN, N. *Studies in cross-cultural psychology.* New York: Academic Press, 1977.

WASTELL, C. (ED.). *Chronic duodenal ulcer.* New York: Appleton-Century-Crofts, 1972.

WATSON, C. G., ET AL. Alpha wave biofeedback training therapy in alcoholics. *Journal of Clinical Psychology,* 1977, **33,** 292–299.

WECHSLER, H., ET AL. (EDS.). *Social psychology and mental health.* New York: Holt, Rinehart and Winston, 1970.

WEINBERG, M. S., AND WILLIAMS, C. J. *Male homosexuals.* New York: Penguin, 1975.

WENER, A. E., AND REHM, L. P. Depressive affect: A test of a behavioral hypothesis. *Journal of Abnormal Psychology,* 1975, **84,** 221–227.

WENNERHOLM, M. A., AND ZARLE, T. H. Internal-external control, defensiveness and anxiety in hypertensive patients. *Journal of Clinical Psychology,* 1976, **32,** 644–648.

WEST, N. D. Sex in geriatrics. *Journal of the American Geriatric Society,* 1975, **23,** 551–552.

WHEATLEY, O. Evaluation of trazodone in the treatment of anxiety. *Current Therapy Research,* 1976, **20,** 74–83.

WHITE, R. B., AND GILLILAND, R. M. *Elements of psychopathology: The mechanisms of defense.* New York: Grune and Stratton, 1975.

WHITEHOUSE, D. Behavior and learning problems in epileptic children. *Behavioral Neuropsychiatry,* 1976, **7,** 23–29,

WICKRAMASEKERA, I. Aversive behavior rehearsal for sexual exhibitionism. *Behavior Therapy,* 1976, **7,** 167–176.

WILBER, C. G. (ED.). *Contemporary violence: A multidisciplinary examination.* Springfield, Ill.: Charles C Thomas, 1975.

WILSON, R. S. Twins: Early mental development. *Science,* 1972, **175,** 914–917.

WILSON, S., ET AL. *Human sexuality.* New York: West, 1977.

WING, L., ET AL. Prevalence of early childhood autism. *Psychological Medicine,* 1976, **6,** 89–100.

WINICK, D., AND KINSIE, P. *The lively commerce: Prostitution in the United States.* New York: Quadrangle, 1971.

WINOKUR, G., AND TSUANG, M. The Iowa 500: Suicide in mania, depression and schizophre-

nia. *American Journal of Psychiatry,* 1975, **132,** 650–651.

WITTKOWER, E. D., AND PRINCE, R. A. A review of transcultural psychiatry. In S. Arieti (Ed.), *American psychiatry.* New York: Basic Books, 1974.

WOLKIND, S. N. The components of "affectionless psychotherapy" in institutionalized children. *Journal of Child Psychology and Psychiatry,* 1974, **15,** 215–220.

WOLPE, J. *The practice of behavior therapy.* Elmsford, N.Y.: Pergamon, 1973.

WOODRUFF, JR., R. A., ET AL. Suicide attempts and psychiatric diagnosis. *Diseases of the Nervous System,* 1972, **33,** 617–621.

WOODRUFF, JR., R. A. ET AL. Anxiety neurosis among psychiatric outpatients. *Comparative Psychiatry,* 1972, **13,** 165–170.

WOODRUFF, JR., R. A., ET AL. Psychiatric diagnoses within a group of adolescent outpatients. In R. D. Wirt, et al., *Life history research in psychopathology.* Minneapolis: University of Minnesota Press, 1975.

WOODRUFF, JR., R. A., ET AL. *Psychiatric diagnosis.* New York: Oxford, 1974.

WOODRUFF, JR., R. A., ET AL. Manic depressive illness and social achievement. *Acta Psychiatrica Scandinavia,* 1971, **47,** 237–249.

WOOLEY, D. W. *The biochemical bases of psychoses.* New York: Wiley, 1962.

WOOLSEY, R. M. Hysteria: 1875 to 1975. *Diseases of the Nervous System,* 1976, **37,** 379–386.

WORICK, W., AND SCHALLER, W. *Alcohol, tobacco and drugs.* Englewood Cliffs, N.J.: Prentice-Hall, 1977.

WHO (WORLD HEALTH ORGANIZATION). *Expert committee on mental health* (report series). Geneva: WHO, 1968–1976.

WHO. *Advances in the drug therapy of mental illness.* Geneva: WHO, 1976.

WHO. *A manual on drug dependence.* Geneva: WHO, 1975.

WHO. *Schizophrenia: A multinational study.* Geneva: WHO, 1975.

WHO. *Suicide and attempted suicide.* Geneva: WHO, 1974.

WHO. *World health statistics.* Geneva: WHO, 1972–1976.

WHO. *Vital statistics and causes of death.*

Geneva: WHO, 1978.

WYATT, R. J., ET AL. Dopamine B hydroxylase activity in the brains of chronic schizophrenic patients. *Science,* 1975, **187,** 368–370.

YANKELOVICH, D. *The new morality: A profile of American youth in the seventies.* New York: McGraw-Hill, 1974.

YARVIS, R. M. Crisis intervention as a first line of defense. *Psychiatric Annals,* 1975, **5,** 195–197.

ZBOROWSKI, M. Cultural components in response to pain. *Journal of Social Issues,* 1952, 8, 16–30.

ZEICHNER, A., ET AL. A comparison between drug-abusers and non-drug-abusers on measures of social skills. *Journal of Clinical Psychology,* 1977, **33,** 585–590.

ZIMERING, S., AND CALHOUN, J. F. Is there an alcoholic personality? *Journal of Drug Education,* 1976, **6,** 97–103.

ZITRIN, A., ET AL. Crime and violence among mental patients. *American Journal of Psychiatry,* 1976, **133,** 142–149.

ZUBIN, J., AND SPRING, B. Vulnerability—A new view of schizophrenia. *Journal of Abnormal Psychology,* 1977, **86,** 103–126.

NAME INDEX

SUBJECT INDEX

[Note: Page numbers in italics refer to illustrations; references with asterisks refer to insert box]

DSM-II Diagnoses*

MENTAL RETARDATION

310.   Borderline
311.   Mild
312.   Moderate
313.   Severe
314.   Profound
315.   Unspecified

With each: Following or associated with
  .00   Infection or intoxication
  .10   Trauma or physical agent
  .20   Disorders of metabolism, growth or nutrition
  .30   Gross brain disease (postnatal)
  .40   Unknown prenatal influence
  .50   Chromosomal abnormality
  .60   Prematurity
  .70   Major psychiatric disorder
  .80   Psycho-social (environmental) deprivation
  .90   Other condition

ORGANIC BRAIN SYNDROMES (OBS)
A   PSYCHOSES
Senile and Pre-senile Dementia

290.00   Senile dementia
290.10   Pre-senile dementia

Alcoholic Psychosis

291.00   Delirium tremens
291.10   Korsakov's psychosis
291.20   Other alcoholic hallucinosis
291.30   Alcohol paranoid state
291.40   Acute alcohol intoxication
291.50   Alcoholic deterioration
291.60   Pathological intoxication
291.90   Other alcoholic psychosis

Psychosis Associated with Intracranial Infection

292.00   General paralysis

292.10   Syphilis of central nervous system
292.20   Epidemic encephalitis
292.30   Other and unspecified encephalitis
292.90   Other intracranial infection

Psychosis Associated with Other Cerebral Condition

293.00   Cerebral arteriosclerosis
293.10   Other cerebrovascular disturbance
293.20   Epilepsy
293.30   Intracranial neoplasm
293.40   Degenerative disease of the CNS
293.50   Brain trauma
293.90   Other cerebral condition

Psychosis Associated with Other Physical Condition

294.00   Endocrine disorder
294.10   Metabolic or nutritional disorder
294.20   Systemic infection
294.30   Drug or poison intoxication (other than alcohol)
294.40   Childbirth
294.80   Other and unspecified physical condition

B   NON-PSYCHOTIC OBS

309.00   Intracranial infection
309.13   Alcohol (simple drunkenness)
309.14   Other drug, poison, or systemic intoxication
309.20   Brain trauma
309.30   Circulatory disturbance
309.40   Epilepsy
309.50   Disturbance of metabolism, growth or nutrition
309.60   Senile or pre-senile brain disease
309.70   Intracranial neoplasm
309.80   Degenerative disease of the CNS
309.90   Other physical condition

PSYCHOSES NOT ATTRIBUTED TO PHYSICAL CONDITIONS LISTED PREVIOUSLY
Schizophrenia

295.00   Simple
295.10   Hebephrenic
295.20   Catatonic
295.23   Catatonic type, excited
295.24   Catatonic type, withdrawn
295.30   Paranoid
295.40   Acute schizophrenic episode
295.50   Latent
295.60   Residual
295.70   Schizo-affective
295.73   Schizo-affective, excited
295.74   Schizo-affective, depressed
295.80   Childhood
295.90   Chronic undifferentiated
295.99   Other schizophrenic

Major Affective Disorders

296.00   Involutional melancholia
296.10   Manic-depressive illness, manic
296.20   Manic-depressive illness, depressed
296.30   Manic-depressive illness, circula
296.33   Manic-depressive, circular, man
296.34   Manic-depressive, circular, depressed
296.80   Other major affective disorder

Paranoid States

297.00   Paranoia
297.10   Involutional paranoid state
297.90   Other paranoid state

Other Psychoses

298.00   Psychotic depressive reaction